Psychology
of Learning:
Readings

Psychology of Learning:
Readings

William L. Mikulas
Editor

Nelson-Hall, Chicago

Library of Congress Cataloging in Publication Data
Main entry under title:

Psychology of learning.

Bibliography: p. 586
1. Learning, Psychology of. I. Mikulas, William L.
[DNLM: 1. Learning. 2. Psychology, Educational.
LB1051 P974]
LB1051.P72938   370.15'2   77-8234
ISBN 0-88229-226-9 (*cloth*)
ISBN 0–88229–519–5 (*paper*)
Copyright © 1977 by William L. Mikulas

Manufactured in the United States of America

To Benita and our Parents

Contents

Preface

The psychology of learning spans many levels, from changes in the nervous system and related molecules to applications of learning-based technology for the modification of human or animal behavior. Yet this very breadth poses problems for the student of learning. No single source comprehensively covers all the different levels; and if such a source existed, it would be impractically large. Thus, no text covers all the areas that interest different instructors and students. Most learning texts omit any discussion of the physiology of learning, while many others omit the applications of learning principles to the problems of human behavior.

The intent of this book of readings, then, is to provide the reader a sample of the thinking and research in various areas of the psychology of learning. It is hoped these readings will supplement various different learning texts and instructors. The readings include some "classic" reports, some relatively recent papers that have strongly influenced the psychology of learning and some lesser known papers that might stimulate some new ideas. For me these are appetizers in an area where I enjoy the banquet.

Introduction:
The Nature of Learning

Knowledge of the phenomena and principles of learning is critical to our understanding of the behavior of people and animals. As we learn more about the processes of learning we can devise better education systems, deal more effectively with many forms of mental illness, train parents in child-rearing practices, and help people learn how to better control their own behavior. Research into the physiology of learning may help us overcome forms of mental deficiency, develop memory pills to facilitate learning, and reduce some of the mental deterioration that accompanies senility. The applications and importance of learning principles could be continued considerably more, for learning is the vehicle by which almost all behaviors are acquired.

An unfortunate result of the breadth of learning is that there is no agreed upon definition of *learning*. There is no definition that theorists agree includes all the phenomena they wish to call learning and excludes all other phenomena. The following is a fairly good definition: Learning is a more or less permanent change in behavior potential that occurs as a result of practice; it is not a change due to motivational factors, sensory adaptation, fatigue, maturation, senescence, or stimulus change. Let us examine this definition. It begins with a more or less permanent change. This means learning refers to relatively stable changes within the organism, as opposed to more transient states such as moods. A popular assumption is that once something has been learned it is fairly permanent in the system. Forgetting, then, is due to problems in retrieving information from within the system, not the information being lost from the system.

Defining learning as a change in behavior potential points out the distinction between *performance* and *learning*. Learning is a hypothetical limit, it partially determines what the organism is capable of doing. Performance is what the organism actually does. For example, a student might have learned a set of multiplication tables, but when asked the product of 6 and 7 by a substitute teacher, he claims he doesn't know. Learning provided the behavior potential to answer 42, but the actual performance was saying he did not know the answer. It is often motivational variables that keep performance below potential. Thus the student's peer group might discourage him from giving correct answers to substitute teachers.

Performance can be thought of as a function of the interaction of learning and motivation. Unfortunately, it is often hard to determine whether a variable affected learning or only performance. Also learning and motivation interact in complex ways that are difficult to separate.

In the definition it was stated that learning occurs as a result of practice. This is the most ambiguous part. It refers to most theorists' belief that for learning to occur the organism must somehow actively participate in the learning experience, as opposed to such hypothetical situations as having memories biochemically implanted in the brain. However, practice has not been specified much past this point and includes such disparate phenomena as an actor learning his lines by saying them over and over, a student learning while quietly sitting and listening, and a rat learning an avoidance task after one trial.

The last half of the definition simply lists a number of variables that affect performance changes but are to be excluded from learning. Motivation refers to temporary states (drives and incentives) that tend to activate behaviors. Sensory adaptation refers to changes in the organism's behavior toward stimulus situations due to relatively simple changes in the sensory systems. For example, seeing improves as you adapt to a dark room and hearing changes as you adapt to a constant sound. Fatigue is the tendency to stop responding merely as a function of the act of responding itself. Maturation refers to changes in behavior due to early aging processes of the organism. Senescence is the deterioration that often comes with old age. Finally, stimulus change refers to the fact that if a response is learned to one stimulus situation and tested in a different stimulus situation, there will be a decrement in the response. Generally, the bigger the difference between situations, the greater the decrement in the response.

It appears most of learning can be subsumed under two basic rubrics: operant conditioning (also called instrumental conditioning) and respondent conditioning (also called classical or Pavlovian conditioning). In operant conditioning the critical contingency is between the response of the organism and a subsequent event. If the event results in an increase in the rate or probability of the response, the event is called a reinforcer. If the event results in a decrease in the rate or probability, the event is called a punisher. Thus if when a rat starts pressing a bar the event of receiving food is contingent upon bar pressing (e.g., the rat must press the bar to get the food), the rate of bar pressing will increase as it is reinforced by the food. Conversely, if pressing the bar resulted in electric shock, the bar pressing rate would decrease as shock is a punisher.

In respondent conditioning the critical contingency is the pairing of stimuli. Two stimuli, both of which elicit responses, are paired until both stimuli elicit a response similar to a response that was previously only elicited by one of the stimuli. For example, an electric shock, but not a light, might make a dog jump. By appropriate pairing of the light and shock, soon just turning on the light could cause the dog to jump.

Section One
Operant Conditioning

Operant conditioning is the learning rubric based on a contingency between a response of the organism and some event. That is, if the organism makes a specified response, then there will be a change in some contingent event. If a rat presses the bar, then a food pellet will drop into the food dish. If the child pulls the plug on the television, then the television will go off. In operant conditioning emphasis is on the rate of responding, that is, how often the response is made during some unit of time. If the contingent event results in an increase in the rate of responding, the event is called *reinforcement*. If the contingent event results in a decrease in the rate of responding, the event is called *punishment*.

The change in the contingent event may be an increase (positive) or a decrease (negative). This results in four combinations: positive reinforcement, negative reinforcement, positive punishment, and negative punishment. Positive reinforcement is an event whose onset or increase results in an increase in the rate of the response it is contingent on. If the rat presses the bar, there is an increase in the food in the dish; so the rate of bar pressing increases. Therefore, the food in this case is a positive reinforcement. Negative reinforcement is a contingent event whose offset or decrease results in an increase in the rate of response. If by pressing the bar the rat can turn off an electric shock on the grid floor, there will be an increase in the rate at which the rat presses the bar when the foot-shock is on. Here the offset of the foot-shock is negative reinforcement.

Positive punishment is a contingent event whose onset or increase results in a decrease in the rate of response. If when a rat presses a bar, he receives a foot-shock, the rate of bar pressing will probably decrease. If so, the onset of the foot-shock is positive punishment. Negative punishment is a contingent event whose offset or decrease results in a decrease in the rate of response. If when the rat presses the bar, food is taken away from the rat, the bar-pressing rate will probably decrease. Here the decrease in the food is negative punishment.

It can be seen that the onset of an event can have one effect, while the offset another. The onset of food can be positive reinforcement, while the offset is negative punishment. The onset of shock can be positive punishment, while the offset is negative reinforcement. The effect is due to whether the onset or offset is contingent on a particular response.

Extinction in operant conditioning generally refers to a reduction in the rate of response due to the termination of the contingency between the response and reinforcement. If the rat were pressing the bar to receive food and a change was made so food was no longer contingent on pressing the bar (i.e., pressing the bar would not produce food), the rate of bar pressing would decrease. This decrease is called extinction.

There have been many attempts to formalize exactly what types of events will function as reinforcement. The simplest is the empirical approach which identifies an event as reinforcement if it does what reinforcements are defined to do, that is, increase the rate of the response. Many psychologists, however, have sought more general theoretical analyses of reinforcement. A few of these are given below.

Some theorists, mostly coming from the influence of Clark Hull (e.g., Hull, 1943), identify reinforcement as an event that reduces the need or drive. When an animal is deprived of food there is an increase in drive. This drive might be conceptualized as specific to food or more general and nonspecific. A nonspecific drive is one that receives input from a number of different sources such as hunger, thirst, and sex. The rat's bar pressing for food is assumed to be reinforced because eating the food reduces the drive that was at least partially elicited by food deprivation. A main issue for this orientation is identifying the variables that elicit the original increases in drive. Sheffield (1966a, 1966b), on the other hand, argues for a drive-induction theory of reinforcement. According to this theory, animals learn responses that arouse motivation. If a rat receives food for turning right in a maze but not for turning left, the consummatory response of eating becomes conditioned to the cues of the right side. Now when the animal approaches the choice point, the right side stimuli tend to elicit the consummatory response, but the rat can't consume until it gets to the food. This consummatory stimulation without consummation is drive induction and motivates the rat to turn right, because turning right is the response that in the past preceded the consummatory response. Although Sheffield's theory was at one time more general, now it is basically applied only to consummatory situations, as opposed to punishment situations, for example. Also the consummatory response may be a central response, that is, a response within the organism without overt behaviors.

Miller (1963) suggests there are one or more *go-mechanisms* activated by reinforcements such as drive reduction or the removal of discrepancy between intention and achievement. Activation of a go-mechanism is then postulated to intensify the ongoing responses to the present stimuli. The go-mechanism also becomes conditioned to the occurrence of the response so that future occurrences of the stimuli elicit both the response and the excitatory state. Similar to Miller's orientation is a theory offered by Landauer (1969). According to Landauer a reinforcement is any event that strengthens response tendencies, such as contingent food or a CS-UCS pairing in respondent conditioning. The reinforcement then facilitates the consolidation of learning, where *consolidation* refers to "the creation of the lasting neural change which underlies learning."

Quite a different approach to reinforcement is that suggested by Premack (1959). As originally stated the necessary and sufficient conditions for reinforcement were as follows: "Any response A will reinforce any other response B if and only if the independent rate of A is greater than that of B." Thus, according to Premack, responses reinforce responses. To determine which responses will reinforce which responses it is necessary to measure their independent rates, the rates at which there is no contingency between the responses. From these independent rates it can be predicted that a response can reinforce any other response if the independent rate of the first is higher than that of the second. For example, if a hungry rat is put in an apparatus where he can eat food and press a bar (where pressing the bar does not yield anything), the rat's independent rate of eating will be higher than the independent rate of bar pressing. Therefore, when eating food is made contingent on bar pressing, it will function as reinforcement.

Premack (1965) later expanded his principle of reinforcement to take into account positive and negative reinforcement. Now the principle is that if the onset or offset of one response is more probable than the onset or offset of another, the former will reinforce the latter positively if the superiority is for "on" probability and negatively if for the "off" probability. This more complex principle is illustrated in the reading by Hundt and Premack in which running in a wheel is the basis for both positive and negative reinforcement.

Although punishment is simply defined as a contingent event that results in a decrease in the frequency of a response, the mechanisms by which it produces this effect are greatly debated (cf. Campbell & Church, 1968; Church, 1963; Dunham, 1971). For example, the punishment may elicit an emotional response such as fear and/or some other response such as jumping back. These elicited responses, then, might become conditioned to the situation where the punishment occurred and/or any existing agent that administered the punishment. To the extent that these conditioned responses are elicited by the situation and are incompatible with the punished response, their occurrence may result in a decrease in the frequency of the punished response. Church (1963) refers to the "fear hypothesis" where the emphasis is on the conditioned fear and the "competing response hypothesis" where the emphasis is on the competing conditioned skeletal responses.

If the onset of an event is positive punishment, the offset will probably be negative reinforcement. Thus, if an animal is punished for response A and the punishment causes him to make response B, response B might be negatively reinforced by the off-set of the aversive event. To the extent that responses A and B are incompatible, reinforcing B may result in a decrease in the frequency of A. For example, Church (1963) mentions the "escape hypothesis," which emphasizes the escape response to the punishment which is negatively reinforced.

Dunham (1971) suggests two basic rules of punishment due to shock:

1) That particular response in the organism's repertoire which is most frequently associated with the onset of shock and/or predicts it within a shorter time than other responses will decrease in probability and remain below its operant baseline.

2) That particular response in the organism's repertoire which is most frequently associated with the absence of the onset of shock and/or predicts the absence of it for a longer period of time than other responses will increase in probability and remain above its operant baseline.

In the second reading Solomon discusses a wide range of effects punishment might have and some of the variables that determine the effect of punishment.

If a neutral stimulus is paired with a reinforcement, the neutral stimulus may acquire reinforcing properties. If it does, it is then called a *secondary reinforcement* or a *conditioned reinforcement*. If when a rat presses a bar he hears a click and receives a food pellet, the click by being paired with the food acquires conditioned reinforcing properties. The rat might now make a new response simply in order to hear the click. There are both positive conditioned reinforcements (e.g., approval and money) and negative conditioned reinforcements (e.g., criticism and fines).

For awhile there were basically two theories of conditioned reinforcement: the S-S hypothesis and the discriminative stimulus hypothesis (cf. Hendry, 1969). The S-S hypothesis, as advocated by theorists such as Hull, suggested that one stimulus acquires reinforcing properties simply by being paired (occurring in close temporal contiguity) with a reinforcing stimulus. The discriminative stimulus hypothesis, suggested by Skinner, argues that only discriminative stimuli become conditioned reinforcers, the stimulus must gain discriminative control over a reinforced response in order to become a conditioned reinforcement. In other words, for a stimulus to acquire conditioned reinforcing properties it must be a cue to which the organism makes a response that is reinforced. For example, if when a red light came on the rat had learned to press the bar for food, the red light would become a conditioned reinforcement.

The discriminative stimulus hypothesis has not held up well because it appears that simple pairing of a stimulus with a reinforcement is often sufficient. And the article by Egger and Miller raises problems for the S-S hypothesis. Egger and Miller showed that an important variable in conditioned reinforcement is the amount of information the stimulus provides about the onset of the reinforcement. For example, if when a light comes on it is followed by a tone and then food, the light will become a stronger conditioned reinforcement than the tone, even though the tone is temporally closer to the food. For the light gives the most information about the food; when the light comes on food is known to follow. The tone, on the other hand, is redundant; it provides no information not already supplied by the light.

Operant conditioning, as discussed above, is concerned with contingent events. Reinforcement and punishment are also often dependent events; they don't occur unless a specified response occurs. Many events, however, are nondependent; they occur almost regardless of the behavior of the organism. If the nondependent event is a reinforcement, the animal might "learn" to make whatever response he just happened to be doing when the nondependent event occurred. This is called *superstitious behavior*. For example, a device might just drop a food pellet into an operant unit at random intervals, independent of what the rat is doing. If the rat happens to be chewing on the food dish when food drops in, he might learn to chew on the dish in an attempt to get food.

If the nondependent event is aversive, such as inescapable shock, the animal might develop learned helplessness. The animal might learn there is no correlation between what he does and the onset or offset of the aversive event. This might result in the animal's simply passively accepting whatever happens to him. The genesis and treatment of learned helplessness are discussed in the article by Seligman, Maier, and Geer.

Until fairly recently it was generally held that autonomic responses such as blood pressure and heart rate could be conditioned respondently, but not operantly. Then in a series of experiments, primarily under the influence of Neal Miller, it was found that many autonomic responses including heart rate, intestinal contractions, urine formation by the kidney, and specific brain waves can be operantly conditioned. In the fifth article Miller discusses this very important research and some of its implications for areas such as psychosomatic illnesses.

The various applications of operant conditioning procedures are impressively extensive. Included are such diverse areas as programmed instruction, design of communities, teaching people how to control their blood pressure, and training circus animals. Animals have been trained to perform a number of tasks. For example, Verhave (1966) trained two pigeons to inspect pills for a drug company, and the article by Skinner describes how pigeons were trained to fly missiles.

An important area of application of operant techniques is in the modification of human behavior (cf. Mikulas, 1972, 1974; Whaley & Malott, 1971). The basic strategy is to withhold reinforcement from undesirable behaviors or in some situations punish them, while simultaneously reinforcing approximations to desirable behaviors. In the seventh article Ayllon shows the applications of operant procedures in a mental hospital. Dealing with a forty-seven-year-old female schizophrenic, Ayllon decreased her food stealing by using negative punishment (withdrawal of a meal). The patient's towel hoarding was decreased by flooding her with towels. This procedure, called "stimulus satiation," decreases the reinforcing value of the towels by extinguishing their conditioned reinforcing value and/or by conditioning in aversive elements to the towels. Finally, the excessive amount of clothes the patient wore was gradually decreased with food reinforcement (although the procedure also has aspects of negative punishment, missing a meal).

Running as Both a Positive and Negative Reinforcer

ALAN G. HUNDT and DAVID PREMACK, *University of Missouri*

Rats were required to press a bar to activate a motor-driven wheel that forced them to run and subsequently to drink to turn off the wheel. Barpressing and licking increased, showing the onset and offset of running to be positively and negatively reinforcing, respectively. The experimental control of the offset of running, in contrast to the traditional control for onset only, served to demonstrate that since organisms stop such behaviors as they start, self-initiated behaviors will act as negative as well as positive reinforcers.

The traditional use of two kinds of events for positive and negative reinforcement, respectively, creates the impression that the environment of a species divides naturally into discrete classes of positive and negative events. In fact, this division results more from an experimenter convention than from a relation between the species and its environment. Specifically, it results from the fact that experimenters instrument only the onset of some behaviors and only the offset of others, rather than using both the onset and offset of any one behavior.

For example, although organisms both initiate and terminate eating, only initiation is used in reinforcement. In the standard food reinforcement case, the organism is required to make

Hundt, A. G. & Premack, D. Running as both a positive and negative reinforcer. *Science,* 1963, *142,* 1087–1088. Copyright 1963 by the American Association for the Advancement of Science.

an arbitrary response (for example, bar-press) to produce food and thus eat; but it is not required to make an additional response to turn food off and thus stop eating. On the contrary, the food delivered per reinforcement is less than the organism normally eats per burst of eating, and thus the usual disposition to terminate eating does not arise.

On the other side of the coin, only the organism's tendency to turn off (for example) electric shock is used. But will organisms initiate contact with shock and other supposedly negative events? Recent work[1] shows that rats initiate contact with electric shock, and fail to do so only at "high" voltages. Except for the "high-intensity" cases, organisms apparently initiate and terminate responding for all stimuli to which they respond. That is, they not only initiate the traditional positives, and terminate the traditional negatives, but rather initiate and terminate both. Indeed, all free responding is highly discontinuous, there being apparently characteristic burst length and interburst length distributions for each behavior.[2] Accordingly, to demonstrate the positive and negative capacities of one and the same event requires that there be experimental control of both onset and offset, not one or the other as has been the case.

Of the three cases for which we are currently attempting to establish control of both onset and offset, the one reported here is locomotion. Two findings aided the implementation of this case. (i) Rats choose to press a bar that causes a wheel to rotate and force themselves to run. That is, for the rat, the opportunity to force itself to run is reinforcing; the frequency of the bar-press is increased by such a contingency. (ii) The rat is able to drink while running. These findings led to the following procedure. The rat is placed in a modified Wahmann activity wheel that contains a bar and a drinkometer.[3] The wheel is not free to move but is connected to a variable-speed motor. When the rat presses the bar, the motor is activated, the wheel rotates, and the rat is forced to run. It must continue running until it licks the drinkometer a predetermined number of times, which turns off the motor, stops the wheel, and allows the rat to stop. The rat thus both starts and stops running, the former by the bar-press, the latter by licking.

The base measure for the bar-press is the usual number of

bar-presses when the bar-press does not turn on the wheel. The base measure for licking is the duration of licking when licks do not turn the wheel off. That is, in determining the base lick rate, the bar-press turns the wheel on, so that the rat runs, but drinking does not turn the wheel off; instead, the experimenter turns the wheel off after each 5-second interval of running. The base condition was designed as a control for the possibility that running might either induce licking or interfere with and reduce it. In fact, running tends to reduce drinking: the rat drinks most when running is totally precluded.[4] Because of this decremental relation, we used the 5-second running burst in the base condition; this value leads to a total duration of running per session (under 200 seconds) that is close to, but less than, the smallest amount of running found in any of the experimental conditions (see Fig. 1). Accordingly, increments in licking computed relative to this base err conservatively, that is, underestimate the increment.

Three female albino rats, about 180 days old, Sprague-Dawley strain, were used. They were maintained on free food and water. An additional question was answered by using a fixed-ratio schedule in conjunction with the "off" response. How does the "difficulty" of turning off a response affect the likelihood of its being turned on? All animals were trained with fixed-ratio lick requirements of 1, 3, 9, 19, and 13, in the order stated. That is, on different sessions the rat was required to complete a different, predetermined number of licks in order to turn the wheel off. On all sessions the drinking tube contained 8 percent sucrose by weight; sucrose was used to facilitate the drinking response. One bar-press always turned the wheel on. All sessions lasted 20 minutes and took place daily.

Figure 1 shows the principal results for one subject, results for the other two being the same in all essentials. Shown as a function of the fixed-ratio requirement on the off-response are (i) frequency of the on-response, (ii) duration of the off-response, (iii) duration of running. The onset of running clearly increased the frequency of the bar-presses. The base frequency or operant level was zero for all three rats, in contrast to the average of 20 bar-presses that occurred for the minimal offset requirement. Increase in the bar-press was less evident when the "off" requirement was high: in general, frequency of the on-response was inversely proportional to magnitude of the off requirement. Thus, the rat turned the wheel on only about twice per session when it took 19 licks to turn it off, and turned it on about 20 times per session when it took only one lick to turn it off.

The average duration of licking per session, shown in the broken line in Fig. 1, increased moderately with the off requirement. Comparison with the point to the left of the curve, which gives the duration of licking when licks had no effect upon the wheel (base duration), shows that offset of running increased the duration of licking at all values of the fixed ratio. Furthermore, the increase is entirely in instrumental licking. The rat does two kinds of licking in this situation, some when it is running, which is instrumental to turning off the wheel, and some when it is not running, which amounts to drinking-to-drink and which is the kind of drinking that occurs in the base condition. The curve for licking in Fig. 1 includes both kinds; if only instrumental licking were shown the curve would rise still more

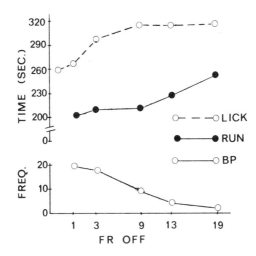

Fig. 1. Shown as a function of the number of licks required to turn off the wheel (fixed ratio off) are (i) average number of bar presses per session, (ii) average duration of licking per session, and (iii) average duration of running per session. The point to the left of the lick curve gives the base duration of licking. Data are for one rat.

steeply. That is, since running reduces drinking, and running increased over the fixed ratio, drinking-to-drink actually declined over the same variable. Thus, the increase in purely instrumental licking is somewhat greater than is indicated by Fig. 1, particularly at the larger fixed-ratio values.

The total duration of running per session is shown by the dark line in Fig. 1. Interestingly, it increased with the magnitude of the off requirement despite the fact that the number of times the rat turned the wheel on decreased as a function of the same variable. This is accounted for by the fact that the average burst of running was far longer in the case of the 19-lick off requirement than in the case of the one-lick requirement—an average of 140 seconds versus 10 seconds. That is, a high off requirement led to a few extremely long bursts of running, whereas the low off requirement led to numerous short bursts of running, the total duration of running being notably greater for the large than for the small requirement. This difference did not result from the rat "trying" but failing to turn the wheel off in the case of the high off requirement. From the time the animal started running to the occurrence of the *first* lick averaged only about 10 seconds for the one-lick requirement versus about 134 seconds for the 19-lick requirement. Thus, when faced with a large off requirement, the animal did not "try" and fail, but rather ran continuously for an unusually long period before even initiating the off response. This delay may amount to a fixed-ratio pause for the off-response, analogous to the classical increase in delay of the instrumental response that is produced by increasing the fixed ratio for the on-response.

That subjects would work to turn on and off the same stimulation had, prior to the present data, been shown only for intracranial self stimulation[5]. Indeed, the first on-off reinforcement system was discovered with intracranial stimulation, on the basis of the originally puzzling finding that subjects would learn to escape but not to avoid the stimulation.[6] Not surprisingly, we find the same relation here: the rat can be trained to escape the already-moving wheel but not to avoid its onset. The formal parallel between the neural and behavioral evidence is thus increased by the present data. More important, since all self-initiated behaviors—for example, eating, drinking, and copulation, as well as running—are also self-terminated, it is likely that merely technical difficulties will impede showing that all such behaviors are on-off systems, capable of generating both positive and negative reinforcement.

These results indicate how a generalization that was stated originally for positive reinforcement may now be broadened to include negative reinforcement as well. Originally, the generalization read: for any pair of responses, the more probable one will reinforce the less probable one.[7] But this fails to distinguish between the onset and offset of an event. The generalization should now read: if the onset or offset of one response is more probable than the onset or offset of another, the former will reinforce the latter—positively, if the superiority is for "on" probability, and negatively, if for the "off" probability. Four reinforcement paradigms can be identified on the basis of the completed generalization: on-on, on-off, off-off, off-on, where the terms of each pair refer to the instrumental and contingent responses, respectively. Thus, the first two paradigms were instanced here by bar-press-run onset and lick-run offset, and represent positive and negative cases, respectively; the other two paradigms remain to be investigated.[8]

NOTES

1. G. M. Harrington and W. K. Linder. *J. Comp. Physiol. Psychol.* 55. 1014 (1962).
2. D. Premack and G. Collier. *Psychol. Monogr.* 76. 5 (whole No. 524) (1962): _____ and R. W. Schaeffer. *J. Exptl, Anal. Behav.* 5, 89 (1962); *ibid.* 6. 473 (1963); _____ and W. Kintsch. unpublished data presented at the Psychonomic Society, Phila., 1963.
3. D. Premack, *Science* 136, 255 (1962).
4. A. Hundt, thesis, University of Missouri (1963).
5. W. W. Roberts, *J. Comp. Physiol. Psychol.* 51, 400 (1958).
6. An exception is an on-off technique used by R. B. Lockhard with the light-contingent bar press. *J. Comp. Physiol. Psychol.* 55. 1118 (1962).
7. D. Premack. *Psychol. Rev.* 66, 219 (1959): *J. Exptl. Psychol.* 61, 163 (1961): *J. Exptl. Anal. Behav.* 6, 81 (1963): *Science* 139, 1062 (1963).
8. Aided by grant G-19574 from the National Science Foundation and by grant M-5798 from the National Institutes of Health, 30 September 1963.

Punishment[1]

Richard L. Solomon, *University of Pennsylvania*

First, an introduction: I will attempt to achieve three goals today. (a) I will summarize some *empirical generalizations and problems* concerning the effects of punishment on behavior; (b) I will give some demonstrations of the *advantages of a two-process learning theory* for suggesting new procedures to be tried out in punishment experiments; and (c) finally, I shall take this opportunity today to *decry some unscientific legends* about punishment, and to do a little pontificating—a privilege that I might be denied in a journal such as the *Psychological Review*, which I edit!

Now, for a working definition of punishment: The definition of a punishment is not operationally simple, but some of its attributes are clear. A punishment is a noxious stimulus, one which will support, by its termination or omission, the growth of new escapes or avoidance responses. It is one which the subject will reject, if given a choice between the punishment and no stimulus at all. Whether the data on the behavioral effects of such noxious stimuli will substantiate our commonsense view of what constitutes an effective punishment, depends on a wide variety of conditions that I shall survey. Needless to say, most of

Solomon, R. L. Punishment. *American Psychologist*, 1964, *19*: 239–253. Copyright 1964 by the American Psychological Association, and reproduced by permission.

these experimental conditions have been studied with infra-human subjects rather than with human subjects.

Let us first consider two sample experiments. Imagine a tra-ditional alley runway, 6 feet long, with its delineated goal box and start box, and an electrifiable grid floor. In our first experi-ment, a rat is shocked in the start box and alley, but there is no shock in the goal box. We can quickly train the rat to run down the alley, if the shock commences as the start-box gate is raised and persists until the rat enters the goal box. This is *escape* train-ing. If, however, we give the rat 5 seconds to reach the goal box after the start-box gate is raised, and only then do we apply the shock, the rat will usually learn to run quickly enough to avoid the shock entirely. This procedure is called *avoidance* training, and the resultant behavior change is called *active* avoidance learning. Note that the response required, either to terminate the shock or to remove the rat from the presence of the dangerous start box and alley, is well specified, while the behavior leading to the onset of these noxious stimulus conditions is left vague. It could be any item of behavior coming *before* the opening of the gate, and it would depend on what the rat happened to be doing when the experimenter raised the gate.

In our second sample experiment, we train a hungry rat to run to the goal box in order to obtain food. After performance appears to be asymptotic, we introduce a shock, both in the alley and goal box, and eliminate the food. The rat quickly stops run-ning and spends its time in the start box. This procedure is called the *punishment procedure,* and the resultant learning-to-stay-in-the-start-box is called *passive* avoidance learning. Note that, while the behavior *producing* the punishment is well speci-fied, the particular behavior *terminating* the punishment is left vague. It could be composed of any behavior that keeps the rat in the start box and out of the alley.

In the first experiment, we were teaching the rat *what to do,* while in the second experiment we were teaching him exactly *what not to do;* yet in each case, the criterion of learning was correlated with the rat's receiving *no* shocks, in contrast to its previous experience of receiving several shocks in the same experimental setting. One cannot think adequately about punishment without considering what is known about the outcomes of both procedures. Yet most reviews of the aversive control of behavior emphasize active avoidance learning and ignore passive avoidance learning. I shall, in this talk, emphasize the similarities, rather than the differences between active and passive avoidance learning. I shall point out that there is a rich store of knowledge of active avoidance learning which, when applied to the punishment procedure, increases our understanding of some of the puzzling and sometimes chaotic results obtained in punishment experiments.

But first, I would like to review some of the empirical generalities which appear to describe the outcomes of experiments on *punishment* and passive avoidance learning. For this purpose, I divide the evidence into 5 classes: (a) the effects of punishment on behavior previously established by *rewards* or positive reinforcement, (b) the effects of punishment on *consummatory* responses, (c) the effects of punishment on complex, sequential patterns of *innate* responses, (d) the effects of punishment on discrete reflexes, (e) the effects of punishment on responses previously established by punishment—or, if you will, the effects of punishment on active escape and avoidance responses. The effectiveness of punishment will be seen to differ greatly across these five classes of experiments. For convenience, I mean by *effectiveness* the degree to which a punishment procedure produces *suppression* of, or facilitates the *extinction* of, existing response patterns.

Now, let us look at punishment for *instrumental responses or habits previously established by reward or positive reinforcers.* First, the outcomes of punishment procedures applied to previously rewarded habits are strongly related to the *intensity* of the punishing agent. Sometimes intensity is independently defined and measured, as in the case of electric shock. Sometimes we have qualitative evaluations, as in the case of Maier's (1949) rat bumping his nose on a locked door, or Masserman's (Masserman & Pechtel, 1953) spider monkey being presented with a toy snake, or Skinner's (1938) rat receiving a slap on the paw from a lever, or my dog receiving a swat from a rolled-up newspaper. As the intensity of shock applied to rats, cats, and dogs is increased from about .1 milliampere to 4 milliamperes, these orderly results can be obtained: (a) *detection* and *arousal,* wherein the punisher can be used as a cue, discriminative stimulus, response intensifier, or even as a secondary reinforcer; (b) *temporary suppression,* wherein punishment results in suppression of the punished response, followed by complete recovery, such that the subject later appears unaltered from his prepunished state; (c) *partial suppression,* wherein the subject always displays some lasting suppression of the punished response, without total recovery; and (d) finally, there is *complete suppression,* with no observable recovery. Any of these outcomes can be produced, other things being equal, by merely varying the intensity of the noxious stimulus used (Azrin & Holz, 1961), when we punish responses previously established by reward or positive reinforcement. No wonder different experimenters report incomparable outcomes. Azrin (1959) has produced a response-rate *increase* while operants are punished. Storms, Borozci, and Broen (1962) have produced long-lasting suppression of operants in rats.[2] Were punishment intensities different? Were punishment durations different? (Storms, Borozci & Broen, 1963, have shown albino rats to be more resistant to punishment than are hooded rats, and this is another source of discrepancy between experiments.)

But other variables are possibly as important as punishment intensity, and their operation can make it unnecessary to use *intense* punishers in order to produce the effective suppression of a response previously established by positive reinforcement. Here are some selected examples:

1. *Proximity* in time and space to the punished response determines to some extent the effectiveness of a punishment. There is a response-suppression gradient. This has been demonstrated in the runway (Brown, 1948; Karsh, 1962), in the lever box (Azrin, 1956), and in the shuttle box (Kamin, 1959). This phenomenon has been labeled the gradient of temporal delay of punishment.

2. The conceptualized *strength* of a response, as measured by its resistance to extinction after omission of positive reinforcement, predicts the effect of a punishment contingent upon the response. Strong responses, so defined, are more resistant to the suppressive effects of punishment. Thus, for example, the over-

training of a response, which often decreases ordinary resistance to experimental extinction, also increases the effectiveness of punishment (Karsh, 1962; Miller, 1960) as a response suppressor.

3. *Adaptation* to punishment can occur, and this *decreases* its effectiveness. New, intense punishers are better than old, intense punishers (Miller, 1960). Punishment intensity, if slowly increased, tends not to be as effective as in the case where it is introduced initially at its high-intensity value.

4. In general, resistance to extinction is decreased whenever a previously reinforced response is punished. However, if the subject is habituated to receiving shock together with positive reinforcement during reward training, the relationship can be reversed, and punishment during extinction can actually increase resistance to extinction (Holz & Azrin, 1961). Evidently, punishment, so employed, can functionally operate as a *secondary reinforcer,* or as a cue for reward, or as an arouser.

5. Punishments become extremely effective when the response-suppression period is tactically used as an aid to the reinforcement of new responses that are topographically *incompatible* with the punished one. When new instrumental acts are established which lead to the old goal (a new *means* to an old *end*), a punishment of very low intensity can have very long-lasting suppression effects. Whiting and Mowrer (1943) demonstrated this clearly. They first rewarded one route to food, then punished it. When the subjects ceased taking the punished route, they provided a new rewarded route. The old route was not traversed again. This reliable suppression effect also seems to be true of temporal, discriminative restraints on behavior. The suppression of urination in dogs, under the control of *indoor stimuli,* is extremely effective in housebreaking the dog, as long as urination is allowed to go unpunished under the control of *outdoor stimuli.* There is a valuable lesson here in the effective use of punishments in producing *impulse control.* A *rewarded alternative,* under discriminative control, makes passive avoidance training a potent behavioral influence. It can produce a highly reliable dog or child. In some preliminary observations of puppy training, we have noted that puppies raised in the lab, if punished by the swat of a newspaper for eating horsemeat, and rewarded for eating pellets, will starve themselves to death when

only given the opportunity to eat the taboo horsemeat. They eagerly eat the pellets when they are available.

It is at this point that we should look at the experiments wherein punishment appears to have only a temporary suppression effect. Most of these experiments offered the subject *no* rewarded alternative to the punished response in attaining his goal. In many such experiments, it was a case of take a chance or go hungry. Hunger-drive strength, under such no-alternative conditions, together with punishment intensity, are the crucial variables in predicting recovery from the suppression effects of punishment. Here, an interesting, yet hard-to-understand phenomenon frequently occurs, akin to Freudian "reaction formation." If a subject has been punished for touching some manipulandum which yields food, he may stay nearer to the manipulandum under low hunger drive and move farther away from it under high hunger drive, even though the probability of finally touching the manipulandum increases as hunger drive increases. This phenomenon is complex and needs to be studied in some detail. Our knowledge of it now is fragmentary. It was observed by Hunt and Schlosberg (1950) when the water supply of rats was electrified, and we have seen it occur in approach-avoidance conflict experiments in our laboratory, but we do not know the precise conditions for its occurrence.

Finally, I should point out that the attributes of effective punishments vary *across species* and *across stages in maturational development* within species. A toy snake can frighten monkeys. It does not faze a rat. A loud noise terrified Watson's little Albert. To us it is merely a Chinese gong.

I have sketchily reviewed some effects of punishment on *instrumental* acts established by *positive reinforcers*. We have seen that any result one might desire, from response enhancement and little or no suppression, to relatively complete suppression, can be obtained with our current knowledge of appropriate experimental conditions. Now let us look at the effects of punishment on *consummatory acts*. Here, the data are, to me, surprising. One would think that consummatory acts, often being of biological significance for the survival of the individual and the species, would be highly resistant to suppression by punishment. The *contrary* appears to be so. Male sexual behavior may be seriously suppressed by weak punishment (Beach, Conovitz, Steinberg, & Goldstein, 1956; Gantt, 1944). Eating in dogs and cats can be permanently suppressed by a moderate shock delivered through the feet or through the food dish itself (Lichtenstein, 1950; Masserman, 1943). Such suppression effects can lead to fatal self-starvation. A toy snake presented to a spider monkey while he is eating can result in self-starvation (Masserman & Pechtel, 1953).

The interference with consummatory responses by punishment needs a great deal of investigation. Punishment seems to be especially effective in breaking up this class of responses, and one can ask *why*, with some profit. Perhaps the intimate temporal connection between drive, incentive, and punishment results in drive or incentive becoming conditioned-stimulus (CS) patterns for aversive emotional reactions when consummatory acts are punished. Perhaps this interferes with vegetative activity: i.e., does it "kill the appetite" in a hungry subject? But, one may ask why the same punisher might not appear to be as effective when made contingent on an *instrumental* act as contrasted with a consummatory act. Perhaps the nature of operants is such that they are separated in time and space and response topography from consummatory behavior and positive incentive stimuli, so that appetitive reactions are not clearly present during punishment for operants. We do not know enough yet about such matters, and speculation about it is still fun.

Perhaps the most interesting parametric variation one can study, in experiments on the effects of punishment on consummatory acts, is the *temporal order* of rewards and punishments. If we hold hunger drive constant, shock-punishment intensity constant, and food-reward amounts constant, a huge differential effect can be obtained when we reverse the order of reward and punishment. If we train a cat to approach a food cup, its behavior in the experimental setting will become quite stereotyped. Then, if we introduce shock to the cat's feet while it is eating, the cat will vocalize, retreat, and show fear reactions. It will be slow to recover its eating behavior in this situation. Indeed, as Masserman (1943) has shown, such a procedure is likely, if repeated a few times, to lead to self-starvation. Lichtenstein (1950) showed the same phenomenon in dogs. Contrast this outcome with that found when the temporal order of food and shock is *reversed*. We now use shock as a discriminative stimulus to signalize the availability of food. When the cat is performing well, the shock may produce eating with a latency of less than 5 seconds. The subject's appetite does not seem to be disturbed. One cannot imagine a more dramatic difference than that induced by reversing the temporal order of reward and punishment (Holz & Azrin, 1962; Masserman, 1943).

Thus, the effects of punishment are partly determined by those events that directly precede it and those that directly follow it. A punishment is not just a punishment. It is an event in a temporal and spatial flow of stimulation and behavior, and its effects will be produced by its temporal and spatial point of insertion in that flow.

I have hastily surveyed some of the effects of punishment when it has been made contingent either on rewarded *operants* and instrumental acts or on *consummatory* acts. A third class of behaviors, closely related to consummatory acts, but yet a little different, are *instinctive act sequences:* the kinds of complex, innately governed behaviors which the ethologists study, such as nest building in birds. There has been little adequate experimentation, to my knowledge, on the effects of punishment on such innate behavior sequences. There are, however, some hints of interesting things to come. For example, sometimes frightening events will produce what the ethologists call displacement reactions—the expression of an inappropriate behavior pattern of an innate sort. We need to experiment with such phenomena in a systematic fashion. The best example I could find of this phenomenon is the imprinting of birds on moving objects, using the locomotor following response as an index. Moltz, Rosenblum, and Halikas (1959), in one experiment, and Kovach and Hess (1963; see also Hess, 1959a, 1959b) in another, have shown that the punishment of such imprinted behavior sometimes depresses its occurrence. However, if birds are punished prior to the presentation of an imprinted object, often the following response will be energized. It is hard to understand what this finding means, except that punishment can either arouse or inhibit such behavior, depending on the manner of presentation of punishment. The suggestion is that imprinting is partially a function of fear or distress. The effectiveness of punishment also is found to be related to the critical period for imprinting (Kovach & Hess, 1963).

However, the systematic study of known punishment parameters as they affect a wide variety of complex sequences of innate behaviors is yet to be carried out. It would appear to be a worthwhile enterprise, for it is the type of work which would enable us to make a new attack on the effects of experience on innate behavior patterns. Ultimately the outcomes of such experiments *could* affect psychoanalytic conceptions of the effects of trauma on impulses of an innate sort.[3]

A fourth class of behavior upon which punishment can be made contingent, is the simple, discrete reflex. For example, what might happen if a conditioned or an unconditioned knee jerk were punished? We are completely lacking in information on this point. Can subjects be trained to inhibit reflexes under aversive motivation? Or does such motivation sensitize and enhance reflexes? Some simple experiments are appropriate, but I was unable to find them in the published work I read.

A fifth class of behavior, upon which punishment can be made contingent, is behavior *previously established by punishment procedures*: in other words, the effect of passive avoidance training on existing, active avoidance learned responses. This use of punishment produces an unexpected outcome. In general, if the same noxious stimulus is used to punish a response as was used to establish it in the first place, the response becomes strengthened during initial applications of punishment. After several such events, however, the response may weaken, but not always. The similarity of the noxious stimulus used for active avoidance training to that used for punishment of the established avoidance response can be of great importance. For example, Carlsmith (1961) has shown that one can increase resistance to extinction by using the same noxious stimuli for both purposes and yet decrease resistance to extinction by using equally noxious, but discriminatively different, punishments. He trained some rats to run in order to avoid shock, then punished them during extinction by blowing a loud horn. He trained other rats to run in order to avoid the loud horn, then during extinction he punished them by shocking them for running. In two control groups, the punisher stimulus and training stimulus were the same. The groups which were trained and then punished by different noxious stimuli extinguished more rapidly during punishment than did the groups in which the active avoidance training unconditioned stimulus (US) was the same as the passive avoidance training US. Thus, punishment for responses established originally by punishment may be ineffective in eliminating the avoidance responses they are supposed to eliminate. Indeed, the punishment may strengthen the responses. We need to know more about this puzzling phenomenon. It is interesting to me that in Japan, Imada (1959) has been systematically exploring shock intensity as it affects this phenomenon.

Our quick survey of the effects of punishment on five classes of responses revealed a wide variety of discrepant phenomena. Thus, to predict in even the grossest way the action of punishment on a response, one has to know *how* that particular response was originally inserted in the subject's response repertoire. Is the response an instrumental one which was strengthened by reward? Is it instead of consummatory response? Is it an innate sequential response pattern? Is it a discrete reflex? Was it originally established by means of punishment? *Where,* temporally, in a behavior sequence, was the punishment used? How *intense* was it? These are but a few of the relevant, critical questions, the answers to which are necessary in order for us to make reasonable predictions about the effects of punishment. Thus, to conclude, as some psychologists have, that the punishment procedure is typically either effective or ineffective, typically either a temporary suppressor or a permanent one, is to oversimplify irresponsibly a complex area of scientific knowledge, one still containing a myriad of intriguing problems for experimental attack.

Yet, the complexities involved in ascertaining the effects of punishment on behavior *need not* be a bar to useful speculation ultimately leading to experimentation of a fruitful sort. The complexities should, however, dictate a great deal of caution in making dogmatic statements about whether punishment is effective or ineffective as a behavioral influence, or whether it is good or bad. I do *not* wish to do that. I would like now to speculate about the data-oriented theories, rather than support or derogate the dogmas and the social philosophies dealing with punishment. I will get to the dogmas later.

THEORY

Here is a theoretical approach that, for me, has high pragmatic value in stimulating new lines of experimentation. Many psychologists today consider the punishment procedure to be a special case of avoidance training, and the resultant learning processes to be theoretically identical in nature. Woodworth and Schlosberg (1954) distinguish the two training procedures, *"punishment for action"* from *"punishment for inaction,"* but assume that the same theoretical motive, a "positive incentive value of safety" can explain the learning produced by both procedures. Dinsmoor (1955) argues that the facts related to both procedures are well explained by simple stimulus-response (S-R) principles of avoidance learning. He says:

> If we punish the subject for making a given response or sequence of responses—that is, apply aversive stimulation, like shock—the cues or discriminative stimuli for this response will correspond to the warning signals that are typically used in more direct studies of avoidance training. By his own response to these stimuli, the subject himself produces the punishing stimulus and pairs or correlates it with these signals. As a result, they too become aversive. In the meantime, any variations in the subject's behavior that interfere or conflict with the chain of reactions leading to the punishment delay the occurrence of the final response and the receipt of the stimulation that follows it. These variations in behavior disrupt the discriminative stimulus pattern for the continuation of the punished chain, changing the current stimulation from an aversive to a nonaversive compound; they are conditioned, differentiated, and maintained by the reinforcing effects of the change in stimulation [p. 96].

The foci of the Dinsmoor analysis are the processes whereby: (a) discriminative stimuli become aversive, and (b) instrumental acts are reinforced. He stays at the quasi-descriptive level. He uses a peripheralistic, S-R analysis, in which response-produced proprioceptive stimuli and exteroceptive stimuli serve to hold behavior chains together. He rejects, as unnecessary, concepts such as fear or anxiety, in explaining the effectiveness of punishment.

Mowrer (1960) also argues that the facts related to the two training procedures are explained by a common set of principles, but Mowrer's principles are somewhat different than those of either Woodworth and Schlosberg, or Dinsmoor, cited above. Mowrer says:

> In both instances, there is fear conditioning; and in both instances a way of behaving is found which eliminates or controls the fear. The only important distinction, it seems is that the stimuli to which the fear gets connected are different. In so-called punishment, these stimuli are produced by (correlated with) the behavior, or response, which we wish to block; whereas, in so-called avoidance learning, the fear-arousing stimuli are not response-produced—they are, so to say, extrinsic rather than intrinsic, independent rather than response-dependent. But in both cases there is avoidance and in both cases there is its antithesis, punishment; hence the impropriety of referring to the one as "punishment" and to the other as "avoidance learning." Obviously precision and clarity of understanding are better served by the alternative terms here suggested, namely, passive avoidance learning and active avoidance learning, respectively. . . . But, as we have seen, the two phenomena involve exactly the same basic principles of fear conditioning and of the reinforcement of whatever action (or inaction) eliminates the fear [pp. 31–32].

I like the simple beauty of each of the three unifying positions; what holds for punishment and its action on behavior should hold also for escape and avoidance training, and vice versa. Generalizations about one process should tell us something about the other. New experimental relationships discovered in the one experimental setting should tell us how to predict a new empirical event in the other experimental setting. A brief discussion of a few selected examples can illustrate this possibility.

APPLICATIONS OF THEORY

I use a case in point stemming from work done in our own laboratory. It gives us new hints about some hidden sources of effectiveness of punishment. Remember, for the sake of argument, that we are assuming many important similarities to exist between active and passive avoidance-learning processes. Therefore, we can look at active avoidance learning as a theoretical device to suggest to us new, unstudied variables pertaining to the effectiveness of punishment.

Turner and I have recently published an extensive monograph (1962) on human traumatic avoidance learning. Our experiments showed that when a very reflexive, short-latency, skeletal response, such as a toe twitch, was used as an escape and avoidance response, grave difficulties in active avoidance learning were experienced by the subject. Experimental variations which tended to render the escape responses more emitted, more deliberate, more voluntary, more operant, or less reflexive, tended also to render the avoidance responses easier to learn. Thus, when a subject was required to move a knob in a slot in order to avoid shock, learning was rapid, in contrast to the many failures to learn with a toe-flexion avoidance response.

There are descriptions of this phenomenon already available in several published experiments on active avoidance learning, but their implications have not previously been noted. When Schlosberg (1934) used for the avoidance response a highly reflexive, short-latency, paw-flexion response in the rat, he found active avoidance learning to be unreliable, unstable, and quick to extinguish. Whenever the rats made active avoidance flexions, a decrement in response strength ensued. When the rats were shocked on several escape trials, the avoidance response tended to reappear for a few trials. Thus, learning to avoid was a tortuous, cyclical process, never exceeding 30% success. Contrast these results with the active avoidance training of nonreflexive, long-latency operants, such as rats running in Hunter's (1935) circular maze. Hunter found that the occurrence of avoidance responses tended to produce more avoidance responses. Omission of shock seemed to reinforce the avoidance running response. Omission of shock seemed to extinguish the avoidance paw flexion. Clearly the operant-respondent distinction has predictive value in active avoidance learning.

The same trend can be detected in experiments using dogs as subjects. For example, Brogden (1949), using the forepaw-flexion response, found that meeting a 20/20 criterion of avoidance learning was quite difficult. He found that 30 dogs took from approximately 200–600 trials to reach the avoidance criterion. The response used was, in our language, highly reflexive—it was totally elicited by the shock on escape trials with a very short latency, approximately .3 second. Compare, if you will, the learning of active avoidance by dogs in the shuttle box with that found in the forelimb-flexion experiment. In the shuttle box, a large number of dogs were able to embark on their criterion trials after 5–15 active avoidance-training trials. Early escape response latencies were long. Resistance to extinction is, across these two types of avoidance responses, inversely related to trials needed for a subject to achieve criterion. Conditions leading to quick acquisition are, in this case, those conducive to slow extinction. Our conclusion, then, is that high-probability, short-latency, *respondents* are not as good as medium-probability, long-latency operants when they are required experimentally to function as active avoidance responses. This generalization seems to hold for rats, dogs, and college students.

How can we make the inferential leap from such findings in active avoidance training to possible variations in punishment experiments? It is relatively simple to generalize across the two kinds of experiments in the case of CS-US interval, US intensity, and CS duration. But the inferential steps are not as obvious in the case of the operant-respondent distinction. So I will trace out the logic in some detail. If one of the major effects of punishment is to motivate or elicit new behaviors, and reinforce them through removal of punishment, and thus, as Dinsmoor describes, establish avoidance responses incompatible with a punished response, how does the operant-respondent distinction logically enter? Here, Mowrer's two-process avoidance-learning theory can suggest a possible answer. Suppose, for example, that a hungry rat has been trained to lever press for food and is performing at a stable rate. Now we make a short-duration, high-intensity pulse of shock contingent upon the bar press. The pulse elicits a startle pattern that produces a release of the lever in .2 second, and the shock is gone. The rat freezes for a few seconds, breathing heavily, and he urinates and defecates. It is our supposition that a conditioned emotional reaction (CER) is thereby established, with its major stimulus control coming from the sight of the bar, the touch of the bar, and proprioceptive stimuli aroused by the lever-press movements themselves. This is, as Dinsmoor describes it, the development of acquired aversiveness of stimuli; or, as Mowrer describes it, the acquisition of conditioned fear reactions. Therefore, Pavlovian conditioning variables should be the important ones in the development of this process. The reappearance of lever pressing in this punished rat would thus depend on the extinction of the CER and skeletal freezing. If no further shocks are administered, then the CER should extinguish according to the laws of Pavlovian extinction, and reappearance of the lever press should not take long, even if the shock-intensity level were high enough to have been able to produce active avoidance learning in another apparatus.

Two process avoidance theory tells us that something very important for successful and durable response suppression was missing in the punishment procedure we just described. What was lacking in this punishment procedure was a good operant to allow us to reinforce a reliable avoidance response. Because the reaction to shock was a respondent, was highly *reflexive,* and was quick to occur, I am led to argue that the termination of shock will *not* reinforce it, nor will it lead to stable avoidance responses. This conclusion follows directly from our experiments on human avoidance learning. If the termination of shock is made contingent on the occurrence of an operant, especially an operant topographically incompatible with the lever press, an active avoidance learning process should then ensue. So I will now propose that we shock the rat until he huddles in a corner of the box. The rat will have learned to *do* something arbitrary whenever the controlling CSs reappear. Thus, the rat in the latter procedure, if he is to press the lever again, must undergo *two* extinction processes. The CER, established by the pairing of CS patterns and shock, must become weaker. Second, the learned huddling response must extinguish. This combination of requirements should make the effect of punishment more lasting, if my inferences are correct. Two problems must be solved by the subject, not one. The experiments needed to test these speculations are, it would appear, easy to design, and there is no reason why one should not be able to gather the requisite information in the near future. I feel that there is much to be gained in carrying on theoretical games like this, with the major assumptions being (a) that active and passive avoidance learning are similar processes, ones in which the same variables have analogous effects, and, (b) that two processes, the conditioning of fear reactions, and the reinforcement of operants incompatible with the punished response, may operate in punishment experiments.

There is another gain in playing theoretical games of this sort. One can use them to question the usual significance imputed to past findings. Take, for example, the extensive studies of Neal Miller (1959) and his students, and Brown (1948) and his students, on gradients of approach and avoidance in conflict situations. Our foregoing analysis of the role of the operant-respondent distinction puts to question one of their central assumptions — that the avoidance gradient is unconditionally steeper than is the approach gradient in approach-avoidance conflicts. In such experiments, the subject is typically trained while hungry to run down a short alley to obtain food. After the running is reliable, the subject is shocked, usually near the goal, in such a way that entering the goal box is discouraged temporarily. The subsequent behavior of the typical subject consists of remaining in the start box, making abortive approaches to the food box, showing hesitancy, oscillation, and various displacement activities, like grooming. Eventually, if shock is eliminated by the experimenter, the subject resumes running to food. The avoidance tendency is therefore thought to have extinguished sufficiently so that the magnitude of the conceptualized approach gradient exceeds that of the avoidance gradient at the goal box. The steepness of the avoidance gradient as a function of distance from the goal box is inferred from the behavior of the subject *prior* to the extinction of the avoidance tendencies. If the subject stays as far away from the goal box as possible, the avoidance gradient may be inferred to be either displaced upward, or if the subject slowly creeps up on the goal box from trial to trial, it may be inferred to be less steep than the approach gradient. Which alternative is more plausible? Miller and his collaborators very cleverly have shown that the latter alternative is a better interpretation.

The differential-steepness assumption appears to be substantiated by several studies by Miller and his collaborators (Miller & Murray, 1952; Murray and Berkun, 1955). They studied the displacement of conflicted approach responses along both spatial and color dimensions, and clearly showed that the approach responses generalized more readily than did the avoidance responses. Rats whose running in an alley had been completely suppressed by shock punishment showed recovery of running in a similar alley. Thus the inference made was that the avoidance gradient is steeper than is the approach gradient; avoidance tendencies weaken more rapidly with changes in the external environmental setting than do approach tendencies. On the basis of the analysis I made of the action of punishment, both as a US for the establishment of a Pavlovian CER and as a potent event for the reinforcement of instrumental escape and avoidance responses, it seems to me very likely that the approach-avoidance conflict experiments have been carried out in such a way as to produce inevitably the steeper avoidance gradients. In other words, these experiments from my particular viewpoint have been inadvertently biased, and they were not appropriate for testing hypotheses about the gradient slopes.

My argument is as follows: Typically, the subject in an approach-avoidance experiment is trained to perform a specific sequence of responses under reward incentive and appetitive drive conditions. He runs to food when hungry. In contrast, when the shock is introduced into the runway, it is usually placed near the goal, and no specific, long sequence of instrumental responses is required of the subject before the shock is terminated. Thus, the initial strengths of the approach and avoidance instrumental responses (which are in conflict) are not equated by analogous or symmetrical procedures. Miller has thoroughly and carefully discussed this, and has suggested that the avoidance gradient would not have as steep a slope if the shock were encountered by the rat early in the runway in the case where the whole runway is electrified. While this comment is probably correct, it does not go far enough, and I would like to elaborate on it. I would argue that if one wants to study the relative steepnesses of approach and avoidance responses in an unbiased way, the competing instrumental responses should be established in a *symmetrical* fashion. After learning to run down an alley to food, the subject should be shocked near the goal box or in it, and the shock should not be terminated until the subject has escaped all the way into the start box. Then one can argue that two conflicting instrumental responses have been established. First, the subject runs one way for food; now he runs the same distance in the opposite direction in order to escape shock. When he stays in the start box, he avoids ˌshock entirely. Then the generalization or displacement of the approach and avoidance responses can be fairly studied.

I am arguing that we need *instrumental*-response balancing, as well as *Pavlovian*-conditioning balancing, in such conflict experiments, if the slopes of gradients are to be determined for a test of the differential-steepness assumption. Two-process avoidance-learning theory requires such a symmetrical test. In previous experiments, an aversive CER and its respondent motor pattern, not a well-reinforced avoidance response, has been pitted against a well-reinforced instrumental-approach response. Since the instrumental behavior of the subject is being used subsequently to test for the slope of the gradients, the usual asymmetrical procedure is, I think, not appropriate. My guess is that, if the symmetrical procedure I described is actually used, the slopes of the two gradients will be essentially the same, and the recovery of the subject from the effects of punishment will be seen to be nearly all-or-none. That is, the avoidance gradient, as extinction of the CER proceeds in time, will drop below the approach gradient, and this will hold all along the runway if the slopes of the two gradients are indeed the same. Using the test of displacement, subjects should stay in the starting area of a similar alley on initial tests and when they finally move forward they should go all the way to the goal box.

The outcomes of such experiments would be a matter of great interest to me, for, as you will read in a moment, I feel that the suppressive power of punishment over instrumental acts has been understated. The approach-avoidance conflict experiment is *but one* example among many wherein the outcome *may have been* inadvertently biased in the direction of showing reward-training influences to be superior, in some particular way, to punishment-training procedures. Now let us look more closely at this matter of bias.

LEGENDS

Skinner, in 1938, described the effect of a short-duration slap on the paw on the extinction of lever pressing in the rat. Temporary suppression of lever-pressing rate was obtained.

When the rate increased, it exceeded the usual extinction performance. The total number of responses before extinction occurred was not affected by the punishment for lever pressing. Estes (1944) obtained similar results, and attributed the temporary suppression to the establishment of a CER (anxiety) which dissipated rapidly. Tolman, Hall, and Bretnall (1932) had shown earlier that punishment could enhance maze learning by serving as a cue for correct, rewarded behavior. Skinner made these observations (on the seemingly ineffective nature of punishment as a response weakener) the basis for his advocacy of a positive reinforcement regime in his utopia, *Walden Two*. In *Walden Two*, Skinner (1948), speaking through the words of Frazier, wrote: "We are now discovering at an untold cost in human suffering—that in the long run punishment doesn't reduce the probability that an act will occur [p. 260]." No punishments would be used there, because they would produce poor behavioral control, he claimed.

During the decade following the publication of *Walden Two*, Skinner (1953) maintained his position concerning the effects of punishment on instrumental responses: Response suppression is but temporary, and the side effects, such as fear and neurotic and psychotic disturbances, are not worth the temporary advantages of the use of punishment. He said:

> In the long run, punishment, unlike reinforcement works to the disadvantage of both the punished organism and the punishing agency [p. 183].
>
> The fact that punishment does not permanently reduce a tendency to respond is in agreement with Freud's discovery of the surviving activity of what he called repressed wishes [p. 184].
>
> Punishment, as we have seen, does not create a negative probability that a response will be made but rather a positive probability that incompatible behavior will occur [p. 222].

It must be said in Skinner's defense, that in 1953 he devoted about 12 pages to the topic of punishment in his introductory textbook. Other texts had devoted but a few words to this topic.

In Bugelski's (1956) words about the early work on punishment: "The purport of the experiments mentioned above appears to be to demonstrate that punishment is ineffective in eliminating behavior. This conclusion appears to win favor with various sentimentalists [p. 275]." Skinner (1961) summarized his position most recently in this way:

> Ultimate advantages seem to be particularly easy to overlook in the control of behavior, where a quick though slight advantage may have undue weight. Thus, although we boast that the birch rod has been abandoned, most school children are still under aversive control—not because punishment is more effective in the long run, but because it yields immediate results. It is easier for the teacher to control the student by threatening punishment than by using positive reinforcement with its *deferred, though more powerful,* effects [p. 36.08, italics mine].

Skinner's conclusions were drawn over a span of time when, just as is the case *now,* there was no conclusive evidence about the supposedly more powerful and long-lasting effects of positive reinforcement. I admire the humanitarian and kindly dispositions contained in such writings. But the scientific basis for the conclusions therein was shabby, because, even in 1938, there were conflicting data which demonstrated the great effectiveness of punishment in controlling instrumental behavior. For example, the widely cited experiments of Warden and Aylesworth (1927) showed that discrimination learning in the rat was more rapid and more stable when incorrect responses were punished with shock than when reward alone for the correct response was used. Later on, avoidance-training experiments in the 1940s and 1950s added impressive data on the long-lasting behavioral control exerted by noxious stimuli (Solomon & Brush, 1956). In spite of this empirical development, many writers of books in the field of learning now devote but a few lines to the problem of punishment, perhaps a reflection of the undesirability of trying to bring satisfying order out of seeming chaos. In this category are the recent books of Spence, Hull, and Kimble. An exception is Bugelski (1956) who devotes several pages to the complexities of this topic. Most contemporary *introductory psychology* texts devote but a paragraph or two to punishment as a scientific problem. Conspicuously, George Miller's new book, *Psychology, the Science of Mental Life,* has no discussion of punishment in it.

The most exhaustive textbook treatment today is that of Deese (1958), and it is a thoughtful and objective evaluation, a singular event in this area of our science. The most exhaustive journal article is that by Church (1963), who has thoroughly summarized our knowledge of punishment. I am indebted to Church for letting me borrow freely from his fine essay in pre-publication form. Without this assistance, the organization of this paper would have been much more difficult, indeed.

Perhaps one reason for the usual textbook relegation of the topic of punishment to the fringe of experimental psychology is the wide-spread belief that punishment is unimportant because *it does not really weaken habits;* that it pragmatically is a *poor controller* of behavior; that it is extremely *cruel* and unnecessary; and that it is a technique leading to *neurosis* and worse, This legend, and it is a legend without sufficient empirical basis, probably arose with Thorndike (1931). Punishment, in the time of Thorndike, used to be called punishment, not passive avoidance training. The term referred to the use of noxious stimuli for the avowed purpose of discouraging some selected kind of behavior. Thorndike (1931) came to the conclusion that punishment did not really accomplish its major purpose, the destruction or extinction of habits. In his book, *Human Learning,* he said:

> Annoyers do not act on learning in general by weakening whatever connection they follow. If they do anything in learning, they do it indirectly, by informing the learner that such and such a response in such and such a situation brings distress, or by making the learner feel fear of a certain object, or by making him jump back from a certain place, or by some other definite and specific change which they produce in him [p. 46].

This argument is similar to that of Guthrie (1935), and of Wendt (1936), in explaining the extinction of instrumental acts and conditioned reflexes. They maintained that extinction was not the weakening of a habit, but the replacement of a habit by a new one, even though the new one might only be sitting still and doing very little.

When Thorndike claimed that the effects of punishment were indirect, he was emphasizing the power of punishment to evoke behavior other than that which produced the punishment;

in much the same manner, Guthrie emphasized the extinction procedure as one arousing competing responses. The competing-response theory of extinction today cannot yet be empirically chosen over other theories such as Pavlovian and Hullian inhibition theory, or the frustration theories of Amsel or Spence. The Thorndikian position on punishment is limited in the same way. It is difficult to designate the empirical criteria which would enable us to know, on those occasions when punishment for a response results in a weakening of performance of that response, whether a habit was indeed weakened or not. How can one tell whether competing responses have displaced the punished response, or whether the punished habit is itself weakened by punishment? Thorndike could not tell, and neither could Guthrie. Yet a legend was perpetuated. Perhaps the acceptance of the legend had something to do with the lack of concerted research on punishment from 1930–1955. For example, psychologists were not then particularly adventuresome in their search for experimentally effective punishments.

Or, in addition to the legend, perhaps a bit of softheartedness is partly responsible for limiting our inventiveness. (The Inquisitors, the Barbarians, and the Puritans could have given us some good hints! They did not have electric shock, but they had a variety of interesting ideas, which, regrettably, they often put to practice.) We clearly need to study new kinds of punishments in the laboratory. For most psychologists, a punishment in the laboratory means electric shock. A few enterprising experimenters have used air blasts, the presentation of an innate fear releaser, or a signal for the coming omission of reinforcement, as punishments. But we still do not know enough about using these stimuli in a controlled fashion to produce either behavior suppression, or a CER effect, or the facilitation of extinction. Many aversive states have gone unstudied. For example, conditioned nausea and vomiting is easy to produce, but it has not been used in the role of punishment. Even the brain stimulators, though they have since 1954 tickled brain areas that will instigate active escape learning, have not used this knowledge to study systematically the punishing effects of such stimulation on existing responses.

While the more humanitarian ones of us were bent on the

discovery of new positive reinforcers, there was no such concerted effort on the part of the more brutal ones of us. Thus, for reasons that now completely escape me, some of us in the past were thrilled by the discovery that, under some limited conditions, either a light onset or a light termination could raise lever-pressing rate significantly, though trivially, above operant level. If one is looking for agents to help in the task of getting strong predictive power, and strong control of behavior, such discoveries seem not too exciting. Yet, in contrast, discoveries *already have* been made of the powerful aversive control of behavior. Clearly, we have been afraid of their implications. Humanitarian guilt and normal kindness are undoubtedly involved, as they should be. But I believe that one reason for our fear has been the widespread implication of the *neurotic syndrome* as a *necessary* outcome of all severe punishment procedures. A second reason has been the general acceptance of the behavioral phenomena of rigidity, inflexibility, or narrowed cognitive map, as *necessary* outcomes of experiments in which noxious stimuli have been used. I shall question *both* of these conclusions.

If one should feel that the Skinnerian generalizations about the inadequate effects of punishment on instrumental responses are tinged with a laudable, though thoroughly incorrect and unscientific, sentimentalism and softness, then, in contrast, one can find more than a lurid tinge in discussions of the effects of punishment on the *emotional* balance of the individual. When punishments are asserted to be ineffective controllers of instrumental behavior, they are, in contrast, often asserted to be devastating controllers of emotional reactions, leading to neurotic and psychotic symptoms, and to general pessimism, depressiveness, constriction of thinking, horrible psychosomatic diseases, and even death! This is somewhat of a paradox, I think. The convincing part of such generalizations is only their face validity. There *are* experiments, many of them carefully done, in which these neurotic outcomes were clearly observed. Gantt's (1944) work on neurotic dogs, Masserman's (1943) work on neurotic cats and monkeys, Brady's (1958) recent work on ulcerous monkeys, Maier's (1949) work on fixated rats, show some of the devastating consequences of the utilization of punishment to control behavior. The side effects are frightening, indeed, and should *not* be ignored! But there *must be* some rules, some principles, governing the appearance of such side effects, for they *do not* appear in all experiments involving the use of strong punishment or the elicitation of terror. In Yates' (1962) new book, *Frustration and Conflict,* we find a thorough discussion of punishment as a creator of conflict. Major attention is paid to the instrumental-response outcomes of conflict due to punishment. Phenomena such as rigidity, fixation, regression, aggression, displacement, and primitivization are discussed. Yates accepts the definition of neurosis developed by Maier and by Mowrer: self-defeating behavior oriented toward no goal, yet compulsive in quality. The behavioral phenomena that reveal neuroses are said to be fixations, regressions, aggressions, or resignations. But we are not told the necessary or sufficient experimental conditions under which these dramatic phenomena emerge.

Anyone who has tried to train a rat in a T maze, using food reward for a correct response, and shock to the feet for an incorrect response, knows that there *is* a period of emotionality during early training, but that, thereafter, the rat, when the percentage of correct responses is high, looks like a hungry, well-motivated, happy rat, eager to get from his cage to the experimenter's hand, and thence to the start box. Evidently, merely going through conflict is not a condition for neurosis. The rat is reliable, unswerving in his choices. Is he neurotic? Should this be called subservient resignation? Or a happy adjustment to an inevitable event? Is the behavior constricted? Is it a fixation, an evidence of behavioral rigidity? The criteria for answering such questions are vague today. Even if we should suggest some specific tests for rigidity, they lack face validity. For example, we might examine *discrimination reversal* as a test of *rigidity.* Do subjects who have received reward for the correct response, and punishment for the incorrect response, find it harder to reverse when the contingencies are reversed, as compared with subjects trained with reward alone? Or, we might try a *transfer test,* introducing our subject to a new maze, or to a new jumping stand. Would the previously punished subject generalize more readily than one not so punished? And if he did, would he then be *less discriminating* and thus neurotic? Or, would the previously punished subject generalize poorly and hesitantly, thus being *too discriminating,* and thus neurotic, too? What are the criteria for behavioral *malfunction* as a consequence of the use of punishment? When instrumental responses are used as the indicator, we are, alas, left in doubt!

The most convincing demonstrations of neurotic disturbances stemming from the use of punishment are seen in Masserman's (Masserman & Pechtel, 1953) work with monkeys. But here the criterion for neurosis is *not* based on instrumental responding. Instead, it is based on emotionality expressed in consummatory acts and innate impulses. Masserman's monkeys were frightened by a toy snake while they were eating. Feeding inhibition, shifts in food preferences, odd sexual behavior, tics, long periods of crying, were observed. Here, the criteria have a face validity that is hard to reject. Clearly, punishment was a dangerous and disruptive behavioral influence in Masserman's experiments. Such findings are consonant with the Freudian position postulating the pervasive influences of traumatic experiences, permeating all phases of the affective existence of the individual, and persisting for long time periods.

To harmonize all of the considerations I have raised concerning the conditions leading to neurosis due to punishment is a formidable task. My guess at the moment is that neurotic disturbances arise often in those cases where *consummatory* behavior or *instinctive* behavior is punished, and punished under *nondiscriminatory* control. But this is merely a guess, and in order for it to be adequately tested, Masserman's interesting procedures would have to be repeated, using discriminative stimuli to signalize when it is safe and not safe for the monkey. Such experiments should be carried out if we are to explore adequately the possible effects of punishment on emotionality. Another possibility is that the number of rewarded behavior alternatives in an otherwise punishing situation will determine the emotional aftereffects of punishments. We have seen that Whiting and Mowrer (1943) gave their rats a rewarding alternative, and the resulting behavior was highly reliable. Their rats remained easy to handle and eager to enter the experimental situation. One guess is that increasing the number of behavioral alternatives leading to a consummatory response will, in a situation where only one behavior alternative is being punished, result in reliable behavior and the absence of neurotic emotional manifestations. However, I suspect that matters cannot be that simple. If our animal subject is punished for Response A, and the punishment quickly elicits Response B, and then Response B is 'quickly rewarded, we have the stimulus contingencies for the establishment of a masochistic habit. Reward follows punishment quickly. Perhaps the subject would then persist in performing the punished Response A? Such questions need to be worked out empirically, and the important parameters must be identified. We are certainly in no position today to specify the necessary or sufficient conditions for experimental neurosis.

I have, in this talk, decried the stultifying effects of legends concerning punishment. To some extent, my tone was reflective of bias, and so I overstated some conclusions. Perhaps now it would be prudent to soften my claims.[4] I must admit that all is not lost! Recently, I have noted a definite increase in good parametric studies of the effects of punishment on several kinds of behavior. For example, the pages of the *Journal of the Experimental Analysis of Behavior* have, in the last 5 years, become liberally sprinkled with reports of punishment experiments. This is a heartening development, and though it comes 20 years delayed, it is welcome.

SUMMARY

I have covered a great deal of ground here, perhaps too much for the creation of a clear picture. The major points I have made are as follows: *First, the effectiveness of punishment as a controller of instrumental behavior varies with a wide variety of kown parameters.* Some of these are: (a) intensity of the punishment stimulus, (b) whether the response being punished is an instrumental one or a consummatory one, (c) whether the response is instinctive or reflexive, (d) whether it was established originally by reward or by punishment, (e) whether or not the punishment is closely associated in time with the punished response, (f) the temporal arrangements of reward and punishment, (g) the strength of the response to be punished, (h) the familiarity of the subject with the punishment being used, (i) whether or not a reward alternative is offered during the behavior-suppression period induced by punishment, (j) whether a distinctive, incompatible avoidance response is strengthened by omission of punishment, (k) the age of the subject, and (l) the strain and species of the subject.

Second, I have tried to show the theoretical virtues of considering active and passive avoidance learning to be similar processes, and have shown the utility of a two-process learning theory. I have described some examples of the application of findings in active avoidance-learning experiments to the creation of new punishment experiments and to the reanalysis of approach-avoidance conflict experiments.

Third, I have questioned persisting legends concerning both the ineffectiveness of punishment as an agent for behavioral change as well as the inevitability of the neurotic outcome as a legacy of all punishment procedures.

Finally, I have indicated where new experimentation might be especially interesting or useful in furthering our understanding of the effects of punishment.

If there is one idea I would have you retain, it is this: Our laboratory knowledge of the effects of punishment on instrumental and emotional behavior is still rudimentary—much too rudimentary to make an intelligent choice among conflicting ideas about it. The polarized doctrines are probably inadequate and in error. The popularized Skinnerian position concerning the inadequacy of punishment in suppressing *instrumental* behavior is, if correct at all, only conditionally correct. The Freudian position, pointing to pain or trauma as an agent for the pervasive and long-lasting distortion of *affective* behavior is equally questionable, and only conditionally correct.

Happily, there is now growing attention being paid to the effects of punishment on behavior, and this new development will undoubtedly accelerate, because the complexity of our current knowledge, and the perplexity it engenders, are, I think, exciting and challenging.

Notes

1. This is a slightly revised text of the author's Presidential Address to the Eastern Psychological Association, New York City, April 1963. The research associated with this address was supported by Grant No. M-4202 from the United States Public Health Service.
2. Since the delivery of this address, several articles have appeared concern-

ing the punishment intensity problem. See especially Karsh (1963),
Appel (1963), and Walters and Rogers (1963). All these studies support
the conclusion that shock intensity is a crucial variable, and high intensities produce lasting suppression effects.

3. Since the delivery of this address, an article has appeared on this specific
problem. See Adler and Hogan (1963). The authors showed that the
gill-extension response of *Betta splendens* could be conditioned to a previously neutral stimulus by a Pavlovian technique, and it could also be
suppressed by electric-shock punishment. This is an important finding,
because there are very few known cases where the same response can be
both conditioned and trained. Here, the gill-extension response is typically elicited by a rival fish, and is usually interpreted to be aggressive or
hostile in nature.

4. Presidential addresses sometimes produce statements that may be plausible at the moment, but on second thought may seem inappropriate. In
contrast to my complaints about inadequate research on punishment and
the nature of active and passive avoidance learning are Hebb's (1960)
recent remarks in his APA Presidential Address. He said: "The choice
is whether to prosecute the attack, or to go on with the endless and
trivial elaboration of the same set of basic experiments (on pain avoidance for example); trivial because they have added nothing to knowledge
for some time, though the early work was of great value [p. 740]."

REFERENCES

Adler, N., & Hogan, J. A. Classical conditioning and punishment of an instinctive response in *Betta splendens*. *Anim. Behav.*, 1963, 11, 351–354.

Appel, J. B. Punishment and shock intensity. *Science*, 1963, 141, 528–529.

Azrin, N. H. Some effects of two intermittent schedules of immediate and non-
immediate punishment. *J. Psychol.*, 1956, 42, 8–21.

Azrin, N. H. Punishment and recovery during fixed-ratio performance. *J. exp.
Anal. Behav.*, 1959, 2, 301–305.

Azrin, N. H., & Holz, W. C. Punishment during fixed-interval reinforcement.
J. exp. Anal. Behav., 1961, 4, 343–347.

Beach, F. A., Conovitz, M. W., Steinberg, F., & Goldstein, A. C. Experimental
inhibition and restoration of mating behavior in male rats. *J. genet. Psychol.*,
1956, 89, 165–181.

Brady, J. V. Ulcers in "executive monkeys." *Scient. American*, 1958, 199, 95–103.

Brogden, W. J. Acquisition and extinction of conditioned avoidance response
in dogs. *J. comp. physiol. Psychol.*, 1949, 42, 296–302.

Brown, J. S. Gradients of approach and avoidance responses and their relation
to level of motivation. *J. comp. physiol, Psychol.*, 1948, 41, 450–465.

Bugelski, B. R. *The psychology of learning.* New York: Holt, 1956.

Carlsmith, J. M. The effect of punishment on avoidance responses: The use
of different stimuli for training and punishment. Paper read at Eastern
Psychological Association, Philadelphia, April 1961.

Church, R. M. The varied effects of punishment on behavior. *Psychol. Rev.*,
1963, 70, 369–402.

Deese, J. *The psychology of learning.* New York: McGraw-Hill, 1958.

Dinsmoor, J. A. Punishment: II. An interpretation of empirical findings.
Psychol. Rev., 1955, 62, 96–105.

Estes, W. K. An experimental study of punishment. *Psychol. Monogr.*, 1944, 57 (3, Whole No. 263) .

Gantt, W. H. *Experimental basis for neurotic behavior.* New York: Hoeber, 1944.

Guthrie, E. R. *The psychology of learning.* New York: Harper, 1935. (Rev. ed., 1952) .

Hebb, D. O. The American revolution. *Amer. Psychologist*, 1960, 15, 735–745.

Hess, E. H. Imprinting. *Science*, 1959, 130, 133–141. (a)

Hess, E. H. Two conditions limiting critical age for imprinting. *J. comp. physiol. Psychol.*, 1959, 52, 515–518. (b)

Holz, W., & Azrin, N. H. Discriminative properties of punishment. *J. exp. Anal. Behav.*, 1961, 4, 225–232.

Holz, W. C., & Azrin, N. H. Interactions between the discriminative and aversive properties of punishment. *J. exp. Anal. Behav.*, 1962, 5, 229–234.

Hunt, J. McV., & Schlosberg, H. Behavior of rats in continuous conflict. *J. comp. physiol. Psychol.*, 1950, 43, 351–357.

Hunter, W. S. Conditioning and extinction in the rat. *Brit. J. Psychol.*, 1935, 26, 135–148.

Imada, M. The effects of punishment on avoidance behavior. *Jap. Psychol. Res.*, 1959, 1, 27–38.

Kamin, L. J. The delay-of-punishment gradient. *J. comp. physiol. Psychol.*, 1959, 52, 434–437.

Karsh, E. B. Effects of number of rewarded trials and intensity of punishment on running speed. *J. comp. physiol. Psychol.*, 1962, 55, 44–51.

Karsh, E. B. Changes in intensity of punishment: Effect on runway behavior of rats. *Science*, 1963, 140, 1084–1085.

Kovach, J. K., & Hess, E. H. Imprinting: Effects of painful stimulation upon the following response. *J. comp. physiol. Psychol.*, 1963, 56, 461–464.

Lichtenstein, F. E. Studies of anxiety: I. The production of a feeding inhibition in dogs. *J. comp. physiol. Psychol.*, 1950, 43, 16–29.

Maier, N. R. F. *Frustration: The study of behavior without a goal.* New York: McGraw-Hill, 1949.

Masserman, J. M. *Behavior and neurosis.* Chicago: Univer. Chicago Press, 1943.

Masserman, J. M., & Pechtel, C. Neurosis in monkeys: A preliminary report of experimental observations. *Ann. N. Y. Acad. Sci.*, 1953, 56, 253–265.

Miller, N. E. Liberalization of basic S-R concepts: Extensions to conflict behavior, motivation, and social learning. In S. Koch (Ed.) , *Psychology: A study of a science.* Vol. 2. *Sensory, perceptual, and physiological formulations.* New York: McGraw-Hill, 1959. Pp. 196–292.

Miller, N. E. Learning resistance to pain and fear: Effects of overlearning, exposure, and rewarded exposure in context. *J. exp. Psychol.*, 1960, 60, 137–145.

Miller, N. E., & Murray, E. J. Displacement and conflict-learnable drive as a basis for the steeper gradient of approach than of avoidance. *J. exp. Psychol.*, 1952, 43, 227–231.

Moltz, H., Rosenblum, L., & Halikas, N. Imprinting and level of anxiety. *J. comp. physiol. Psychol.*, 1959, 52, 240–244.

Mowrer, O. H. *Learning theory and behavior.* New York: Wiley, 1960.

Murray, E. J., & Berkun, M. M. Displacement as a function of conflict. *J. abnorm. soc. Psychol.*, 1955, 51, 47–56.

Schlosberg, H. Conditioned responses in the white rat. *J. genet. Psychol.*, 1934, 45, 303–335.

Skinner, B. F. *The behavior of organisms.* New York: Appleton-Century, 1938.

Skinner, B. F. *Walden Two.* New York: Macmillan, 1948.

Skinner, B. F. *Science and human behavior.* New York: Macmillan, 1953.

Skinner, B. F. *Cumulative record.* New York: Appleton-Century-Crofts, 1961.

Solomon, R. L. & Brush, F. S. Experimentally derived conceptions of anxiety and aversion. In M. R. Jones (Ed.), *Nebraska Symposium on Motivation: 1956.* Lincoln: Univer. Nebraska Press, 1956.

Storms, L. H., Boroczi, C., & Broen, W. E. Punishment inhibits on instrumental response in hooded rats. *Science,* 1962, 135, 1133–1134.

Storms, L. H., Boroczi, C., & Broen, W. E. Effects of punishment as a function of strain of rat and duration of shock. *J. comp. physiol. Psychol.,* 1963, 56, 1022–1026.

Thorndike, E. L. *Human learning.* New York: Appleton-Century-Crofts, 1931.

Tolman, E. C., Hall, C. S., & Bretnall, E. P. A disproof of the law of effect and a substitution of the laws of emphasis, motivation, and disruption. *J. exp. Psychol.,* 1932, 15, 601–614.

Turner, L. H., & Solomon, R. L. Human traumatic avoidance learning: Theory and experiments on the operant-respondent distinction and failures to learn. *Psychol. Monogr.,* 1962, 76 (40, Whole No. 559).

Walters, G. C., & Rogers J. V. Aversive stimulation of the rat: Long term effects on subsequent behavior. *Science,* 1963, 142, 70–71.

Warden, C. J., & Aylesworth, M. The relative value of reward and punishment in the formation of a visual discrimination habit in the white rat. *J. comp. Psychol.,* 1927, 7, 117–127.

Wendt, G. R. An interpretation of inhibition of conditioned reflexes as competition between reaction systems. *Psychol. Rev.,* 1936, 43, 258–281.

Whiting, J. W. M., & Mowrer, O. H. Habit progression and regression—a laboratory study of some factors relevant to human socialization. *J. comp. Psychol.,* 1943, 36, 229–253.

Woodworth, R. S., & Schlosberg, H. *Experimental psychology.* New York: Holt, 1954.

Yates, A. J. *Frustration and conflict.* New York: Wiley, 1962.

Secondary Reinforcement in Rats as a Function of Information Value and Reliability of the Stimulus[1]

M. DAVID EGGER and NEAL E. MILLER, *Yale University*

Although secondary reinforcement has been of major importance to behavior theory, especially in explanations of complex learning phenomena (e.g., Hull, 1943; Miller, 1951; Skinner, 1938), little is known about the conditions for its occurrence in any but the simplest situations. The first hypothesis explored in the experiments reported here is that in a situation in which there is more than one stimulus predicting primary reinforcement, e.g., food, the more informative stimulus will be the more effective secondary reinforcer. Further it is asserted that a necessary condition for establishing any stimulus as a secondary reinforcer is that the stimulus provide information about the occurrence of primary reinforcement; a redundant predictor of primary reinforcement should not acquire secondary reinforcement strength.

A possible situation in which to test this hypothesis is the following: a short stimulus always precedes the delivery of food. But it is made essentially redundant by being overlapped by a longer

Egger, M. D. & Miller, N. E. Secondary reinforcement in rats as a function of information value and reliability of the stimulus. *Journal of Experimental Psychology*, 1962, *64*, 97–104. Copyright 1962 by the American Psychological Association, and reproduced by permission.

stimulus of slightly earlier onset which is also invariably followed
by food. This situation is summarized in Fig. 1. The longer stimulus is labeled S_1 and the shorter, S_2. For an S trained with this
series of stimulus events, S_2 is a reliable but redundant, i.e., non-
informative, predictor of food. Hence, according to our hypothesis, S_1 should be an effective secondary reinforcer; S_2 should acquire little or no secondary reinforcing strength, even though
it is closer in time to the occurrence of food, and therefore in
a more favorable position than is S_1 on the gradient of delay of
reinforcement.

There is a way, however, to make S_2 informative. If S_1 occurs
a number of times without S_2, unaccompanied by the food pellet,
and randomly interspersed with occurrences of the stimulus sequence shown at the bottom of Fig. 1, then S_2, when it occurs, is
no longer redundant; for now S_2 is the only reliable predicator of

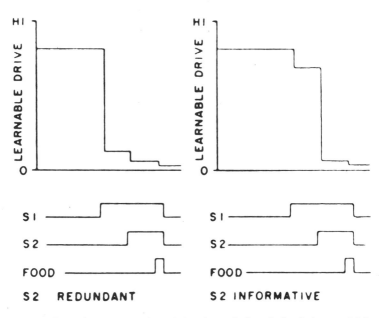

Fig. 1.   Schematic representation of the theoretical analysis of the two Main
Experiment groups according to a strict interpretation of the drive-reduction
hypothesis.

food. Thus, it is predicted that for a group of rats who receive the stimulus sequence depicted in Fig. 1 interspersed with occurrences of S_1 alone, S_2 will be a considerably more effective secondary reinforcer than for the group of rats who receive only the stimulus sequence depicted in Fig. 1.

It should be noted that both groups will receive exactly the same number of pairings of S_2 with food and in exactly the same immediate stimulus context, so that if a difference were found between the groups in the secondary reinforcing value of S_2, it could not be due to simple patterning, stimulus-generalization decrement, or differences in association with food.

Our predicted results would be compatible with a strict interpretation of the drive-reduction hypothesis of reinforcement (Miller, 1959). Such a theoretical analysis is represented schematically in the upper portion of Fig. 1. According to the drive-reduction hypothesis, a stimulus acquires secondary reinforcing value by acquiring the ability to elicit a drive-reducing response. The left side of Fig. 1 illustrates that if most of the learnable drive already has been reduced by S_1, little drive-reduction remains to be conditioned to S_2. On the other hand, if S_1 sometimes fails to predict food, some of the conditioned drive-reduction to it should extinguish. Hence, as is depicted on the right side of Fig. 1, more of the drive-reduction should occur to, and be conditioned to, S_2.

From Fig. 1, one can also see that the drive-reduction analysis also demands that the secondary reinforcing value of S_1 should be greater when it is a reliable predictor (making S_2 redundant) than when it is an unreliable predictor (making S_2 informative). Thus we are led to our second hypothesis, namely, that in a situation in which a predictor of primary reinforcement exists which is both reliable and informative, this predictor should become a more effective secondary reinforcer than an unreliable predictor. Note that here we predict the opposite of a partial-reinforcement effect, which would be expected to increase the resistance to extinction of the unreliable predictor, that is, the stimulus which had been paired with food only part of the time. In any prolonged test for secondary reinforcement, this increased resistance to extinction should show up as a greater total secondary-reinforcing effect.

Method

Subjects. The Ss were 88 male rats of the Sprague-Dawley strain who were approximately 90 days old at the beginning of their experimental training. Owing to deaths and equipment failures, the data from 4 Ss were lost, and the data from another 4, selected at random, were discarded in order to have equal sized groups for an analysis of variance. The Ss, fed once daily following the experimental session, were maintained at approximately 80 percent of their ad lib. weight.

Apparatus. The apparatus consisted of two identical Skinner boxes, 19 in. long, 8 in. wide, and 6¾ in. high (inside dimensions). The floors of the boxes consisted of six ½ in. diameter rods running parallel to the side containing the Plexiglas door. Each box was enclosed in a large, light-proof, sound-deadened crate into which a stream of air was piped for ventilation and masking noise. Inside each of the Skinner boxes were two lights, one located 2 in. above the food cup, another located in the middle of the long back wall, opposite the Plexiglas door. The food cup was in the center of the front, 8-in. wall; the bar, a bent steel strip 1½ in. wide, protruded ½ in. into the inner chamber of the box. The entire bar assembly was removable and, when withdrawn, its opening was sealed with a metal panel. The bar was located to the right of and slightly above the food cup. A downward force of at least 12 gm. on the bar activated a microswitch normally connected in the circuit of a Gerbrands feeder which delivered a standard .045-gm. Noyes pellet into the food cup. A loudspeaker was located 3 in. behind and slightly to the left of the front wall of the Skinner box. Both flashing lights (12 per sec.) and tones (750 cps) were used as stimuli.

Procedure. All training sessions lasted 25 min. per day. During the first three sessions, Ss were magazine-trained in the absence of the bar. Then the bar was inserted, and, for two sessions, each bar press was followed by a pellet of food. A few rats who did not spontaneously learn to press were given an extra remedial session during which bar pressing was "shaped." Over the next four sessions the required ratio of responses to reinforcements was gradually increased to 4:1.

Then, for the subsequent five sessions, the bar was removed, and Ss were randomly assigned to Group A (for whom S_2 was reliable but *redundant*) and Group B (for whom S_2 was reliable and *informative*). Group A received the following sequence of events during each of its five "stimulus-training" sessions: once every 56 sec. on the average, a pellet of food was delivered into the food cup. The pellet was inevitably preceded by 2 sec. of S_1 and 1½ sec. of S_2. Both stimuli overlapped the delivery of the food pellet by ¼ sec., and both terminated together.

Group B also received this stimulus sequence immediately preceding the delivery of the food pellet. But in addition, Group B Ss received aperiodically, interspersed with the stimulus-food sequence, 2 sec. of S_1 alone. The events for Group B occurred on the average of once every 30 sec.

For half the Ss in each group, S_1 was a flashing light and S_2 was a tone, and for the other half, the conditions were reversed: S_1 was a tone and S_2 was a flashing light.

During 5 days of such training, each group received 135 pairings of S_1 and S_2 with food, and Group B received in addition about 110 occurrences of S_1 alone. Thus for both groups S_2 was followed 100 percent of the time by food, while S_1 was followed by food 100 percent of the time for Group A, but only 55 percent of the time for Group B.

The above description of training applies to all but 16 Ss, 8 Group B and 8 Group A. For these Ss, training was exactly as described above except that the stimulus-food pairings occurred for both groups on the average of one every 75 sec. instead of 56 sec., and Group B received a stimulus event on the average of once every 15 sec. instead of 30 sec., so that S_1 was followed by food only 20 percent of the time for Group B. These 16 Ss were given seven 25-min. "stimulus-training" sessions. The data from these Ss were analyzed separately and not included in the overall analysis of variance.

Testing. On the day following the final stimulus-training session, Ss were tested as follows: the bar was reinserted and Test Session 1 began with each S pressing for food pellets on a fixed ratio of 3:1. The retraining presses continued until S had received 30 pellets. At this point the bar was disconnected and 10 min. of extinction ensued.

At the end of the 10 min., the bar was reconnected, not to the feeder, but to a timer which delivered on the same 3:1 schedule 1 sec. of whatever stimulus was being tested for secondary reinforcing strength. The test session continued until 25 min. had elapsed since the beginning of the extinction period, or until 10 min. after the first occurrence of a stimulus, whichever was longer.

In the foregoing procedure, relearning following experimental extinction was used as the measure of secondary reinforcing strength on the assumption that it would be more rapid and less variable than would de novo learning of the skill of pressing the bar. A preliminary study had validated this technique showing that in such a test more bar presses would occur when followed by a stimulus previously associated with food than when the stimulus had not been associated with food.

After an interval of 1 day, Test Session 2 was conducted, identical to the first, except that this time the stimulus delivered following the 10-min. extinction period was the opposite from that tested in Test Session 1: for half of the Ss, S_2 was tested in Test Session 1 and S_1 was tested in Session 2; for the other half of the Ss, trained and tested subsequent to the first half, the stimuli were tested in the opposite order.

For Ss tested first with S_2 and then with S_1, Test Session 3 followed another intervening day, this time with Ss pressing for S_2 again. Throughout the course of the 10-min. extinction and ensuing "pressing for stimuli" period, the cumulative total number of bar presses for each S was recorded each minute.

Response measures. The total number of bar presses in a 10-min. period following the first occurrence of the stimulus was the measure of secondary reinforcing strength. Since there were significant between-S and within-S correlations ($\tau_b = .53$; $\tau_w = .34$) of this measure with the total number of bar presses in the 10-min. extinction periods, this total number of bar presses in extinction was used as a control variable in analyses of covariance. (It should be noted that most of the bar presses during extinction occurred within the first 2–4 min. of the 10-min. extinction period.)

Furthermore, since it was found that in no case would analyses based only on data from Test Session 1 have led to any substantially different conclusions from those reported below, the means and results of analyses reported (unless otherwise noted) are based on combined data from Test Sessions 1 and 2.

Since by Test Session 3, there no longer appeared to be any differences between the experimental groups, the data from this session were not included in the final analyses.

Results

Overall analysis. Neither of the hypotheses being tested depended upon the significance of the main effects of the overall analysis, but instead upon comparisons between the means shown in specific subcells of Table 1. The marginal entries in Table 1 give the overall means for Groups A and B (rows), and for S_1 and S_2 (columns). The overall mean for each group is based on data from 32 Ss each tested with S_1 and with S_2; the overall mean for each stimulus position is based on data from all 64 Ss. As seen from an inspection of Tables 1 and 2, Group A responded significantly more than Group B and the position of S_1 was reliably more effective than that of S_2.

TABLE 1
Mean responses during 10 min. of extinction and 10 min. of "pressing for stimuli"

Group	S_1		S_2		$S_1 + S_2$
	Ext.	Pressing	Ext.	Pressing	
A	110.8	115.1	101.9	65.8	90.5
B	112.1	76.1	112.0	82.6	79.4
A + B		95.6		74.2	

Note.—Test Sessions 1 and 2 combined.

It should be noted that although the groups were identically treated in all other respects, the 32 Ss tested with S_1 first and S_2 second were run subsequent to the 32 Ss tested with S_2 first and with S_1 second. No significant differences between these groups existed in the control variable, total presses in 10 min. of extinction. Nor did an analysis of covariance reveal any significant effects of order of testing (O), or of the interaction of order of testing with experimental group (G), or with stimulus position (P) (see Table 2).

TABLE 2
Summary of analysis of variance and covariance: Test sessions 1 and 2 combined

Source	Analysis of Variance			Analysis of Covariance		
	df	MS	F	df	MS	F
Between S_s						
Experimental Group (G)	1	3,916.12	2.36	1	6,062.17	4.98*
Modality of S_1 (M)	1	7,938.00	4.79*	1	4,792.37	3.93
Order of S_1,S_2 (O)	1	435.13		1	709.44	
G x M	1	2,907.03	1.75	1	573.36	
G x O	1	2,329.03	1.41	1	50.93	
M x O	1	9.03		1	37.41	
G x M x O	1	1,624.50		1	1,382.64	1.14
Error (b)	56	1,657.19		55	1,218.04	$(r_b = .53)$
Within S_s						
Stimulus Position (P)	1	14,663.28	10.83**	1	12,168.39	9.97**
P x G	1	24,864.50	18.36***	1	21,613.81	17.71***
P x M = St	1	15,664.50	11.56**	1	10,316.32	8.45**
P x O = T	1	52,650.13	38.87***	1	1,594.90	1.31
P x G x M	1	87.78		1	546.78	
P x M x O	1	35.13		1	16.45	
P x G x O	1	5,330.28	3.94	1	3,168.95	2.60
P x G x M x O	1	5,781.27	4.27*	1	6,720.79	5.51*
Error (w)	56	1,354.57		55	1,220.64	$(r_w = .34)$

Note.—St = modality of stimulus tested; T = test session (1 or 2).

*$P < .05$.
**$P < .01$.
***$P < .001$.

52

Across all groups, the Ss responded more for the flashing lights than for the tones ($F = 8.45$; $df = 1/55$; $P < .01$, analysis of covariance).

Examination of the minute-by-minute response totals during the "pressing for stimuli" period revealed that the differences between groups tested at 10 min. had generally begun to appear after 3–5 min., and continued to increase out to 15 min., which was the longest period any S was permitted to bar press for stimuli during a given test session.

As expected from our hypotheses, the (P × G) interaction was highly significant ($F = 17.71$; $df = 1/55$; $P < .001$, analysis of covariance). Hence, we were justified in making within experimental group and stimulus position comparisons.

S_2: *Group B vs. Group A.* On the basis of our first hypothesis, we expected that Group B Ss, for whom S_2 was informative, should press more for S_2 than Group A Ss, for whom S_2 was redundant. The difference between the group means on the secondary reinforcing measure was in the predicted direction and significant beyond the .05 level ($F = 4.03$; $df = 1/56$). (The means are given in Table 1.) However, the effect was not statistically reliable in an analysis of covariance.

As mentioned above, 16 Ss, 8 each in Groups A and B, were trained with the number of occurrences of S_1 alone for Group B increased so that 80 percent of the stimulus events for Group B were unaccompanied occurrences of S_1. For these Ss, tested with S_2 in Test Session 1, the means on the secondary reinforcing measure were in the predicted direction, 97.5 vs. 88.0, but the difference was short of statistical significance. However, when these data were analyzed in an analysis of covariance and combined by means of a critical ratio test with the data discussed above, the predicted effect was significant beyond the .05 level. ($CR = 1.97$ if the data from these 16 Ss are combined with those from the 64 Ss tested with S_2 in Test Session 1 or Test Session 2; $CR = 2.02$ if the data are combined with those from the 32 Ss tested with S_2 in Test Session 1 only.)

S_1: *Group A vs. Group B.* Our second hypothesis predicted that S_1 would be a more effective secondary reinforcer for Group A, for whom it was reliable and informative, than for Group B,

for whom it was unreliable. This prediction was borne out by
the data beyond the .001 level ($F = 15.71$; $df = 1/55$; analysis
of covariance).

Group A: S_1 *vs.* S_2. As predicted from our first hypothesis,
S_1 was a much more effective secondary reinforcer than S_2 for
Group A. The difference between the means for these two stimulus positions, 115.1 vs. 65.8, was significant beyond the .001 level
($F = 26.35$; $df = 1/27$; analysis of covariance).

CONTROL EXPERIMENTS

Pseudoconditioned and unconditioned control. Fourteen Ss,
male albino rats, handled exactly as in the Main Experiment,
were trained in groups of 7 Ss each with stimulus sequences identical to those of Groups A and B, except that the stimuli were
never paired with the occurrence of food, which was delivered
at least 10 sec. after the occurrence of the stimuli. The two different patterns of stimuli used in training had no effect upon the
pseudoconditioned rate of bar pressing. The mean for the 14 Ss
with both test sessions combined with 64.3. These 14 Ss bar
pressed for the stimuli significantly less in both Test Session 1
($t = 3.41$; $df = 28$; $P < .005$) and Test Session 2 ($t = 2.72$;
$df = 28$; $P = < .02$) than did the 16 Group A Ss bar pressing
for the informative stimulus (S_1) in each of the Main Experiment test sessions. Hence, in a group predicted to show a large
secondary reinforcing effect, we did indeed find such an effect
produced by our training procedure.

Eight Ss were exposed to the stimuli during training exactly
as described above, except that the food pellets were eliminated
entirely. The unconditioned rate of pressing for the stimuli was
comparable to that of the pseudoconditioned group ($M = 73.4$).

The mean for the total group of pseudoconditioned and
unconditioned Ss with both test sessions combined was 67.6, indicating that the secondary reinforcing value of the redundant
stimulus for Group A of the Main Experiment ($M = 65.8$),
once the unconditioned rate of pressing for stimuli is taken into
account, was small, if not zero, as we predicted from our first
hypothesis. The estimates of the pseudoconditioned and unconditioned scores may be somewhat high, however, since these Ss

tended to have higher 10-min. extinction scores than did Ss of the Main Experiment.

Activation control. To test whether the effects studied in the Main Experiment were related to secondary reinforcement or only to a possible activation effect of a stimulus formerly associated with food (Wyckoff, Sidowski, & Chambliss, 1958), 10 additional Ss were trained exactly as in the Main Experiment, 5 as in Group A and 5 as in Group B. However, during the testing of these Ss, the bar remained nonfunctional once it was disconnected from the feeder. Each S was tested at the same time as an identically trained S used in the Main Experiment. The yoked Activation Control S received only the stimuli earned by his Main Experiment partner. If the Main Experiment S pressed for a stimulus within $7\frac{1}{2}$ sec. of a yoked Activation Control S's response, the stimulus for the Activation Control S was delayed so that it was not delivered until $7\frac{1}{2}$ sec. after his response. Hence spurious pairings of stimuli and pressing could not occur.

Thus, for these 10 Ss, any pressing which occurred during the retraining test period could have been due only to the activation effects of the stimuli plus remaining operant level; the possibility of secondary reinforcement was eliminated.

In Test Session 1, all 10 of the Activation Control Ss pressed less than did their secondary-reinforced partners ($P <$ .002, binomial test, two-tailed). In Test Session 2, 9 out of 10 pressed less than did their yoked partners ($P <$ .02, binomial test, two-tailed). Hence, we are quite certain that in the Main Experiment we were indeed studying secondary reinforcement.

Partial reinforcement effect control. In the Main Experiment we had found that in the presence of a reliable predictor (S_2), training with partial reinforcement of S_1 produced less total pressing for S_1 as a secondary reinforcer than did 100 percent reinforcement. This confirmed our hypothesis but was opposite to the effect of increased resistance to extinction usually found with partial reinforcement. In order to see whether the presence of the reliable predictor was indeed the crucial factor, we ran two special control groups of 8 Ss each, one with the usual partial reinforcement procedure and one with 100 percent reinforcement. These groups were identical in all respects to those of the

Main Experiment, except that the reliable predictor, S_2, was omitted. When these groups were tested, the partial reinforcement group tended to press more for the stimuli than did the continuous reinforcement group (though the difference between the group means, 128.6 vs. 115.6, was not statistically significant). However, the difference between these two groups was in the opposite direction and significantly different ($F = 5.71$; $df = 1/35$; $P < .025$) from the difference found between Test Session 1 means of the 32 Ss of the Main Experiment tested with S_1 during Test Session 1. Thus it appears that the presence of S_2, the reliable predictor of food, did play the crucial role in determining the direction of the results obtained in our tests of the secondary reinforcing value of S_1.

DISCUSSION

Our situation differed from those in which the effect of partial reinforcement on the establishment of secondary reinforcement has been studied (e.g., Klein, 1959; Zimmerman, 1957, 1959) in that during training all our Ss had a reliable predictor of food. The seemingly crucial importance of the presence or absence of a reliable predictor during training may help to explain the apparently conflicting results obtained from single-group vs. separate-group experimental designs in determining the effects of partial reinforcement on the strength of a secondary reinforcer (e.g., D'Amato, Lachman, & Kivy, 1958). It may be that partial reinforcement will increase resistance to extinction of a secondary reinforcer only if training occurs in the absence of a reliable predictor.

It should be noted that our formulation of the conditions necessary for the establishment of a secondary reinforcer is compatible with the well-known "discriminative stimulus hypothesis" of secondary reinforcement (Keller & Schoenfeld, 1950; Schoenfeld, Antonitis, & Bersh, 1950). Furthermore, our results with respect to S_2: Group B vs. Group A could perhaps be considered analogous to those reported by Notterman (1951) in studies using rats as Ss in both a Skinner box and a straight alley.

SUMMARY

Albino rats ($N = 88$, male) were trained to press a bar for food, then divided randomly into two groups and trained as follows for 135 trials in the same Skinner boxes with the bars removed: two stimuli, when paired, ended together and always preceded food. For Group A, the second, shorter stimulus (S_2) was always redundant because the first stimulus (S_1) had already given reliable information that food was to come. But for Group B, S_2 was informative, because for them S_1 also occurred sometimes alone without food.

After the training sessions, the bars were reinserted, bar pressing was retained with food pellets, extinguished, and then retrained again, this time using 1 sec. of one of the training stimuli as a secondary reinforcer in place of the food. The total number of bar presses in 10 min. following the first occurrence of the secondary reinforcing stimulus was used as the measure of secondary reinforcing strength. The testing procedure was repeated after 48 hr. using the other training stimulus as secondary reinforcer, so that all Ss were tested with both stimuli in a balanced sequence.

Control experiments were run to provide baseline levels for pseudoconditioned and unconditioned rates of pressing, and for any activating effect of the stimuli.

As predicted, S_2 was a stronger secondary reinforcer when it was informative than when it was redundant; S_1 was a more effective secondary reinforcer than S_2 in that group for which S_2 was a redundant predictor of primary reinforcement. In addition, S_1 was a more effective secondary reinforcer when it had been a reliable predictor of food.

NOTE

1. This study was supported by funds from Grant MY647 from the National Institute of Mental Health, United States Public Health Service. We wish to thank Elizabeth Sherwood for her assistance in running the animals.

A portion of the data reported in this paper was presented by Neal Miller in his Presidential Address to the American Psychological Association.

REFERENCES

D'Amato, M. R., Lachman, R., & Kivy, P. Secondary reinforcement as affected by reward schedule and the testing situation. *J. comp. physiol. Psychol.,* 1958, 51, 737–741.

Hull, C. L. *Principles of behavior.* New York: Appleton-Century, 1943.

Keller, F. S., & Schoenfeld, W. N. *Principles of psychology.* New York: Appleton-Century-Crofts, 1950.

Klein, R. M. Intermittent primary reinforcement as a parameter of secondary reinforcement. *J. exp. Psychol.,* 1959, 58, 423–427.

Miller, N. E. Learnable drives and rewards. In S. S. Stevens (Ed.), *Handbook of experimental psychology*. New York: Wiley, 1951. Pp. 435–472.

Miller, N. E. Liberalization of basic S-R concepts: Extensions to conflict behavior, motivation and social learning. In S. Koch (Ed.), *Psychology: A study of a science*. Vol. 2. New York: McGraw-Hill, 1959. Pp. 196–292.

Miller, N. E. Analytical studies of drive and reward. *Amer. Psychologist,* 1961, 16, 739–754.

Notterman, J. M. A study of some relations among aperiodic reinforcement, discrimination training, and secondary reinforcement. *J. exp. Psychol.,* 1951, 41, 161–169.

Schoenfeld, W. N., Antonitis, J. J., & Bersh, P. J. A preliminary study of training conditions necessary for secondary reinforcement. *J. exp. Psychol.,* 1950, 40, 40–45.

Skinner, B. F. *The behavior of organisms*. New York: Appleton-Century, 1938.

Wyckoff, L. B., Sidowski, J., & Chambliss, D. J. An experimental study of the relationship between secondary reinforcing and cue effects of a stimulus. *J. comp. physiol. Psychol.,* 1958, 51, 103–109.

Zimmerman, D. W. Durable secondary reinforcement: Method and theory. *Psychol. Rev.,* 1957, 64, 373–383.

Zimmerman, D. W. Sustained performance in rats based on secondary reinforcement. *J. comp. physiol. Psychol.,* 1959, 52, 353–358.

Alleviation of
Learned Helplessness in the Dog[1]

MARTIN E. P. SELIGMAN,[2] *Cornell University;*
STEVEN F. MAIER,[3] *University of Pennsylvania;* and
JAMES H. GEER, *State University of New York at Stony Brook*

Dogs given inescapable shock in a Pavlovian harness later seem to "give up" and passively accept traumatic shock in shuttlebox escape/avoidance training. A theoretical analysis of this phenomenon was presented. As predicted by this analysis, the failure to escape was alleviated by repeatedly compelling the dog to make the response which terminated shock. This maladaptive passive behavior in the face of trauma may be related to maladaptive passive behavior in humans. The importance of instrumental control over aversive events in the cause, prevention, and treatment of such behaviors was discussed.

This paper discusses a procedure that produces a striking behavior abnormality in dogs, outlines an analysis which predicts a method for eliminating the abnormality, and presents data which support the prediction. When a normal, naïve dog receives escape/avoidance training in a shuttlebox, the following behavior typically occurs: At the onset of electric shock, the dog runs frantically about, defecating, urinating, and howling, until it scrambles over the barrier and so escapes from shock. On the

Seligman, M. E. P., Maier, S. F. & Geer, J. H. Alleviation of learned helplessness in the dog. *Journal of Abnormal Psychology*, 1968, *73*, 256–262. Copyright 1968 by the American Psychological Association, and reproduced by permission.

next trial, the dog, running and howling, crosses the barrier more quickly, and so on until efficient avoidance emerges. See Solomon and Wynne (1953) for a detailed description.

Overmier and Seligman (1967) have reported the behavior of dogs which had received *inescapable* shock while strapped in a Pavlovian harness 24 hr. before shuttlebox training. Typically, such a dog reacts *initially* to shock in the shuttlebox in the same manner as the naïve dog. However, in dramatic contrast to the naïve dog, it soon stops running and remains silent until shock terminates. The dog does not cross the barrier and escape from shock. Rather, it seems to "give up" and passively "accept" the shock. On succeeding trials, the dog continues to fail to make escape movements and thus takes 50 sec. of severe, pulsating shock on each trial. If the dog makes an escape or avoidance response, this does not reliably predict occurrence of future responses, as it does for the normal dog. Pretreated dogs occasionally escape or avoid by jumping the barrier and then revert to taking the shock. The behavior abnormality produced by prior inescapable shock is highly maladaptive: a naïve dog receives little shock in shuttlebox training because it escapes quickly and eventually avoids shock altogether. A dog previously exposed to inescapable shock, in contrast, may take unlimited shock without escaping or avoiding at all.

Aside from establishing the existence of this interference effect, the experiments of Overmier and Seligman (1967) and Seligman and Maier (1967) have pointed to the variables controlling this phenomenon. Three hypotheses concerning the necessary conditions under which this phenomenon occurs have been disconfirmed, and one has been confirmed.

Overmier and Seligman (1967) tested two hypotheses which had been advanced to explain similar phenomena: a competing-motor-response hypothesis (Carlson & Black, 1960) and an adaptation hypothesis (MacDonald, 1946). The competing-response hypothesis holds that, in the harness, the dog learned some motor response which alleviated shock. When placed in the shuttlebox, the dog performed this response, which was antagonistic to barrier jumping, and thus was retarded in its acquisition of barrier jumping. This hypothesis was tested in the following way: Dogs, whose skeleto-musculature was paralyzed by curare (eliminating the possibility of the execution of overt motor responses), received inescapable shock in the harness. These dogs subsequently failed to escape in the shuttlebox. Dogs, paralyzed by curare, but not given inescapable shock, escaped normally. These results disconfirmed the competing-response hypothesis. The adaptation hypothesis holds that the dogs adapted to shock in the harness and therefore were not motivated enough to escape shock in the shuttlebox. Overmier and Seligman (1967) found that dogs failed to escape in the shuttlebox, even when the shock intensity was increased to a point just below which some dogs arc tctanized and thus physically prevented from jumping the barrier. These results are inconsistent with the adaptation hypothesis.

Seligman and Maier (1967) presented and tested an analysis of the phenomenon in terms of learned independence between shock termination and instrumental responding. Learning theory has traditionally stressed that two relationships between events produce learning: explicit contiguity (acquisition) and explicit dissociation (extinction). Seligman and Maier (1967) suggested that organisms are sensitive to a third relationship: independence between events. In particular, they proposed that, during inescapable shock in the harness, the dogs learned that shock termination occurred independently of their responses. Conventional learning theory allows that animals are sensitive to the conditional probability of shock termination given any specific response, and are also sensitive to the conditional probability of shock termination not given that response. In the special case in which these two probabilities are equal (independence), it is suggested that the animal *integrates* these two experiences. Thus, learning that shock termination is independent of a response reduces to learning that shock termination follows the response with a given probability, that shock termination occurs with a given probability if the response does not occur, and that these two probabilities do not differ. Such an integration could be called an expectation that shock termination is independent of responding. Seligman and Maier (1967) further proposed that one condition for the emission of active responses in the presence of electric shock is the expectation that responding leads to shock termination. In the absence of such an expectation, emitted responding should be less likely. When the dogs are subsequently placed in the shuttlebox, shock mediates the generalization of the initial learning to the new situation, and the probability of escape responding is thereby decreased.

This analysis was tested by varying the dogs' control over shock termination in their initial experience with shock. For one group (Escape), pressing panels located about 3 in. from either side of their heads terminated shock. Another group (Yoked) received the identical shock, but shock termination occurred independently of its responses (since shock duration was determined by the responses of the Escape group). The Escape group escaped normally in the shuttlebox, while the Yoked group failed to escape in the shuttlebox. This result confirmed the hypothesis that the learning of independence of shock termination and instrumental responding is a necessary condition for the interference effect. It disconfirmed a punishment interpretation of interference to the effect that the dogs failed to escape in the shuttlebox because they had been punished in the harness by the onset of shock for active responding. This experiment equated the groups for punishment by the onset of shock; the groups differed only with respect to the independence and nonindependence of shock termination and the head-turning response. This theoretical analysis, as noted below, predicts that failure to escape shock should be *eliminable* by compelling the dog to respond in a situation in which its responses terminate shock. Repeated exposure to the response-relief contingency should replace the expectation that shock termination is independent of responding with the expectation that responding produces shock termination.

Learned "helplessness" was defined as the learning (or perception) of independence between the emitted responses of the organism and the presentation and/or withdrawal of aversive events. This term is not defined as the occurrence of a subjective feeling of helplessness (although such a possibility is not excluded), nor is it to be taken as a description of the appearance of the organism. Such learning seems to be a necessary condition for the occurrence of the interference effect. That such learning occurs, moreover, seems to be a necessary premise for any systematic explication of the concept of "hopelessness" advanced by Mowrer (1960, p. 197) and by Richter (1957), the concept of "helplessness" advanced by Cofer and Appley (1964, p. 452), and the concept of "external control of reinforcement" of Lefcourt (1966).

Overmier and Seligman (1967) found that if 48 hr. elapsed between the inescapable shock in the harness and escape/avoidance training in the shuttlebox, dogs did not show the interference effect. Thus, although experience with inescapable trauma might be a necessary precondition for such maladaptive behavior, it was not a sufficient condition. However, Seligman and Maier (1967) found that the interference effect could be prolonged, perhaps indefinitely. If 24 hr. after inescapable shock in the harness the dog passively accepted shock in the shuttlebox, the dog again failed to escape after further rests of 168 hr. or longer. Thus, chronic failure to escape occurred when an additional experience with nonescaped shock followed the first experience.

Other work with infrahumans also suggests that lack of control (the independence of response and reinforcement) over the important events in an animal's environment produces abnormal behavior. Richter (1957) reported that wild rats rapidly gave up swimming and drowned when placed in tanks of water from which there was no escape. If, however, the experimenter (*E*) repeatedly placed the rats in the tank and then took them out, or if *E* allowed them repeatedly to escape from his grasp, they swam for approximately 60 hr. before drowning. Richter concluded that loss of hope was responsible for the sudden deaths. Maier (1949) reported that rats showed positional fixations when they were given insoluble discrimination problems (problems in which the responses of the rat and the outcome are independent). Making the problems soluble, alone, did not break up these fixations. But the "therapeutic" technique of forcing the rats to jump to the nonfixated side when the problem was soluble eliminated the fixations. Liddell (1956) reported that inescapable shocks produced experimental "neurosis" in lambs. Masserman (1943, pp. 79–85) reported that cats which instrumentally controlled the presentation of food were less prone to experimental neurosis than cats which did not have such control.

The maladaptive failure of dogs to escape shock resembles some human behavior disorders in which individuals passively

accept aversive events without attempting to resist or escape. Bettelheim (1960) described the reaction of certain prisoners to
the Nazi concentration camps:

> Prisoners who came to believe the repeated statements of the
> guards—that there was no hope for them, that they would never leave
> the camp except as a corpse—who came to feel that their environment
> was one over which they could exercise no influence whatsoever,
> these prisoners were in a literal sense, walking corpses. In the camps
> they were called "moslems" (*Müselmänner*) because of what we er-
> roneously viewed as a fatalistic surrender to the environment, as
> Mohammedans are supposed to blandly accept their fate.
> . . . they were people who were so deprived of affect, self-esteem,
> and every form of stimulation, so totally exhausted, both physically
> and emotionally, that they had given the environment total power
> over them [pp. 151–152].

Bleueler (1950, p. 40) described the passive behavior of
some of his patients:

> The sense of self-preservation is often reduced to zero. The patients
> do not bother anymore about whether they starve or not, whether
> they lie on a snowbank or on a red-hot oven. During a fire in the
> hospital, a number of patients had to be led out of the threatened
> area; they themselves would never have moved from their places;
> they would have allowed themselves to be burned or suffocated
> without showing an affective response.

It is suggested that an explanation which parallels the analysis of the interference effect in dogs may hold for such psychopathological behavior in humans. Consider an individual who
has learned that his responses and the occurrence and withdrawal of traumatic events are independent. If a necessary condition for the initiation of responding is the expectation that his
responses may control the trauma, such an individual should react passively in the face of trauma.

The time course of the interference effect found with dogs
suggests that such human disorders may also be subject to temporal variables. Experience with traumatic inescapable shock produces interference with subsequent escape learning. This interference dissipates over time. Traumatic events must *intervene*
if permanent failure to escape shock is to occur. This suggests
that one traumatic experience may be sufficient to predispose

an individual to future maladaptive behavior, producing, perhaps, a temporary disturbance which Wallace (1957) has called the "disaster syndrome." In order for this experience to be translated into a chronic disorder, however, subsequent traumatic events may have to occur.

Because the interference effect in dogs and these forms of human psychopathology may be acquired in similar ways, information about the modification of the interference effect may lead to insights concerning the treatment of such psychopathological behavior in humans. Two categories of treatment could be attempted: prevention or "immunization" against the effects of future inescapable shock (proactive), or modification of maladaptive behavior after inescapable shock has had its effect (retroactive). Seligman and Maier (1967) reported that prior experience with *escapable* shock immunizes dogs against the effects of later *inescapable* shock. Thus, preventive steps have been shown to be effective.

The above analysis of the interference effect predicts that by exposing a dog to the contingent relationship of shock termination and its responses the interference effect established by prior exposure to unavoidable shock should be eliminated. This experiment reports an elimination of learned "helplessness" in dogs that had chronically failed to escape from traumatic shock. Such retroactive treatment resembles the traditional treatment of human psychopathology more than does the preventive procedure.

METHOD

Subjects

The Ss were four mongrel dogs. They weighed 25–29 lb., were 15–19 in. high at the shoulder, and were housed in individual cages with food and water freely available. Each dog chronically failed to escape shock (see Procedure) as a result of receiving inescapable shock in Experiment I of Seligman and Maier (1967).

Apparatus

The apparatus is described fully by Overmier and Seligman (1967). In brief, it consisted of two separate units: a Pavlovian harness, in which initial exposure to inescapable shock occurred, and a dog shuttlebox, in which escape/avoidance training and modification of the failure to escape were carried out.

The unit in which each S was exposed to inescapable shock was a rubberized cloth hammock located inside a shielded white sound-reducing cubicle. The hammock was constructed so that S's legs hung down below his body through four holes. The S's legs were secured in this position, and S was strapped into the hammock. The S's head was held in position by panels placed on either side and a yoke between them across S's neck. Shock was applied from a 500-VAC transformer through a fixed resistor of 20,000 ohms. The shock was applied to S through brass-plate electrodes coated with electrode paste and taped to the foot-pads of S's hind feet. The shock intensity was 6.0 ma.

The unit in which S received escape/avoidance trials was a two-way shuttlebox with two black compartments separated by an adjustable barrier. Running along the upper part of the front of the shuttlebox were two one-way mirror windows, through which E could observe and which E could open. The barrier was set at S's shoulder height. Each compartment was illuminated by two 50-w. and one 7½-w. lamps. The CS consisted of turning off the four 50-w. lamps which resulted in a sharp decrease in illumination. The UCS was 4.5-ma. electric shock applied through the grid floors from a 500-VAC source. The polarity pattern of the grid bars was scrambled four times a second. Whenever S crossed from one side of the shuttlebox to the other, photocell beams were interrupted, and the trial was terminated. Latency of crossing was measured from CS onset to the nearest .01 sec. by an electric clock. Seventy decibels (SPL) white noise was present in both units.

Procedure

Inescapable shock exposure. Each S was strapped into the harness and given 64 trials of inescapable shock. The shocks were presented in a sequence of trials of diminishing duration. The mean intershock interval was 90 sec. with a 60–120 sec. range. Each S received a total of 226 sec. of shock.

Instrumental escape/avoidance training. Twenty-four hours after inescapable shock exposure, Ss received 10 trials of instrumental escape/avoidance training in the shuttlebox. The onset of the CS (dimmed illumination) initiated each trial, and the CS remained on until trial termination. The CS–UCS onset interval was 10 sec. If S crossed to the other compartment during the interval, the CS terminated, and no shock was presented. If S did not cross during the CS–UCS interval, shock came on and remained on until S crossed. If no response occurred within 60 sec. of CS onset, the trial was automatically terminated, and a 60-sec. latency was recorded. The average intertrial interval was 90 sec. with a 60–120 sec. range.

All four Ss failed to escape shock on each of the 10 trials. Thus each S took 500 sec. of shock during the first escape/avoidance session.

Testing for chronic failure to escape. Seven days later, Ss were again placed in the shuttlebox and given 10 further escape/avoidance trials. Again, each S failed to escape shock on every trial (although one S avoided shock once, on the fifth trial). By this time, each S was failing to make any escape movements and was remaining silent during shock on every trial. Previous work has shown that when a dog remains silent and fails to make escape movements during shock, this reliably predicts that the dog will continue to fail to escape and avoid.

Treatment. The attempt at behavioral modification consisted of two distinct phases: all Ss received Phase I; if Phase I succeeded, as it did with one of the four dogs, no further treatment was given, and "recovery" (see Recovery section below) was begun. The other three Ss received Phase II following Phase I.

Phase I: no barrier, calling. At intervals ranging from 4 to 25 days following the demonstration that the interference was chronic, Ss were again placed in the shuttlebox. The escape/avoidance contingencies used previously remained in effect during Phase I and II trials. The barrier dividing the two sides of the shuttlebox (formerly set at shoulder height) was removed. Thus in order to escape or avoid, S had only to step over the remaining 5-in. high divider. In addition, E opened the observation window on the side of the shuttlebox opposite the side S was on and called to S ("Here, boy") during shock and during the CS–UCS interval. The rationale for such treatment was to encourage S to make the appropriate response on its own, thus exposing itself to the response-reinforcement contingency. One

S responded to this treatment and began to escape and avoid. The remaining Ss then received Phase II.

Phase II: forced escape/avoidance exposure. Phase II began when it was clear that Phase I would not produce escape and avoidance in the remaining three Ss since they remained silent and motionless during Phase I. The S was removed from the shuttlebox, and two long leashes were tied around its neck. The S was put back into the shuttlebox, and escape/avoidance trials continued. The end of each leash was brought out at opposite ends of the shuttlebox. Thus, two Es were able to drag S back and forth across the shuttlebox by pulling one of the leashes. Phase II consisted of pulling S across to the safe side on each trial during shock or during the CS–UCS interval. A maximum of 25 Phase II trials per day were given. The rationale for Phase II was to force S to expose himself to the response-reinforcement contingency. Such "directive therapy" continued until S began to respond without being pulled by E.

Recovery. Following Phase II (for three dogs) and Phase I (for the other dog), each S received further escape/avoidance trials. The barrier height was gradually increased over the course of 15 trials until shoulder height had been reached. Ten further escape/avoidance trials were then given. The last five of these recovery trials (with the barrier at shoulder height) were administered from 5 to 10 days following the first five trials with the barrier at this height. This tested the durability of the recovery.

RESULTS

Figure 1 presents the results of this study. It is clear that the procedures employed in Phases I and II of treatment were wholly successful in breaking up the maladaptive failure to escape and avoid shock. With the single exception of one S on one trial, the dogs had not escaped or avoided the intense shock prior to treatment. This is indicated by the mean percentage of escape or avoidance responses present at or near zero during the pretreatment phase. Following Phase I (no barrier, calling) and Phase II (forced escape/avoidance exposure) of treatment, posttreatment recovery trials without forcing or calling were given to determine the effectiveness of the treatment. All Ss escaped or avoided on every recovery trial.

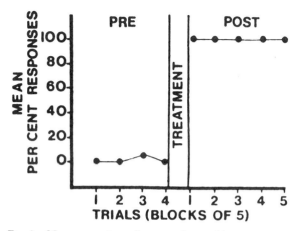

Fig. 1. Mean percentage of escape plus avoidance responses before treatment and during posttreatment recovery trials.

The behavior of one S was successfully modified by Phase I of treatment. After sporadic failures to escape shock during this phase, it began to escape and avoid reliably after 20 Phase I trials. With the barrier increased to shoulder height, it continued to avoid reliably. The other three dogs all responded to treatment in a fashion similar to one another: after failing to respond to Phase I, each of these dogs began to respond on its own after differing numbers of Phase II trials on which it had to be pulled to safety. One of the Phase II Ss required 20 forced exposures to escape and avoid in Phase II before it began to respond without being pulled; the other two required 35 and 50 such trials. During the course of Phase II trials, progressively less forceful pulls were required before S crossed to the safe side. With the barrier increased to shoulder height following Phase II, each S escaped and avoided efficiently. At this stage, the dogs responded like normal dogs at or near asymptotic avoidance performance.

DISCUSSION

The chronic failure of dogs to escape shock can be eliminated by physically compelling them to engage repeatedly in the response which terminates shock. Solomon, Kamin, and Wynne (1953) also attenuated maladaptive behavior in dogs by forcing them to expose themselves to the experimental contingencies. They reported that dogs continued to make avoidance responses long after shock was no longer present in the situation. A glass barrier, which prevented the dogs from making the response and forced them to "reality test," attenuated the persistent responding somewhat. Such "directive therapy" also is similar to Maier and Klee's (1945) report that abnormal positional fixations in rats were eliminated by forcing the rat to respond to the nonfixated side, and to Masserman's (1943, pp. 76–77) report that "neurotic" feeding inhibition could be overcome by forcing the cat into close proximity with food.

Seligman and Maier (1967) suggested that during its initial experience with inescapable shock, S learns that its responses are independent of shock termination. They further suggested that this learning not only reduces the probability of response initiation to escape shock, but also inhibits the formation of the response-relief association if S does make an escape or avoidance response in the shuttlebox. That the dogs escaped and avoided at all after being forcibly exposed to the response-relief contingency confirmed the suggestion that they had initially learned that their responses were independent of shock termination and that this learning was contravened by forcible exposure to the contingency. The finding that so many forced exposures to the contingency were required before they responded on their own (before they "caught on") confirmed the suggestion that the initial learning inhibited the formation of a response-relief association when the dog made a relief-producing response.

The perception of degree of control over the events in one's life seems to be an important determinant of the behavior of human beings. Lefcourt (1966) has summarized extensive evidence which supports this view. Cromwell, Rosenthal, Shakow, and Kahn (1961), for example, reported that schizophrenics perceive reinforcement to be externally controlled (reinforcement occurs independently of their responses) to a greater extent than normals. Such evidence, along with the animal data cited above, suggests that lack of control over reinforcement may be of widespread importance in the development of psychopathology in both humans and infrahumans.

In conclusion, one might speculate that experience with

traumatic events in which the individual can do nothing to eliminate or mitigate the trauma results in passive responding to future aversive events in humans. The findings of Seligman and Maier (1967) suggest that an individual might be immunized against the debilitating effects of uncontrollable trauma by having had prior experience with instrumental control over the traumatic events. Finally, the findings suggest that the pathological behavior resulting from inescapable trauma might be alleviated by repeated exposure of the individual to the trauma under conditions in which his responses were instrumental in obtaining relief. It has been demonstrated that normal escape/avoidance behavior can be produced in "passive" dogs by forcibly exposing them to relief-producing responses.

NOTES

1. This research was supported by grants to R. L. Solomon from the National Science Foundation (GB-2428) and the National Institute of Mental Health (MH-04202). The authors are grateful to him for his advice in the conduct and reporting of this experiment. The authors also thank J. P. Brady and J. Mecklenburger for their critical readings of the manuscript.
2. At the time this work was carried out, the first author was a National Science Foundation predoctoral fellow at the University of Pennsylvania.
3. National Institute of Mental Health predoctoral fellow.

REFERENCES

Bettelheim, B. *The informed heart.* New York: Free Press of Glencoe, 1960.

Bleueler, E. *Dementia praecox or the group of schizophrenics.* New York: International Universities Press, 1950.

Carlson, N. J., & Black, A. H. Traumatic avoidance learning: The effect of preventing escape responses. *Canadian Journal of Psychology,* 1960, 14, 21–28.

Cofer, C. N., & Appley, M. A. *Motivation: Theory and research.* New York: Wiley, 1964.

Cromwell, R., Rosenthal, D., Shakow, D., & Kahn, T. Reaction time, locus of control, choice behavior and descriptions of parental behavior in schizophrenic and normal subjects. *Journal of Personality,* 1961, 29, 363–380.

Lefcourt, H. M. Internal versus external control of reinforcement: A review. *Psychological Bulletin,* 1966, 65, 206–221.

Liddell, H. S. *Emotional hazards in animals and man.* Springfield, Ill.: Charles C. Thomas, 1956.

MacDonald, A. Effect of adaptation to the unconditioned stimulus upon the formation of conditional avoidance responses. *Journal of Experimental Psychology,* 1946, 36, 11–12.

Maier, N., & Klee, J. Studies of abnormal behavior in the rat: XVII. Guidance versus trial and error in the alteration of habits and fixations. *Journal of Psychology*, 1945, 19, 133–163.

Maier, N. R. F. *Frustration: The study of behavior without a goal*. New York: McGraw-Hill, 1949.

Masserman, J. H. *Behavior and neurosis*. Chicago: University of Chicago Press, 1943.

Mowrer, O. H. *Learning theory and behavior*. New York: Wiley, 1960.

Overmier, J. B., & Seligman, M. E. P. Effects of inescapable shock upon subsequent escape and avoidance responding. *Journal of Comparative and Physiological Psychology*, 1967, 63, 28–33.

Richter, C. On the phenomenon of sudden death in animals and man. *Psychosomatic Medicine*, 1957, 19, 191–198.

Seligman, M. E. P., & Maier, S. F. Failure to escape traumatic shock. *Journal of Experimental Psychology*, 1967, 74, 1–9.

Solomon, R. L., Kamin, L., & Wynne, L. C. Traumatic avoidance learning: The outcomes of several extinction procedures with dogs. *Journal of Abnormal and Social Psychology*, 1953, 48, 291–302.

Solomon, R. L., & Wynne, L. C. Traumatic avoidance learning: Acquisition in normal dogs. *Psychological Monographs*, 1953, 67 (4, Whole No. 354).

Wallace, A. F. C. Mazeway disintegration: The individual's perception of sociocultural disorganization. *Human Organization*, 1957. 16, 23–27.

Learning of Visceral
and Glandular Responses

NEAL E. MILLER, *Yale University*

There is a strong traditional belief in the inferiority of the autonomic nervous system and the visceral responses that it controls. The recent experiments disproving this belief have deep implications for theories of learning, for individual differences in autonomic responses, for the cause and the cure of abnormal psychosomatic symptoms, and possibly also for the understanding of normal homeostasis. Their success encourages investigators to try other unconventional types of training. Before describing these experiments, let me briefly sketch some elements in the history of the deeply entrenched, false belief in the gross inferiority of one major part of the nervous system.

HISTORICAL ROOTS AND
MODERN RAMIFICATIONS

Since ancient times, reason and the voluntary responses of the skeletal muscles have been considered to be superior, while emotions and the presumably involuntary glandular and visceral responses have been considered to be inferior. This invidious

Miller, N. E. Learning of visceral and glandular responses. *Science,* 1969, *163,* 434–445. Copyright 1969 by the American Association for the Advancement of Science.

73

dichotomy appears in the philosophy of Plato,[1] with his superior rational soul in the head above the inferior souls in the body below. Much later, the great French neuroanatomist Bichat[2] distinguished between the cerebrospinal nervous system of the great brain and spinal cord, controlling skeletal responses, and the dual chain of ganglia (which he called "little brains") running down on either side of the spinal cord in the body below and controlling emotional and visceral responses. He indicated his low opinion of the ganglionic system by calling it "vegetative"; he also believed it to be largely independent of the cerebrospinal system, an opinion which is still reflected in our modern name for it, the autonomic nervous system. Considerably later, Cannon[3] studied the sympathetic part of the autonomic nervous system and concluded that the different nerves in it all fire simultaneously and are incapable of the finely differentiated individual responses possible for the cerebrospinal system, a conclusion which is enshrined in modern textbooks.

Many, though not all, psychiatrists have made an invidious distinction between the hysterical and other symptoms that are mediated by the cerebrospinal nervous system and the psychosomatic symptoms that are mediated by the autonomic nervous system. Whereas the former are supposed to be subject to a higher type of control that is symbolic, the latter are presumed to be only the direct physiological consequences of the type and intensity of the patient's emotions.[4]

Similarly, students of learning have made a distinction between a lower form, called classical conditioning and thought to be involuntary, and a superior form variously called trial-and-error learning, operant conditioning, type II conditioning, or instrumental learning and believed to be responsible for voluntary behavior. In classical conditioning, the reinforcement must be by an unconditioned stimulus that already elicits the specific response to be learned; therefore, the possibilities are quite limited. In instrumental learning, the reinforcement, called a reward, has the property of strengthening any immediately preceding response. Therefore, the possibilities for reinforcement are much greater; a given reward may reinforce any one of a number of different responses, and a given response may be reinforced by any one of a number of different rewards.

Finally, the foregoing invidious distinctions have coalesced into the strong traditional belief that the superior type of instrumental learning involved in the superior voluntary behavior is possible only for skeletal responses mediated by the superior cerebrospinal nervous system, while, conversely, the inferior classical conditioning is the only kind possible for the inferior, presumably involuntary, visceral and emotional responses mediated by the inferior autonomic nervous system. Thus, in a recent summary generally considered authoritative, Kimble[5] states the almost universal belief that "for autonomically mediated behavior, the evidence points unequivocally to the conclusion that such responses can be modified by classical, but not instrumental, training methods." Upon examining the evidence, however, one finds that it consists only of failure to secure instrumental learning in two incompletely reported exploratory experiments and a vague allusion to the Russian literature.[6] It is only against a cultural background of great prejudice that such weak evidence could lead to such a wrong conviction.

The belief that instrumental learning is possible only for the cerebrospinal system and, conversely, that the autonomic nervous system can be modified only by classical conditioning has been used as one of the strongest arguments for the notion that instrumental learning and classical conditioning are two basically different phenomena rather than different manifestations of the same phenomenon under different conditions. But for many years I have been impressed with the similarity between the laws of classical conditioning and those of instrumental learning, and with the fact that, in each of these two situations, some of the specific details of learning vary with the specific conditions of learning. Failing to see any clear-cut dichotomy, I have assumed that there is only one kind of learning[7]. This assumption has logically demanded that instrumental training procedures be able to produce the learning of any visceral responses that could be acquired through classical conditioning procedures. Yet it was only a little over a dozen years ago that I began some experimental work on this problem and a somewhat shorter time ago that I first, in published articles,[8] made specific sharp challenges to the traditional view that the instrumental learning of visceral responses is impossible.

SOME DIFFICULTIES

One of the difficulties of investigating the instrumental learning of visceral responses stems from the fact that the responses that are the easiest to measure—namely, heart rate, vasomotor responses, and the galvanic skin response—are known to be affected by skeletal responses, such as exercise, breathing, and even tensing of certain muscles, such as those in the diaphragm. Thus, it is hard to rule out the possibility that, instead of directly learning a visceral response, the subject has learned a skeletal response the performance of which causes the visceral change being recorded.

One of the controls I planned to use was the paralysis of all skeletal responses through administration of curare, a drug which selectively blocks the motor end plates of skeletal muscles without eliminating consciousness in human subjects or the neural control of visceral responses, such as the beating of the heart. The muscles involved in breathing are paralyzed, so the subject's breathing must be maintained through artificial respiration. Since it seemed unlikely that curarization and other rigorous control techniques would be easy to use with human subjects, I decided to concentrate first on experiments with animals.

Originally I thought that learning would be more difficult when the animal was paralyzed, under the influence of curare, and therefore I decided to postpone such experiments until ones on nonparalyzed animals had yielded some definitely promising results. This turned out to be a mistake because, as I found out much later, paralyzing the animal with curare not only greatly simplifies the problem of recording visceral responses without artifacts introduced by movement but also apparently makes it easier for the animal to learn, perhaps because paralysis of the skeletal muscles removes sources of variability and distraction. Also, in certain experiments I made the mistake of using rewards that induced strong unconditioned responses that interfered with instrumental learning.

One of the greatest difficulties, however, was the strength of the belief that instrumental learning of glandular and visceral responses is impossible. It was extremely difficult to get students to work on this problem, and when paid assistants were assigned to it, their attempts were so half-hearted that it soon became more economical to let them work on some other problem which they could attack with greater faith and enthusiasm. These difficulties and a few preliminary encouraging but inconclusive early results have been described elsewhere.[9]

Success with Salivation

The first clear-cut results were secured by Alfredo Carmona and me in an experiment on the salivation of dogs. Initial attempts to use food as a reward for hungry dogs were unsuccessful, partly because of strong and persistent unconditioned salivation elicited by the food. Therefore, we decided to use water as a reward for thirsty dogs. Preliminary observations showed that the water had no appreciable effects one way or the other on the bursts of spontaneous salivation. As an additional precaution, however, we used the experimental design of rewarding dogs in one group whenever they showed a burst of spontaneous salivation, so that they would be trained to increase salivation, and rewarding dogs in another group whenever there was a long interval between spontaneous bursts, so that they would be trained to decrease salivation. If the reward had any unconditioned effect, this effect might be classically conditioned to the experimental situation and therefore produce a change in salivation that was not a true instance of instrumental learning. But in classical conditioning the reinforcement must elicit the response that is to be acquired. Therefore, conditioning of a response elicited by the reward could produce either an increase or a decrease in salivation, depending upon the direction of the unconditioned response elicited by the reward, but it could not produce a change in one direction for one group and in the opposite direction for the other group. The same type of logic applies for any unlearned cumulative aftereffects of the reward; they could not be in opposite directions for the two groups. With instrumental learning, however, the reward can reinforce any response that immediately precedes it; therefore, the same reward can be used to produce either increases or decreases.

The results are presented in Fig. 1, which summarizes the effects of 40 days of training with one 45-minute training session per day. It may be seen that in this experiment the learning

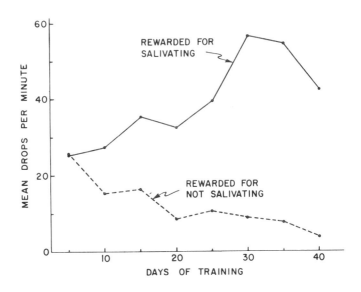

Fɪɢ. 1. Learning curves for groups of thirsty dogs rewarded with water for either increases or decreases in spontaneous salivation. [From Miller and Carmona (*10*)]

proceeded slowly. However, statistical analysis showed that each of the trends in the predicted rewarded direction was highly reliable.[10]

Since the changes in salivation for the two groups were in opposite directions, they cannot be attributed to classical conditioning. It was noted, however, that the group rewarded for increases seemed to be more aroused and active than the one rewarded for decreases. Conceivably, all we were doing was to change the level of activation of the dogs, and this change was, in turn, affecting the salivation. Although we did not observe any specific skeletal responses, such as chewing movements or panting, which might be expected to elicit salivation, it was difficult to be absolutely certain that such movements did not occur. Therefore, we decided to rule out such movements by paralyzing the dogs with curare, but we immediately found that curare had two effects which were disastrous for this experiment: it elicited such copious and continuous salivation that there were no changes in salivation to reward, and the salivation was so viscous that it almost immediately gummed up the recording apparatus.

HEART RATE

In the meantime, Jay Trowill, working with me on this problem, was displaying great ingenuity, courage, and persistence in trying to produce instrumental learning of heart rate in rats that had been paralyzed by curare to prevent them from "cheating" by muscular exertion to speed up the heart or by relaxation to slow it down. As a result of preliminary testing, he selected a dose of curare (3.6 milligrams of d-tubocurarine chloride per kilogram, injected intraperitoneally) which produced deep paralysis for at least 3 hours, and a rate of artificial respiration (inspiration-expiration ratio 1:1; 70 breaths per minute; peak pressure reading, 20 cm-H_2O) which maintained the heart at a constant and normal rate throughout this time.

In subsequent experiments, DiCara and I have obtained similar effects by starting with a smaller dose (1.2 milligrams per kilogram) and constantly infusing additional amounts of the drug, through intraperitoneal injection, at the rate of 1.2 milligrams per kilogram per hour, for the duration of the experiment. We have recorded, electromyographically, the response of the muscles, to determine that this dose does indeed produce a complete block of the action potentials, lasting for at least an hour after the end of infusion. We have found that if parameters of respiration and the face mask are adjusted carefully, the procedure not only maintains the heart rate of a 500-gram control animal constant but also maintains the vital signs of temperature, peripheral vasomotor responses, and the pCO_2 of the blood constant.

Since there are not very many ways to reward an animal completely paralyzed by curare, Trowill and I decided to use direct electrical stimulation of rewarding areas of the brain. There were other technical difficulties to overcome, such as devising the automatic system for rewarding small changes in heart rate as recorded by the electrocardiogram. Nevertheless, Trowill at last succeeded in training his rats.[11] Those rewarded for an increase in heart rate showed a statistically reliable increase, and those rewarded for a decrease in heart rate showed a statistically reliable decrease. The changes, however, were disappointingly small, averaging only 5 percent in each direction.

The next question was whether larger changes could be achieved by improving the technique of training. DiCara and I used the technique of shaping—in other words, of immediately rewarding first very small, and hence frequently occurring, changes in the correct direction and, as soon as these had been learned, requiring progressively larger changes as the criterion for reward. In this way, we were able to produce in 90 minutes of training changes averaging 20 percent in either direction.[12]

KEY PROPERTIES OF LEARNING: DISCRIMINATION AND RETENTION

Does the learning of visceral responses have the same properties as the learning of skeletal responses? One of the important characteristics of the instrumental learning of skeletal responses is that a discrimination can be learned, so that the responses are more likely to be made in the stimulus situations in which they are rewarded than in those in which they are not. After the training of the first few rats had convinced us that we could produce large changes in heart rate, DiCara and I gave all the rest of the rats in the experiment described above 45 minutes of additional training with the most difficult criterion. We did this in order to see whether they could learn to give a greater response during a "time-in" stimulus (the presence of a flashing light and a tone) which indicated that a response in the proper direction would be rewarded than during a "time-out" stimulus (absence of light and tone) which indicated that a correct response would not be rewarded.

Figure 2 shows the record of one of the rats given such training. Before the beginning of the special discrimination training it had slowed its heart from an initial rate of 350 beats per minute to a rate of 230 beats per minute. From the top record of Fig. 2 one can see that, at the beginning of the special discrimination training, there was no appreciable reduction in heart rate that was specifically associated with the time-in stimulus. Thus it took the rat considerable time after the onset of this stimulus to meet the criterion and get the reward. At the end of the discrimination training the heart rate during time-out remained approximately the same, but when the time-in light and tone came on, the heart slowed down and the criterion was promptly met. Although the other rats showed less change than this, by the end of the relatively short period of discrimination training their heart rate did change reliably ($P < .001$) in the predicted direction when the time-in stimulus came on. Thus, it is clear that instrumental visceral learning has at least one of the important properties of instrumental skeletal learning—namely, the ability to be brought under the control of a discriminative stimulus.

Another of the important properties of the instrumental learning of skeletal responses is that it is remembered. DiCara and I performed a special experiment to test the retention of learned changes in heart rate.[13] Rats that had been given a single training session were returned to their home cages for 3 months without further training. When curarized again and returned to the experimental situation for nonreinforced test trials, rats in both the "increase" and the "decrease" groups showed good retention by exhibiting reliable changes in the direction rewarded in the earlier training.

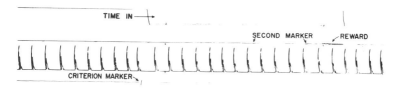

BEGINNING OF DISCRIMINATION TRAINING

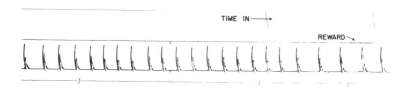

AFTER 45 MINUTES OF DISCRIMINATION TRAINING

FIG. 2. Electrocardiograms at the beginning and at the end of discrimination training of curarized rat rewarded for slow heart rate. Slowing of heart rate is rewarded only during a "time-in" stimulus (tone and light). [From Miller and DiCara (12)]

ESCAPE AND AVOIDANCE LEARNING

Is visceral learning by any chance peculiarly limited to reinforcement by the unusual reward of direct electrical stimulation of the brain, or can it be reinforced by other rewards in the same way that skeletal learning can be? In order to answer this question, DiCara and I[14] performed an experiment using the other of the two forms of thoroughly studied reward that can be conveniently used with rats which are paralyzed by curare—namely, the chance to avoid, or escape from, mild electric shock. A shock signal was turned on; after it had been on for 10 seconds it was accompanied by brief pulses of mild electric shock delivered to the rat's tail. During the first 10 seconds the rat could turn off the shock signal and avoid the shock by making the correct response of changing its heart rate in the required direction by the required amount. If it did not make the correct response in time, the shocks continued to be delivered until the rat escaped them by making the correct response, which immediately turned off both the shock and the shock signal.

For one group of curarized rats, the correct response was an increase in heart rate; for the other group it was a decrease. After the rats had learned to make small responses in the proper direction, they were required to make larger ones. During this training the shock signals were randomly interspersed with an equal number of "safe" signals that were not followed by shock; the heart rate was also recorded during so-called blank trials—trials without any signals or shocks. For half of the rats the shock signal was a tone and the "safe" signal was a flashing light; for the other half the roles of these cues were reversed.

The results are shown in Fig. 3. Each of the 12 rats in this experiment changed its heart rate in the rewarded direction. As training progressed, the shock signal began to elicit a progressively greater change in the rewarded direction than the change recorded during the blank trials; this was a statistically reliable trend. Conversely, as training progressed, the "safe" signal came to elicit a statistically reliable change in the opposite direction, toward the initial base line. These results show learning when escape and avoidance are the rewards; this means that visceral responses in curarized rats can be reinforced by rewards other than direct electrical stimulation of the brain. These rats also discriminate between the shock and the "safe" signals. You will remember that, with noncurarized thirsty dogs, we were able to use yet another kind of reward, water, to produce learned changes in salivation.

In the experiments discussed above, paralysis of the skeletal muscles by curare ruled out the possibility that the subjects were learning the overt performance of skeletal responses which were indirectly eliciting the changes in the heart rate. It is barely conceivable, however, that the rats were learning to send out from the motor cortex central impulses which would have activated the muscles had they not been paralyzed. And it is barely conceivable that these central impulses affected heart rate by means either of inborn connections or of classically conditioned ones that had been acquired when previous exercise had been accompanied by an increase in heart rate and relaxation had been accompanied by a decrease. But, if the changes in heart rate were produced in this indirect way, we would expect that, during a

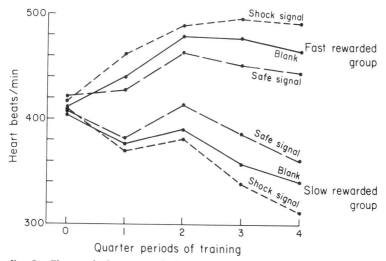

Fig. 3. Changes in heart rate during avoidance training. [From DiCara and Miller (14)]

subsequent test without curare, any rat that showed learned changes in heart rate would show the movements in the muscles that were no longer paralyzed. Furthermore, the problem of whether or not visceral responses learned under curarization carry over to the noncurarized state is of interest in its own right.

In order to answer this question, DiCara and I[15] trained two groups of curarized rats to increase or decrease, respectively, their heart rate in order to avoid, or escape from, brief pulses of mild electric shock. When these rats were tested 2 weeks later in the noncurarized state, the habit was remembered. Statistically reliable increases in heart rate averaging 5 percent and decreases averaging 16 percent occurred. Immediately subsequent retraining without curare produced additional significant changes of heart rate in the rewarded direction, bringing the total overall increase to 11 percent and the decrease to 22 percent. While, at the beginning of the test in the noncurarized state, the two groups showed some differences in respiration and activity, these differences decreased until, by the end of the retraining, they were small and far from statistically reliable $(t = 0.3$ and 1.3, respectively). At the same time, the difference between the two groups with respect to heart rate was increasing, until it became large and thus extremely reliable $(t = 8.6$, d.f. $= 12$, $P < .001)$.

In short, while greater changes in heart rate were being learned, the response was becoming more specific, involving smaller changes in respiration and muscular activity. This increase in specificity with additional training is another point of similarity with the instrumental learning of skeletal responses. Early in skeletal learning, the rewarded correct response is likely to be accompanied by many unnecessary movements. With additional training during which extraneous movements are not rewarded, they tend to drop out.

It is difficult to reconcile the foregoing results with the hypothesis that the differences in heart rate were mediated primarily by a difference in either respiration or amount of general activity. This is especially true in view of the research, summarized by Ehrlich and Malmo,[16] which shows that muscular activity, to affect heart rate in the rat, must be rather vigorous.

While it is difficult to rule out completely the possibility that changes in heart rate are mediated by central impulses to skeletal muscles, the possibility of such mediation is much less attractive for other responses, such as intestinal contractions and the formation of urine by the kidney. Furthermore, if the learning of these different responses can be shown to be specific in enough visceral responses, one runs out of different skeletal movements each eliciting a specific different visceral response.[17] Therefore, experiments were performed on the learning of a variety of different visceral responses and on the specificity of that learning. Each of these experiments was, of course, interesting in its own right, quite apart from any bearing on the problem of mediation.

SPECIFICITY:
INTESTINAL VERSUS CARDIAC

The purpose of our next experiment was to determine the specificity of visceral learning. If such learning has the same properties as the instrumental learning of skeletal responses, it should be possible to learn a specific visceral response independently of other ones. Furthermore, as we have just seen, we might expect to find that, the better the rewarded response is learned, the more specific is the learning. Banuazizi and I worked on this problem.[18] First we had to discover another visceral response that could be conveniently recorded and rewarded. We decided on intestinal contractions, and recorded them in the curarized rat with a little balloon filled with water thrust approximately 4 centimeters beyond the anal sphincter. Changes of pressure in the balloon were transduced into electric voltages which produced a record on a polygraph and also activated an automatic mechanism for delivering the reward, which was electrical stimulation of the brain.

The results for the first rat trained, which was a typical one, are shown in Fig. 4. From the top record it may be seen that, during habituation, there were some spontaneous contractions. When the rat was rewarded by brain stimulation for keeping contractions below a certain amplitude for a certain time, the number of contractions was reduced and the base line was lowered. After the record showed a highly reliable change indicating that relaxation had been learned (Fig. 4, second record from the top), the conditions of training were reversed and the reward was delivered whenever the amplitude of contractions rose above a certain level. From the next record (Fig. 4, middle) it may be seen that this

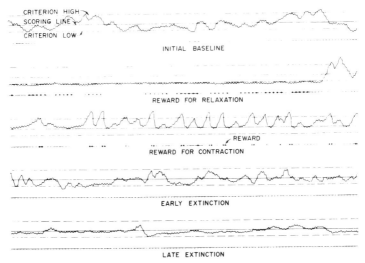

Fɪɢ. 4. Typical samples of a record of instrumental learning of an intestinal response by a curarized rat. (From top to bottom) Record of spontaneous contraction before training; record after training with reward for relaxation; record after training with reward for contractions; records during nonrewarded extinction trials. [From Miller and Banuazizi (18)]

type of training increased the number of contractions and raised the base line. Finally (Fig. 4, two bottom records) the reward was discontinued and, as would be expected, the response continued for a while but gradually became extinguished, so that the activity eventually returned to approximately its original baseline level.

After studying a number of other rats in this way and convincing ourselves that the instrumental learning of intestinal responses was a possibility, we designed an experiment to test specificity. For all the rats of the experiment, both intestinal contractions and heart rate were recorded, but half the rats were rewarded for one of these responses and half were rewarded for the other response. Each of these two groups of rats was divided into two subgroups, rewarded, respectively, for increased and decreased response. The rats were completely paralyzed by curare, maintained on artificial respiration, and rewarded by electrical stimulation of the brain.

The results are shown in Figs. 5 and 6. In Fig. 5 it may be

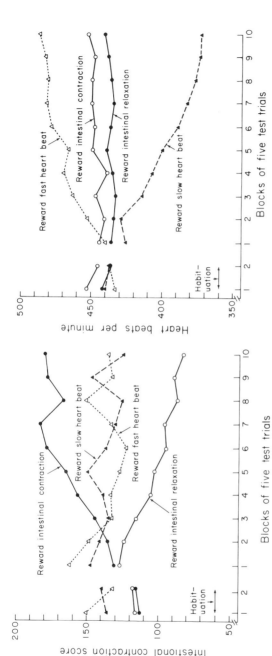

FIG. 5 (left). Graph showing that the intestinal contraction score is changed by rewarding either increases or decreases in intestinal contractions but is unaffected by rewarding changes in heart rate. [From Miller and Banuazizi (18)] FIG. 6 (right). Graph showing that the heart rate is changed by rewarding either increases or decreases in heart rate but is unaffected by rewarding changes in intestinal contractions. Comparison with FIG. 5 demonstrates the specificity of visceral learning. [From Miller and Banuazizi (18)]

seen that the group rewarded for increases in intestinal contractions learned an increase, the group rewarded for decreases learned a decrease, but neither of these groups showed an appreciable change in heart rate. Conversely (Fig. 6), the group rewarded for increases in heart rate showed an increase, the group rewarded for decreases showed a decrease, but neither of these groups showed a change in intestinal contractions.

The fact that each type of response changed when it was rewarded rules out the interpretation that the failure to secure a change when that change was not rewarded could have been due to either a strong and stable homeostatic regulation of that response or an inability of our techniques to measure changes reliably under the particular conditions of our experiment.

Each of the 12 rats in the experiment showed statistically reliable changes in the rewarded direction; for 11 the changes were reliable beyond the $P < .001$ level, while for the 12th the changes were reliable only beyond the .05 level. A statistically reliable negative correlation showed that the better the rewarded visceral response was learned, the less change occurred in the other, nonrewarded response. This greater specificity with better learning is what we had expected. The results showed that visceral learning can be specific to an organ system, and they clearly ruled out the possibility of mediation by any single general factor, such as level of activation or central commands for either general activity or relaxation.

In an additional experiment, Banuazizi[19] showed that either increases or decreases in intestinal contractions can be rewarded by avoidance of, or escape from, mild electric shocks, and that the intestinal responses can be discriminatively elicited by a specific stimulus associated with reinforcement.

Kidney Function

Encouraged by these successes, DiCara and I decided to see whether or not the rate of urine formation by the kidney could be changed in the curarized rat rewarded by electrical stimulation of the brain.[20] A catheter, permanently inserted, was used to prevent accumulation of urine by the bladder, and the rate of urine formation was measured by an electronic device for counting minute drops. In order to secure a rate of urine forma-

tion fast enough so that small changes could be promptly detected and rewarded, the rats were kept constantly loaded with
water through infusion by way of a catheter permanently inserted in the jugular vein.

All of the seven rats rewarded when the intervals between
times of urine-drop formation lengthened showed decreases in
the rate of urine formation, and all of the seven rats rewarded
when these intervals shortened showed increases in the rate of
urine formation. For both groups the changes were highly reliable $(P < .001)$.

In order to determine how the change in rate of urine formation was achieved, certain additional measures were taken.
As the set of bars at left in Fig. 7 shows, the rate of filtration,
measured by means of ^{14}C-labeled inulin, increased when increases in the rate of urine formation were rewarded and decreased when decreases in the rate were rewarded. Plots of the
correlations showed that the changes in the rates of filtration
and urine formation were not related to changes in either blood
pressure or heart rate.

The middle set of bars in Fig. 7 shows that the rats rewarded
for increases in the rate of urine formation had an increased rate
of renal blood flow, as measured by ^{3}H-p-aminohippuric acid,
and that those rewarded for decreases had a decreased rate of
renal blood flow. Since these changes in blood flow were not accompanied by changes in general blood pressure or in heart rate,
they must have been achieved by vasomotor changes of the renal
arteries. That these vasomotor changes were at least somewhat
specific is shown by the fact that vasomotor responses of the tail,
as measured by a photoelectric plethysmograph, did not differ
for the two groups of rats.

The set of bars at right in Fig. 7 shows that when decreases
in rate of urine formation were rewarded, a more concentrated
urine, having higher osmolarity, was formed. Since the slower
passage of urine through the tubules would afford more opportunity for reabsorption of water, this higher concentration does
not necessarily mean an increase in the secretion of antidiuretic
hormone. When an increased rate of urine formation was rewarded, the urine did not become more diluted—that is, it showed
no decrease in osmolarity; therefore, the increase in rate of urine

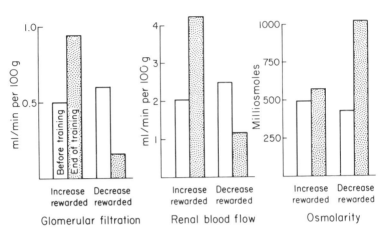

Fig. 7. Effects of rewarding increased rate of urine formation in one group and decreased rate in another on measures of glomerular filtration, renal blood flow, and osmolarity. [From data in Miller and DiCara (20)]

formation observed in this experiment cannot be accounted for in terms of an inhibition of the secretion of antidiuretic hormone.

From the foregoing results it appears that the learned changes in urine formation in this experiment were produced primarily by changes in the rate of filtration, which, in turn, were produced primarily by changes in the rate of blood flow through the kidneys.

GASTRIC CHANGES

In the next experiment, Carmona, Demierre, and I used a photoelectric plethysmograph to measure changes, presumably in the amount of blood, in the stomach wall.[21] In an operation performed under anesthesia, a small glass tube, painted black except for a small spot, was inserted into the rat's stomach. The same tube was used to hold the stomach wall against a small glass window inserted through the body wall. The tube was left in that position. After the animal had recovered, a bundle of optical fibers could be slipped snugly into the glass tube so that the light beamed through it would shine out through the unpainted spot in the tube inside the stomach, pass through the stomach wall, and be recorded by a photocell on the other side of the glass window. Preliminary tests indicated that, as would be expected, when the amount of blood in the stomach wall increased, less light would pass through. Other tests showed that stomach contractions elicited by injections of insulin did not affect the amount of light transmitted.

In the main experiment we rewarded curarized rats by enabling them to avoid or escape from mild electric shocks. Some were rewarded when the amount of light that passed through the stomach wall increased, while others were rewarded when the amount decreased. Fourteen of the 15 rats showed changes in the rewarded direction. Thus, we demonstrated that the stomach wall, under the control of the autonomic nervous system, can be modified by instrumental learning. There is strong reason to believe that the learned changes were achieved by vasomotor responses affecting the amount of blood in the stomach wall or mucosa, or in both.

In another experiment, Carmona[22] showed that stomach contractions can be either increased or decreased by instrumental learning.

It is obvious that learned changes in the blood supply of internal organs can affect their functioning—as, for example, the rate at which urine was formed by the kidneys was affected by changes in the amount of blood that flowed through them. Thus, such changes can produce psychosomatic symptoms. And if the learned changes in blood supply can be specific to a given organ, the symptom will occur in that organ rather than in another one.

PERIPHERAL VASOMOTOR RESPONSES

Having investigated the instrumental learning of internal vasomotor responses, we next studied the learning of peripheral ones. In the first experiment, the amount of blood in the tail of a curarized rat was measured by a photoelectric plethysmograph, and changes were rewarded by electrical stimulation of the brain.[23] All of the four rats rewarded for vasoconstriction showed that response, and, at the same time, their average core temperature, measured rectally, decreased from 98.9° to 97.9°F. All of the four rats rewarded for vasodilatation showed that response and,

at the same time, their average core temperature increased from
99.9° to 101°F. The vasomotor change for each individual rat
was reliable beyond the $P < .01$ level, and the difference in
change in temperature between the groups was reliable beyond
the .01 level. The direction of the change in temperature was
opposite to that which would be expected from the heat conservation caused by peripheral vasoconstriction or the heat loss
caused by peripheral vasodilatation. The changes are in the direction which would be expected if the training had altered the
rate of heat production, causing a change in temperature which,
in turn, elicited the vasomotor response.

The next experiment was designed to try to determine the
limits of the specificity of vasomotor learning. The pinnae of
the rat's ears were chosen because the blood vessels in them are
believed to be innervated primarily, and perhaps exclusively,
by the sympathetic branch of the autonomic nervous system, the
branch that Cannon believed always fired nonspecifically as a
unit.[23] But Cannon's experiments involved exposing cats to extremely strong emotion-evoking stimuli, such as barking dogs,
and such stimuli will also evoke generalized activity throughout
the skeletal musculature. Perhaps his results reflected the way
in which sympathetic activity was elicited, rather than demonstrating any inherent inferiority of the sympathetic nervous
system.

In order to test this interpretation, DiCara and I[24] put photocells on both ears of the curarized rat and connected them to a
bridge circuit so that only differences in the vasomotor responses
of the two ears were rewarded by brain stimulation. We were
somewhat surprised and greatly delighted to find that this experiment actually worked. The results are summarized in Fig.
8. Each of the six rats rewarded for relative vasodilatation of the
left ear showed that response, while each of the six rats rewarded
for relative vasodilatation of the right ear showed that response.
Recordings from the right and left forepaws showed little
if any change in vasomotor response.

It is clear that these results cannot be by-products of changes
in either heart rate or blood pressure, as these would be expected
to affect both ears equally. They show either that vasomotor re-

sponses mediated by the sympathetic nervous system are capable of much greater specificity than has previously been believed, or that the innervation of the blood vessels in the pinnae of the ears is not restricted almost exclusively to sympathetic-nervous-system components, as has been believed, and involves functionally significant parasympathetic components. In any event, the changes in the blood flow certainly were surprisingly specific. Such changes in blood flow could account for specific psychosomatic symptoms.

BLOOD PRESSURE INDEPENDENT
OF HEART RATE

Although changes in blood pressure were not induced as by-products of rewarded changes in the rate of urine formation, another experiment on curarized rats showed that, when changes in systolic blood pressure are specifically reinforced, they can be learned.[25] Blood pressure was recorded by means of a catheter permanently inserted into the aorta, and the reward was avoidance of, or escape from, mild electric shock. All seven rats rewarded for increases in blood pressure showed further increases, while all seven rewarded for decreases showed decreases, each of the changes, which were in opposite directions, being reliable beyond the $P < .01$ level. The increase was from 139 mm-Hg, which happens to be roughly comparable to the normal systolic blood presssure of an adult man, to 170 mm-Hg, which is on the borderline of abnormally high blood pressure in man.

Each experimental animal was "yoked" with a curarized partner, maintained on artificial respiration and having shock electrodes on its tail wired in series with electrodes on the tail of the experimental animal, so that it received exactly the same electric shocks and could do nothing to escape or avoid them. The yoked controls for both the increase-rewarded and the decrease-rewarded groups showed some elevation in blood pressure as an unconditioned effect of the shocks. By the end of training, in contrast to the large difference in the blood pressures of the two groups specifically rewarded for changes in opposite directions, there was no difference in blood pressure between the yoked control partners for these two groups. Furthermore, the

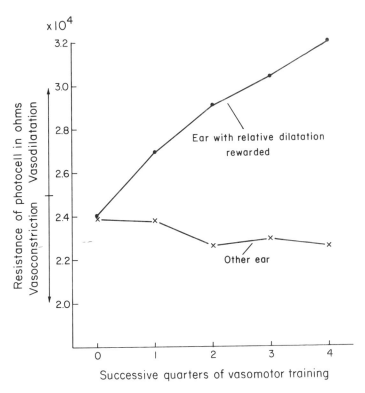

FIG. 8. Learning a difference in the vasomotor responses of the two ears in the curarized rat. [From data in DiCara and Miller (24)]

increase in blood pressure in these control groups was reliably less (P < .01) than that in the group specifically rewarded for increases. Thus, it is clear that the reward for an increase in blood pressure produced an additional increase over and above the effects of the shocks per se, while the reward for a decrease was able to overcome the unconditioned increase elicited by the shocks.

For none of the four groups was there a significant change in heart rate or in temperature during training: there were no significant differences in these measures among the groups. Thus, the learned change was relatively specific to blood pressure.

Transfer from Heart Rate
to Skeletal Avoidance

Although visceral learning can be quite specific, especially if only a specific response is rewarded, as was the case in the experiment on the two ears, under some circumstances it can involve a more generalized effect.

In handling the rats that had just recovered from curarization, DiCara noticed that those that had been trained, through the avoidance or escape reward, to increase their heart rate were more likely to squirm, squeal, defecate, and show other responses indicating emotionality than were those that had been trained to reduce their heart rate. Could instrumental learning of heart-rate changes have some generalized effects, perhaps on the level of emotionality, which might affect the behavior in a different avoidance-learning situation? In order to look for such an effect, DiCara and Weiss[26] used a modified shuttle avoidance apparatus. In this apparatus, when a danger signal is given, the rat must run from compartment A to compartment B. If he runs fast enough, he avoids the shock; if not, he must run to escape it. The next time the danger signal is given, the rat must run in the opposite direction, from B to A.

Other work had shown that learning in this apparatus is an inverted U-shaped function of the strength of the shocks, with shocks that are too strong eliciting emotional behavior instead of running. DiCara and Weiss trained their rats in this apparatus with a level of shock that is approximately optimum for naive rats of this strain. They found that the rats that had been rewarded for decreasing their heart rate learned well, but that those that had been rewarded for increasing their heart rate learned less well, as if their emotionality had been increased. The difference was statistically reliable $(P < .001)$. This experiment clearly demonstrates that training a visceral response can affect the subsequent learning of a skeletal one, but additional work will be required to prove the hypothesis that training to increase heart rate increases emotionality.

Visceral Learning without Curare

Thus far, in all of the experiments except the one on teaching thirsty dogs to salivate, the initial training was given when the animal was under the influence of curare. All of the experiments, except the one on salivation, have produced surprisingly rapid learning—definitive results within 1 or 2 hours. Will learning in the normal, noncurarized state be easier, as we originally thought it should be, or will it be harder, as the experiment on the noncurarized dogs suggests? DiCara and I have started to get additional evidence on this problem. We have obtained clearcut evidence that rewarding (with the avoidance or escape reward) one group of freely moving rats for reducing heart rate and rewarding another group for increasing heart rate produces a difference between the two groups.[27] That this difference was not due to the indirect effects of the overt performance of skeletal responses is shown by the fact that it persisted in subsequent tests during which the rats were paralyzed by curare. And, on subsequent retraining without curare, such differences in activity and respiration as were present earlier in training continued to decrease, while the differences in heart rate continued to increase. It seems extremely unlikely that, at the end of training, the highly reliable differences in heart rate $(t = 7.2; P < .0001)$ can be explained by the highly unreliable differences in activity and respiration $(t = .07$ and 0.2, respectively).

Although the rats in this experiment showed some learning when they were trained initially in the noncurarized state, this learning was much poorer than that which we have seen in our other experiments on curarized rats. This is exactly the opposite of my original expectation, but seems plausible in the light of hindsight. My hunch is that paralysis by curare improved learning by eliminating sources of distraction and variability. The stimulus situation was kept more constant, and confusing visceral fluctuations induced indirectly by skeletal movements were eliminated.

LEARNED CHANGES IN BRAIN WAVES

Encouraged by success in the experiments on the instrumental learning of visceral responses, my colleagues and I have attempted to produce other unconventional types of learning. Electrodes placed on the skull or, better yet, touching the surface of the brain record summative effects of electrical activity over a considerable area of the brain. Such electrical effects are called brain waves, and the record of them is called an electroencephalogram. When the animal is aroused, the electroencephalogram consists of fast, low-voltage activity; when the animal is drowsy or sleeping normally, the electroencephalogram consists of considerably slower, higher-voltage activity. Carmona attempted to see whether this type of brain activity, and the state of arousal accompanying it, can be modified by direct reward of changes in the brain activity.[28,29]

The subjects of the first experiment were freely moving cats. In order to have a reward that was under complete control and that did not require the cat to move, Carmona used direct electrical stimulation of the medial forebrain bundle, which is a rewarding area of the brain. Such stimulation produced a slight lowering in the average voltage of the electroencephalogram and an increase in behavioral arousal. In order to provide a control for these and any other unlearned effects, he rewarded one group for changes in the direction of high-voltage activity and another group for changes in the direction of low-voltage activity.

Both groups learned. The cats rewarded for high-voltage activity showed more high-voltage slow waves and tended to sit like sphinxes, staring out into space. The cats rewarded for low-voltage activity showed much more low-voltage fast activity, and appeared to be aroused, pacing restlessly about, sniffing, and looking here and there. It was clear that this type of training had modified both the character of the electrical brain waves and the general level of the behavioral activity. It was not clear, however, whether the level of arousal of the brain was directly modified and hence modified the behavior; whether the animals learned specific items of behavior which, in turn, modified the arousal of the brain as reflected in the electroencephalogram; or whether both types of learning were occurring simultaneously.

In order to rule out the direct sensory consequences of changes in muscular tension, movement, and posture, Carmona performed the next experiment on rats that had been paralyzed by means of curare. The results, given in Fig. 9, show that both rewarded groups showed changes in the rewarded direction; that a subsequent nonrewarded rest increased the number of high-voltage responses in both groups; and that, when the conditions of reward were reversed, the direction of change in voltage was reversed.

At present we are trying to use similar techniques to modify

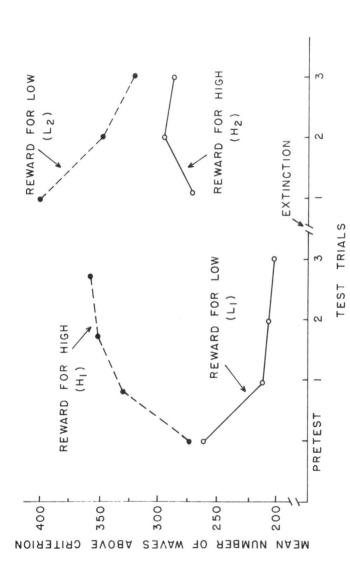

Fig. 9. Instrumental learning by curarized rats rewarded for high-voltage or for low-voltage electroencephalograms recorded from the cerebral cortex. After a period of nonrewarded extinction, which produced some drowsiness, as indicated by an increase in voltage, the rats in the two groups were then rewarded for voltage changes opposite in direction to the changes for which they were rewarded earlier. [From Carmona (29)]

98

the functions of a specific part of the vagal nucleus, by recording and specifically rewarding changes in the electrical activity there. Preliminary results suggest that this is possible. The next step is to investigate the visceral consequences of such modification. This kind of work may open up possibilities for modifying the activity of specific parts of the brain and the functions that they control. In some cases, directly rewarding brain activity may be a more convenient or more powerful technique than rewarding skeletal or visceral behavior. It also may be a new way to throw light on the functions of specific parts of the brain.[30]

HUMAN VISCERAL LEARNING

Another question is that of whether people are capable of instrumental learning of visceral responses. I believe that in this respect they are as smart as rats. But, as a recent critical review by Katkin and Murray[31] points out, this has not yet been completely proved. These authors have comprehensively summarized the recent studies reporting successful use of instrumental training to modify human heart rate, vasomotor responses, and the galvanic skin response. Because of the difficulties in subjecting human subjects to the same rigorous controls, including deep paralysis by means of curare, that can be used with animal subjects, one of the most serious questions about the results of the human studies is whether the changes recorded represent the true instrumental learning of visceral responses or the unconscious learning of those skeletal responses that can produce visceral reactions. However, the able investigators who have courageously challenged the strong traditional belief in the inferiority of the autonomic nervous system with experiments at the more difficult but especially significant human level are developing ingenious controls, including demonstrations of the specificity of the visceral change, so that their cumulative results are becoming increasingly impressive.

POSSIBLE ROLE IN HOMEOSTASIS

The functional utility of instrumental learning by the cerebrospinal nervous system under the conditions that existed during mammalian evolution is obvious. The skeletal responses mediated by the cerebrospinal nervous system operate on the external environment, so that there is survival value in the ability to learn responses that bring rewards such as food, water, or escape from pain. The fact that the responses mediated by the autonomic nervous system do not have such direct action on the external environment was one of the reasons for believing that they are not subject to instrumental learning. Is the learning ability of the autonomic nervous system something that has no normal function other than that of providing my students with subject matter for publications? Is it a mere accidental by-product of the survival value of cerebrospinal learning, or does the instrumental learning of autonomically mediated responses have some adaptive function, such as helping to maintain that constancy of the internal environment called homeostasis?

In order for instrumental learning to function homeostatically, a deviation away from the optimum level will have to function as a drive to motivate learning, and a change toward the optimum level will have to function as a reward to reinforce the learning of the particular visceral response that produced the corrective change.

When a mammal has less than the optimum amount of water in his body, this deficiency serves as a drive of thirst to motivate learning; the overt consummatory response of drinking functions as a reward to reinforce the learning of the particular skeletal responses that were successful in securing the water that restored the optimum level. But is the consummatory response essential? Can restoration of an optimum level by a glandular response function as a reward?

In order to test for the possible rewarding effects of a glandular response, DiCara, Wolf, and I[32] injected albino rats with antidiuretic hormone (ADH) if they chose one arm of a T-maze and with the isotonic saline vehicle if they chose the other, distinctively different, arm. The ADH permitted water to be reabsorbed in the kidney, so that a smaller volume of more concentrated urine was formed. Thus, for normal rats loaded in advance with H_2O, the ADH interfered with the excess-water excretion required for the restoration of homeostasis, while the control injection of isotonic saline allowed the excess water to be excreted. And, indeed, such rats learned to select the side of the maze that assured them an injunction of saline so that their glandular response could restore homeostasis.

Conversely, for rats with diabetes insipidus, loaded in advance with hypertonic NaCl, the homeostatic effects of the same two injections were reversed; the ADH, causing the urine to be more concentrated, helped the rats to get rid of the excess NaCl, while the isotonic saline vehicle did not. And, indeed, a group of rats of this kind learned the opposite choice of selecting the ADH side of the maze. As a further control on the effects of the ADH per se, normal rats which had not been given H_2O or NaCl exhibited no learning. This experiment showed that an excess of either H_2O or NaCl functions as a drive and that the return to the normal concentration produced by the appropriate response of a gland, the kidney, functions as a reward.

When we consider the results of this experiment together with those of our experiments showing that glandular and visceral responses can be instrumentally learned, we will expect the animal to learn those glandular and visceral responses mediated by the central nervous system that promptly restore homeostasis after any considerable deviation. Whether or not this theoretically possible learning has any practical significance will depend on whether or not the innate homeostatic mechanisms control the levels closely enough to prevent any deviations large enough to function as a drive from occurring. Even if the innate control should be accurate enough to preclude learning in most cases, there remains the intriguing possibility that, when pathology interferes with innate control, visceral learning is available as a supplementary mechanism.

IMPLICATIONS AND SPECULATIONS

We have seen how the instrumental learning of visceral responses suggests a new possible homeostatic mechanism worthy of further investigation. Such learning also shows that the autonomic nervous system is not as inferior as has been so widely and firmly believed. It removes one of the strongest arguments for the hypothesis that there are two fundamentally different mechanisms of learning, involving different parts of the nervous system.

Cause of Psychosomatic Symptoms

Similarly, evidence of the instrumental learning of visceral responses removes the main basis for assuming that the psychosomatic symptoms that involve the autonomic nervous system are fundamentally different from those functional symptoms, such as hysterical ones, that involve the cerebrospinal nervous system. Such evidence allows us to extend to psychosomatic symptoms the type of learning-theory analysis that Dollard and I [7,33] have applied to other symptoms.

For example, suppose a child is terror-striken at the thought of going to school in the morning because he is completely unprepared for an important examination. The strong fear elicits a variety of fluctuating autonomic symptoms, such as a queasy stomach at one time and pallor and faintness at another; at this point his mother, who is particularly concerned about cardiovascular symptoms, says, "You are sick and must stay home." The child feels a great relief from fear, and this reward should reinforce the cardiovascular responses producing pallor and faintness. If such experiences are repeated frequently enough, the child, theoretically, should learn to respond with that kind of symptom. Similarly, another child whose mother ignored the vasomotor responses but was particularly concerned by signs of gastric distress would learn the latter type of symptom. I want to emphasize, however, that we need careful clinical research to determine how frequently, if at all, the social conditions sufficient for such theoretically possible learning of visceral symptoms actually occur. Since a given instrumental response can be reinforced by a considerable variety of rewards, and by one reward on one occasion and a different reward on another, the fact that glandular and visceral responses can be instrumentally learned opens up many new theoretical possibilities for the reinforcement of psychosomatic symptoms.

Furthermore, we do not yet know how severe a psychosomatic effect can be produced by learning. While none of the 40 rats rewarded for speeding up their heart rates have died in the course of training under curarization, 7 of the 40 rats rewarded for slowing down their heart rates have died. This statistically reliable difference (chi square $= 5.6$, $P < .02$) is highly suggestive, but it could mean that training to speed up the heart helped the rats resist the stress of curare rather than that the reward for slowing down the heart was strong enough to overcome innate regulatory mechanisms and induce sudden death. In either event the visceral learning had a vital effect. At present, DiCara and I are trying to see whether or not the learning of visceral responses can be carried far enough in the noncurarized animal to produce physical damage. We are also investigating the possibility that there may be a critical period in early infancy during which visceral learning has particularly intense and long-lasting effects.

Individual and Cultural Differences

It is possible that, in addition to producing psychosomatic symptoms in extreme cases, visceral learning can account for certain more benign individual and cultural differences. Lacey and Lacey[34] have shown that a given individual may have a tendency, which is stable over a number of years, to respond to a variety of different stresses with the same profile of autonomic responses, while other individuals may have statistically reliable tendencies to respond with different profiles. It now seems possible that differential conditions of learning may account for at least some of these individual differences in patterns of autonomic response.

Conversely, such learning may account also for certain instances in which the same individual responds to the same stress in different ways. For example, a small boy who receives a severe bump in rough-and-tumble play may learn to inhibit the secretion of tears in this situation since his peer group will punish crying by calling it "sissy." But the same small boy may burst into tears when he gets home to his mother, who will not punish weeping and may even reward tears with sympathy.

Similarly, it seems conceivable that different conditions of reward by a culture different from our own may be responsible for the fact that Homer's adult heroes so often "let the big tears fall." Indeed, a former colleague of mine, Herbert Barry III, has analyzed cross-cultural data and found that the amount of crying reported for children seems to be related to the way in which the society reacts to their tears.[35]

I have emphasized the possible role of learning in producing the observed individual differences in visceral responses to stress, which in extreme cases may result in one type of psychosomatic symptom in one person and a different type in another. Such learning does not, of course, exclude innate individual differences in the susceptibility of different organs. In fact, given social conditions under which any form of illness will be rewarded, the symptoms of the most susceptible organ will be the most likely ones to be learned. Furthermore, some types of stress may be so strong that the innate reactions to them produce damage without any learning. My colleagues and I are currently investigating the psychological variables involved in such types of stress.[36]

Therapeutic Training

The experimental work on animals has developed a powerful technique for using instrumental learning to modify glandular and visceral responses. The improved training technique consists of moment-to-moment recording of the visceral function and immediate reward, at first, of very small changes in the desired direction and then of progressively larger ones. The success of this technique suggests that it should be able to produce therapeutic changes. If the patient who is highly motivated to get rid of a symptom understands that a signal, such as a tone, indicates a change in the desired direction, that tone could serve as a powerful reward. Instruction to try to turn the tone on as often as possible and praise for success should increase the reward. As patients find that they can secure some control of the symptom, their motivation should be strengthened. Such a procedure should be well worth trying on any symptom, functional or organic, that is under neural control, that can be continuously monitored by modern instrumentation, and for which a given direction of change is clearly indicated medically—for example, cardiac arrhythmias, spastic colitis, asthma, and those cases of high blood pressure that are not essential compensation for kidney damage.[37] The obvious cases to begin with are those in which drugs are ineffective or contraindicated. In the light of the fact that our animals learned so much better when under the influence of curare and transferred their training so well to the normal, nondrugged state, it should be worth while to try to use hypnotic suggestion to achieve similar results by enhancing the reward effect of the signal indicating a change in the desired direction, by producing relaxation and regular breathing, and by removing interference from skeletal responses and distraction by irrelevant cues.

Engel and Melmon[38] have reported encouraging results in the use of instrumental training to treat cardiac arrhythmias of organic origin. Randt, Korein, Carmona, and I have had some success in using the method described above to train epileptic patients in the laboratory to suppress, in one way or another, the abnormal paroxysmal spikes in their electroencephalogram. My colleagues and I are hoping to try learning therapy for other symptoms—for example, the rewarding of high-voltage electroencephalograms as a treatment for insomnia. While it is far too early to promise any cures, it certainly will be worth while to investigate thoroughly the therapeutic possibilities of improved instrumental training techniques.

NOTES

1. *The Dialogues of Plato,* B. Jowett, Transl., (Univ. of Oxford Press, London, ed. 2, 1875), vol. 3, "Timaeus."
2. X. Bichat, *Recherches Physiologiques sur la Vie et le Mort* (Brosson, Gabon, Paris, 1800).
3. W. B. Cannon, *The Wisdom of the Body* (Norton, New York, 1932).
4. F. Alexander, *Psychosomatic Medicine: Its Principles and Applications* (Norton, New York, 1950), pp. 40–41.
5. G. A. Kimble, *Hilgard and Marquis' Conditioning and Learning* (Appleton-Century-Crofts, New York, ed. 2, 1961), p. 100.
6. B. F. Skinner, *The Behavior of Organisms* (Appleton-Century, New York, 1938); O. H. Mowrer, *Harvard Educ. Rev.* 17, 102 (1947).
7. N. E. Miller and J. Dollard, *Social Learning and Imitation* (Yale Univ. Press, New Haven, 1941); J. Dollard and N. E. Miller, *Personality and Psychotherapy* (McGraw-Hill, New York, 1950); N. E. Miller, *Psychol. Rev.* 58, 375 (1951).
8. N. E. Miller, *Ann. N.Y. Acad. Sci.* 92, 830 (1961); _____, in *Nebraska Symposium on Motivation,* M. R. Jones, Ed. (Univ. of Nebraska Press, Lincoln, 1963); _____, in *Proc. 3rd World Congr. Psychiat., Montreal, 1961* (1963), vol. 3, p. 213.
9. _____, in "Proceedings, 18th International Congress of Psychology, Moscow, 1966," in press.
10. _____ and A. Carmona, *J. Comp. Physiol. Psychol.* 63, 1 (1967).
11. J. A. Trowill, *ibid.,* p. 7.
12. N. E. Miller and L. V. DiCara, *ibid.,* p. 12.
13. L. V. DiCara and N. E. Miller, *Commun. Behav. Biol.* 2, 19 (1968).
14. _____, *J. Comp. Physiol. Psychol.* 65, 8 (1968).
15. _____, *ibid.,* in press.
16. D. J. Ehrlich and R. B. Malmo, *Neuropsychologia* 5, 219 (1967).
17. "It even becomes difficult to postulate enough different thoughts each arousing a different emotion, each of which in turn innately elicits a specific visceral response. And if one assumes a more direct specific connection between different thoughts and different visceral responses, the notion becomes indistinguishable from the ideo-motor hypothesis of the voluntary movement of skeletal muscles." [W. James, *Principles of Psychology* (Dover, New York, new ed., 1950), vol. 2, chap. 26.]
18. N. E. Miller and A. Banuazizi, *J. Comp. Physiol. Psychol.* 65, 1 (1968).
19. A. Banuazizi, thesis, Yale University (1968).

20. N. E. Miller and L. V. DiCara, *Amer. J. Physiol.* 215, 677 (1968).
21. A. Carmona, N. E. Miller, T. Demierre, in preparation.
22. A. Carmona, in preparation.
23. L. V. DiCara and N. E. Miller, *Commun. Behav. Biol.* 1, 209 (1968).
24. _____, *Science* 159, 1485 (1968).
25. _____, *Psychosom. Med.* 30, 489 (1968).
26. L. V. DiCara and J. M. Weiss, *J. Comp. Physiol. Psychol.*, in press.
27. L. V. DiCara and N. E. Miller, *Physiol. Behav.*, in press.
28. N. E. Miller, *Science* 152, 676 (1966).
29. A. Carmona, thesis, Yale University (1967).
30. For somewhat similar work on the single-cell level, see J. Olds and M. E. Olds, *in Brain Mechanisms and Learning*, J. Delafresnaye, A. Fessard, J. Konorski, Eds. (Blackwell, London, 1961).
31. E. S. Katkin and N. E. Murray, *Psychol. Bull.* 70, 52 (1968); for a reply to their criticisms, see A. Crider, G. Schwartz, S. Shnidman, *ibid.*, in press.
32. N. E. Miller, L. V. DiCara, G. Wolf, *Amer. J. Physiol.* 215, 684 (1968).
33. N. E. Miller, in *Personality Change*, D. Byrne and P. Worchel, Eds. (Wiley, New York, 1964), p. 149.
34. J. I. Lacey and B. C. Lacey, *Amer. J. Psychol.* 71, 50 (1958); *Ann. N.Y. Acad. Sci.* 98, 1257 (1962).
35. H. Barry III, personal communication.
36. N. E. Miller, *Proc. N.Y. Acad. Sci.*, in press.
37. Objective recording of such symptoms might be useful also in monitoring the effects of quite different types of psychotherapy.
38. B. T. Engel and K. T. Melmon, personal communication.
39. The work described is supported by U.S. Public Health Service grant MH 13189.

Pigeons in a Pelican

B. F. SKINNER, *Harvard University*

This is the history of a crackpot idea, born on the wrong side of the tracks intellectually speaking, but eventually vindicated in a sort of middle class respectability. It is the story of a proposal to use living organisms to guide missiles—of a research program during World War II called "Project Pigeon" and a peacetime continuation at the Naval Research Laboratory called "ORCON," from the words "organic control." Both of these programs have now been declassified.

Man has always made use of the sensory capacities of animals, either because they are more acute than his own or more convenient. The watchdog probably hears better than his master and in any case listens while his master sleeps. As a detecting system the dog's ear comes supplied with an alarm (the dog need not be taught to announce the presence of an intruder), but special forms of reporting are sometimes set up. The tracking behavior of the bloodhound and the pointing of the hunting dog are usually modified to make them more useful. Training is sometimes quite explicit. It is said that seagulls were used to detect submarines in the English Channel during World War I.

Skinner, B. F. Pigeons in a pelican. *American Psychologist*, 1960, *15*, 28–37. Copyright 1960 by the American Psychological Association, and reproduced by permission.

The British sent their own submarines through the Channel releasing food to the surface. Gulls could see the submarines from the air and learned to follow them, whether they were British or German. A flock of gulls, spotted from the shore, took on special significance. In the seeing-eye dog the repertoire of artificial signaling responses is so elaborate that it has the conventional character of the verbal interchange between man and man.

The detecting and signaling systems of lower organisms have a special advantage when used with explosive devices which can be guided toward the objects they are to destroy, whether by land, sea, or air. Homing systems for guided missiles have now been developed which sense and signal the position of a target by responding to visible or invisible radiation, noise, radar reflections, and so on. These have not always been available, and in any case a living organism has certain advantages. It is almost certainly cheaper and more compact and, in particular, is especially good at responding to patterns and those classes of patterns called "concepts." The lower organism is not used because it is more sensitive than man—after all, the kamikaze did very well—but because it is readily expendable.

PROJECT PELICAN

The ethical question of our right to convert a lower creature into an unwitting hero is a peacetime luxury. There were bigger questions to be answered in the late thirties. A group of men had come into power who promised, and eventually accomplished, the greatest mass murder in history. In 1939 the city of Warsaw was laid waste in an unprovoked bombing, and the airplane emerged as a new and horrible instrument of war against which only the feeblest defenses were available. Project Pigeon was conceived against that background. It began as a search for a homing device to be used in a surface-to-air guided missile as a defense against aircraft. As the balance between offensive and defensive weapons shifted, the direction was reversed, and the system was to be tested first in an air-to-ground missile called the "Pelican." Its name is a useful reminder of the state of the missile art in America at that time. Its detecting and servomechanisms took up so much space that there was no room for explosives: hence the resemblance to the pelican "whose beak can hold more than its belly can." My title is perhaps now clear.

At the University of Minnesota in the spring of 1940 the capacity of the pigeon to steer toward a target was tested with a moving hoist. The pigeon, held in a jacket and harnessed to a block, was immobilized except for its neck and head. It could eat grain from a dish and operate a control system by moving its head in appropriate directions. Movement of the head operated the motors of the hoist. The bird could ascend by lifting its head, descend by lowering it, and travel from side to side by moving appropriately. The whole system, mounted on wheels, was pushed across a room toward a bull's-eye on the far wall. During the approach the pigeon raised or lowered itself and moved from side to side in such a way as to reach the wall in position to eat grain from the center of the bull's-eye. The pigeon learned to reach any target within reach of the hoist, no matter what the starting position and during fairly rapid approaches.

The experiment was shown to John T. Tate, a physicist, then Dean of the Graduate School at the University of Minnesota, who brought it to the attention of R. C. Tolman, one of a group of scientists engaged in early defense activities. The result was the first of a long series of rejections. The proposal "did not warrant further development at the time." The project was accordingly allowed to lapse. On December 7, 1941, the situation was suddenly restructured; and, on the following day, with the help of Keller Breland, then a graduate student at Minnesota, further work was planned. A simpler harnessing system could be used if the bomb were to rotate slowly during its descent, when the pigeon would need to steer in only one dimension: from side to side. We built an apparatus in which a harnessed pigeon was lowered toward a large revolving turntable across which a target was driven according to contacts made by the bird during its descent. It was not difficult to train a pigeon to "hit" small ship models during fairly rapid descents. We made a demonstration film showing hits on various kinds of targets, and two psychologists then engaged in the war effort in Washington, Charles Bray and Leonard Carmichael, undertook to look for government support. Tolman, then at the Office of Scientific Research

FIG. 1. Thirty-two pigeons, jacketed for testing.

FIG. 2. Nose of the Pelican, showing lenses.

110

and Development, again felt that the project did not warrant support, in part because the United States had at that time no missile capable of being guided toward a target. Commander (now Admiral) Luis de Florez, then in the Special Devices Section of the Navy, took a sympathetic view. He dismissed the objection that there was no available vehicle by suggesting that the pigeon be connected with an automatic pilot mounted in a small plane loaded with explosives. But he was unable to take on the project because of other commitments and because, as he explained, he had recently bet on one or two other equally long shots which had not come in.

The project lapsed again and would probably have been abandoned if it had not been for a young man whose last name I have ungratefully forgotten, but whose first name—Victor—we hailed as a propitious sign. His subsequent history led us to refer to him as Vanquished; and this, as it turned out, was a more reliable omen. Victor walked into the Department of Psychology at Minnesota one day in the summer of 1942 looking for an animal psychologist. He had a scheme for installing dogs in antisubmarine torpedoes. The dogs were to respond to faint acoustic signals from the submarine and to steer the torpedo toward its goal. He wanted a statement from an animal psychologist as to its feasibility. He was understandably surprised to learn of our work with pigeons but seized upon it eagerly, and citing it in support of his contention that dogs could be trained to steer torpedoes he went to a number of companies in Minneapolis. His project was rejected by everyone he approached; but one company, General Mills, Inc., asked for more information about our work with pigeons. We described the project and presented the available data to Arthur D. Hyde, Vice-President in Charge of Research. The company was not looking for new products, but Hyde thought that it might, as a public service, develop the pigeon system to the point at which a governmental agency could be persuaded to take over.

Breland and I moved into the top floor of a flour mill in Minneapolis and with the help of Norman Guttman, who had joined the project, set to work on further improvements. It had been difficult to induce the pigeon to respond to the small angular displacement of a distant target. It would start working dangerously late in the descent. Its natural pursuit behavior was not appropriate to the characteristics of a likely missile. A new system was therefore designed. An image of the target was projected on a translucent screen as in a camera obscura. The pigeon, held near the screen, was reinforced for pecking at the image on the screen. The guiding signal was to be picked up from the point of contact of screen and beak.

In an early arrangement the screen was a translucent plastic plate forming the larger end of a truncated cone bearing a lens at the smaller end. The cone was mounted, lens down, in a gimbal bearing. An object within range threw its image on the translucent screen; and the pigeon, held vertically just above the plate, pecked the image. When a target was moved about within range of the lens, the cone continued to point to it. In another apparatus a translucent disk, free to tilt slightly on gimbal bearings, closed contacts operating motors which altered the position of a large field beneath the apparatus. Small cutouts of ships and other objects were placed on the field. The field was constantly in motion, and a target would go out of range unless the pigeon continued to control it. With this apparatus we began to study the pigeon's reactions to various patterns and to develop sustained steady rates of responding through the use of appropriate schedules of reinforcement, the reinforcement being a few grains occasionally released onto the plate. By building up large extinction curves a target could be tracked continuously for a matter of minutes without reinforcement. We trained pigeons to follow a variety of land and sea targets, to neglect large patches intended to represent clouds of flak, to concentrate on one target while another was in view, and so on. We found that a pigeon could hold the missile on a particular street intersection in an aerial map of a city. The map which came most easily to hand was of a city which, in the interests of international relations, need not be identified. Through appropriate schedules of reinforcement it was possible to maintain longer uninterrupted runs than could conceivably be required by a missile.

We also undertook a more serious study of the pigeon's behavior, with the help of W. K. Estes and Marion Breland who joined the project at this time. We ascertained optimal conditions of deprivation, investigated other kinds of deprivations, studied the effect of special reinforcements (for example, pigeons were said to find hemp seed particularly delectable), tested the effects of energizing drugs and increased oxygen pressures, and so on. We differentially reinforced the force of the pecking response and found that pigeons could be induced to peck so energetically that the base of the beak became inflamed. We investigated the effects of extremes of temperature, of changes in atmospheric pressure, of accelerations produced by an improvised centrifuge, of increased carbon dioxide pressure, of increased and prolonged vibration, and of noises such as pistol shots. (The birds could, of course, have been deafened to eliminate auditory distractions, but we found it easy to maintain steady behavior in spite of intense noises and many other distracting conditions using the simple process of adaptation.) We investigated optimal conditions for the quick development of discriminations and began to study the pigeon's reactions to patterns, testing for induction from a test figure to the same figure inverted, to figures of different sizes and colors, and to figures against different grounds. A simple device using carbon paper to record the points at which a pigeon pecks a figure showed a promise which has never been properly exploited.

We made another demonstration film and renewed our contact with the Office of Scientific Research and Development. An observer was sent to Minneapolis, and on the strength of his report we were given an opportunity to present our case in Washington in February 1943. At that time we were offering a homing device capable of reporting with an on-off signal the orientation of a missile toward various visual patterns. The capacity to respond to pattern was, we felt, our strongest argument, but the fact that the device used only visible radiation (the same form of information available to the human bombardier) made it superior to the radio controlled missiles then under development because it was resistant to jamming. Our film had some effect. Other observers were sent to Minneapolis to see the demonstration itself. The pigeons, as usual, behaved beautifully. One of them held the supposed missile on a particular intersection of streets in the aerial map for five minutes although the target would have been lost if the pigeon had paused for a second or two. The observers returned to Washington, and two weeks later we were asked to supply data on (*a*) the population of pigeons in the United States (fortunately, the census bureau has some figures) and (*b*) the accuracy with which pigeons struck a point on a plate. There were many arbitrary conditions to be taken into account in measuring the latter, but we supplied possibly relevant data. At long last, in June 1943, the Office of Scientific Research and Development awarded a modest contract to General Mills, Inc. to "develop a homing device."

At that time we were given some information about the missile the pigeons were to steer. The Pelican was a wing steered glider, still under development and not yet successfully steered by any homing device. It was being tested on a target in New Jersey consisting of a stirrup shaped pattern bulldozed out of the sandy soil near the coast. The white lines of the target stood out clearly against brown and green cover. Colored photographs were taken from various distances and at various angles, and the verisimilitude of the reproduction was checked by flying over the target and looking at its image in a portable camera obscura.

Because of security restrictions we were given only very rough specifications of the signal to be supplied to the controlling system in the Pelican. It was no longer to be simply on-off; if the missile was badly off target, an especially strong correcting signal was needed. This meant that the quadrant-contact system would no longer suffice. But further requirements were left mainly to our imagination. The General Mills engineers were equal to this difficult assignment. With what now seems like unbelievable speed, they designed and constructed a pneumatic pickup system giving a graded signal. A lens in the nose of the missile threw an image on a translucent plate within reach of the pigeon in a pressure sealed chamber. Four air valves resting against the edges of the plate were jarred open momentarily as the pigeon pecked. The valves at the right and left admitted air to chambers on opposite sides of one tambour, while the valves at the top and bottom admitted air to opposite sides of another. Air on all sides was exhausted by a Venturi cone on the side of the missile. When the missile was on target, the pigeon pecked the center of the plate, all valves admitted equal amounts of air, and the tambours remained in neutral positions. But if the image moved as little as a quarter of an inch off-center, corresponding to a very small angular displacement of the target, more air was admitted by the valves on one side, and the resulting displacement of the tambours sent appropriate correcting orders directly to the servosystem.

The device required no materials in short supply, was relatively foolproof, and delivered a graded signal. It had another advantage. By this time we had begun to realize that a pigeon was more easily controlled than a physical scientist serving on a committee. It was very difficult to convince the latter that the former was an orderly system. We therefore multiplied the probability of success by designing a multiple bird unit. There was adequate space in the nose of the Pelican for three pigeons each with its own lens and plate. A net signal could easily be generated. The majority vote of three pigeons offered an excellent guarantee against momentary pauses and aberrations. (We later worked out a system in which the majority took on a more characteristically democratic functon. When a missile is falling toward *two* ships at sea, for example, there is no guarantee that all three pigeons will steer toward the same ship. But at least two must agree, and the third can then be punished for his minority opinion. Under proper contingencies of reinforcement a punished bird will shift immediately to the majority view. When all three are working on one ship, any defection is immediately punished and corrected.)

The arrangement in the nose of the Pelican is shown in Figure 3. Three systems of lenses and mirrors, shown at the left, throw images of the target area on the three translucent plates shown in the center. The ballistic valves resting against the edges of these plates and the tubes connecting them with the manifolds leading to the controlling tambours may be seen. A pigeon is being placed in the pressurized chamber at the right.

The General Mills engineers also built a simulator—a sort of Link trainer for pigeons—designed to have the steering characteristics of the Pelican, in so far as these had been communicated to us. Like the wing steered Pelican, the simulator tilted and turned side to side. When the three-bird nose was attached to it, the pigeons could be put in full control—the "loop could be closed"—and the adequacy of the signal tested under pursuit conditions. Targets were moved back and forth across the far

Fig. 3.   Demonstration model of the three-pigeon guidance system.

wall of a room at prescribed speeds and in given patterns of oscillation, and the tracking response of the whole unit was studied
quantitatively.

   Meanwhile we continued our intensive study of the behavior
of the pigeons. Looking ahead to combat use we designed methods for the mass production of trained birds and for handling
large groups of trained subjects. We were proposing to train certain birds for certain *classes* of targets, such as ships at sea,
while special squads were to be trained on special targets, photographs of which were to be obtained through reconnaissance.
A large crew of pigeons would then be waiting for assignment,
but we developed harnessing and training techniques which
should have solved such problems quite esaily.

   In a multiple unit trainer each box contains a jacketed pigeon held at an angle of 45° to the horizontal and perpendicular

to an 8″ × 8″ translucent screen. A target area is projected on each screen. Two beams of light intersect at the point to be struck. All on-target responses of the pigeon are reported by the interruption of the crossed beams and by contact with the translucent screen. Only a four-inch, disk shaped portion of the field is visible to the pigeon at any time, but the boxes move slowly about the field, giving the pigeon an opportunity to respond to the target in all positions. The positions of all reinforcements are recorded to reveal any weak areas. A variable-ratio schedule is used to build sustained, rapid responding.

By December 1943, less than six months after the contract was awarded, we were ready to report to the Office of Scientific Research and Development. Observers visited the laboratory and watched the simulator follow a target about a room under the control of a team of three birds. They also reviewed our tracking data. The only questions which arose were the inevitable consequence of our lack of information about the signal required to steer the Pelican. For example, we had had to make certain arbit-

FIG. 4. Simulator for testing the adequacy of the pigeon signal.

Fig. 5.   A trainer for four pigeons.

rary decisions in compromising between sensitivity of signal and its integration or smoothness. A high vacuum produced quick, rather erratic movements of the tambours, while a lower vacuum gave a sluggish but smooth signal. As it turned out, we had not chosen the best values in collecting our data, and in January 1944 the Office of Scientific Research and Development refused to extend the General Mills contract. The reasons given seemed to be due to misunderstandings or, rather, to lack of communication. We had already collected further data with new settings of the instruments, and these were submitted in a request for reconsideration.

We were given one more chance. We took our new data to the radiation lab at the Massachusetts Institute of Technology where they were examined by the servospecialists working on the Pelican controls. To our surprise the scientist whose task it was to predict the usefulness of the pigeon signal argued that our data were inconsistent with respect to phase lag and certain other characteristics of the signal. According to his equations, our device could not possibly yield the signals we reported. We knew, of course, that it had done so. We examined the supposed inconsistency and traced it, or so we thought, to a certain nonlinearity in our system. In pecking an image near the edge of the plate, the pigeon strikes a more glancing blow; hence the air admitted at the valves is not linearly proportional to the displacement of the target. This could be corrected in several ways: for example, by using a lens to distort radial distances. It was our understanding that in any case the signal was adequate to control the Pelican. Indeed, one servo authority, upon looking at graphs of the performance of the simulator, exclaimed: "This is better than radar!"

Two days later, encouraged by our meeting at MIT, we reached the summit. We were to present our case briefly to a committee of the country's top scientists. The hearing began with a brief report by the scientist who had discovered the "inconsistency" in our data, and to our surprise he still regarded it as unresolved. He predicted that the signal we reported would cause the missile to "hunt" wildly and lose the target. But his prediction should have applied as well to the closed loop simulator. Fortunately another scientist was present who had seen the simulator performing under excellent control and who could confirm our report of the facts. But reality was no match for mathematics.

The basic difficulty, of course, lay in convincing a dozen distinguished physical scientists that the behavior of a pigeon could be adequately controlled. We had hoped to score on this point by bringing with us a demonstration. A small black box had a round translucent window in one end. A slide projector placed some distance away threw on the window an image of the New Jersey target. In the box, of course, was a pigeon—which, incidentally, had at that time been harnessed for 35 hours. Our intention was to let each member of the committee observe the response to the target by looking down a small tube; but time was not available for individual observation, and we were asked to take the top off the box. The translucent screen was flooded with so much light that the target was barely visible, and the peering scientists offered conditions much more unfamiliar and threatening than those likely to be encountered in a missile. In spite of this the pigeon behaved perfectly, pecking steadily and energetically at the image of the target as it moved about on the plate. One scientist with an experimental turn of mind intercepted the beam from the projector. The pigeon stopped instantly. When the image again appeared, pecking began within a fraction of a second and continued at a steady rate.

It was a perfect performance, but it had just the wrong effect. One can talk about phase lag in pursuit behavior and discuss mathematical predictions of hunting without reflecting too closely upon what is inside the black box. But the spectacle of a living pigeon carrying out its assignment, no matter how beautifully, simply reminded the committee of how utterly fantastic our proposal was. I will not say that the meeting was marked by unrestrained merriment, for the merriment was restrained. But it was there, and it was obvious that our case was lost.

Hyde closed our presentation with a brief summary: we were offering a homing device, unusually resistant to jamming, capable of reacting to a wide variety of target patterns, requiring no materials in short supply, and so simple to build that production could be started in 30 days. He thanked the committee, and we left. As the door closed behind us, he said to me: "Why don't you go out and get drunk!"

Official word soon came: "Further prosecution of this project would seriously delay others which in the minds of the Division would have more immediate promise of combat application." Possibly the reference was to a particular combat application at Hiroshima a year and a half later, when it looked for a while as if the need for accurate bombing had been eliminated for all time. In any case we had to show, for all our trouble, only a loftful of curiously useless equipment and a few dozen pigeons with a strange interest in a feature of the New Jersey coast. The equipment was scrapped, but 30 of the pigeons were kept to see how long they would retain the appropriate behavior.

In the years which followed there were faint signs of life. Winston Churchill's personal scientific advisor, Lord Cherwell, learned of the project and "regretted its demise." A scientist who had had some contact with the project during the war, and who evidently assumed that its classified status was not to be taken seriously, made a good story out of it for the *Atlantic Monthly*, names being changed to protect the innocent. Other uses of animals began to be described. The author of the *Atlantic Monthly* story also published an account of the "incendiary bats." Thousands of bats were to be released over an enemy city, each carrying a small incendiary time bomb. The bats would take refuge, as is their custom, under eaves and in other out-of-the-way places; and shortly afterwards thousands of small fires would break out practically simultaneously. The scheme was never used because it was feared that it would be mistaken for germ warfare and might lead to retaliation in kind.

Another story circulating at the time told how the Russians trained dogs to blow up tanks. I have described the technique elsewhere (Skinner, 1956). A Swedish proposal to use seals to achieve the same end with submarines was not successful. The seals were to be trained to approach submarines to obtain fish attached to the sides. They were then to be released carrying magnetic mines in the vicinity of hostile submarines. The required training was apparently never achieved. I cannot vouch for the authenticity of probably the most fantastic story of this sort, but it ought to be recorded. The Russians were said to have trained sea lions to cut mine cables. A complicated device attached to the sea lion included a motor driven cable-cutter, a tank full of small fish, and a device which released a few fish into a muzzle covering the sea lion's head. In order to eat, the sea lion had to find a mine cable and swim along side it so that the cutter was automatically triggered, at which point a few fish were released from the tank into the muzzle. When a given number of cables had been cut, both the energy of the cutting mechanism and the supply of fish were exhausted, and the sea lion received a special stimulus upon which it returned to its home base for special reinforcement and reloading.

ORCON

The story of our own venture has a happy ending. With the discovery of German accomplishments in the field of guided missiles, feasible homing systems suddenly became very important. Franklin V. Taylor of the Naval Research Laboratory in Washington, D.C. heard about our project and asked for further details. As a psychologist Taylor appreciated the special capacity of living organisms to respond to visual patterns and was aware of recent advances in the control of behavior. More important, he was a skillful practitioner in a kind of control which our project had conspicuously lacked: he knew how to approach the people who determine the direction of research. He showed our demonstration film so often that it was completely worn out—but to good effect, for support was eventually found for a thorough investigation of "organic control" under the general title ORCON. Taylor also enlisted the support of engineers in obtaining a more effective report of the pigeon's behavior. The translucent plate upon which the image of the target was thrown had a semiconducting surface, and the tip of the bird's beak was covered with a gold electrode. A single contact with the plate sent an immediate report of the location of the target to the controlling mechanism. The work which went into this system contributed to the so-called Pick-off Display Converter developed as part of the Naval Data Handling System for human observers. It is no longer necessary for the radar operator to give a verbal report of the location of a pip on the screen. Like the pigeon, he has only to touch the pip with a special contact. (He holds the contact is his hand.)

At the Naval Research Laboratory in Washington the responses of pigeons were studied in detail. Average peck rate, average error rate, average hit rate, and so on were recorded under various conditions. The tracking behavior of the pigeon was analyzed with methods similar to those employed with human operators. Pattern perception was studied, including generalization from one pattern to another. A simulator was constructed in which the pigeon controlled an image projected by a moving-picture film of an actual target: for example, a ship at sea as seen from a plane approaching at 600 miles per hour.

The publications from the Naval Research Laboratory which report this work (Chernikoff & Newlin, 1951; Conklin, Newlin, Taylor, & Tipton, 1953; Searle & Stafford, 1950; Taylor, 1949; White, 1952) provide a serious evaluation of the possibilities of organic control. Although in simulated tests a single pigeon occasionally loses a target, its tracking characteristics are surprisingly good. A three- or seven-bird unit with the same individual consistency should yield a signal with a reliability which is at least of the order of magnitude shown by other phases of guided missiles in their present stage of development. Moreover, in the seven

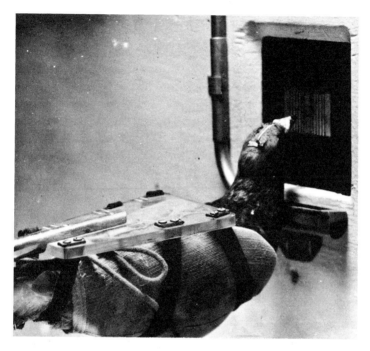

FIG. 6.   Arrangement for studying pursuit movements.

years which have followed the last of these reports, a great deal of relevant information has been acquired The color vision of the pigeon is now thoroughly understood; its generalization along single properties of a stimulus has been recorded and analyzed; and the maintenance of behavior through scheduling of reinforcement has been drastically improved, particularly in the development of techniques for pacing responses for less erratic and steadier signals (Skinner, 1957). Tests made with the birds salvaged from the old Project Pigeon showed that even after six years of inactivity a pigeon will immediately and correctly strike a target to which it has been conditioned and will continue to respond for some time without reinforcement.

The use of living organisms in guiding missiles is, it seems fair to say, no longer a crackpot idea. A pigeon is an extraordi-

FIG. 7. Frames from a simulated approach.

124

narily subtle and complex mechanism capable of performances which at the moment can be equalled by electronic equipment only of vastly greater weight and size, and it can be put to reliable use through the principles which have emerged from an experimental analysis of its behavior. But this vindication of our original proposal is perhaps the least important result. Something happened during the brief life of Project Pigeon which it has taken a long time to appreciate. The practical task before us created a new attitude toward the behavior of organisms. We had to maximize the probability that a given form of behavior would occur at a given time. We could not enjoy the luxury of observing one variable while allowing others to change in what we hoped was a random fashion. We had to discover all relevant variables and submit them to experimental control whenever possible. We were no doubt under exceptional pressure, but vigorous scientific research usually makes comparable demands. Psychologists have too often yielded to the temptation to be content with hypothetical processes and intervening variables rather than press for rigorous experimental control. It is often intellectual laziness rather than necessity which recommends the *a posteriori* statistical treatment of variation. Our task forced us to emphasize prior experimental control, and its success in revealing orderly processes gave us an exciting glimpse of the superiority of laboratory practice over verbal (including some kinds of mathematical) explanation.

THE CRACKPOT IDEA

If I were to conclude that crackpot ideas are to be encouraged, I should probably be told that psychology has already had more than its share of them. If it has, they have been entertained by the wrong people. Reacting against the excesses of psychological quackery, psychologists have developed an enormous concern for scientific respectability. They constantly warn their students against questionable facts and unsupported theories. As a result the usual PhD thesis is a model of compulsive cautiousness, advancing only the most timid conclusions thoroughly hedged about with qualifications. But it is just the man capable of displaying such admirable caution who needs a touch of uncontrolled speculation. Possibly a generous exposure to psychological science fiction would help. Project Pigeon might be said to support that view. Except with respect to its avowed goal, it was, as I see it, highly productive; and this was in large measure because my colleagues and I knew that, in the eyes of the world, we were crazy.

One virtue in crackpot ideas is that they breed rapidly and their progeny show extraordinary mutations. Everyone is talking about teaching machines nowadays, but Sidney Pressey can tell you what it was like to have a crackpot idea in that field 40 years ago. His self-testing devices and self-scoring test forms now need no defense, and psychomotor training devices have also achieved a substantial respectability. This did not, however, prepare the way for devices to be used in verbal instructions—that is, in the kinds of teaching which are the principal concern of our schools and colleges. (I can quote official opinion to that effect from high places.) Even five short years ago that kind of instruction by machine was still in the crackpot category. Now, there is a direct genetic connection between teaching machines and Project Pigeon. We had been forced to consider the mass education of pigeons. True, the scrap of wisdom we imparted to each was indeed small, but the required changes in behavior were similar to those which must be brought about in vaster quantities in human students. The techniques of shaping behavior and of bringing it under stimulus control which can be traced, as I have suggested elsewhere (Skinner, 1958), to a memorable episode on the top floor of that flour mill in Minneapolis needed only a detailed reformulation of verbal behavior to be directly applicable to education.

I am sure there is more to come. In the year which followed the termination of Project Pigeon I wrote *Walden Two* (Skinner, 1948), a utopian picture of a properly engineered society. Some psychotherapists might argue that I was suffering from personal rejection and simply retreated to a fantasied world where everything went according to plan, where there never was heard a discouraging word. But another explanation is, I think, equally plausible. That piece of science fiction was a declaration of confidence in a technology of behavior. Call it a crackpot idea if you will; it is one in which I have never lost faith. I still believe that the same kind of wide-ranging speculation about human affairs, supported by studies of compensating rigor, will make a substantial contribution toward that world of the future in which, among other things, there will be no need for guided missiles.

REFERENCES

Chernikoff, R., & Newlin, E. P. ORCON. Part III. Investigations of target acquisition by the pigeon. *Naval Res. Lab. lett. Rep.*, 1951, No. S-3600-629a/51 (Sept. 10).

Conklin, J. E., Newlin, E. P., Jr., Taylor, F. V., & Tipton, C. L. ORCON. Part IV. Simulated flight tests. *Naval Res. Lab. Rep.*, 1953, No. 4105.

Searle, L. V., & Stafford, B. H. ORCON. Part II. Report of phase I research and bandpass study. *Naval Res. Lab. lett. Rep.*, 1950, No. S-3600-157/50 (May 1).

Skinner, B. F. *Walden two.* New York: Macmillan, 1948.

Skinner, B. F. A case history in scientific method. *Amer. Psychologist,* 1956, 11, 221–233.

Skinner, B. F. The experimental analysis of behavior. *Amer. Scient.,* 1957, 45, 343–371.

Skinner, B. F. Reinforcment today. *Amer. Psychologist,* 1958, 13, 94–99.

Taylor, F. V. ORCON. Part I. Outline of proposed research. *Naval Res. Lab. lett. Rep.*, 1949, No. S-3600-157/50 (June 17).

White, C. F. Development of the NRL ORCON tactile missile simulator. *Naval Res. Lab. Rep.*, 1952, No. 3917.

Intensive Treatment of Psychotic Behaviour by Stimulus Satiation and Food Reinforcement[1]

T. AYLLON, *Anna State Hospital, Illinois*

This investigation demonstrates that extensive and effective behavioural modification is feasible without costly and lengthy psychotherapeutic treatment. In addition, the often heard notion that another undesirable type of behaviour will replace the original problem behaviour is not supported by the findings to date.

INTRODUCTION

Until recently, the effective control of behaviour was limited to the animal laboratory. The extension of this control to human behaviour was made when Lindsley successfully adapted the methodology of operant conditioning to the study of psychotic behaviour (Lindsley, 1956). Following Lindsley's point of departure other investigators have shown that, in its essentials, the behaviour of mental defective individuals (Orlando and Bijou, 1960), stutterers (Flanagan, Goldiamond and Azrin, 1958), mental patients (Hutchinson and Azrin, 1961), autistic (Ferster and

Ayllon, T. Intensive treatment of psychotic behaviour by stimulus satiation and food reinforcement. *Behavior Research and Therapy*, 1963, *1*, 53–61. Photographs of the subject, present in the original article, were omitted in this reproduction. Additional information and related research can be found in The Token Economy: A Motivational System for Therapy and Rehabilitation by T. Ayllon and N. H. Azrin, published by Appleton Century-Crofts, 1968.

DeMyer, 1961), and normal children (Bijou, 1961; Azrin and Lindsley, 1956) is subject to the same controls.

Despite the obvious implications of this research for applied settings there has been a conspicuous lag between the research findings and their application. The greatest limitation to the direct application of laboratory principles has been the absence of control over the subjects' environment. Recently, however, a series of applications in a regulated psychiatric setting has clearly demonstrated the possiblities of behavioural modification (Ayllon and Michael, 1959; Ayllon and Haughton, 1962). Some of the behaviour studied has included repetitive and highly stereotyped responses such as complaining, pacing, refusal to eat, hoarding and many others.

What follows is a demonstration of behaviour techniques for the intensive individual treatment of psychotic behaviour. Specific pathological behaviour patterns of a single patient were treated by manipulating the patient's environment.

The Experimental Ward and
Control Over the Reinforcement

This investigation was conducted in a mental hospital ward, the characteristics of which have been described elsewhere (Ayllon and Haughton, 1962). Briefly, this was a female ward to which only authorized personnel were allowed access. The ward staff was made up of psychiatric nurses and untrained aides who carried out the environmental manipulations under the direction of the experimenter. Using a time-sample technique, patients were observed daily every 30 minutes from 7:00 a.m. to 11:00 p.m.

The dining room was the only place where food was available and entrance to the dining room could be regulated. Water was freely available at a drinking fountain on the ward. None of the patients had ground passes or jobs outside the ward.

Subject

The patient was a 47-year-old female diagnosed as a chronic schizophrenic. The patient had been hospitalized for 9 years. Upon studying the patient's behaviour on the ward, it became apparent that the nursing staff[2] spent considerable time caring for her. In particular, there were three aspects of her behaviour which seemed to defy solution. The first was stealing food. The second was the hoarding of the ward's towels in her room. The third undesirable aspect of her behaviour consisted in her wearing excessive clothing, e.g., a half-dozen dresses, several pairs of stockings, sweaters, and so on.

In order to modify the patient's behaviour systematically, each of these three types of behaviour (stealing food, hoarding, and excessive dressing) was treated separately.

EXPERIMENT I

Control of Stealing Food by Food Withdrawal

The patient had weighed over 250 pounds for many years. She ate the usual tray of food served to all patients, but, in addition, she stole food from the food counter and from other patients. Because the medical staff regarded her excessive weight as detrimental to her health, a special diet had been prescribed for her. However, the patient refused to diet and continued stealing food. In an effort to discourage the patient from stealing, the ward nurses had spent considerable time trying to persuade her to stop stealing food. As a last resort, the nurses would force her to return the stolen food.

To determine the extent of food stealing, nurses were instructed to record all behaviour associated with eating in the dining room. This record, taken for nearly a month, showed that the patient stole food during two thirds of all meals.

Procedure

The traditional methods previously used to stop the patient from stealing food were discontinued. No longer were persuasion, coaxing, or coercion used.

The patient was assigned to a table in the dining room, and no other patients were allowed to sit with her. Nurses removed the patient from the dining room when she approached a table other than her own, or when she picked up unauthorized food from the dining room counter. In effect, this procedure resulted in the patient missing a meal whenever she attempted to steal food.

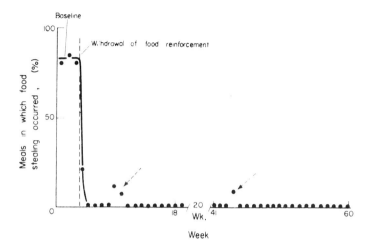

Fig. 1. A response, food stealing, is eliminated when it results in the withdrawal of food reinforcement. The dotted arrows indicate the rare occasions when food stealing occurred. For purposes of presentation a segment comprising 20 weeks during which no stealing occurred is not included.

Results

Figure 1 shows that when withdrawal of positive reinforcement (i.e. meal) was made dependent upon the patient's 'stealing', this response was eliminated in two weeks. Because the patient no longer stole food, she ate only the diet prescribed for her. The effective control of the stealing response is also indicated by the gradual reduction in the patient's body weight. At no time during the patient's 9 years of hospitalization had she weighed less than 230 pounds. Figure 2 shows that at the conclusion of this treatment her weight stabilized at 180 pounds or 17 percent loss from her original weight. At this time, the patient's physical condition was regarded as excellent.

Discussion

A principle used in the laboratory shows that the strength of a response may be weakened by the removal of positive reinforcement following the response (Ferster, 1958). In this case, the response was food-stealing and the reinforcer was access to

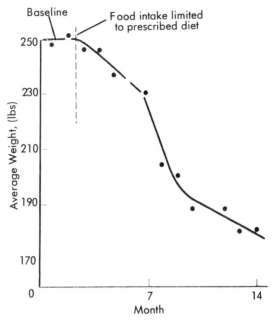

Fɪɢ. 2. The effective control of food stealing results in a notable reduction in body weight. As the patient's food intake is limited to the prescribed diet her weight decreases gradually.

meals. When the patient stole food she was removed from the dining room and missed her meal.

After one year of this treatment, two occasions of food stealing occurred. The first occasion, occurring after one year of not stealing food, took the nurses by surprise and, therefore the patient 'got away' with it. The second occasion occurred shortly thereafter. This time, however, the controlling consequences were in force. The patient missed that meal and did not steal again to the conclusion of this investigation.

Because the patient was not informed or warned of the consequences that followed stealing, the nurses regarded the procedure as unlikely to have much effect on the patient's behaviour. The implicit belief that verbal instructions are indispensable for learning is part of present day psychiatric lore. In keeping with this notion, prior to this behaviour treatment, the nurses had tried to persuade the patient to co-operate in dieting. Because there were strong medical reasons for her losing weight, the patient's refusal to follow a prescribed diet was regarded as further evidence of her mental illness.

EXPERIMENT II

Control of One Form of Hoarding
Behavior through Stimulus Satiation

During the 9 years of hospitalization, the patient collected large numbers of towels and stored them in her room. Although many efforts had been made to discourage hoarding, this behaviour continued unaltered. The only recourse for the nursing staff was to take away the patient's towels about twice a week.

To determine the degree of hoarding behaviour, the towels in her room were counted three times a week, when the patient was not in her room. This count showed that the number of towels kept in her room ranged from 19 to 29 despite the fact that during this time the nurses continued recovering their towel supply from the patient's room.

Procedure

The routine removal of the towels from the patient's room was discontinued. Instead, a programme of stimulus satiation was carried out by the nurses. Intermittently, throughout the day, the nurses took a towel to the patient when she was in her room and simply handed it to her without any comment. The first week she was given an average of 7 towels daily, and by the third week this number was increased to 60.

Results

The technique of satiation eliminated the towel hoarding. Figure 3 shows the mean number of towels per count found in the patient's room. When the number of towels kept in her room reached the 625 mark, she started taking a few of them out. Thereafter, no more towels were given to her. During the next 12 months the mean number of towels found in her room was 1.5 per week.

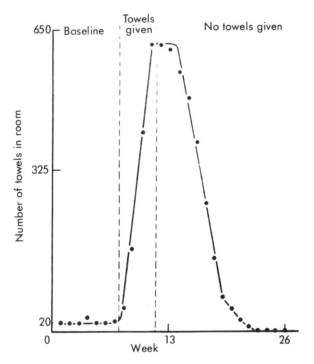

FIG. 3. A response, towel hoarding, is eliminated when the patient is given towels in excess. When the number of towels reaches 625 the patient starts to discard them. She continues to do so until the number found in her room averages 1 to 5 compared to the previous 20 towels per week.

Discussion

The procedure used to reduce the amount of towel hoarding bears resemblance to satiation of a reinforcer. A reinforcer loses its effect when an excessive amount of that reinforcer is made available. Accordingly, the response maintained by that reinforcer is weakened. In this application, the towels constituted the reinforcing stimuli. When the number of towels in her room reached 625, continuing to give her towels seemed to make their collection aversive. The patient then proceeded to rid herself of the towels until she had virtually none.

During the first few weeks of satiation, the patient was observed patting her cheeks with a few towels, apparently enjoying them. Later, the patient was observed spending much of her time folding and stacking the approximately 600 towels in her room. A variety of remarks were made by the patient regarding receipt of towels. All verbal statements made by the patient were recorded by the nurse. The following represent typical remarks made during this experiment. First week: As the nurse entered the patient's room carrying a towel, the patient would smile and say, "Oh, you found it for me, thank you." Second week: When the number of towels given to patient increased rapidly, she told the nurses, "Don't give me no more towels. I've got enough." Third week: "Take them towels away .... I can't sit here all night and fold towels." Fourth and fifth weeks: "Get these dirty towels out of here." Sixth week: After she had started taking the towels out of her room, she remarked to the nurse, "I can't drag any more of these towels, I just can't do it."

The quality of these remarks suggests that the initial effect of giving towels to the patient was reinforcing. However, as the towels increased they ceased to be reinforcing, and presumably became aversive.

The ward nurses, who had undergone a three year training in psychiatric nursing, found it difficult to reconcile the procedure in this experiment with their psychiatric orientation. Most nurses subscribed to the popular psychiatric view which regards hoarding behaviour as a reflection of a deep 'need' for love and security. Presumably, no 'real' behavioural change was possible without meeting the patient's 'needs' first. Even after the patient discontinued hoarding towels in her room, some nurses predicted that the change would not last and that worse behaviour would replace it. Using a time-sampling technique the patient was under continuous observation for over a year after the termination of the satiation programme. Not once during this period did the patient return to hoarding towels. Furthermore, no other behaviour problem replaced hoarding.

EXPERIMENT III

Control of an additional form
of hoarding through food reinforcement

Shortly after the patient had been admitted to the hospital she wore an excessive amount of clothing which included several

sweaters, shawls, dresses, undergarments and stockings. The clothing also included sheets and towels wrapped around her body,
and a turban-like head-dress made up of several towels. In
addition, the patient carried two to three cups on one hand while
holding a bundle of miscellaneous clothing, and a large purse
on the other.

To determine the amount of clothing worn by the patient,
she was weighed before each meal over a period of two weeks.
By subtracting her actual body weight from that recorded when
she was dressed, the weight of her clothing was obtained.

Procedure

The response required for reinforcement was stepping on
a scale and meeting a predetermined weight. The requirement
for reinforcement consisted of meeting a single weight (i.e. her
body weight plus a specified number of pounds of clothing). Initially she was given an allowance of 23 pounds over her current
body weight. This allowance represented a 2 pound reduction
from her usual clothing weight. When the patient exceeded
the weight requirement, the nurse stated in a matter-of-fact manner, "Sorry, you weigh too much, you'll have to weigh less." Failure to meet the required weight resulted in the patient missing
the meal at which she was being weighed. Sometimes, in an effort
to meet the requirement, the patient discarded more clothing
than she was required. When this occurred the requirement was
adjusted at the next weighing-time to correspond to the limit set
by the patient on the preceding occasion.

Results

When food reinforcement is made dependent upon the removal of superfluous clothing the response increases in frequency.
Figure 4 shows that the patient gradually shed her clothing to
meet the more demanding weight requirement until she dressed
normally. At the conclusion of this experiment her clothes
weighed 3 pounds compared to the 25 pounds she wore before
this treatment.

Some verbal shaping was done in order to encourage the patient to leave the cups and bundles she carried with her. Nurses
stopped her at the dining room and said, "Sorry, no things are

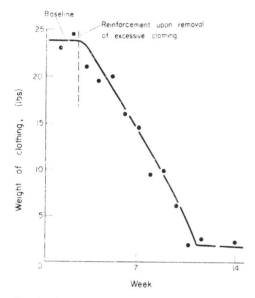

Fig. 4. A response, excessive dressing, is eliminated when food reinforcement is made dependent upon removal of superfluous clothing. Once the weight of the clothing worn by the patient drops to 3 pounds it remains stable.

allowed in the dining room." No mention of clothing or specific items was made to avoid focusing undue attention upon them. Within a week, the patient typically stepped on the scale without her bundle and assorted objects. When her weight was over the limit, the patient was informed that she weighed "too much". She then proceeded to take off a few clothes, stepped on the scale again, and upon meeting the weight requirement, gained access to the dining room.

Discussion

According to the principle of reinforcement a class of responses is strengthened when it is followed by reinforcement. A reinforcer is such when it results in a response increase. In this application the removal of excessive clothing constituted the response and the reinforcer was food (i.e. access to meals). When the patient met the weight requirement she was reinforced by being given access to meals.

At the start of this experiment, the patient missed a few meals because she failed to meet the weight requirement, but soon thereafter she gradually discarded her superfluous clothing. First, she left behind odd items she had carried in her arms, such as bundles, cups and handbags. Next she took off the elaborate headgear and assorted "capes" or shawls she had worn over her shoulders. Although she had worn 18 pairs of stockings at one time, she eventually shed these also.

During the initial part of this experiment, the patient showed some emotional behaviour, e.g. crying, shouting and throwing chairs around. Because nurses were instructed to "ignore" this emotional behaviour, the patient obtained no sympathy or attention from them. The withholding of social reinforcement for emotional behaviour quickly led to its elimination.

At the conclusion of this behaviour treatment, the patient typically stepped on the scale wearing a dress, undergarments, a pair of stockings and a pair of light shoes. One of the behavioural changes concomitant with the current environmental manipulation was that as the patient began dressing normally she started to participate in small social events in the hospital. This was particularly new to the patient as she had previously remained seclusive spending most of the time in her room.

About this time the patient's parents came to visit her and insisted on taking her home for a visit. This was the first time during the patient's 9 years of hospitalization that her parents had asked to take her out. They remarked that previously they had not been interested in taking her out because the patient's excessive dressing in addition to her weight made her look like a "circus freak".

CONCLUSIONS

The research presented here was conducted under nearly ideal conditions. The variables manipulated (i.e. towels and food) were under full experimental control. Using a time-sample technique the patient was observed daily every 30 minutes from 7:00 a.m. to 11:00 p.m. Nurses and aides carried out these observations which were later analysed in terms of gross behaviour categories. These observations were in force for over a year during which time these three experiments were conducted. The results of these observations indicate that none of the three pathological behaviour patterns (i.e. food stealing, hoarding and excessive dressing) exhibited by the patient were replaced by any undesirable behaviour.

The patient displayed some emotional behaviour in each experiment, but each time it subsided when social reinforcement (i.e. attention) was not forthcoming. The patient did not become violent or seclusive as a consequence of these experiments. Instead, she became socially more accessible to patients and staff. She did not achieve a great deal of social success but she did begin to participate actively in social functions.

A frequent problem encountered in mental hospitals is overeating. In general this problem is solved by prescribing a reduction diet. Many patients, however, refuse to take a reduction diet and continue overeating. When confronted with this behaviour, psychiatric workers generally resort to two types of explanations.

One explanation of overeating points out that only with the active and sincere cooperation of the patient can weight reduction be accomplished. When the patient refuses to cooperate he is regarded as showing more signs of mental illness and all hopes of eliminating overeating come to an end.

Another type of explanation holds that overeating is not the behaviour to be concerned with. Instead, attention is focused on the psychological 'needs' of the patient. These 'needs' are said to be the cause of the observable behaviour, overeating. Therefore the emphasis is on the removal of the cause and not on the symptom or behaviour itself. Whatever theoretical merit these explanations may have, it is unfortunate that they fail to suggest practical ways of treating the behaviour itself. As a consequence, the patient continues to overeat often to the detriment of his health.

The current psychiatric emphasis on the resolution of the mental conflict that is presumably at the basis of the symptoms, is perhaps misplaced. What seems to have been forgotten is that behaviour problems such as those reported here, prevent the patient from being considered for discharge not only by the hospital personnel but also by the patient's relatives. Indeed, as far as the patient's relatives are concerned, the index of improvement or deterioration is the readily observable behaviour and not a detailed account of the mechanics of the mental apparatus.

Many individuals are admitted to mental hospitals because of one or more specific behaviour difficulties and not always because of a generalized 'mental' disturbance. For example, an individual may go into a mental hospital because he has refused to eat for several days, or because he talks to himself incessantly. If the goal of therapy were behavioral rehabilitation, these problems would be treated and normal eating and normal talking reinstated. However, the current emphasis in psychotherapy is on 'mental-conflict resolution' and little or no attention is given to dealing directly with the behavioural problems which prevent the patient from returning to the community.

NOTES

1. This report is based, in part, on a two-year research project (1959–1961), conducted by the author at the Saskatchewan Hospital, Weyburn, Saskatchewan, Canada, and supported by a grant from the Commonwealth Fund. Grateful acknowledgment is due to H. Osmond and I. Clancey of the Saskatchewan Hospital. The author also thanks E. Haughton who assisted in the conduct of this investigation, and N. Azrin and W. Holtz for their critical reading of the manuscript.
2. As used in this paper, 'nurse' is a generic term including all those who actually work on the ward (attendants, aides, psychiatric and registered nurses).

REFERENCES

Ayllon, T. and Michael, J. (1959) The psychiatric nurse as a behavioural engineer. *J. exp. anal. Behav.* 2, 323–334.

Ayllon, T. and Haughton, E. (1962) Control of the behaviour of schizophrenic patients by food. *J. exp. anal. Behav.* 5, 343–352.

Azrin, N. and Lindsley, O. (1956) The reinforcement of cooperation between children. *J. abnorm. (soc.) Psychol.* 52, 100–102.

Bijou, S. (1961) Discrimination performance as a baseline for individual analysis of young children. *Child Develpm.* 32, 163–170.

Ferster, C. B. (1958) Control of behaviour in chimpanzees and pigeons by time out from positive reinforcement. *Psychol. Monogr.* 72, 1–38.

Ferster, C. and DeMyer, M. (1961) The development of performances in autistic children in an automatically controlled environment. *J. chron. Dis.* 13, 312–345.

Flanagan, B., Goldiamond, I. and Azrin, N. (1958) Operant stuttering: The control of stuttering behaviour through response-contingent consequences. *J. exp. anal. Behav.* 56, 49–56.

Hutchinson, R. R. and Azrin, N. H. (1961) Conditioning of mental hospital patients to fixed-ratio schedules of reinforcement. *J. exp. anal. Behav.* 4, 87–95.

Lindsley, O. R. (1956) Operant conditioning methods applied to research in chronic schizophrenia. *Psychiat. Res. Rep.* 5, 118–139.

Orlando, R. and Bijou, S. (1960) Single and multiple schedules of reinforcement in developmentally retarded children. *J. exp. anal. Behav.* 3, 339–348.

Section Two

Respondent Conditioning

In respondent conditioning we begin with an unconditioned stimulus (called UCS or US) that elicits an unconditioned response (UCR). "Unconditioned" does not mean that the UCS innately elicits the UCR, but only that at the present time the UCS elicits the UCR, either innately or because of previous learning. In experiments with humans a popular UCS is a puff of air to the eye with the resulting UCR of an eye-blink. A second stimulus is chosen, the conditioned stimulus (CS), which does not elicit a response similar to the UCR. The CS elicits some response, but the response is different than the UCR and usually chosen to be a weaker response than the UCR. In the eye-blink example a CS of a tone might be chosen. The response elicited by the tone is usually just an orienting to the source of the tone.

Respondent conditioning consists of pairing the CS and UCS, until the CS elicits a conditioned response (CR) that is similar to the UCR. Generally, the most effective way to do this pairing is to have the CS come on first and then the UCS about one-half second later. For example, the tone would come on, followed by the puff of air to the eye. This would be continued until the tone by itself was capable of eliciting an eye-blink. Although the CR and UCR are similar responses, they are generally not identical. They usually differ by magnitude, with the UCR a stronger response than the CR.

Extinction in respondent conditioning is accomplished by terminating the CS-UCS contingency, that is, by stopping pairing the CS and UCS. Thus if we keep presenting the tone to the person and no longer pairing it with the air puff, eventually the CR will extinguish, the tone will no longer elicit an eye-blink.

Theories of respondent conditioning emphasize different relationships that result from pairing the CS and UCS. Most theories, however, center around one or both of the following two possible relationships: First, there is the CS-UCS contiguity relationship, the fact that the CS and UCS might become associated because they occur closely together in time. Guthrie (1935) emphasized this association. Second, there is a CR-UCS reinforcement relationship. That is, when the CR begins to occur and when it precedes the UCS, the UCS might reinforce the CR. If the UCS is a pleasant stimulus, such as wet food powder to a hungry dog, the onset of the UCS might be reinforcing. If the UCS is an unpleasant stimulus, such as the air-puff to the eye, it might be the offset of the UCS that is the reinforcement. Spence (1956) was a theorist who emphasized the reinforcing role of the UCS. Occasionally theorists also include the CS-UCR S-R relationship where the stimulus CS simply by being paired with the response of the UCR results in an association between the CS and UCR.

Some theories involve a combination of relationships. Joan E. Jones (1962) suggested that in early stages of some conditioning the major variable is the CS-UCR relationship, while later in conditioning it is the CR-UCS relationship.

In the first reading Rescorla discusses different theoretical models of respondent conditioning in the context of describing adequate control procedures. One theoretical orientation emphasizes the number of times the CS and UCS have actually been paired. That is, respondent conditioning basically reduces to the number of times the CS has been closely followed by the UCS. An alternative orientation, which Rescorla favors, emphasizes the contingency between the CS and UCS. The subject learns not only what is paired with the CS, but also what is not paired. Instead of just simple pairings, the subject is learning causal relationships between stimulus events. From this latter orientation the ideal control group for respondent conditioning is what Rescorla calls the "truly random" control procedure. In this procedure the CS and UCS are presented randomly to each other; that is, there is no contingency between the CS and UCS although there may be some chance pairings.

An important theoretical question is whether the subject is more disposed to learn the association between one CS-UCS as opposed to another. The reading by Garcia and Koelling suggests this might be the case. They found that rats readily learned the association between audiovisual stimuli and electric shock and between gustatory stimuli (taste) and toxins and x-rays that cause gastrointestinal problems, but not conversely. The rats did not readily learn associations between gustatory stimuli and electric shock or between the audiovisual stimuli and the nausea producing stimuli. Similar types of findings are discussed in a later reading by Seligman.

In human respondent conditioning the CR might be considered undersirable. After being knocked down a few times by a dog, a child might develop a conditioned fear of dogs that carries into later life when the fear is no longer functional or desirable. One way of changing an undesired CR is by means of *counter-conditioning*, the respondent conditioning of a desired response in place of an undesired response (cf. Mikulas, 1972, p. 32–38). The readings by Davison and by Bandura, Blanchard, and Ritter show variations of the counterconditioning procedure.

Davison describes the case of a college male who was sexually aroused by imagining sadistic scenes but not by "normal" sexual fantasies or activities. This situation was reversed by procedures that were primarily counterconditioning. To condition in the desired responses, heterosexual stimuli (CS) such as pictures from *Playboy* were paired with stimuli (UCS) from masturbation that produced a sexual response (UCR). Similarly to weaken the sexually arousing effects of the sadistic fantasies, sadistic images (CS) were paired with imagined scenes (UCS) that produced disgusting nauseous feelings (UCR). The idea of gradually conditioning in sexual responses appears to be one of the major variables underlying the procedures Masters and Johnson (1970) outline for treatment of sexual inadequacies.

The reading by Bandura, Blanchard, and Ritter describes a number of procedures for treating snake phobias. The procedure of desensitization, as developed by Wolpe (1958), generally requires the subject, while being kept relaxed, to imagine scenes that gradually approximate the feared object. Although the mechanisms underlying desensitization are greatly debated, the most common explanation is that the relaxation responses gradually become conditioned (counterconditioning) to the stimuli that previously elicited anxiety. Another explanation (e.g., Wilson and Davison, 1971) is that desensitization is basically respondent extinction, where the relaxation facilitates extinction of the anxiety from the feared stimulus.

The second procedure used in the Bandura study is *modeling*. Here it has been shown (Bandura, 1969, chapter 3) that simply having a subject with a snake phobia watch an appropriate model approach and interact with the snake will tend to reduce the subject's fear of snakes. The third procedure, *contact desensitization* (live modeling combined with guided participation), is essentially a combination of parts of desensitization with modeling.

The general findings of the Bandura study were that all the procedures were effective in reducing anxiety and changing related attitudes, with contact desensitization the most effective.

Pavlovian Conditioning and Its Proper Control Procedures[1]

ROBERT A. RESCORLA, *Yale University*

The traditional control procedures for Pavlovian conditioning are examined and each is found wanting. Some procedures introduce nonassociative factors not present in the experimental procedure while others transform the excitatory, experimental CS–US contingency into an inhibitory contingency. An alternative control procedure is suggested in which there is no contingency whatsoever between CS and US. This "truly random" control procedure leads to a new conception of Pavlovian conditioning postulating that the contingency between CS and US, rather than the pairing of CS and US, is the important event in conditioning. The fruitfulness of this new conception of Pavlovian conditioning is illustrated by 2 experimental results.

The operations performed to establish Pavlovian conditioned reflexes require that the presentation of an unconditioned stimulus be contingent upon the occurrence of a conditioned stimulus. Students of conditioning have regarded this contingency between CS and US as vital to the definition of conditioning and have rejected changes in the organism not dependent

Rescorla, R. A. Pavlovian conditioning and its proper control procedures. *Psychological Review*, 1967, *74*, 71–80. Copyright 1967 by the American Psychological Association, and reproduced by permission.

upon this contingency (such as sensitization or pseudoconditioning) as not being "true" conditioning (i.e., associative). Therefore, in order to identify the effects due uniquely to the contingency between CS and US, a variety of control procedures have been developed. Each of these procedures attempts to retain some features of the Pavlovian conditioning situation while eliminating the CS–US contingency.

This paper argues that, in fact, none of the conventional control procedures for nonassociative effects is adequate, either taken alone or in combination; it further argues that a new type of "random stimulus" control procedure does enable one to identify the role of the CS–US contingency in Pavlovian conditioning.

TRADITIONAL CONTROL PROCEDURES

The conventional control procedures for Pavlovian conditioning are quite familiar, so they will be described only briefly. In all of these descriptions, we assume that the conditioning or control treatment is administered, and then all groups are tested with a single (unreinforced) CS presentation. It is only the results of the test trial that are of interest. (Similar descriptions could be given when anticipatory CRs rather than test trial CRs are used as the index of conditioning.)

The various control treatments which are administered prior to the test trial in place of Pavlovian conditioning are listed below together with examples of their use.

1. CS-alone control. In this procedure a control subject (S) receives the same number of CS presentations as does an experimental S; however, no US is administered. This control is designed to evaluate the effects of familiarity with the CS and any changes in the organism due solely to that familiarity (Rodnick, 1937; Thompson & McConnell, 1955).

2. Novel CS control. In this procedure, no CS is given prior to the test trial. The test trial gives an estimate of the unconditioned effects of the CS (Rodnick, 1937; Wickens & Wickens, 1940).

3. US-alone control. Repeated presentations of the US alone are made in order to control for sensitization by, or habituation to, the US (Notterman, Schoenfeld, & Bersh, 1952; Wickens & Wickens, 1940).

4. Explicitly unpaired control (sometimes called the random control). In this procedure, S receives unpaired presentations of CS and US. This can be done in a variety of ways, but the most typical is presentation of both CS and US in the same session in random order but never close together in time (Bitterman, 1964; Harris, 1943).

5. Backward conditioning. The CS and US are paired, but the US is always presented prior to the CS (Kalish, 1954; Spence & Runquist, 1958).

6. Discriminative conditioning. One stimulus (CS+) is paired with the US and the other (CS−) is not. In this way CS− receives a treatment similar to that of CS+ except that the contingency with the US is an "explicitly unpaired" one. Differences between the reactions to CS+ and CS− are taken to indicate Pavlovian conditioning (Solomon & Turner, 1962).

The very variety of control procedures which have been developed attests to the inadequacy of any one. But it may be worthwhile to point briefly to the pitfalls of each procedure because some of these have not been widely recognized. We take as the logical criterion for an adequate control procedure that it retain as many features as possible of the experimental procedure while excluding the CS–US contingency. In general, each of the control procedures, although attempting to eliminate the CS–US contingency, can be shown to do considerably more. The result is that a variety of other differences, both associative and nonassociative, between experimental and control procedures is confounded with the absence of the CS–US contingency. Some of the confoundings are pointed out below.

1. CS-alone control. Quite obviously, an S treated in this way does not have the same number of US experiences as the experimental S does; therefore, any differences between Ss can be attributed to this difference in experience with the US. But worse, repeated CS presentations in the absence of all USs may not lead to the same rate of CS habituation as does repeated CS presentation in a chamber in which the US also occurs.

2. Novel CS control. It is useful to know the unconditioned properties of the CS, but it is not clear what relevance this has for identifying "true" Pavlovian conditioning. The experimental S *has* experienced the CS a large number of times prior to the

test trial and it is no longer novel to him. Why compare him to an *S* for whom the CS is novel? Comparison with a novel CS group allows one to assess the total change in reaction to the CS produced by the conditioning procedure but does not permit isolation of those changes due uniquely to the occurrence of Pavlovian conditioning.

3. US-alone control. This procedure has faults similar to those of the novel CS procedure. An *S* with this procedure receives a novel CS at the time of test, while the experimental *S* receives a CS which it has experienced many times.

4. Explicitly unpaired control. In many ways this procedure comes closest to being an appropriate control, and it has become increasingly popular in recent years. However, it contains flaws which cannot be overlooked. Although it escapes the criticisms of Procedures 1, 2, and 3, it, too, does not simply remove the contingency between CS and US; rather, it introduces instead a *new* contingency, such that the US *cannot* follow the CS for some minimum time interval. Instead of the CS being a signal for the US, it can become a signal for the *absence* of the US. Although this is an interesting procedure in itself, it does not allow a comparison between two groups, one with a CS–US contingency and one without it. We are, instead, in the position of having two different CS–US contingencies which may yield different results. How can we know which group showed Pavlovian conditioning?

5. Backward conditioning. The relevance of this procedure rests upon the assumption that in Pavlovian conditioning not only the CS–US contingency but also their temporal order of presentation is important. It is not clear whether this should be taken as part of the definition of Pavlovian conditioning or as an empirical result. Nevertheless, some investigators have suggested comparison with a backward conditioning group to evaluate the traditional experimental group. For the purposes of analysis, let us assume that the CS and US do not overlap in this procedure. We then have a sequence of events: US–CS ... US–CS ... US–CS ... in conditioning. This procedure produces the same difficulty as does the explicitly unpaired procedure: The occurrence of the CS predicts a period *free from the US*. Again, presentation of the US *is* contingent upon CS occurrence but the contingency is a *negative* one. Of course, if the CS begins during the

US in this procedure, CS occurrence predicts the *termination* of the US, which, in turn, introduces another contingency and further complications. It is worth noting that Konorski (1948) considered the backward conditioning paradigm as the prime example of an inhibitory conditioning procedure.

6. Discriminative conditioning. By now it should be clear that this control procedure falls prey to the same criticisms as do Procedures 5 and 6. CS— is explicitly unpaired with the US. In fact, the discriminative conditioning procedure can be viewed as the simultaneous administration to the same S of the experimental procedure and Control Procedure 4.

We can conclude that each of the proposed control procedures either confounds some important nonassociative change with the disruption of the CS–US contingency or changes the contingency from a positive to a negative one. Furthermore, there is no obvious way in which combined control procedures can be used to eliminate confoundings. Therefore, we are in the unfortunate position of being unable to evaluate "true" Pavlovian conditioning by the use of any or all of the conventional control procedures.

An Adequate Alternative

There is, however, a control procedure which solves the problems raised above. We shall call this procedure the "truly random" control procedure. In this procedure, both the CS and the US are presented to S but there is *no contingency whatsoever* between them. That is, the two events are programmed entirely randomly and independently in such a way that some "pairings" of CS and US may occur by chance alone. All CS and US occurrences for the control group are the same as for the experimental group except that the regular temporal contingency between CS and US is eliminated. The occurrence of the CS provides *no information* about subsequent occurrences of the US. This procedure is similar in conception to the explicitly unpaired procedure, (4), except that it eliminates the contingency of that procedure which allows the CS to signal nonoccurrence of the US.[2]

There are a variety of ways of arranging a truly random control condition. Two major alternatives are: (a) Present the CS as

in the experimental group but randomly distribute USs throughout the session; (b) conversely, present USs as in the experimental group but randomly distribute CSs. Note that, in order for
there to be *no* contingency, the distributions must be such that
CS occurrences do not predict the occurrence of USs at *any* time
in the remainder of the session. If the CS predicts the occurrence
of a US 30 minutes later in the session, an appropriate random
control condition has not been achieved.

Despite the apparent adequacy of these alternatives, they
actually add other confoundings. In the usual Pavlovian conditioning procedure, several time intervals other than the CS–US
interval are kept relatively constant. Thus time intervals between
successive CSs and successive USs are of some (relatively large)
minimum value. Each of the two truly random controls would
violate one of these relations and thus introduce changes other
than removal of the CS–US contingency. Fortunately, this can
be avoided if we depart from the traditional conditioning procedures and use a wide variety of intertrial intervals for the experimental *S*s. Then it is possible to arrange truly random presentations of CS and US for the control *S*s while preserving the inter-
US and inter-CS intervals of the experimental condition. For instance, one could program CS–US pairings for the experimental
group with a random-interval programmer. Then a truly random
control would be arranged by using two independent random-
interval programmers with the same parameters as that of the
experimental group—one to deliver CSs and one to deliver USs.

We do not wish to understate the importance of a variety
of nonassociative factors which do occur in Pavlovian conditioning. It is respect for their effects that leads to the advocacy of the
truly random control for contingency-produced effects. One great
advantage of the truly random control is that it holds constant
between the experimental and control procedures *all* of the factors extraneous to the CS–US contingency *without demanding
that we be able to specify in advance what factors might be operating*. In contrast, the customary control procedures have often
been developed only to deal with one supposed nonassociative
factor.

It is also important to realize that the actual results obtained
with the truly random control procedure are irrelevant to the

present argument. It may be that in some conditioning situations, Ss treated with the truly random control procedure will show strong changes in behavior when the CS is presented. This simply means that important changes not dependent upon a CS–US contingency occur in this situation; effects due to that contingency still must be evaluated as deviations from the effects produced by the truly random procedure.

Traditionally, the prime concern of American investigators has been the excitatory processes, and the inadequate conventional control procedures have reflected this concern. As noted above, many of these control procedures are biased toward the inhibitory side because of the explicit nonpairings of the CS and US. But the inhibitory effects of conditioning deserve attention in their own right. Clearly, we need an appropriate base condition against which to compare *both* the inhibitory and excitatory kinds of conditioning relations. The truly random sequence of CSs and USs provides an unbiased control procedure for both positive and negative contingencies between CS and US. In fact, if we are going to retain the conceptual terms "conditioned excitatory" and "conditioned inhibitory" stimuli, the truly random control procedure will provide a base line against which to *define* these effects.

In addition to serving as a control condition for Pavlovian conditioning, the truly random presentation of CS and US provides an unbiased *extinction* procedure. To the degree that our concern in extinction of Pavlovian CRs is with how the animal loses its *associative* connection, simply removing the US from the situation is an inappropriate extinction procedure. Simple removal of the US eliminates not only the CS–US contingency but also whatever nonassociative effects the US might have. However, using the truly random presentation of CS and US as an extinction procedure permits examination of the loss of contingency-dependent learning independently of these other effects. Furthermore, the truly random procedure serves as an unbiased procedure for extinction of *both* excitation and inhibition. If inhibition can be acquired it seems reasonable that it can be extinguished. The truly random presentation of CS and US is the most natural extinction procedure for inhibitory as well as excitatory effects.

OBJECTIONS TO THE "TRULY
RANDOM" PROCEDURE: TWO
THEORETICAL VIEWS OF CONDITIONING

It seems certain that our arguments will not be entirely convincing. All conventional control procedures have a common feature: They never allow forward pairings of the control CS and US. The reluctance which one might feel toward accepting a truly random control procedure stems in part from the close temporal pairings of CS and US which *will occur by chance* in that condition. One may thus argue that the truly random control procedure itself allows Pavlovian conditioning because of those few chance trials which pair CS and US; if so, it can hardly be considered a "pure" control condition. According to such an argument, the same processes may be operative in both the experimental and control procedures, but to a lesser degree in the latter.

This objection runs deep and is worthy of extensive examination. It rests upon an assumption, often not made explicit, that the temporal *pairing* of CS and US is the sufficient condition for "true" Pavlovian conditioning. It views Pavlovian conditioning as a one-sided affair in which conditioning is either absent or excitatory; the number of CS–US pairings determines the degree to which conditioning is excitatory. It is this view which dominates American notions of conditioning and which has been influential in preventing inhibitory processes from playing a major role in our thinking. A good example of this position is the Guthrian claim that the reinforcing event in Pavlovian conditioning is simple contiguity between CS and US. From this point of view, a reasonable control procedure for Pavlovian conditioning is one in which S "is not taught that the US follows the CS." This has been interpreted to include the possibly quite different learning that "the CS is *not* followed by the US." With this type of bias, it might be reasonable to conclude that the "explicitly unpaired" and the discriminative conditioning procedure are appropriate controls for Pavlovian conditioning.

An alternative theoretical view of Pavlovian conditioning, and one which has not often been distinguished from that in the previous paragraph, is that the temporal *contingency* between CS and US is the relevant condition. The notion of *contingency* differs from that of *pairings* in that the former includes not only what *is* paired with the CS but also what *is not* paired with the CS. Thus the truly random procedure contains *no* contingency between the CS and US, even though it does contain some chance CS–US pairings. From this point of view the appropriate control condition for Pavlovian conditioning is one in which the animal is taught that "the CS is irrelevant to the US." Deviations from this base conditioning can be either positive (CS is followed by US) or negative (CS is followed by absence of US). This view of conditioning has the advantage of separating out, from the simple absence of conditioning, a conceptualized inhibitory process which has a status equal to that of excitatory processes. Intuitively it seems clear that learning that the US does not follow the CS is different from failing to learn that the US follows the CS or learning that the CS is irrelevant to the US. In this sense, at least, the contingency view of conditioning, and the truly random control procedure which it generates, is more in the spirit of Pavlovian theory.[3]

The idea of contingency used here needs explication. By it we mean the degree of dependency which presentation of the US has upon prior presentation of the CS. This is clearly a function of the relative proportion of US events which occur during or at some specified time following the CS. Thus, in the truly random condition no dependency exists, but in the standard Pavlovian conditioning situation the dependence is complete. The control condition is brought closer to the experimental condition as we increase the proportion of USs occurring in the presence of the CS. When, at the other extreme, all USs occur in the absence of the CS, the inhibitory end of the continuum is reached. These proportions can be stated in terms of the probability of a US occurring given the presence of a CS (or given that the CS occurred at some designated prior time), and the probability of a US occurring given the absence of the CS (cf. Prokasy, 1965). The dimension of contingency is then a function of these two probabilities; if Pavlovian conditioning is dependent upon the contingency between CS and US, it, too, will be a function of these two probabilities. However, no attempt is made here to specify a particular function which relates these two probabilities to a continuum of contingencies.[4]

If two conditioning procedures have the same probability

of reinforcement in the absence of the CS, but have different prob-abilities in the presence of the CS, they differ in what is usually called the degree of partial reinforcement. Whether or not this affects the degree of contingency depends upon the function of these two probabilities that we choose to describe degree of con-tingency. We suggest that the contingency dimension, rather than the number of CS–US pairings, is the theoretically fruitful dimen-sion in Pavlovian conditioning.

As soon as one admits a symmetry of inhibition and excita-tion in the Pavlovian conditioning situation, the CS–US pairing view of conditioning begins to lose appeal. Pavlovian condition-ing consists of a sequence of CSs and USs arranged in a particular temporal pattern. Suppose, now, that one is primarily interested not in excitatory processes but in inhibitory processes, or in how an animal learns that the CS signals a period free from the US. From the point of view that the pairing of CS and US is the im-portant Pavlovian event, the truly random control procedure is inadequate for a reason that is exactly the opposite to what it was for excitatory conditioning; now it contains a number of *nonpairings* of CS and US. Therefore, from such a view we are forced to conclude that the symmetrical control procedure for the study of inhibitory processes is to consistently *pair* CS and US. This, it seems, is less than sensible.

It may also be argued that the truly random control proce-dure does more than simply remove the contingency of Pavlovian conditioning. It might, for instance, introduce a new process of its own such as increasing the likelihood that S will ignore or habituate to the CS since it bears no relation to the US. This is, of course, possible; but it means that the arrangement of a contin-gency affects the rate at which S comes to "ignore" a CS. Thus this ignoring of a CS is governed by its associative relation to the US and is a proper part of the development of a CR. From the point of view of this paper, then, the truly random control proce-dure still provides the appropriate control.

Another objection to the truly random control procedure rests again upon the notion that the pairing of CS and US is the significant event for Pavlovian conditioning. One can claim "what is random for the experimenter may not be random for S." Such an objection argues that if we use the truly random control, we should arrange it so that the relation between the CS and US is phenomenally random. One suspects that, at least in part, this objection is based upon the notion of pairing of CS and US. The statement implies that even though CS and US are not related, S will behave as if the CS predicts the US. Those who make this claim are rarely concerned that S will behave as if the CS predicts no US!

It is, of course, possible that some process which normally produces Pavlovian conditioning when the US is made contingent upon the CS is operative even when the CS and US are presented in random fashion. Such a process might fail to operate only when there is a slight inhibitory, or only when there is a slight excitatory, contingency between CS and US. In its most general form, this argument says that the limits of our operational procedures do not necessarily define the limits of psychological processes in the organism. It is difficult to disagree. On the other hand, this is not an objection which applies uniquely to the truly random control procedure. For instance, it applies also to the traditional controls for Pavlovian conditioning: What is explicitly unpaired for E may not be explicitly unpaired for S. A solution to this problem requires an ability, which we do not yet have, to identify psychological processes; until we do, there is little choice but to associate psychological processes in Pavlovian conditioning with experimental operations.

A major advantage of the contingency view of Pavlovian conditioning is that it provides a continuum of CS–US contingencies along which a zero point can be located. In the long run, the location of this zero with respect to process is not crucial; if we discover that the assumed correspondence between experimental contingency and psychological process is in error, it may be that results can be brought into line by relocating the point of "zero contingency."

Two Experimental Predictions

The truly random control has led to the consideration of two theoretical views of Pavlovian conditioning, the pairing view and the contingency view. The difference between these two theoretical conceptions of Pavlovian conditioning is partly semantic. From our present knowledge it is arbitrary whether we wish to have a point of "zero" conditioning with deviations on both sides or a zero point from which deviations can occur only in one direction. On the other hand, the difference is also partly empirical, and in this framework the question is whether the *number* of CS–US pairings, or the *relative probabilities* of US in the presence and absence of CS, is the determinant of Pavlovian conditioning. A comprehensive empirical answer to this question requires an extensive program of research, but two specific predictions can be extracted for illustrative purposes. .

The area of most blatant disagreement between the two conceptions of conditioning is the notion of inhibition. (a) The *pairing* viewpoint fails to distinguish between Ss failing to learn and Ss learning that the CS and US are explicitly unpaired. Experimentally, in accord with the pairing view, a CS which has been repeatedly presented alone should not differ from one which has been explicitly unpaired with the US. (This simple statement of the prediction neglects the operation of such factors as sensitization which would produce more CRs in the explicitly unpaired condition.) (b) From the viewpoint that CS–US *contingencies* are the important determinants of Pavlovian conditioning, repeated CS presentations may result in failure to condition; but, explicitly unpairing CS and US should lead to the development of inhibitory phenomena. Thus, under some circumstances, the contingency viewpoint predicts a difference between the outcomes of these two treatments and the pairing view does not. But it is important to note that the contingency approach *only* predicts this difference when the CS is tested in the presence of some other excitatory stimulus. Inhibitory effects can be measured only when there is some level of excitation to be reduced. Again, at the risk of being pedantic, it is important not to confuse the question of the presence or absence of inhibition with the question of the ability to measure inhibitory effects.

The conditions for testing the empirical fruitfulness of the contingency view were met in an experiment by Rescorla and LoLordo (1965). In that experiment, two groups of dogs were trained on a Sidman avoidance task. Both groups were then confined and given Pavlovian conditioning treatments. While confined, one group received repeated tone presentations without any shock USs, while the other group received tones and shocks explicitly unpaired in the manner of Procedure 4 above. Later presentation of these tonal stimuli during the Sidman avoidance performance led to a substantial reduction in avoidance rate during the CS in the explicitly unpaired group and little change in rate during the CS for the group that received only tones. Because previous experiments supported the assumption that avoidance rate is in part a function of the level of fear, these results were interpreted to indicate that explicitly unpairing the CS and US led to the development of Pavlovian inhibitory processes capable of reducing fear. Merely presenting the tones did not lead to this result. The outcome of this experiment is consistent with the theoretical view that CS–US contingency, rather than simply CS–US pairing determines the outcome of Pavlovian conditioning procedures.

The two contrasting views of Pavlovian conditioning also make differential predictions for the outcomes of excitatory conditioning procedures. Suppose that we condition one group of Ss with a type of truly random conditioning procedure in which USs are delivered on a variable interval schedule and CSs are randomly distributed throughout the session. A second (experimental) group receives the identical treatment except that the preprogrammed USs are allowed to reach S only if they come in a 30-second period following a CS onset. Thus, for this group a switch permits the delivery of the independently programmed USs only for a period just after each CS. USs which are programmed for the truly random Ss during other periods of the session never occur for the experimental group. The Ss in this experimental group receive at least as many CS–US pairings as do Ss in the truly random group, but USs can occur *only* following CSs. If the number of CS–US *pairings* is important, then this procedure should produce results similar to those of the truly random control. However, if the CS–US *contingencies* are important, then a considerably greater number of CRs should occur in the experimental group.

This conditioning procedure was used in a paradigm like that of the Rescorla and LoLordo experiment (Rescorla, 1966). All dogs were trained on a Sidman avoidance schedule. Then, separately, half of the animals received the truly random control treatment while the other half received the modified treatment of the experimental group described above. Shock was the US and tones served as CSs. After these conditioning treatments, the tones were presented during performance of the avoidance response. The CS of the truly random group had little effect upon performance, while the CS of the experimental group showed marked fear-producing properties, increasing the avoidance response rate. Again, this result supports the view that the important dimension in Pavlovian conditioning is the CS–US contingency rather than CS–US pairing.

These are but two examples of the kinds of experiments which the contingency view of Pavlovian conditioning generates. The fact that the results of these experiments support the fruitfulness of the contingency view suggests a program of research varying the relative probabilities which form the basis of the CS–US contingencies. In this way we can explore the relations between CS–US contingencies and Pavlovian conditioning.

In summary, we have argued that the conventional control procedures for Pavlovian conditioning are inadequate in a variety of ways. An alternative procedure, in which the CS and US bear no relation to each other, was proposed, It was argued that the failure previously to use this procedure stems from a particular, and probably inadequate, conception of Pavlovian conditioning. Taking seriously the truly random control procedure, we proposed an alternative theoretical view of Pavlovian conditioning in which the CS–US contingency is important rather than the CS–US pairing. The empirical usefulness of this alternative view has been illustrated.

NOTES

1. The preparation of this paper and the experimental work related to it were aided by United States Public Health Service Grant MH–04202 and National Science Foundation Grant GB–2428 to Richard L. Solomon and by a National Science Foundation predoctoral fellowship to the author. The author would like to express his appreciation to Vincent M. LoLordo and Richard L. Solomon for their advice and criticism of the ideas presented in this paper.
2. A similar control procedure has been suggested by Jensen (1961) and by Prokasy (1965).
3. It is worth pointing out that the argument advanced in this paper has direct analogues for instrumental training. Whatever faults it might have, the yoked-control procedure was introduced precisely to determine what

effects are uniquely due to instrumental reinforcement contingencies. Similarly, the distinction between pairing and contingency views has recently been examined for operant conditioning by Premack (1965).

4. These probabilities can be calculated whatever the number of CS and US events. If, for instance, there is only one CS–US pairing, there is a high degree of contingency since the probability of a US following a CS is one and the probability of a US in the absence of the CS is zero. However, it may turn out empirically that with only a few CS and US events the relative importance of single pairings is greater.

REFERENCES

Bitterman, M. E. Classical conditioning in the goldfish as a function of the CS–US interval. *Journal of Comparative and Physiological Psychology*, 1964, 58, 359–366.

Harris, J. D. Studies of nonassociative factors inherent in conditioning. *Comparative Psychological Monographs*, 1943, 18 (1, Whole No. 93).

Jensen, D. D. Operationism and the question "Is this behavior learned or innate?" *Behavior*, 1961, 17, 1–8.

Kalish, H. I. Strength of fear as a function of the number of acquisition and extinction trials. *Journal of Experimental Psychology*, 1954, 47, 1–9.

Konorski, J. *Conditioned reflexes and neuron organization.* New York: Cambridge University Press, 1948.

Notterman, J. M., Schoenfeld, W. N., & Bersh, P. J. Partial reinforcement and conditioned heart rate response in human subjects. *Science*, 1952, 115, 77–79.

Premack, D. Reinforcement theory. In D. Levine (Ed.), *Nebraska symposium on motivation: 1965.* Lincoln: University of Nebraska Press, 1965. Pp. 123–180.

Prokasy, W. F. Classical eyelid conditioning: Experimenter operations, task demands, and response shaping. In W. F. Prokasy (Ed.), *Classical conditioning.* New York: Appleton-Century-Crofts, 1965.

Rescorla, R. A. Predictability and number of pairings in Pavlovian fear conditioning. *Psychonomic Science*, 1966, 4, 383–384.

Rescorla, R. A., & LoLordo, V. M. Inhibition of avoidance behavior. *Journal of Comparative and Physiological Psychology*, 1965, 59, 406–412.

Rodnick, E. H. Does the interval of delay of conditioned responses possess inhibitory properties? *Journal of Experimental Psychology*, 1937, 20, 507–527.

Solomon, R. L., & Turner, L. H. Discriminative classical conditioning in dogs paralyzed by curare can later control discriminative avoidance responses in the normal state. *Psychological Review*, 1962, 69, 202–219.

Spence, K. W., & Runquist, W. N. Temporal effects of conditioned fear on the eyelid reflex. *Journal of Experimental Psychology*, 1958, 55, 613–616.

Thompson, R., & McConnell, J. Classical conditioning in the planarian. *Dugesia dorotocephala. Journal of Comparative and Physiological Psychology*, 1955, 48, 65–68.

Wickens, D. D., & Wickens, C. A study of conditioning in the neonate. *Journal of Experimental Psychology*, 1940, 26, 94–102.

Relation of Cue to
Consequence in Avoidance Learning[1]

JOHN GARCIA and ROBERT A. KOELLING, *Harvard Medical School and Massachusetts General Hospital*

An audiovisual stimulus was made contingent upon the rat's licking at the water spout, thus making it analogous with a gustatory stimulus. When the audiovisual stimulus and the gustatory stimulus were paired with electric shock the avoidance reactions transferred to the audiovisual stimulus, but not the gustatory stimulus. Conversely, when both stimuli were paired with toxin or x-ray the avoidance reactions transferred to the gustatory stimulus, but not the audiovisual stimulus. Apparently stimuli are selected as cues dependent upon the nature of the subsequent reinforcer.

A great deal of evidence stemming from diverse sources suggests an inadequacy in the usual formulations concerning reinforcement. Barnett (1963) has described the "bait-shy" behavior of wild rats which have survived a poisoning attempt. These animals utilizing olfactory and gustatory cues, avoid the poison bait which previously made them ill. However, there is no evidence that they avoid the "place" of the poisoning.

In a recent volume (Haley & Snyder, 1964) several authors have discussed studies in which ionizing radiations were employed

Garcia, J. and Koelling, R. A. Relation of cue to consequence in avoidance learning. *Psychonomic Science,* 1966, *4,* 123–124.

as noxious stimulus to produce avoidance reactions in animals. Ionizing radiation like many poisons produces gastrointestinal disturbances and nausea. Strong aversions are readily established in animals when distinctively flavored fluids are conditionally paired with x-rays. Subsequently, the gustatory stimulus will depress fluid intake without radiation. In contrast, a distinctive environmental complex of auditory, visual, and tactual stimuli does not inhibit drinking even when the compound stimulus is associated with the identical radiation schedule. This differential effect has also been observed following ingestion of a toxin and the injection of a drug (Garcia & Koelling, 1965).

Apparently this differential effectiveness of cues is due either to the nature of the reinforcer, i.e., radiation or toxic effects, or to the peculiar relation which a gustatory stimulus has to the drinking response, i.e., gustatory stimulation occurs if and only if the animal licks the fluid. The environmental cues associated with a distinctive place are not as dependent upon a single response of the organism. Therefore, we made an auditory and visual stimulus dependent upon the animal's licking the water spout. Thus, in four experiments reported here "bright-noisy" water, as well as "tasty" water was conditionally paired with radiation, a toxin, immediate shock, and delayed shock, respectively, as reinforcers. Later the capacity of these response-controlled stimuli to inhibit drinking in the absence of reinforcement was tested.

METHOD

The apparatus was a light and sound shielded box (7 in. × 7 in. × 7 in.) with a drinking spout connected to an electronic drinkometer which counted each touch of the rat's tongue to the spout. "Bright-noisy" water was provided by connecting an incandescent lamp (5 watts) and a clicking relay into this circuit. "Tasty" water was provided by adding flavors to the drinking supply.

Each experimental group consisted of 10 rats (90 day old Sprague-Dawley males) maintained in individual cages without water, but with *Purina Laboratory chow ad libidum.*

The procedure was: A. One week of habituation to drinking in the apparatus without stimulation. B. Pretests to measure intake of bright-noisy water and tasty water prior to training. C. Acquisition training with: (1) reinforced trials where these stimuli were paired with reinforcement during drinking, (2) nonreinforced trials where rats drank water without stimuli or reinforcement. Training terminated when there was a reliable difference between water intake scores on reinforced and nonreinforced trials. D. Post-tests to measure intake of bright-noisy water and tasty water after training.

In the x-ray study an audiovisual group and a gustatory group were exposed to an identical radiation schedule. In the other studies reinforcement was contingent upon the rat's response. To insure that both the audiovisual and the gustatory stimuli received equivalent reinforcement, they were combined and simultaneously paired with the reinforcer during acquisition training. Therefore, one group serving as its own control and divided into equal subgroups, was tested in balanced order with an audiovisual and a gustatory test before and after training with these stimuli combined.

One 20-min. reinforced trial was administered every three days in the x-ray and lithium chloride studies. This prolonged intertrial interval was designed to allow sufficient time for the rats to recover from acute effects of treatment. On each interpolated day the animals received a 20-min. nonreinforced trial. They were post-tested two days after their last reinforced trial. The x-ray groups received a total of three reinforced trials, each with 54 r of filtered 250 kv x-rays delivered in 20 min. Sweet water (1 gm saccharin per liter) was the gustatory stimulus. The lithium chloride group had a total of five reinforced trials with toxic salty water (.12 M lithium chloride). Nontoxic salty water (.12 M sodium chloride) which rats cannot readily distinguish from the toxic solution was used in the gustatory tests (Nachman, 1963).

The immediate shock study was conducted on a more orthodox avoidance schedule. Tests and trials were 2 min. long. Each day for four consecutive acquisition days, animals were given two nonreinforced and two reinforced trials in an NRRN, RNNR pattern. A shock, the minimal current required to interrupt drinking (0.5 sec. at 0.08–0.20 ma), was delivered through a floor grid 2 sec. after the first lick at the spout.

The delayed shock study was conducted simultaneously with

the lithium chloride on the same schedule. Non-toxic salty water
was the gustatory stimulus. Shock reinforcement was delayed during first trials and gradually increased in intensity (.05 to .30
ma) in a schedule designed to produce a drinking pattern during
the 20-min. period which resembled that of the corresponding
animal drinking toxic salty water.

RESULTS AND DISCUSSION

The results indicate that all reinforcers were effective in producing discrimination learning during the acquisition phase (see
Fig. 1), but obvious differences occurred in the post-tests. The
avoidance reactions produced by x-rays and lithium chloride are
readily transferred to the gustatory stimulus but not to the audiovisual stimulus. The effect is more pronounced in the x-ray study,

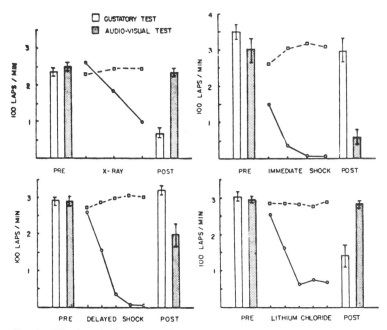

FIG. 1.   The bars indicate water intake ($\pm$ St. Error) during a gustatory test
(a distinctive taste) and an audiovisual test (light and sound contingent
upon licking) before and after conditional pairing with the reinforcers indicated. The curves illustrate mean intake during acquisition.

perhaps due to differences in dose. The x-ray animals received a constant dose while the lithium chloride rats drank a decreasing amount of the toxic solution during training. Nevertheless, the difference between post-test scores is statistically significant in both experiments ($p < 0.01$ by ranks test).

Apparently when gustatory stimuli are paired with agents which produce nausea and gastric upset, they acquire secondary reinforcing properties which might be described as "conditioned nausea." Auditory and visual stimulation do not readily acquire similar properties even when they are contingent upon the licking response.

In contrast, the effect of both immediate and delayed shock to the paws is in the opposite direction. The avoidance reactions produced by electric shock to the paws transferred to the audio-visual stimulus but not to the gustatory stimulus. As one might expect the effect of delayed shocks was not as effective as shocks where the reinforcer immediately and consistently followed licking. Again, the difference between post-test intake scores is statistically significant in both studies ($p < 0.01$ by ranks test). Thus, when shock which produces peripheral pain is the reinforcer, "conditioned fear" properties are more readily acquired by auditory and visual stimuli then by gustatory stimuli.

It seems that given reinforcers are not equally effective for all classes of discriminable stimuli. The cues, which the animal selects from the welter of stimuli in the learning situation, appear to be related to the consequences of the subsequent reinforcer. Two speculations are offered: (1) Common elements in the time-intensity patterns of stimulation may facilitate a cross modal generalization from reinforcer to cue in one case and not in another. (2) More likely, natural selection may have favored mechanisms which associate gustatory and olfactory cues with internal discomfort since the chemical receptors sample the materials soon to be incorporated into the internal environment. Krechevsky (1933) postulated such a genetically coded hypothesis to account for the predispositions of rats to respond systematically to specific cues in an insoluble maze. The hypothesis of the sick rat, as for many of us under similar circumstances, would be, "It must have been something I ate."

NOTE

1. This research stems from doctoral research carried out at Long Beach V. A. Hospital and supported by NIH No. RH00068. Thanks are extended to Professors B. F. Ritchie, D. Krech and E. R. Dempster, U. C. Berkeley, California.

REFERENCES

Barnett, S. A. *The rat: a study in behavior*. Chicago: Aldine Press. 1963.

Garcia, J., & Koelling, R. A. A comparison of aversions induced by x-rays, toxins, and drugs in the rat. *Radiat. Res.*, in press, 1965.

Haley, T. J., & Snyder, R. S. (Eds.) *The response of the nervous system to ionizing radiation*. Boston: Little, Brown & Co., 1964.

Krechevsky, I. The hereditary nature of 'hypothesis'. *J. comp. Psychol.*, 1932, 16, 99–116.

Nachman, M. Learned aversion to the taste of lithium chloride and generalization to other salts. *J. comp. physiol. Psychol.*, 1963, 56, 343–349.

Elimination of a Sadistic Fantasy by a Client-Controlled Counterconditioning Technique: A Case Study[1]

GERALD C. DAVISON, *State University of New York at Stony Brook*

To the best of the author's knowledge, this is the 1st report of the elimination of a sadistic fantasy by conditioning methods, as well as the 1st to describe a client-controlled technique for counterconditioning sexual responses. The mainstay of the therapy entailed client-controlled masturbation sessions, in which strong sexual feelings were paired with pictures and images of females in nonsadistic contexts. This presumed positive counterconditioning was supplemented in the consulting room by imaginal aversive counterconditioning ("covert sensitization"), whereby an extremely disgusting scene was paired in imagination with a typical sadistic fantasy. Furthermore, therapeutic change seemed to be facilitated through the client's reconstruction of his problem in conditioning terms, rather than in terms of mental illness and putative unconscious processes.

The modification of deviant sexual behavior has been approached largely through the contiguous pairing of a primary aversive stimulus with a stimulus eliciting an undesirable response (the "symptom"), the goal being to endow the inappropri-

Davison, G. C. Elimination of a sadistic fantasy by a client-controlled counterconditioning technique: a case study. *Journal of Abnormal Psychology*, 1968, 73, 84–90. Copyright 1968 by the American Psychological Association, and reproduced by permission.

ate stimulus with negative properties, or at least to eliminate the unwanted positive attributes. Many such cases have been reviewed by Bandura (in press), Feldman (1966), Grossberg (1964), Kalish (1965), Rachman (1961), and Ullmann and Krasner (1965). Therapy of fetishism, homosexuality, and transvestism has tended to follow this counterconditioning model (e.g., Blakemore, Thorpe, Barker, Conway, & Lavin, 1963; Davies & Morgenstern, 1960; Freund, 1960; Lavin, Thorpe, Barker, Blakemore, & Conway, 1961; Raymond, 1956; Thorpe, Schmidt, Brown, & Castell, 1964). In addition, several workers have introduced complementary procedures in attempts to endow suitable social stimuli with the positive attributes necessary to make less likely a reversion to the inappropriate goal-object. Thus, for example, Freund (1960) gave his male homosexuals not only aversion conditioning trials to pictures of men, but also exposures to pictures of nude women after injection of male hormones. Similar procedures have been employed by Thorpe, Schmidt, and Castell (1963) and Feldman and MacCulloch (1965).

Of particular relevance to the present study is the work of Thorpe et al. (1963). These writers report therapeutic benefit following presumably counterconditioning sessions during which efforts were made to pair female pictures with orgasm from masturbation. It was assumed that this intensely pleasurable sexual response counterconditioned the aversion to females which appeared to play a crucial role in the behavior of the homosexuals. These authors recognized the importance of a person's fantasy life to his overt behavioral adjustment, and they assumed that beneficial generalization would occur from pictorial to the real-life situation, similar to the assumptions made for systematic desensitization (Davison, in press; Wolpe, 1958). Although the therapeutic outcomes reported by Thorpe and his co-workers are equivocal in respect to actual sexual behavior, the procedures did have considerable effect on fantasies.

The possibility of extending this kind of work to an outpatient setting presented itself to the author during the course of his private practice. Various modifications of procedures used by Thorpe et al. (1963) were employed, apparently to good effect. In addition, other important issues became evident in the course of therapy, which required fewer than 5 consulting-room hours over a span of 10 wk., and it is for these heuristic reasons that the following is reported.

CASE STUDY

The client was a 21-year-old unmarried white male college senior majoring in history. The university counseling center had received an anxious letter from his parents, requesting help for their son in treating his introversion, procrastination, and "masochism." After working with the student for a few weeks on his tendency to wait until the last minute in his academic work, the psychologist at the center referred him to the author for help with his sexual difficulties.

Mr. M's statement of the problem was: "I'm a sadist." There followed a rather troubled account of a complete absence of "normal" sexual fantasies and activities since age 11. Masturbating about five times a week, the client's fantasies had been exclusively sadistic ones, specifically, inflicting tortures on women. He declared emphatically that he had never been sexually aroused by any other kind of image. Although generally uninterested in dating girls, he felt no aversion to them; on the contrary, he sometimes felt a "warm glow" when near them, but did not describe this at all in sexual terms. Because of his extreme concern over the content of his fantasies, however, he had dated very little and expressed no interest in the co-eds at the college. He recalled having kissed only two girls in his life, with no sexual arousal accompanying these fleeting episodes. He had never engaged in any homosexual activities or fantasies. Although expressing no guilt about his problem, he was very much worried about it inasmuch as he felt it impossible to ever contemplate marriage. This concern had recently been markedly increased upon reading an account of a Freudian interpretation of "sado-masochism." He was especially perturbed about the poor prognosis for this "illness."

Because his concern over the gravity and implications of his problem seemed at least as disruptive as the problem itself, the therapist spent most of the first session raising arguments against a disease interpretation of unusual behavior. Psychoanalytic notions were critically reviewed, and attention was directed especially to the intestability of many Freudian concepts (Levy,

1963). Instances in the therapist's own clinical work were cited to illustrate the liberating effects observed in many people when they interpret their maladaptive behavior as determined by "normal" psychological processes rather than by insidious disease processes (cf. Davison, 1966; Glaser, 1965; Maher, 1966; Mainford, 1962). Mr. M frequently expressed relief at these ideas, and the therapist, indeed, took full advantage of his prestigious position to reinforce these notions.

At the end of the session, the counterconditioning orientation which would be followed was explained (Davison, in press; Guthrie, 1935; Wolpe, 1958), as well as the specific activities which he was to engage in during the coming week. When assured of privacy in his dormitory room (primarily on the weekend), he was first to obtain an erection by whatever means possible—undoubtedly with a sadistic fantasy, as he indicated. He was then to begin to masturbate while looking at a picture of a sexy, nude woman (the "target" sexual stimulus); *Playboy* magazine was suggested to him as a good source. If he began losing the erection, he was to switch back to his sadistic fantasy until he could begin masturbating effectively again. Concentrating again on the *Playboy* picture, he was to continue masturbating, using the fantasy only to regain erection. As orgasm was approaching, he was at all costs to focus on the *Playboy* picture, even if sadistic fantasies began to intrude. It was impressed on him that gains would ensue only when sexual arousal was associated with the picture, and that he need not worry about indulging in sadistic fantasies at this point. The client appeared enthusiastic and hopeful as he left the office. (Table 1 summarizes the client-controlled masturbation assignments following this and succeeding consulting-room sessions.)

At the second session he reported success with the assignment: he had been able to masturbate effectively and enjoyably three times over the weekend to a particular picture from *Playboy* without once having to use a sadistic fantasy; however, it did take significantly longer to climax with the *Playboy* photograph than with the usual kind of sadistic fantasy. During the rest of the week, when he had not had enough privacy for real-life visual stimulation, he had "broken down" a few times and used his sadistic fantasies.

TABLE 1
"Target" and "Back-Up" Sexual Stimuli for Client-Controlled
Masturbation Sessions

Week	Target stimulus	Back-up stimulus
1	*Playboy*, real stimulus	Sadistic fantasy
2	Bathing-suit, real stimulus	*Playboy*, real stimulus
	Playboy, imaginal stimulus	Sadistic fantasy
3	Same as Week 2	Same as Week 2
4	Bathing suit, real stimulus	*Playboy*, real stimulus
	Playboy, imaginal stimulus	None

Much of this session was then spent in talking to him about some of the social-sexual games which most males play in our culture, especially the "mental undressing" of attractive women. The purpose was to engage him in the kind of "stud" conversation which he had never experienced and which, it was felt, would help to change his orientation toward girls. The therapist reassured him that the first direct contacts with girls are sometimes disappointing; he had to admit, however, that his extreme sensitivity about the sadistic fantasies had severely limited his experience.

During the coming week he was, first of all, to ask out on a coffee date any girl whom he felt he *might* find attractive, even for a sadistic fantasy. He was also to spend some time between classes just looking at some of the co-eds and noting some of their more remarkable attributes. Finally, his masturbation sessions were to be structured as follows: The real-life pictorial stimuli were to be girls either in bathing suits or lingerie, used in the same way as the *Playboy* picture the preceding week; this latter stimulus was to be used as "back-up" stimulus, replacing the sadistic fantasies in the event that he was losing his erection. Attention was also to be directed to imaginal sexual stimuli, and when masturbating in this way he was to use the *Playboy* image, with a sadistic fantasy as back-up.

The third session lasted half an hour. He had procrastinated so long in asking for a date that the girls he contacted had already made other plans; the therapist expressed his disappointment quite openly and urged him even more strongly to follow through with this task. He had managed to spend some time looking at girls but did not note significant sexual arousal, except when a sadistic fantasy crept in occasionally. He had masturbated only once to real-life stimuli, using some bathing-suit pictures from a weekly national news magazine; this was successful, though it took longer even than when the *Playboy* material was used previously. When masturbating to imaginal sexual stimuli, he had relied almost exclusively on his sadistic fantasies rather than utilizing the *Playboy* picture in imagination as he had in real life 1 wk. earlier.

His reluctance to give up the sadistic fantasies prompted the use of the following procedure, the idea for which had been obtained from Lazarus (1958). With his eyes closed, he was instructed to imagine a typical sadistic scene, a pretty girl tied to stakes on the ground and struggling tearfully to extricate herself. While looking at the girl, he was told to imagine someone bringing a branding iron toward his eyes, ultimately searing his eyebrows. A second image was attempted when this proved abortive, namely, being kicked in the groin by a ferocious-looking karate expert. When he reported himself indifferent to this image as well, the therapist depicted to him a large bowl of "soup," composed of steaming urine with reeking fecal boli bobbing around on top. His grimaces, contortions, and groans indicated that an effective image had been found, and the following 5 min. were spent portraying his drinking from the bowl, with accompanying nausea, at all times while peering over the floating debris at the struggling girl. After opening his eyes at the end of the imaginal ordeal, he reported spontaneously that he felt quite nauseated, and some time was spent in casual conversation in order to dispel the mood.

His assignments for masturbation during the coming week entailed increasing the frequency of his real-life masturbatory exposures to bathing-suit pictures, along with concerted efforts to use the *Playboy* stimuli in imagination as he had in real life 2 wk. earlier, resorting to sadistic fantasies if necessary.

The fourth session lasted only 15 min. He had managed to arrange a date for the coming weekend and found himself almost looking forward to it. Again, he had masturbated several times to a real-life picture of a bathing beauty. In fantasy he had managed to use the *Playboy* girl exclusively two out of five times, with no noticeable diminution in enjoyment.

He was to continue using the bathing-suit pictures while masturbating to real-life stimuli, but to avoid sadistic fantasies altogether, the idea being that any frustration engendered by this deprivation would simply add to his general sexual arousal and thereby make it all the easier to use the *Playboy* stimuli in imagination.

The fifth session, also lasting only 15 min., opened with Mr. M animatedly praising the efficacy of the therapy. He had masturbated several times, mostly to real-life bathing-suit pictures, with no problems and, most importantly, had found himself *unable* to obtain an erection to a sadistic fantasy. In fact, he even had difficulty conjuring up an image. He had also spent considerable time with two girls, finding himself at one point having to resist an urge to hug one of them—a totally new experience for him. He enthusiastically spoke of how different he felt about "normal dating," and a 1-mo. period without interviews was decided upon to let him follow his new inclinations.

The sixth session, 1 mo. later, revealed that his sadistic fantasies had not reappeared, and that he had been masturbating effectively to both real-life and imaginal appropriate sexual stimuli. He had not, however, been dating, and some time was spent stressing the importance of seeking "normal" sexual outlets. He felt strongly, however, that the sexual problem had been successfully handled and requested that his procrastination problem be taken up. Two sessions were subsequently devoted to following the same general strategy that had been adopted, with some success, by the college counselor, that is, arranging for various rewards to be made contingent upon certain academic task-performances. Mr. M did report doing "an enormous amount of work" during 1 wk.—out of fear of having to admit to the therapist that he had been loafing. Practical considerations, however, made it clear that this handling of the problem, even if it should prove effective, was not as realistic as his facing the reality that there was no "magic pill" to eliminate his procrastination. Therapy, therefore, was terminated, with no sadistic fantasies having occurred for over 1 mo., and with the problem of procrastination left more or less untouched.

A follow-up of 1 mo. was obtained by telephone. Mr. M reported that there was still no sign of sadistic fantasies and that, indeed, he was no longer even thinking about the issue. He had still not "gotten around" to asking any girl out on a date, and the therapist urged him in no uncertain terms to tackle this aspect of his procrastination problem with the vigor that he had shown in regard to his studies (where significant improvement had been made). Extensive and persistent questioning failed to evoke any reported aversion to girls as the basis of his reluctance to ask them out.

DISCUSSION

As with every case study, one must necessarily speculate, to a large extent, on the "active ingredients." Hypotheses are not readily strengthened from such data. As a demonstration of various strategies, however, the present report does seem to be of heuristic value.

1. The first significant event in therapy was the author's general reaction to the client's statement of the problem, "I'm a sadist." After Mr. M had recounted the horror with which he had read about his mysterious "illness" in Freudian terms, the therapist countered with a logical attack that made the hour take on more the characteristics of a graduate seminar than a psychotherapy session, except perhaps for the warmth, support, and acceptance which were deliberately conveyed. A key factor in this initial phase was an attempt to change the client's general orientation to his problem. As this writer has usually found, the client had been regarding himself as "sick," qualitatively different from so-called "normals." Furthermore, the idea that much of his behavior was determined by forces working in devious ways in his "unconscious" was quite troubling, as was the poor prognosis. As reported in the case material, these issues were dealt with immediately, and significant relief was afforded the young man simply by reconstructing the problem for him in conditioning terms. It would, indeed, have been interesting and valuable to attempt some sort of assessment of improvement at this very point.

2. Inextricably intertwined with the foregoing was the outlining of a therapeutic strategy: his sadistic fantasies were to be attacked by procedures aimed at counterconditioning the maladaptive emotional reactions to specific kinds of stimuli. The client perceived the theoretical rationale as reasonable and was satisfied with the actual techniques which would be employed. Furthermore, being able to buttress the plan with both clinical and experimental data added to its credibility. It must be emphasized that whether the data cited, or the explanation offered, are valid is an irrelevant question in the present situation. The important point is that the client's enthusiastic participation was enlisted in a therapeutic regime which, by all counts, was to be highly unconventional.

3. A third conceivably relevant variable was the "older brother" type of relationship which the therapist established in talking with Mr. M about conventional sex. Clearly the client had missed this part of the average American male's upbringing and, as has been reported, much time was spent in deliberately provocative "locker-room talk," not as an end in itself, but rather as a means of exposing him to the kinds of heterosexual ideations which seemed to the author useful in promoting nonsadistic fantasies about girls.

4. It is likely that the two positive exposures to actual women contributed to therapeutic improvement. Mr. M, having been goaded into direct social contact with girls, was fortunately able to appreciate the enjoyment that can come from a satisfactory relationship with a woman, albeit on nonsexual terms. In addition, having felt a very strong urge to hug one of them, in a nonsadistic fashion, was reported by the client as a highly significant event and must surely have fostered some change in his concept of himself as a sexual misfit. Furthermore, aside from any alleged counterconditioning with respect to appropriate stimuli (see below), it is also suggested that a favorable change in self-concept developed as he saw himself able to respond sexually to imaginal and pictorial stimuli that had previously left him unaroused.

5. It is assumed that the most important variable in therapy was the masturbation sessions which the client carried out privately. As discussed by Thorpe et al. (1963), it was felt that more

appropriate social-sexual behavior would probably follow upon a change in sexual fantasies; in the present case a focus on the fantasies seemed all the more reasonable in view of the fact that *they formed the basis of the referral.* According to the client, it was his fantasy life which had retarded his sexual development, and it was this that he was most worried about. It was assumed that generalization to real-life girls would be effected in a fashion similar to the generalization which has been reported for Wolpe's technique of systematic desensitization (Davison, in press; Lang & Lazovik, 1963; Lang, Lazovik, & Reynolds, 1965; Lazarus, 1961; Paul, 1966; Paul & Shannon, 1966; Rachman, 1966; Schubot, 1966; Wolpin & Raines, 1966; Zeisset, 1966). Of course, whether Mr. M would actually begin dating regularly, or at all, would seem to depend importantly on factors other than those dealt with in this brief therapy, for example, the client's physical attractiveness, his conversational and sexual techniques, the availability of women attractive to him, and so forth. The generalization spoken of here, then, is best restricted to the thoughts and feelings which he had about women and about the prospects of relating to them nonsadistically; the case-study data contain ample verification for this.

The actual procedure followed was unique in that control of the pairing was vested entirely in the client, as is done in the use of differential relaxation with in vivo exposures to aversive stimuli (Davison, 1965; Wolpe & Lazarus, 1966). The sadistic fantasies were used initially to enable Mr. M to obtain and maintain an erection. During this arousal, he looked at culture-appropriate sexual stimuli (a nude *Playboy* photo) and masturbated. The assumption is made (and must obviously be investigated experimentally) that the pairing of masturbatory arousal with the *Playboy* picture served to replace neutral emotional responses to the picture with intensely pleasurable sexual responses. In succeeding sessions the content of the new sexual stimuli was changed to less openly provocative female pictures (bathing-suit photographs), with the already established *Playboy* picture used as backup. Then the stimuli were made solely imaginal in similar fashion. Obviously, if this procedure worked for counterconditioning reason, the client exhibited considerable control over the content of his fantasies, switching back and forth as he had been directed.

This control of imagery is a central issue in desensitization research as well (Davison, in press).

6. Probably very instrumental in changing the content of his fantasies was the intensive "imaginal aversive counterconditioning" (or "covert sensitization," viz, Cautela, 1966; Lazarus, 1958) conducted by the therapist, in which extreme feelings of disgust were generated by fantasy and then related to the sadistic image. One can fruitfully compare this technique with the "emotive imagery" procedure described by Lazarus and Abramovitz (1962), in which pleasant images were generated in fearful children and then related by the therapist to conditioned aversive stimuli. The procedure was resorted to in the present case because the client appeared unable to give up the sadistic fantasy solely on the basis of beginning to find the nonsadistic pictures and images effective in maintaining erection and leading to orgasm.

The assessment of therapeutic outcome poses some difficulty here, as indeed it does for any therapy. Explicitly rejected as criteria of "cure" are the client's "self-actualization," "mental health," "ego strength," or other vague notions. While the intention is not simply to beg the question, it does seem more appropriate for the present case report to restrict judgment to the problem as presented by the client, namely, the sadistic fantasies and the attendant worry and doubt about suitability for normal human intercourse.

The clinical data on change in fantasy are self-reports, supplemented by the therapist's inference of the client's credibility. The orderliness of response to therapy, along with the enthusiasm which accompanied the progress reports, serves to bolster the conclusion that Mr. M did, in fact, give up his sadistic fantasies of 10 years' standing in favor of the kinds of fantasies which he felt were a sine qua non for appropriate sociosexual behavior. Both preceding and accompanying these changes was the radical difference in outlook. Simply stated, Mr. M stopped worrying about himself as an "oddball," doomed to a solitary life, and did make some initial attempts to establish appropriate relationships with girls. That he has not yet done so (as of this writing) may, indeed, be due to a return of the original problem; however, this alternative seems less likely than that verbalized by the client, namely, that he has always had trouble doing what he knows he ought to do, and that, above all, being a so-called sexual deviate has ceased being an issue for him. Moreover, as mentioned above, variables other than the content of fantasies would seem to bear importantly on the matter of overt sexual behavior. Clearly, if usual dating habits were to be used as a criterion for outcome, the therapy must be considered a failure—although this would qualify many a young adult as "maladjusted" or "abnormal." Be that as it may, a relevant, well-established class of behaviors was modified, setting the stage for a social adjustment from which the client had initially seen himself utterly alienated.

Supplementary Follow-Up Data

A follow-up report was received by mail 16 mo. following termination. The client reported that, since the therapy had so readily eliminated the arousal from sadistic fantasies, and, most importantly, had altered his outlook for "normal" sexual behavior, he allowed himself, "premeditatedly," to return to the use of the sadistic fantasies 6 mo. after termination, ". . . resolving to enjoy my fantasies until June 1, and then to reform once more. This I did. On June 1 [1967], right on schedule, I bought an issue of *Playboy* and proceeded to give myself the treatment again. Once again, it worked like a charm. In two weeks, I was back in my reformed state, where I am now [August 1967]. I have no need for sadistic fantasies . . . I have [also] been pursuing a vigorous (well, vigorous for *me*) program of dating. In this way, I have gotten to know a lot of girls of whose existence I was previously only peripherally aware. As you probably know, I was very shy with girls before; well, now I am not one-fifth as shy as I used to be. In fact, by my old standards, I have become a regular rake!"

A telephone call was made to obtain more specific information about his return to the sadistic fantasies. He reported that the return was "fairly immediate," with a concomitant withdrawal of interest in conventional sexual stimuli. His self-administered therapy in June 1967 followed the gradual pattern of the original therapy, although progress was much faster. The author advised him not to make any more "premeditated" returns, rather to consolidate his gains in dating and other conventional hetero-sexual activities and interests. The client indicated that this plan could and would be readily implemented.

Of the past 16 mo., then, the client has been free of the sa-distic fantasies for 7 mo., the other 9 mo. involving what he terms a willful return for sexual stimulation while masturbating. Con-stant throughout this follow-up period has been the relief which he derived from finding himself able to respond sexually to con-ventional sexual stimuli. Additional gains are his dating activi-ties, which, it will be recalled, were not in evidence while the writer was in direct contact with him.

Still aware of the limitations of these case-study data, it does seem noteworthy and possibly quite important that the client's self-initiated partial "relapse" took place in a step-wise fashion, that is, without a *gradual* reorientation to the sadistic fantasies: he reported himself almost immediately excited by them once he had made the decision to become so. This sudden shift raises questions as to whether "aversive counterconditioning" underlay the indifference to the fantasies which was effected during ther-apy. This surprising finding also underlines the probable impor-tance of other-than-conditioning variables in the treatment.

NOTE

1. This paper was written during a postdoctoral traineeship at the Veterans Administration Hospital, Palo Alto, California. For critical comments and helpful suggestions, the author thanks Walter Mischel, Arnold A. Lazarus, David Fisher, and Thomas J. D'Zurilla.

REFERENCES

Bandura, A. *Principles of behavior modification*, New York: Holt, Rinehart & Winston, in press.

Blakemore, C. B., Thorpe, J. G., Barker, J. C., Conway, C. G., & Lavin, N. I. The application of faradic aversion conditioning in a case of transvestism. *Behaviour Research and Therapy*, 1963, 1, 29–34.

Cautela, J. R. Treatment of compulsive behavior by covert sensitization. *The Psychological Record*, 1966, 16, 33–41.

Davies, B., & Morgenstern, F. A case of cysticercosis, temporal lobe epilepsy, and transvestism. *Journal of Neurological and Neurosurgical Psychiatry*, 1960, 23, 247–249.

Davison, G. C. Relative contributions of differential relaxation and graded exposure to in vivo desensitization of a neurotic fear. *Proceedings of the 73rd annual convention of the American Psychological Association*, 1965, 209–210.

Davison, G. C. Differential relaxation and cognitive restructuring in therapy with a "paranoid schizophrenic" or "paranoid state." *Proceedings of the 74th annual convention of the American Psychological Association*, 1966, 2, 177–178.

Davison, G. C. Systematic desensitization as a counterconditioning process. *Journal of Abnormal Psychology*, 1968, in press.

Feldman, M. P. Aversion therapy for sexual deviations: A critical review. *Psychological Bulletin*, 1966, 65, 65–79.

Feldman, M. P., & MacCulloch, M. J. The application of anticipatory avoidance learning to the treatment of homosexuality: I. Theory, technique and preliminary results. *Behaviour Research and Therapy*, 1965, 2, 165–183.

Freund, K. Some problems in the treatment of homosexuality. In H. J. Eysenck (Ed.), *Behaviour therapy and the neurosis*. London: Pergamon, 1960. Pp. 312–326.

Glasser, W. *Reality therapy: A new approach to psychiatry*. New York: Harper & Row, 1965.

Grossberg, J. M. Behavior therapy: A review. *Psychological Bulletin*, 1964, 62, 73–88.

Guthrie, E. R. *The psychology of learning*. New York: Harper, 1935.

Kalish, H. I. Behavior therapy. In B. B. Wolman (Ed.), *Handbook of clinical psychology*. New York: McGraw-Hill, 1965, Pp. 1230–1253.

Lang, P. J., & Lazovik, A. D. Experimental desensitization of a phobia. *Journal of Abnormal and Social Psychology*, 1963, 66, 519–525.

Lang, P. J., Lazovik, A. D., & Reynolds, D. J. Desensitization, suggestibility, and pseudotherapy. *Journal of Abnormal Psychology*, 1965, 70, 395–402.

Lavin, N. I., Thorpe, J. G., Barker, J. C., Blakemore, C. B., & Conway, C. G. Behavior therapy in a case of transvestism. *Journal of Nervous and Mental Disease*, 1961, 133, 346–353.

Lazarus, A. A. New methods in psychotherapy: A case study. *South African Medical Journal*, 1958, 33, 660–663.

Lazarus, A. A. Group therapy of phobic disorders by systematic desensitization. *Journal of Abnormal and Social Psychology*, 1961, 63, 504–510.

Lazarus, A. A., & Abramovitz, A. The use of "emotive imagery" in the treatment of children's phobias. *Journal of Mental Science*, 1962, 108, 191–195.

Levy, L. H. *Psychological interpretation*. New York: Holt, Rinehart & Winston, 1963.

Maher, B. A. *Principles of psychopathology: An experimental approach*. New York: McGraw-Hill, 1966.

Mainord, W. A. A therapy. *Research Bulletin*, Mental Health Research Institute, Ft. Steilacom, Washington, 1962, 5, 85–92.

Paul, G. L. *Insight vs. desensitization in psychotherapy: An experiment in anxiety reduction*. Stanford: Stanford University Press, 1966.

Paul, G. L., & Shannon, D. T. Treatment of anxiety through systematic desensitization in therapy groups. *Journal of Abnormal Psychology*, 1966, 71, 124–135.

Rachman, S. Sexual disorders and behaviour therapy. *American Journal of Psychiatry*, 1961, 118, 235–240.

Rachman, S. Studies in desensitization—III: Speed of generalization. *Behaviour Research and Therapy*, 1966, 4, 7–15.

Raymond, M. J. Case of fetishism treated by aversion therapy. *British Medical Journal*, 1956, 2, 854–857.

Schubot, E. The influence of hypnotic and muscular relaxation in systematic desensitization of phobias. Unpublished doctoral dissertation, Stanford University, 1966.

Thorpe, J. G., Schmidt, E., Brown, P. T., & Castell, D. Aversion-relief therapy: A new method for general application. *Behaviour Research and Therapy,* 1964, 2, 71–82.

Thorpe, J. G., Schmidt, E., & Castell, D. A comparison of positive and negative (aversion) conditioning in the treatment of homosexuality. *Behaviour Research and Therapy,* 1963, 1, 357–362.

Ullmann, L., & Krasner, L. P. (Eds.) *Case studies in behavior modification.* New York: Holt, Rinehart & Winston, 1965.

Wolpe, J. *Psychotherapy by reciprocal inhibition.* Stanford: Stanford University Press, 1958.

Wolpe, J., & Lazarus, A. A. *Behavior therapy techniques.* New York: Pergamon, 1966.

Wolpin, M., & Raines, J. Visual imagery, expected roles and extinction as possible factors in reducing fear and avoidance behavior. *Behaviour Research and Therapy,* 1966, 4, 25–37.

Zeisset, R. M. Desensitization and relaxation in the modification of psychiatric patients' interview behavior. Unpublished doctoral dissertation, University of Illinois, 1966.

Relative Efficacy of Desensitization and Modeling Approaches for Inducing Behavioral, Affective, and Attitudinal Changes[1]

ALBERT BANDURA, EDWARD B. BLANCHARD, and BRUNHILDE RITTER, *Stanford University*

The present study investigated basic change processes accompanying several social-learning procedures from the perspective of a dual-process theory of avoidance behavior. Snake-phobic subjects were administered either symbolic desensitization, symbolic modeling, live modeling combined with guided participation (contact desensitization), or they received no treatment. All three approaches produced generalized and enduring reductions in fear arousal and avoidance behavior as well as positive changes in attitudes. Of the three methods, modeling with guided participation proved most powerful, achieving virtually complete extinction of phobic behavior in every subject. Moreover, those who attained only partial improvement through the other treatments displayed total extinction of phobic behavior after a brief period of modeling with guided participation. Consistent with social-learning theory, the favorable changes produced toward the phobic object were accompanied by fear reduction toward threatening situations beyond the specifically treated phobia, the decrements being roughly proportional to the potency of the treatments employed. Moderately high positive correlations were found between behavioral and attitudinal changes. Some evidence was

Bandura, A., Blanchard, E. B., & Ritter, B. Relative efficacy of desensitization and modeling approaches for inducing behavioral, affective, and attitudinal changes. *Journal of Personality and Social Psychology*, 1969, *3*, 173–199. Copyright 1969 by the American Psychological Association, and reproduced by permission. Photographs of modeling deleted in this reproduction.

obtained that modeling procedures expedite behavioral changes through vicarious extinction of fear arousal to aversive stimuli below the threshold for activating avoidance responses, thus enabling persons to perform approach behaviors. Direct contact with threats that are no longer objectively justified provides new experiences that further extinguish residual anxiety and augment attitudinal changes.

Psychological approaches to the modification of human behavior have relied heavily upon verbal influence procedures. It would appear from the results of psychotherapy outcome studies that the popularity of such methods is attributable more to their ease of application than to their demonstrated effectiveness. Recent years have witnessed a rapid growth of new treatment approaches that achieve psychological changes mainly through guided learning experiences (Bandura, 1969a). The present experiment was principally designed to assess the differential efficacy of several of these approaches for inducing behavioral, affective, and attitudinal changes in phobic subjects, and to investigate certain issues pertaining to basic change processes.

The research reported in this paper is guided by the dual-process theory of avoidance behavior. According to this view, threatening stimuli evoke emotional arousal which has both autonomic and central components. It is further assumed that these arousal processes, operating primarily at the central level, exercise some degree of control over instrumental avoidance responding.

The influential role of arousal mediators in avoidance behavior is most clearly demonstrated by Solomon and his colleagues (Rescorla & Solomon, 1967; Solomon & Turner, 1962). In these studies, which use a three-stage paradigm, animals first learn to make an avoidance response to a light stimulus. They are then skeletally immobilized by curare to prevent avoidance responses from being conditioned directly to external stimuli, and shock is paired with one tone, while a contrasting tone is never associated with aversive stimulation. In subsequent tests the animals display essentially the same degree of avoidance in response to the negatively valenced tone and the light, both of which evoke common arousal reactions, whereas avoidance responses rarely occur to the neutral tone. Considering that the light and the tones were never associated, and assuming that the curare blocked all skeletal activity (Black, 1967), thus precluding any differential conditioning of avoidance responses to the tones, the controlling power of the aversive auditory stimulus must be mediated either through events in central systems or through autonomic feedback mechanisms.

There is evidence that avoidance responses can be acquired and maintained in sympathectomized animals (Wynne & Solomon, 1955), and that avoidance behavior persists long after autonomic responses have been extinguished (Black, 1959; Notterman, Schoenfeld, & Bersh, 1952). Moreover, the latency of autonomic reactions is much longer than that of skeletal responding; consequently, avoidance behavior is typically executed before autonomic reactions could possibly be elicited. Findings of the preceding studies indicate that behavior is in large part centrally regulated rather than under autonomic control, as is commonly assumed in peripheral theories of anxiety.

It would follow from the dual-process theory that if the arousal capacity of subjectively threatening events is extinguished, then both the motivation and one set of controlling simuli for avoidance behavior are removed. Black (1958) has shown in experiments with curarized subjects that neutralization of an aversive stimulus through repeated presentation without any accompanying adverse experiences markedly facilitates elimination of avoidance behavior. The psychological procedures investigated in the present study are likewise predicated on the assumption that extinction of fear arousal will reduce phobic behavior.

The method of systematic desensitization (Wolpe, 1958) attempts to eliminate fear arousal through repeated pairing of imaginal representations of threatening situations with deep relaxation. Wolpe explains the effects of this form of treatment in terms of reciprocally inhibitory processes occurring at the level of the autonomic nervous system. These theoretical speculations about the mechanisms governing the counterconditioning process are largely disputed by empirical findings (Bandura, 1969a); nevertheless, numerous well-designed experiments (Davison, 1968; Krapil 1967; Lang, Lazovik & Reynolds, 1965; Mealiea, 1967; H. R. Miller, 1967; Moore, 1965; Paul, 1966; Paul & Shannon, 1966; Schubot, 1966) have shown that the systematic desensitization procedure produces significant reduction in avoidance behavior.

Fear arousal can also be eliminated on a vicarious basis. These vicarious extinction effects are achieved by having persons observe models performing fear-provoking behavior without any adverse consequences accruing to the performers (Bandura, 1968). The absence of anticipated negative consequences is a requisite condition for fear extinction. Hence, the modeled displays most likely to have strong effects on phobic observers are ones in which performances they regard as hazardous are repeatedly shown to be safe under a variety of threatening circumstances. However, presentation of modeled approach responses toward the most aversive situations at the outset is apt to generate in observers high levels of emotional arousal that can impede vicarious extinction.

Avoidance responses can be extinguished with minimal distress if persons are exposed to a graduated sequence of modeling activities beginning with displays that have low arousal value (Bandura, Grusec, & Menlove, 1967; Bandura & Menlove, 1968). After emotional reactions to attenuated threats have been extinguished, progressively more aversive modeling events, which are weakened by generalization of fear extinction from preceding displays, are gradually introduced and neutralized. Stimulus graduation is not a necessary condition for vicarious extinction, but it permits greater control over the change process and it entails less fear elicitation than approaches involving repeated exposure to modeling events having high threat value.

When fear arousal is extinguished to symbolic representations of threats, as in systematic desensitization and symbolic modeling, one would expect some loss in generalization of fear reduction to actual events because they constitute more severe threats. In instances where fear arousal is not reduced below the threshold for activating avoidance behavior, persons will be unable to perform highly threatening approach responses even though their fear has been extinguished to the symbolic equivalents. One might expect less transfer loss when fear arousal is extinguished through both vicarious and direct experiences with the actual threatening events. However, when desired behavior is severely inhibited active response guidance procedures may be required, in addition to graduated modeling, to reinstate approach behavior.

The third approach consists of a form of treatment combining graduated live modeling with guided participation. The principal elements of this method were originally applied by Ritter (1965) and further developed as contact desensitization (Ritter, 1968a, 1968b, 1969a). In the procedure employed in the present study, the model initially demonstrates the desired behavior under secure observational conditions, after which individuals are aided through further demonstration and joint performance to execute progressively more difficult responses. Whenever subjects are unable to perform a given behavior upon demonstration alone they are assisted physically by enacting the activities concurrently with the model. The physical guidance is then gradually reduced until all subjects are able to perform the behavior without assistance.

In the present experiment subjects who suffered from snake phobias received either systematic desensitization, symbolic modeling, live modeling with guided participation,[2] or were assigned to a nontreated control group. Prior to, and upon completion of, their respective treatment programs subjects were administered a behavioral avoidance test to measure the strength of their fear and avoidance of snakes. In addition they completed a comprehensive fear inventory to determine whether extinction of fear of snakes is associated with changes in other areas of anxiety. Attitude measures were also included to furnish information regarding the interesting but inadequately explored attitudinal effects of behavioral changes induced through social-learning procedures.

It was predicted that all three treatment approaches would extinguish both fear arousal and avoidance behavior, but that live modeling combined with guided participation would prove superior in this respect. No predictions were advanced, however, concerning the relative efficacy of systematic desensitization and symbolic modeling.

Psychodynamic theories generally assume that anxieties are internally generated by arousal of repressed impulses which are then displaced and projected onto environmental events. External phobic objects are therefore regarded as pseudoevocative stimuli.

Thus, for example, snake phobias are believed to reflect phallic anxieties (Fenichel, 1945). From this point of view, direct neutralization of a given phobic stimulus should either have no lasting effect, or result in the emergence of new phobic disorders because the underlying source of anxiety has not been eliminated.

According to social-learning theory, extinction of the arousal potential of a phobic stimulus should produce not only stable decreases in avoidance behavior, but some reduction in anxiety in other areas of functioning on the basis of stimulus generalization. The transfer of extinction effects would be expected to vary as a function of level of fear extinction achieved toward the treated phobic stimuli and the degree of similarity between the neutralized and the other sources of anxiety.

Considering both the extensive research on attitude change and the powerful controlling functions that are often conferred upon attitudes, there has been surprisingly little investigation of the relationship between attitudinal and behavioral change. A thorough search of the literature by Festinger (1964) yielded only a few studies which disclose that changes in attitudes produced by persuasive communications have little or no effect upon the performance of corresponding actions. There is some reason to suppose that the degree of relationship between attitudinal and behavioral change may be partly determined by the affective and social consequences of the behavior being modified and by the method of influence used to bring about the change.

One can distinguish among three basic modes of attitude change. The *cognitive-oriented* approach attempts to modify persons' attitudes by altering their beliefs about the attitude object through various forms of persuasive communications. As noted above, this method can produce changes in attitudes but it often has little effect upon overt actions. A second general strategy involves an *affect-oriented* approach wherein both evaluations of, and behavior toward, particular attitude objects are modified by altering their emotion-arousing properties, usually through direct or vicarious conditioning procedures. The third approach relies upon a *behavior-oriented* strategy. Results of the latter procedure provide considerable evidence that attitudinal changes can be successfully achieved by getting a person to engage in new behavior in relation to the attitude object without untoward consequences.

The relative modifiability of attitudes and actions, and the degree of correspondence obtained between changes in these two sets of events, may vary with the affective consequences accompanying the behavior. A given social influence might produce analogous changes in both attitude and action when persons are indifferent to, or favorably disposed toward, performing the advocated activities. Most attempts to control consumer behavior through persuasive communications, for example, would fall in this category. The process is much more complicated, however, when persons resist advocated behavior that they can perform because it results in self-devaluation, or when they are amenable to engaging in the desired activities but are unable to do so because of strong fears and inhibitions. In the latter instances, a weak method may alter responses that are readily susceptible to change, such as verbal evaluations, but fail to modify overt behavior which is rendered intractable by its adverse consequences. A relatively powerful influence would be required to achieve correlative changes.

Two of the treatment procedures investigated in the present experiment, namely systematic desensitization and symbolic modeling, are designed to produce changes primarily by extinguishing emotional arousal to symbolic representations of the phobic object. Modeling with guided participation, on the other hand, eliminates emotional arousal to actual threats and it also provides new direct experiences with the previously avoided object that can serve as a further basis for modifying attitudes. It was predicted that all three treatment procedures would produce favorable changes in attitudes. On the assumption that a method operating through behavior change furnishes an objective and genuine basis for new evaluations, it was expected that modeling with participation would achieve the greater modification in attitudes.

There is some evidence from laboratory studies of counterconditioning processes (Gale, Sturmfels, & Gale, 1966; Poppen, 1968) that the aversive properties of threatening stimuli can be extinguished more effectively when administered in conjunction with anxiety-neutralizing events than when presented alone. In the present experiment the symbolic modeling treatment was administered in conjunction with relaxation procedures. Several investigators have also demonstrated that relaxation can reduce physiological arousal to both imagined and external threats (Grings & Uno, 1968; Paul, 1969), and that it increases tolerance of psychologically aversive stimuli (Davison, 1968; Schubot, 1966). In order to evaluate the contribution of relaxation to changes accompanying symbolic modeling, after the posttreatment assessment was completed, subjects in the control group received the symbolic modeling treatment except that they did not utilize relaxation to counteract fear arousal. It was hypothesized that symbolic modeling combined with relaxation would achieve more rapid vicarious extinction of fear arousal, and greater changes in behavior, attitudes, and emotional responsiveness, than symbolic modeling alone.

Under conditions where a given influence procedure exercises weak behavioral control, other variables (e.g., personality characteristics of change agents, attributes of the recipients, and minor variations in the procedure) are likely to emerge as influential determinants of change. However, if a method is sufficiently powerful it should be able to override such influences. In order to demonstrate that in cases exhibiting only partial improvement the major deficits may reside in the method rather than in the recipient, all subjects who failed to achieve terminal performances, including the treated controls, were subsequently administered the treatment combining live modeling with guided participation. Upon completion of this supplementary treatment program, each subject was again administered the regular assessment procedures. Approximately 1 month after subjects concluded their treatment they returned for a follow-up assessment to evaluate the durability of the established changes.

METHOD

Subjects

Subjects were recruited through an advertisement placed in community newspapers. The advertisement requested volunteers to participate in an experiment testing procedures designed to eliminate fear of snakes. The sample also contained a small number of students recruited from an introductory course in psychology.

Of the total number of 48 subjects who qualified for inclusion in the study on the basis of a behavioral avoidance test, 5 were males and 43 were females. They varied in age from 13 to 59 years, with a mean age of 27 years.

In virtually all cases the phobia unnecessarily restricted subjects' activities and adversely affected their psychological functioning in various ways. Some of the people were unable to perform their occupational duties in situations where there was any remote possibility that they might come into contact with snakes; others could not take part in recreational activities such as hunting, camping, hiking, or gardening, because of their dread of snakes; and still others avoided purchasing homes in rustic areas, or experienced marked distress whenever they would be unexpectedly confronted with pet snakes in the course of their social or occupational activities.

In the preliminary assessment subjects completed a questionnaire in which they were asked to describe any direct or vicarious aversive experiences that they or members of their families had had in relation to snakes, to indicate the onset of their fear, and to note any familial modeling of snake phobic behavior.

Pretreatment Measurement of Attitudes

In the present study attitudes are conceptualized as evaluative responses. Subjects' attitudes toward snakes were measured in two ways. First, they were administered six attitude scales describing various encounters with snakes such as visiting a reptile exhibit, being unexpectedly shown a documentary film on the habits of snakes, encountering a snake on a hike, keeping snakes in the home, and handling snakes and caring for them. Subjects were instructed to rate each item on a 7-point scale which indicates strong enjoyment at one end, strong dislike on the other, and indifference at the midpoint. The mean of the six ratings constituted the attitude score.

Subjects' attitudes toward snakes were also assessed in terms of evaluative dimensions of the semantic differential technique. The form used consisted of eight bipolar adjective rating scales using the following pairs of contrasting adjectives: good-bad, clean-dirty, ugly-beautiful, belligerent-peaceful, interesting-dull, worthless-valuable, nice-awful, and pleasant-unpleasant. The pooled ratings obtained from these scales were averaged to provide a summary evaluative score.

Behavioral Avoidance Test

The test of avoidance behavior, which was similar to the one employed by Schubot (1966), consisted of a graded series of 29 performance tasks involving increasingly more threatening interactions with a 4-foot king snake. The tasks required subjects to approach the snake in an enclosed glass cage, to look down at it, to touch and hold the snake with gloved and then bare hands, to let it loose in the room and then to replace it in the cage, to hold it within 5 inches of their faces, and finally to tolerate the snake crawling in their laps while they held their hands passively at their sides.

Prior to the test of avoidance behavior subjects were given some factual information about the characteristics of reptiles. They were told that snakes are dry rather than slimy, that they feel cool to the touch because they are cold-blooded and take on the temperature of their surroundings, and that they often flick their tongues because they have faulty vision and use the tongue to explore their environment. This information was provided in order to exclude moderately fearful subjects who might achieve performance gains on the basis of incidental information alone derived from testing and treatment experiences. Moreover, by introducing informational factors prior to measurement of the behavioral base line their potential influence was eliminated from the effects produced by the treatment operations.

Subjects were tested individually by a female experimenter. Those who were unable to enter the room containing the snake were given a score of zero; subjects who could go in were asked to perform the items in the graded series of tasks. To control for any possible influence of expressive and postural cues from the experimenter, she stood behind the subject and read aloud the approach responses to be performed. She also rated the snake's activity level and recorded whether or not the subject successfully completed each test item. In order to evaluate scorer reliability

17 of the behavioral tests, randomly selected from pretreatment, posttreatment, and follow-up phases of the experiment, were scored simultaneously but independently by another rater who observed the test sessions through a one-way mirror. The interrater agreement was 100 percent for approach responses and 92 percent for snake activity level.

The subject's score on the behavioral test was the number of approach tasks he was able to perform. Those who succeeded in lifting the snake inside the cage with a gloved hand for 5 seconds or more were eliminated from the experiment. On the basis of this selection criterion, 38 percent of the subjects who had defined themselves as snake phobic proved, much to their surprise, relatively fearless in the behavioral test. Subjects were excluded only on the basis of approach behavior without regard to any other psychological characteristics so as to increase generality of the findings.

Fear Arousal Accompanying Approach Responses

In addition to measuring the attitudinal and behavioral effects of the different treatment approaches, their efficacy in eliminating the fear arousal potential of phobic objects was also assessed. During the behavioral test subjects were asked to rate orally, in terms of a 10-interval scale, the intensity of the fear they experienced when each snake approach response was described to them and again while they were performing the corresponding behavior. The scores, averaged across the responses that each subject was able to complete, served as measures of anticipatory fear arousal and performance-related fear.

Immediately after the behavioral avoidance test was completed subjects were readministered the attitude scales and the semantic differential to obtain a new attitudinal base line reflecting any changes resulting from receipt of factual information and exposure to an actual snake.

Appraisal of Fear Proneness

As the final task in the pretreatment assessment subjects completed a comprehensive fear inventory to determine whether elimination of fears concerning snakes is associated with concomitant changes in other areas of anxiety. The inventory, which contained

100 items, included 72 from the test developed by Wolpe and Lang (1964) plus an additional 28 items designed to provide 20 items in each of the following five fear categories: animals; social situations and interpersonal behavior; physical afflictions and injuries; classical phobias; and a group of miscellaneous fears.

Subjects were asked to rate their emotional responses to each object or situation in terms of a 5-point scale describing increasing degrees of fearfulness. Two sets of scores were derived from this test. One was the number of situations that were rated as fear-provoking and the other was a fear-intensity measure obtained by assigning to each item numerical values ranging from 0 to 4 depending upon the level of fear checked. Number and intensity of fear scores were determined separately for each of the five categories and summed across all the items to provide an overall index of susceptibility to fear arousal.

It should be noted in passing that attitudes, defined as evaluative responses, are differentiated from fear arousal. These two sets of measures are distinguished on the grounds that people can be attracted to things they fear, as evident in approach-avoidance conflicts; conversely, it is not uncommon for people to dislike things they do not fear.

Treatment Conditions

Subjects were individually matched on the basis of their pretreatment avoidance behavior and then randomly assigned to one of four conditions. Each group contained 12 subjects. All treatments were administered individually.

One group of subjects received the standard form of systematic desensitization treatment originally devised by Wolpe (1958). In this procedure deep relaxation was successively paired with imaginal representations of snakes arranged in order of increasing aversiveness. During the first of two sessions subjects received training in muscular relaxation and in the use of positive imagery to diminish emotional arousal. In subsequent sessions, after being deeply relaxed, subjects were asked by the experimenter to visualize the least threatening item in the hierarchy of emotion-arousing scenes involving snakes that they had previously ranked from least to most aversive. This anxiety hierarchy contained a total of 34 scenes ranging from relatively innocuous activities such as looking at pictures and toy replicas of snakes to handling live snakes in ways that would be fear provoking. Whenever subjects signaled anxiety to visualization of a threatening scene it was promptly withdrawn, relaxation was reinstated, and then the item was repeatedly presented until it ceased to evoke anxiety. If relaxation remained unimpaired in the imagined presence of the threat, subjects' emotional responses to the next item in the hierarchy were extinguished and so on throughout the graduated series until the most threatening events were completely neutralized.

A second group of subjects participated in a self-administered symbolic modeling treatment in which they observed a graduated film depicting young children, adolescents, and adults engaging in progressively more threatening interactions with a snake. The colored film, which was approximately 35 minutes long, began with scenes showing the fearless models handling plastic snakes and proceeded through displays in which they touched and held a large king snake, draped it around their necks, and let it crawl freely over their bodies.

To further increase the efficacy of this method two other features were added: First, subjects were taught to induce and to maintain anxiety-neutralizing relaxation throughout the period of exposure. The second factor concerned the control of stimulus presentation. A self-regulated modeling treatment would be expected to permit greater control over extinction outcomes than one in which subjects were exposed to a sequence of aversive modeling stimuli without regard to their anxiety responses. Therefore, the rate of presentation of modeling stimuli was regulated by subjects through a Kodak analyst projector equipped with remote control starting and reversing devices. Subjects were instructured to stop the film whenever a particular model performance was anxiety provoking, to reverse the film to the beginning of the aversive sequence, and to reinduce deep relaxation. They then reviewed the threatening scene repeatedly in this manner until it was completely neutralized before proceeding to the next item in the graduated sequence. After subjects became skillful in handling the projector controls and the self-induction of relaxation, the experimenter absented himself from the situation so that the subjects themselves conducted their own treatment until their anxieties to the depicted scenes were thoroughly extinguished. Treatment was terminated when they could view the entire film without experiencing any emotional arousal.

During the symbolic modeling treatment subjects rated on a 10-point scale the intensity of their emotional responses to each scene and to subsequent reexposures to the same items. These data were collected to provide information on the course of vicarious extinction of emotional arousal as a function of repeated observation of modeled approach responses.

Subjects assigned to the third group received the treatment combining graduated live modeling with guided participation. After observing intimate snake-interaction behavior repeatedly modeled by the experimenter, subjects were aided through demonstration and joint participation to perform progressively more threatening approach responses toward the king snake. In the initial procedure subjects observed through a one-way mirror the experimenter perform a series of threatening activities with the king snake that provided striking demonstrations that close interaction with the snake does not have harmful consequences. During this period, which lasted approximately 15 minutes, the experimenter held the snake close to his face, allowed it to crawl over his body at will, and let it loose to slither about the room. After returning the snake to its glass cage, the experimenter invited the subject to join him in the room and to be seated in one of four chairs placed at varying distances from the experimenter's chair. The experimenter then removed the snake from the cage and commenced the treatment, beginning with relatively nonthreatening performance tasks and proceeding through increasingly fear-provoking activities. This treatment was conducted without the use of relaxation procedures.

At each step the experimenter himself performed fearless behavior and gradually led subjects into touching, stroking, and then holding the midsection of the snake's body with gloved and then bare hands while the experimenter held the snake securely by the head and tail. Whenever a subject was unable to perform the behavior upon demonstration alone she was asked to place her hand on the experimenter's and to move her hand down gradually until it touched the snake's body. After subjects no longer felt any apprehension about touching the snake under these secure conditions, anxieties about contact with the snake's head area and entwining tail were extinguished. The experimenter again performed the tasks fearlessly, and then he and the subject enacted the responses jointly; as subjects became less fearful the experimenter gradually reduced his participation and control over the snake until eventually subjects were able to hold the snake in their laps without assistance, to let the snake loose in the room and to retrieve it, and to let it crawl freely over their bodies. Progress through the graded approach tasks was paced according to the subjects' apprehensiveness. The threat value of the activities for each subject determined the particular order in which they were performed. When they reported being able to perform one activity with little or no fear, they were eased into a more difficult interaction. Treatment was terminated when subjects were able to execute all the snake interaction tasks independently.

Subjects assigned to the control condition participated in all of the assessment procedures without receiving any intervening treatment. This group primarily furnished a control for changes resulting from repeated measurements. A pseudotherapy was not employed because several previous investigations (Davison, 1968; Krapfl, 1967; Lang et al., 1965) have shown that snake avoidance behavior is unaffected by such experiences. In addition, the controls were subsequently used to test the efficacy of symbolic modeling without relaxation.

To evaluate the reliability of treatment outcomes the procedures were administered by two experimenters, one female and one male. Each experimenter applied each of the three treatments to half the subjects. The experimenters received no information about subjects' pretreatment performances on any of the measures so as not to alter the manner in which they administered the procedures.

The treatments, which were typically scheduled twice a week, continued until subjects either achieved the terminal criterion specified for each condition or the maximum time allotment for 5.25 hours of treatment (not counting relaxation training) was completed. Maximum contact with snakes, either in live or symbolic form, was thus equated across conditions. The average dura-

tion of treatment required for the different methods was 2 hours,
10 minutes for contact desensitization, 2 hours, 46 minutes for
symbolic modeling, and 4 hours, 32 minutes for systematic desensitization. The latter method required more treatment time
than the two modeling procedures, which did not differ significantly from each other. These treatment durations do not include
the time devoted to relaxation training in the symbolic modeling
and systematic desensitization conditions.

Several subjects who were originally selected for the experiment had to be replaced by subjects with comparable avoidant
tendencies because of various difficulties that precluded their
participation. A male subject who was making satisfactory progress in the contact desensitization treatment had to discontinue
the program when an occupational change made it difficult for
him to meet the required schedule; and a female subject in this
same condition had to be replaced because she was afflicted
with mononucleosis; two controls moved to distant cities during
the waiting period, and one dropped out after the pretreatment
assessment.

Posttreatment Assessment

Following completion of the treatment series the assessment
procedures employed in the pretreatment phase of the study were
readministered to all subjects. As in the pretest, the attitude measures were administered prior to and following the behavioral
avoidance test to permit evaluation of the reciprocal interaction
between attitudinal and behavioral changes.

In order to determine the generality of extinction effects,
half the subjects in each of the conditions were tested initially
with the familiar brown-striped king snake and then with an unfamiliar crimson-splotched corn snake that was strikingly different in coloration; the remaining subjects were tested with the
two snakes in the reverse order. Two groups of 12 students,
drawn from an introductory psychology course, were tested with
either the king snake or the corn snake to compare their aversive
properties. Except for a slight tendency for the corn snake to
evoke more negative evaluation on the semantic differential
$(t = 2.33, p < .05)$, both snakes produced equivalent approach

behavior, fear arousal accompanying specific approach responses, and negative attitudes toward reptiles.

The same female experimenter who conducted the pretreatment assessment administered the posttreatment measures. To control for any possible bias, she was provided with no information about the conditions to which the subjects were assigned.

RESULTS

Differences in approach behavior toward the two snakes were evaluated separately for each treatment condition. Although subjects in the contact desensitization and systematic desensitization treatments performed more approach responses toward the familiar king snake than toward the generalization snake, none of the differences reached the .05 significance level. Nor did subjects experience differential levels of fear arousal while performing specific approach responses toward the two snakes. The two sets of scores were, therefore, averaged across snakes for evaluating the results of the experiment.

The data were analyzed using analysis of covariance in which pretreatment measurements served as the covariates. Separate three-way analyses were computed for each independent variable with treatment conditions, experimenters, and snake order representing the three factors.

Table 1 shows the significance levels of the treatment effects, the differences between pairs of treatment conditions, and the changes that occurred within each group on each of 17 measures. The order in which the snake tests were administered did not in itself produce any significant differences, and except for one instance which will be discussed later, the two experimenters achieved equivalent results. In the numerous analyses only three significant interaction effects were obtained that will be discussed when results are reported separately for each measure.

Approach Behavior

The mean approach responses performed by subjects in each of the four conditions at the pretreatment and posttreatment phases of the experiment are presented in Figure 1. As depicted in Table 1, subjects in the control group showed no change in

TABLE 1

Significance of Treatment Effects, Intergroup Differences, and Within-Group Changes for Each of Several Measures

Response measure	Treatment effect (F test)	Comparison of pairs of treatment conditions (F test)						Within-group changes (t test)			
		Modeling with participation vs. symbolic modeling	Modeling with participation vs. systematic desensitization	Modeling with participation vs. control	Symbolic modeling vs. systematic desensitization	Symbolic modeling vs. control	Systematic desensitization vs. control	Modeling with participation	Symbolic modeling	Systematic desensitization	Control
Approach behavior	16.70***	8.24**	11.75**	34.54***	.79	9.04**	6.00*	11.07***	3.97**	3.36**	.17
Fear arousal											
Initial approach	16.73***	2.30	10.71**	52.83***	22.93***	77.18***	19.95***	6.05***	7.69***	5.73***	3.03*
Total approach	14.61***	.12	15.82***	47.73***	18.66***	52.57***	8.59**	6.00***	7.35***	4.36***	1.73
Attitude scores	22.84***	7.36***	22.27***	64.34***	4.02	28.17***	10.90***	11.84***	5.53***	3.64***	.79
Semantic differential	26.33***	6.05*	17.78***	70.76***	3.90	35.42***	17.60***	9.53***	4.95***	2.70*	1.68
Total number	.85							3.27**	1.59	.56	1.59
Total intensity	1.23							5.13***	3.41**	.93	.57
Number animal	1.84							1.99	3.89***	1.52	1.03
Intensity animal	4.06*	1.54	.004	4.18*	1.71	10.08**	3.91	5.56***	6.14***	3.85***	.39
Number social	.63							1.29	1.01	.93	1.34
Intensity social	1.90							3.49**	2.36*	.48	.09
Number injury	.47							2.77*	.63	1.02	1.64
Intensity injury	.42							2.57*	2.13	.85	.84
Number classical	.48							1.68	.85	.24	1.52
Intensity classical	1.02							1.92	1.59	.12	.21
Number miscellaneous	1.66							2.92*	.27	.39	.96
Intensity miscellaneous	1.10							4.82***	1.82	.14	1.36

*p < .05. **p < .01. ***p < .001.

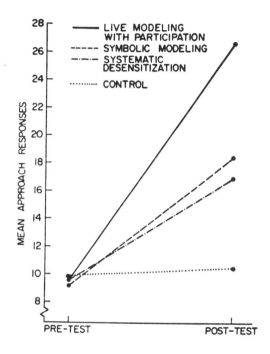

FIG. 1. Mean number of approach responses performed by subjects before and after receiving their respective treatments.

their avoidance behavior. On the other hand, all three treatments produced substantial reductions in avoidance behavior and they differed significantly in this respect from the control condition. Symbolic modeling and systematic desensitization proved equally efficacious in restoring approach behavior. As predicted, subjects who received live modeling combined with guided participation achieved the greatest performance gains. The analysis disclosed no significant experimenter differences or interaction effects.

A more stringent criterion of extinction of avoidance behavior is the percentage of subjects in each condition who were able to perform the terminal approach task with at least one snake.

The rates were 92 percent for modeling with participation, 33 percent for symbolic modeling, 25 percent for systematic desensitization, and 0 percent for the controls. These differential rates of terminal performances were highly significant ($\chi^2 = 23.14$, $p < .001$).

As noted earlier, the behavior changes produced by the treatment procedures generalized extensively to the unfamiliar snake that subjects encountered for the first time in the posttreatment assessment. However, some of the subjects whose avoidance behavior was thoroughly extinguished in relation to the familiar king snake were nevertheless unwilling to perform the terminal task with the corn snake. Among subjects who achieved terminal performances with the king snake, the percentage showing complete transfer to the other reptile was 55 percent, 100 percent, and 0 percent for contact desensitization, symbolic modeling, and systematic desensitization, respectively. When approach scores are considered for all subjects, regardless of whether or not they achieved terminal performances with the experimental snake, the contact desensitization treatment of course produced greater approach behavior ($M = 24.6$) toward the generalization snake than either symbolic modeling (18.0) or systematic desensitization (15.8).

Fear Arousal Accompanying Approach Responses

The degree of fear arousal evoked by approach responses is partly dependent on the threat value of the behavior being performed. That is, looking at a caged snake is a much less fear-provoking activity than holding a writhing snake close to one's face. The degree of fear extinction was measured by comparing the mean level of fear arousal accompanying approach responses that subjects performed before treatment with the fear levels reported in the posttreatment period for the same subset of approach responses and for all of the approach behavior that subjects successfully executed. If, for example, a given subject successfully completed 5 approach responses in the pretest and 20 responses in the posttreatment phase, the fear decrement for initial approach responses was based on differences in mean fear scores for the same 5 responses in the two assessments; the fear decrement for total approach behavior was measured in terms of differences between mean fear scores for the 5 pretest responses and for the 20 responses performed in the posttreatment period.

The fear extinction data are depicted graphically in Figure 2. Since anticipatory and performance fear arousal did not differ significantly, these two sets of ratings were averaged for statistical analyses. The results are shown in Table 1.

Fear evoked by initial approach responses. With regard to the pretreatment subset of approach responses, subjects in all conditions, including the controls, experienced less fear the second time they performed the same behavior. The treatment conditions, however, produced more marked fear decrements. Further comparisons among means revealed that the magnitude of fear reduction achieved by subjects who received systematic desensitization was significantly less than that shown by subjects in the two modeling conditions, which did not differ from each other.

The analysis disclosed a Treatment × Order interaction effect at a borderline level of significance $(F = 2.97, p < .05)$. Subjects who received the modeling treatments achieved greatest

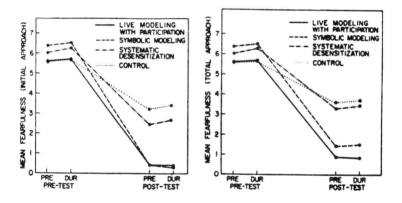

FIG. 2. Mean level of fear arousal associated with approach responses that subjects performed before treatment and the fear levels reported in the post-treatment period for the same subset of approach responses (left figure) and for all the approach responses (right figure) that subjects successfully performed. (*Pre* refers to the intensity of fear subjects experienced when each snake approach response was described to them, and *Dur* signifies the fear level they reported while actually performing the corresponding behavior.)

decrements in fear arousal when they were tested first with the unfamiliar snake, systematic desensitization subjects displayed greatest fear reduction when they were tested initially with the familiar snake, while the order of the behavioral test had no differential effects on fear arousal in control subjects. The results also yielded a significant triple interaction effect $(F = 5.96, p < .01)$ that is not easily interpretable.

Fear evoked by total approach responses. Further evidence for the differential efficacy of the treatment procedures in extinguishing fear arousal is provided in comparisons of fear level experienced in relation to pretreatment approach responses with fear arousal accompanying total approach behavior. On this measure, control subjects showed no significant fear reduction even though their posttreatment performances did not differ much from their initial approach behavior. Subjects in the treatment conditions, on the other hand, experienced significantly less fear in connection with far more threatening performances. Except for the significant treatment effect none of the other main effects or interactions between variables were significant.

As was the case with fear reduction in relation to pretreatment level performances, the two modeling conditions did not differ from each other, but both produced greater fear extinction for total approach behavior than did systematic desensitization. Considering, however, that the mean fear level for contact desensitization is based upon more fear-provoking behavior in posttreatment than the mean for symbolic modeling, the data for the latter two groups are not entirely comparable. A supplementary analysis was therefore performed which compared the level of fear associated with the last approach response that the more timorous member of each matched pair was able to perform. That is, if a pair of matched subjects in the contact desensitization and symbolic modeling treatments completed 29 and 25 approach responses, respectively, the comparison included the fear level accompanying the twenty-fifth response they performed in common. In this analysis subjects receiving symbolic modeling experienced far greater fear arousal $(M = 4.21)$ than their counterparts in contact desensitization $(M = .69)$, a difference that is highly significant $(t = 3.29, p < .01)$.

Attitudinal Changes

The changes in attitudes produced by the various treatment procedures are shown graphically in Figure 3 and evaluated statistically in Table 1. Both measures—based on the attitude scales and the semantic differential—yielded comparable results. There are no differences on either measures between the two attitude assessments conducted in the pretreatment phase (Pre$_2$ − Pre$_1$). For the types of subjects included in this experiment, apparently factual information about snakes and exposure to a snake in the behavioral test did not alter their negative evaluations of reptiles. The refractory quality of these negative attitudes is further shown by the control subjects whose attitudes remained unaltered in the posttreatment assessment as well.

Analysis of changes in attitude scores obtained between the pretreatment behavioral test and following the treatment phase (Post$_1$ − Pre$_2$) reveals a highly significant treatment effect for both measures. Subjects in all three experimental conditions displayed favorable changes in their evaluation of reptiles. Individual comparisons among the means for the different conditions show that modeling combined with participation produced the greatest attitudinal changes, the two modeling procedures were

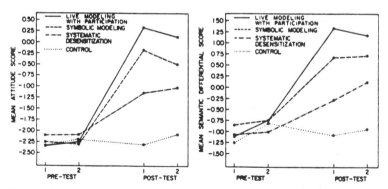

FIG. 3. Attitudes displayed by subjects on the attitude scales (left figure) and the semantic differential (right figure) before and after receiving their respective treatments. (The numeral 1 indicates subjects' attitudes prior to the behavioral test, and the numeral 2 shows their attitudes immediately after the test of avoidance behavior.)

superior to systematic desensitization, and all three treatment conditions differed significantly in this respect from the nontreated control group. It is interesting to note that subjects showed no additional attitudinal changes as measured immediately after the posttreatment behavioral test $(Post_2 - Post_1)$.

The results revealed two additional significant effects. Subjects treated by the female experimenter displayed greater changes on the semantic differential than those treated by the male $(F = 7.75, p < .01)$. A significant Treatment × Order interaction effect $(F = 3.08, p < .05)$ was obtained in the analysis of data from the attitude scales. The behavioral test order in which the familiar snake was presented first produced more favorable changes in attitudes of subjects receiving the modeling treatments, but variation in snake order had no differential effects on subjects in the systematic desensitization and control groups.

Fear Inventory

The changes in the number and intensity of fears in each of the five areas measured are given in Figure 4. Results of the statistical evaluation of these scores are summarized in Table 1. The analysis of covariance indicates no significant difference between groups except for intensity of animal fears. Further comparison of pairs of means shows that subjects in the two modeling conditions experienced a greater reduction in the degree to which they feared animals than did the controls.

Analysis of change scores within groups reveals some degree of fear reduction toward situations beyond the specifically treated phobia, the decrements being roughly proportional to the potency of the treatments employed (Table 1). Nontreated controls showed no changes in either the number or intensity of fears; systematic desensitization produced a decrease only in severity of fears toward other animals; and symbolic modeling was accompanied by reduction in the intensity of fear of animals and social events. Contact desensitization, on the other hand, effected the most widespread fear reductions in relation to a variety of threats including animals, physical injury, interpersonal situations, and miscellaneous events.

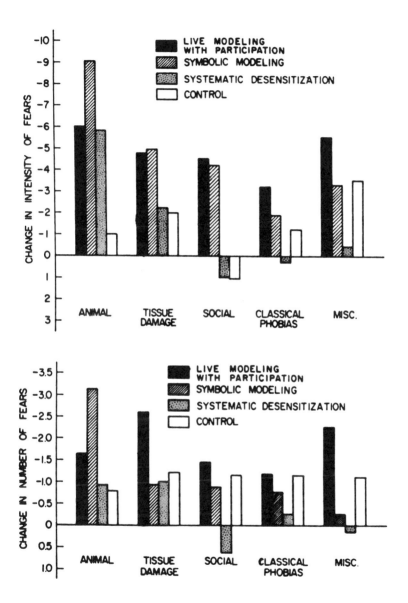

FIG. 4. Changes in the mean number and intensity of fear shown by groups of subjects in each of the five areas measured.

Relationship between Attitudinal and Behavioral Changes

Pretest attitudes and behavior were correlated to assess the degree of relationship that ordinarily exists between these two responses classes. Attitudes were highly positively related to approach behavior for the unselected group of subjects who were used to measure the aversiveness of the snakes. Approach scores correlated .73 with attitudes prior to the behavior test and .87 immediately after the behavior test. The corresponding relationships between the attitude measures based on the semantic differential and approach behavior were .56 and .70, respectively. These correlations are all significant beyond the .01 level.

Similar product-movement correlations were calculated for the phobic subjects as well, although coefficients based on these data are less informative because the range of approach scores for this sample is considerably curtailed. Nevertheless, approach behavior correlated positively with attitudes prior to $(r = .48)$ and after $(r = .56)$ the behavior test. The data also reveal moderately high positive relationships between approach behavior and evaluative responses on the semantic differential as measured before $(r = .44)$ and after $(r = .60)$ the behavior test. All of the preceding correlation coefficients exceed the .01 level of significance.

In order to determine whether the treatment procedures produced analogous changes in attitude and behavior, correlations were computed on amount of change obtained between pretest and posttreatment scores for these sets of measures. Since the corresponding correlations computed separately for data from the different treatment conditions were in the same direction and did not differ significantly, they were averaged by means of an r to z transformation.

Behavior change is positively correlated with attitude change $(\text{Post}_1 - \text{Pre}_2)$ as measured by both the semantic differential $(r = .39, p < .05)$ and the attitude scales $(r = .59, p < .01)$. Moderately high positive relationships are likewise obtained between these measures when the attitude change scores are based on differences between pretest attitudes and those exhibited in posttreatment following the behavioral avoidance test $(\text{Post}_2 - \text{Pre}_2)$.

The correlations of changes in behavior with changes in semantic differential and attitude scores are $r = .55$ $(p < .01)$ and $r = .58$ $(p < .01)$, respectively.

The correlational analysis disclosed no relationship between degree of behavioral change and either initial number or intensity of fears in other areas of functioning. Thus, the effectiveness of the treatment procedures was not diminished by the presence of generalized anxiety. Nor did subjects' initial attitudes toward snakes affect the degree of behavioral improvement achieved by the different treatment methods.

Although attitudes were not predictors of behavioral change, the initial severity of avoidance behavior was a significant predictor of degree of attitude change as measured by both the attitude scales $(r = -.43;$ $p < .01)$ and the semantic differential $(r = -.42;$ $p < .01)$. The more avoidant subjects were to begin with, the less they altered their evaluations of reptiles in the positive direction. Moreover, within the two modeling treatments, degree of attitude change on the attitude scales correlated negatively with numbers of fears $(r = -.40;$ $p < .05)$, and anxiety about physical injury $(r = -.54;$ $p < .01)$.

Treated Controls

Following completion of the posttreatment assessment, subjects in the control group received the symbolic modeling treatment without the relaxation component. They simply reviewed threatening scenes repeatedly until completely neutralized, and recorded their level of fear arousal during each exposure. Except for one subject who had to discontinue toward the end of the treatment to undergo major surgery, all of the controls completed this second phase of the experiment. They were then readministered the same sets of measures used in the preceding assessments.

In evaluating the efficacy of symbolic modeling without relaxation, t tests for correlated means were computed on changes in the performances of control subjects after they had received the treatment relative to their posttest scores. As shown in Table 2, symbolic modeling alone increased subjects' approach behavior. In fact, 45 percent of the subjects exhibited terminal performances toward both snakes. This treatment also produced fa-

TABLE 2

Significance of Supplemental Treatments and Temporal Changes for Each of Several Measures

Response measure	Treated controls	Treated controls vs. symbolic modeling	Changes following modeling with participation			Group differences at multiple treatment (F test)	Post treatment vs. follow-up (t test)	Group differences at follow-up (F test)
			Symbolic modeling n = 8	Systematic desensitization n = 9	Treated controls n = 6			
Approach behavior	5.65***	.46	18.50***	18.36***	9.58***	.15	.50	.12
Fear arousal								
Initial approach	5.35***	2.04*	1.91	7.19***	2.12	1.32	2.65*	.72
Total approach	2.92*	3.00**	3.39*	5.96***	2.16	1.46	4.21**	1.68
Attitude scores	3.73**	2.09*	8.26***	3.12*	3.47*	2.36	2.12*	1.30
Semantic differential	5.29***	2.71*	4.09**	1.49	1.80	3.30*	2.24*	3.68*
Fear inventory								
Total number	4.78***	.62	3.21*	.24	4.89**	1.45	2.13*	1.33
Total intensity	6.43***	.45	6.52**	.71	1.97	1.19	2.80**	1.50
Number animal	3.68**	.62	3.97**	.00	1.23	1.61	1.83	2.72
Intensity animal	4.55**	.74	4.95**	.45	1.95	1.19	3.07*	2.06
Number social	3.99**	1.22	4.41**	1.00	.00	1.18	.40	.52
Intensity social	2.85*	.04	5.34**	1.43	.72	1.13	.63	.66
Number injury	1.79	.34	1.25	2.03	.80	2.11	3.66**	1.42
Intensity injury	2.39*	.93	3.81**	.69	2.43	1.50	2.87**	1.43
Number classical	2.39*	.22	3.00*	.12	4.39**	1.97	.95	2.16
Intensity classical	5.02***	.71	4.58**	.32	2.76*	2.10	1.33	2.51
Number miscellaneous	2.60*	1.98	1.75	.23	2.42	1.48	2.24*	.80
Intensity miscellaneous	3.60**	.17	2.44*	.79	1.29	.94	2.43*	1.08

*p < .05. **p < .01. ***p < .001.

vorable attitudinal changes, and it reduced fear arousal to both snake approach behavior and a variety of other potentially threatening situations measured by the fear inventory (Table 2).

Statistical comparisons were made of the changes achieved by control subjects through symbolic modeling alone and by experimental subjects who received symbolic modeling with relaxation. No differences were found between the groups either in approach behavior or in generalized anxiety (Table 2). However, subjects who paired aversive modeling cues with relaxation subsequently experienced significantly less fear arousal while performing snake-approach responses, and they showed greater positive changes in their attitude toward snakes.

Vicarious Extinction of Fear Arousal to Modeled Events

As was mentioned earlier, subjects receiving film-mediated treatment rated the degree of fear arousal evoked by the modeled scenes initially and by each subsequent reexposure to the same scenes. These ratings were averaged across subjects and scenes at each exposure to provide an index of the rate with which fear arousal was extinguished in subjects who observed the modeled events with and without the benefit of relaxation. The data are plotted in Figure 5 for the first six exposures since subjects rarely required more than six presentations to neutralize any given scene. The vicarious extinction data for the subject who had to discontinue before completing the final portion of the treatment and the fear arousal ratings of the matched subject for the same duration of treatment were included in the statistical analysis.

Both groups of subjects showed a progressive decline in fear arousal with each successive exposure to modeled approach behavior. Separate comparisons of scores between adjacent points reveals that the fear decrements with each reexposure are highly significant for both sets of data.

Although repeated observation of nonreinforced approach behavior eliminated fear arousal, the addition of relaxation did not have a strong facilitative effect on the rate of vicarious fear extinction. The two groups did not differ significantly in level of fear arousal on first exposure to each modeled scene, but sub-

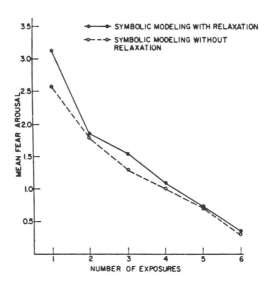

Fɪɢ. 5. Mean level of fear arousal evoked by the modeling stimuli initially and by each subsequent reexposure to the same scenes in subjects receiving symbolic modeling with relaxation and symbolic modeling alone.

jects who combined modeling with relaxation experienced a greater reduction in fear on the second exposure to the aversive scenes than their counterparts who received modeling alone ($t =$ 1.80, $p < .05$) ; on subsequent reexposures, however, the rate of fear extinction was essentially the same. Subjects who paired modeling with relaxation required fewer reexposures ($M = 24$) than the modeling-alone group ($M = 58$) to achieve complete extinction of fear arousal, but there was considerable variability and the difference is significant only at a borderline level of significance ($t = 1.66$, $.10 < p < .05$).

Changes Following Supplementary Treatment with Contact Desensitization

A total of 23 subjects from the symbolic modeling, systematic desensitization, and treated control groups who failed to attain terminal performances received live modeling with guided participation. Although there was some variability, the average

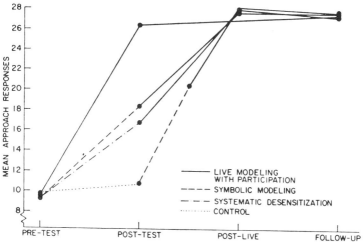

FIG. 6. Mean number of approach responses performed by subjects before and after receiving their respective treatments (posttest). (Control subjects subsequently received symbolic modeling without relaxation. The postlive point combines the scores of subjects in each condition who required no additional treatment and those who were later given the supplementary treatment combining modeling with guided participation. The approach behavior in all four groups was measured again in the follow-up study conducted one month later.)

length of this supplementary treatment was approximately 1 hour and 20 minutes. After these subjects completed their treatment they were administered the regular assessment procedures.

As shown in Figure 6 and Table 2, subjects in all three groups displayed further significant increases in approach behavior. The data of this subgroup combined and those who required no additional treatment reveals that 96 percent of all the subjects who participated in the study achieved terminal performances with the experimental snake, while 70 percent showed complete extinction of avoidance behavior toward the generalization snake as well. These behavioral changes were maintained at the same level over the follow-up period, with the terminal performances being 96 percent and 67 percent for the experimental and generalization snakes, respectively. At the various test periods subjects in the different treatment conditions who failed to complete the final approach response usually successfully performed the remaining tasks, which explains why differences in approach scores based on the two snakes do not reach statistical significance.

Subjects' attitudes and level of fear arousal at the different assessment periods are summarized graphically in Figures 7 and 8. The significance of the changes on these and other measures by the subgroup of subjects receiving the supplementary treatment is presented in Table 2.

Of the three groups of subjects, those who originally received symbolic modeling paired with relaxation benefited most from live modeling with guided participation. In addition to the increases in approach behavior previously reported, they showed further improvements in attitude, additional fear extinction, and generalized reduction of anxiety in all five areas of functioning measured by the fear inventory (Table 2). Following the supplementary treatment, control subjects, who previously received symbolic modeling alone, displayed a significant reduction in avoidance behavior, positive changes on the attitude measure, and a significant decrease in the total number of fears.

The supplementary treatment likewise produced behavioral and attitudinal improvements in the systematic desensitization subgroup. In addition, subjects in this condition, who originally achieved the smallest decrement in fear arousal compared to the other methods, showed marked extinction of fear arousal. However, the supplementary treatment did not produce any further change in their fear of other potential threats. The fact that subjects receiving the symbolic modeling treatment originally achieved greater decrements in fear arousal than either the treated controls or the systematic desensitization subjects might explain why the former group showed the most generalized reduction in other fears following the treatment combining modeling with participation.

Separate analyses of variance were computed on the 17 measures after subjects attained terminal performances either through their regular treatment alone or combined with modeling and participation. At this phase of the experiment there were no significant differences between the groups on any of the measures except the semantic differential administered before the behav-

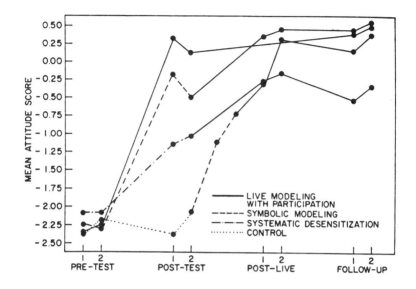

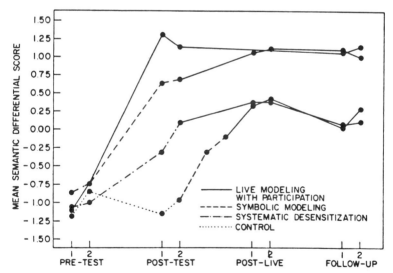

FIG. 7. Attitudes exhibited by subjects in each of the four groups before treatment (pretest); following their respective treatments (posttest); after supplementary treatment of the subgroups of subjects with modeling and participation (postlive); and at the follow-up period.

215

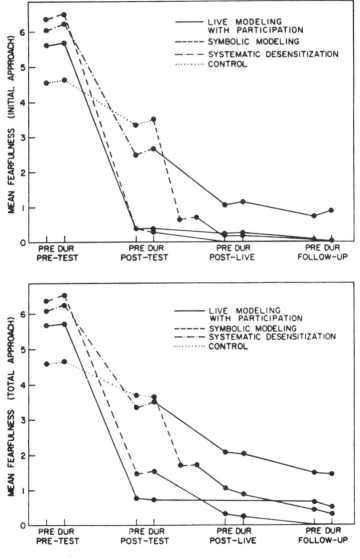

Fig. 8. Mean level of fear arousal displayed by subjects in each of the four groups before treatment (pretest); following their respective treatments (post-test); after supplementary treatment of the subgroup of subjects with modeling and guided participation (postlive); and at the follow-up period.

216

ioral avoidance test (Table 2). Subjects who received modeling with participation exhibited greater changes than their counterparts in either the control ($F = 6.10$, $p < .05$) or the systematic desensitization ($F = 5.05$, $p < .05$) conditions. The symbolic modeling group also manifested more positive evaluative responses than the controls ($F = 4.64$, $p < .05$), but it did not differ significantly from the systematic desensitization group. No significant group differences were found, however, either on attitude scores ($F = .54$) or semantic differential scores ($F = 1.45$) obtained immediately after the behavioral avoidance test.

Maintenance of Psychological Changes

In order to evaluate the durability of induced changes subjects returned for an additional evaluation approximately 1 month after they had concluded their final treatment. t tests were calculated on differences between performances for the total sample of subjects in their last posttreatment test and in the follow-up assessment. Results of these statistical analyses for the combined sample are given in Table 2.

Subjects not only maintained the same level of bold approach behavior, but they experienced significantly less fear arousal while performing the same approach responses in the follow-up assessment. However, subjects showed a small but nevertheless significant decrease in positive attitudes toward snakes over the follow-up period. As can be seen from Figures 8 and 9, subjects in the systematic desensitization ($t = 2.34$, $p < .05$) and control ($t = 1.93$, $p < .10$) conditions accounted mainly for the change in attitude scores; control subjects ($t = 2.82$, $p < .02$) also contributed largely to the change on the semantic differential.

Analysis of fear inventory scores revealed that subjects either maintained their gains or showed further reductions in their fear of potential threats in other areas of functioning (Table 2). Specifically, they reported fewer fears and a significant diminution in the intensity of their subjective reactions to threats. The greatest fear reduction over the follow-up period occurred in relation to animals and apprehension over physical injury. In addition, subjects reported decrements in various miscellaneous fears.

Separate analyses of variance were also performed on the 17 measures at the follow-up period to determine whether sub-

jects in the different conditions retained their comparable improvements. As in the final posttreatment assessment, there were
no significant differences between the groups on any of the measures, except the semantic differential obtained prior to the behavioral avoidance test (Table 2). Individual comparisons of
pairs of means shows the control group as having lower positive
evaluations of snakes than subjects in either the contact desensitization ($F = 7$, $p < .05$) or symbolic modeling ($F = 8.54$, $p < .01$)
conditions. However, control subjects significantly increased
their valuations of snakes after the behavioral avoidance test and
no significant group differences were found ($F = 1.70$) on the
final semantic differential score.

Antecedents of Snake-Phobic Behavior

As was previously mentioned, at the beginning of the experiment subjects were administered a questionnaire measuring both
direct and vicarious aversive experiences with snakes and the incidence of familial modeling of snake phobic behavior. Although
not a single subject had ever been physically injured by a snake,
they reported a variety of frightening experiences involving reptiles. For example, 68 percent of the subjects were frightened in
childhood by surprise encounters with snakes on walks, coiled
up under rocks, under household furniture, in boats, in tents,
and in other unexpected places. Some subjects described revolting
child experiences in which they witnessed snakes viciously beaten
to death. To a young child incidents of this type would tend to
convey the impression that snakes must be exceedingly dangerous
to warrant such extreme onslaughts.

In 62 percent of the cases, fear of snakes was further reinforced through pranks involving live or dead snakes and toy specimens. In their childhood years the subjects were chased by other
children brandishing snakes menacingly, they had dead snakes
thrown at them, or hidden in their lunch baskets, in beds, in tents,
in closets, and in grocery bags. Those who were most apprehensive
about snakes were selected as the favorite targets in such pranks.

Traumatic vicarious experiences that often resulted in recur-
rent nightmares were also reported by 58 percent of the sample.
The episodes that subjects found most shocking were sequences
in movies or television programs in which snakes were shown

stalking their prey, crawling menacingly toward sleeping people, wrapping themselves around animals or people and slowly crushing them to death, or where persons were thrown into a pit of writhing snakes.

Familial modeling of snake-phobic behavior also occurred with relatively high frequency (56 percent) in this sample. The vast majority of cases (85 percent) reported having experienced two or more of these different forms of fear arousal (i.e., direct, vicarious, and familial modeling influences). Although these findings cannot be fully interpreted in the absence of comparative data from a nonphobic sample, they nevertheless reveal that subjects in the present study had undergone numerous frightening experiences capable of endowing snakes with strong aversive properties.

At the conclusion of the experiment subjects filled out a questionnaire that asked them, among other things, to describe their reaction when they first learned about the type of treatment that they would be receiving and their confidence in the method; and to indicate whether the treatment experiences in any way enhanced or hindered their functioning. These results are reported next.

Therapeutic Expectations

The treatment procedures were presented to subjects as experimental approaches, without any claims made for their efficacy. Questionnaire results disclose that when subjects first learned about the type of treatment they were to receive, 67 percent did not expect to benefit from the program, 16 percent were uncertain about what to expect, while 16 percent believed that they would achieve beneficial results. Subjects in the symbolic modeling and systematic desensitization conditions were skeptical that even if the treatment eliminated their fears toward symbolic representation of snakes, the extinction effects would transfer to actual snakes.

> I felt totally unconfident that it would work on me. I thought I could probably get used to seeing snakes, but I never thought that I could be able to pick one up calmly ... I did not see how just imagining snakes could help me. I did not have much confidence in the method.

Most subjects in the contact desensitization condition, on the other hand, had serious doubts that they could ever perform the snake approach responses required by the treatment ("I was appalled and determined I could never handle a snake.").

The skepticism regarding these more direct treatment approaches also stemmed in part from the widespread belief that anxiety conditions can be successfully modified only through verbal interpretive means. This attitude is reflected in the following comments of one of the subjects:

> When I heard that it would be all involvement with snakes, I didn't think it would be successful in my case. I had expected and hoped for more discussion about snakes. However, I now realize that this would not have solved my problem. Rather, it would have been a waste of time.

Positive Transfer to Naturalistic Situations

During the follow-up period 47 percent of the subjects reported encounters with snakes in one form or another. In each case they reported that the reduction in fear of snakes achieved in treatment generalized to snakes in naturalistic situations. The subjects no longer experienced marked distress when unexpectedly confronted with snakes in the course of their social or occupational activities; they could visit reptile exhibits and look at pictorial displays of snakes without trepidation; they were able to handle harmless snakes, and a few even served as model therapists for their own children and faint-hearted friends.

Other subjects, though they had no contact with snakes, were nevertheless able to participate in recreational activities such as hunting, camping, picnicking and hiking, which they had formerly avoided because of their dread of snakes. As one subject explained, "I am no longer harassed by walking through grassy areas in fear of running across a snake."

DISCUSSION

Results of the present experiment provide further evidence that treatment approaches based on social-learning principles can be highly efficacious in producing generalized and enduring psychological changes. Of the three methods investigated, modeling combined with guided participation was most successful in eliminating phobic behavior, in extinguishing fear arousal, and in creating favorable attitudes. The generality of these findings is increased by the additional evidence that subjects who achieved only partial improvement through other treatments displayed substantial changes after a brief period of contact desensitization.

It would appear from these laboratory findings that a powerful form of treatment is one in which therapeutic agents themselves model the desired behavior and arrange optimal conditions for clients to engage in similar activities until they can perform the behavior skillfully and fearlessly.

Comparison of symbolic desensitization and symbolic modeling shows both procedures to be equally effective in extinguishing avoidance behavior; however, symbolic modeling produced greater reduction in both fear arousal and negative attitudes, and the behavioral changes it achieved appear to be more generalized. Indeed, findings of the present study and those reported by Blanchard (1969) disclose that subjects who attain terminal performances through modeling alone show almost complete transfer on behavioral generalization tests.

Although the foregoing results demonstrate that significant psychological changes can be reliably achieved by extinguishing the arousal potential of aversive stimuli presented in symbolic form, they also indicate that such treatment approaches have certain limitations if used alone. Virtually all subjects who received systematic desensitization or symbolic modeling displayed behavioral improvements that surpassed either their pretreatment performances (96 percent) or the changes exhibited by matched nontreated controls (91 percent). Nevertheless, most subjects in these treatment conditions were unable to perform terminal-level activities that had been thoroughly neutralized in symbolic form. Other investigators (Agras, 1967; Hoenig & Reed, 1966) have found a similar discrepancy between symbolic desensitization and actual performance.

From knowledge of stimulus generalization one would ordinarily expect some transfer loss in symbolically oriented treatments. A major advantage of modeling with participation is that fear is eliminated toward actual threats. In clinical practice, of course, symbolic desensitization is typically supplemented with graded performance tasks that are executed in real life situations, with active positive reinforcement of approach behavior to overcome initial reluctance of phobic persons to reexpose themselves to feared situations, and with modeling procedures to further augment change in behavior. In laboratory investigations, these various "extraneous" influences are intentionally excluded.

The prediction that relaxation would augment the effects of symbolic modeling was only partially corroborated. Modeling coupled with relaxation produced greater decrements in fear accompanying approach responses, more favorable attitudes, and more rapid vicarious extinction of fear arousal on initial reexposure to the modeled events. The groups did not differ, however, in approach behavior. These results, while interesting, must be accepted with reservation because subjects who received modeling without the benefit of relaxation required significantly more observational trials to extinguish their fearful reactions to the modeled approach responses. It is conceivable that if these treatments were limited to the same number of observational extinction trials, the obtained differences would have been even larger and a difference in approach behavior might also have emerged. This expectation receives some support from a recent study (Spiegler, Liebert, McMains, & Fernandez, 1969) demonstrating that relaxation facilitates vicarious fear extinction under conditions where subjects receive only a single exposure to the modeled approach behavior.

It is of interest that the efficacy of the treatment procedures was in no way limited by subjects' general level of anxiety. The correlational data from the present study are somewhat at variance with previous findings (Bandura & Menlove, 1968) that susceptibility to emotional arousal in children is inversely related to degree of vicarious extinction achieved through film-mediated modeling. Several factors might have accounted for these divergent results. The two experiments differ in the age of the subjects and in the type of phobic behavior being modified. Another possible explanation is in terms of markedly different ways in which the modeling treatments were conducted. The earlier study involved only a single exposure to modeling stimuli without regard to subjects' fear arousal, whereas the present experiment utilized a self-regulated modeling procedure which permitted subjects the opportunity to review threatening scenes repeatedly until thoroughly neutralized. Under conditions where aversive modeling stimuli are presented only once, anxiety proneness in observers is more likely to serve as a determinant of vicarious extinction.

It is also noteworthy that the various treatments were equally effective when applied by experimenters differing widely in personality characteristics. These findings are consistent with those of Paul (1966) and Mann and Rosenthal (1969), showing that changes produced by systematic desensitizations are not differentially affected by variations in experimenter characteristics. Further evidence that socially conducted and self-administered systematic desensitization achieves equivalent results (Donner, 1967; Krapfl, 1967; Melamed & Lang, 1967) suggests that social variables are not appreciable contributors to the measured outcomes. Ideally, psychological treatment methods should be sufficiently powerful to achieve consistent changes by different therapists, just as one would not be content with medical procedures whose effects depended heavily upon the bedside manner of physicians.

Further research is needed to isolate the factors in modeling cues that govern fear reduction in observers. There is some reason to expect that the affective expressions accompanying a model's behavior may exercise some degree of control over vicarious extinction. It has been shown in studies of vicarious emotional arousal in primates (R. E. Miller, 1967; Miller, Banks, & Ogawa, 1962; Miller, Murphy, & Mirsky, 1959) and in human subjects (Bandura & Rosenthal, 1966; Berger, 1962), that negative affective expressions by others can serve as powerful cues for arousing fear and avoidance in observers. In fact, Miller and his colleagues (Miller et al., 1959) have shown that exposure to a subject reacting in an apprehensive or fearful manner could reinstate avoidance responses in observers even after such responses had been completely extinguished.

The foregoing research suggests that modeled approach responses accompanied by positive affective expressions would engender less fear arousal in observers and hence faster vicarious extinction, than if models manifested fearful reactions while performing the same approach behavior. In the present experiment the models frequently expressed pleasant emotional reactions as they performed approach responses in a relaxed manner.

It is generally assumed in theories of identification that similarity of the model to the observer enhances response matching. However, it remains an open question whether utilization of fearful models would facilitate or hinder the reduction of phobic behavior. According to the theory of identification presented by Bandura (1969b), response consequences to models generally outweigh their characteristics in producing indentificatory behavior in observers. Thus, for example, witnessing a similar model bitten by a snake would in all likelihood increase snake avoidance behavior, whereas seeing a dissimilar model handle a snake without any untoward consequences would weaken avoidance responses. The treatment film included not only fearless adult models but also several young children, on the assumption that their lack of fear while performing responses that adult observers regarded as hazardous would provide the most dramatic disconfirmation of anticipated aversive consequences. It would be of considerable interest to investigate systematically the degree to which model-subject similarity on a relevant dimension (i.e., fearfulness) and also on irrelevant dimensions (i.e., attitudes, interests, general background) affects the rate of vicarious extinction of phobic behavior.

The results show that applications of social-learning procedures have important attitudinal consequences. Both symbolic modeling and systematic desensitization, which operate primarily through extinction of negative affect aroused by aversive stimuli, produced favorable changes in attitudes toward snakes. Consistent with expectation, the treatment condition that reduced the fear-arousing properties of snakes and enabled subjects to engage in intimate interactions with snakes achieved the greatest attitudinal changes. These findings are sufficiently promising to warrant more extensive use of social-learning procedures for studying theoretical issues concerning the development, modification, and functional role of attitudes.

It will be recalled that previous research, though admittedly meager, found changes in attitude and actions to be essentially unrelated. More recently, Greenwald (1965a) reported a positive, but low, correlation between these measures on an academic activity that does not have much affective impact. However, for subjects who expressed their negative attitude prior to the influence attempt, persuasive communications changed their attitudes but not their behavior (Greenwald, 1965b). In contrast to these results, desensitization and modeling treatments produced corresponding changes in both attitudes and behavior even though all subjects initially committed themselves to a strong loathing for snakes. In a study employing similar procedures, Blanchard (1969) also found a high positive correlation $(r = .72)$ between changes in attitude and behavior as induced through modeling influences.

The correlated changes produced by social-learning procedures in different response systems may be interpreted in several different ways. According to most contemporary attitude theories (Abelson, Aronson, McGuire, Newcomb, Rosenberg, & Tannenbaum, 1968), there exists a strong drive for consistency among beliefs, feelings, and actions. A change in any one of the components will, therefore, engender congruous modification in the other constituents. In these consistency models, changes in attitudes or behavior are treated, not simply as consequent events, but as causal factors affecting other classes of behavior. An alternative interpretation is that social influences have similar but independent effects on attitudes, behavior, and emotional arousal. In this view, attitude-behavior consistencies represent correlated coeffects rather than outcomes of a process in which modification of one type of behavior forces changes in other forms of responding to eliminate cognitive disequilibrium.

Definitive tests of the parallel effects and consistency explanations of change processes are precluded by the absence of a methodology that would permit simultaneous measurement of attitudes, affect, and actions. If incongruity creates an internal stimulus for psychological change then a sequential testing procedure unavoidably confounds the effects of external influences and the consistency drive. Conversely, a given environmental influence could have analogous effects on different classes of response that would be erroneously attributed to the operation of a consistency drive. These alternative formulations perhaps should be regarded as complementary rather than competing.

Under most conditions, powerful social influences produce corresponding changes in different modes of responding, and performance of new behavior is likely to have additional cognitive and emotional consequences.

The findings of the present study also have implications for different theoretical formulations regarding the conditions governing phobic behavior. Contrary to expectation from psychodynamic theory, extinction of emotional responses toward the phobic object not only enduringly eliminated fear arousal and phobic avoidance of snakes, but the treatments produced significant reductions in anxiety in other areas of functioning not specifically treated. These findings are in accord with numerous studies demonstrating that direct extinction of phobic behavior is typically accompanied by generalized anxiety reduction as measured by self-ratings (Lang, et al., 1965; Mealiea, 1967; H. R. Miller, 1967; Paul, 1966, 1967, 1968; Paul & Shannon, 1966) and behavioral avoidance tests (Mealiea, 1967).

The positive transfer obtained in the present experiment probably reflects the operation of at least two somewhat different processes. The first involves generalization of fear extinction effects from stimuli that were neutralized by the treatments to related anxiety sources. Analysis of differences between groups and changes within treatment conditions revealed that the greatest fear decrements occurred in relation to similar phobic objects such as other animals, which would be expected from knowledge of stimulus generalization. The second process entails positive reinforcement of a sense of capability through success which can mitigate emotional arousal to potentially threatening situations. Having successfully eliminated a phobia that had plagued them for most of their lives, a number of subjects reported increased confidence that they could cope effectively with other fear-provoking events. As one subject explained it, "My success in gradually overcoming this fear of snakes has contributed to a greater feeling of confidence generally in my abilities to overcome any other problem which may arise. I have more faith in myself." Others stated that their treatment experiences not only changed their views about the modifiability of personality patterns, but provided them with a means of eliminating other unwarranted fears.

Within the treatment combining modeling and guided participation several factors are operative that might contribute to the psychological changes accompanying this method. These component influences include observation of fearless approach behavior repeatedly modeled without any unfavorable consequences to the performer, incidental information received about the feared objects, and guided interaction with threatening objects that engender no adverse effects. Results of experiments subsequently conducted by Blanchard (1969) and Ritter (1969a, 1969b) throw some light on the relative influence of these component variables.

In a comparative study of the effects of modeling, informational factors, and guided participation, Blanchard (1969) found that modeling accounted for approximately 60 percent of the behavior change and 80 percent of the change in attitudes and fear arousal; guided participation contributed the remaining increment. Informational influences, on the other hand, had no effect on any of the three classes of responses.

As mentioned earlier, the guided participation component of the procedure under discussion involves both enactment of progressively more difficult responses and physical assistance in performing the required behavior. In a study designed to evaluate the influence of these elements, Ritter (1969c) found that modeling accompanied by physically guided performance produced greater changes in acrophobic subjects than modeling with verbally guided enactment which, in turn, was superior to demonstration alone.

Ritter (1968a) gave special emphasis to the anxiety-reducing effects of physical contact. In addition, when persons are physically assisted in performing the behavior required at each step in the graded sequence, their fears and inhibitions may be reduced to some degree by the added protection that the model's behavior provides. An experiment is needed to determine whether the facilitative effects of physical guidance derive from interpersonal contact, from protection against potential injurious consequences, or, as seems most likely, from both factors.

Further research is needed to clarify the mechanisms through which modeling combined with guided participation achieves such uniformly powerful extinction effects. Results of modeling procedures, particularly those based on a nonresponse extinction paradigm, are consistent with the dual-process theory of avoidance behavior. Data from subjects in the symbolic modeling condition demonstrate that emotional arousal can be effectively extinguished on a vicarious basis simply by having observers witness models exhibit approach responses toward feared objects without experiencing any adverse consequences. It has been further shown by Blanchard (1969) that the more thoroughly emotional arousal to aversive modeling stimuli is vicariously extinguished the greater is the reduction in avoidance behavior and the more generalized are the changes.

In accordance with the above findings the change process associated with the powerful procedure involving modeling with guided participation may be conceptualized as follows: Repeated modeling of approach responses and the anxiety-mitigating influence of physical contact and physical protection decrease the arousal potential of aversive stimuli below the threshold for activating avoidance responses, thus enabling persons to engage, albeit somewhat anxiously, in approach behavior. The favorable outcomes resulting from direct contact with threats that are no longer objectively justified further extinguish any residual anxiety and avoidance tendencies. Without the benefit of prior vicarious extinction, the reinstatement of severely inhibited behavior generally requires a tedious and protracted program. After approach behavior toward formerly avoided objects has been fully restored the resultant new experiences give rise to substantial reorganization of attitudes.

NOTES

1. This research was supported by Public Health Research Grant M-5162 from the National Institute of Mental Health. The authors are indebted to Antonette Raskoff, Patricia Baker, and Robert O'Connor for their generous assistance with various aspects of this research.
2. The terms modeling with participation and contact desensitization are used interchangeably to refer to the treatment condition.

REFERENCES

Abelson, R. P., Aronson, E., McGuire, W. J., Newcomb, T. M., Rosenberg, M. J., & Tannenbaum, P. H. *Theories of cognitive consistency: A sourcebook.* Chicago: Rand McNally, 1968.

Agras, W. S. Transfer during systematic desensitization therapy. *Behaviour Research and Therapy,* 1967, 5, 193–199.

Bandura, A. Modelling approaches to the modification of phobic disorders. In R. Porter (Ed.), *Ciba foundation symposium. The role of learning in psychotherapy*. London: Churchill, 1968.

Bandura, A. *Principles of behavior modification*. New York: Holt, Rinehart & Winston, 1969. (a)

Bandura, A. Social-learning theory of identificatory processes. In D. A. Goslin (Ed.), *Handbook of socialization theory and research*. Chicago: Rand McNally, 1969. (b)

Bandura, A., Grusec, J. E., & Menlove, F. L. Vicarious extinction of avoidance behavior. *Journal of Personality and Social Psychology*, 1967, 5, 16–23.

Bandura, A., & Menlove, F. L. Factors determining vicarious extinction of avoidance behavior through symbolic modeling. *Journal of Personality and Social Psychology*, 1968, 8, 99–108.

Bandura, A., & Rosenthal, T. L. Vicarious classical conditioning as a function of arousal level. *Journal of Personality and Social Psychology*, 1966, 3, 54–62.

Berger, S. M. Conditioning through vicarious investigation. *Psychological Review*, 1962, 69, 450–466.

Black, A. H. The extinction of avoidance responses under curare. *Journal of Comparative and Physiological Psychology*, 1958, 51, 519–524.

Black, A. H. Heart rate changes during avoidance learning in dogs. *Canadian Journal of Psychology*, 1959, 13, 229–242.

Black, A. H. Transfer following operant conditioning in the curarized dog. *Science*, 1967, 155, 201–203.

Blanchard, E. B. The relative contributions of modeling, informational influences, and physical contact in the extinction of phobic behavior. Unpublished doctoral dissertation, Stanford University, 1969.

Davison, G. C. Systematic desensitization as a counterconditioning process. *Journal of Abnormal Psychology*, 1968, 73, 91–99.

Donner, L. Effectiveness of a preprogrammed group desensitization treatment for test anxiety with and without a therapist present. Unpublished doctoral dissertation, Rutgers University, 1967.

Fenichel, O. *The psychoanalytic theory of neurosis*. New York: Norton, 1945.

Festinger, L. Behavioral support for opinion change. *Public Opinion Quarterly*, 1964, 28, 404–417.

Gale, D. S., Sturmfels, G., & Gale, E. N. A comparison of reciprocal inhibition and experimental extinction in the psychotherapeutic process. *Behaviour Research and Therapy*, 1966, 4, 149–155.

Greenwald, A. G. Behavior change following a persuasive communication. *Journal of Personality*, 1965, 33, 370–391. (a)

Greenwald, A. G. Effects of prior commitment on behavior change after a persuasive communication. *Public Opinion Quarterly*, 1965, 29, 595–601. (b)

Grings, W. W., & Uno, T. Counterconditioning: Fear and relaxation. *Psychophysiology*, 1968, 4, 479–485.

Hoenig, J., & Reed, G. F. The objective assessment of desensitization. *British Journal of Psychiatry*, 1966, 112, 1279–1283.

Krapfl, J. E. Differential ordering of stimulus presentation and semiautomated versus live treatment of the systematic desensitization of snake phobia. Unpublished doctoral dissertation, University of Missouri, 1967.

Lang, P. J., Lazovik, A. D., & Reynolds, D. J. Desensitization, suggestibility and pseudotherapy. *Journal of Abnormal Psychology*, 1965, 70, 395–402.

Mann, J., & Rosenthal, T. L., Vicarious and direct counterconditioning of test anxiety through individual and group desensitization. *Behaviour Research and Therapy*, 1969, in press.

Mealiea, W. L., Jr. The comparative effectiveness of systematic desensitization and implosive theory in the elimination of snake phobia. Unpublished doctoral dissertation, University of Missouri, 1967.

Melamed, B., & Lang, P. J. Study of the automated desensitization of fear. Paper presented at the meeting of the Midwestern Psychological Association, Chicago, May 1967.

Miller, H. R. The role of control of aversive stimulus termination in the systematic desensitization of snake phobic subjects. Unpublished doctoral dissertation, University of Missouri, 1967.

Miller, R. E. Experimental approaches to the physiological and behavioral concomitants of affective communication in rhesus monkeys. In S. A. Altmann (Ed.), *Social communication among primates.* Chicago: University of Chicago Press, 1967.

Miller, R. E., Banks, J. H., Jr., & Ogawa, N. Communication of affect in "cooperative conditioning" of rhesus monkeys. *Journal of Abnormal and Social Psychology,* 1962, 64, 343–348.

Miller, R. E., Murphy, J. V., & Mirsky, I. A. Nonverbal communication of affect. *Journal of Clinical Psychology,* 1959, 15, 155–158.

Moore, N. Behavior therapy in bronchial asthma: A controlled study. *Journal of Psychosomatic Research,* 1965, 9, 257–276.

Notterman, J. M., Schoenfeld, W. N., & Bersch, P. J. A comparison of three extinction procedures following heart rate conditioning. *Journal of Abnormal and Social Psychology,* 1952, 47, 674–677.

Paul, G. L., *Insight vs. desensitization in psychotherapy.* Stanford, Calif.: Stanford University Press, 1966.

Paul, G. L. Insight versus desensitization in psychotherapy two years after termination. *Journal of Consulting Psychology,* 1967, 31, 333–348.

Paul, G. L. Two-year follow-up of systematic desensitization in therapy groups. *Journal of Abnormal Psychology,* 1968, 73, 119–130.

Paul, G. L. Physiological effects of relaxation training and hypnotic suggestion. *Journal of Abnormal Psychology,* 1969, in press.

Paul, G. L., & Shannon, D. T. Treatment of anxiety through systematic desensitization in therapy groups. *Journal of Abnormal Psychology,* 1966, 71, 124–135.

Poppen, R. L. Counterconditioning of conditioned suppression. Unpublished doctoral dissertation, Stanford University, 1968.

Rescorla, R. A., & Solomon, R. L. Two-process learning theory: Relationships between Pavlovian conditioning and instrumental learning. *Psychological Review,* 1967, 74, 151–182.

Ritter, B. The treatment of a dissection phobia. Unpublished manuscript, Queens College, 1965.

Ritter, B. The effect of contact desensitization on avoidance behavior, fear ratings, and self-evaluative statements. *Proceedings of the 76th Annual Convention of the American Psychological Association,* 1968, 3, 527–528. (a)

Ritter, B. The group treatment of children's snake phobias using vicarious and contact desensitization procedures. *Behaviour Research and Therapy,* 1968, 6, 1–6. (b)

Ritter, B. Eliminating excessive fears of the environment through contact desensitization. In J. B. Krumboltz & C. E. Thoresen (Eds.), *Behavioral counseling: Cases and techniques.* New York: Holt, Rinehart & Winston, 1969. (a)

Ritter, B. Treatment of acrophobia with contact desensitization. *Behaviour Research and Therapy*, 1969, 7, 41–45. (b)

Ritter, B. The use of contact desensitization, demonstration-plus-participation, and demonstration alone in the treatment of acrophobia. *Behaviour Research and Therapy*, 1969, 7, 157–164. (c)

Schubot, E. D. The influence of hypnotic and muscular relaxation in systematic desensitization of phobic behavior. Unpublished doctoral dissertation, Stanford University, 1966.

Solomon, R. L., & Turner, L. H. Discriminative classical conditioning in dogs paralyzed by curare can later control discriminative avoidance responses in the normal state. *Psychological Review*, 1962, 69, 202–219.

Spiegler, M. D., Liebert, R. M., McMains, M. J., & Fernandez, L. E. Experimental development of a modeling treatment to extinguish persistent avoidance behavior. In R. D. Rubin & C. M. Franks (Eds.), *Advances in behavior therapy*. New York: Academic Press, 1969.

Wolpe, J. *Psychotherapy by reciprocal inhibition*. Stanford, Calif.: Stanford University Press, 1958.

Wolpe, J., & Lang, P. J. A fear survey schedule for use in behaviour therapy. *Behaviour Research and Therapy*, 1964, 1, 27–30.

Wynne, L. C., & Solomon, R. L. Traumatic avoidance learning: Acquisition and extinction in dogs deprived of normal peripheral autonomic function. *Genetic Psychology Monographs*, 1955, 52, 241–284.

Section Three

General Issues

Operant conditioning and respondent conditioning have been discussed separately. However, in most behavior there is a significant interaction between operant and respondent variables. Sources of motivation, such as learned drives, might be established by respondent conditioning, while the response made under such motivation is an operant. Also an operant response might be reinforced by a conditioned reinforcement that was established under respondent conditioning. For example, a boy who had unpleasant experiences in school now feels anxious when in the school (respondent conditioning). By skipping his last class and leaving early (operant) he feels a reduction in his anxiety (negative reinforcement from a reduction of a respondently established source of anxiety).

The two-process theory, as discussed in the reading by Rescorla and Solomon, assumes that respondent CRs serve as mediators of operant behavior, functioning as instigators and/or sources of reinforcement. The Rescorla and Solomon article describes many of the comparisons between respondent conditioning and operant conditioning and how the different processes interact.

As operant and respondent variables interact in most situations, so learning and motivation variables interact to produce performance. In the reading by Spence, it is argued that anxiety, as measured by the Taylor Manifest Anxiety scale, feeds into a nonspecific drive. This drive, a key motivational variable in the Hull and Spence theories, affects the performance of subjects in learning tasks. Specifically, Spence argues that human subjects with high manifest anxiety have better performance in respondent eyelid conditioning than subjects low in manifest anxiety.

In the reading by Kleinsmith and Kaplan the motivational variable of arousal is suggested to affect the retrieval of learned information. It is hypothesized that after learning trials the learned information goes into a reverberatory neural network that is responsible for producing the physiological change that underlies long-term memory. Short-term memory depends on how accessible for retrieval the information is while it is reverberating. Kleinsmith and Kaplan suggest that the more arousal during learning the less accessible the information will be during short-term memory, but long-term memory will be better since the increased reverberation produces greater long-term memory.

The above conceptualization has recently been revised by Kaplan and his associates (e.g., Pomerantz, Kaplan, and Kaplan, 1969). It is now suggested that the initial unavailability is not due simply to the reverberation, but due to neural fatigue generated by the reverberation. The higher the arousal the more the reverberation, hence more fatigue masking short-term memory but also more activity producing better long-term memory.

There is a tendency for some works in learning to treat principles of learning as if they apply equally to almost all animals. However, differences between species often affect these principles of learning. The reading by Breland and Breland describes some failures in trying to condition different animals operantly. Instinctual behavioral patterns of the animals often interfered with the behavior the Brelands were trying to condition. This does not mean that operant conditioning principles are not applicable to these animals; it means that species-specific behaviors interact with learning.

In the next article Bitterman describes a number of differences between species in various learning tasks. Bitterman has been able to identify some general trends along a dimension of complexity of the animals' nervous systems (the phyletic scale). The reader must be careful not to equate changes along this scale with evolutionary trends (cf. Hodos and Campbell, 1969). For it is generally inappropriate to discuss evoluntionary effects among species all of which are currently alive. Evolutionary trends must include common ancestors, many of which no longer exist.

A number of comparisons (e.g., Kellogg, 1968) have been made between the learning capabilities of chimpanzees and humans. Although chimps readily learn things such as to wear clothes, sleep in beds, eat with silverware, work faucets, and use toilets, they are quite poor at learning to speak. However, chimps are generally not vocal animals unless disturbed. Therefore, to study language learning in chimps it would be better to use non-vocal language. The reading by Gardner and Gardner describes successfully teaching a chimpanzee sign language. This becomes particularly important as the chimp eventually starts combining words in novel ways to generate new "thoughts." Similar results have been reported by Premack (1970) who trained a chimp to use plastic figures on a board to represent words. Premack's chimp Sarah has a vocabulary of more than 120 words and can form fairly complex sentences.

The last reading by Seligman reviews a number of interspecies differences in learning and what evolutionary functions these differences might serve. Seligman argues that animals differ in the degree to which they are "prepared" to learn different associations.

Two-Process Learning Theory: Relationships Between Pavlovian Conditioning and Instrumental Learning[1]

ROBERT A. RESCORLA,[2] *Yale University;* and
RICHARD L. SOLOMON,[3] *University of Pennsylvania*

The history of 2-process learning theory is described, and the logical and empirical validity of its major postulates is examined. The assumption of 2 acquisition processes requires the demonstration of an empirical interaction between 2 types of reinforcement contingencies and (a) response classes, (b) reinforcing stimulus classes, or (c) characteristics of the learned behavior itself. The mediation postulates of 2-process theory which argue that CRs are intimately involved in the control of instrumental responding are emphasized, and 2 major lines of evidence that stem uniquely from these postulates are examined: (a) the concurrent development and maintenance of instrumental responses and conditioned reflexes, and (b) the interaction between separately conducted Pavlovian conditioning contingencies and instrumental training contingencies in the control of instrumental behavior. The evidence from concurrent measurement studies provides, at the very best, only weak support for the mediational hypotheses of 2-process theory. In contrast, the evidence from interaction studies shows the strong mediating control of instrumental responses by Pavlovian conditioning procedures, and demonstrates the surprising power of Pavlovian concepts in predicting the outcomes of many kinds of interaction experiments.

Rescoral, R. A. & Solomon, R. L. Two-process learning theory: relationships between Pavlovian conditioning and instrumental learning. *Psychological Review*, 1967, *74*, 151–182. Copyright 1967 by the American Psychological Association, and reproduced by permission.

The procedures which the experimenter (*E*) carries out in the Pavlovian, or classical, conditioning experiment are quite different from those he carries out in a Thorndikian, or instrumental, training experiment. In the Pavlovian conditioning experiment, *E* ideally has full control over all experimental events; he determines the time of occurrence and the duration of a trial without any regard to the animal's behavior. That is, *E* arranges relations between *stimulus* events which he controls. In contrast, in the Thorndikian training experiment, *E* only arranges it such that the animal's behavior at specified times will yield predetermined environmental changes; *E* arranges relations between the animal's *behavior* and future stimulus events.

Because the laws of learning are stated as interrelationships between experimental operations and consequent behavioral changes, the laws of conditioning and those of learning must be different at a descriptive level. This would be so even though the behavioral changes were identical in the two cases. On the other hand, if some theoretical system could be developed to unify the different empirical laws, to reduce them to the same general underlying principles, then the laws of behavioral modification would deduce the outcomes of both types of experiment. In an important sense, the history of learning theories is a succession of attempts to specify the relation between the outcomes of the two types of experiment.

Most learning theorists have attempted to reduce the outcomes of these two experimental procedures to a common underlying learning principle. Such attempts led to a period of vigorous experimenting, in order to see which of several competing theories of learning would survive the data of both conditioning and training experiments. Pavlov's (1932), Hull's (1943), Tolman's (1932) and Guthrie's (1935) theories are well enough known in the history of learning theory to excuse us from detailed discussion of them. Suffice to say, these single-process theories challenged each other during the period 1930–1950. Then, in recent years, interest in the all-encompassing, "single, sovereign principle" theories declined as *E*s more and more explained their findings in terms of limited, more specific "miniature models." Thus, for example, theories of the partial reinforcement effect have multiplied and have been refined to account for a single phenomenon rather than all learning phenomena. In the same way, theories of extinction have proliferated, until now there are at least seven distinct accounts of the phenomenon. Grand theory testing, in the sense of seeking a crucial experimental test of whole theoretical systems, has clearly subsided.

In contrast, two-process learning theory has persisted as a systematic influence since 1928, and interest in it has increased rather than decreased. Lacking the elegance and simplicity of a postulated, single learning process and the parsimony of a single reinforcement principle, as well as the proselytizing influence of a vigorous "school of thought," two-process learning theory nevertheless has been a major heuristic tool in the stimulation of new conditioning and training experiments.

History

How did two-process learning theory arise, and what stages of development has it undergone? Two Polish investigators, Konorski and Miller, stated in 1928 that the facts of Pavlovian conditioning and Thorndikian learning required the postulation of two underlying associative processes for adequate explanation; the facts of one could not be explained by the inferred processes of the other (Miller & Konorski, 1928). They distinguished between responses yielding rich sensory feedback and those yielding little or no sensory feedback. They assumed that Pavlovian conditioned reflexes yield poor sensory or proprioceptive feedback; but, in contrast, Thorndikian response learning involves extensive and intricate feedback mechanisms. The associative processes operating for responses with poor feedback were postulated to be those of an S–S nature: the linking of afferent processes set up by the conditioned stimulus (CS) and the unconditioned stimulus (US). In contrast, for responses yielding rich feedback, the feedback itself was postulated to be a part of the associative process, and subjects (Ss) learn an S–R relationship only insofar as the feedback from R is distinctive and powerful. There was, however, no postulation of a law of effect for such feedback-rich responses (Miller & Konorski, 1928).

Thorndike (1932) believed that Pavlovian conditioned reflexes do not reflect the general laws of ordinary trial-and-error learning. Perhaps, he speculated, Pavlovian conditioned responses

(CRs) are a special case of some subclass of learning? Writing in this vein in the early 1930s, Thorndike had, however, no alternative to his own law of effect to propose in order to account for Pavlovian phenomena. Relegating such phenomena to a limited subclass did not solve the theoretical problem, and he candidly said so.

Skinner (1935) arrived at a two-experiment and two-response classification, emphasizing that the operations of E differ between the Pavlovian and Thorndikian experiment. He proposed that there are two types of conditioned reflex, Type S and Type R, and two types of response, the operant and respondent. However, Skinner did not postulate two separate associative processes to explain the two sets of conditioning facts, nor did he infer two distinctly different theoretical reinforcement processes for them. His distinction between the respondent and the operant paralleled, but was not identical to, Miller and Konorski's (1928) distinction between poor and elaborated feedback.

Konorski and Miller felt that Skinner's distinction was superficial. In 1937, they argued that Skinner had not completely specified all of the differences between the two types of conditioned reflexes, and they pointed out that Skinner's operant conditioned reflex ". . . is confined exclusively to striped muscles, while the classical type has no restrictions laid on effectors and includes among them, besides striped muscles, smooth muscles and glands [Konorski & Miller, 1937b, p. 271]." They further argued that: "Being a glandular reaction, salivation cannot by any means be made a conditioned reaction of the new type [p. 271]." Konorski and Miller were thus speculating that respondents *cannot* be brought under the control of the law of effect.

It is one matter to argue that temporal contingency between CS and US onsets is *sufficient* for conditioning, or that the response-reward temporal contingency is *sufficient* for instrumental learning. Here, however, Konorski and Miller were arguing for a *strong* two-process law: that the contingency sufficient for law of effect learning *cannot* reinforce a CS–CR relationship of the Pavlovian type. Though the converse was not stated at the time, we might suppose that Konorski and Miller believed it to be so (i.e., instrumental responses *cannot* be conditioned by a Pavlovian procedure). Their emphasis was on Pavlovian conditioning, and, indeed, they anticipated Mowrer (1947) in thinking that Pavlovian CRs might strongly influence instrumental responding; however, they did not have in mind a concept like that of mediation.

The first explicit statement of a complete two-process learning theory came in 1937, in a paper by Schlosberg entitled, "The Relationship between Success and the Laws of Conditioning." This paper was the basis for most of the more recent elaborations of two-process learning theory. In it, Schlosberg distinguished between (a) the *experimenter operations* of Pavlovian conditioning and Thorndikian training, (b) the postulated *associative processes* set up by the two different procedures, and (c) the theoretical *reinforcement mechanisms* appropriate for the two processes. He argued that the empirical laws of Pavlovian conditioning implied that the associations formed are those between stimulus-related or contiguous perceptual processes, and that the reinforcement mechanism is brought into play by the initiation of a US. He further claimed that the empirical laws of Pavlovian conditioning are the laws of conditioning of diffuse, preparatory responses of an *emotional* type. In contrast, he stated that the empirical laws of Thorndikian learning imply that the major associative process is that linking stimulus and precise, adaptive, motor response, and that the reinforcement process is that of "success" or an improvement of the *hedonic state of the S*.

Actually, even though Schlosberg was aware of Konorski and Miller's two-response idea, Skinner's operant and respondent, and Type S and Type R conditioning procedures, he was much more influenced by W. J. Brogden's 1936 APA paper than he was by the published papers of Konorski and Miller and of Skinner. Brogden, at that time, reported on the work later to be incorporated into the article by Brogden, Lipman, and Culler (1938), the widely cited work showing that omission of shock could reinforce running by guinea pigs in a running wheel, in contrast to the poor and unreliable running obtained with a Pavlovian, inevitable presentation of the shock. Brogden suggested that the underlying reinforcing mechanism for Pavlovian conditioning might be different from that for Thorndikian learning. He contrasted forepaw conditioning, relatively successful with a Pavlovian procedure, with the conditioning of running, relatively unsuccessful with a Pavlovian procedure, and speculated about possible theoretical reasons for such a discrepancy.

Schlosberg developed a novel theoretical explanation for the discrepancy. He pointed out that some diffuse motor responses are composed of *reflexes* within an *emotionality* pattern. These are conditionable *only* by Pavlovian methods. If one tries to make use of such motor responses as operants, one will not be able to train them as such because the law of effect will not "work" with such reflexes. Pavlov's laws will. (Konorski & Miller, 1937a, 1937b, at about the same time, made the same claim about visceral, glandular reflexes.)

Schlosberg's (1937) clearly stated two-process theory was listened to, digested, and acknowledged. Yet it did not effectively enter into the arena of the theory-testing giants, those single-process theories struggling against each other during the 1930s and 1940s. There was no two-process "school" to match the Hullian, Yale-Iowa group, or the Tolmanian group at Berkeley, or the Guthrie group at the University of Washington. Instead, due note of the reasonableness of the two-process idea appeared here and there, in sporadic fashion. For example, Hilgard and Marquis (1940) in their influential book, *Conditioning and Learning*, distinguished between classical and instrumental conditioning, preferring to use the term "conditioning" for both the Pavlovian and Thorndikian experiment. Maier and Schnierla (1942) espoused a distinction between two acquisition processes, but preferred to classify the Pavlovian processes as those for perceptual reorganization and the Thorndikian processes as those for biologically adaptive behavior. Later Tuttle (1946), in a rarely cited paper, argued for the existence of associative conditioning and law of effect learning as two completely distinct processes. Birch and Bitterman (1949) noted the usefulness of the two-process distinctions.

Mowrer (1947) published what was at the time the longest, most tightly reasoned, and most persuasive argument for two-process theory. He added precision to Schlosberg's (1937) specifications, refined the theoretical relationships between inferred processes and experimental operations, and developed the conception of CRs as *motivational mediators* of instrumental responding. Mowrer argued that the laws of Pavlovian conditioning are applicable only to visceral responses. The Thorndikian law of effect applies only to the training of skeletal motor responses. The specific controlling relationship for the establishment of *conditioned emotional reactions* is the temporal contiguity between CS onset and US onset. (US termination conditions are irrelevant to this process.) Mowrer called this process the *problem-posing* process. Previously neutral environmental events come to have the conditioned power to evoke visceral responses. These visceral responses create emotional and motivational tensions which then must be resolved by *problem-solving behavior*. The problem-solving is done by skeletal motor responses alone, as reinforced by drive-reduction (in Mowrer's terms, reduction of visceral tension-states). Therefore, conditioned reflexes are powerful *mediators* of instrumental responses. Mowrer argued that, in signalized avoidance experiments, the CS and US are paired on early trials, and this established CS anxiety, a type of conditioned fear. The anxiety has the properties earlier assigned to it by Miller (1941); that is, it is both a response and an acquired drive. As a response, it is a pattern of conditioned visceral reactions. The drive properties come from response-produced feedback stimulation arising from visceral reactions. Therefore, if CRs can produce drive, they can strongly influence instrumental responses. The more intense the conditioned anxiety, the more vigorous are avoidance responses, and the shorter are their latencies in the presence of fear-producing CSs. The more drive-arousing the CS, the more reinforcing would be a response that terminated the CS. Avoidance responses are reinforced by anxiety-reduction. Thus did Mowrer provide both a motivational and a reinforcement principle for avoidance learning. Although Mowrer believed that the mediational principles would apply to appetitive CRs and reward learning, he did not develop this idea, perhaps because at that time the relevant observations were missing.

Because Mowrer's mediational hypotheses were so important in the development of and testing of two-process theory, we shall emphasize the experiments relevant to them. Slight modifications and expansions were made by other investigators, but the major ideas remained, and they served as the basis for a large number of experiments appearing in the 1950s, experiments which presented grave problems for all of the single-process theories (see Solomon & Brush, 1956).

Then some notable desertions from single-process learning theory occurred. Tolman (1949) argued that there might be as many as six kinds of learning, each with its own reinforcement principle. Spence (1956) acknowledged the possibility that there might be two reinforcement processes, one for instrumental learning and one for classical conditioning. However, Spence turned things around. He tentatively suggested that if he were to adopt a two-process theory, he would argue that classical conditioning is a habit acquired by reinforcement of an appetitional or aversive sort, whereas instrumental learning is acquired by contiguity principles without a specific reinforcing event. Spence's important idea from our particular point of view was the postulation of a mediational relationship between the Pavlovian, conditioned r_g and instrumental responding. This mediational process is the appetitive counterpart of Mowrer's description of aversively motivated behavior.

The manifestations of two-process learning theory have recently become difficult to follow. On the one hand, we have Spence's view of two-process theory, arguing that Pavlovian conditioning is reinforced by the law of effect. On the other hand, heavily influenced by Schlosberg (1937), Solomon and Wynne (1954) extended Mowrer's (1947) postulates to cover the conditioning of skeletal-motor reflexes by Pavlovian processes, rather than confining Pavlovian conditioning to visceral responses. In other respects, Solomon and Wynne (1954) and Solomon and Brush (1956) have held faithfully to the Schlosberg-Mowrer concepts, and their experiments have been guided by these concepts. Yet, in contrast, Mowrer himself has steadily abandoned his original two-process conception of learning. In the most recent statement of his position, Mowrer (1960) has proposed a learning theory which employs only one underlying learning process with two major types of reinforcing event. Although Mowrer continues to call this a "two-factor" theory, it clearly does not involve two learning processes in the same sense as do previous theories. This latest version of Mowrer's theory has not yet been widely used to generate new types of experimentation. In contrast, the number of experiments instigated by the Schlosberg-Mowrer type of two-process theory has increased steadily. It is this latter type of two-process theory that we shall discuss in detail.

The Scope of this Paper

In this paper we analyze the two major questions posed by various two-process learning theories: (a) Are there two acquisition processes, a conditioning process and a learning process, each with its own set of distinct laws? (b) Does the conditioning process serve a mediating function in the control of instrumentally learned responses?

Our main emphasis will be upon the second, mediational, question. In examining the mediation role of conditioning processes in the control of instrumentally learned responses, we will discuss two major research strategies: (a) The first is the *concomitant measurement* of Pavlovian CRs and instrumental responses during the course of acquisition and extinction of instrumental behavior. The question of interest here is to what degree the two classes of behavior are correlated. (b) The *interaction* of independently established Pavlovian CSs with instrumental behavior and the effectiveness of such CSs in controlling that behavior. In assessing both of these research strategies we concentrate upon the role of Pavlovian conditioning processes in evoking instrumental behavior. The establishment of reinforcers of behavior by Pavlovian processes is beyond the scope of this paper.

Although the mediational question is our main concern, it seems appropriate to deal first with the logically prior question of whether there are really two kinds of learning. It is obviously not possible to deal with this vastly complex question in all of its ramifications; however, in the next section we do attempt to lay out a logical framework within which the question can be answered.

Are There Two Acquisition Processes?

A variety of two-process theories have been mentioned in the previous section. In attempting to specify the domain of the two processes, each theory has made a number of logical and empirical assertions. This section attempts a classification of the distinctions drawn by two-process theories and attempts to specify the kinds of evidence that may be taken as supporting the proposition that there are two acquisition processes. We will not attempt an exhaustive review of the relevant literature; rather we wish to make explicit the logical structure of the evidence that would be relevant to the two-process proposition.

All two-process theories emphasize the basic operational difference between the Thorndikian and Pavlovian experiment. In the former, E's presentation of the reinforcer is dependent upon the organism's behavior, but in the latter it is independent of that behavior. In Pavlovian conditioning the reinforcement is made contingent upon the occurrence of a stimulus; in instrumental training it is made contingent upon the occurrence of an arbitrarily selected response.

In general, this operational distinction has not been thought sufficient to justify by itself the assertion of two different learning processes. Theorists have felt that only if the difference between response-contingent (instrumental) and stimulus-contingent (Pavlovian) reinforcement has important implications for the way in which behavior is modified would we want to identify these two operations with different underlying processes. Therefore, the assertion of two separate learning processes has rested upon an assumed interaction between reinforcement contingency and other variables in producing behavior change. In particular, two-process theories have pointed to three sets of such variables (a) response class, (b) reinforcement class, and (c) characteristics of the products of learning. The claim is that the class of responses affected, the effective reinforcers, and the results of learning, all depend upon whether response- or stimulus-contingencies are employed.

Response Distinctions

Theorists have tried to separate those responses subject to modification by stimulus- and response-contingencies in a variety of different ways. Some of the proposed response distinctions have been: (a) ANS (visceral or glandular) responses as contrasted with somatic (skeletal) responses (Mowrer, 1947) ; (b) operant (emitted) responses as contrasted with respondent (elicited) responses (Skinner, 1938) ; (c) voluntary responses versus involuntary responses (Schlosberg, 1937) ; (d) so-called "lightweight" responses as contrasted with "heavy-weight" responses (Miller & Konorski, 1928; Osgood, 1953); (e) diffuse, emotional responses as against precise, adaptive responses (Schlosberg, 1937); and (f) responses high in reflexiveness as contrasted with those low in reflexiveness (Turner & Solomon, 1962).

We do not wish to review in detail the evidence for and against the ability of each of these distinctions to discriminate between responses subject to modification by the two reinforcement contingencies. Instead, we will take as an example the autonomic-skeletal distinction to illustrate the logic and problems of testing the propositions of two-process theory. The autonomic-skeletal distinction has the advantage of being the easiest distinction to make with precision.

The assertion central to some versions of two-process theory is that skeletal responses are subject to instrumental reinforcement contingencies but not to Pavlovian reinforcement contingencies, while autonomic responses are only subject to Pavlovian contingencies. It is worth pointing out that the autonomic-skeletal distinction is typical of all response-class distinctions in relating response classes and reinforcement contingencies in a one-to-one manner. This particular form of interaction between response class and reinforcement contingency is, however, not a logical requirement of the two-process approach. The separation of response classes would be no less important if, for example, several classes of responses were subject to modification by one reinforcement contingency while only one class contained responses affected also by the other contingency.

Thus the question of theoretical interest is whether *any* autonomic responses are subject to instrumental training procedures and whether *any* skeletal responses are subject to modification by Pavlovian conditioning procedures. If both of these possibilities occur, we cannot rely on the interaction of reinforcement contingency with the autonomic-skeletal distinction to justify the theoretical separation of the effects of stimulus- and response-contingent reinforcement.

At least three skeletal responses have been successfully brought under the control of Pavlovian procedures. Schlosberg (1928) found patellar reflex conditioning in humans; a number of investigators have demonstrated conditioned paw flexion in dogs (e.g., Konorski & Szwejsowska, 1956); and human eyelid conditioning has become a standard procedure for the investigation of acquisition processes. However, in trying to interpret these results we meet a problem typical of attempts to bring under Pavlovian control responses in any class supposedly not subject to Pavlovian conditioning. We must be able to assure ourselves that unwanted response-contingencies are not producing the results. There is a common way in which such contingencies often enter; occurrence of the CR may influence the effect of the US, thus converting presumed Pavlovian to actual instrumental contingencies. For example, the inevitable occurrence of the shock US to a dog's paw may be less aversive when the paw is in a flexed position. Schlosberg (1937) was the first to discuss this kind of possibility in detail. The typical way of dealing with this problem is to try to arrange a situation in which such an argument seems, at a common-sense level, implausible. However, an alternative procedure would be to give S the choice (following conditioning) between (a) presenting himself with the CS (and thus the CR) followed by the US or (b) presenting himself with the US alone (or followed by the CS). Presumably, if the role of the CR in altering the effect of the US is important, a clear preference would be demonstrated. A similar design has been suggested for this purpose by Wagner (1966) who used it to detect instrumental reinforcement in cortical conditioning experiments. Without this kind of evidence we must reserve judgment on supposed demonstrations of the Pavlovian conditioning of skeletal responses.

There is also evidence suggesting that autonomic responses can come under response-contingent control. Although Mowrer (1938) and Skinner (1938) reported failure to train autonomic responses instrumentally, more recent investigators have reported success. Fowler and Kimmel (1962), Kimmel and Kimmel (1963) and Crider, Shapiro, and Tursky (1966) have all reported successful instrumental training of the galvanic skin response (GSR). Lisina (reported by Razran, 1961) trained vasodilation as an escape response, and Shearn (1962) obtained suggestive evidence that heart-rate changes can be used as avoidance responses. Although Sheffield (1965) found the salivary response insensitive to instrumental contingencies, using food as the reinforcer, Miller and Carmona (1967) were able to reinforce salivary responses in thirsty dogs when water was used as the reinforcer.

The interpretative problem that arises in this sort of experiment concerns the need to rule out mediating operants. We must be sure that some unnoticed skeletal response is not being learned and is not directly producing the observed autonomic changes. The most effective argument against this possibility would be the successful replication of these experiments while S is immobilized by curare agents. This type of experiment has recently been reported. Trowill (1967) and Miller and DiCara (1967) produced heart-rate changes in curarized rats using positive brain stimulation as the instrumental reinforcer. Birk, Crider, Shapiro, and Tursky (1966) partially curarized a human S and were able to produce GSR changes using instrumental avoidance contingencies. And yet there is the disturbing possibility that even the use of curare agents may not permit us to rule out operant mediators. Curare only precludes peripheral skeletal mediators and allows central responses to occur. Thus, even while paralyzed, a human can think of emotional events which will reflexly produce peripheral respondent events. It is not at all clear whether such "thoughts," or brain events which are clearly subject to response-contingent reinforcement, should be considered to be "skeletal" or not. Possibly the distinction is better made between types of brain events than between types of peripheral nervous system association.

These brief comments give an idea of the logic and problems involved in testing the assertion that the autonomic-skeletal distinction is identical with the distinction between responses subject to modification by stimulus- and response-contingencies.

The kinds of experiments and problems generated by other response-class distinctions are similar. The most frequently mentioned of these other distinctions is the operant-respondent distinction. According to Skinner (1938, pp. 20, 21) "behavior that is correlated with specific eliciting stimuli may be called *respondent* behavior . . ." (elicited behavior) and an operant is identified by the fact that "no correlated stimulus can be detected upon occasions when it is observed to occur" (emitted behavior). A two-process position then asserts that respondents are subject only to stimulus-contingencies and operants can only be taught by response-contingent reinforcement. One can then attempt to test these notions, as in the case of the autonomic-skeletal distinction.

The operant-respondent distinction raises special problems of its own. Although, for many common responses, there is no practical difficulty in identifying which are operants and which are respondents, there are, unfortunately, cases where this is extremely difficult. Many responses seem at times to be operants and at other times to be respondents. This observation suggested to Turner and Solomon (1962) that we examine a *continuous dimension,* which they called "reflexiveness," on which operants and respondents are located. This modification of two-process theory claims that the relative effectiveness of response- and stimulus-contingent reinforcement would vary along this response dimension, each contingency being maximally effective at one end; it has yet to receive any extensive empirical analysis.

The two remaining, commonly made, response-class distinctions are very difficult to make empirically. Schlosberg suggested that responses subject to stimulus-contingencies were "preparatory-diffuse" responses while those affected by response-contingencies were "precise-adaptive" responses. The other response-class distinction is that between voluntary and involuntary behavior. Reliable ways of distinguishing between these latter types of behavior are few. One suspects that attempts to classify responses into voluntary and involuntary are not entirely independent of reinforcement-contingency distinctions. Thus, the most reasonable objective criterion of whether or not a response is voluntary may be just whether or not it is subject to modification by response-contingent reinforcement contingencies. If a response-contingent reinforcement procedure will not modify a response, it is involuntary.

Although these different categorizations of response are far from identical, they all seem to be attempting to embody the idea that behavior subject to modification through instrumental contingencies is somehow "freer," more varied, and "adaptive," while the responses which are conditionable by Pavlovian procedures are more "rigid," more "specialized," and more automatic or "reflexive." In general, many results support this correlation between response-class and reinforcement contingency. However, considerably more analytic experiments are needed before a precise statement about the nature of the response-class distinction involved can be made.

Reinforcement Class

Instead of asking whether the class of responses subject to modification varies with type of reinforcement contingency, one can ask whether the events which serve as reinforcers differ when response- and stimulus-contingent delivery of reinforcement are used. Clearly, reinforcers for Pavlovian conditioning experiments are closely related to reinforcers for instrumental training. For example, food serves both as a US for the conditioning of salivation through stimulus-contingent reinforcement and as a reward for the training of bar-pressing through response-contingent reinforcement. But are there reinforcers which will function only in conjunction with one or the other contingency?

Two-process theories have generated several theoretical attempts to specify differences between reinforcement classes. Both Schlosberg (1937) and Mowrer (1947) have argued that the reinforcement event for instrumental training must have some *affective* character but, in contrast, the simple contingency of CS and US is sufficient for Pavlovian conditioning. In the instrumental case, the reinforcer must be pleasant or unpleasant, whereas for Pavlovian conditioning it is sufficient that the reinforcer regularly elicit the unconditioned response (UR). But such a characterization is probably not precise enough to be helpful. Even our intuitive notions of affect seem strained by such instrumental reinforcers as light onset (Kiernan, 1964) or the opportunity to run in a running wheel (Hundt & Premack, 1963). It is equally easy, in the case of almost all Pavlovian reinforcers, to become convinced that they produce a modicum of affect.

An alternative specification of the difference between instrumental and Pavlovian reinforcers has been suggested by Mowrer (1947): Instrumental reinforcers are drive-reducers, whereas Pavlovian reinforcers do not necessarily reduce drives and, indeed, may even increase drive level. A typical example of the latter is Pavlovian fear conditioning, for which there is now excellent evidence (Mowrer & Aiken, 1954; Mowrer & Solomon, 1954;

Overmier, 1966) that the effective US is shock onset, a drive-increasing stimulus. Unfortunately, there is no guarantee that all instrumental reinforcers are drive-reducing; indeed, many examples of reinforcers (brain stimulation, light onset, novelty, etc.) strain this notion. Furthermore, such drive inducers as shock onset are often instrumental reinforcers—albeit negative ones (punishers). Thus the notion of drive-reduction does not seem helpful in separating Pavlovian and instrumental reinforcers.

Perhaps a more fruitful, if more limited, approach is simply to examine empirically the degree to which the two classes of reinforcers overlap. "Reinforcer" is used here in both the positive and negative sense, that is, punishers are instrumental reinforcers, and Pavlovian CRs involving reduction in behavioral output are treated in the same way as those involving increment. Thus, in order to demonstrate that a given stimulus reinforces when used with one contingency, and does not do so when used with the other contingency, it is not sufficient to show that it has incremental effects in one case and decremental effects in the other. We here require that a stimulus have *no effects* when used with one contingency or the other. Of course, it is necessary to employ appropriate control procedures in making this assessment. A particular stimulus may have nonassociative effects upon a response which are not dependent upon the particular contingency with which it is used. Thus, to show that a given stimulus is an effective reinforcer in stimulus-contingent presentation, it is necessary to demonstrate, through appropriate control procedures, that the changes which it produces depend upon the contingency arranged. The problem of control procedures for Pavlovian conditioning has been discussed in detail by Rescorla (1967b). Similarly, to demonstrate that a stimulus is a reinforcer when used in a response-contingent fashion requires suitable control procedures.

It seems likely, as has been implied by the various theoretical attempts to separate the two kinds of reinforcers, that the class of Pavlovian reinforcers is larger than that of instrumental reinforcers, and in fact includes as a subclass the set of events which serve as instrumental reinforcers. With this in mind, we may ask whether there is *any* stimulus event which will reinforce behavior when made contingent upon prior stimulus presentation but *not* when made contingent upon a response. Unfortunately, this question, though basic to the two-process approach, seems to have received relatively little direct experimental attention; but there are a few hints available. One of the earliest USs to be used in Pavlovian conditioning was a tap on the patellar tendon; there is considerable evidence that this is an adequate stimulus to establish a Pavlovian conditioned knee-jerk (e.g., Schlosberg, 1928). Yet, if the US is administered properly, Ss report being "neutral" toward it. It would be of considerable interest to see whether this patellar tap could be used to reinforce instrumental behavior in a situation comparable to that in which it conditions the knee-jerk. A second, promising source of "pure" Pavlovian reinforcers is the class of interoceptive USs described by Bykov (1957). Many of the internal USs used to produce Pavlovian conditioning would most likely go completely unnoticed in an instrumental training situation. However, we do not yet know whether or not such internal USs can serve as instrumental reinforcers. This would certainly be an important type of investigation to pursue.

Another example comes closer to fulfilling our experimental requirements. Doty and Giurgea (1961) have recently provided considerable evidence that direct stimulation of the motor cortex will serve as a US for limb-flexion conditioning. Yet, when the same US is made contingent upon ongoing operant behavior, in many cases it produces no change in that behavior. Although one would like similar demonstrations with a large number of operants, the Doty and Giurgea findings indicate that this type of brain stimulation is indeed a Pavlovian reinforcer with no instrumental rewarding or punishing properties. Likewise, Malmo (1965) has reported a few cases of septal stimulation which serve as USs for heart-rate conditioning in rats but which will not maintain operant bar-pressing.

However, recent evidence presented by Wagner (1966) indicates the presence of instrumental reinforcement in such experiments. Paw flexion was conditioned in dogs, using a motor center brain stimulation as US. When the CS was presented, the dogs appeared to be positioning themselves in such a way as to modify the effect of the US. When the dogs were later given a choice between signaled and unsignaled presentations of the US, they chose the signaled US. This indicates that this type of experiment may not be a pure case of Pavlovian conditioning.

Finally, experiments directed toward examination of sensory preconditioning (which fits the Pavlovian, stimulus contingency paradigm) provide some support for the separation of Pavlovian and instrumental reinforcers. Unfortunately, such experiments have failed to include direct evidence that the neutral "US" used for the sensory preconditioning is not also an instrumental reinforcer. Furthermore, the demonstration that sensory preconditioning has actually occurred is often less than convincing.

We can only conclude that the evidence on the overlap of Pavlovian and instrumental reinforcers is scanty. Despite the fact that most Pavlovian reinforcers seem also to be instrumental rewards or punishments, the evidence does imply that the overlap is not complete. To the degree that Pavlovian and Thorndikian reinforcers are different, a two-process theory receives strong support. Clearly, this is one of the most exciting areas of research suggested by a two-process theory of learning, and considerable work remains to be done.

Characteristics of the Learned Behavior

It is often thought that the product of the learning process differs across stimulus- and response-reinforcement contingencies. Several attempts have been made to specify how the result of learning is different in the Pavlovian and Thorndikian experiments.

S–S versus S–R connections. The first distinction is theoretical. Both Schlosberg (1937) and Maier and Schneirla (1942) believed that Pavlovian conditioning procedures established S–S connections; at the same time they suggested that instrumental learning consists of acquired S–R bonds. Other authors have made similar claims in describing conditioning as stimulus-substitution and instrumental learning as response-substitution (Hilgard & Marquis, 1940). Both of these distinctions arise as direct consequences of the contingencies of reinforcement which E arranges; however, they imply that a difference beyond that of experimental manipulation is involved.

Two types of experiment have been thought to bear on these theoretical distinctions. First, a number of investigators have shown that Pavlovian conditioning is possible even when peripheral responding has been prevented. Salivary conditioning is possible when salivation is blocked by atropine (Crisler, 1930; Finch, 1938) and Pavlovian fear conditioning occurs while S is paralyzed by curare (Solomon & Turner, 1962). To the degree that the S–R bond is conceived to require peripheral skeletal responding for its establishment, the S–S alternative is favored for Pavlovian conditioning.

The second line of evidence stems from the use of direct motor-cortex stimulation as a US for Pavlovian conditioning. Loucks' (1935) failure to obtain conditioning using such a US was taken as evidence that Pavlovian conditioning involves S–S connections. However, Brogden and Gantt (1937) obtained conditioning with direct stimulation of the cerebellum as the US. And Doty and Giurgea (1961) were able to obtain Pavlovian conditioning with electrical stimulation of the motor-cortex as the US. If the S–S and S–R notions are given physiological interpretation as sensory- and motor-cortex connections, this result suggests that Pavlovian conditioning may not be S–S in nature. We can conclude that the present evidence does not support a sharp distinction between Pavlovian conditioning and instrumental training in terms of hypothetical S–S and S–R connections.

Similarity of CR and UR. Greater similarity of the CR to the UR is often mentioned as setting Pavlovian conditioning apart from instrumental learning. However, the CR is by no means identical with the UR, even for Pavlovian conditioning; indeed, many have suggested that the CR is preparatory for the US or that it is a fractional part of the UR. But there *is* a gross similarity of the CR and UR in Pavlovian conditioning, at least to the extent that they usually involve the same response system. This is in general *not* true in instrumental training situations, where, for example, the response may be bar-pressing, which bears no fixed relation to the UR, ingestion of a food pellet.

It is possible that the more valuable distinction here rests in the relation of the CR to the US. Skinner has pointed out that in Pavlovian conditioning, once the US is selected, E is no longer free to select the CR at will (except in the trivial sense that he chooses to ignore parts of the behavior pattern). In instrumental training, selection of the US does not uniquely determine the CR which is acquired; E is free to select arbitrarily the response he will reinforce. Thus, it may be that the apparent CR–UR relationship results from the added constraint which selection of the US places upon Pavlovian conditioning but not upon instrumental training. The US may uniquely determine *both* the UR and the Pavlovian CR, even though the learned and unlearned responses are quite different.

Sensitivity to parametric variations. Finally, the Pavlovian CR may differ from the instrumentally trained response in its sensitivity to a variety of parametric variations. In general, as Kimble (1961) points out, there is a striking resemblance in the reaction of the two kinds of learning to such variables as amount of reinforcement, delay of reinforcement, etc. However, Kimble suggests one possible difference. Instrumentally trained responses consistently show greater resistance to extinction following partial reinforcement; this may not be the case for Pavlovian CRs. The evidence on this point is far from clear-cut. However, a sharp difference in the sensitivity of Pavlovian conditioned responses and instrumental behavior to such a parametric variation would give strong support to the distinctions of two-process theories. The investigation of such parameters seems to us to be a fruitful area for future research.

Conclusion

We have argued that the basic operational distinction between response- and stimulus-contingent reinforcement may interact with various other variables in such a way as to justify the claim that two independent processes are acting. In general, the results relevant to such interactions are still inadequate. Our attempt therefore has been not so much to marshal all the evidence in support of such interactions as to point out the kinds of evidence which *would* be relevant. The questions we have raised here have often not received explicit experimental attention, although to our minds these are basic questions in the study of behavior modification.

EXPERIMENTAL APPROACHES
GENERATED BY
TWO-PROCESS THEORY

In addition to asserting the existence of two independent acquisition processes, two-process theories have postulated inter-relationships between the two processes in the control of behavior. They usually assert that Pavlovian CRs serve as *mediators* of instrumental behavior, functioning as either instigators or reinforcers. Such assumptions have given rise to two research strategies: (a) concurrent measurement of the development and maintenance of conditioned reflexes and instrumental responses within instrumental learning situations; and (b) testing the interaction between separately conducted Pavlovian conditioning contingencies and instrumental contingencies in the control of instrumental behavior.

It should be mentioned at the outset that the claim that instrumental behavior is mediated by Pavlovian CRs is by no means a unitary theoretical idea. As is pointed out below, different theorists have emphasized different aspects of the mediational process. But their ideas also differ on the precise role that CRs play in mediating instrumental behavior. Some propose that the observed CR itself, or sensory feedback from it, is an event which elicits and/or reinforces a particular instrumental act. In this case, the research strategy is to seek out and vary those particular CRs which one suspects are mediating the instrumental behavior. As we will conclude below, this approach does not seem to have been a fruitful one, because the attempts to find specific mediating CRs have been generally without success. A more viable claim is that operant behavior is mediated by a complex of CRs, both autonomic and skeletal; no one of these may be necessary for operant behavior, but each contributes to that behavior. This position suggests an extension of the concurrent measurement research strategy to the study of more complex CRs.

Still another position is that the observed Pavlovian CRs are not themselves mediators of instrumental behavior but rather are merely an index of a central nervous system state which does mediate that behavior. This position leads to a research strategy reviewed in the final section of this paper.

It is often difficult to tell which of these positions an author intends when he describes the mediation of instrumental behavior by Pavlovian CRs, so it is well to keep these distinctions in mind.

CONCURRENT MEASUREMENT OF
PAVLOVIAN CONDITIONING AND
INSTRUMENTAL LEARNING

Any instrumental training situation has within it the conditions favoring the development of Pavlovian conditioned responses. In the discriminated operant paradigm there is a regular sequence of S^d and the reinforcement; in nondiscriminated operant behavior, feedback from various responses leading to reward is also regularly followed by reward. To the degree that the stimulus event maintaining the operant behavior is also a Pavlovian reinforcer, we would expect the development of Pavlovian CRs in addition to the acquisition of instrumental behavior. Given that food is both a Pavlovian and an instrumental reinforcer, we would expect that its use in an instrumental training situation would also lead to the development of Pavlovian CRs such as salivation, cardiac changes, licking, swallowing, etc.

However, two-process theories make the still stronger assertion that these Pavlovian CRs are somehow crucial to the maintenance of instrumental behavior. Two different mediational roles have been assigned to Pavlovian CRs. Some authors have emphasized their *motivational* role. This conception seems to have originated, at least for aversively motivated behavior, with Miller (1948), who postulated that emotional reactions become associated with previously neutral stimuli by the action of drive reduction. The emotional reactions give rise to immediate sensory feedback, having both cue and drive properties. Thus the "acquired drive state" is a complex of emotional reactions and then correlated perceptual events. Such mediators have been given either or both of two properties, motivational or reinforcing. The two-process theories of Spence (1956) and Mowrer (1947) have likewise emphasized the motivating function of conditioned reflexes, arguing that such CRs as salivation or cardiac change may reflect the level of motivation or incentive in instrumental training situations. Conditioned responses are assigned the role of instigators (or indexes of instigators) of instrumental behavior.

These theories, therefore, predict a close correspondence between the occurrence or nonoccurrence of Pavlovian CRs and the magnitude or probability of specific instrumental responses.

On the other hand, Konorski (1948), Soltysik (1963), and Mowrer (1960) have emphasized the rewarding functions of mediating respondents. Thus the reduction of heart-rate or the increase in salivary flow may be thought to reflect a state which is instrumentally rewarding. For these theories the important changes in conditioned reflexes reflect instrumental reinforcement and thus occur following instrumental behavior. Again, a close relation between conditioned reflexes and learned instrumental behavior is predicted.

The instigating and rewarding functions of conditioned reflexes in maintaining instrumental behavior are by no means incompatible. For instance, conditioned cardiac acceleration may reflect the motivation for an avoidance response while cardiac deceleration following the response may reflect a reward. This is roughly the picture of avoidance behavior which Mowrer (1947) drew. For appetitive behavior, it is not clear whether salivation should be treated as reflecting a motivating or a rewarding state; in the former case, we might expect salivation to precede the operant (Spence, 1956), while in the latter it should follow the operant (Konorski, 1948).

The dual role which two-process theories assign to conditioning processes leads naturally to an examination of the *sequence* of CRs and instrumental responses in instrumental training situations. One research strategy for studying these temporal sequences is to allow the normal instrumental sequence to be established while taking simultaneous measures of various CRs and operants.

The degree to which the various theories are bound by these predictions depends upon the precise role which the theory assigns to mediating CRs. In the preceding few paragraphs we have purposely been vague on this role, using such phrases as "the CR reflects a motivational state." It is clear that a theory which claims that a particular CR or complex of CRs is itself mediating the instrumental behavior predicts a closer correspondence between the CR and instrumental behavior than does a theory which assigns to the CR the role of indexing a central mediator.

Thus the experiments to be described below are particularly relevant to the view that the CR itself (or its associated feedback) is mediating the instrumental behavior.

Appetitive Behavior

It is probably no accident that the first experiment using the concurrent measurement technique was performed by Konorski and Miller (1930), who were the first to propose a two-process theory. They trained a dog to lift his paw when a signal sounded, in order to obtain food. They found a close relation between the occurrence of the paw movement and the magnitude of conditioned salivation. But for them the important finding was that the operant consistently *preceded* increased salivary flow. Working in Konorski's laboratory some years later, Wolf (1963) found similar results using a fixed ratio (FR) schedule of reinforcement. These findings have been substantiated by similar results of Williams (1965) for FR, and of Shapiro (1961) and Kintsch and Witte (1962) for fixed interval (FI) performance and extinction. In addition, Kintsch and Witte found that the characteristic FI scallop developed prior to a similar temporal discrimination in the salivary response.

These studies suggest that, at least under some circumstances, conditioned salivation does not provide the essential motivating state which instigates operant behavior. Rather, they support the notion that operant behavior precedes (and possibly serves as a CS for) conditioned salivation. The observed temporal sequence of events is that predicted by Konorski's (1948) notion that salivation indexes a state of excitation which serves to reinforce instrumental behavior.

But results inconsistent with this conclusion have also been obtained by Shapiro (1962), who trained dogs to obtain food by pressing a panel on a differential reinforcement of low rates (DRL) schedule. On this schedule, bursts of salivation regularly *preceded* the operant, even though the occurrence of the operant itself generally led to a further increment in salivation. Evidently the temporal sequence of CRs and instrumental behavior is not fixed, but depends upon the relations which the E arranges between instrumental response and reinforcement. A dramatic demonstration of this dependence is provided by Ellison and Konorski (1964). They trained dogs to panel-press on an FR, the completion of which initiated an 8-second waiting period at the end of which food was delivered. Using this technique, panel-pressing and salivation were kept almost completely separate temporally, the first occurring only during the FR requirement and the second only following its completion.

It thus appears that although salivation and operant behavior may bear a gross relation to each other in typical instrumental training situations, the details of this relation are not constant. Salivation consistently represents neither Spence's r_g nor Konorski's alimentary excitation; salivation must neither precede nor consistently follow operant behavior in order for that behavior to be maintained.

Similar conclusions are in order for other "mediating" CRs. Both Soltysik (1960) and Wenzel (1961) have found a gross temporal correspondence between cardiac acceleration and performance on a motor response reinforced by food. Further, Soltysik found that cardiac acceleration occurred prior to the motor behavior, suggesting that it may be involved in instigating that behavior. But Wenzel found, upon administration of reserpine to her cats, that the heart-rate response was markedly reduced with no effect upon operant behavior. We need further research, detailing the relation between food-motivated behavior and conditioned cardiac changes; but at the present time the evidence does not suggest that cardiac changes are necessary mediators for operant behavior.

Another possible CR, licking, has been studied by Miller and DeBold (1965). Using a discriminated bar-press operant reinforced by intraoral liquid, and simultaneously measuring intraoral licking, these investigators found that although licking was more probable just *prior* to a bar-press than at other times, it was maximal just *following* an unreinforced bar-press. To the degree that the licking response is under the control of Pavlovian contingencies, this parallels the case of salivation; neither the notion that the operant leads to the respondent, nor the notion that the respondent must occur prior to the operant, can alone encompass the data. This empirical conclusion proves to be an interesting problem for those two-process theories that postulate the mediation of instrumental responses by action of peripheral Pavlovian CRs (and their associated feedback).

Aversive Behavior

Two-process theories of avoidance learning have typically ascribed motivating and rewarding properties to autonomic responses and their afferent feedback. In a standard, discriminative avoidance training situation, the pairing of a CS with electric shock leads to the development of a conditioned "fear" reaction. Increase in sensory feedback from that "fear" reaction is postulated to instigate the instrumental avoidance response while reduction in the feedback rewards it. Various CR indexes of this fear-state have been suggested: heart-rate increase, blood-pressure increase, pupillary dilation, GSR, defecation, urination, suppression of appetitive behavior, etc. If two-process conceptions of avoidance behavior are adequate, and if the various indexes of emotionality reflect adequately the level of conditioned fear, a close correspondence between the occurrence of instrumental avoidance behavior and these indexes is clearly predicted.

Some of the relations which two-process theories require are the following: (a) Conditioned fear should increase in the early stages of avoidance training; (b) acquisition of the fear reaction should precede acquisition of a reliable avoidance response, and extinction of the avoidance response should occur concurrently with, or follow, extinction of the fear reaction; (c) during avoidance responding, fear should be greater preceding successful avoidance responses than on other trials; (d) fear should decrease following the avoidance response; and finally (e) physiological manipulation such as administration of drugs or sympathectomy which may directly affect the level of conditioned autonomic responses should likewise indirectly affect the avoidance behavior.

The two most often used indexes of the conditioned fear reaction used to test these predictions are heart-rate and suppression of appetitive behavior (conditioned emotional response, or CER, technique) by a CS. The evidence on cardiac conditioning is more extensive, and we will examine it first.

1. Cardiac CRs —acquisition. Changes in cardiac responding during acquisition of an avoidance response provide some support for the two-process position. Both Gantt and Dykman (1957) using paw flexion and Black (1959) using a panel-press response found general increases in heart-rate during instrumental avoidance training in dogs. Furthermore, both reported the development of conditioned heart-rate increases during the S^d for the avoidance response. Typically, heart-rate conditioning occurred *prior* to acquisition of the avoidance reaction. But one of Black's more detailed findings contradicts at least one form of a two-process position; maximum heart-rate occurred *following* the avoidance response, and it was only some seconds later that the rate declined. This is in disagreement with the two-process requirement of rapid reduction in fear as a reinforcement for the avoidance response. It may be that the influence of the skeletal avoidance movement and respiratory changes upon heart-rate makes cardiac change suspect as an index of conditioned fear in such situations. The possibility of artifact from movement is especially great when instrumental responses are required or possible.

Performance. The evidence relating heart-rate to avoidance behavior during continued performance of the avoidance response is conflicting. Soltysik (1960), using a paw-placement response with dogs, obtained results which fit quite closely with two-process predictions. In well-trained animals, an increase in heart-rate preceded the avoidance response and a decrease followed it. Furthermore, heart-rate CRs and avoidance responses were brought under parallel, discriminative stimulus control. The conditioned heart-rate was maintained through continued, long-term avoidance. In contrast to Black's findings, Soltysik found that maximum heart-rate occurred *prior* to the avoidance response. The avoidance response was followed by sharp cardiac deceleration. Bersh, Notterman, and Schoenfeld (1956), in disagreement with Soltysik, found that with continued avoidance performance, human Ss showed no heart-rate acceleration to the S^d for avoidance. That is, avoidance behavior was maintained in the absence of conditioned fear, as indexed by cardiac acceleration. Using cats, which show cardiac deceleration as a CR when shock is the US, Wenzel (1961) found a gross relation between magnitudes of deceleration and the latency of a bar-press avoidance response. However, the introduction of reserpine left unaffected the conditioned cardiac deceleration although it disrupted the avoidance behavior. McCleary's (1960) failure to demonstrate interocular transfer of avoidance responding in fish in spite of good interocular transfer of Pavlovian cardiac conditioning also questions the role of cardiac responses in the mediation of avoidance behavior.

Extinction. Several relations have been found between heart-rate and avoidance responding during extinction of the avoidance response. Gantt and Dykman (1957) found extinction of the instrumental response long before extinction of the cardiac CR. In contrast, Soltysik's dogs showed parallel extinction of the cardiac CR and the avoidance response, including trial-by-trial correspondence. To further complicate matters, Black (1959) found more rapid extinction of the cardiac CR than of the instrumental response, and no relation between the rates of extinction for the cardiac CR and the avoidance response in individual Ss. Furthermore, Black (1958) found that extinction trials under curare facilitated extinction of the avoidance response without affecting that of the heart-rate CR.

It is clear that the relation between cardiac changes and avoidance behavior is not well understood. The sharp disagreements in findings suggest that the relation, if any really exists, is easily disturbed by yet unidentified variables. Most likely we have been naïve in selecting a single aspect of cardiovascular change as an index of conditioned "emotionality." The cardiovascular system is a highly complex one with many self-regulatory mechanisms. To expect simple heart-rate changes, which are only a small portion of this system, to mirror adequately a state such as "fear" is to oversimplify hopelessly the operation of the cardiovascular system. When we apply stress to an organism, we affect not only the heart rate but also a number of other aspects of the circulatory system, such as blood pressure, peripheral vessel resistance, stroke volume, etc. Many of these have intricate interrelations such that they can compensate for and change the action of each other within a fraction of a second. It is clear that we cannot look at only heart rate in isolation, but must examine the entire cardiovascular system if we hope to establish a fruitful peripheral index of a motivational state.

2. *Conditioned suppression.* If a stimulus associated with the onset of shock is sounded while a hungry rat is pressing a bar

to obtain food, it produces a marked decrement in bar-pressing. This is usually interpreted to mean that the stimulus has produced a CER which is incompatible with bar-pressing. This CER is not specified precisely, but is usually thought to be due to a pattern of Pavlovian CRs, identical to the conditioned fear reaction postulated by two-process theories of avoidance learning. Thus, the degree of conditioned suppression, like changes in the heart rate, can be used to assess the amount of fear elicited by the S^d from a signaled avoidance situation.

The suppression measure is not entirely unrelated to conditioned heart-rate changes. Stebbins and Smith (1964) found a positive relation between the occurrence of CER suppression and heart-rate acceleration in monkeys. But, more recently, deToledo and Black (1966) have found slower acquisition for cardiac CRs than for CER suppression in a simple Pavlovian conditioning situation.

Hoffman and Fleshler (1962) attempted concurrent measurement of avoidance behavior and conditioned suppression. While rats pedal-pushed for food, an avoidance S^d was sounded, during which they had to press a nearby bar to avoid shock. Suppression of pedal-pushing during the avoidance S^d was greater on successful avoidance trials, in agreement with two-process predictions. However, only with further training was conditioned suppression less following the avoidance response than it was during the S^d. Fear reduction, as indexed by conditioned suppression, did not seem to be the reinforcement for early avoidance responses.

Kamin, Brimer, and Black (1963) used a procedure similar to that of Hoffman and Fleshler. However, they separated the avoidance training and conditioned suppression situations. After training rats to various criteria of avoidance acquisition and extinction, Kamin et al. imposed the avoidance S^d upon food-motivated bar-pressing. They found that as extinction of the avoidance response proceeded, conditioned suppression was reduced. However, during avoidance acquisition, conditioned suppression produced by the avoidance S^d first increased and then decreased as avoidance training proceeded. If a conditioned fear reaction indexed by conditioned suppression was maintaining the avoidance behavior, this later result is difficult to understand. It is not entirely consistent with that of Hoffman and Fleshler who found continued conditioned suppression with long-term avoidance behavior. It may be that the suppression found by Hoffman and Fleshler resulted from the incompatibility of the avoidance response with the appetitive bar-press, rather than from some conditioned emotional state.

Like heart-rate changes, conditioned suppression does not reflect a mediating fear reaction in a manner completely consistent with two-process theories. However, there are two alternative interpretations of the CER experiments which might make the results compatible with a two-process description of avoidance learning. First, it may be that the role of the fear reaction in maintaining avoidance behavior is different from its role in the establishment and extinction of avoidance behavior. Thus the failure of a CS for a well-learned avoidance response to produce conditioned suppression may indicate that the CS is not producing fear in the avoidance situation and that the traditional two-process account of avoidance learning does not apply to maintained avoidance behavior. A second possibility is that the CER experiment is not an adequate index of the conditioned fear reaction. After all, there does not exist a closely reasoned account of the fact that the CER procedure produces *suppression* of the appetitively maintained operant. Why should we not instead find rate increases?

3. Physiological manipulations. Another method can be used to examine the interrelations between Pavlovian CRs and instrumental responses. If we suspect that a specific set of CRs is mediating instrumental behavior, we can simply eliminate those CRs and observe the effects upon the instrumental behavior. Solomon and his co-workers have pursued this line of research for various classes of CRs.

Using sympathectomized dogs, Wynne and Solomon (1955) have demonstrated that although removal of *peripheral autonomic CRs* impairs avoidance learning, it does not prevent it; nor does such removal facilitate extinction of avoidance. Sympathectomy after avoidance learning does not impair performance in dogs. Presumably, sympathectomy combined with vagal blocking as used by Wynne and Solomon eliminates cardiac and blood-pressure changes. Following the same strategy, Auld (1951) used tetraethylammonium (TEA) to block sympathetic autonomic nervous system (ANS) reactions, and found results perfectly paralleling those of Wynne and Solomon. There followed a long series of experiments, too numerous to describe here, in which barbiturates, autonomic blocking agents, stimulants, and tranquilizers were used to study the relationship between autonomic CRs and avoidance behavior. They did not importantly affect the conclusion that autonomic CRs are not necessary mediators of avoidance behavior.

Similarly, the transfer of Pavlovian fear conditioning from the curarized to the normal state, demonstrated by Solomon and Turner (1962) shows that *peripheral skeletal* CRs are not required for avoidance behavior. (These experiments are described in detail in the next section.) Both the sympathectomy and the curarization preparations eliminate broad classes of peripheral CRs as necessary mediators of avoidance behavior.

In summary, we have not yet identified any peripheral CRs which are necessary to mediate avoidance behavior. From this review of both aversively and appetitively motivated behavior, the simple idea that some peripherally observed CR is essential in the mediation of operant behavior seems implausible. In no case that we have studied does a peripheral CR seem to bear the required strong relation to the instrumental behavior. However, the two alternative views of the mediational process, (a) that a complex of autonomic and skeletal CRs is the mediator, and (b) that the peripheral CRs are simply indexes of central events, still seem to be reasonable. Both views permit some slippage between instrumental behavior and CRs. That we are not measuring complex enough peripheral behavior is difficult to refute; on the other hand, it is a relatively unattractive position because it suggests little that is new by way of experimentation except the recording of a larger number of CR measures.

However, consider a third view, (c), that what concomitance we do observe between instrumental behavior and peripheral CRs is due to mediation by a common central state. Then the concurrent measurement of instrumental behavior and Pavlovian CRs is not the optimal experimental strategy. Indeed, it becomes an irrelevant strategy.

Accepting the third view, then to find that a particular CR

does not control operant behavior is hardly a refutation of a general two-process approach; indeed, it would be surprising if we should be able to select from the complex instrumental situation the few controlling CRs. Rather, the *essential postulate of two-process theory will then be that manipulation of Pavlovian conditioning procedures should have important effects upon instrumental behavior.* Although we may not be able to identify the precise Pavlovian CRs which affect instrumental behavior, we can demonstrate that Pavlovian conditioning procedures exert strong influences over instrumental behavior in the absence of changes in instrumental contingencies. Such studies are reviewed in the next section.

MANIPULATION OF INSTRUMENTAL BEHAVIOR BY SEPARATELY CONDUCTED PAVLOVIAN CONDITIONING PROCEDURES

It is one matter to lift Pavlovian *concepts* out of Pavlovian theory and experiments, as Hull and Spence did, and use them to explain instrumental behavior. It is quite another matter to employ the *procedures* of Pavlovian conditioning in order to influence already established, or to-be-established, instrumental behavior. The latter strategy is generated by two-process theory, because it assumes that Pavlovian conditioning and instrumental learning are two distinct processes, each governed by its own appropriate sets of operations and laws, and it is typified by the experiment of Solomon and Turner (1962). They avoidance-trained dogs in a panel-pressing apparatus with a visual S^d. The dogs were then completely paralyzed by d-tubocurarine, and were subjected to purely Pavlovian, discriminative conditioning procedures, with tone CSs and a shock US. When Ss were later tested in the panel-pressing apparatus, they retained their avoidance response to the visual S^d. In addition, they showed reliable panel-pressing responses to the tone paired with shock (CS+) during Pavlovian conditioning, but these responses were weak or absent when the tone not paired with shock (CS−) was presented. Thus, the postulated two processes were seen to interact in a particular way, such that the instrumental panel-pressing was immediately elicited by the introduction of a Pavlovian CS+, even though

S had never before pressed a panel in the presence of CS+. This experiment can be analyzed in terms of two propositions of two-process learning theory: (a) Pavlovian association processes precede the acquisition of emotional reactions to previously neutral stimuli; and (b) these emotional reactions have motivational properties that can influence instrumental responding. It follows that *any empirical or theoretical law of Pavlovian conditioning has profound implications for the control of instrumental responding* when the two processes are interactively combined by E's procedures.

What are some of these Pavlovian laws (see Pavlov, 1927), and how would they be expected to reveal their impact?

1. The Law of Excitation. A CS consistently paired with a US acquires excitatory properties. Previously neutral stimuli, originally unable to elicit salivary responses in the dog, come to do so after several temporal pairings with meat powder on the tongue (the US for salivation). Irradiation of excitation should occur, and so stimuli similar to the CS should elicit the CR.

2. The Law of Internal Inhibition. (a) *Differential inhibition.* If a CS+ is consistently paired with a US on one-half of the conditioning trials, and a CS− is consistently presented unpaired with the US on the other half of the conditioning trials, the last phases of the conditioning show "differentiation"; that is, S gives a reliable CR to each CS+ presentation but not to CS−. Differential inhibition is postulated to *suppress actively* the CR in the presence of CS−. Salivation is not merely failing to occur in response to CS−; it is being suppressed. That CS− actually has inhibitory powers can be demonstrated by presenting it along with an effective CS+. When we do this, a CR that normally would have a specific magnitude will occur in markedly reduced magnitude. (b) *Conditioned inhibition.* If a compound CS is used as CS−, and one segment of the compound CS is used as the CS+, we meet the conditions for producing a conditioned inhibitor. For example, on half of the conditioning trials we present CS_1, paired with the US, and on the other half of the trials we present CS_2 and CS_1 in sequence, unpaired with the US. Then, eventually, good CRs will emerge in the presence of CS_1, and no CRs in the presence of CS_2–CS_1 sequence. We can test the properties of CS_1 and CS_2 by presenting each one in a

test trial together with some effective CS+. CS_1 with CS+ will lead to an enhanced CR, but CS_2 with CS+ will lead to a diminished CR. Therefore, CS_2 is a conditioned inhibitor. It has acquired the property of *actively suppressing* a CR that would have occurred in greater magnitude; it is no longer neutral. (c) *Inhibition by temporal delay.* We carry out the conditioning of the salivary reflex under a procedure that delays the onset of the US long after the CS+ has begun. For example, a tone comes on and remains on for 30 seconds before the meat powder is delivered to the dog's tongue. When this conditioning technique is used, the excitatory CR at the end of many conditioning trials has a long latency, "crowding" the end of the CS–US interval. Pavlov supposed that the CR was actively inhibited during the early moments of presentation of CS+ and that this inhibition dissipated in time, allowing the excitatory influence of CS+ to appear. The CR is thus temporarily paced by an inhibition process. A similar phenomenon occurs if a trace conditioning procedure is used with a long CS–US interval. (d) *Extinctive inhibition.* If a dog is given 50 conditioning trials with CS+ always paired with the US, and then the CS+ is presented unpaired with the US for several hundred trials, the CR, previously measurable after 50 trials, will disappear. This extinction procedure, according to Pavlov, does not merely reduce the excitatory power of CS+ but rather builds up its inhibitory power. Thus, if CS+ is presented along with another CS+ which normally elicits a CR, the CR should be diminished in magnitude. The extinguished CS+ is then labeled an extinctive inhibitor, with power to suppress CRs. (e) *Induction.* During the course of establishing a differential CR, when CS+ clearly produces a CR of greater magnitude than does CS−, a few CS− trials will often produce an enhanced CR on the next CS+ trial. This phenomenon is called positive induction. Conversely, a few CS+ trials are thought to produce a diminished CR on the next CS− trial. This is called negative induction.

3. The Law of External Inhibition. Novel or distracting stimuli, whether weak or unusually intense, can temporarily diminish the magnitude of a CR. Thus, when an effective CS+ is presented, the occurrence of a loud noise will diminish the CR magnitude. Conversely, novel, distracting, or unusually intense

stimuli can destroy temporarily the inhibitory power of a CS–. Any inhibitory process is thought to be susceptible to disruption by an external inhibitor. This is called *disinhibition*. Repeated presentation of an external inhibitor diminishes its inhibitory and disinhibitory power.

We have reviewed in some detail a few of the major laws of Pavlovian conditioning. What does two-process theory do with such laws? First, it assumes that these laws of Pavlovian conditioning of the salivary reflex are probably *the laws of emotional conditioning or laws of acquired drive states*. Second, it assumes that conditioned emotional states change S's motivation level and thus *can serve either as motivators or reinforcers* of instrumental responses.

Table 1 provides a convenient summary of the variety of ways in which Pavlovian conditioned emotional states can interact with instrumental learning to produce changes in instrumental responding.

TABLE 1
Combinations of Separately Conducted Pavlovian Procedures and Instrumental Training Procedures

Pavlovian conditioning		Instrumental training			
		Appetitive		Aversive	
		no S^d	S^d–S^Δ	no S^d	S^d–S^Δ
Appetitive (alimentary)	CS+	1 ↑	5 ↑	9	13
	CS–	2 ↓	6 ↓	10	14
Aversive (defensive)	CS+	3 ↓	7	11 ↑	15 ↑
	CS–	4 ↑	8	12 ↓	16 ?

Note.— ↑ and ↓ refer to the effect of the conditioning-training combination on amount of instrumental response.

Note that Table 1 accomplishes three purposes. First, it allows us to classify and organize the existing knowledge about interactions between the two hypothetical processes. Second, it dramatizes the absence of certain kinds of knowledge, thus pointing to new experiments which need to be done. And third, it raises new and interesting theoretical questions concerning the outcomes of the experiments in the table.

The Solomon and Turner (1962) experiment, which we have already described, can be located in Table 1 in the following manner. In this experiment, the US for fear conditioning was aversive (shock) as was the reinforcer for avoidance behavior. In addition, the Pavlovian conditioning was discriminative, and the Ss were tested with independent presentations of CS+ and CS−. The instrumental training was discriminative, since Ss learned to respond by panel-pressing in the presence of S^d. This allows us to insert the results of the Solomon and Turner experiment in Cells 15 and 16. We arbitrarily use a ($\uparrow$) sign in Cell 15 to indicate that the Pavlovian CS+ produced an enhancement of *instrumental* responding. CS−, on the other hand, had little or no effect, and so we have inserted a (?) in Cell 16.

The traditional CER experiment falls into Cell 3. The S is trained to perform some instrumental response reinforced by some appetitive stimulus. Pavlovian conditioning is carried out with an aversive US. The S is tested with presentations of CS+ while performing the instrumental response. The usual finding is that the response rate is suppressed by CS+, and so Cell 3 contains a ($\downarrow$).

Now we can examine the laws of Pavlovian conditioning as they are reflected in the interactions contained in Table 1. In all cases, the dependent variable is some measure of instrumental responding. Yet the independent variables, the influence of which is being tested, are those contained in the Pavlovian conditioning experiment.

EXCITATION AND INHIBITION

1. Differential Excitation and Inhibition.

Rescorla and LoLordo (1965) gave dogs discriminative conditioning with an aversive US (shock). A Pavlovian law predicts that the stimulus not paired with shock (CS−) will become a differential inhibitor—that is, it will have the capacity to suppress actively *whatever emotional reflex pattern is usually elicited by CS+*. Thus, CS− should be able to inhibit "fear of shock." Prior to discriminative fear conditioning, the dogs had been trained so that they reliably responded on a Sidman avoidance schedule at a rate of seven jumps per minute in a dog shuttlebox. While Ss were jumping, short presentations of CS+ and CS− were given in some random sequence.

Two-process theory leads to the following expectations. If CS+ is a Pavlovian excitor, then conditioned fear should be augmented by its presence, and the instrumental responding rate should increase above the normal rate. In contrast, if CS− is a Pavlovian differential inhibitor, then it should actively suppress conditioned fear and the instrumental responding rate should decrease below the normal rate.

Rescorla and LoLordo (1965) found that the presentation of the CS+ resulted in a doubling of the Sidman jumping rate, but the presentation of the CS− resulted in a large reduction in the Sidman jumping rate. It seems clear that CS− had acquired inhibitory properties. The Rescorla and LoLordo experiment can be inserted in Cells 11 and 12 in Table 1. They represent the intersection of aversive, discriminative Pavlovian conditioning preceded by unsignalized (Sidman) aversive training, with no S^d.

Another example of differential Pavlovian conditioning combined with instrumental training is the experiment by Ray and Stein (1959) who trained hungry rats to bar-press for milk on a VI–2 schedule. Then, when the rats attained a steady response rate, an 1800 cps tone was presented for 5 minutes and it terminated with shock to the feet. A contrasting 200 cps tone was presented at other times, but it terminated without shock. Eventually, the 1800 cps tone acquired the capacity to suppress bar-pressing completely. In contrast, presentation of the 200 cps tone (CS−) often produced increases in the bar-pressing rate *above* the normal base-line rate, though this difference was not a large one (see Cells 3 and 4, Table 1).

Hoffman and Fleshler (1964) have carried out a series of experiments similar to that of Ray and Stein. In general, their findings paralleled those of Ray and Stein with regard to the CER suppression effect of CS+ presentations. However, unlike Ray and Stein they did not find the enhancement of instrumental responding in the presence of CS−. Hammond (1966) repeated and extended the results of Ray and Stein. He further showed that enhancement of bar-pressing rate by presentation of CS− occurred only when the base-line responding rate was below normal.

These interesting findings raise the *possibility* that a Pavlovian differential inhibitor established by *aversive* conditioning can enhance instrumental responding established by an *appetitive* reinforcer. But what could the finding, that an inhibitor of fear enhances appetitively maintained behavior, mean? One possibility is that reflex interrelations exist between appetitively and aversively based incentive states. The occurrence of an elicitor or inhibitor of a fear state may reflexly depress or enhance positive incentive motivation. On the other hand, it may be that an inhibitor of fear has no effect upon an appetitive motivation state. Instead, there may be a general level of fear produced by the experimental situation; since such fear presumably reduces the response rate, an inhibitor of that fear would lead to a rate enhancement. The Hammond experiment strongly supports such an interpretation. These findings are of considerable importance to a theory of incentive motivation.

So far, we have concerned ourselves with aversive Pavlovian conditioning, and have traced the effects of CS+ and CS−, in their roles as differential excitors and inhibitors, on both aversive and appetitive instrumental responding. There is, in addition, a series of experiments in which *appetitive,* discriminative conditioning procedures are combined with appetitive instrumental training procedures. These experiments come out of the Skinnerian tradition. A prototype experiment is that of Estes (1948), and it was probably the first of its kind to be successful in showing that a CS+, previously paired with food presentations, could enhance, during extinction, the rate of an operant previously reinforced by food presentations. As is the case in all of the experiments subsequently using the Estes paradigm, CS+ presentations are in reality being paired not only with food presentations, but also with magazine approach responses. This is inevitable, because the conditioning procedure in these experiments is done through magazine training. In order to get the food, Ss must make instrumental responses. Even though this procedure is not "pure" Pavlovian conditioning, it resembles it to the extent that the approach response cannot produce the food US; only the CS+ can produce it. Neither can the approach response produce the CS+. (The procedure can be described in Skinnerian terminology as a "discriminated operant.")

Morse and Skinner (1958) trained pigeons to approach a magazine for food in the presence of one color (CS+), but the food never was presented in the presence of a contrasting color

(CS−). The behavior of S was irrelevant for the occurrence of magazine operation. Then, in the second stage of the experiment, Ss learned to peck at a white key for food. Finally, extinction was instituted, during which there were test periods in which CS+ and CS− were alternately presented. The pecking rate was higher in the presence of CS+ than it was when CS− was present. There was, however, no control for normal extinction in white light alone, so we cannot tell whether CS− was inhibitory, or the CS+ excitatory, or both. We know CS+ showed differential excitatory properties when compared to CS−, and this confirms Estes' (1948) findings, but it leaves in doubt the proper sign to put in Cells 1 and 2 of Table 1. It is our guess that Cell 1 should contain a (↑) sign, and Cell 2 a (↓) sign, but in the absence of the proper controls we cannot be sure. A recent experiment by Bower and Kaufman (1963) confirms the finding by Morse and Skinner of a difference between the effects of CS+ and CS−.

Most of the earlier experiments showing the differential excitatory and inhibitory effects of CS+ and CS− on instrumental responding have used *extinction* responding as a base line. Recently, however, there have been several experiments exploring the effects of differential Pavlovian conditioning procedures on subsequent *learning* of discriminative instrumental responses. For example, Bower and Grusec (1964) used thirsty rats, conditioning them by having tone S_1 paired with water reinforcements and tone S_2 occurring without water reinforcements. The rats had previously been trained to press a lever to get water, but this early training was not discriminative (no S^d). Then, in a third stage of the experiment, the rats were given discriminative instrumental training. One group was trained with its CS+ from the conditioning phase now the S^d for the operant, and its CS− as S^Δ, while in contrast, another group had its CS+ from the conditioning phase now the S^Δ for the operant and its CS− as S^d. Thus, in one group the CS/S^d relationship was consistent, but in the other group the CS/S^d relationship was inconsistent. Bower and Grusec found that the acquisition of the S^d–S^Δ discrimination was enhanced for the consistent group but was interfered with in the inconsistent group. There was, however, no way of ascertaining whether or not CS− had true differential inhibitory properties because there was no control group that learned the S^d–S^Δ discrimination without prior conditioning with CS+ and CS−.

We can speculate, however, that learning was interfered with whenever CS− inhibited conditioned appetitive reactions in the presence of S^d, and learning was facilitated whenever CS+ facilitated excitatory appetitive reactions in the presence of S^d.

More recently, Trapold (1966) has shown that inconsistent differential conditioning can actually facilitate reversal learning of a discriminative instrumental response. Rats were first trained, in an operant discrimination, to press a lever for food in the presence of S_1 but to refrain from pressing in the presence of S_2. Then the lever was removed, and S_2 was paired with food presentation while S_1 was paired with absence of food. Later, when the rats were presented again with the lever, they were required to reverse the original operant discrimination and press in the presence of S_2. They learned this reversal more rapidly than a group that had not received pairings of S_2 with food presentation. Thus, Pavlovian contingencies were powerful enough to assist the instrumental discrimination reversal.

2. Conditioned Inhibition.

Rescorla and LoLordo (1965) trained dogs in our laboratory on a Sidman avoidance contingency in the shuttlebox, until the dogs performed the avoidance response at a stable rate. Then they subjected some of the dogs to a Pavlovian fear conditioning procedure in which CS+ was followed 2–8 seconds later by shock on one-half of the trials, but on the other half of the trials CS+ was followed 2–8 seconds later by CS− and no shock. Other dogs, after learning the Sidman avoidance response, were subjected to a Pavlovian fear conditioning procedure in which CS+ was followed by shock on one-half of the trials, but on the other half of the trials CS− was inserted 5 seconds prior to CS+ and no shock followed. CS− in both procedures was shown to have inhibitory properties. Test presentations of CS− reduced the Sidman avoidance response rate significantly. Rescorla and LoLordo infer that conditioned fear was inhibited by their CS−. In contrast, fear was aroused by CS+.

3. Inhibition by Temporal Delay.

Rescorla (1967a) trained dogs in our laboratory in a Sidman avoidance response in the dog shuttlebox. When the dogs had acquired a stable jumping rate, they were subjected to a Pavlovian fear conditioning procedure in which only a long-delay CS+ was used. A 30-second tone was followed by shock on all conditioning trials. Then later, when the dogs were performing their avoidance response in the shuttlebox, the 30-second tone was presented from time to time. Rescorla found that the *onset* of the tone produced a *decrease* in jumping rate, and the rate thereafter increased until, at about 20-second duration, the jumping rate went above normal, increasing steadily to the end of the interval. Cessation of the tone produced a decrease in jumping rate to a below-base-line level, followed by slow recovery to the base-line rate. Here is a case where onset of a "danger signal" resulted in a temporary *decrease* of avoidance responding. This is what one would expect from Pavlovian experiments on long duration CSs. CS onset is never closely paired with shock, and so it serves as a CS−, an inhibitor of conditioned reflexes. In the Rescorla experiment, we can infer that CS+ onset inhibited fear.

Recently, Trapold, Carlson, and Myers (1965) have shown how Pavlovian inhibition by temporal delay can operate in an appetitive situation. They conditioned rats with either fixed or variable temporal delay intervals between food US presentations, in the absence of any CS (temporal conditioning). Then they gave the rats FI training with food reward in a bar-press situation. They found that when the temporal interval between US presentations previously used in Pavlovian conditioning was the same as that used in the subsequent FI training, the development of a sharp FI "scallop" was facilitated. Evidently the delivery of a US can serve as a stimulus which temporarily inhibits an appetitive state that mediates bar-pressing for food. The temporal pacing of instumental behavior, as in FI contingencies, can be "sharpened" by Pavlovian conditioning treatments of the proper sort. This is evidence quite compatible with that of Pavlovian experiments.

4. Induction.

Not much is known about the operation of the Pavlovian induction phenomenon as it influences instrumental responding. Rescorla (1967a) and Rescorla and LoLordo (1965) found that termination of an aversive CS+ during instrumental avoidance responding reduced the response rate for a few seconds. This, however, is not the only way of showing induction. One might explore the increase in jumping rate produced by a CS+ presentation that followed a CS− presentation, as compared with one that followed another CS+ presentation, in order to measure positive induction. This has not been done. Neither has negative induction been studied in such a way. In order to do this, one would compare responding to CS− when it has recently been preceded by a CS+ presentation, as compared with being preceded by a CS− presentation.

5. External Inhibition and Disinhibition.

The effects of extraneous stimuli upon CSs imposed on ongoing instrumental behavior have been little studied. It would be of interest to see whether a novel stimulus could disrupt the effect which a CS+ has upon instrumental behavior (external inhibition). Likewise, we would like to know whether we can remove the inhibitory effect which a CS− has upon instrumental behavior by presentation of a novel stimulus (disinhibition). Preliminary experimentation with dogs (Rescorla, 1967a) suggests that disinhibition of inhibition of temporal delay can be produced with fear conditioning; however, no evidence was found for external inhibition.

We have covered many of the experiments showing how Pavlovian procedures, interacting with Thorndikian (or Skinnerian) procedures, can influence instrumental responding. In doing so, it became clear that many of the cells in Table 1 are empty. Some of the empty cells are as interesting as the filled ones. For example, take Cell 9. This cell would require the testing of the effect of an appetitive CS+ on unsignaled avoidance responding. What would happen? Would the "irrelevancy" of the fear that mediates avoidance to the appetitive CRs elicited by CS+ mean that avoidance rate would be unaffected by CS+? Or is there a matrix of interrelationships among emotional-motivational states that requires that appetitive CRs interfere with or inhibit *all* aversive states to some extent? Perhaps, instead, the Spence (1956) view of "generalized D" would be correct, and *any* excitatory CS+ would enhance *any* response mediated by *any* excitatory state in the presence of S^d. CER experimentation (see Cell 3) would argue against this expectation, but perhaps it is too early to be certain. Certainly, much work is needed in this area of ignorance.

Another interesting cell is No. 10. Suppose a dog has acquired a stable Sidman avoidance response in the shuttlebox. He is then given test presentations with a CS− previously established in an *appetitive* Pavlovian conditioning procedure. What might be expected to happen? Would CS− be "irrelevant" for fear level, and therefore leave jumping rate unaffected? Or would CS−, being a signal for the nonoccurrence of an appetitive US, be "disturbing" in some way, thus "adding to" fear level and increasing the avoidance response rate? Is there a dimension of "pessimism" established in the emotional life of laboratory animals, such that a signal that says "food won't come," although it may superficially seem irrelevant for fear motivated avoidance responding, nevertheless is a "bad" event, just as shock is also a "bad" event? Amsel (1965) and Brown and Wagner (1964) have recently shown the generality of a "perseverance" attribute for laboratory Ss given special types of partial reinforcement experiences. Perhaps "pessimism" can be similarly established by appropriate Pavlovian and Thorndikian treatments, such that *all* CS−'s for *appetitive* differential conditioning, and all CS+'s for *aversive* differential conditioning, can enhance *all* instrumental responses reinforced by the avoidance of *aversive* USs of *any* type. It certainly would be valuable to know how these interactions work. The techniques for getting this information have already been worked out.[4]

There are other cells in Table 1 that command attention, but the reader can now generate his own experiments to fill them. We should note, however, that Table 1 does not exhaust the possibilities for analysis of interactions between Pavlovian and Thorndikian processes. The Pavlovian conditioning procedures can either precede, or be preceded by, the instrumental training procedures (thus focusing attention on order effects in the interaction of the two processes). Or the Pavlovian conditioning procedures can be carried out either within the situation used for instrumental training or in another situation as distinctively different as possible from the instrumental training situation. This variation focuses attention upon situational stimuli as a factor in the interaction of the two processes. Intrasituational Pavlovian conditioning can, in turn, either be carried out "on the base line," that is, while the instrumental behavior to be influenced is occurring; or, in contrast, it can be carried out "off the base line," that is, when instrumental responding is impossible.

Up to this point we have talked only of variations in the Pavlovian conditioning parameters. Another strategy is to vary the instrumental training parameters while holding the Pavlovian conditioning constant. For example, would Pavlovian conditioned stimuli based on a shock US have the same effect on an S during asymptotic, reinforced, operant performance as it would have during the first moments of extinction of that operant? Such a question has implications for any theory that argues for the importance of emotion in the control of instrumental responding, since presumably different emotions are present in training and extinction. It seems clear that systematic variations of both the Pavlovian and instrumental operations in Table 1 would be valuable in extending our understanding of the emotional control of instrumental behavior.

The many possible variations in procedure will complicate Table 1 and expand it to almost unmanageable proportions. Nevertheless, such variations must be kept in mind, because we already know that they are important. For example, the effects of the order of Pavlovian conditions and instrumental training are subtle and interesting. Overmier and Leaf (1965), working in our laboratory, found that the discriminative control of avoidance responding by a Pavlovian CS+ and CS− was poorer when the conditioning preceded avoidance training than when the reverse order was used. However, there is nothing in two-process theory that predicts an order effect. This result indicates that two-process theory is rapidly generating new data requiring further refinement and extension of such theory while not requiring the abandonment of the approach.

We can conclude that, following one strategy suggested by two-process theory, Pavlovian conditioning procedures can readily be used to control instrumental responding. Furthermore, it might very well turn out that instrumental responding is as sensitive, or perhaps even more sensitive, a measure of the effects of Pavlovian conditioning procedures than are the traditionally measured conditioned visceral or motor reflexes themselves. If this should turn out to be true, it would constitute a major heuristic, albeit somewhat ironic, contribution of two-process learning theory.

Finally, we point to the success achieved in controlling instrumental responding by means of a wide variety of Pavlovian procedures, contrasted with the failure to establish definitive relationships between CRs (as mediators) and concurrent instrumental responses. Such success gives support to the version of two-process theory postulating that the concomitance we do observe between CRs and instrumental responding is mediated by a common central state, and the changes in that state are subject to the laws of Pavlovian conditioning.

Notes

1. The research leading to this paper was supported by Grants MH-04202 from the United States Public Health Service and GB-2428 from the National Science Foundation.

   Parts of this paper were delivered in a Harold Schlosberg Memorial Symposium address, Eastern Psychological Association, Atlantic City, April 1965. This paper is dedicated to the memory of Harold Schlosberg.
2. National Science Foundation Predoctoral Fellow.
3. The authors would like to thank Otello L. Desiderato, Henry Gleitman, Francis W. Irwin, and Vincent M. LoLordo for their extensive comments on an earlier draft of this paper.
4. After the completion of this manuscript LoLordo (1966) showed that the summation of fear of two different aversive events is reflected in instrumental responding. He trained dogs to avoid shock by pressing a panel, with an unsignalized (Sidman) procedure. He then exposed the dogs to a Pavlovian conditioning experience during which the CS+ was paired with a loud blast from a horn and CS— was explicitly unpaired with the horn blast. Later, in a test session, 5-second presentations of CS+ and CS— were imposed on Sidman responding. The CS+ elicited an increase in the pressing rate, but the CS— did not produce an inhibitory effect on the pressing rate. Such a result indicates that the generalization of fear excitation as a mediator is probably quite great (from noise to shock), but perhaps the generalization of fear inhibition is not very great.

References

Amsel, A., & Ward, J. S. Frustration and persistence: Resistance to discrimination following prior experience with the discriminanda. *Psychological Monographs*, 1965, 79 (4, Whole No. 597).

Auld, F. The effects of tetraethylammonium on a habit motivated by fear. *Journal of Comparative and Physiological Psychology,* 1951, 44, 565–574.

Bersh, P. J., Notterman, J. M., & Schoenfeld, W. N. Extinction of a human cardiac-response during avoidance-conditioning. *American Journal of Psychology,* 1956, 59, 244–251.

Birch, H. G., & Bitterman, M. E. Reinforcement and learning: The process of sensory integration. *Psychological Review,* 1949, 56, 292–308.

Birk, L., Crider, A., Shapiro, D., & Tursky, B. Operant electrodermal conditioning under partial curarization. *Journal of Comparative and Physiological Psychology,* 1966, 62, 165–166.

Black, A. H. The extinction of avoidance responses under curare. *Journal of Comparative and Physiological Psychology,* 1958, 51, 519–525.

Black, A. H. Heart rate changes during avoidance learning in dogs. *Canadian Journal of Psychology,* 1959, 13, 229–242.

Bower, G., & Grusec, T. Effect of prior Pavlovian discrimination training upon learning an operant discrimination. *Journal of the Experimental Analysis of Behavior,* 1964, 7, 401–404.

Bower, G., & Kaufman, R. Transfer across drives of the discriminative effect of a Pavlovian conditioned stimulus. *Journal of the Experimental Analysis of Behavior,* 1963, 6, 445–448.

Brogden, W. J., & Gantt, W. H. Cerebellar conditioned reflexes. *American Journal of Physiology,* 1937, 119, 277–278.

Brogden, W. J., Lipman, E. A., & Culler, E. The role of incentive in conditioning and extinction. *American Journal of Psychology,* 1938, 51, 109–117.

Brown, R. T., & Wagner, A. R. Resistance to punishment and extinction following training with shock or nonreinforcement. *Journal of Experimental Psychology,* 1964, 68, 503–507.

Bykov, K. M. *The cerebral cortex and the internal organs.* (Trans. & ed. by W. H. Gantt) New York: Chemical Publishing Co., 1957.

Crider, A., Shapiro, D., & Tursky, B. Reinforcement of spontaneous electrodermal activity. *Journal of Comparative and Physiological Psychology,* 1966, 61, 20–27.

Crisler, G. Salivation is unnecessary for the establishment of the salivary conditioned reflex induced by morphine. *American Journal of Physiology,* 1930, 44, 553–556.

DeToledo, L., & Black, A. H. Heart-rate changes during conditioned suppression in rats. Paper read at Eastern Psychological Association, New York, April 1966.

Doty, R. W., & Giurgea, C. Conditioned reflexes established by coupling electrical excitation of two cortical areas. In J. Delafresnaye (Ed.), *Brain mechanisms and learning.* London: Blackwell Scientific Publications, 1961. Pp. 133–151.

Ellison, G. D., & Konorski, J. Separation of the salivary and motor responses in instrumental conditioning. *Science,* 1964, 146, 1071–1072.

Estes, W. K. Discriminative conditioning. II. Effects of a Pavlovian conditioned stimulus upon a subsequently established operant response. *Journal of Experimental Psychology,* 1948, 38, 173–177.

Finch, G. Salivary conditioning in atropinized dogs. *American Journal of Physiology,* 1938, 124, 136–141.

Fowler, R. L., & Kimmel, H. D. Operant conditioning of the GSR. *Journal of Experimental Psychology,* 1962, 63, 563–567.

Gantt, W. H., & Dykman, R. A. Experimental psychogenic tachycardia. In P. H. Hock & J. Zubin (Eds.), *Experimental psychopathology*. New York: Grune & Stratton, 1957.

Guthrie, E. R. *The psychology of learning*. New York: Harper, 1935.

Hammond, L. J. Increased responding to CS— in differential CER. *Psychonomic Science*, 1966, 5, 337–338.

Hilgard, E. R., & Marquis, D. G. *Conditioning and learning*. New York: Appleton-Century-Crofts, 1940.

Hoffman, H. S., & Fleshler, M. The course of emotionality in the development of avoidance. *Journal of Experimental Psychology*, 1962, 64, 288–294.

Hoffman, H. S., & Fleshler, M. Stimulus aspects of aversive controls: Stimulus generalization of conditioned suppression following discrimination training. *Journal of the Experimental Analysis of Behavior*, 1964, 7, 233–239.

Hull, C. L. *Principles of behavior*. New York: Appleton-Century-Crofts, 1943.

Hundt, A. G., & Premack, D. Running as both a positive and negative reinforcer. *Science*, 1963, 142, 1087–1088.

Kamin, L. J., Brimer, C. J., & Black, A. H. Conditioned suppression as a monitor of fear of the CS in the course of avoidance training. *Journal of Comparative and Physiological Psychology*, 1963, 56, 497–501.

Kiernan, C. C. Positive reinforcement by light. *Psychological Bulletin*, 1964, 62, 551–557.

Kimble, G. A. *Hilgard and Marquis' conditioning and learning*. (2nd ed.) New York: Appleton-Century-Crofts, 1961.

Kimmel, E., & Kimmel, H. D. A replication of operant conditioning of the GSR. *Journal of Experimental Psychology*, 1963, 65, 212–213.

Kintsch, W., & Witte, R. S. Concurrent conditioning of bar press and salivation responses. *Journal of Comparative and Physiological Psychology*, 1962, 55, 963–968.

Konorski, J. *Conditioned reflexes and neuron organization*. New York: New Cambridge University Press, 1948.

Konorski, J., & Miller, S. Méthode d'examen de l'analysateur moteur par les réactions salivomatrices. *Compte Rendu Hebdomadaire des Séances et Mémoires de la Société de Biologie*, 1930, 104, 907–910.

Konorski, J., & Miller, S. Further remarks on two types of conditioned reflex. *Journal of Genetic Psychology*, 1937, 17, 405–407. (a)

Konorski, J., & Miller, S. On two types of conditioned reflex. *Journal of Genetic Psychology*, 1937, 16, 264–272. (b)

Konorski, J., & Szwejkowska, G. Reciprocal transformations of heterogeneous conditioned reflexes. *Acta Biologicae Experimentalis*, 1956, 18, 142–165.

LoLordo, V. M. Summation of fear of different aversive events. Unpublished doctoral dissertation, University of Pennsylvania, 1966.

Loucks, R. B. The experimental delimitation of neural structures essential for learning: The attempt to condition striped muscle responses to faradization of the signoid gyri. *Journal of Psychology*, 1935, 1, 5–44.

Maier, N. R. F., & Schneirla, T. C. Mechanisms in conditioning. *Psychological Review*, 1942, 49, 117–134.

Malmo, R. B. Classical and instrumental conditioning with septal stimulation as reinforcement. *Journal of Comparative and Physiological Psychology*, 1965, 60, 1–8.

McCleary, R. A. Type of response as a factor in interocular transfer in the fish. *Journal of Comparative and Physiological Psychology*, 1960, 53, 311–321.

Miller, N. E. An experimental investigation of acquired drives. *Psychological Bulletin*, 1941, 38, 534–535.

Miller, N. E. Studies of fear as an acquirable drive: I. Fear as motivation and fear reduction as reinforcement in the learning of new responses. *Journal of Experimental Psychology*, 1948, 38, 89–101.

Miller, N. E., & Carmona, A. Modification of visceral response, salivation in thirsty dogs, by instrumental training with water reward. *Journal of Comparative and Physiological Psychology*, 1967, 63, 1–6.

Miller, N. E., & DeBold, R. C. Classically conditioned tongue-licking and operant bar pressing recorded simultaneously in the rat. *Journal of Comparative and Physiological Psychology*, 1965, 59, 109–111.

Miller, N. E., & DiCara, L. Instrumental learning of heart-rate changes in curarized rats: Shaping and specificity to discriminative stimulus. *Journal of Comparative and Physiological Psychology*, 1967, 63, 12–19.

Miller, S., & Konorski, J. Sur une forme particuliere des reflexes conditionnels. *Compte Rendu Hebdomadaire des Séances et Mémoires de la Société de Biologie*, 1928, 99, 1151–1157.

Morse, W. E., & Skinner, B. F. Some factors involved in the stimulus control of operant behavior. *Journal of the Experimental Analysis of Behavior*, 1958, 1, 103–107.

Mowrer, O. H. Preparatory set (expectancy) —a determinant in motivation and learning. *Psychological Review*, 1938, 45, 62–91.

Mowrer, O. H. On the dual nature of learning—a re-interpretation of "conditioning" and "problem-solving." *Harvard Educational Review*, 1947, 17, 102–148.

Mowrer, O. H. *Learning theory and behavior*. New York: Wiley, 1960.

Mowrer, O. H., & Aiken, E. G. Contiguity vs. drive-reduction in conditioned fear: Temporal variations in conditioned and unconditioned stimulus. *American Journal of Psychology*, 1954, 67, 26–38.

Mowrer, O. H., & Solomon, L. N. Contiguity vs. drive-reduction in conditioned fear: The proximity and abruptness of drive-reduction. *American Journal of Psychology*, 1954, 67, 15–25.

Osgood, C. E. *Method and theory in experimental psychology*. Oxford University Press, 1953.

Overmier, J. B. Instrumental and cardiac indices of Pavlovian fear conditioning as a function of US duration. *Journal of Comparative and Physiological Psychology*, 1966, 62, 15–20.

Overmier, J. B., & Leaf, R. C. Effects of discriminative Pavlovian fear conditioning upon previously or subsequently acquired avoidance responding. *Journal of Comparative and Physiological Psychology*, 1965, 60, 213–217.

Pavlov, I. P. *Conditioned reflexes*. London: Oxford University Press, 1927.

Pavlov, I. P. The reply of a physiologist to psychologists. *Psychological Review*, 1932, 39, 91–127.

Ray, O. S., & Stein, L. Generalization of conditioned suppression. *Journal of the Experimental Analysis of Behavior*, 1959, 2, 357–361.

Razran, G. The observable unconscious and the inferable conscious in current Soviet psychophysiology: Interoceptive conditioning, semantic conditioning, and the orienting reflex. *Psychological Review*, 1961, 68, 81–147.

Rescorla, R. A. Inhibition of delay in Pavlovian fear conditioning. *Journal of Comparative and Physiological Psychology*, 1967, in press. (a)

Rescorla, R. A. Pavlovian conditioning and its proper control procedures. *Psychological Review*, 1967, 74, 71–80. (b)

Rescorla, R. A., & LoLordo, V. M. Inhibition of avoidance behavior. *Journal of Comparative and Physiological Psychology*, 1965, 59, 406–412.

Schlosberg, H. A study of the conditioned patellar reflex. *Journal of Experimental Psychology*, 1928, 11, 468–494.

Schlosberg, H. The relationship between success and the laws of conditioning. *Psychological Review*, 1937, 44, 379–394.

Shapiro, M. M. Salivary conditioning in dogs during fixed-interval reinforcement contingent upon lever pressing. *Journal of the Experimental Analysis of Behavior*, 1961, 4, 361–364.

Shapiro, M. M. Temporal relationship between salivation and lever pressing with differential reinforcement of low rates. *Journal of Comparative and Physiological Psychology*, 1962, 55, 567–571.

Shearn, D. W. Operant conditioning of heart rate. *Science*, 1962, 137, 530–531.

Sheffield, F. D. Relation between classical conditioning and instrumental learning. In W. F. Prokasy (Ed.), *Classical conditioning*. New York: Appleton-Century-Crofts, 1965. Pp 302–322.

Skinner, B. F. Two types of conditioned reflex and a pseudo type. *Journal of Genetic Psychology*, 1935, 12, 66–77.

Skinner, B. F. *The Behavior of organisms: An experimental analysis*. New York: Appleton-Century-Crofts, 1938.

Solomon, R. L., & Brush, E. S. Experimentally derived conceptions of anxiety and aversion. In M. R. Jones (Ed.), *Nebraska symposium on motivation: 1956*. Lincoln: University of Nebraska Press, 1956. Pp. 212–305.

Solomon, R. L., & Turner, L. H. Discriminative classical conditioning in dogs paralyzed by curare can later control discriminative avoidance responses in the normal state. *Psychological Review*, 1962, 69, 202–219.

Solomon, R. L., & Wynne, L. C. Traumatic avoidance learning: The principles of anxiety conservation and partial irreversibility, *Psychological Review*, 1954, 61, 353–385.

Soltysik, S. Inhibitory feedback in avoidance conditioning. *Boletin del Instituto de Estudios Médicos y Biológicos, Universidad Nacional de Mexico*, 1963, 21, 433.

Soltysik, S. Studies on the avoidance conditioning: II. Differentiation and extinction of avoidance reflexes. *Acta Biologiae Experimentalis*, 1960, 20, 171–182.

Spence, K. W. *Behavior theory and conditioning*. New Haven: Yale University Press, 1956.

Stebbins, W. C., & Smith, O. A. Cardiovascular concomitants of the conditioned emotional response in the monkey. *Science*, 1964, 144, 881–882.

Thorndike, E. L. *The fundamentals of learning*. New York: Columbia University, 1932.

Tolman, E. C. *Purposive behavior in animals and men*. New York: Appleton-Century, 1932.

Tolman, E. C. There is more than one kind of learning. *Psychological Review*, 1949, 56, 144–155.

Trapold, M. A. Reversal of an operant discrimination by non-contingent discrimination reversal training. *Psychonomic Science*, 1966, 4, 247–248.

Trapold, M. A., Carlson, J. G., & Myers, W. A. The effect of non-contingent fixed- and variable-interval reinforcement upon subsequent acquisition of the fixed-interval scallop. *Psychonomic Science*, 1965, 2, 261–262.

Trowill, J. A. Instrumental conditioning of the heart rate in the curarized rat. *Journal of Comparative and Physiological Psychology*, 1967, 63, 7–11.

Turner, L. H., & Solomon, R. L. Human traumatic avoidance learning: Theory and experiments on the operant-respondent distinction and failures to learn. *Psychological Monographs*, 1962, 76 (40, Whole No. 559).

Tuttle, H. S. Two kinds of learning. *Journal of Psychology*, 1946, 22, 267–277.

Wagner, A. R. Instrumental-motivational processes in the classical conditioning of skeletal behavior. Paper read at the XVIII International Congress of Psychology, Moscow, August 1966.

Wenzel, B. M. Changes in heart rate associated with responses based on positive and negative reinforcement. *Journal of Comparative and Physiological Psychology*, 1961, 54, 638–644.

Williams, D. R. Classical conditioning and incentive motivation. In W. F. Prokasy (Ed.), *Classical conditioning*. New York: Appleton-Century-Crofts, 1965. Pp. 340–357.

Wolf, K. Properties of multiple conditioned reflex type II activity. *Acta Biologiae Experimentalis*, 1963, 23, 133–150.

Wynne, L. C., & Solomon, R. L. Traumatic avoidance learning: Acquisition and extinction in dogs deprived of normal peripheral autonomic function. *Genetic and Psychological Monographs*, 1955, 52, 241–284.

Anxiety (Drive) Level and Performance in Eyelid Conditioning[1]

KENNETH W. SPENCE, *University of Iowa*

Studies from the Iowa laboratory and elsewhere that have involved a comparison of the eyelid conditioning performance of *S*s scoring at the extremes of the Taylor Manifest Anxiety (MA) scale are reviewed. In 21 of 25 independent comparisons, differences between groups were in favor of the high anxiety (HA) *S*s, with the majority being statistically significant. Although these data provide substantial confirmation of the implication of the drive interpretation of MA scale that HA *S*s should exhibit a higher level of performance than LA *S*s, an attempt was made to ascertain what factors might be responsible for failure of the difference to occur in some studies. The major factors appeared to be small numbers of *S*s and the presence of "voluntary form" responders in the samples. Significant differences appear to be related to the degree of experimental naiveté of the *S*s and the extent to which the experimental situation is designed to arouse some degree of apprehensiveness.

Recently King, Kimble, Gorman, and King (1961) reported failure to find a significant relation between level of emotionality as measured by the Taylor Manifest Anxiety (*MA*) scale and performance in aversive (eyelid) conditioning. In the light of the previous evidence, this finding was rather surprising and the

Spence, K. W. Anxiety (drive) level and performance in eyelid conditioning. *Psychological Bulletin*. 1964, *61*, 129–139. Copyright 1964 by the American Psychological Association, and reproduced by permission.

authors were able to conclude only that emotionality or anxiety must be an interacting variable that is related to conditioning under certain as yet unknown conditions and not under others. The purpose of the present article is (a) to review the data bearing on the relation between the MA scale and aversive conditioning, only a small fraction of which was cited by King et al., and (b) to examine this evidence in detail in an attempt to suggest what the factors are that might be responsible for the failure of the relationship to appear in some studies.

In presenting these data, the results of studies comparing performance in simple conditioning of Ss preselected on the basis of extreme MA scale scores will first be summarized. The second group of studies to be reviewed also involves comparison of the performance of preselected Ss but in differential conditioning. Thirdly, the results of a number of previously unpublished comparisons based on simple conditioning data from studies conducted in the Iowa laboratory for other purposes will be presented. The Ss serving in these latter studies were unselected with respect to the MA scale. Since their scores on the test were available, it was possible to determine the differences in the conditioning performance between Ss who scored at the extremes of the scale.

STUDIES INVOLVING PRESELECTED
EXTREME GROUPS

Simple Conditioning.

The findings of the previously published Iowa studies and one unpublished study directly concerned with comparing the conditioning performance of preselected high and low anxiety (HA and LA) Ss are summarized in Table 1. The criteria of selection of Ss in these studies varied slightly, ranging from raw scores of 20 to 24 as the lower limit of the HA Ss and from 7 to 9 as the upper limit of the LA Ss. These scores roughly mark the upper and lower twentieth to twenty-fifth percentiles of the distribution of MA scale scores made by students in the introductory course in psychology at Iowa. Shown in the successive columns of the table are: (a) the reference studies, (b) the number of trials over which the conditioning measures were obtained, (c)

TABLE 1

Iowa Studies of Conditioning Performance of Preselected HA and LA Scale Ss

Iowa experiments	No. trials	Ready signal	UCS (psi)	No. Ss	Percent CR		Difference (H-L)	p
					HA	LA		
1. Taylor (1951)	80	Yes	1.6	60	59.6	27.9	21.7	.001
2. Spence-Taylor (1951)	100	Yes	.6	50	48.2	33.8	14.4	.05[a]
	100	Yes	2.0	50	55.0	41.7	13.3	.05
3. Spence-Farber (1953)	60	Yes	1.0	64	48.8	34.1	14.7	.05
4. Spence-Beecroft (1954)	50	Yes	1.0	45	56.5	36.3	20.2	.02
5. Spence-Weyant (1960)	100	No	.25	36	41.8	28.6	13.2	.10[b]
	100	No	2.0	36	65.4	53.2	12.2	.10
6. Spence (unpublished)	80	Yes	.25	60	36.5	21.6	14.9	.02[c]
	80	Yes	1.50	60	48.0	38.8	9.2	.02

[a]The F value based on all groups provided a p value < .01.
[b]The F value based on all groups provided a p value < .05.
[c]The F value based on all groups provided a p value < .01.

TABLE 2

Non-Iowa Studies of Conditioning Performance of HA and LA Scale Ss

Non-Iowa experiments	No. trials	Ready signal	UCS (psi)	No. Ss	Percent CR		Difference (H-L)	p
					HA	LA		
1. Hilgard et al. (1951)	60	Yes	1.6	20	35.2	32.4	2.8	—
2. Prokasy-Truax (1959)	20	No	3.0	20	36.0	48.0	-12.0	—
3. Baron-Conner (1960)	80	No	1.6	36	44.9	27.8	17.1	.01
4. King et al. (1961)	80	Yes	1.5	32	37.4	51.6	-14.2	—
5. King et al. (1961)	80	No	1.5	32	66.8	64.0	2.8	—
6. King et al. (1961)	80	Yes	1.14	30	49.0	51.3	-2.3	—

the use or nonuse of a ready signal, (d) the strength of the UCS (air puff) employed, (e) the total number of Ss in the two groups, (f) the mean percentage of CRs made by the HA group of Ss, (g) the mean percentage of responses made by LA Ss, (h) the difference in percentage of CRs given by the two groups, and (i) the significance level of the differences between the groups expressed in terms of p (two-tailed test).

As may be seen, the six Iowa studies provided nine independent comparisons of HA and LA groups at UCS intensities ranging from very weak (.25 psi) to moderately strong ones (2.0 psi). In every study HA Ss responded with a higher percentage of CRs over the conditioning period than did the LA Ss and in each the difference was significant at the .05 level or better. Since the conditioning curves of the HA and LA groups tended to diverge, it is apparent that the differences in their performance at the end of training were even larger than those shown in Table 1. Thus in the case of these six studies the differences were approximately 20 percent larger over the last 20 conditioning trials than for all trials. These larger differences also tended to be slightly more significant. Attention should also be directed to the fact that the numbers of Ss on which the significance values obtained in these studies were based are relatively large, ranging from a minimum of 45 in studies with two groups to a maximum of 120 when four groups were used.

In turning to the non-Iowa studies in Table 2, it will be seen that not a single one of the comparisons involved as many as 50 Ss. The study (No. 3) with the largest number of Ss (36), it is worthy of note, did give results in line with those obtained in the Iowa laboratory. In this study, conducted at Kent State University, HA Ss responded at a significantly higher level (.01) than LA Ss. The remaining comparisons in this portion of the table, however, failed to support such a finding, that is, there were no significant differences between groups. The first two of the studies probably should not be taken too seriously as they involved only 10 Ss in each extreme group. The variability of conditioning performance among individual Ss is so great that such results would not be unexpected with so few Ss. However, the final three comparisons, all of which were reported by King, Kimble, and their students (1961) present a more formidable array of evidence that is quite contrary to the findings of the Iowa laboratory. Not only did they fail to obtain a significant difference in favor of the HA Ss, but two of the differences, though not significant, were actually in favor of the LA Ss. While only 30–32 Ss were involved in each experiment, the results as a whole are clearly opposed to the Iowa findings.

In addition to the experiments contained in Tables 1 and 2, the findings of three further published studies that bear on the relation between the *MA* scale and performance in simple conditioning should be mentioned. In each of these investigations unselected Ss were run in the experiment and comparisons were subsequently made between Ss who scored in the upper and lower *halves* of the distribution of scores on the *MA* scale: Two of these studies were primarily interested in the effects of administrating shocks on the level of conditioning performance. In the first, Spence, Farber, and Taylor (1954) found that HA Ss ($N =$ 15) responded at a significantly higher level in Trials 1–40 than LA Ss ($N = 25$) under the shock condition ($p < .01$). Under no shock HA Ss also gave more CRs than LA Ss, but with only 10 Ss per group the difference was not significant. In a partial replication of this experiment carried out at Peabody College, Caldwell and Cromwell (1959) compared Ss, 30 from the upper and 30 from the lower halves of the distribution of *MA* scale scores and obtained a significant relation (.05 level) with conditioning performance over Trials 1–40. In each of these experiments, however, conditioning performance over Trials 41–80 was not related either to shock-no shock or to anxiety level. The third and final study that compared above and below average Ss on the *MA* scale was conducted with students from the evening classes of Northwestern University (Spence & Taylor, 1953). Over the 80 conditioning trials, 22 HA Ss averaged 32.2 percent CRs, 21 LA Ss, 18.2 percent. The difference was significant at the .04 level.

Differential Conditioning.

Table 3 presents the data from two reported investigations of the relation between the *MA* scale and level of performance to the *positive* CS in differential conditioning. As in the studies of Table 1, HA and LA groups represent roughly the upper and lower quartiles on the *MA* scale. Spence and Farber (1953, 1954) conducted two separate experiments differing slightly in conditioning methodology. The data presented in the table show the level of response to the positive CS over the last 20 reinforced trials (31–50). As may be seen, in the first experiment, the HA group gave significantly more CRs than the LA group. The second experiment of Spence and Farber, as originally reported, included Ss on the basis of a forced-choice version of the scale or on the basis of the *MA* scale. The data presented here are based only on Ss who were identified as high or low on the *MA* scale. Again, as may be seen from the table, HA Ss responded at a higher level than LA Ss. The difference was not significant at the .05 level by a two-tailed test, but was on the basis of a one-tailed test.

Using a factorial design, Prokasy and Whaley (1962) investigated whether the relation between performance on the *MA* scale and differential conditioning was a function of the presence or absence of a ready signal in the experimental procedure. Table 3 presents the percentage of CRs given to the positive CS on the last 20 reinforced trials (26–45). As may be seen, when a ready signal was employed HA Ss gave a significantly larger number of CRs than did LA Ss. In the absence of a signal, however, the superiority of the HA group was small and not significant.

Unpublished Data Involving
Unselected Subjects

The third set of studies providing relevant evidence is presented in Table 4. Included in this group are the findings of two previously published studies (No. 1 & 2) that were concerned with investigating among unselected Ss the relation between conditioning measures and physiological indices of emotionality (e.g., heart rate changes, GSR, and muscle action potential). As the scores on the *MA* scale were available it was possible to examine the conditioning performance of Ss who scored in the upper and lower quartiles of the distribution of scores on the scale. As the table shows, HA Ss gave a significantly greater number of CRs than LA Ss in both of these studies.

The remaining data presented in Table 4 come from three as yet unpublished studies from the Iowa laboratory. Each is

TABLE 3

Studies of Performance of HA and LA Scale Ss to Positive CS in Differential Conditioning

Study	No. trials	Ready signal	No. Ss	Percent CR HA	Percent CR LA	Difference (H-L)	p
1. Spence-Farber (1953)	31–50	Yes	36	50.0	39.7	10.3	.05
2. Spence-Farber (1954)	31–50	Yes	52	41.1	31.7	9.4	.09
3. Prokasy-Whaley (1962)	26–45	Yes	60	54.5	39.5	15.0	.05
4. Prokasy-Whaley (1962)	26–45	No	70	60.2	56.7	3.5	—

TABLE 4

Iowa Studies Involving Unpublished Data from Postselected Ss.

Study	No. trials	Ready signal	UCS (psi)	No. Ss	Percent CR HA	Percent CR LA	Difference (H-L)	p
1. Runquist & Ross (1959)	41–80	+	1.0	27	70.0	44.3	25.7	.05
2. Runquist & Spence (1959)	41–80	+	1.0	34	57.0	38.2	18.8	.05
3. Individual differences: (unpubl.)	1–80	+	1.0	52	41.8	45.5	−3.7	—
4. Extinction: (unpubl.)	1–30	—	2.0	39	64.3	53.6	10.7	.05
5a. Conditioning problem: Male (unpubl.)	31–60	—	.6	67	61.8	47.6	14.2	.05
5b. Conditioning problem: Female (unpubl.)	31–60	—	.6	31	71.0	59.0	12.0	—

identified by a word or label describing the primary interest of the study. In each of these investigations a fairly large number of Ss, the MA scale scores of whom were available after completion of the experiment, were conditioned under identical circumstances. Again, the findings reported are for Ss who scored in the upper and lower quartiles of the MA scale distribution. As may be seen, the three comparisons (No. 4, 5a, & 5b) provided by the last two experiments once again show that HA Ss responded at a higher level than LA Ss. Two of these differences were significant, while the third (that involving the smallest number of Ss) was not. Attention should be directed to the fact that a ready signal was not employed in these latter studies. The relation of the use or nonuse of a ready signal to the findings of these studies will be discussed in a later section.

The final item of note in Table 4 is the negative difference found in the study entitled "Individual Differences" (No. 3). This is the only instance among a total of 17 comparisons of HA and LA Ss provided by our Iowa studies in which LA Ss gave a larger number of CRs than HA Ss. The small difference is not, of course, significant.

DISCUSSION

Looking at the findings of the studies included in Tables 1, 2, 3, and 4 as a whole, a number of characteristics may be noted. First, the proportion of instances in which the conditioning performance of the HA group was higher than that of the LA group is much greater than one would expect by chance. Thus, the results of 21 of 25 comparisons were in this direction. If there actually were no relation between the MA scale and conditioning performance, the probability of obtaining such a percentage of differences (84 percent) in the same direction by chance is less than .01.

Secondly, it is clearly evident that the studies with relatively large numbers of Ss tended to provide significant differences in favor of HA Ss, whereas those with smaller numbers did not. Thus, in the case of comparisons involving 36 or more Ss, 65 percent (11/17) of the comparisons were significant at the .05 level or better on the basis of a two-tailed test. On the other hand, in studies involving fewer than 36 Ss only two of the eight compari-

sons provided a significant result. Moreover, all of the 13 significant differences were in the direction of higher conditioning performance on the part of the HA Ss, whereas none of the four obtained differences in favor of the LA Ss were significant.

As was mentioned earlier, intersubject variability in eyelid
conditioning is exceedingly great. In our experiments the percentages of CRs given by individuals customarily range all the way
from zero to very high values. The standard deviations of these
percentage measures vary roughly between 20 and 25 percent.
Under such circumstances it is readily apparent that fairly large
numbers of Ss must be sampled if an adequate test as to whether
the manipulated variable produces a difference is to be made.
This is particularly the case if the size of the difference is not
large relative to the variance of the measures. Apparently, degree
of emotionality, as specified in terms of extreme scores on the
MA scale, is a relatively minor factor or variable among all those
contributing to the intersubject variance of conditioning performance. In this connection, it is interesting to note that in two
studies in which emotionality differences and differences in UCS
(puff) strength were both variables, the differences between the
conditioning performances of the HA and LA Ss were of about
the same order of magnitude as those obtained between relatively
weak and strong puff intensities (.25 vs. 1.5 psi and .6 vs. 2.0 psi).
In the case of both types of comparison, individual performances
ranged from very low to high levels in the groups being compared
and the overlap was considerable.

In the light of these considerations, it is not at all surprising
to find such divergent findings among studies that employ such
small numbers of Ss, nor is it difficult to understand why the
Iowa studies, with their relatively larger samples, have tended
to be more consistent and to give a higher proportion of significant differences in favor of the HA Ss.

A third characteristic of the data provided by these studies
is that the relation between the MA scale and conditioning does
appear to vary from one laboratory to another. This fact is clearly
revealed in Table 5, which presents an analysis of the data in
terms of their source. As may be seen, we have divided the studies
into three groups, those carried out in the Iowa laboratory and
those from other laboratories. The latter, in turn, have been

TABLE 5
Comparison of Differences between HA and LA Ss' Conditioning
Performance Obtained in Different Laboratories

Laboratory	No. comparisons	Mean No. Ss	Percent HA $>$ LA	Percent significant (.05)
Iowa	17	47.0	94	60
Non-Iowa I[a]	5	41.2	80	40
Non-Iowa II[b]	3	31.3	33	0

[a]Obtained in the university laboratories of Stanford, Wisconsin, Pennsylvania State, and Kent State.
[b]Obtained in the university laboratories of Duke and North Carolina.

broken down into two subgroups, primarily on the basis of the strikingly different findings obtained in them.

It is clearly evident from the data of Table 5 that the Iowa studies have most consistently demonstrated a relation between conditioning performance and emotionality (*MA* scale). Thus 16 (94 percent) of the 17 comparisons gave differences in favor of the HA Ss, with 10 (60 percent) of these differences being significant at the .05 level or better. Contrasting most sharply with these findings are those obtained in the subgroup of non-Iowa studies from Duke and North Carolina. These studies, carried out or supervised by Kimble and his associates, failed to find a significant difference in three comparisons of the HA and LA Ss and, moreover, found that LA Ss responded at a higher level than HA Ss in two of their three experiments. Falling in between, but closer to the results of the Iowa studies, are the findings from the four other non-Iowa laboratories. Thus, in four of five comparisons, HA Ss gave more CRs than LA groups, with two of these being significant. Recalling that two of the studies in this latter group had only 10 Ss per group, we see that two of the three experiments that had groups of 36 or more obtained significant differences.

In summary, we see that when studies with a reasonably large number of Ss (36 or more) are considered, the experiments conducted in the Iowa laboratory and those from laboratories *other* than Duke and North Carolina tend to be in close agreement with each other in pointing to a genuine difference in the conditioning performance of the HA and LA Ss. The studies of Kimble and his associates, on the other hand, do not.

In an effort to ascertain what factors might be responsible for these contrasting findings a comparison was made of the experimental conditions under which the studies were conducted. For this purpose a more detailed description of the experimental situation, procedures, and experiences of the Ss was obtained through correspondence with the investigators involved.

With respect to the conditions under which the experiments were conducted at Iowa, we were greatly influenced by the writer's theoretical interpretation as to why HA Ss could be expected to perform at a higher level than LA Ss. According to this theory, the differences in conditioning performance of these two groups of Ss reflect differences in their level of generalized drive (D), which, in turn, are assumed to be the result of differences in their level of emotional reactivity to the experimental situation and procedures. Accordingly, a deliberate attempt was made in the Iowa studies to provide conditions in the laboratory that might elicit some degree of emotionality. Thus, the experimenter was instructed to be impersonal and quite formal in greeting S and in giving the necessary instructions. On coming into the experiment, S at first saw an impressive array of electronic recording equipment and was then led into an adjoining room in which was located an isolated, screened cubicle. The latter contained a dental chair (sic) in which S was seated in a reclining position, while a headband was placed on his head and a plastic piece was fastened to his upper eyelid. After completing the instructions, the illumination in the cubicle was reduced to a low level of semi-darkness and S was informed that, if the need arose, he could get in touch with E by means of a microphone placed on a stand within his reach. The door to the cubicle and the door leading to the adjoining room in which E worked were then closed and S was left in isolation.

To say the least, these conditions were unusual and strange for Ss. Furthermore, in order to maximize the likelihood that they would have a tendency to arouse some degree of apprehensiveness, only individuals who had no previous experience as an S in psychological laboratory experiments were used in all but one of our studies in Tables 1, 2, and 3. It has been our experience that students are much more likely to be concerned and apprehensive in the first experiment in which they serve. After one or two experiences they become much less fearful and, all too often, quite bored and blasé. Some experimental evidence, that the amount of such previous experience is a factor in experiments comparing the performances of the HA and LA Ss, has been provided by an experiment reported by Mednick (1957). The latter found that experimentally naive HA Ss showed more stimulus generalization of a response than LA Ss, whereas no such difference was obtained in the case of Ss who had served in from two to three previous psychological experiments.

It is evident from this account that the conditions under which our experiments were conducted were designed to arrange for some degree of situation-aroused anxiety or emotionality. While one version of our theory hypothesized that differences in emotionality of the HA and LA Ss might be chronic, an alternative possibility was that it was dependent upon some degree of stress being present in the situation. We were primarily interested in testing the theory under conditions that maximized the likelihood of differences in the emotional reactions of the two groups of Ss.

In the light of the above discussion, it is interesting to compare the conditions and procedures employed by Kimble and King with those employed at Iowa. First, with respect to physical conditions, there are a number of differences. The two Duke experiments were conducted in a cubicle within a room in which E was located. However, instead of being semidark, the cubicle was rather brightly lighted (23 apparent foot-candles). The experiment at the University of North Carolina was also conducted under bright illumination with S and E being in the same room on the opposite sides of a partition. In place of a dental chair, Ss in the Duke experiments were seated on a secretarial-type chair, with chin in a headrest. At North Carolina, S sat in a straight desk chair with head free. In addition to these physical differences, most Ss in the Kimble-King experiments had already been in one or two experiments prior to serving in the conditioning experiment.

Considering the differences in the two laboratories in terms of the use of different degrees of isolation of S from E, semidark-ness versus well-lighted room, dental chair (emotionally condi-tioned cue) versus neutral-type chair, and experimentally naive versus sophisticated Ss, it would seem quite plausible to suspect that the differences in the findings could, in part at least, be due to the fact that the experimental conditions at Duke and North Carolina were not as emotion arousing as those employed in the Iowa experiments. Further experimentation is needed, of course, to check on the role of such factors for there are other differences between the two sets of experiments that might have played im-portant roles. One important one that should be investigated is the possibility that cultural backgrounds of southern and north-ern students may lead to a difference in the manner in which they respond to the different items in the MA scale.

Still another variable is the E-S interaction. Our Es were not acquainted with Ss and we have attempted to instill in them an attitude of being quite impersonal at the beginning of the experi-ment and to avoid making any particular attempt to put S at ease or allay any expressed fears. Undoubtedly Es differ greatly in the degree to which they are able to achieve and maintain this objective. It is interesting to note that the person who served as one of two Es in the single Iowa study that gave negative results (LA > HA) has recently completed a doctoral dissertation in which there again was little difference between HA and LA Ss. Unfortunately, there were only a small number of the HA and LA Ss under each of the different conditions of this experiment and the proportion of male and female Ss was not equated so the results are not very helpful. This is, nevertheless, a poten-tially important variable and should be investigated further, pos-sibly by deliberately manipulating the behavior of E. It has re-cently been shown experimentally that one can markedly increase the conditioning performance of Ss by emotion producing in-structions (Spence & Goldstein, 1961).

A final variable to be considered is the presence or absence of a ready signal. In a recent article Prokasy and Whaley (1962) have proposed that the use or nonuse of a "ready-blink" signal is a possible factor with which emotionality might be interacting in these conditioning studies. In support of this notion these in-vestigators found, as is shown in Table 2, that in differential conditioning, their HA Ss gave a significantly larger number of CRs to the positive CS than LA Ss when a ready-blink signal was used, whereas only a small, insignificant difference was obtained in its absence. However, before this study even appeared there was evidence against the notion that the difference in conditioning performance of the HA and LA Ss was a function of the presence or absence of a ready signal. As Table 1 reveals, Baron and Conner (1960) had reported a highly significant difference ($p < .01$), while Spence and Weyant (1960) also obtained a significant F ($<.05$ level) for HA and LA Ss in experiments that did not employ a ready signal. Further evidence against this view that a ready signal is a necessary condition for the difference to occur is provided by the findings of recent experiments from our laboratory presented in Table 4. As the last three items in this table show, three comparisons between HA and LA Ss in which there was no ready signal all gave differences in favor of the HA group with the two comparisons that involved more than 35 Ss being significant at the .05 level.

Unfortunately, a serious methodological error is present in the early studies that did not employ a ready signal. As Hartman and Ross (1961) have recently demonstrated the latency criterion employed in the Iowa laboratory (Spence & Ross, 1959; Spence & Taylor, 1951) to identify and eliminate "voluntary" responders from the data sample is not applicable when a ready signal is not employed. The use of this criterion was originally based on the finding in experiments using a ready signal and a CS-UCS interval of 500 milliseconds that the latency distribution of responses judged to be similar in form to voluntary eyelid closures did not overlap to any great extent with that for CRs, which are very different in form. Thus, it was possible to employ this more convenient latency property as the index of whether a response was a voluntary response or a CR. As employed in these studies all responses with latencies between 300 and 500 milliseconds were counted as CRs, while responses whose latencies fell between 150 milliseconds (tone CS) or 200 milliseconds (light CS) and 300 milliseconds were counted as voluntary responses. The Ss who gave 50 percent or more responses in the voluntary category were eliminated from the sample data.

The reason for so doing was that the behavior of such Ss appeared to obey quite different laws from those holding for Ss who gave few such voluntary responses. Among the differences importantly related to our present concern are (a) the tendency to respond at an extremely high level (approaching 100 percent) once the first such anticipatory voluntary response is made and (b) the lack of any relation whatever between the frequency of responses given by such Ss and the level of the MA scale score. The effect of both of these tendencies is clearly that of reducing the likelihood of obtaining a significant difference in the conditioning performance of the HA and LA Ss, the first by greatly increasing the variance of the conditioning scores and the second by reducing the difference between groups that contained a number of such Ss.

Unfortunately, investigators who did not use a ready signal took over the latency criterion to identify voluntary responders without checking its appropriateness, with the consequence that all such Ss probably were not eliminated from their samples. The Prokasy and Truax (1959) study is especially suspect in this regard as it involved a very strong puff (3.0 psi), a condition that produces a high incidence of such voluntary responders. When one considers the small number of Ss (10 per group) in this experiment, the negative difference obtained is not too surprising. The presence of one or two more high responding voluntary Ss in the LA group than in the HA group could easily have produced this result. The findings obtained with the no-signal groups in the later study of Prokasy and Whaley (1962) and one of the Duke studies also may be suspected of being affected by the presence of a number of voluntary responders who were not detected by the inappropriate latency criterion that was employed.

An example of the effects of including the data of voluntary responders in a sample is provided by the recent studies (Table 4) from the Iowa laboratory that did not employ a ready signal. Having confirmed the findings of Hartman and Ross (1961) that latency does not differentiate voluntary form responses from CRs when a ready signal is absent, the identification of voluntary Ss in these studies was made in terms of the form of the eyelid responses. If, instead, the latency criterion had been employed none of the voluntary responders detected by the form criteria would have been identified and thus would have been included in the samples. It is worthy of note that the inclusion of six voluntary responders (three in each group) in the case of the comparison involving the male Ss of our most recent experiment (Table 4, No. 5a) would have reduced the reported difference of 14.2 percent between HA and LA Ss to 11.0 percent. Correspondingly, the significance of the difference would have been reduced from the .05 level to one of .16. In other words, the addition of only six voluntary Ss to the sample of 67 would have changed the conclusion from one that the difference is significant to one that it is not.

In concluding this discussion, attention should especially be directed to the point that the behavior of human Ss in classical eyelid conditioning, while simple in form, is complexly determined. Recent research in this and other laboratories has revealed that higher mental processes (inhibitory and facilitatory sets, etc.) play a much more prominent role in human conditioning than has sometimes been realized. Moreover, our lack of knowledge concerning these factors has precluded our controlling them in any satisfactory manner with the result that the intersubject variance of conditioning performance is extremely large. This state of affairs has unfortunate consequences for the testing of simple theories of behavior which specify only associational and motivational constructs (e.g., H and D) as determiners of excitatory strength of the conditioned responses. Obviously, the additional uncontrolled variables minimize the role of these basic theoretical factors, tending to hide their effects. Under such circumstances it is necessary to have reasonably large samples so that the effects of these confounding variables are more likely to be equalized in the comparison groups. On the basis of the writer's experience with conditioning data, experiments of the type discussed here should be required to have groups of at least 25 Ss. Unhappily, as we have seen, this has all too frequently not been the case.

NOTE

1. This study was carried out as part of a project concerned with the influence of motivation on performance in learning under Contract Nonr-1509 (04), Project NR 154–107 between the University of Iowa and the Office of Naval Research.

REFERENCES

Baron, M. R., & Conner, J. P. Eyelid conditioned responses with various levels of anxiety. *J. exp. Psychol.*, 1960, 60, 310–313.

Caldwell, D. F., & Cromwell, R. L. Replication report: The relation of manifest anxiety and electric shock to eyelid conditioning. *J. exp. Psychol.*, 1959, 57, 348–349.

Hartman, T. F., & Ross, L. E. An alternative criterion for the elimination of "voluntary" responses in eyelid conditioning. *J. exp. Psychol.*, 1961, 61, 334–338.

Hilgard, E. R., Jones, L. V., & Kaplan, S. J. Conditioned discrimination as related to anxiety. *J. exp. Psychol.*, 1951, 42, 94–99.

King, M. S., Kimble, G. A., Gorman, J., & King, R. A. Replication report: Two failures to reproduce effects of anxiety on eyelid conditioning. *J. exp. Psychol.*, 1961, 62, 532–533.

Mednick, S. A. Generalization as a function of manifest anxiety and adaptation of psychological experiments. *J. consult. Psychol.*, 1957, 21, 491–494.

Prokasy, W. F., & Truax, C. B. Reflex and conditioned responses as a function of manifest anxiety. *Amer. J. Psychol.*, 1959, 72, 262–264.

Prokasy, W. F., & Whaley, F. L. Manifest anxiety scale score and the ready signal in classical conditioning. *J. exp. Psychol.*, 1962, 63, 119–124.

Runquist, W. N., & Ross, L. E. The relation between physiological measures of emotionality and performance in eyelid conditioning. *J. exp. Psychol.*, 1959, 57, 329–332.

Runquist, W. N., & Spence, K. W. Performance in eyelid conditioning related to changes in muscular tension and physiological measures of emotionality. *J. exp. Psychol.*, 1959, 58, 417–422.

Spence, K. W., & Beecroft, R. S. Differential conditioning and level of anxiety. *J. exp. Psychol.*, 1954, 48, 399–403.

Spence, K. W., & Farber, I. E. Conditioning and extinction as a function of anxiety. *J. exp. Psychol.*, 1953, 45, 116–119.

Spence, K. W., & Farber, I. E. The relation of anxiety to differential eyelid conditioning. *J. exp. Psychol.*, 1954, 47, 127–134.

Spence, K. W., Farber, I. E., & Taylor, E. The relation of electric shock and anxiety to level of performance in eyelid conditioning. *J. exp. Psychol.*, 1954, 48, 404–408.

Spence, K. W., & Goldstein, H. Eyelid conditioning performance as a function of emotion-producing instructions. *J. exp. Psychol.*, 1961, 62, 291–294.

Spence, K. W., & Ross, L. E. A methodological study of the form and latency of eyelid responses in conditioning. *J. exp. Psychol.*, 1959, 58, 376–381.

Spence, K. W., & Taylor, J. A. Anxiety and strength of UCS as determinants of amount of eyelid conditioning. *J. exp. Psychol.*, 1951, 42, 183–188.

Spence, K. W., & Taylor, J. A. The relation of conditioned response strength to anxiety in normal, neurotic, and psychotic subjects. *J. exp. Psychol.*, 1953, 45, 265–272.

Spence, K. W., & Weyant, G. F. Conditioning performance of high- and low-anxious Ss in the absence of a warning signal. *J. exp. Psychol.* 1960, 60, 146–149.

Taylor, J. A. The relationship of anxiety to the conditioned eyelid response. *J. exp. Psychol.*, 1951, 41, 81–92.

Paired-Associate Learning as a Function of Arousal and Interpolated Interval[1]

Lewis J. Kleinsmith and Stephen Kaplan,
University of Michigan

This experiment tested the hypothesis that due to the phenomenon of perseverative consolidation, a pattern perceived under high arousal should show stronger permanent memory and weaker immediate memory than a pattern accompanied by low arousal. While recording skin resistance as a measure of arousal, 48 Ss were presented 8 paired associates for learning. The Ss were tested at various time intervals: 2 min., 20 min., 45 min., 1 day, and 1 wk. The results confirmed the hypothesis (p = .001). Paired associates learned under low arousal exhibited high immediate recall value and rapid forgetting. High arousal paired associates exhibited a marked reminiscence effect, that is, low immediate recall and high permanent memory.

There is growing evidence that perseverative consolidation of the memory trace can last over a considerable period of time. Glickman (1961) provides an extensive review of the literature in this area. Still more recently, Paré (1961), by the use of drugs, has shown that arousal plays an important role in the consolidation process. A stimulant administered immediately following a learning trial increases retention, while a depressant has the opposite effect.

Kleinsmith, L. J. & Kaplan, S. Paired-associate learning as a function of arousal and interpolated interval. *Journal of Experimental Psychology*, 1963, 65, 190–193. Copyright 1963 by the American Psychological Association, and reproduced by permission.

As Paré has indicated, reverberating neural circuits (Hebb, 1958) provide a mechanism to explain the effect of arousal on consolidation. Under conditions of low arousal, relatively little nonspecific neural activity will be available to support the reverberating trace, resulting in little consolidation and poor long-term retention. On the other hand, under conditions of high arousal the increased nonspecific neural activity will result in more reverberation, and thus retention should be better.

While reverberation is taking place, however, one might expect the trace to be relatively unavailable to the organism, resulting in poor recall of the consolidating material during this interval. Such unavailability follows from a consideration of the difficulties in refiring a neuron which is already firing repeatedly in a reverberating circuit. Hodgkin (1948) has shown that neurons are sharply limited in their maximum rate of firing. Thus under high arousal, perseverative consolidation should be effective both in strengthening the memory trace and in making the memory difficult to evoke until the perseveration terminates.

In the present study Ss were asked to learn a set of paired associates composed of words as stimuli and single-digit numbers as responses. The words were chosen to differ in their arousal value (as measured by galvanic skin response). In terms of the hypothesis, word-number pairs of high arousal value should be recalled poorly at first, but should be recalled well at a later time. Low arousal pairs, by contrast, should be remembered better at first and should show a gradual decay (forgetting) with time.

METHOD

Subjects.

The Ss were 48 University of Michigan undergraduates obtained from introductory courses in psychology. They were run in six subgroups of 8 Ss each.

Procedure.

The Ss were given a single learning trial with a list of eight word-number pairs. Eight words expected to produce different arousal levels were chosen as stimulus words. These were KISS,

RAPE, VOMIT, EXAM, DANCE, MONEY, LOVE, SWIM. The response items were single digits from 2 to 9.

A slide projector with an exposure time of 4 sec. was used to present the stimuli. During the training trial S first saw the stimulus word alone, and then saw the word repeated with a single digit response. To separate the arousal effects from one set of pairings to the next, two slides containing four colors each were inserted between the paired associates, and S was instructed to name the colors. (Red, green, blue, black, yellow, and orange were used randomly on these slides.) The S was instructed to "concentrate carefully on both colors and word-number pairs" as he called them out loud, but to avoid rehearsal S was not specifically told that he would be tested for recall.

In order to determine the arousal effects of each stimulus word, skin resistance was recorded during learning. The electrodes were of the zinc variety described by Lykken (1959). To insure constancy of conditions, electrodes and recording apparatus were also used during the recall session.

During the recall session S was instructed to indicate the correct number for each stimulus word as it appeared. The correct numbers were not repeated. Colors were used as an interpolated task as before.

Design.

The six groups were tested one at each of the following recall intervals: immediate (about 2 min.), 20 min., 45 min., 1 day, and 1 wk. Two groups were run at the first recall interval.

To correct for serial order effects eight different training lists were used for each group, designed so that each of the eight words appeared in each position in the list once (Fisher & Yates, 1938). The order of the recall lists was varied in the same manner.

Data analysis.

Any drop in S's skin resistance which occurred within 4 sec. of presentation of a given word was considered an arousal deflection; these were converted to percent deflections. Each S's eight GSR deflections were then ranked. (In case of ties, absolute skin resistance level was used to break them. A deflection occurring at a low level of absolute skin resistance was considered higher arousal than a similar deflection occurring at a higher absolute level.) The three highest deflections for each S were designated "high arousal learning," and the three lowest were designated "low arousal learning."

RESULTS

Figure 1 illustrates the relationship between high and low arousal recall as a function of time. At immediate recall, numbers associated with low arousal words are recalled five times as often as numbers associated with high arousal words. The capacity to recall numbers associated with low arousal words decreases as a function of time in a normal forgetting curve pattern. On the other hand, the capacity to recall numbers associated with high arousal words shows a considerable reminiscence effect. After 20 min., the increase is more than 100 percent, and after 45 min. it has increased 400 percent. This high capacity for recall of high arousal pairs persists for at least a week—the longest interval employed.

Analysis of variance (Lindquist, 1953) for correct responses confirms the trends in the figure at $p < .001$ (Table 1). The significant interaction is primarily attributable to the effect of

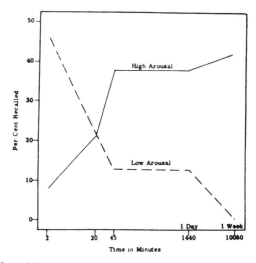

Fig. 1. Differential recall of paired associates as a function of arousal level.

the immediate condition, $F(1, 15) = 11.36$, p < .005, and the 1-wk. condition, $F(1,7) = 11.67$, $p < .025$. Thus at immediate recall, low arousal learning is significantly greater than high arousal learning; after 1 wk., the situation has reversed and high arousal recall is significantly better than low arousal recall.

As can be seen in Table 2 the distribution of items at different times sampled forms no systematic patterns that might account for the results obtained. This table shows the proportion of each of the eight items at each time sampled for both high and low arousal learning.

DISCUSSION

The increase in the capacity to recall items learned under conditions of high arousal in contrast to items learned under low arousal conditions provides further support for the theory of reverberating neural circuits. A somewhat simplified physiological explanation of the processes involved may be pictured as follows. When a person perceives a pattern, a closed, reverberating neural circuit is set up in his brain corresponding to this pattern. The more nonspecific neural activity or arousal present, the greater the number of times which the trace is likely to reverberate. And the greater this perseverative consolidation of the neural trace, the stronger the permanent memory.

However the apparent paradox is that while perseveration is taking place, recall ability is poor. This follows from the hypothesis that at any given instant the neurons involved in the perseverating trace are either already in the process of firing, or are in an absolute refractory state, or may be in a state of slowly developing subthreshold activity (Hodgkin, 1948) ; thus the trace would be relatively unavailable to the organism. With greater arousal there will be increased perseveration and thus poorer immediate performance.

This explanation coincides with the empirical findings. High arousal learning showed poor immediate recall due to the hypothesized period of unavailability of the trace, while recall was better under low arousal, for this immediate period. The long-term effects are, as predicted, in the opposite direction. There was significantly poorer long-term retention under low arousal and superior long-term retention under high arousal. This is in keeping

TABLE 1

Analysis of Variance of Recall Scores

Source	df	MS	F
Between Ss	47		
Conditions (B)	4	0.1459	.27
Error (b)	43	0.5377	
Within Ss	48		
Arousal level (A)	1	0.1667	.27
A x B	4	5.7396	9.45***
Error (w)	43	0.6076	
Total	95		

***$p < .001$.

TABLE 2

Distribution of Items at Different Times Sampled

Item	High Arousal					Low Arousal				
	2 Min.	20 Min.	45 Min.	Day	Wk.	2 Min.	20 Min.	45 Min.	Day	Wk.
DANCE	.06	.08	.13	.08	.13	.13	.08	.21	.21	.17
EXAM	.13	.04	.17	.08	.13	.15	.13	.08	.17	.21
KISS	.10	.13	.08	.17	.08	.15	.08	.08	.04	.17
LOVE	.10	.13	.13	.13	.17	.17	.17	.13	.17	.08
MONEY	.10	.17	.08	.04	.08	.08	.17	.17	.21	.13
RAPE	.27	.13	.21	.21	.25	.04	.17	.04	.08	.04
SWIM	.10	.13	.13	.08	.08	.15	.13	.13	.08	.13
VOMIT	.13	.21	.08	.21	.08	.15	.08	.17	.04	.08

with the expectation that there would be more consolidation and thus better learning under high arousal.

Reminiscence has become so rare in recent years that Underwood (1953) has wondered if it might not be a prewar phenomenon. This study suggests that methodological considerations might be an important factor in the return of reminiscence. The innovation in this experiment consisted of measuring arousal during learning and thus independently determining in advance which items should show reminiscence effects and which should not. When recall as a function of time is plotted for all items at once, little reminiscence is evident.

NOTE

1. This investigation was supported in part by a research grant (M4239) from the National Institutes of Health, Public Health Service. The Ss in this study were run by Robert D. Tarte, research assistant on this project.

REFERENCES

Fisher, R. A., & Yates, F. *Statistical tables for biological agricultural, and medical research.* London: Oliver and Boyd, 1938.

Glickman, S. E. Perseverative neural processes and consolidation of the memory trace. *Psychol. Bull.,* 1961, 58, 218–233.

Hebb, D. O. *A textbook of psychology.* Philadelphia: Saunders, 1958.

Hodgkin, A. L. The local electric changes associated with repetitive action in a nonmedullated axon. *J. Physiol.,* 1948, 107, 165–181.

Lindquist, E. F. *Design and analysis of experiments in psychology and education.* Boston: Houghton Mifflin, 1953.

Lykken, D. T. Properties of electrodes used in electrodermal measurement. *J. comp. physiol. Psychol.,* 1959, 52, 629–644.

Paré, W. The effect of caffeine and seconal on a visual discrimination task. *J. comp. physiol. Psychol.,* 1961, 54, 506–509.

Underwood, B. J. Learning. *Annu. Rev. Psychol.,* 1953, 4, 31–58.

The Misbehavior of Organisms

KELLER BRELAND and MARIAN BRELAND,
Animal Behavior Enterprises, Hot Spring, Arkansas

There seems to be a continuing realization by psychologists that perhaps the white rat cannot reveal everything there is to know about behavior. Among the voices raised on this topic, Beach (1950) has emphasized the necessity of widening the range of species subjected to experimental techniques and conditions. However, psychologists as a whole do not seem to be heeding these admonitions, as Whalen (1961) has pointed out.

Perhaps this reluctance is due in part to some dark precognition of what they might find in such investigations, for the ethologists Lorenz (1950, p. 233) and Tinbergen (1951, p. 6) have warned that if psychologists are to understand and predict the behavior of organisms, it is essential that they become thoroughly familiar with the instinctive behavior patterns of each new species they essay to study. Of course, the Watsonian or neobehavioristically oriented experimenter is apt to consider "instinct" an ugly word. He tends to class it with Hebb's (1960) other "seditious notions" which were discarded in the behavioristic revolution, and he may have some premonition that he will encounter this bete noir in extending the range of species and situations studied.

Breland, K. & Breland, M. The misbehavior of organisms. *American Psychologist*, 1961, *16*, 681–684. Copyright 1961 by the American Psychological Association, and reproduced by permission.

We can assure him that his apprehensions are well grounded. In our attempt to extend a behavioristically oriented approach to the engineering control of animal behavior by operant conditioning techniques, we have fought a running battle with the seditious notion of instinct.[1] It might be of some interest to the psychologist to know how the battle is going and to learn something about the nature of the adversary he is likely to meet if and when he tackles new species in new learning situations.

Our first report (Breland & Breland, 1951) in the *American Psychologist,* concerning our experiences in controlling animal behavior, was wholly affirmative and optimistic, saying in essence that the principles derived from the laboratory could be applied to the extensive control of behavior under nonlaboratory conditions throughout a considerable segment of the phylogenetic scale.

When we began this work, it was our aim to see if the science would work beyond the laboratory, to determine if animal psychology could stand on its own feet as an engineering discipline. These aims have been realized. We have controlled a wide range of animal behavior and have made use of the great popular appeal of animals to make it an economically feasible project. Conditioned behavior has been exhibited at various municipal zoos and museums of natural history and has been used for department store displays, for fair and trade convention exhibits, for entertainment at tourist attractions, on television shows, and in the production of television commercials. Thirty-eight species, totaling over 6,000 individual animals, have been conditioned, and we have dared to tackle such unlikely subjects as reindeer, cockatoos, raccoons, porpoises, and whales.

Emboldened by this consistent reinforcement, we have ventured further and further from the security of the Skinner box. However, in this cavalier extrapolation, we have run afoul of a persistent pattern of discomforting failures. These failures, although disconcertingly frequent and seemingly diverse, fall into a very interesting pattern. They all represent breakdowns of conditioned operant behavior. From a great number of such experiences, we have selected, more or less at random, the following examples.

The first instance of our discomfiture might be entitled,

What Makes Sammy Dance? In the exhibit in which this occurred, the casual observer sees a grown bantam chicken emerge from a retaining compartment when the door automatically opens. The chicken walks over about 3 feet, pulls a rubber loop on a small box which starts a repeated auditory stimulus pattern (a four-note tune). The chicken then steps up onto an 18-inch, slightly raised disc, thereby closing a timer switch, and scratches vigorously, round and round, over the disc for 15 seconds, at the rate of about two scratches per second until the automatic feeder fires in the retaining compartment. The chicken goes into the compartment to eat, thereby automatically shutting the door. The popular interpretation of this behavior pattern is that the chicken has turned on the "juke box" and "dances."

The development of this behavioral exhibit was wholly unplanned. In the attempt to create quite another type of demonstration which required a chicken simply to stand on a platform for 12–15 seconds, we found that over 50 percent developed a very strong and pronounced scratch pattern, which tended to increase in persistence as the time interval was lengthened. (Another 25 percent or so developed other behaviors—pecking at spots, etc.) However, we were able to change our plans so as to make use of the scratch pattern, and the result was the "dancing chicken" exhibit described above.

In this exhibit the only real contingency for reinforcement is that the chicken must depress the platform for 15 seconds. In the course of a performing day (about 3 hours for each chicken) a chicken may turn out over 10,000 unnecessary, virtually identical responses. Operant behaviorists would probably have little hesitancy in labeling this an example of Skinnerian "superstition" (Skinner, 1948) or "mediating" behavior, and we list it first to whet their explanatory appetite.

However, a second instance involving a raccoon does not fit so neatly into this paradigm. The response concerned the manipulation of money by the raccoon (who has "hands" rather similar to those of the primates). The contingency for reinforcement was picking up the coins and depositing them in a 5-inch metal box.

Raccoons condition readily, have good appetites, and this one was quite tame and an eager subject. We anticipated no trouble. Conditioning him to pick up the first coin was simple. We started out by reinforcing him for picking up a single coin. Then the metal container was introduced, with the requirement that he drop the coin into the container. Here we ran into the first bit of difficulty: he seemed to have a great deal of trouble letting go of the coin. He would rub it up against the inside of the container, pull it back out, and clutch it firmly for several seconds. However, he would finally turn it loose and receive his food reinforcement. Then the final contingency: we put him on a ratio of 2, requiring that he pick up both coins and put them in the container.

Now the raccoon really had problems (and so did we). Not only could he not let go of the coins, but he spent seconds, even minutes, rubbing them together (in a most miserly fashion), and dipping them into the container. He carried on this behavior to such an extent that the practical application we had in mind— a display featuring a raccoon putting money in a piggy bank— simply was not feasible. The rubbing behavior became worse and worse as time went on, in spite of nonreinforcement.

For the third instance, we return to the gallinaceous birds. The observer sees a hopper full of oval plastic capsules which contain small toys, charms, and the like. When the S_D (a light) is presented to the chicken, she pulls a rubber loop which releases one of these capsules onto a slide, about 16 inches long, inclined at about 30 degrees. The capsule rolls down the slide and comes to rest near the end. Here one or two sharp, straight pecks by the chicken will knock it forward off the slide and out to the observer, and the chicken is then reinforced by an automatic feeder. This is all very well—most chickens are able to master these contingencies in short order. The loop pulling presents no problems; she then has only to peck the capsule off the slide to get her reinforcement.

However, a good 20 percent of all chickens tried on this set of contingencies fail to make the grade. After they have pecked a few capsules off the slide, they begin to grab at the capsules and drag them backwards into the cage. Here they pound them up and down on the floor of the cage. Of course, this results in no reinforcement for the chicken, and yet some chickens will pull in over half of all the capsules presented to them.

Almost always this problem behavior does not appear until after the capsules begin to move down the slide. Conditioning is begun with stationary capsules placed by the experimenter. When the pecking behavior becomes strong enough, so that the chicken is knocking them off the slide and getting reinforced consistently, the loop pulling is conditioned to the light. The capsules then come rolling down the slide to the chicken. Here most chickens, who before did not have this tendency, will start grabbing and shaking.

The fourth incident also concerns a chicken. Here the observer sees a chicken in a cage about 4 feet long which is placed alongside a miniature baseball field. The reason for the cage is the interesting part. At one end of the cage is an automatic electric feed hopper. At the other is an opening through which the chicken can reach and pull a loop on a bat. If she pulls the loop hard enough the bat (solenoid operated) will swing, knocking a small baseball up the playing field. If it gets past the miniature toy players on the field and hits the back fence, the chicken is automatically reinforced with food at the other end of the cage. If it does not go far enough, or hits one of the players, she tries again. This results in behavior on an irregular ratio. When the feeder sounds, she then runs down the length of the cage and eats.

Our problems began when we tried to remove the cage for photography. Chickens that had been well conditioned in this behavior became wildly excited when the ball started to move. They would jump up on the playing field, chase the ball all over the field, even knock it off on the floor and chase it around, pecking it in every direction, although they had never had access to the ball before. This behavior was so persistent and so disruptive, in spite of the fact that it was never reinforced, that we had to reinstate the cage.

The last instance we shall relate in detail is one of the most annoying and baffling for a good behaviorist. Here a pig was conditioned to pick up large wooden coins and deposit them in a large "piggy bank." The coins were placed several feet from the bank and the pig required to carry them to the bank and deposit them, usually four or five coins for one reinforcement. (Of course, we started out with one coin, near the bank.)

Pigs condition very rapidly, they have no trouble taking ratios, they have ravenous appetites (naturally), and in many ways are among the most tractable animals we have worked with. However, this particular problem behavior developed in pig after pig, usually after a period of weeks or months, getting worse every day. At first the pig would eagerly pick up one dollar, carry it to the bank, run back, get another, carry it rapidly and neatly, and so on, until the ratio was complete. Thereafter, over a period of weeks the behavior would become slower and slower. He might run over eagerly for each dollar, but on the way back, instead of carrying the dollar and depositing it simply and cleanly, he would repeatedly drop it, root it, drop it again, root it along the way, pick it up, toss it up in the air, drop it, root it some more, and so on.

We thought this behavior might simply be the dilly-dallying of an animal on a low drive. However, the behavior persisted and gained in strength in spite of a severely increased drive—he finally went through the ratios so slowly that he did not get enough to eat in the course of a day. Finally it would take the pig about 10 minutes to transport four coins a distance of about 6 feet. This problem behavior developed repeatedly in successive pigs.

There have also been other instances: hamsters that stopped working in a glass case after four or five reinforcements, porpoises and whales that swallow their manipulanda (balls and inner tubes), cats that will not leave the area of the feeder, rabbits that will not go to the feeder, the great difficulty in many species of conditioning vocalization with food reinforcement, problems in conditioning a kick in a cow, the failure to get appreciably increased effort out of the ungulates with increased drive, and so on. These we shall not dwell on in detail, nor shall we discuss how they might be overcome.

These egregious failures came as a rather considerable shock to us, for there was nothing in our background in behaviorism to prepare us for such gross inabilities to predict and control the behavior of animals with which we had been working for years.

The examples listed we feel represent a clear and utter failure of conditioning theory. They are far from what one would normally expect on the basis of the theory alone. Furthermore, they are definite, observable; the diagnosis of theory failure does not depend on subtle statistical interpretations or on semantic legerdemain—the animal simply does not do what he has been conditioned to do.

It seems perfectly clear that, with the possible exception of the dancing chicken, which could conceivably, as we have said, be explained in terms of Skinner's superstition paradigm, the other instances do not fit the behavioristic way of thinking. Here we have animals, after having been conditioned to a specific learned response, gradually drifting into behaviors that are entirely different from those which were conditioned. Moreover, it can easily be seen that these particular behaviors to which the animals drift are clear-cut examples of instinctive behaviors having to do with the natural food getting behaviors of the particular species.

The dancing chicken is exhibiting the gallinaceous birds' scratch pattern that in nature often precedes ingestion. The chicken that hammers capsules is obviously exhibiting instinctive behavior having to do with breaking open of seed pods or the killing of insects, grubs, etc. The raccoon is demonstrating so-called "washing behavior." The rubbing and washing response may result, for example, in the removal of the exoskeleton of a crayfish. The pig is rooting or shaking—behaviors which are strongly built into this species and are connected with the food getting repertoire.

These patterns to which the animals drift require greater physical output and therefore are a violation of the so-called "law of least effort." And most damaging of all, they stretch out the time required for reinforcement when nothing in the experimental setup requires them to do so. They have only to do the little tidbit of behavior to which they were conditioned—for example, pick up the coin and put it in the container—to get reinforced immediately. Instead, they drag the process out for a matter of minutes when there is nothing in the contingency which forces them to do this. Moreover, increasing the drive merely intensifies this effect.

It seems obvious that these animals are trapped by strong instinctive behaviors, and clearly we have here a demonstration of the prepotency of such behavior patterns over those which have been conditioned.

We have termed this phenomenon "instinctive drift." The general principle seems to be that wherever an animal has strong instinctive behaviors in the area of the conditioned response, after continued running the organism will drift toward the instinctive behavior to the detriment of the conditioned behavior and even to the delay or preclusion of the reinforcement. In a very boiled-down, simplified form, it might be stated as "learned behavior drifts toward instinctive behavior."

All this, of course, is not to disparage the use of conditioning techniques, but is intended as a demonstration that there are definite weaknesses in the philosophy underlying these techniques. The pointing out of such weaknesses should make possible a worthwhile revision in behavior theory.

The notion of instinct has now become one of our basic concepts in an effort to make sense of the welter of observations which confront us. When behaviorism tossed out instinct, it is our feeling that some of its power of prediction and control were lost with it. From the foregoing examples, it appears that although it was easy to banish the Instinctivists from the science during the Behavioristic Revolution, it was not possible to banish instinct so easily.

And if, as Hebb suggests, it is advisable to reconsider those things that behaviorism explicitly threw out, perhaps it might likewise be advisable to examine what they tacitly brought in—the hidden assumptions which led most disastrously to these breakdowns in the theory.

Three of the most important of these tacit assumptions seem to us to be: that the animal comes to the laboratory as a virtual *tabula rasa,* that species differences are insignificant, and that all responses are about equally conditionable to all stimuli.

It is obvious, we feel, from the foregoing account, that these assumptions are no longer tenable. After 14 years of continuous conditioning and observation of thousands of animals, it is our reluctant conclusion that the behavior of any species cannot be adequately understood, predicted, or controlled without knowledge of its instinctive patterns, evolutionary history, and ecological niche.

In spite of our early successes with the application of behavioristically oriented conditioning theory, we readily admit now that ethological facts and attitudes in recent years have done more to advance our practical control of animal behavior than recent reports from American "learning labs."

Moreover, as we have recently discovered, if one begins with evolution and instinct as the basic format for the science, a very illuminating viewpoint can be developed which leads naturally to a drastically revised and simplified conceptual framework of startling explanatory power (to be reported elsewhere).

It is hoped that this playback on the theory will be behavioral technology's partial repayment to the academic science whose impeccable empiricism we have used so extensively.

NOTE

1. In view of the fact that instinctive behaviors may be common to many zoological species, we consider *species specific* to be a sanitized misnomer, and prefer the possibly septic adjective *instinctive*.

REFERENCES

Beach, F. A. The snark was a boojum. *Amer. Psychologist,* 1950, 5, 115–124.
Breland, K., & Breland, M. A field of applied animal psychology. *Amer. Psychologist,* 1951, 6, 202–204.
Hebb, D. O. The American revolution. *Amer. Psychologist,* 1960, 15, 735–745.
Lorenz, K. Innate behaviour patterns. In *Symposia of the Society for Experimental Biology.* No. 4, *Physiological mechanisms in animal behaviour.* New York: Academic Press, 1950.
Skinner, B. F. Superstition in the pigeon. *J. exp. Psychol.,* 1948, 38, 168–172.
Tinbergen, N. *The study of instinct.* Oxford: Clarendon, 1951.
Whalen, R. E. Comparative psychology. *Amer. Psychologist,* 1961, 16, 84.

Phyletic Differences in Learning[1]

M. E. Bitterman, *Bryn Mawr College*

One way to study the role of the brain in learning is to compare the learning of animals with different brains. Differences in brain structure may be produced by surgical means, or they may be found in nature—as when the learning of different species is compared. Of these two approaches the first (the neurosurgical approach) has been rather popular, but the potentialities of the second still are largely unexplored. Students of learning in animals have been content for the most part to concentrate their attention on a few closely related mammalian forms, chosen largely for reasons of custom and convenience, which they have treated as representative of animals in general. Their work has been dominated almost from its inception by the hypothesis that the laws of learning are the same for all animals—that the wide differences in brain structure which occur in the animal series have a purely quantitative significance.

The hypothesis comes to us from Thorndike (1911), who more than any other man may be credited with having brought the study of animal intelligence into the laboratory. On the basis of his early comparative experiments, Thorndike decided that

Bitterman, M. E. Phyletic differences in learning. *American Psychologist*, 1965, *20*, 396–410. Copyright 1965 by the American Psychological Association, and reproduced by permission.

however much animals might differ in "what" they learned (which could be traced, he thought, to differences in their sensory, motor, and motivational properties), or in the "degree" of their learning ability (some seemed able to learn more than others, and more quickly), the principles which governed their learning were the same. Thorndike wrote:

> If my analysis is true, the evolution of behavior is a rather simple matter. Formally the crab, fish, turtle, dog, cat, monkey and baby have very similar intellects and characters. All are systems of connections subject to change by the laws of exercise and effect [p. 280].

Although Thorndike's hypothesis was greeted with considerable skepticism, experiments with a variety of animals began to turn up functional similarities far more impressive than differences, and before long there was substantial disagreement only as to the *nature* of the laws which were assumed to hold for all animals. As acceptance of the hypothesis grew, the range of animals studied in experiments on learning declined—which, of course, was perfectly reasonable. If the laws of learning were the same everywhere in the animal series, there was nothing to be gained from the study of many different animals; indeed, standardization offered many advantages which it would be foolish to ignore. As the range of animals declined, however, so also did the likelihood of discovering any differences which might in fact exist.

It is difficult for the nonspecialist to appreciate quite how restricted has been the range of animals studied in experiments on animal learning because the restriction is so marked; the novelty of work with lower animals is such that two or three inexpressibly crude experiments with a flatworm may be better publicized than a hundred competent experiments with the rat. Some quantitative evidence on the degree of restriction was provided about 20 years ago by Schneirla, whose conclusion then was that "we do not have a comparative psychology [Harriman, 1946, p. 314]." Schneirla's analysis was carried further by Beach (1950), who plotted the curves which are reproduced in Figure 1. Based on a count of all papers appearing between 1911 and 1948 in the *Journal of Animal Behavior* and its successors, the *Journal of Comparative Psychology,* and the *Journal of Comparative and Physiological Psychology,* the curves show how interest

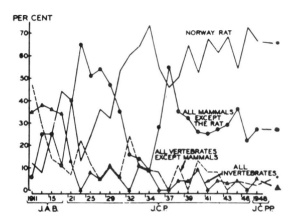

Fig. 1. Percentage of papers dealing with animals in each of four categories which appeared between 1911 and 1948 in the *Journal of Animal Behavior,* the *Journal of Comparative Psychology,* and the *Journal of Comparative and Physiological Psychology* (Beach, 1950). (The points at right, for the decade after 1949, were added by me.)

in the rat mounted while interest in submammalian forms declined. By the '30s, a stable pattern had emerged: about 60 percent of papers on the rat, 30 percent on other mammals (mostly primates), and 10 percent on lower forms. The set of points at the extreme right, which I have added for the decade after 1948, shows no change in the pattern. You will note that these curves are based on papers published only in a single line of journals, and on all papers in those journals—not only the ones which deal with learning; but most of the papers *do* deal with learning, and I know of no other journal which is a richer source of information about learning in submammalians or which, if included in the tabulation, would alter the conclusion that what we know about learning in animals we know primarily from the intensive study of a small number of mammalian forms.

How widespread is the acceptance of Thorndike's hypothesis by contemporary theorists and systematists may be judged from a set of writings recently assembled by Koch (1959). Skinner is quite explicit in his assumption that which animal is studied "doesn't matter." When due allowance has been made for differences in sensory and motor characteristics, he explains, "what remains of . . . behavior shows astonishingly similar properties [Koch, 1959, p. 375]." Tolman, Miller, Guthrie, Estes, and Logan (representing Hull and Spence) rest their perfectly general conclusions about the nature of learning on the data of experiments with a few selected mammals—mostly rat, monkey, and man—skipping lightly back and forth from one to another as if indeed structure did not matter, although Miller "does not deny the possibility that men may have additional capacities which are much less well developed or absent in the lower mammals [Koch, 1959, p. 204]." Harlow alone makes a case for species differences in learning, pointing to the unequal rates of improvement shown by various mammals (mostly primates) trained in long series of discriminative problems, but he gives us no reason to believe that the differences are more than quantitative. While he implies clearly that the capacity for interproblem transfer may be absent entirely in certain lower animals—in the rat, he says, it exists only in a "most rudimentary form [Koch, 1959, p. 505]"—submammalian evidence is lacking.

Although I have been considering thus far only the work of the West, I do not think that things have been very different on the other side of the Curtain. The conditioning has been "classical" rather than "instrumental" in the main, and the favored animal has been the dog rather than the rat, but the range of animals studied in any detail has been small, at least until quite recently, and the principles discovered have been generalized widely. In the words of Voronin (1962), the guiding Pavlovian propositions have been that

> The conditioned reflex is a universal mechanism of activity acquired in the course of the organism's individual life . . . . [and that] In the course of evolution of the animal world there took place only a quantitative growth or complication of higher nervous activity [pp. 161–162].

These propositions are supported, Voronin believes, by the results of some recent Russian comparisons of mammalian and submammalian vertebrates. On the basis of these results, he defines three stages in the evolution of intelligence which are distinguished in terms of the increasing role of learning in the life of the individual organism, and in terms of the precision and delicacy of the learning process. He hastens to assure us, however, that there is nothing really new even at the highest stage, which differs from the others only quantitatively.

The results of the experiments which I shall now describe support quite another view. I began these experiments without very much in the way of conviction as to their outcome, although the formal attractions of the bold Thorndikian hypothesis were rather obvious, and I should have been pleased on purely esthetic grounds to be able to accept it. I was convinced only that the hypothesis had not yet received the critical scrutiny it seemed to warrant, and that it was much too important to be taken any longer on faith. With the familiar rat as a standard, I selected for comparative study another animal—a fish—which I thought similar enough to the rat that it could be studied in analogous experiments, yet different enough to afford a marked neuroanatomical contrast. I did not propose to compare the two animals in terms of numerical scores, as, for example, the number of trials required for (or the number of errors made in) the mastery of some problem, because such differences would not necessarily imply the operation of different learning processes. I proposed instead of compare them in terms of *functional relations*—to find out whether their performance would be affected in the same way by the same variables (Bitterman, 1960). Why I chose to begin with certain variables rather then others probably is not worth considering—the choice was largely intuitive; whatever the reasons, the experiments soon turned up some substantial differences in the learning of fish and rat. I shall describe here two of those differences, and then present the results of some further experiments which were designed to tell us what they mean.

One of the situations developed for the study of learning in the fish is illustrated in Figure 2. The animal is brought in its individual living tank to a black Plexiglas enclosure. The manipulanda are two Plexiglas disks (targets) at which the animal is trained to strike. The targets are mounted on rods set into the needle holders of phonograph cartridges in such a way that when the animal makes contact with one of the targets a voltage is generated across its cartridge. This voltage is used to operate a set of relays which record the response and control its consequences. The targets are illuminated with colored lights or patterns projected upon them from behind; on any given trial, for example, the left target may be green and the right one red, or the left target may show a triangle and the right one a circle. The reward for correct choice is a *Tubifex* worm discharged into the water through a small opening at the top of the enclosure—the worm is discharged from an eye-dropper whose bulb is compressed by a pair of solenoid-operated jaws. When a worm is dropped, a magazine light at the rear of the enclosure is turned on for a few seconds, which signals that a worm has been dropped and provides some diffuse illumination which enables the animal to find it. All of the events of training are programed automatically and recorded on tape.[2]

I shall talk about two kinds of experiments which have been done in this situation. The first is concerned with *habit reversal*. Suppose an animal is trained to choose one of two stimuli, either for a fixed number of trials or to some criterion level of correct choice, and then the positive and negative stimuli are reversed; that is, the previously unrewarded stimulus now is rewarded, and the previously rewarded stimulus is unrewarded. After the same number of trials as were given in the original problem, or when the original criterion has been reached in the first reversal, the positive and negative stimuli are reversed again—and so forth.

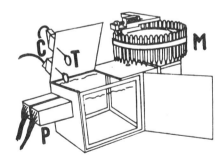

FIG. 2. A situation for the study of discrimination in the fish. (T, targets which are lowered into the water as the cover of the enclosure is brought down; C, phonograph cartridges which hold the targets and register contacts with them; P, projectors for projecting various stimuli on the targets; M, live-worm dispenser.)

In such an experiment, the rat typically shows a dramatic improvement in performance. It may make many errors in the early reversals, but as training proceeds it reverses more and more readily.

In Figure 3, the performance of a group of African mouthbreeders is compared with that of a group of rats in a series of spatial reversals. (In a spatial problem, the animal chooses between a pair of stimuli which differ only with respect to their position in space, and reinforcement is correlated with position, e.g., the stimulus on the left is reinforced.) The apparatus used for the rat was analogous to the apparatus for the fish which you have already seen. On each trial, the animal was offered a choice between two identically illuminated panels set into the wall of the experimental chamber. It responded by pressing one of the panels, and correct choice operated a feeder which discharged a pellet of food into a lighted food cup. The fish were trained in an early version of the apparatus which you have already seen. For both species, there were 20 trials per day to the criterion of 17 out of 20 correct choices, positive and negative positions being reversed for each animal whenever it met that criterion. Now consider the results. The upper curve of the pair you see here is quite representative of the performance of rats in such a problem—rising at first, and then falling in negatively accelerated fashion to a low level; with a little more training than is shown here, the animals reverse after but a single error. The lower curve is quite representative of the performance of fish in such a problem—there is no progressive improvement, but instead some tendency toward progressive deterioration as training continues.

How is this difference to be interpreted? We may ask first whether the results indicate anything beyond a quantitative difference in the learning of the two animals. It might be contended that reversal learning simply goes on more slowly in the fish than in the rat—that in 10 or 15 more reversals the fish, too, would have shown progressive improvement. In fact, however, the training of fish has been carried much further in later experiments, some animals completing more than 150 reversals without any sign of improvement. I invite anyone who remains skeptical on this point to persist even longer in the search for improvement.

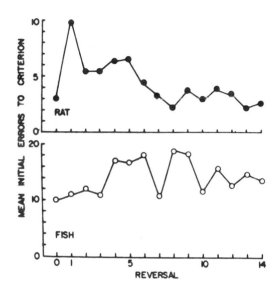

Fig. 3. Spatial habit reversal in fish and rat. (The fish data are taken from Bitterman, Wodinsky, & Candland, 1958; the rat data are from Gonzalez, Roberts, & Bitterman, 1964.)

Another possibility to be considered is that the difference between fish and rat which is reflected in these curves is not a difference in learning at all, but a difference in some confounded variable—sensory, motor, or motivational. Who can say, for example, whether the sensory and the motor demands made upon the two animals in these experiments were exactly the same? Who can say whether the fish were just as hungry as the rats, or whether the bits of food given the fish were equal in reward value to those given the rats? It would, I must admit, be a rare coincidence indeed if the conditions employed for the two animals were exactly equal in all of these potentially important respects. How, then, is it possible to find out whether the results obtained are to be attributed to a difference in learning, or to a difference in sensory, or in motor, or in motivational factors? A frank critic might say that it was rather foolish to have made the comparison in the first place, when a moment's thought would have shown that it could not possibly have any meaningful outcome. It is interesting to note that neither Harlow nor Voronin shows any appreciation of this problem. We may doubt, then, whether they have evidence even for quantitative differences in the *learning* of their various animals.

I do not, of course, know how to arrange a set of conditions for the fish which will make sensory and motor demands exactly equal to those which are made upon the rat in some given experimental situation. Nor do I know how to equate drive level or reward value in the two animals. Fortunately, however, meaningful comparisons still are possible, because for *control by equation* we may substitute what I call *control by systematic variation*. Consider, for example, the hypothesis that the difference between the curves which you see here is due to a difference, not in learning, but in degree of hunger. The hypothesis implies that there is a level of hunger at which the fish *will* show progressive improvement, and, put in this way, the hypothesis becomes easy to test. We have only to vary level of hunger widely in different groups of fish, which we know well how to do. If, despite the widest possible variation in hunger, progressive improvement fails to appear in the fish, we may reject the hunger hypothesis. Hypotheses about other variables also may be tested by systematic variation. With regard to the question of reversal learning, I shall simply say here that progressive improvement has appeared in the rat under a wide variety of experimental conditions—it is difficult, in fact, to find a set of conditions under which the rat does not show improvement. In the fish, by contrast, reliable evidence of improvement has failed to appear under a variety of conditions.

I cannot, of course, prove that the fish is incapable of progressive improvement. I only can give you evidence of failure to find it in the course of earnest efforts; and the point is important enough, perhaps, that you may be willing to look at some more negative results. The curves of Figure 4 summarize the outcome of an experiment in which the type of problem was varied. Three groups of mouthbreeders were given 40 trials per day and reversed daily, irrespective of their performance. In the visual problem, reinforcement was correlated with color and independent of position, which varied randomly from trial to trial; e.g., red positive on odd days and green positive on even days. In the confounded problem, reinforcement was correlated both with color and position; e.g., red always on the left, green always on the right, with red-left positive on odd days and green-right posi-

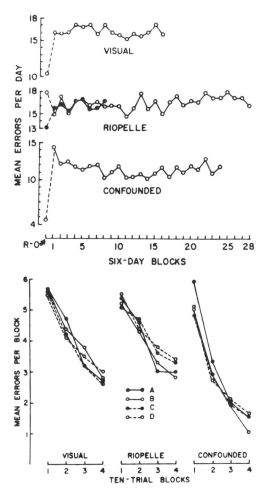

Fig. 4. Visual habit reversal in the fish. (The upper curves show between-sessions performance in each of three problems; the lower curves show within-sessions performance at various stages of training—A, early, D, late—in each problem. These data are taken from some as yet unpublished experiments by Behrend, Domesick, and Bitterman.)

tive on even days. The Riopelle problem was like the visual problem, except that each day's colors were chosen from a group of four, with the restriction that there be no more than partial reversal from one day to the next; i.e., yesterday's negative now positive with a "new" color negative, or yesterday's positive now negative with a "new" color now positive. The upper curves show that there was no improvement over days in any of the three problems (the suggestion of an initial decline in the confounded curve is not statistically reliable). The lower curves show that there was a considerable amount of learning over the 40 trials of each day in each problem and at every stage of training, but that the pattern of improvement over trials did not change as training continued. Negative results of this sort now have been obtained under a variety of conditions wide enough, I think, that the burden of proof now rests with the skeptic. Until someone produces positive results, I shall assume that the fish is incapable of progressive improvement, and that we have come here upon a difference in the learning of fish and rat.

Experiments on *probability learning* also have given different results for rat and fish. Suppose that we train an animal in a choice situation with a ratio of reinforcement other than 100:0; that is, instead of rewarding one alternative on 100 percent of trials and the other never, we reward one alternative on, say, a random 70 percent of trials and the other on the remaining 30 percent of trials, thus constituting what may be called a *70:30 problem*. Under some conditions, rat and fish both "maximize" in such a problem, which is to say that they tend always to choose the more frequently reinforced alternative. Under other conditions—specifically, under conditions in which the distribution of reinforcements is exactly controlled—the rat continues to maximize, but the fish "matches," which is to say that its distribution of choices approximates the distribution of reinforcements: In a 70:30 problem, it chooses the 70 percent alternative on about 70 percent of trials and the 30 percent alternative on the remaining trials.

Figure 5 shows some sample data for a visual problem in which the discriminanda were horizontal and vertical stripes. In the first stage of the experiment, response to one of the stripes was rewarded on a random 70 percent of each day's 20 trials, and

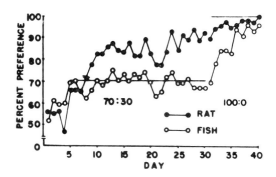

FIG. 5. Visual probability learning in fish and rat (from Bitterman, Wodinsky, & Candland, 1958).

response to the other stripe was rewarded on the remaining 30 percent of the trials—a 70:30 problem. In the second stage of the experiment the ratio of reinforcement was changed to 100:0, response to the 70 percent stripe of the first stage being consistently rewarded. The curves shown are plotted in terms of the percentage of each day's responses which were made to the more frequently rewarded alternative. The fish went rapidly from a near-chance level of preference for the 70 percent stimulus to about a 70 percent preference, which was maintained from Day 5 until Day 30. With the beginning of the 100:0 training, the preference shifted rapidly upward to about the 95 percent level. The preference of the rats for the more frequently reinforced stimulus rose gradually from a near-chance level at the start of the 70:30 training to about the 90 percent level on Day 30. In the 10 days of 100:0 training, this preference continued to increase gradually, as it might have done irrespective of the shift from inconsistent to consistent reinforcement. Some further evidence of the close correspondence between choice ratio and reward ratio, which is easy to demonstrate in the fish, is presented in Figure 6. The upper portion shows the performance of two groups of mouth-breeders; one trained on a 100:0 and the other on a 70:30 confounded (black-white) problem, and both then shifted to the 0:100 problem (the less frequently rewarded alternative of the first phase now being consistently rewarded). The lower portion

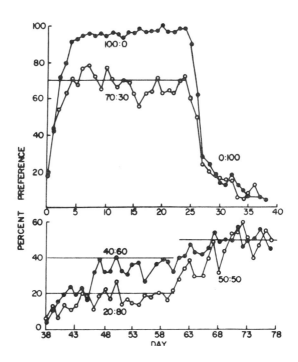

Fig. 6. Probability matching in the fish (from Behrend & Bitterman, 1961).

shows what happened when one group then was shifted to 40:60 and the other to 20:80, after which both were shifted to 50:50.

Two characteristics of these data should be noted. First, the probability matching which the fish curves demonstrate is an individual, not a group phenomenon—that is, it is not an artifact of averaging. All the animals in the group behave in much the same way. I make this obvious point because some averaged data which have been taken as evidence of matching in the rat are indeed unrepresentative of individual performances.[3] Second, the matching shown by the fish is random rather than systematic. The distribution of choices recorded in the 70:30 problem looks like the distribution of colors which might be obtained by drawing marbles at random from a sack of black and white marbles with a color ratio of 70:30—that is, no sequential dependency is to be found in the data. While the rat typically maximizes, it may on occasion show a correspondence of choice ratio and reward ratio which can be traced to some systematic pattern of choice, like the patterns which are displayed in analogous experiments by human subjects. For example, a correspondence reported by Hickson (1961) has been traced to a tendency in his rats to choose on each trial the alternative which had been rewarded on the immediately preceding trial. Quite the opposite tendency, which also tends to produce a correspondence between choice ratio and reinforcement ratio, has been found in the monkey—a tendency to *avoid* the rewarded alternative of the preceding trial (Wilson, Oscar, & Bitterman, 1964a, 1964b). The matching shown by the fish, which I shall call *random matching*, is a very different sort of thing.

Here then, are two striking differences between rat and fish. In experiments on habit reversal, the rat shows progressive improvement while the fish does not. In experiments on probability learning, the fish shows random matching while the rat does not. These results suggest a number of interesting questions, of which I shall raise here only two: First, there is the question of how the two differences are related. From the point of view of parsimony, the possibility must be considered that they reflect a single underlying difference in the functioning of the two animals—one which has to do with adjustment to inconsistent reinforcement. Inconsistency of reinforcement certainly is involved in both kinds of experiment, between sessions in reversal learning and within sessions in probability learning. It also is possible, however, that the results for reversal learning reflect one functional difference and the results for probability learning quite another. A second question concerns the relation between the observed differences in behavior and differences in brain structure. We may wonder, for example, to what extent the cortex of the rat is responsible for its progressive improvement in habit reversal, or for its failure to show random matching. In an effort to answer such questions we have begun to do some experiments, analogous to those which differentiate fish and normal rat, with a variety of other animals, and with rats surgically deprived in infancy of relevant brain tissues.

I shall describe first some results for extensively decorticated

rats (Gonzalez et al., 1964). The animals were operated on at
the age of 15 or 16 days in a one-stage procedure which resulted
in the destruction of about 70 percent of the cortex. Two sample
lesions, one relatively small and one relatively large, are shown
in Figure 7. The experimental work with the operates, like the
work with normals, was begun after they had reached maturity—
at about 90 days of age. From the methodological viewpoint, work
with a brain-injured animal is perfectly equivalent to work with
a normal animal of another species, and rats operated in our standard fashion are treated in all respects as such, with systematic
variation employed to control for the effects of sensory, motor,
and motivational factors. The substantive relation of the work
with decorticated rats to the work with normal animals of different species is obvious: We are interested in whether extensive

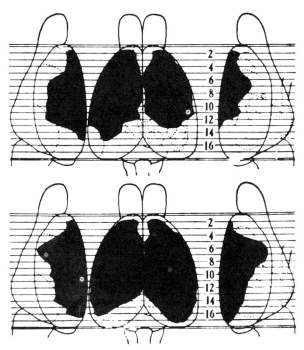

Fig. 7. Extent of cortical destruction in two rats operated at the age of 15
days and sacrificed at the age of 150 days. (The two brains are selected to
illustrate the range and general locus of injury produced by the operation.
From Gonzalez, Robert, & Bitterman, 1964.)

cortical damage will produce in the rat the kinds of behavior which are characteristic of precortical animals, such as the fish, or of animals with only very limited cortical development.

The results for decorticated rats emphasize the importance of the distinction between spatial and visual problems. In a pure spatial problem, you will remember, the two alternatives are identical except for position in space, and reinforcement is correlated with position, e.g., the alternative on the left is reinforced. In a pure visual problem, the two alternatives are visually differentiated, each occupying each of the two positions equally often, and reinforcement is correlated with visual appearance— e.g., the green alternative is reinforced independently of its position. The behavior of the decorticated rat is indistinguishable from that of the normal rat in spatial problems, but in visual problems it differs from the normal in the same way as does the fish.

The criterion-reversal performance of a group of decorticated rats trained in a spatial problem is shown in Figure 8 along with that of a group of normal controls. There were 20 trials per day by the correction method, and the criterion of learning was 17 out of 20 correct choices. As you can see, the performance of the two groups was very much the same in the original problem. In the first 10 reversals the operates made more errors than did the normals, but (like the normals) they showed progressive improvement, and in the last 10 reversals, there was no difference between the two groups. The results for two additional groups, decorticated and normal, trained under analogous conditions in a visual problem (a brightness discrimination) are plotted in Figure 9. Again, the performance of normals and operates was much the same in the original problem. In the subsequent reversals, the error scores of the normal animals rose at first and then declined in characteristic fashion, but the error scores of the operates rose much more markedly and showed no subsequent tendency to decline.

In spatial probability learning the performance of the operates was indistinguishable from that of normals, but in visual probability learning the operates showed random matching. The asymptotic preferences of operates and normals, first in a 70:30 and then in a 50:50 brightness discrimination, are shown in

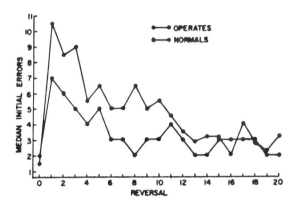

Fig. 8. Spatial habit reversal in normal rats and in rats extensively decorticated in infancy (from Gonzalez, Roberts, & Bitterman, 1964).

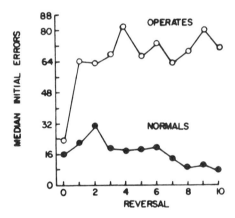

Fig. 9. Visual habit reversal in normal rats and in rats extensively decorticated in infancy (from Gonzalez, Roberts, & Bitterman, 1964).

Table 1. In the 70:30 problem, the operates came to choose the 70 percent stimulus on about 70 percent of trials (the mean was 71.7 percent); in the 50:50 problem they chose the two stimuli about equally often (the mean preference for the former 70 percent stimulus was 53.7 percent). No sequential dependencies could be found in their behavior. By contrast, the normal animals tended

TABLE 1

Preferences of Decorticated Rats (O) and Normal Controls (N) for the
More Frequently Reinforced Alternative in a 70:30 Visual Problem
and for the Same Alternative in a Subsequent 50:50 Problem.

Subject	70:30 problem	50:50 problem
O-1	68.0	49.5
O-2	69.5	53.0
O-3	71.5	47.0
O-4	73.5	57.0
O-5	76.0	62.0
N-1	64.5	CP
N-2	79.0	CP
N-3	89.5	86.0
N-4	90.0	CP
N-5	90.0	80.0

Note.—CP means choice of one position on 90% or more of trials. Data
from Gonzalez, Roberts, and Bitterman (1964).

to maximize in the 70:30 problem. The two whose preferences
came closest to 70 percent adopted rigid position habits (CP)
in the 50:50 problem, while one of the others also responded to
position, and two continued in the previously established preference. In both spatial experiments, then, the decorticated rats behaved like normal rats, while in both visual experiments they
behaved like fish.

These results are compatible with the hypothesis that the
cortex of the rat is responsible in some measure for its progressive
improvement in habit reversal and for its failure to show random
probability matching, at least in visual problems. They are compatible also with the hypothesis that the behavioral differences
between fish and rat which appear in the two kinds of experiment are reflections of a single functional difference between
the two species. The latter hypothesis is contradicted, however,
by some results for the pigeon which I shall now describe. I need
not go into any detail about the experimental situation, because
it is a fairly familiar one. Suffice it to say that the Skinnerian
key-pecking apparatus was adapted for discrete-trials choice experiments directly analogous to those done with fish and rat. The
bird, in a darkened enclosure, pecks at one of two lighted keys,
correct choice being rewarded by access to grain. Contingencies
are programed automatically, and responses are recorded on tape.

In experiments on habit reversal, both visual and spatial, the pigeon behaves like the rat; that is, it gives clear evidence of progressive improvement (Bullock & Bitterman, 1962a). Shown in Figure 10 is the criterion-reversal performance of a group of pigeons trained in a blue-green discrimination. There were 40 trials per day to the criterion of 34 correct choices in the 40 trials, with positive and negative colors reversed for each animal whenever it met that criterion. The results look very much like those obtained in analogous experiments with the rat: There is an initial increase in mean errors to criterion, followed by a progressive, negatively accelerated decline. Now what can we say of the behavior of the pigeon in experiments on probability learning? Figure 11 gives evidence of a correspondence between choice ratio and reward ratio as close in the pigeon as in the fish, and statistical analysis shows that the matching is random. The points for the pigeon, like those for the fish, represent the pooled results of a variety of experiments, both published and unpublished, which were carried out in my laboratory. Unlike the points for the fish, however, the points for the pigeon are based only on *visual* data, because the pigeon shows random matching only in visual problems; in spatial problems it tends to maximize (Bullock & Bitterman, 1962; Graf, Bullock, & Bitterman, 1964).

The results for the pigeon, then, are in a sense intermediate between those for the rat and for the fish. Like the rat, the pigeon shows progressive improvement in habit reversal, but, like the fish, it shows random probability matching—in visual problems if not in spatial ones. One conclusion which may be drawn from these results is that experiments on habit reversal and experiments on probability learning tap somewhat different processes. If the processes were the same, any animal would behave either like the fish, or like the rat, in both kinds of experiment. We have, then, been able to separate the processes underlying the two phenomena which differentiate fish and rat by a method which might be called *phylogenetic filtration*. It is interesting, too, that the visual-spatial dichotomy which appeared in work with the decorticated rat appears again in the probability learning of the pigeon. In experiments on habit reversal, the pigeon behaves like a normal rat; in experiments on probability learn-

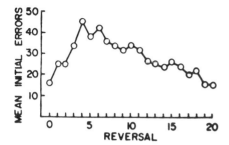

Fig. 10. Visual habit reversal in the pigeon (from Stearns & Bitterman, 1965).

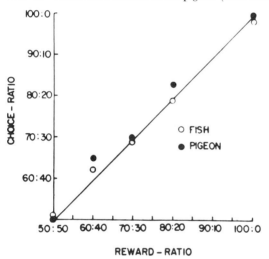

Fig. 11. Probability matching in fish and pigeon. (The points for the fish are based both on spatial and on visual data, while those for the pigeon are based only on visual data.)

ing, the pigeon behaves, not like a fish, but like an extensively decorticated rat.

Now let me show you some comparable data for several other species. Being very much interested in the reptilian brain, which is the first to show true cortex, I have devoted a good deal of ef-

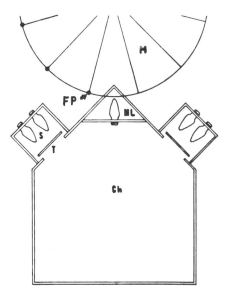

FIG. 12. A situation for the study of discrimination in the turtle. (Ch, animal's chamber; T, target; S, lamps for projecting colored lights on the targets; M, feeder which rotates a pellet of food, FP, into the chamber; ML, magazine lamp which is turned on to signal the presentation of food. From Bitterman, 1964.)

fort to the development of a satisfactory technique for the study of learning in the painted turtle. After some partial success with a primitive T maze (Kirk & Bitterman, 1963), I came finally to the situation diagramed in Figure 12. As in our latest apparatus for monkey, rat, pigeon, and fish, the turtle is presented with two differentially illuminated targets between which it chooses by pressing against one of them. Correct choice is rewarded with a pellet of hamburger or fish which is rotated into the chamber on a solenoid-driven tray. Some experiments on habit reversal now under way in this situation have yielded the data plotted in Figure 13. One group of turtles was trained on a spatial problem (both targets the same color) and another group on a visual problem (red versus green). There were 20 trials per day, with reversal after every 4 days. As you can see, progressive improvement has appeared in the spatial problem, but not in the visual

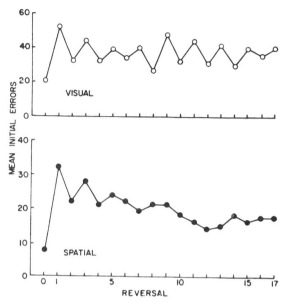

FIG. 13. Visual and spatial habit reversal in the turtle. (The data are taken from some as yet unpublished experiments by Holmes and Bitterman.)

problem. Some experiments on probability learning also are under way in this situation. In spatial problems, only maximizing and nonrandom matching (reward following) have been found, but in visual problems, random matching has begun to appear. This pattern of results, you will remember, is exactly that which was found in decorticated rats. Insofar as performance in these tests is concerned, then, extensive decortication in infancy turns rats into turtles.

I come now to some work with invertebrates. Diagramed in Figure 14 is a Y maze for the cockroach used in the experiments of Longo (1964). The technique is a much cruder one than those used for vertebrates, but it represents, I think, a considerable advance over anything that has yet been done with the cockroach. The motive utilized is shock avoidance: Ten seconds after the animal is introduced into the starting box, shock is turned on, and remains on, until the animal enters the goal box,

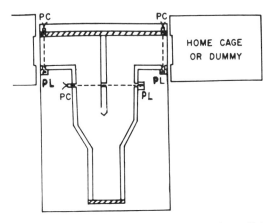

FIG. 14. A Y maze for the cockroach. (PC, photocell; PL, photocell lamp; S, starting compartment. From Longo, 1964.)

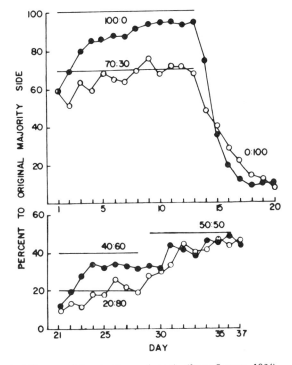

FIG. 15. Spatial probability matching in the cockroach (from Longo, 1964).

which is its home cage; if the animal reaches the goal box in less than 10 seconds, it avoids shock entirely. Choices are detected objectively by photocells, but complete automation is not possible, because no satisfactory alternative to handling the animal has been found. The results of an experiment on spatial probability learning in the cockroach, which was patterned after those done with vertebrates, are plotted in Figure 15. Like the fish— but *unlike any higher vertebrate*—the cockroach shows random matching under spatial conditons. The results of an experiment on spatial habit reversal in the cockroach are plotted in Figure 16. Three groups of animals were given 10 trials per day—one group reversed each day, another group reversed every 4 days, and a control group never reversed during the stage of the experiment for which data are plotted. Although the 4-day group showed no significant improvement (its curve hardly declines at all beyond the first point, which is for the original problem), the daily group did show significant improvement (its curve declining in much the same way as that of the control group). What does this result mean? Have we found in the primitive

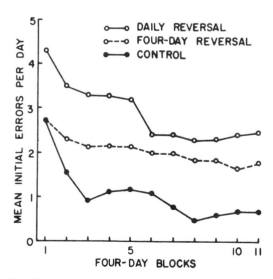

Fig. 16. Spatial habit reversal in the cockroach (from Longo, 1964).

cockroach a capability which does not exist in the fish? A consideration of some results for the earthworm will help to answer this question.

Diagramed in Figure 17 is a T maze developed for the earthworm by Datta (1962). The stem of the maze is bright, warm, and dry, and the animal occasionally is shocked in it. A correct turn at the choice point carries the animal to its dark, moist, cool, shock-free home container, while an incorrect turn is punished with shock from a metal door which converts one arm of the maze into a cul. When the animal is shocked for contact with the door, a sensitive relay in the circuit is energized, thereby providing an objective index of error. This technique, again, is a crude one by vertebrate standards, but it seems to give reliable results. Some sample data on spatial habit reversal are plotted in Figure 18. The worms were given five trials per day and reversed every 4 days. Note that the mean number of errors rose in the first reversal, and thereafter declined progressively, the animals doing better in the fourth and fifth reversals than in the original problem. In a further experiment, however, this improvement was found to be independent of reversal training per se and a function only of general experience in the maze: A control group, trained always to the same side while an experimental group was reversed repeatedly, did not differ from the experimental group when eventually it, too, was reversed. This test for the effects of general experience is feasible in the earthworm, because the turning preferences which it develops do not persist from session to session. The analysis of the progressive improvement shown by the cockroach is, however, a more difficult matter, and I must be content here simply to state Longo's opinion that it reflects, as in the earthworm, not an improvement in reversal capability, but an improved adjustment to the maze situation. The course of that general improvement is traced by the curve for the control group, which parallels that of the daily group. Nonspecific improvement probably is not as evident in the vertebrate data because general adjustment to the experimental situation proceeds rapidly and is essentially complete at the end of pretraining.[4]

The results of these experiments on habit reversal and probability learning in a variety of animals are summarized in Table

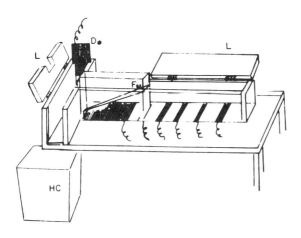

FIG. 17.   A T maze for the earthworm. (L, lid; Do, metal door which converts one arm of the maze into a cul and delivers shock for erroneous choice; Fu, funnel to reduce retracing; HC, home container. From Datta, 1962.)

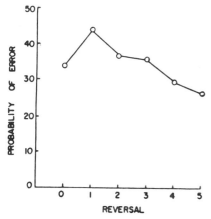

FIG. 18.   Spatial habit reversal in the earthworm (from Datta, 1962).

2. Spatial and visual problems are categorized separately because they give different results. The rows for all the subjects except one are ordered in accordance with the conventional scale of complexity—monkey at the top and earthworm at the bottom. The only subject whose place in the table is not based on preconceived

M. E. Bitterman

complexity is the decorticated rat, whose placement (with the turtle, between the pigeon and the fish) is dictated by experimental outcomes. The differences between fish and rat which provided points of departure for the subsequent work with other

TABLE 2
Behavior of a Variety of Animals in Four Classes of Problem which Differentiate Rat and Fish Expressed in Terms of Similarity to the Behavior of One or the Other of These Two Reference Animals

Animal	Spatial problems		Visual problems	
	Reversal	Probability	Reversal	Probability
Monkey	R	R	R	R
Rat	R	R	R	R
Pigeon	R	R	R	F
Turtle	R	R	F	F
Decorticated rat	R	R	F	F
Fish	F	F	F	F
Cockroach	F	F	—	—
Earthworm	F	—	—	—

Note.—F means behavior like that of the fish (random probability matching and failure of progressive improvement in habit reversal). R means behavior like that of the rat (maximizing or nonrandom probability matching and progressive improvement in habit reversal). Transitional regions are connected by the stepped line. The brackets group animals which have not yet been differentiated by these problems.

organisms also provide a frame of reference for reading the table: R means that the results obtained in a given kind of experiment with a given subject are like those for the rat (that is, progressive improvement in habit reversal and failure of random matching), while F means that the results obtained are like those for the fish (that is, random matching and failure of progressive improvement). It should be understood that these entries are made with varying degrees of confidence. Where there are no data, there are no entries, but an entry is made even where, as in the case of the turtle, the data are yet fragmentary and incomplete. All entries are based on data from my laboratory, except those for reversal learning in the monkey, which are based on the literature.

The table is an orderly one. In each column there is a single transition from F to R as the scale of subjects is ascended, although the point of transition varies from column to column, suggesting a certain functional independence: Rat-like behavior in spatial problems of both kinds appears first in decorticated rat and turtle, rat-like behavior in visual reversal learning appears first in pigeon, and rat-like behavior in visual probability learning appears first in rat. The eight subjects fall into four different groupings: monkey and rat in one; pigeon in a second; turtle and decorticated rat in a third; fish, cockroach, and earthworm in a fourth. Monkey and rat fall into the same grouping because they are not differentiated by these experiments when all failures of random probability matching are classified as R. The data for the two mammals do, however, show different kinds of sequential dependency in experiments on probability learning, reward following in the rat giving way in the monkey to the opposite strategy (avoiding the rewarded alternatives of the preceding trial). It is interesting to note that this new strategy of the monkey has been manifested thus far only with respect to the spatial locus of reward, even when the alternatives have been visually distinct. This finding fits the generalization suggested at other points in the table: that as we ascend the phyletic scale new modes of adjustment appear earlier in spatial than in visual contexts.

It is of some interest to ask whether R modes of adjustment are in any sense more effective than F modes, and for habit reversal, at least, the answer is clear. Progressive improvement is on its face a superior adjustment, representing a flexibility that cannot help but be of value in an animal's adjustment to changing life circumstances. The answer for probability learning is less clear, although it can be said that maximizing produces a higher percentage of correct choice than does matching. In a 70:30 problem, for example, the probability of correct choice is .70 for maximizing but only .58— $(.70 \times .70) + (.30 \times .30)$ — for matching. Nonrandom matching is no more successful than random matching by this criterion, but we know that in human subjects it is the outcome of an effort to find a principle that will permit 100 percent correct choice; the hypotheses tested reflect the observed reward ratio, and they produce a corresponding choice ratio. To the degree that nonrandom matching in infrahuman subjects is based on an emerging hypothetical or strategic capability, it represents a considerable functional advance over random matching.

The table does, of course, have certain obvious limitations. Clearly, I should like to be able to write *bird* rather than *pigeon*, I should like by *fish* to mean more than *mouthbreeder*, and so forth. It will be interesting to discover how representative of their classes are the particular species studied in these experiments—whose choice was dictated largely by practical considerations—and to extend the comparisons to other classes and phyla. I can say, too, that the behavioral categories used in the table almost certainly will need refining; already the R-F dichotomy is strained by the data on probability learning (with R standing for maximizing, for near maximizing, and for nonrandom matching of several different kinds), while better techniques must be found for isolating the various constituents of progressive improvement in habit reversal. The uncontaminated linear order which now appears in the table, while undeniably esthetic, is rather embarrassing from the standpoint of the far-from-linear evolutionary relationships among the species studied; nonlinearities are perhaps to be expected as the behavioral categories are refined and as the range of tests is broadened.

Whatever its limitations, the table is useful, I think, not only as a summary of results already obtained, but as a guide to further research. Almost certainly, the order in the table will permit us to reduce the amount of parametric variation which must be done before we are satisfied that some phenomenon for which we are looking in a given animal is not to be found. Suppose, for example, that we had begun to work with the turtle before the pigeon, and suppose that we had sought persistently, but in vain, for evidence of random matching in spatial probability learning, being satisfied at last to enter an R for the turtle in the second column of the table. Turning then to the pigeon, we should be prepared after many fewer unsuccessful efforts to enter an R. I do not mean, of course, that systematic parametric variation is no longer important in comparative research; we must continue to do a great deal of it, especially at points of transition in the table, and wherever the entries fail to reflect gross discontinuities in the evolutionary histories of the organisms concerned.

I do think, however, that the table will save us some parametric effort *in certain regions*—effort which may be diverted to the task of increasing the range of organisms and the range of tests represented. It does not seem unreasonable to expect that, thus expanded, the table will provide some useful clues to the evolution of intelligence and its relation to the evolution of the brain.

NOTES

1. This paper was presented in March 1964, under the auspices of the National Science Foundation and of the National Institute of Mental Health, at the Institut de Psychologie in Paris, the Institute of Experimental Psychology in Oxford, the Institut für Hirnforschung in Zurich, and the Nencki Institute of Experimental Biology in Warsaw. The research described was supported by Grant MH-02857 from the National Institute of Mental Health and by Contract Nonr 2829 (01) with the Office of Naval Research.

2. The response-detection system and a dry-pellet feeder are described in Longo and Bitterman (1959). The live-worm dispenser—which makes it possible to extend the work to species (like the goldfish) that do not take an abundance of dry food—is described in Longo and Bitterman (1963). Programing procedures are described in my chapter on "Animal Learning" in Sidowski (1965). The fully automated technique was developed only after some years of work with less elegant ones which did not permit the complete removal of the experimenter from the experimental situation. The advantages of such removal, from the standpoint of efficiency and of objectivity, should be obvious; yet I have encountered, especially in Europe, a good deal of hostility toward automation. In almost every audience, someone can be counted on to say, rather self-righteously, "*I* like to *watch* my animals." I explain that the automated techniques were developed after a good deal of watching to determine what was worth watching, and that they simply transfer a good part of the watching function to devices more sensitive and reliable than the experimenter, but that they do not rule out the possibility of further watching. In fact, freed of the necessity of programing trials and of recording data, the experimenter now can watch more intently than ever before. The United States has seen great advances in mammalian technique during recent years, while submammalian technique (except for the Skinnerian work with pigeons) has remained terribly primitive. A systematic comparative psychology will require some parallel advances in submammalian technique.

3. The averaged data are cited by Estes (1957). The distribution of individual performances is given by Bitterman, Wodinsky, and Candland (1958).

4. A possibility to be considered is that a portion at least of the cockroach's improvement was due to improvement in the experimenter, of whom the conduct of the experiment required considerable skill. The same may be said of the first in the series of experiments with the fish by Wodinsky and Bitterman (1957) which was the only one to show anything like progressive improvement and whose results have not been replicated in work with automated equipment; the pattern of improvement was, in-

cidentally, quite unlike that found in mammals. A study of another arthropod (the Bermuda land crab) in a simple escape situation, by Datta, Milstein, and Bitterman (1960), gave no evidence of improvement.

REFERENCES

Beach, F. A. The snark was a boojum. *American Psychologist*, 1950, 5, 115–124.

Behrend, E. R., & Bitterman, M. E. Probability-matching in the fish. *American Journal of Psychology*, 1961, 74, 542–551.

Bitterman, M. E. Toward a comparative psychology of learning. *American Psychologist*, 1960, 15, 704–712.

Bitterman, M. E. An instrumental technique for the turtle. *Journal of the Experimental Analysis of Behavior*, 1964, 7, 189–190.

Bitterman, M. E., Wodinsky, J., & Candland, D. K. Some comparative psychology. *American Journal of Psychology*, 1958, 71, 94–110.

Bullock, D. H., & Bitterman, M. E. Habit reversal in the pigeon. *Journal of Comparative and Physiological Psychology*, 1962, 55, 958–962. (a)

Bullock, D. H., & Bitterman, M. E. Probability-matching in the pigeon. *American Journal of Psychology*, 1962, 75, 634–639. (b)

Datta, L. G. Learning in the earthworm, *Lumbricus terrestris*. *American Journal of Psychology*, 1962, 75, 531–553.

Datta, L. G., Milstein, S., & Bitterman, M. E. Habit reversal in the crab. *Journal of Comparative and Physiological Psychology*, 1960, 53, 275–278.

Estes, W. K. Of models and men. *American Psychologist*, 1957, 12, 609–616.

Gonzalez, R. C., Roberts, W. A., & Bitterman, M. E. Learning in adult rats with extensive cortical lesions made in infancy. *American Journal of Psychology*, 1964, 77, 547–562.

Graf, V., Bullock, D. H., & Bitterman, M. E. Further experiments on probability-matching in the pigeon. *Journal of Experimental Analysis of Behavior*, 1964, 7, 151–157.

Harriman, P. L. (Ed.) *Twentieth century psychology.* New York: Philosophical Library, 1946.

Hickson, R. H. Response probability in a two-choice learning situation with varying probability of reinforcement. *Journal of Experimental Psychology*, 1961, 62, 138–144.

Kirk, K. L., & Bitterman, M. E. Habit reversal in the turtle. *Quarterly Journal of Experimental Psychology*, 1963, 15, 52–57.

Koch, S. *Psychology: A study of a science.* Vol. 2. *General systematic formulations, learning, and special processes.* New York: McGraw-Hill, 1959.

Longo, N. Probability-learning and habit-reversal in the cockroach. *American Journal of Psychology*, 1964, 77, 29–41.

Longo, N., & Bitterman, M. E. Improved apparatus for the study of learning in fish. *American Journal of Psychology*, 1959, 72, 616–620.

Longo, N., & Bitterman, M. E. An improved live-worm dispenser. *Journal of the Experimental Analysis of Behavior*, 1963, 6, 279–280.

Sidowski, J. (Ed.) *Experimental methods and instrumentation in psychology.* New York: McGraw-Hill, 1965.

Stearns, E. M., & Bitterman, M. E. A comparison of key-pecking with an ingestive technique for the study of discriminative learning in pigeons. *American Journal of Psychology*, 1965, 78, in press.

Thorndike, E. L. *Animal intelligence.* New York: Macmillan, 1911.

Voronin, L. G. Some results of comparative-physiological investigations of higher nervous activity. *Psychological Bulletin*, 1962, 59, 161–195.

Wilson, W. A., Jr., Oscar, M., & Bitterman, M. E. Probability learning in the monkey. *Quarterly Journal of Experimental Psychology*, 1964, 16, 163–165. (a)

Wilson, W. A., Jr., Oscar, M., & Bitterman, M. E. Visual probability-learning in the monkey. *Psychonomic Science*, 1964, 1, 71–72. (b)

Wodinsky, J., & Bitterman, M. E. Discrimination-reversal in the fish. *American Journal of Psychology*, 1957, 70, 569–576.

Teaching Sign Language to a Chimpanzee

R. Allen Gardner and Beatrice T. Gardner,
University of Nevada

The extent to which another species might be able to use human language is a classical problem in comparative psychology. One approach to this problem is to consider the nature of language, the processes of learning, the neural mechanisms of learning and of language, and the genetic basis of these mechanisms, and then, while recognizing certain gaps in what is known about these factors, to attempt to arrive at an answer by dint of careful scholarship.[1] An alternative approach is to try to teach a form of human language to an animal. We chose the latter alternative and, in June 1966, began training an infant female chimpanzee, named Washoe, to use the gestural language of the deaf. Within the first 22 months of training it became evident that we had been correct in at least one major aspect of method, the use of a gestural language. Additional aspects of method have evolved in the course of the project. These and some implications of our early results can now be described in a way that may be useful in other studies of communicative behavior. Accordingly, in this article we discuss the considerations which led us to use the chimpanzee as a subject and American Sign Language (the lan-

Gardner, R. A. & Gardner, B. T. Teaching sign language to a chimpanzee. *Science,* 1969, *165,* 664–672. Copyright 1969 by the American Association for the Advancement of Science.

guage used by the deaf in North America) as a medium of communication; describe the general methods of training as they were initially conceived and as they developed in the course of the project; and summarize those results that could be reported with some degree of confidence by the end of the first phase of the project.

PRELIMINARY CONSIDERATIONS

The Chimpanzee as a Subject.

Some discussion of the chimpanzee as an experimental subject is in order because this species is relatively uncommon in the psychological laboratory. Whether or not the chimpanzee is the most intelligent animal after man can be disputed; the gorilla, the orangutan, and even the dolphin have their loyal partisans in this debate. Nevertheless, it is generally conceded that chimpanzees are highly intelligent, and that members of this species might be intelligent enough for our purposes. Of equal or greater importance is their sociability and their capacity for forming strong attachments to human beings. We want to emphasize this trait of sociability; it seems highly likely that it is essential for the development of language in human beings, and it was a primary consideration in our choice of a chimpanzee as a subject.

Affectionate as chimpanzees are, they are still wild animals, and this is a serious disadvantage. Most psychologists are accustomed to working with animals that have been chosen, and sometimes bred, for docility and adaptability to laboratory procedures. The difficulties presented by the wild nature of an experimental animal must not be underestimated. Chimpanzees are also very strong animals; a full-grown specimen is likely to weigh more than 120 pounds (55 kilograms) and is estimated to be from three to five times as strong as a man, pound-for-pound. Coupled with the wildness, this great strength presents serious difficulties for a procedure that requires interaction at close quarters with a free-living animal. We have always had to reckon with the likelihood that at some point Washoe's physical maturity will make this procedure prohibitively dangerous.

A more serious disadvantage is that human speech sounds

are unsuitable as a medium of communication for the chimpanzee. The vocal apparatus of the chimpanzee is very different from that of man.[2] More important, the vocal behavior of the chimpanzee is very different from that of man. Chimpanzees do make many different sounds, but generally vocalization occurs in situations of high excitement and tends to be specific to the exciting situations. Undisturbed, chimpanzees are usually silent. Thus, it is unlikely that a chimpanzee could be trained to make refined use of its vocalizations. Moreover, the intensive work of Hayes and Hayes[3] with the chimpanzee Viki indicates that a vocal language is not appropriate for this species. The Hayeses used modern, sophisticated, psychological methods and seem to have spared no effort to teach Viki to make speech sounds. Yet in 6 years Viki learned only four sounds that approximated English words.[4]

Use of the hands, however, is a prominent feature of chimpanzee behavior; manipulatory mechanical problems are their forte. More to the point, even caged, laboratory chimpanzees develop begging and similar gestures spontaneously,[5] while individuals that have had extensive contact with human beings have displayed an even wider variety of communicative gestures.[6] In our choice of sign language we were influenced more by the behavioral evidence that this medium of communication was appropriate to the species than by anatomical evidence of structural similarity between the hands of chimpanzees and of man. The Hayeses point out that human tools and mechanical devices are constructed to fit the human hand, yet chimpanzees have little difficulty in using these devices with great skill. Nevertheless, they seem unable to adapt their vocalizations to approximate human speech.

Psychologists who work extensively with the instrumental conditioning of animals become sensitive to the need to use responses that are suited to the species they wish to study. Lever-pressing in rats is not an arbitrary response invented by Skinner to confound the mentalists; it is a type of response commonly made by rats when they are first placed in a Skinner box. The exquisite control of instrumental behavior by schedules of reward is achieved only if the original responses are well chosen. We chose a language based on gestures because we reasoned that gestures for the chimpanzee should be analogous to bar-pressing for rats, key-pecking for pigeons, and babbling for humans.

American Sign Language.

Two systems of manual communication are used by the deaf. One system is the manual alphabet, or finger spelling, in which configurations of the hand correspond to letters of the alphabet. In this system the words of a spoken language, such as English, can be spelled out manually. The other system, sign language, consists of a set of manual configurations and gestures that correspond to particular words or concepts. Unlike finger spelling, which is the direct encoding of a spoken language, sign languages have their own rules of usage. Word-for-sign translation between a spoken language and a sign language yields results that are similar to those of word-for-word translation between two spoken languages: the translation is often passable, though awkward, but it can also be ambiguous or quite nonsensical. Also, there are national and regional variations in sign languages that are comparable to those of spoken languages.

We chose for this project the American Sign Language (ASL), which, with certain regional variations, is used by the deaf in North America. This particular sign language has recently been the subject of formal analysis.[7] The ASL can be compared to pictograph writing in which some symbols are quite arbitrary and some are quite representational or iconic, but all are arbitrary to some degree. For example, in ASL the sign for "always" is made by holding the hand in a fist, index finger extended (the pointing hand), while rotating the arm at the elbow. This is clearly an arbitrary representation of the concept "always." The sign for "flower," however, is highly iconic; it is made by holding the fingers of one hand extended, all five fingertips touching (the tapered hand), and touching the fingertips first to one nostril then to the other, as if sniffing a flower. While this is an iconic sign for "flower," it is only one of a number of conventions by which the concept "flower" could be iconically represented; it is thus arbitrary to some degree. Undoubtedly, many of the signs of ASL that seem quite arbitrary today once had an iconic origin that was lost through years of stylized usage. Thus, the signs of ASL are neither uniformly arbitrary nor uniformly iconic; rather the degree of abstraction varies from sign to sign over a wide range. This would seem to be a useful property of ASL for our research.

The literate deaf typically use a combination of ASL and finger spelling: for purposes of this project we have avoided the use of finger spelling as much as possible. A great range of expression is possible within the limits of ASL. We soon found that a good way to practice signing among ourselves was to render familiar songs and poetry into signs; as far as we can judge, there is no message that cannot be rendered faithfully (apart from the usual problems of translation from one language to another). Technical terms and proper names are a problem when first introduced, but within any community of signers it is easy to agree on a convention for any commonly used term. For example, among ourselves we do not finger-spell the words *psychologist* and *psychology,* but render them as "think doctor" and "think science." Or, among users of ASL, "California" can be finger-spelled but is commonly rendered as "golden playland." (Incidentally, the sign for "gold" is made by plucking at the earlobe with thumb and forefinger, indicating an earring—another example of an iconic sign that is at the same time arbitrary and stylized.)

The fact that ASL is in current use by human beings is an additional advantage. The early linguistic environment of the deaf children of deaf parents is in some respects similar to the linguistic environment that we could provide for an experimental subject. This should permit some comparative evaluation of Washoe's eventual level of competence. For example, in discussing Washoe's early performance with deaf parents we have been told that many of her variants of standard signs are similar to the baby-talk variants commonly observed when human children sign.

Washoe.

Having decided on a species and a medium of communication, our next concern was to obtain an experimental subject. It is altogether possible that there is some critical early age for the acquisition of this type of behavior. On the other hand, newborn chimpanzees tend to be quite helpless and vegetative. They are also considerably less hardy than older infants. Nevertheless, we reasoned that the dangers of starting too late were much greater than the dangers of starting too early, and we sought the youngest infant we could get. Newborn laboratory chimpanzees are very scarce, and we found that the youngest laboratory infant we could get would be about 2 years old at the time we planned to start the project. It seemed preferable to obtain a wild-caught infant. Wild-caught infants are usually at least 8 to 10 months old before they are available for research. This is because infants rarely reach the United States before they are 5 months old, and to this age must be added 1 or 2 months before final purchase and 2 or 3 months for quarantine and other medical services.

We named our chimpanzee Washoe for Washoe County, the home of the University of Nevada. Her exact age will never be known, but from her weight and dentition we estimated her age to be between 8 and 14 months at the end of June 1966, when she first arrived at our laboratory. (Her dentition has continued to agree with this initial estimate, but her weight has increased rather more than would be expected.) This is very young for a chimpanzee. The best available information indicates that infants are completely dependent until the age of 2 years and semi-dependent until the age of 4; the first signs of sexual maturity (for example, menstruation, sexual swelling) begin to appear at about 8 years, and full adult growth is reached between the ages of 12 and 16.[8] As for the complete life-span, captive specimens have survived for well over 40 years. Washoe was indeed very young when she arrived; she did not have her first canines or molars, her hand-eye coordination was rudimentary, she had only begun to crawl about, and she slept a great deal. Apart from making friends with her and adapting her to the daily routine, we could accomplish little during the first few months.

Laboratory Conditions.

At the outset we were quite sure that Washoe could learn to make various signs in order to obtain food, drink, and other things. For the project to be a success, we felt that something more must be developed. We wanted Washoe not only to ask for objects but to answer questions about them and also to ask us questions. We wanted to develop behavior that could be described as conversation. With this in mind, we attempted to provide Washoe with an environment that might be conducive to this sort of behavior. Confinement was to be minimal, about the same as that of human infants. Her human companions were to be friends and playmates as well as providers and protectors, and they were to introduce a great many games and activities that would be likely to result in maximum interaction with Washoe.

In practice, such an environment is readily achieved with a chimpanzee; bonds of warm affection have always been established between Washoe and her several human companions. We have enjoyed the interaction almost as much as Washoe has, within the limits of human endurance. A number of human companions have been enlisted to participate in the project and relieve each other at intervals, so that at least one person would be with Washoe during all her waking hours. At first we feared that such frequent changes would be disturbing, but Washoe seemed to adapt very well to this procedure. Apparently it is possible to provide an infant chimpanzee with affection on a shift basis.

All of Washoe's human companions have been required to master ASL and to use it extensively in her presence, in association with interesting activities and events and also in a general way, as one chatters at a human infant in the course of the day. The ASL has been used almost exclusively, although occasional finger spelling has been permitted. From time to time, of course, there are lapses into spoken English, as when medical personnel must examine Washoe. At one time, we considered an alternative procedure in which we would sign and speak English to Washoe simultaneously, thus giving her an additional source of informative cues. We rejected this procedure, reasoning that, if she should come to understand speech sooner or more easily than ASL, then she might not pay sufficient attention to our gestures. Another alternative, that of speaking English among ourselves and signing to Washoe, was also rejected. We reasoned that this would make it seem that big chimps talk and only little chimps sign, which might give signing an undesirable social status.

The environment we are describing is not a silent one. The human beings can vocalize in many ways, laughing and making sounds of pleasure and displeasure. Whistles and drums are sounded in a variety of imitation games, and hands are clapped for attention. The rule is that all meaningful sounds, whether vocalized or not, must be sounds that a chimpanzee can imitate.

TRAINING METHODS

Imitation.

The imitativeness of apes is proverbial, and rightly so. Those who have worked closely with chimpanzees have frequently remarked on their readiness to engage in visually guided imitation. Consider the following typical comment of Yerkes:[9] "Chim and Panzee would imitate many of my acts, but never have I heard them imitate a sound and rarely make a sound peculiarly their own in response to mine. As previously stated, their imitative tendency is as remarkable for its specialization and limitations as for its strength. It seems to be controlled chiefly by visual stimuli. Things which are seen tend to be imitated or reproduced. What is heard is not reproduced. Obviously an animal which lacks the tendency to reinstate auditory stimuli—in other words to imitate sounds—cannot reasonably be expected to talk. The human infant exhibits this tendency to a remarkable degree. So also does the parrot. If the imitative tendency of the parrot could be coupled with the quality of intelligence of the chimpanzee, the latter undoubtedly could speak."

In the course of their work with Viki, the Hayeses devised a game in which Viki would imitate various actions on hearing the command "Do this."[10] Once established, this was an effective means of training Viki to perform actions that could be visually guided. The same method should be admirably suited to training a chimpanzee to use sign language; accordingly we have directed much effort toward establishing a version of the "Do this" game with Washoe. Getting Washoe to imitate us was not difficult, for she did so quite spontaneously, but getting her to imitate on command has been another matter altogether. It was not until the 16th month of the project that we achieved any degree of control over Washoe's imitation of gestures. Eventually we got to a point where she would imitate a simple gesture, such as pulling at her ears, or a series of such gestures—first we make a gesture, then she imitates, then we make a second gesture, she imitates the second gesture, and so on—for the reward of being tickled. Up to this writing, however, imitation of this sort has not been an important method for introducing new signs into Washoe's vocabulary.

As a method of prompting, we have been able to use imitation extensively to increase the frequency and refine the form of signs. Washoe sometimes fails to use a new sign in an appropriate situation, or uses another, incorrect sign. At such times we can make the correct sign to Washoe, repeating the performance until she makes the sign herself. (With more stable signs, more indirect forms of prompting can be used—for example, pointing at, or touching, Washoe's hand or a part of her body that should be involved in the sign; making the sign for "sign," which is equivalent to saying "Speak up"; or asking a question in signs, such as "What do you want?" or "What is it?") . Again, with new signs, and often with old signs as well, Washoe can lapse into what we refer to as poor "diction." Of course, a great deal of slurring and a wide range of variants are permitted in ASL as in any spoken language. In any event, Washoe's diction has frequently been improved by the simple device of repeating, in exaggeratedly correct form, the sign she has just made, until she repeats it herself in more correct form. On the whole, she has responded quite well to prompting, but there are strict limits to its use with a wild animal—one that is probably quite spoiled, besides. Pressed too hard, Washoe can become completely diverted from her original object; she may ask for something entirely different, run away, go into a tantrum, or even bite her tutor.

Chimpanzees also imitate, after some delay, and this delayed imitation can be quite elaborate. The following is a typical example of Washoe's delayed imitation. From the beginning of the project she was bathed regularly and according to a standard routine. Also, from her 2nd month with us, she always had dolls to play with. One day, during the 10th month of the project, she bathed one of her dolls in the way we usually bathed her. She filled her little bathtub with water, dunked the doll in the tub, then took it out and dried it with a towel. She has repeated the entire performance, or parts of it, many times since, sometimes also soaping the doll.

This is a type of imitation that may be very important in the acquisition of language by human children, and many of our procedures with Washoe were revised to capitalize on it. Routine activities—feeding, dressing, bathing, and so on—have been highly ritualized, with appropriate signs figuring prominently in the rituals. Many games have been invented which can be accompanied by appropriate signs. Objects and activities have been named as often as possible, especially when Washoe seemed to be paying particular attention to them. New objects and new examples of familiar objects, including pictures, have been continually brought to her attention, together with the appropriate signs. She likes to ride in automobiles, and a ride in an automobile, including the preparations for a ride, provides a wealth of sights that can be accompanied by signs. A good destination for a ride is a home or the university nursery school, both well stocked with props for language lessons.

The general principle should be clear: Washoe has been exposed to a wide variety of activities and objects, together with their appropriate signs, in the hope that she would come to associate the signs with their referents and later make the signs herself. We have reason to believe that she has come to understand a large vocabulary of signs. This was expected, since a number of chimpanzees have acquired extensive understanding vocabularies of spoken words, and there is evidence that even dogs can acquire a sizable understanding vocabulary of spoken words.[11] The understanding vocabulary that Washoe has acquired, however, consists of signs that a chimpanzee can imitate.

Some of Washoe's signs seem to have been originally acquired by delayed imitation. A good example is the sign for "toothbrush." A part of the daily routine has been to brush her teeth after every meal. When this routine was first introduced Washoe generally resisted it. She gradually came to submit with less and less fuss, and after many months she would even help or sometimes brush her teeth herself. Usually, having finished her meal, Washoe would try to leave her highchair; we would restrain her, signing "First, toothbrushing, then you can go." One day, in the 10th month of the project, Washoe was visiting the Gardner home and found her way into the bathroom. She climbed up on the counter, looked at our mug full of toothbrushes, and signed "toothbrush." At the time, we believed that Washoe understood this sign but we had not seen her use it. She had no reason to ask for the toothbrushes, because they were well within her reach, and it is most unlikely that she was asking to have her teeth brushed. This was our first observation, and one of the clearest examples, of behavior in which Washoe seemed to name an object or an event for no obvious motive other than communication.

Following this observation, the toothbrushing routine at mealtime was altered. First, imitative prompting was introduced. Then as the sign became more reliable, her rinsing-mug and toothbrush were displayed prominently until she made the sign. By the 14th month she was making the "toothbrush" sign at the end of meals with little or no prompting; in fact she has called for her toothbrush in a peremptory fashion when its appearance at the end of a meal was delayed. The "toothbrush" sign is not merely a response cued by the end of a meal; Washoe retained her ability to name toothbrushes when they were shown to her at other times.

The sign for "flower" may also have been acquired by delayed imitation. From her first summer with us, Washoe showed a great interest in flowers, and we took advantange of this by providing many flowers and pictures of flowers accompanied by the appropriate sign. Then one day in the 15th month she made the sign, spontaneously, while she and a companion were walking toward a flower garden. As in the case of "toothbrush," we believed that she understood the sign at this time, but we had made no attempt to elicit it from her except by making it ourselves in appropriate situations. Again, after the first observation, we proceeded to elicit this sign as often as possible by a variety of methods, most frequently by showing her a flower and giving it to her if she made the sign for it. Eventually the sign became very reliable and could be elicited by a variety of flowers and pictures of flowers.

It is difficult to decide which signs were acquired by the method of delayed imitation. The first appearance of these signs is likely to be sudden and unexpected; it is possible that some inadvertent movement of Washoe's has been interpreted as meaningful by one of her devoted companions. If the first observer were kept from reporting the observation and from making any direct attempts to elicit the sign again, then it might be possible to obtain independent verification. Quite understandably, we have been more interested in raising the frequency of new signs than in evaluating any particular method of training.

Babbling.

Because the Hayeses were attempting to teach Viki to speak English, they were interested in babbling, and during the first year of their project they were encouraged by the number and variety of spontaneous vocalizations that Viki made. But, in time, Viki's spontaneous vocalizations decreased further and further to the point where the Hayeses felt that there was almost no vocal babbling from which to shape spoken language. In planning this project we expected a great deal of manual "babbling," but during the early months we observed very little behavior of this kind. In the course of the project, however, there has been a great increase in manual babbling. We have been particularly encouraged by the increase in movements that involve touching parts of the head and body, since these are important components of many signs. Also, more and more frequently, when Washoe has been unable to get something that she wants, she has burst into a flurry of random flourishes and arm-waving.

We have encouraged Washoe's babbling by our responsiveness; clapping, smiling, and repeating the gesture much as you might repeat "goo goo" to a human infant. If the babbled gesture has resembled a sign in ASL, we have made the correct form of the sign and have attempted to engage in some appropriate activity. The sign for "funny" was probably acquired in this way. It first appeared as a spontaneous babble that lent itself readily to a simple imitation game—first Washoe signed "funny," then we did, then she did, and so on. We would laugh and smile during the interchanges that she initiated, and initiate the game ourselves when something funny happened. Eventually Washoe came to use the "funny" sign spontaneously in roughly appropriate situations.

Closely related to babbling are some gestures that seem to have appeared independently of any deliberate training on our part, and that resemble signs so closely that we could incorporate them into Washoe's repertoire with little or no modification. Almost from the first she had a begging gesture—an extension

TABLE 1

Signs used reliably by chimpanzee Washoe within 22 months of the beginning of training. The signs are listed in the order of their original appearance in her repertoire (see text for the criterion of reliability and for the method of assigning the date of original appearance).

Signs	Description	Context
Come-gimme	Beckoning motion, with wrist or knuckles as pivot.	Sign made to persons or animals, also for objects out of reach. Often combined: "come tickle," "gimme sweet," etc.
More	Fingertips are brought together, usually overhead. (Correct ASL form: tips of the tapered hand touch repeatedly.)	When asking for continuation or repetition of activities such as swinging or tickling, for second helpings of food, etc. Also used to ask for repetition of some performance, such as a somersault.
Up	Arm extends upward; index finger may also point up.	Wants a lift to reach objects such as grapes on vine, or leaves; wants to be placed on someone's shoulders; or wants to leave potty-chair.
Sweet	Index or index and second fingers touch tip of wagging tongue. (Correct ASL form: index and second fingers extended side by side.)	For dessert; used spontaneously at end of meal. Also, when asking for candy.
Open	Flat hands are placed side by side, palms down, then drawn apart while rotated to palms up.	At door of house, room, car, refrigerator, or cupboard; on containers such as jars; and on faucets.
Tickle	The index finger of one hand is drawn across the back of the other hand. (Related to ASL "touch.")	For tickling or for chasing games.

364

Sign	Description	Context
Go	Opposite of "come-gimme."	While walking hand-in-hand or riding on someone's shoulders. Washoe usually indicates the direction desired.
Out	Curved hand grasps tapered hand, then tapered hand is withdrawn upward.	When passing through doorways; until recently, used for both "in" and "out." Also, when asking to be taken outdoors.
Hurry	Open hand is shaken at the wrist. (Correct ASL form: index and second fingers extended side by side.)	Often follows signs such as "come-gimme," "out," "open," and "go," particularly if there is a delay before Washoe is obeyed. Also, used while watching her meal being prepared.
Hear-listen	Index finger touches ear.	For loud or strange sounds; bells, car horns, sonic booms, etc. Also, for asking someone to hold a watch to her ear.
Toothbrush	Index finger is used as brush, to rub front teeth.	When Washoe has finished her meal, or at other times when shown a toothbrush.
Drink	Thumb is extended from fisted hand and touches mouth.	For water, formula, soca pop, etc. For soda pop, often combined with "sweet."
Hurt	Extended index fingers are jabbed toward each other. Can be used to indicate location of pain.	To indicate cuts and bruises on herself or on others. Can be elicited by red stains on a person's skin or by tears in clothing.
Sorry	Fisted hand clasps and unclasps at shoulder. (Corect ASL form: fisted hand is rubbed over heart with circular motion.)	After biting someone, or when someone has been hurt in another way (not necessarily by Washoe). When told to apologize for mischief.

TABLE 1 (continued)

Signs	Description	Context
Funny	Tip of index finger presses nose, and Washoe snorts. (Correct ASL form: index and second fingers used; no snort.)	When soliciting interaction play, and during games. Occasionally, when being pursued after mischief.
Please	Open hand is drawn across chest. (Correct ASL form: fingertips used, and circular motion.)	When asking for objects and activities. Frequently combined: "Please go," "Out, please," "Please drink."
Food-cot	Several fingers of one hand are placed in mouth. (Correct ASL form: fingertips of tapered hand touch mouth repeatedly.)	During meals and preparation of meals.
Flower	Tip of index finger touches one or both nostrils. (Correct ASL form: tips of tapered hand touch first one nostril, then the other.)	For flowers.
Cover-blanket	Draws one hand toward self over the back of the other.	At bedtime or naptime, and, on cold days, when Washoe wants to be taken out.
Dog	Repeated slapping on thigh.	For dogs and for barking.
You	Index finger points at a person's chest.	Indicates successive turns in games. Also used in response to questions such as "Who tickle?" "Who brush?"

Sign	Description	Usage
Napkin-bib	Fingertips wipe the mouth region.	For bib, for washcloth, and for Kleenex.
In	Opposite of "out."	Wants to go indoors, or wants someone to join her indoors.
Brush	The fisted hand rubs the back of the open hand several times. (Adapted from ASL "polish.")	For hairbrush, and when asking for brushing.
Hat	Palm pats top of head.	For hats and caps.
I-me	Index finger points at, or touches, chest.	Indicates Washoe's turn, when she and a companion share food, drink, etc. Also used in phrases, such as "I drink," and in reply to questions such as "Who tickle?" (Washoe: "you"); "Who I tickle?" (Washoe: "Me.")
Shoes	The fisted hands are held side by side and strike down on shoes or floor. (Correct ASL form: the sides of the fisted hands strike against each other.)	For shoes and boots.
Smell	Palm is held before nose and moved slightly upward several times.	For scented objects: tobacco, perfume, sage, etc.
Pants	Palms of the flat hands are drawn up against the body toward waist.	For diapers, rubber pants, trousers.

TABLE 1 (continued)

Signs	Description	Context
Clothes	Fingertips brush down the chest.	For Washoe's jacket, nightgown, and shirts; also for our clothing.
Cat	Thumb and index finger grasp cheek hair near side of mouth and are drawn outward (representing cat's whiskers).	For cats.
Key	Palm of one hand is repeatedly touched with the index finger of the other. (Correct ASL form: crooked index finger is rotated against palm.)	Used for keys and locks and to ask us to unlock a door.
Baby	One forearm is placed in the crook of the other, as if cradling a baby.	For dolls, including animal dolls such as a toy horse and duck.
Clean	The open palm of one hand is passed over the open palm of the other.	Used when Washoe is washing or being washed, or when a companion is washing hands or some other object. Also used for "soap."

368

of her open hand, palm up, toward one of us. She made this gesture in situations in which she wanted aid and in situations in which we were holding some object that she wanted. The ASL signs for "give me" and "come" are very similar to this, except that they involve a prominent beckoning movement. Gradually Washoe came to incorporate a beckoning wrist movement into her use of this sign. In Table 1 we refer to this sign as "come-gimme." As Washoe has come to use it, the sign is not simply a modification of the original begging gesture. For example, very commonly she reaches forward with one hand (palm up) while she gestures with the other hand (palm down) held near her head. (The result resembles a classic fencing posture.)

Another sign of this type is the sign for "hurry," which, so far, Washoe has always made by shaking her open hand vigorously at the wrist. This first appeared as an impatient flourish following some request that she had made in signs; for example, after making the "open" sign before a door. The correct ASL for "hurry" is very close, and we began to use it often, ourselves, in appropriate contexts. We believe that Washoe has come to use this sign in a meaningful way, because she has frequently used it when she, herself, is in a hurry—for example, when rushing to her nursery chair.

Instrumental Conditioning.

It seems intuitively unreasonable that the acquisition of language by human beings could be strictly a matter of reiterated instrumental conditioning—that a child acquires language after the fashion of a rat that is conditioned, first, to press a lever for food in the presence of one stimulus, then to turn a wheel in the presence of another stimulus, and so on until a large repertoire of discriminated responses is acquired. Nevertheless, the so-called "trick vocabulary" of early childhood is probably acquired in this way, and this may be a critical stage in the acquisition of language by children. In any case, a minimal objective of this project was to teach Washoe as many signs as possible by whatever procedures we could enlist. Thus, we have not hesitated to use conventional procedures of instrumental conditioning.

Anyone who becomes familiar with young chimpanzees soon learns about their passion for being tickled. There is no doubt that tickling is the most effective reward that we have used with Washoe. In the early months, when we would pause in our tickling, Washoe would indicate that she wanted more tickling by taking our hands and placing them against her ribs or around her neck. The meaning of these gestures was unmistakable, but since we were not studying our human ability to interpret her chimpanzee gestures, we decided to shape an arbitrary response that she could use to ask for more tickling. We noted that, when being tickled, she tended to bring her arms together to cover the place being tickled. The result was a very crude approximation of the ASL sign for "more" (see Table 1). Thus, we would stop tickling and then pull Washoe's arms away from her body. When we released her arms and threatened to resume tickling, she tended to bring her hands together again. If she brought them back together, we would tickle her again. From time to time we would stop tickling and wait for her to put her hands together by herself. At first, any approximation to the "more" sign, however crude, was rewarded. Later, we required closer approximations and introduced imitative prompting. Soon, a very good version of the "more" sign could be obtained, but it was quite specific to the tickling situation.

In the 6th month of the project we were able to get "more" signs for a new game that consisted of pushing Washoe across the floor in a laundry basket. In this case we did not use the shaping procedure but, from the start, used imitative prompting to elicit the "more" sign. Soon after the "more" sign became spontaneous and reliable in the laundry-basket game, it began to appear as a request for more swinging (by the arms)—again, after first being elicited with imitative prompting. From this point on, Washoe transferred the "more" sign to all activities, including feeding. The transfer was usually spontaneous, occurring when there was some pause in a desired activity or when some object was removed. Often we ourselves were not sure that Washoe wanted "more" until she signed to us.

The sign for "open" had a similar history. When Washoe wanted to get through a door, she tended to hold up both hands and pound on the door with her palms or her knuckles. This is the beginning position for the "open" sign (see Table 1). By waiting for her to place her hands on the door and then lift them, and also by imitative prompting, we were able to shape a good approximation of the "open" sign, and would reward this by opening the door. Originally she was trained to make this sign for three particular doors that she used every day. Washoe transferred this sign to all doors; then to containers such as the refrigerator, cupboards, drawers, briefcases, boxes, and jars; and eventually—an invention of Washoe's—she used it to ask us to turn on water faucets.

In the case of "more" and "open" we followed the conventional laboratory procedure of waiting for Washoe to make some response that could be shaped into the sign we wished her to acquire. We soon found that this was not necessary; Washoe could acquire signs that were first elicited by our holding her hands, forming them into the desired configuration, and then putting them through the desired movement. Since this procedure of guidance is usually much more practical than waiting for a spontaneous approximation to occur at a favorable moment, we have used it much more frequently.

RESULTS

Vocabulary.

In the early stages of the project we were able to keep fairly complete records of Washoe's daily signing behavior. But, as the amount of signing behavior and the number of signs to be monitored increased, our initial attempts to obtain exhaustive records became prohibitively cumbersome. During the 16th month we settled on the following procedure. When a new sign was introduced we waited until it had been reported by three different observers as having occurred in an appropriate context and spontaneously (that is, with no prompting other than a question such as "What is it?" or "What do you want?"). The sign was then added to a checklist in which its occurrence, form, context, and the kind of prompting required were recorded. Two such checklists were filled out each day, one for the first half of the day and one for the second half. For a criterion of acquisition we chose a reported frequency of at least one appropriate and spontaneous occurrence each day over a period of 15 consecutive days.

In Table 1 we have listed 30 signs that met this criterion

by the end of the 22nd month of the project. In addition, we have listed four signs ("dog," "smell," "me," and "clean") that we judged to be stable, despite the fact that they had not met the stringent criterion before the end of the 22nd month. These additional signs had, nevertheless, been reported to occur appropriately and spontaneously on more than half of the days in a period of 30 consecutive days. An indication of the variety of signs that Washoe used in the course of a day is given by the following data: during the 22nd month of the study, 28 of the 34 signs listed were reported on at least 20 days, and the smallest number of different signs reported for a single day was 23, with a median of 29.[12]

The order in which these signs first appeared in Washoe's repertoire is also given in Table 1. We considered the first appearance to be the date on which three different observers reported appropriate and spontaneous occurrences. By this criterion, 4 new signs first appeared during the first 7 months, 9 new signs during the next 7 months, and 21 new signs during the next 7 months. We chose the 21st month rather than the 22nd month as the cutoff for this tabulation so that no signs would be included that do not appear in Table 1. Clearly, if Washoe's rate of acquisition continues to accelerate, we will have to assess her vocabulary on the basis of sampling procedures. We are now in the process of developing procedures that could be used to make periodic tests of Washoe's performance on samples of her repertoire. However, now that there is evidence that a chimpanzee can acquire a vocabulary of more than 30 signs, the exact number of signs in her current vocabulary is less significant than the order of magnitude—50, 100, 200 signs, or more—that might eventually be achieved.

Differentiation.

In Table 1, column 1, we list English equivalents for each of Washoe's signs. It must be understood that this equivalence is only approximate, because equivalence between English and ASL, as between any two human languages, is only approximate, and because Washoe's usage does differ from that of standard ASL. To some extent her usage is indicated in the column labeled "Context" in Table 1, but the definition of any given sign must always depend upon her total vocabulary, and this has been continually changing. When she had very few signs for specific things, Washoe used the "more" sign for a wide class of requests. Our only restriction was that we discouraged the use of "more" for first requests. As she acquired signs for specific requests, her use of "more" declined until, at the time of this writing, she was using this sign mainly to ask for repetition of some action that she could not name, such as a somersault. Perhaps the best English equivalent would be "do it again." Still, it seemed preferable to list the English equivalent for the ASL sign rather than its current referent for Washoe, since further refinements in her usage may be achieved at a later date.

The differentiation of the signs for "flower" and "smell" provides a further illustration of usage depending upon size of vocabulary. As the "flower" sign became more frequent, we noted that it occurred in several inappropriate contexts that all seemed to include odors; for example, Washoe would make the "flower" sign when opening a tobacco pouch or when entering a kitchen filled with cooking odors. Taking our cue from this, we introduced the "smell" sign by passive shaping and imitative prompting. Gradually Washoe came to make the appropriate distinction between "flower" contexts and "smell" contexts in her signing, although "flower" (in the single-nostril form) (see Table 1) has continued to occur as a common error in "smell" contexts.

Transfer

In general, when introducing new signs we have used a very specific referent for the initial training—a particular door for "open," a particular hat for "hat." Early in the project we were concerned about the possibility that signs might become inseparable from their first referents. So far, however, there has been no problem of this kind: Washoe has always been able to transfer her signs spontaneously to new members of each class of referents. We have already described the transfer of "more" and "open." The sign for "flower" is a particularly good example of transfer, because flowers occur in so many varieties, indoors, outdoors, and in pictures, yet Washoe uses the same sign for all. It is fortunate that she has responded well to pictures of objects. In the case of "dog" and "cat" this has proved to be important because live dogs and cats can be too exciting, and we have had to use pictures to elicit most of the "dog" and "cat" signs. It is noteworthy that Washoe has transferred the "dog" sign to the sound of barking by an unseen dog.

The acquisition and transfer of the sign for "key" illustrates a further point. A great many cupboards and doors in Washoe's quarters have been kept secure by small padlocks that can all be opened by the same simple key. Because she was immature and awkward, Washoe had great difficulty in learning to use these keys and locks. Because we wanted her to improve her manual dexterity, we let her practice with these keys until she could open the locks quite easily (then we had to hide the keys). Washoe soon transferred this skill to all manner of locks and keys, including ignition keys. At about the same time, we taught her the sign for "key," using the original padlock keys as a referent. Washoe came to use this sign both to name keys that were presented to her and to ask for the keys to various locks when no key was in sight. She readily transferred the sign to all varieties of keys and locks.

Now, if an animal can transfer a skill learned with a certain key and lock to new types of key and lock, it should not be surprising that the same animal can learn to use an arbitrary response to name and ask for a certain key and then transfer that sign to new types of keys. Certainly, the relationship between the use of a key and the opening of locks is as arbitrary as the relationship between the sign for "key" and its many referents. Viewed in this way, the general phenomenon of transfer of training and the specifically linguistic phenomenon of labeling become very similar, and the problems that these phenomena pose for modern learning theory should require similar solutions. We do not mean to imply that the problem of labeling is less complex than has generally been supposed; rather, we are suggesting that the problem of transfer of training requires an equally sophisticated treatment.

Combinations

During the phase of the project covered by this article we made no deliberate attempts to elicit combinations or phrases, although we may have responded more readily to strings of two or more signs than to single signs. As far as we can judge, Washoe's early use of signs in strings was spontaneous. Almost as soon as she had eight or ten signs in her repertoire, she began to use them two and three at a time. As her repertoire increased, her tendency to produce strings of two or more signs also increased, to the point where this has become a common mode of signing for her. We, of course, usually signed to her in combinations, but if Washoe's use of combinations has been imitative, then it must be a generalized sort of imitation, since she has invented a number of combinations, such as "gimme tickle" (before we had ever asked her to tickle us), and "open food drink" (for the refrigerator—we have always called it the "cold box").

Four signs—"please," "come-gimme," "hurry," and "more"—used with one or more other signs, account for the largest share of Washoe's early combinations. In general, these four signs have functioned as emphasizers, as in "please open hurry" and "gimme drink please."

Until recently, five additional signs—"go," "out," "in," "open," and "hear-listen"—accounted for most of the remaining combinations. Typical examples of combinations using these four are, "go in" or "go out" (when at some distance from a door), "go sweet" (for being carried to a raspberry bush), "open flower" (to be let through the gate to a flower garden), "open key" (for a locked door), "listen eat" (at the sound of an alarm clock signaling mealtime), and "listen dog" (at the sound of barking by an unseen dog). All but the first and last of these six examples were inventions of Washoe's. Combinations of this type tend to amplify the meaning of the single signs used. Sometimes, however, the function of these five signs has been about the same as that of the emphasizers, as in "open out" (when standing in front of a door).

Toward the end of the period covered in this article we were able to introduce the pronouns "I-me" and "you," so that combinations that resemble short sentences have begun to appear.

CONCLUDING OBSERVATIONS

From time to time we have been asked questions such as, "Do you think that Washoe has language?" or "At what point will you be able to say that Washoe has language?" We find it very difficult to respond to these questions because they are altogether foreign to the spirit of our research. They imply a distinction between one class of communicative behavior that can be called language and another class that cannot. This in turn implies a well-established theory that could provide the distinction. If our objectives had required such a theory, we would certainly not have been able to begin this project as early as we did.

In the first phase of the project we were able to verify the hypothesis that sign language is an appropriate medium of two-way communication for the chimpanzee. Washoe's intellectual immaturity, the continuing acceleration of her progress, the fact that her signs do not remain specific to their original referents but are transferred spontaneously to new referents, and the emergence of rudimentary combinations all suggest that significantly more can be accomplished by Washoe during the subsequent phases of this project. As we proceed, the problems of these subsequent phases will be chiefly concerned with the technical business of measurement. We are now developing a procedure for testing Washoe's ability to name objects. In this procedure, an object or a picture of an object is placed in a box with a window. An observer, who does not know what is in the box, asks Washoe what she sees through the window. At present, this method is limited to items that fit in the box; a more ingenious method will have to be devised for other items. In particular, the ability to combine and recombine signs must be tested. Here, a great deal depends upon reaching a stage at which Washoe produces an extended series of signs in answer to questions. Our hope is that Washoe can be brought to the point where she describes events and situations to an observer who has no other source of information.

At an earlier time we would have been more cautious about suggesting that a chimpanzee might be able to produce extended utterances to communicate information. We believe now that it is the writers—who would predict just what it is that no chimpanzee will ever do—who must proceed with caution. Washoe's accomplishments will probably be exceeded by another chimpanzee, because it is unlikely that the conditions of training have been optimal in this first attempt. Theories of language that depend upon the identification of aspects of language that are exclusively human must remain tentative until a considerably larger body of intensive research with other species becomes available.

SUMMARY

We set ourselves the task of teaching an animal to use a form of human language. Highly intelligent and highly social, the chimpanzee is an obvious choice for such a study, yet it has not been possible to teach a member of this species more than a few spoken words. We reasoned that a spoken language, such as English, might be an inappropriate medium of communication for a chimpanzee. This led us to choose American Sign Language, the gestural system of communication used by the deaf in North America, for the project.

The youngest infant that we could obtain was a wild-born female, whom we named Washoe, and who was estimated to be between 8 and 14 months old when we began our program of training. The laboratory conditions, while not patterned after those of a human family (as in the studies of Kellogg and Kellogg and of Hayes and Hayes), involved a minimum of confinement and a maximum of social interaction with human companions. For all practical purposes, the only verbal communication was in ASL, and the chimpanzee was maximally exposed to the use of this language by human beings.

It was necessary to develop a rough-and-ready mixture of training methods. There was evidence that some of Washoe's early signs were acquired by delayed imitation of the signing behavior of her human companions, but very few if any, of her early signs were introduced by immediate imitation. Manual babbling was directly fostered and did increase in the course of the project. A number of signs were introduced by shaping and instrumental conditioning. A particularly effective and convenient method of shaping consisted of holding Washoe's hands, forming them into a configuration, and putting them through the movements of a sign.

We have listed more than 30 signs that Washoe acquired and could use spontaneously and appropriately by the end of the 22nd month of the project. The signs acquired earliest were simple demands. Most of the later signs have been names for objects, which Washoe has used both as demands and as answers to questions. Washoe readily used noun signs to name pictures of objects as well as actual objects and has frequently called the attention of her companions to pictures and objects by naming them. Once acquired, the signs have not remained specific to the original referents but have been transferred spontaneously to a wide class of appropriate referents. At this writing, Washoe's rate of acquisition of new signs is still accelerating.

From the time she had eight or ten signs in her repertoire, Washoe began to use them in strings of two or more. During the period covered by this article we made no deliberate effort to elicit combinations other than by our own habitual use of strings of signs. Some of the combined forms that Washoe has used may have been imitative, but many have been inventions of her own. Only a small proportion of the possible combinations have, in fact, been observed. This is because most of Washoe's combinations include one of a limited group of signs that act as combiners. Among the signs that Washoe has recently acquired are the pronouns "I-me" and "you." When these occur in combinations the result resembles a short sentence. In terms of the eventual level of communication that a chimpanzee might be able to attain, the most promising results have been spontaneous naming, spontaneous transfer to new referents, and spontaneous combinations and recombinations of signs.

NOTES

1. See, for example, E. H. Lenneberg, *Biological Foundations of Language* (Wiley, New York, 1967).
2. A. L. Bryan, *Curr. Anthropol*, 4, 297 (1963).
3. K. J. Hayes and C. Hayes, *Proc. Amer. Phil. Soc.* 95, 105 (1951).
4. K. J. Hayes, personal communication. Dr. Hayes also informed us that Viki used a few additional sounds which, while not resembling English words, were used for specific requests.
5. R. M. Yerkes, *Chimpanzees* (Yale Univ. Press, New Haven, 1943).
6. K. J. Hayes and C. Hayes, in *The Non-Human Primates and Human Evolution*. J. A. Gavan, Ed. (Wayne Univ. Press, Detroit, 1955), p. 110; W. N. Kellogg and L. A. Kellogg, *The Ape and the Child* (Hafner, New York, 1967; originally published by McGraw-Hill, New York, 1933); W. N. Kellogg, *Science* 162, 423 (1968).
7. W. C. Stokoe, D. Casterline, C. G. Croneberg, *A Dictionary of American Sign Language* (Gallaudet College Press, Washington, D.C., 1965); E. A. McCall, thesis, University of Iowa (1965).

8. J. Goodall, in *Primate Behavior*, I. DeVore, Ed. (Holt, Rinehart & Winston, New York, 1965), p. 425; A. J. Riopelle and C. M. Rogers, in *Behavior of Nonhuman Primates*. A. M. Schrier, H. F. Harlow, F. Stollnitz, Eds. (Academic Press, New York, 1965), p. 449.

9. R. M. Yerkes and B. W. Learned, *Chimpanzee Intelligence and Its Vocal Expression* (William & Wilkins, Baltimore, 1925), p. 53.

10. K. J. Hayes and C. Hayes, *J. Comp. Physiol. Psychol.* 45, 450 (1952).

11. C. J. Warden and L. H. Warner, *Quart. Rev. Biol.* 3, 1 (1928).

12. The development of Washoe's vocabulary of signs is being recorded on motion-picture film. At the time of this writing, 30 of the 34 signs listed in Table 1 are on film.

13. The research described in this article has been supported by National Institute of Mental Health grants MH-12154 and MH-34953 (Research Scientist Development Award to B. T. Gardner) and by National Science Foundation grant GB-7432. We acknowledge a great debt to the personnel of the Aeromedical Research Laboratory, Holloman Air Force Base, whose support and expert assistance effectively absorbed all of the many difficulties attendant upon the acquisition of a wild-caught chimpanzee. We are also grateful to Dr. Frances L. Fitz-Gerald of the Yerkes Regional Primate Research Center for detailed advice on the care of an infant chimpanzee. Drs. Emanuel Berger of Reno, Nevada, and D. B. Olsen of the University of Nevada have served as medical consultants, and we are grateful to them for giving so generously of their time and medical skills. The faculty of the Sarah Hamilton Fleischmann School of Home Economics, University of Nevada, has generously allowed us to use the facilities of their experimental nursery school on weekends and holidays.

On the Generality
of the Laws of Learning[1]

Martin E. P. Seligman, *Cornell University*

That all events are equally associable and obey common laws is a central assumption of general process learning theory. A continuum of preparedness is defined which holds that organisms are prepared to associate certain events, unprepared for some, and contraprepared for others. A review of data from the traditional learning paradigms shows that the assumption of equivalent associability is false: in classical conditioning, rats are prepared to associate tastes with illness even over very long delays of reinforcement, but are contraprepared to associate tastes with footshock. In instrumental training, pigeons acquire key pecking in the absence of a contingency between pecking and grain (prepared), while cats, on the other hand, have trouble learning to lick themselves to escape, and dogs do not yawn for food (contraprepared). In discrimination, dogs are contraprepared to learn that different locations of discriminative stimuli control go–no go responding, and to learn that different qualities control directional responding. In avoidance, responses from the natural defensive repertoire are prepared for avoiding shock, while those from the appetitive repertoire are contraprepared. Language acquisition and the functional autonomy of motives are also viewed using the preparedness continuum. Finally, it is speculated that the laws of learning themselves may vary with the preparedness of the organism for the association and that different physiological and cognitive mechanisms may covary with the dimension.

Sometimes we forget why psychologists ever trained white rats to press bars for little pellets of flour or sounded metronomes

Seligman, M. E. P. On the generality of the laws of learning. *Psychological Review*, 1970, 77, 406–418. Copyright 1970 by the American Psychological Association, and reproduced by permission.

followed by meat powder for domestic dogs. After all, when in the real world do rats encounter levers which they learn to press in order to eat, and when do our pet dogs ever come across metronomes whose clicking signals meat powder? It may be useful now to remind ourselves about a basic premise which gave rise to such bizarre endeavors, and to see if we still have reason to believe this premise.

THE GENERAL PROCESS
VIEW OF LEARNING

It was hoped that in the simple, controlled world of levers and mechanical feeders, of metronomes and salivation, something quite general would emerge. If we took such an arbitrary behavior as pressing a lever and such an arbitrary organism as an albino rat, and set it to work pressing the lever for food, then *by virtue of* the very arbitrariness of the environment, we would find features of the rat's behavior general to real-life instrumental learning. Similarly, if we took a dog, undistracted by extraneous noises and sights, and paired a metronome's clicking with meat, what we found about the salivation of the dog might reveal characteristics of associations in general. For instance, when Pavlov found that salivation stopped occurring to a clicking that used to signal meat powder, but no longer did, he hoped that this was an instance of a *law,* "experimental extinction," which would have application beyond clicking metronomes, meat powder, and salivation. What captured the interest of the psychological world was the possibility that such laws might describe the general characteristics of the behavior acquired as the result of pairing one event with another. When Thorndike found that cats learned only gradually to pull strings to escape from puzzle boxes, the intriguing hypothesis was that animal learning in general was by trial and error. In both of these situations, the very arbitrariness and unnaturalness of the experiment was assumed to guarantee generality, since the situation would be uncontaminated by past experience the organism might have had or by special biological propensities he might bring to it.

The basic premise can be stated specifically: In classical conditioning, the choice of CS, US, and response is a matter of relative indifference; that is, any CS and US can be associated with approximately equal facility, and a set of general laws exist which describe the acquisition, extinction, inhibition, delay of reinforcement, spontaneous recovery, etc., for all CSs and USs. In instrumental learning, the choice of response and reinforcer is a matter of relative indifference; that is, any emitted response and any reinforcer can be associated with approximately equal facility, and a set of general laws exist which describe acquisition, extinction, discriminative control, generalization, etc., for all responses and reinforcers. I call this premise the assumption of equivalence of associability, and I suggest that it lies at the heart of general process learning theory.

This is not a straw man. Here are some quotes from three major learning theorists to document this assumption:

> It is obvious that the reflex activity of any effector organ can be chosen for the purpose of investigation, since signalling stimuli can get linked up with any of the inborn reflexes [Pavlov, 1927, p. 17].
> Any natural phenomenon chosen at will may be converted into a conditional stimulus . . . any visual stimulus, any desired sound, any odor, and the stimulation of any part of the skin [Pavlov, 1928, p. 86].
> All stimulus elements are equally likely to be sampled and the probability of a response at any time is equal to the proportion of elements in S′ that are connected to it . . . On any acquisition trial all stimulus elements sampled by the organism become connected to the response reinforced on that trial [Estes, 1959, p. 399].
> The general topography of operant behavior is not important, because most if not all specific operants are conditioned. I suggest that the dynamic properties of operant behavior may be studied with a single reflex [Skinner, 1938, pp. 45–46].

A Reexamination of
Equivalence of Associability

The premise of equivalence places a special premium on the investigations of arbitrarily related, as opposed to naturally occurring, events. Such events, since they are supposedly uncontaminated by past experience or by special propensities the organism brings to the situation, provide paradigms for the investigations of general laws of learning. More than 60 years of research in both the instrumental and classical conditioning traditions have yielded considerable data suggesting that similar laws hold over a wide range of arbitrarily chosen events; the shape of generalization gradients is pretty much the same for galvanic skin responses classically conditioned to tones when shock is the US (Hovland, 1937), and for salivating to being touched at different points on the back when food is the US (Pavlov, 1927). Partial reinforcement causes greater resistance to extinction than continuous reinforcement regardless of whether rats are bar pressing for water or running down alleyways for food. Examples of analogous generality of laws could be multiplied at great length.

Inherent in the emphasis on arbitrary events, however, is a danger: *that the laws so found will not be general, but peculiar to arbitrary events.*

THE DIMENSION OF PREPAREDNESS

It is a truism that an organism brings to any experiment certain equipment and predispositions more or less appropriate to that situation. It brings specialized sensory and receptor apparatus with a long evolutionary history which has modified it into its present appropriateness or inappropriateness for the experiment. In addition to sensory-motor capacity, the organism brings associative apparatus, which likewise has a long and specialized evolutionary history. For example, when an organism is placed in a classical conditioning experiment, not only may the CS be more or less perceptible and the US more or less evocative of a response, *but also the CS and US may be more or less associable.* The organism may be more or less prepared by the evolution of its species to associate a given CS and US or a given response with an outcome. If evolution has affected the associability of specific events, then it is possible, even likely, that the very *laws* of learning might vary with the preparedness of the organism from one class of situations to another. If this is so, investigators influenced by the general process view may have discovered only a subset of the laws of learning; the laws of learning about arbitrarily concatenated events, those associations which happen in fact to be equivalent.

We can define a continuum of preparedness operationally. Confront an organism with a CS paired with US or with a response which produces an outcome. Depending on the specifics, the organism can be either prepared, unprepared, or contraprepared for learning about the events. *The relative preparedness of an organism for learning about a situation is defined by the amount of input* (e.g., numbers of trials, pairings, bits of information, etc.) *which must occur before that output* (responses, acts, repertoire, etc.), *which is construed as evidence of acquisition, reliably occurs.* It does not matter how input or output are specified, as long as that specification can be used consistently for all points on the continuum. Thus, using the preparedness dimension is independent of whether one happens to be an S-R theorist, a cognitive theorist, an information processing theorist, an ethologist, or what have you. Let me illustrate how one can place an experimental situation at various points on the continuum for classical conditioning. If the organism makes the indicant response consistently from the very first presentation of the CS on, such "learning" represents a clear case of instinctive responding, the extreme of the prepared end of the dimension. If the organism makes the response consistently after only a few pairings, it is somewhat prepared. If the response emerges only after many pairings (extensive input), the organism is unprepared. If acquisition occurs only after very many pairings or does not occur at all, the organism is said to be contraprepared. The number of pairings is the measure that makes the dimension a continuum, and implicit in this dimension is the notion that "learning" and "instinct" are continuous. Typically ethologists have examined situations in the prepared side of the dimension, while general process learning theorists have largely restricted themselves to the unprepared region. The contraprepared part of the dimension has been largely uninvestigated, or at least unpublished.

The dimension of preparedness should not be confused with the notion of operant level. The frequency with which a response is made in a given situation is not necessarily related to the associability of that response with a given outcome. As will be seen later, frequent responses may not be acquired when they are reinforced as readily as infrequent responses. Indeed, some theorists (e.g., Turner & Solomon, 1962) have argued that high-probability, fast-latency responding may actually antagonize operant reinforceability.

The first empirical question with which this paper is concerned is whether sufficient evidence exists to challenge the equivalence of associability. For many years, ethologists and others (for an excellent example, see Breland & Breland, 1966) have gathered a wealth of evidence to challenge the general process view of learning. Curiously, however, these data have had little impact on the general process camp, and while not totally ignored, they have not been theoretically incorporated. In view of differences in methodology, this is perhaps understandable. I do not expect that presenting these lines of evidence here would have any more effect than it has already had. More persuasive to the general process theorist should be the findings which have sprung up within his own tradition. Within traditional conditioning and training paradigms, a considerable body of evidence now exists which challenges the premise. In reviewing this evidence, we shall find the dimension of preparedness to be a useful integrative device. It is not the intent of this article to review exhaustively the growing number of studies which challenge the premise. Rather, we shall look within each of the major paradigms which general process learning theorists have used and discuss one or two clear examples. The theme of these examples is that all events are not equivalent in their associability; that although the organism may have the necessary receptor and effector apparatus to deal with events, there is much variation in its ability to learn about relations between events.

Classical Conditioning.

The investigation of classical aversive conditioning has been largely confined to the unconditioned response of pain caused by the stimulus of electric shock (cf. Campbell & Church, 1969), and the "laws" of classical conditioning are based largely on these findings along with those from salivary conditioning. Recently, Garcia and his collaborators (Garcia, Ervin & Koelling, 1966; Garcia, Ervin, Yorke, & Koelling, 1967; Garcia & Koelling, 1966; Garcia, McGowan, Ervin & Koelling, 1968), and Rozin and his collaborators (Rodgers & Rozin, 1966; Rozin, 1967, 1968, 1969) have used illness as an unconditioned response and reported some intriguing findings. In the paradigm experiment (Garcia & Koelling, 1966), rats received "bright-noisy, saccharin-tasting water." What this meant was that whenever the rat licked a drinking tube containing saccharine-flavored water, lights flashed and a noise source sounded. During these sessions the rats were X-irradiated. X-irradiation makes rats sick, but it should be noted that the illness does not set in for an hour or so following X-raying. Later the rats were tested for acquired aversions to the elements of the compound CS. The rats had acquired a strong aversion to the taste of saccharine, *but had not acquired an aversion to the "bright-noise."* The rats had "associated" the taste with their illness, but not the exteroceptive noise-light stimuli. So that it could not be argued that saccharine is such a salient event that it masked the noise and light, Garcia and Koelling ran the complementary experiment: "Bright and noisy saccharin-tasting water" was again used as a CS, but this time electric shock to the feet was the US. The rats were then tested for aversion to the elements of the CS. In this case, the bright noise became aversive, but the saccharin-tasting water did not. This showed that the bright noise was clearly perceptible; but the rats associated only the bright noise and the exteroceptive US of footshock, and not the taste of saccharin in spite of its also being paired with shock.

In the experiment, we see both ends as well as the middle of the preparedness continuum. Rats are prepared, by virtue of their evolutionary history, to associate tastes with malaise. For in spite of a several-hour delay of reinforcement, and the presence of other perceptible CSs, only the taste was associated with nausea, and light and noise were not. Further, rats are contraprepared to associate exteroceptive events with nausea and contraprepared to associate tastes with footshock. Finally, the association of footshock with light and sound is probably someplace in the unprepared region. The survival advantage of this preparedness seems obvious; organisms who are poisoned by a distinctive food and survive, do well not to eat it again. Selective advantage should accrue, moreover, to those rats whose associative apparatus could bridge a very long CS-US interval and who could ignore contiguous, as well as interpolated, exteroceptive CSs in the case of taste and nausea.

Does such prepared and contraprepared acquisition reflect the evolutionary results of selective pressure or does it result from experience? It is possible that Garcia's rats may have previously learned that tastes were uncorrelated with peripheral pain and that tastes were highly correlated with alimentary consequences. Such an argument involves an unorthodox premise; that rats' capacities for learning set and transfer are considerably broader than previously demonstrated. The difference between a position that invokes selective pressure (post hoc) and the experiential set position is testable: Would mating those rats who were most proficient at learning the taste–footshock association produce offspring more capable of such learning than an unselected population? Conversely, would interbreeding refractory rats select out the facility with which the taste–nausea association is made?

Supporting evidence for preparedness in classical conditioning has come from other recent experiments on specific hungers and poisoning. Rodgers and Rozin (1966) and Rozin (1967, 1968) have demonstrated that at least part of the mechanism of specific hungers (other than sodium) involves conditioned aversion to the taste of the diet the rats were eating as they became sick. Deficient rats spill the old diet and will not eat it, even after they have recovered. The association of the old taste with malaise seems to be made in spite of the long delay between taste of the diet and gradual onset of illness. The place and the container in which the old diet was set, moreover, do not become aversive. The remarkable ability of wild rats who recover from being poisoned by a novel food, and thereafter avoid new tastes (Barnett, 1963; Rozin, 1968), also seems to result from classical conditioning. Note that the wild rat must be prepared to associate the taste with an illness which does not appear for several hours in only one trial; note also that it must be contraprepared to associate some contiguous CSs surrounding the illness with malaise.

Do these findings really show that rats can associate tastes and illness when an interval of many minutes or even hours intervenes or are they merely a subtle instance of contiguity? Peripheral cues coming either from long-lasting aftertastes or from regurgitation might bring the CS and US into contiguity. Rozin (1969) reported evidence against aftertaste mediation; rats received a high concentration of saccharin paired with apomorphine poisoning. Later, the rats were given a choice between the high concentration and a low concentration. The rats preferred the low concentration, even though the aftertaste that was purportedly contiguous with malaise should be more similar to the low concentration (since it had been diluted by saliva) than the high concentration.

Not only do rats acquire an aversion for the old diet, on which they got sick, but they also learn to prefer the taste of a new diet containing the needed substance. This mechanism also seems to involve prepared conditioning of taste to an internal state. Garcia et al. (1967) paired the taste of saccharin with thiamine injections given to thiamine deficient rats, and the rats acquired a preference for saccharin. So both the rejection of old foods and acceptance of new foods in specific hungers can be explained by prepared conditioning of tastes to internal state.

Instrumental Learning.

E. L. Thorndike, the founder of the instrumental learning tradition, was by no means oblivious to the possibility of preparedness in instrumental learning, as we shall see below. He also hinted at the importance of preparedness in one of his discussions of classical conditioning (Thorndike, 1935, pp. 192–197); one of his students (Bregman, 1934) attempted to replicate the results of Watson and Rayner (1920), who found that little Albert became afraid of a white rat, rabbit, and dog which had been paired with a startling noise. Bregman was unable to show any fear conditioning when she paired more conventional CSs, such as blocks of wood and cloth curtains, with startling noise. Thorndike speculated that infants at the age of locomotion were more disposed to manifest fear to objects that wiggle and contort themselves than to motionless CSs.

Thorndike's parallel views on instrumental learning rose from his original studies of cats in puzzle boxes. As every psychologist knows, he put cats in large boxes and investigated the course of learning to pull strings to escape. What is less widely known is that he put his cats in not just one puzzle box, but in a whole series of different ones (incidentally in doing this he seems to have discovered learning set—Thorndike, 1964, pp. 48–50). In one box the cats had to pull a string to get out, in another a button had to be pushed, in another a lever had to be depressed, etc. One of his boxes—Box Z—was curious: it was merely a large box with nothing but a door that the experimenter could open. Thorndike opened the door in Box Z whenever cats licked themselves or scratched themselves. The cat is known to use both of these frequently occurring responses instrumentally: it scratches itself to turn off itches, and licks itself to remove dirt. In addition, Thorndike had established that getting out of a puzzle box was a sufficient reward for reinforcing the acts of string pulling, button pushing, and lever clawing. In spite of this, Thorndike's cats seemed to have a good deal of trouble learning to scratch themselves or lick themselves to get out of the boxes.

A reanalysis of the individual learning curves presented by Thorndike (1964) for each of the seven cats who had experience in Box Z documents the impression: of the 28 learning curves presented for these seven cats in the boxes other than Z, 22 showed faster learning than in Z, three showed approximately equal learning, and only three showed slower learning. While all of the cats eventually showed improved speeds of licking or scratching for escape, such learning was difficult and irregular. Thorndike noted another unusual property of licking and scratching:

> There is in all these cases a noticeable tendency . . . to diminish the act until it becomes a mere vestige of a lick or scratch . . . the licking degenerated into a mere quick turn of the head with one or two motions up and down with tongue extended. Instead of a hearty scratch, the cat waves its paw up and down rapidly for an instant. Moreover, if sometimes you do not let the cat out after the feeble reaction, it does not at once repeat the movement, as it would do if it depressed a thumb piece, for instance, without success in getting the door open [Thorndike, 1964, p. 48].

Contemporary investigators have reported related findings. Konorski (1967, pp 463–467) attempted to train "reflex" movements, such as anus licking, scratching, and yawning, with food reinforcement. While reporting success with scratching and anus licking, like Thorndike, he observed spontaneous simplification and arrhythmia in the responses. More importantly, he reported that reinforcement of "true yawning" with food is very difficult, if not impossible. Bolles and Seelbach (1964) reported that rearing could be reinforced by noise offset, but not punished by noise onset, exploration could be modified by both, and grooming by neither. This difference could not be accounted for by difference in operant level, which is substantial for all these behaviors of the rat.

Thorndike (1964) speculated that there may be some acts which the organism is not neurally prepared to connect to some sense impressions:

> If the associations in general were simply between situation and impulse to act, one would suppose that the situation would be associated with the impulse to lick or scratch as readily as with the impulse to turn a button or claw a string. Such is not the case. By comparing the curves for Z on pages 57–58 with the others, one sees that for so simple an act it takes a long time to form the association. This is not the final reason, for lack of attention, a slight increase in the time taken to open the door after the act was done, or *an absence of preparation in the nervous system for connections between these particular acts and definite sense impressions* [italics added] may very well have been the cause of the difficulty in forming the associations [p. 113].

This speculation seems reasonable; after all, in the natural history of cats, only behavior such as manipulating objects which maximized chances for escaping traps would be selected, and licking is not in the repertoire which maximizes escape. At minimum, Thorndike demonstrated that the emission of licking paired with an event which could reinforce other emitted acts was not sufficient to reinforce licking equally well. In the present terms, Thorndike had discovered a particular instrumental training situation for which cats are relatively contraprepared.

Brown and Jenkins (1968, Experiment 6) have reported findings which appear to come from the opposite end of the dimension. Pigeons were exposed to a lighted key which was paired with grain delivered in a lighted food hopper below the key. But unlike the typical key-pecking situation, the pigeons' pecking the key did not produce food. Food was contingent only on the key's being lit, not on pecking the key. In spite of this, all pigeons began pecking the key after exposure to the lighted key, followed by grain. Moreover, key pecking was maintained even though it had no effect on food. One can conclude from these "autoshaping results" that the pigeon is highly prepared for associating the pecking of a lighted key with grain.

There is another curiosity in the history of the instrumental

learning literature which is usefully viewed with the preparedness dimension: the question of why a reinforcer is reinforcing.
For over 20 years, disputes raged about what monolithic principle
described the necessary and sufficient conditions for learning.
Hull (1943) claimed that tissue-need reduction must occur for
learning to take place, while Miller (1951) held that drive reduction was necessary and sufficient. Later, Sheffield, Roby, and
Campbell (1954) suggested that a consummatory response was the
necessary condition. More recently, it has become clear that learning can occur in the absence of any of these (e.g., Berlyne, 1960).
I suggest that when CSs or responses are followed by such biologically important events as need reducers, drive reducers, or
consummatory responses, learning should take place readily because natural selection has prepared organisms for such relationships. The relative preparedness of organisms for these events
accounts for the saliency of such learning and hence the appeal
of each of the monolithic principles. But organisms *can* learn
about bar pressing paired with light onset, etc.; they are merely
less prepared to do so, and hence, the now abundant evidence
against the earlier principles was more difficult to gather.

   Thus, we find that in instrumental learning paradigms, there
are situations which lie on either side of the rat's bar pressing
for food on the preparedness dimension. A typical rat will ordinarily learn to bar press for food after a few dozen exposures to
the bar press—food contingency. But cats, who can use scratching
and licking as instrumental acts in some situations, have trouble
using these acts to get out of puzzle boxes, and dogs do not learn
to yawn for food even after many exposures to the contingency.
On the other hand, pigeons acquire a key peck in a lighted key—
grain situation, even when there is no contingency at all between
key pecking and grain. These three instrumental situations represent unprepared, contraprepared, and prepared contingencies,
respectively. Later we shall discuss the possibility that they obey
different laws as a function of different preparedness.

Discrimination Learning.

   The next two paradigms we consider—discrimination learning and avoidance learning—combine both classical and instrumental procedures. In both of these paradigms, findings have

been reported which challenge the equivalence of associability. We begin with some recent Polish work on discrimination learning in dogs. Lawicka (1964) attempted to train dogs in either a go right–go left differentiation or a go–no go differentiation. Whether such differentiation could be acquired depended on the specific discriminative stimuli used. For the left–right differentiation, if the S− and the S+ differed in location (one speaker above the dog; one speaker below), the dog readily learned which way to go in order to receive food. If, however, the stimuli came from the *same* speaker and differed only in pitch, the left–right differentiation was exceedingly difficult. Topographical differences in stimuli, as opposed to qualitative differences, seem to aid in differentiating two topographically different responses. The dog seems contraprepared, moreover, for making a left–right differentiation to two tones which do not also differ in direction. Lest one argue that the two tones coming out of the same speaker were not discriminable, Lawicka (1964; like Garcia & Koelling, 1966) did the complementary experiment: dogs were trained to go and receive food or stay with two tones coming out of the same speaker. One tone was the S+ and the other tone the S−. The dogs learned this readily. Thus, using the same tones which could not be used to establish a left–right differentiation, a go–no go differentiation was established. The author then attempted to elaborate the go–no go differentiation to the same tone differing in location of speakers. As the reader should expect by now, the dogs had trouble learning the go–no go differentiation to the difference in location of S+ and S−. Dogs, then, are contraprepared for learning about different locations controlling a go–no go differentiation although they are not contraprepared for learning that the same locations control a left–right differentiation. Dogs are contraprepared for learning that qualitative differences of tone from the same location control a left–right differentiation, but not contraprepared for using this difference to govern a go–no go differentiation. Dobrzecka and Konorski (1967, 1968) and Szwejkowska (1967) have confirmed and extended these findings.

Emlen (personal communication, 1969) reported discrimination (or at least perceptual) learning that is prepared. It is known from planetarium experiments that adult indigo buntings use the northern circumpolar constellations for migration, since blocking these from view disrupts directed migration. One might have thought that the actual constellations were represented genetically. If young birds are raised under a sky which rotates around a fictitious axis, however, they use the arbitrarily chosen circumpolar constellations for migration and ignore the natural circumpolar constellations. Thus, it appears that indigo buntings are prepared to pay attention to and learn about those configurations of stars which rotate most slowly in the heavens.

Avoidance Learning.

Data from avoidance learning studies also challenge the equivalence of associability. Rats learn reasonably readily to press bars to obtain food. Rats also learn very readily to jump (Baum, 1969) and reasonably readily to run (Miller, 1941, 1951) from a dangerous place to a safe place to avoid electric shock. From this, the premise deduces that rats should learn readily to press bars to avoid shock. But this is not so (e.g., D'Amato & Schiff, 1964). Very special procedures must be instituted to train rats to depress levers to avoid shock reliably (e.g., D'Amato & Fazzaro, 1966; Fantino, Sharp & Cole, 1966). Similarly, pigeons learn readily to peck lighted keys to obtain grain: too readily, probably, for this to be considered an unprepared or arbitrary response (see Brown & Jenkins, 1968). But it is very difficult to train pigeons with normal laboratory techniques to key peck to avoid shock. Hoffman and Fleshler (1959) reported that key pecking was impossible to obtain with negative reinforcement; Azrin (1959) found only temporary maintenance of key pecking in but one pigeon; and Rachlin and Hineline (1967) needed 10–15 hours of patient shaping to train key pecking to remove shock. This probably attests more to a problem specific to the response and reinforcer than to some inability of the pigeon to learn about avoidance contingencies. Ask anyone who has attempted to kill pigeons (e.g., by electrocution or throwing rocks at them), how good pigeons are at avoiding. Pigeons learn to fly away to avoid noxious events (e.g., Bedford & Anger, 1968; Emlen, 1970). In contrast, it is hard to imagine a pigeon flying *away* from something to obtain food.

Bolles has recently (1970) —and quite persuasively—argued

that avoidance responses as studied in laboratory experiments are not simple, arbitrary operants. In order to produce successful avoidance, Bolles argues, the response must be chosen from among the natural, *species-specific* defensive repertoire of the organism. Thus, it must be a response for which the organism is prepared. Running away for rats and flying away for pigeons make good avoidance responses, while key pecking and bar pressing (which are probably related to the appetitive repertoire) do not.

It might be argued that these difficulties in learning avoidance are not due to contrapreparedness but to competing motor responses. Thus, for example, rats have trouble pressing levers to avoid shock because shock causes them to "freeze" which is incompatible with bar pressing. A word of caution is in order about such hypotheses: I know of no theory which specifies in advance what competes with what; rather, response competition (or facilitation) is merely invoked post hoc. When, and if, a *theory* of topographical incompatibility arises it may indeed provide an *explanation* of contrapreparedness, but at the present time, it does not.

Let us review the evidence against the equivalence of associability premise: in classical conditioning, rats are prepared to associate tastes with nausea and contraprepared to associate taste with footshock. In instrumental learning, different emitted responses are differentially associable with different reinforcers: pigeons are prepared to peck lighted keys for food, since they will acquire this even in the absence of any contingency between key pecking and food. Cats are contraprepared for learning to scratch themselves to escape, and dogs for yawning for food. In discrimination learning, dogs are contraprepared to learn that different locations control a go–no go differentiation, and contraprepared for different qualities controlling a left–right response. In avoidance learning, those responses which come from the natural defensive repertoire of rats and pigeons are prepared (or at least unprepared) for avoiding shock. Those responses from the appetitive repertoire seem contraprepared for avoidance.

Two Failures of General Process Learning Theory:
Language and the Functional Autonomy of Motives.

The interest of psychologists in animal learning theory is on the wane. Although the reasons are many, a prominent one is that such theories have failed to capture and bring into the laboratory phenomena which provide fertile models of complex human learning. This failure may be due in part to the equivalence premise. By concentrating on events for which organisms have been relatively unprepared, the laws and models which general process learning theories have produced may not be applicable beyond the realm of arbitrary events, arbitrarily connected. This would not be an obstacle if all of human learning consisted of learning about arbitrary events. But it does not. *Homo sapiens* has an evolutionary history and a biological makeup which has made it relatively prepared to learn some things and relatively contraprepared to learn others. If learning varies with preparedness, it should not be surprising that the laws for unprepared association between events have not explained such phenomena as the learning of language or the acquisition of motives.

Lenneberg (1967) has recently provided an analysis of language, the minimal conclusion of which is that children do not learn language the way rats learn to press a lever for food. Put more strongly, the set of laws which describe language learning are not much illuminated by the laws of the acquisition of arbitrary associations between events, as Skinner (1957) has argued. Unlike such unprepared contingencies as bar pressing for food, language does not require careful training or shaping for its acquisition. We do not need to arrange sets of linguistic contingencies carefully to get children to speak and understand English. Programmed training of speech is relatively ineffective, for under all but the most impoverished linguistic environments, human beings learn to speak and understand. Children of the deaf make as much noise and have the same sequence and age of onset for cooing as children of hearing parents. Development of language seems roughly the same across cultures which presumably differ widely in the arrangement of reinforcement contingencies, and language skill is not predicted by chronological age but by motor skill (see Lenneberg, 1967, especially pp. 125–158, for a fuller discussion).

The acquisition of language, not unlike pecking a lighted key for grain in the pigeon and the acquisition of birdsong (Petrinovich, 1970), is prepared. The operational criterion for the prepared side of the dimension is that minimal input should produce acquisition. One characteristic of language acquisition which separates it from the bar press is just this: elaborate training is not required for its production. From the point of view of this paper, it is not surprising that the traditional analyses of instrumental and classical conditioning are not adequate for an analysis of language. This is not because language is a phenomenon *sui generis,* but because the laws of instrumental and classical conditioning were developed to explain unprepared situations and not to account for learning in prepared situations. This is not to assert that the laws which govern language acquisition will necessarily be the same as those governing the Garcia phenomenon, birdsong, or the key peck, but to say that species-specific, biological analysis might be fruitfully made of these phenomena.

It is interesting to note in this context the recent success that Gardner and Gardner (1970) have had in teaching American sign language to a chimpanzee. The Gardners reasoned that earlier failures to teach spoken English to chimpanzees (Hayes & Hayes, 1952; Kellogg & Kellogg, 1933) did not result from cognitive deficiencies on the part of the subjects, but from the contraprepared nature of vocalization as a trainable response. The great manual dexterity of the chimpanzee, however, suggested sign language as a more trainable vehicle. Hayes (1968) has recently reanalyzed the data from Vicki (the Hayes' chimp) and confirmed the suggestion that chimpanzees' difficulty in using exhalation instrumentally may have caused earlier failures.

Language is not the only example of human learning that has eluded general process theory. The extraordinary persistence of acquired human motives has not been captured in ordinary laboratory situations. People, objects, and endeavors which were once unmotivating to an individual acquire and maintain strongly motivating properties. Fondness for the objects of sexual learning long after sexual desire is gone is a clear example. Acquisition of motives is not difficult to bring into the laboratory, and the extensive literature on acquired drives has often been taken as an analysis of acquired human motivation. A rat, originally unafraid of a tone, is shocked while the tone is played. Thereafter, the rat is afraid of the tone. But the analogy breaks down here; for once the tone is presented several times without shock, the tone loses its fear-inducing properties (Little & Brimer, 1968; Wagner, Siegel & Fein, 1967). (The low resistance to extinction of the conditioned emotional response should not be confused with the high resistance to extinction of the avoidance response. This inextinguishability probably stems from the failure of the organism to stay around in the presence of the CS long enough to be exposed to the fact that shock no longer follows the CS, rather than a failure of fear of the CS to extinguish.) Yet, acquired motivators for humans retain their properties long after the primary motivation with which they were originally paired is absent. Allport (1937) raised the problem for general process theory as the "functional autonomy of motives." But in the 30 years since the problem was posed, the failure of acquired human motives to extinguish remains unanalyzed experimentally.

The notion of preparedness may be useful in analyzing persistent acquired motivation. Typically, investigations of acquired drives have paired arbitrary CSs with arbitrary primary motivators. It seems possible that if more prepared CSs were paired with primary motivators, the motivational properties of such CSs might be unusually resistant to extinction. Seligman, Ives, Ames, and Mineka (1970) conditioned drinking by pairing compound CSs with injections of hypertonic saline-procaine in rats. When the CS consisted only of exteroceptive stimuli (white box, white noise), conditioning occurred, but extinguished in a few days. When the interoceptive CS of one-hour water deprivation was added to the compound, conditioning occurred and persisted unabated for two months. It seems possible that preparedness of mild thirst for association with rapidly induced strong thirst may account for the inextinguishability of acquired drinking.

Are humans prepared to associate a range of endeavors and objects with primary motivators, and are such associations unusually persistent after the original motivators have left the scene? Here, as for language, viewing persistent acquired motives as cases of preparedness may make human motivation—both adaptive and maladaptive—more amenable to study.

Preparedness and the Laws of Learning.

The primary empirical question has been answered affirmatively: The premise of equivalence of associability does not hold,

even in the traditional paradigms for which it was first assumed.
But does this matter? Do the same laws which describe the learning of unprepared events hold for prepared, unprepared, and
contraprepared events? Given that an organism is prepared, and
therefore learns with minimal input, does such learning have
different properties from those unprepared associations that the
organism acquires more painstakingly? Are the same mechanisms
responsible for learning in prepared, unprepared, and relatively
contraprepared situations?

We can barely give a tentative answer to this question, since
it has been largely uninvestigated. Only a few pieces of evidence
have been gathered to suggest that once a relatively prepared
or contraprepared association has been acquired, it may not display the same family of extinction curves, values for delay of reinforcement, punishment effects, etc., as the lever press for food
in the rat. Consider again the Garcia and Koelling (1966) findings: the association of tastes with illness is made with very different delays of reinforcement from ordinary Pavlovian associations. Unlike salivating to sounds, the association will be acquired with delays of up to one hour and more. Detailed studies
which compare directly the delay of reinforcement gradients, extinction functions, etc., for prepared versus unprepared associations are needed. It would be interesting to find that the extinction and inhibition functions for prepared associations were different than for unprepared associations. If preparation underlies
the observations of functional autonomy, prepared associations
might be highly resistant to extinction, punishment, and other
changes in instrumental contingencies. Breland and Breland
(1966) reported that many of the "prepared" behaviors that the
organisms they worked with acquired would persist even under
counterproductive instrumental contingencies. To what extent
would the autoshaped key pecking responses of Brown and Jenkins (1968) be weakened by extinction or punishment, as bar
pressing for food is weakened? Williams and Williams (1969)
reported that autoshaped key-pecking responses persist even when
they actually "cost" the pigeon reinforcement.

Does contraprepared behavior, after being acquired, obey
the same laws as unprepared behavior? Thorndike (1964) reported that when he finally trained licking for escape, the re-

sponse no longer looked like the natural response, but was a pale, mechanical imitation of the natural response. Would the properties of the response differentiation and shaping of such behavior be like those of unprepared responses? The answer to this range of questions is presently unknown.

Preparedness has been operationally defined, and it is possible that different laws of learning may vary with the dimension. How can the dimension be anchored more firmly? Might different cognitive and physiological mechanisms covary with dimension?

Acquired aversions to tastes following illness is commonplace in humans. These Garcia phenomena are not easily modified by cognition in contrast to other classically conditioned responses in humans (e.g., Spence & Platt, 1967). The knowledge that the illness was caused by the stomach flu and not the Sauce Bearnaise does not prevent the sauce from tasting bad in the future. Garcia, Kovner, and Green (1970) reported that distinctive tastes can be used by rats as a cue for shock avoidance in a shuttlebox; but the preference for the taste in the home cage is unchanged. When the taste is paired with illness, however, the preference is reduced in the home cage. Such evidence suggests that prepared associations may not be cognitively mediated, and it is tempting to speculate that cognitive mechanisms (expectation, attention, etc.) come into play with more unprepared or contraprepared situations. If this is so, it is ironic that the "blind" connections which both Thorndike and Pavlov wanted to study lie in the prepared realm and not in the unprepared paradigms they investigated.

We might also ask if different neural structures underlie differently prepared learning. Does elaborate prewiring mediate prepared associations such as taste and nausea, while more plastic structures mediate unprepared and contraprepared associations?

We have defined the dimension of preparedness and given examples of it. To anchor the dimension we need to know the different laws of learning (families of functions) hold along the answers to three questions about what covaries with it: (a) Do dimension? (b) Do different cognitive mechanisms covary with different laws of learning (families of functions) hold along it? (c) Do different physiological mechanisms also covary with preparedness?

Preparation and the General Process View of Learning.

If the premise of equivalence of associability is false, then we have reason to suspect that the laws of learning discovered using lever pressing and salivation may not hold for any more than other simple, unprepared associations. If the laws of learning for unprepared association do not hold for prepared or contraprepared associations, is the general process view salvageable in any form? This is an empirical question. Its answer depends on whether *differences* in learning vary systematically along the dimension of preparedness; the question reduces to whether the preparedness continuum is a nomological continuum. For example, if one finds that the families of extinction functions vary systematically with the dimension, then one might be able to formulate *general* laws of extinction. Thus, if prepared CRs extinguished very slowly, unprepared CRs extinguished gradually, and contraprepared CRs extinguished precipitously, such a systematic, continuous difference in *laws* would be a truly general law of extinction. But before such general laws can be achieved, we must first investigate what the laws of prepared and contraprepared associations actually are. If this were done, then the possibility of general laws of learning would be again alive.

NOTE

1. The preparation of this manuscript was supported in part by National Institute of Mental Health Grant MH 16546-01 to the author. The author gratefully acknowledges the helpful comments of R. Bolles, P. Cabe, S. Emlen, J. Garcia, E. Lenneberg, R. MacLeod, H. Rachlin, D. Regan, R. Rosinski, P. Rozin, T. A. Ryan, R. Solomon, and F. Stollnitz.

REFERENCES

Allport, G. The functional autonomy of motives. *American Journal of Psychology*, 1937, 50, 141–156.
Azrin, N. J. Some notes on punishment and avoidance. *Journal of the Experimental Analysis of Behavior*, 1959, 2, 260.
Barnett, S. *The rat: A study in behavior*. London: Methuen, 1963.
Baum, M. Dissociation of respondent and operant processes in avoidance learning. *Journal of Comparative and Physiological Psychology*, 1969, 67, 83–88.
Bedford, J., & Anger, D. Flight as an avoidance response in pigeons. Paper presented at the meeting of the Psychonomic Society, St. Louis, October 1968.
Berlyne, D. E. *Conflict, arousal, and curiosity*. McGraw-Hill: New York, 1960.

Bolles, R. Effects of escape training on avoidance learning. In F. R. Brush (Ed.), *Aversive conditioning and learning*. New York: Academic Press, 1970, in press.

Bolles, R., & Seelbach, S. Punishing and reinforcing effects of noise onset and termination for different responses. *Journal of Comparative and Physiological Psychology*, 1964, 58, 127–132.

Bregman, E. An attempt to modify the emotional attitude of infants by the conditioned response technique. *Journal of Genetic Psychology*, 1934, 45, 169–198.

Breland, K., & Breland, M. *Animal behavior*. New York: Macmillan, 1966.

Brown, P., & Jenkins, H. Autoshaping of the pigeon's key-peck. *Journal of the Experimental Analysis of Behavior*, 1968, 11, 1–8.

Campbell, E. A., & Church, R. M. *Punishment and aversive behavior*. New York: Appleton-Century-Crofts, 1969.

D'Amato, M. R., & Fazzaro, J. Discriminated lever-press avoidance learning as a function of type and intensity of shock. *Journal of Comparative and Physiological Psychology*, 1966, 61, 313–315.

D'Amato, M. R., & Schiff, J. Long-term discriminated avoidance performance in the rat. *Journal of Comparative and Physiological Psychology*, 1964, 57, 123–126.

Dobrzecka, C., & Konorski, J. Qualitative versus directional cues in differential conditioning. I. Left leg-right leg differentiation to cues of a mixed character. *Acta Biologiae Experimentale*, 1967, 27, 163–168.

Dobrzecka, C., & Konorski, J. Qualitative versus directional cues in differential conditioning. *Acta Biologiae Experimentale*, 1968, 28, 61–69.

Emlen, S. The influence of magnetic information on the orientation of the indigo bunting. *Animal Behavior*, 1970, in press.

Estes, W. K. The statistical approach to learning theory. In S. Koch (Ed.), *Psychology: A study of a science*. Vol. 2. New York: McGraw-Hill, 1959.

Fantino, E., Sharp, D., & Cole, M. Factors facilitating lever press avoidance. *Journal of Comparative and Physiological Psychology*, 1966, 63, 214–217.

Garcia, J., Ervin, F., & Koelling, R. Learning with prolonged delay of reinforcment. *Psychonomic Science*, 1966, 5, 121–122.

Garcia, J., Ervin, F., Yorke, C., & Koelling, R. Conditioning with delayed vitamin injections. *Science*, 1967, 155, 716–718.

Garcia, J., Kovner, R., & Green, K. F. Cue properties versus palatability of flavors in avoidance learning. *Psychonomic Science*, 1970, in press.

Garcia, J., & Koelling, R. Relation of cue to consequence in avoidance learning. *Psychonomic Science*, 1966, 4, 123–124.

Garcia, J., McGowan, B., Ervin, F., & Koelling, R. Cues: Their relative effectiveness as a function of the reinforcer. *Science*, 1968, 160, 794–795.

Gardner, B., & Gardner, A. Two-way communication with an infant chimpanzee. In A. Schrier & F. Stollnitz (Eds.), *Behavior of nonhuman primates*. Vol. 3. New York: Academic Press, 1970, in press.

Hayes, K. J. Spoken and gestural language learning in chimpanzees. Paper presented at the meeting of the Psychonomic Society, St. Louis, October 1968.

Hayes, K. J., & Hayes, C. Imitation in a home-raised chimpanzee. *Journal of Comparative and Physiological Psychology*, 1952, 45, 450–459.

Hoffman, H. S., & Fleshler, M. Aversive control with the pigeon. *Journal of the Experimental Analysis of Behavior*, 1959, 2, 213–218.

Hovland, C. The generalization of conditioned responses. I. The sensory generalization of conditioned responses with varying frequencies of tone. *Journal of Genetic Psychology*, 1937, 17, 279–291.

Hull, C. L. *Principles of behavior*. New York: Appleton-Century-Crofts, 1943.

Kellogg, W. N., & Kellogg, L. A. *The ape and the child*. New York: McGraw-Hill, 1933.

Konorski, J. *Integrative activity of the brain*. Chicago: University of Chicago Press, 1967.

Lawicka, W. The role of stimuli modality in successive discrimination and differentiation learning. *Bulletin of the Polish Academy of Sciences*, 1964, 12, 35–38.

Lenneberg, E. *The biological foundations of language*. New York: Wiley, 1967.

Little, J., & Brimer, C. Shock density and conditioned suppression. Paper presented at the meeting of the Eastern Psychological Association, Washington, D.C., April 1968.

Miller, N. E. An experimental investigation of acquired drives. *Psychological Bulletin*, 1941, 38, 534–535.

Miller, N. E. Learnable drives and rewards. In S. S. Stevens (Ed.), *Handbook of experimental psychology*. New York: Wiley, 1951.

Pavlov, I. P. *Conditioned reflexes*. New York: Dover, 1927.

Pavlov, I. P. *Lectures on conditioned reflexes*. New York: International Publishers, 1928.

Petrinovich, L. Psychobiological mechanisms in language development. In G. Newton & A. R. Riesen (Eds.), *Advances in psychobiology*. New York: Wiley, 1970, in press.

Rachlin, H. C., & Hineline, P. N. Training and maintenance of key pecking in the pigeon by negative reinforcement. *Science*, 1967, 157, 954–955.

Rodgers, W., & Rozin, P. Novel food preferences in thiamine-deficient rats. *Journal of Comparative and Physiological Psychology*, 1966, 61, 1–4.

Rozin, P. Specific aversions as a component in specific hungers. *Journal of Comparative and Physiological Psychology*, 1967, 63, 421–428.

Rozin, P. Specific aversions and neophobia resulting from vitamin deficiency or poisoning in half wild and domestic rats. *Journal of Comparative and Physiological Psychology*, 1968, 66, 82–88.

Rozin, P. Central or peripheral mediation of learning with long CS-US intervals in the feeding system. *Journal of Comparative and Physiological Psychology*, 1969, 67, 421–429.

Seligman, M. E. P., Ives, C. E., Ames, H., & Mineka, S. Conditioned drinking and its failure to extinguish: Avoidance, preparedness, or functional autonomy? *Journal of Comparative and Physiological Psychology*, 1970, 71, 411–419.

Sheffield, F. D., Roby, T. B., & Campbell, B. A. Drive reduction versus consummatory behavior as determinants of reinforcement. *Journal of Comparative and Physiological Psychology*, 1954, 47, 349–354.

Skinner, B. F. *The behavior of organisms*. New York: Appleton-Century-Crofts, 1938.

Skinner, B. F. *Verbal behavior*. New York: Appleton-Century-Crofts, 1957.

Spence, K. W., & Platt, J. R. Effects of partial reinforcement on acquisition and extinction of the conditioned eye blink in a masking situation. *Journal of Experimental Psychology*, 1967, 74, 259–263.

Szwejkowska, G. Qualitative versus directional cues in differential conditioning.

II. Go–no go differentiation to cues of a mixed character. *Acta Biologiae Experimentale*, 1967, 27, 169–175.

Thorndike, E. L. *Animal intelligence*. New York: Hafner, 1964. (Originally published: New York: Macmillan, 1911.)

Thorndike, E. L. *The psychology of wants, interests, and attitudes*. New York: Appleton-Century, 1935.

Turner, L., & Solomon, R. L. Human traumatic avoidance learning: Theory and experiments on the operant-respondent distinction and failures to learn. *Psychological Monographs*, 1962, 76 (40, Whole No. 559) .

Wagner, A., Siegel, L., & Fein, G. Extinction of conditioned fear as a function of the percentage of reinforcement. *Journal of Comparative and Physiological Psychology*, 1967, 63, 160–164.

Watson, J. B., & Rayner, R. Conditioned emotional reactions. *Journal of Experimental Psychology*, 1920, 3, 1–14.

Williams, D. R., & Williams, H. Auto-maintenance in the pigeon: Sustained pecking despite contingent non-reinforcement. *Journal of the Experimental Analysis of Behavior*, 1969, 12, 511–520.

Verbal Learning and Retention

Many theorists have been concerned with applying principles of learning to the understanding of verbal learning and retention (cf. Hall, 1971). Of the theories dealing with retention,
the most popular for quite a while was the *associative interference theory*. According to this theory, retention loss is due to
competition from alternative responses at the time of recall.
Thus, when a person can't remember another person's name,
although he once knew it, it is probably not because the name is
lost from the memory storage. Rather, it is because other responses, such as other names, interfere with the retrieval of the
desired name from the memory. When trying to remember the
name Shirley, names like Shelley might keep interferring.

There are basically two sources of interfering responses, *retroactive inhibition* (RI) and *proactive inhibition* (PI). RI refers
to interference from sources learned *after* the material to be recalled. PI refers to interference from sources learned *before* the
material to be recalled. The reading by Slamecka and Ceraso
summarizes much of the work on RI and PI.

It should be noted that there is considerably more to the
associative interference theory than simply RI and PI. In addition to the specific competition of RI and PI, there is also a generalized competition, a response tendency of the subject to respond with the last learned material. The subject also comes into
the experimental situation with many past learning experiences

that might provide another source of interference, extra-experimental interference. Also in addition to the associations between the material to be learned, the subject also develops associations between the material and the setting where the learning occurs, contextual associations. It also makes a difference how the subject codes and identifies the stimuli (Martin, 1971) and the type of cognitive structure elicited by meaningful material (e.g., Ausubel, Stager, and Garte, 1968). There are, in addition, many other relevant variables.

Distinctions are often made between short-term memory (STM) and long-term memory (LTM). The basic distinction is how long the information is stored, although there is no consensus on the time something can be stored and still be considered STM. Many theorists identify other differences between STM and LTM. Some (e.g., Broadbent, 1963) have suggested that information in STM decays over time, while forgetting in LTM is basically a function of interference due to similarity of material. Another distinction is that STM has a limited storage capacity (how much information it can hold at one time) while LTM, for practical purposes, is not limited (Broadbent, 1963; Waugh and Norman, 1965).

A different orientation, as illustrated in the reading by Melton, argues that STM and LTM are simply different points on the same continuum, and the same basic principles of verbal learning and retention apply to both STM and LTM.

A controversial issue in learning is whether a person's verbal responses can be conditioned without his being aware of the contingencies. In many studies the subject is reinforced for emitting a class of words, such as specific pronouns to complete sentences, with a subtle reinforcement, such as a nod of the experimenter's head or the experimenter saying "good." The subject gradually learns in these situations and the issue is whether he must be aware of the reinforcement contingency in order to learn. Some theorists (e.g., Spielberger and DeNike, 1966) argue that if you have a sensitive enough measure of awareness, which is usually based on questioning the subject, it can be demonstrated that changes in performance occur as the subject becomes aware of the reinforcement contingencies. The problem is that in trying to assess awareness the experimenter helps make the subject aware, thus confounding the issue. The reading by Rosenfeld and Baer shows a clever way to assess awareness in verbal conditioning without making the subject aware.

In the last reading Glucksberg and King show how material associated with unpleasant events is harder to recall than neutral material. This study is important because it shows the role that affect has on retention and suggests an experimental approach to the study of repression, which is an important phenomenon in many clinical models.

Retroactive and Proactive Inhibition of Verbal Learning[1]

NORMAN J. SLAMECKA, *University of Vermont;* and
JOHN CERASO, *Yeshiva University*

The last review of the literature solely devoted to retroactive inhibition (RI) was Swenson's (1941) monograph whose
coverage extended through 1940. The present paper extends the
coverage by presenting a full bibliography and critical analysis
of all published reports on the RI and proactive inhibition (PI)
of verbal learning from 1941 through 1959. Studies of infra-
human Ss and of nonverbal behavior were excluded because of
considerations of length and the fact that, traditionally, RI is
a concept associated with verbal behavior. Excluded also were
studies using interpolated convulsive seizures or surgical procedures because such treatments are qualitatively different from
intervening learning as such and require other theoretical formulations to explain their effects. Following a brief summary of the
field in 1940, subsequent developments will be discussed under
five general headings: Degree of Acquisition, Similarity of Materials, Extrinsic Factors, Temporal Effects, Major Theoretical
Positions.

The dominant theoretical position in 1940 was a transfer
theory, given its fullest exposition by McGeoch and his collaborators. In essence the theory stated that RI could be explained by

Slamecka, N. J. & Ceraso, J. Retroactive and proactive inhibition of verbal
learning, *Psychological Bulletin*, 1960, *57*, 449–475. Copyright 1960 by the
American Psychological Association, and reproduced by permission.

the general principles discovered in the study of transfer. The failure of performance of an old association could be attributed to greater strength of the new association, a mutual blocking of old and new associations, or a confusion between the two.

This theory was capable of handling a great deal of the relevant data and depended largely upon two sources of evidence for empirical support. The first source was the evidence for the effect of similarity of materials upon RI, which supported the contention that RI could be explained by the principles of transfer. The second source was intrusion errors, which are responses from the interpolated learning offered by Ss when they are asked for responses from the original learning. The existence of these errors supported the contention that old responses were not given because new ones had supplanted them.

Much of the subsequent history of RI can be viewed as a process of extension and enlargement of McGeoch's basic position. The four major theories discussed later on in this paper serve as leading examples. The Melton-Irwin two-factor theory enlarged the competition of response theory by postulating an unlearning process in addition to competition of response. Gibson elaborated the theory by placing it within the setting of the conditioning experiment, making available the conceptual apparatus of differentiation and generalization. Underwood's work has concentrated upon clarifying the nature of both unlearning and differentiation, while Osgood has stressed the communality of transfer and RI in his "transfer and retroaction surface."

A consideration of terms is now in order. RI is the decrement in retention attributable to interpolated learning (McGeoch & Irion, 1952), and the operations that define it require a comparison of the retention of some original learning (OL) between two groups that differ in some aspect of the interpolated activity (IL) (Underwood, 1949a). The experimental group has IL, and the control group engages in some non-learning filler task. Better retention in the control group defines RI, and better retention in the experimental group defines retroactive facilitation. Since the control group almost always shows some loss of the OL after its "rest activity," to what can the decrement be attributed: to incidental learning, to loss of set, to sheer metabolic activity (Shaklee & Jones, 1959)? The impossibility of assuring that no interpolated learning takes place for that group introduces an inevitable looseness into the significance of the RI measure. The control group's decrement is sometimes assumed to be due to "natural" forgetting, as distinct from the additional decrement attributed to the specific interfering tasks given the experimental group. But if a strict interference position is to be maintained, the "natural" forgetting must also be attributed to some source of interference, albeit beyond E's control. The fact that different investigators may employ different filler tasks imposes a shifting base against which experimentally induced RI is calculated and renders comparison of results difficult. Osgood (1946, 1948) has dealt with the problem by simply omitting the control group and regarding RI as the difference in performance between the end of OL and the subsequent OL relearning (RL), lumping together both the specific and nonspecific decremental variables operating during the interpolated interval. This, of course, is a measure of total forgetting. Such a straightforward procedure cannot, however, distinguish between RI and retroactive facilitation, as they are usually understood, since facilitation may involve simply less decrement in retention as compared to a control group. Another troublesome problem arises with the other methods of quantifying RI, both of which rely upon control groups. Absolute RI is simply the numerical difference between the retention of the control and experimental groups, and relative RI is the percentage difference between them:

$$\frac{\text{Rest-Work} \times 100}{\text{Rest}}$$

Each of these measures is thus dually dependent upon both the experimental and the control groups' performance, and they may not always give the same pattern of results. This problem becomes especially important in studies of degree of OL upon RI. It is often the case that as OL increases, absolute RI increases, but relative RI decreases (Postman & Riley, 1959). To illustrate, it can be seen that, when degree of OL is low, the control group's retention is low, and even slight departures from this baseline on the part of the experimental group will represent a substantial percentage difference; whereas when the control's recall is high, the same absolute difference will reflect a lesser percentage change, and the relative RI will have decreased, while absolute RI will have remained the same. At present, we can only be alerted to this source of confusion and take it into account when viewing the results of any RI study. The foregoing observations apply just as fully to the quantification of PI, to which we now turn.

The PI paradigm requires a comparison of the retention of some original learning (List 2) between two groups that differ only in some aspect of the activity preceding that learning. The experimental group learns some previous material (List 1), and the control group does not. The same problem with regard to the control group's experience applies here. Better retention in the control group defines PI, and better retention in the experimental group defines proactive facilitation. In addition, the PI design requires that a clear temporal distinction be made between the end of the acquisition phase of List 2 and its subsequent retention test. Minimally, a retention interval longer than the OL intertrial interval is needed. If this is not done, the learning and retention phases would be operationally identical, and the PI design would be indistinguishable from the transfer design.

DEGREE OF ACQUISITION

Swenson's (1941) generalizations about the acquisition variables were as follows:

> [a] ... susceptibility to retroaction does not tend to decrease as the amount of original activity is increased ... (p. 17). [b] ... the greater the degree of learning of the original activity, the less susceptible is the learning to retroactive inhibition (p. 18). [c] ... we may retain the idea of increased retroactive inhibition with increased amount of interpolated activity (p. 19). [d] All measures show an increase in retroactive inhibition with early increases in the degree of interpolated learning and a decrease in retroactive inhibition with every high degrees of interpolated learning (p. 20).

These conclusions have been further amplified through subsequent work. (Unless otherwise noted, the results cited below refer to measures at recall—first relearning trial.)

Several papers have reported the effect of degree of IL upon RI either by varying the number of IL trials (Briggs, 1957; Highland, 1949; Melton, 1941; Postman & Riley, 1959; Slamecka,

1959, 1960a; Thune & Underwood, 1943; Underwood, 1945, 1950b), by setting a performance criterion (Archer & Underwood, 1951; Osgood, 1948; Richardson, 1956), by varying the number of interfering lists (Underwood, 1945), or by analysis of the associative strength of any single IL list item (Runquist, 1957).

Most of the papers agreed that RI of recall showed a negatively accelerated increase with increasing IL, and studies that carried IL to very high degrees also agreed that the curve tended to flatten out or even to decrease (Briggs, 1957; Thune & Underwood, 1943; Underwood, 1945). In general, maximum levels of RI were obtained when the IL practice had somewhat exceeded the OL practice and further IL trials did not serve to increase the RI appreciably. An exception to this was Runquist's (1957) finding that RI of individual items was not a function of the strength of the corresponding interpolated items. Also, in Exp. B of Underwood's (1945) report, there were no significant recall differences among the work groups, nor was there any consistent trend toward a negatively accelerated curve of recall as a function of degree of IL. A possible explanation for this may lie in the fact that the lowest IL degree (8 trials) exceeded the mean OL trials (which averaged about 6). Under these conditions it might well be expected that increasing the IL practice would have no further decremental effect. Increasing the IL levels did, however, produce faster RI dissipation, which gives marginal support to Underwood's differentiation hypothesis. The question of whether degree of IL, measured by trials, or amount of IL, measured by the number of different interpolated lists given, is the more powerful variable in producing RI was also specifically tested by Underwood (1945). Care was taken to equate the amount and degree levels by equal total trials, and the findings showed that RI changed at a faster rate with increases in amount than with increases in degree of IL. Both relative and absolute RI grew steadily as the number of IL lists was increased, but the frequency of overt interlist intrusions remained relatively constant, regardless of the number of lists. This is also consistent with the differentiation hypothesis, since increasing the number of lists should not increase differentiation, whereas increasing the number of trials on a single list should increase it. It is urged that a further comparison of the effect of amount against degree of IL should be made, using yet lower IL levels, so as to fill out that part of the curve at which acquisition is very slight.

Degree of OL was controlled in the following studies by varying the number of trials (Briggs, 1957; Melton, 1941; Postman & Riley, 1959; Shaw, 1942; Slamecka, 1960a), setting a performance criterion (Richardson, 1956), or analyzing individual item strengths (Runquist, 1957). All reports agreed that the susceptibility of the original material to RI was inversely related to its level of acquisition. The well-designed factorial study by Briggs (1957), using four OL and five IL levels (2, 5, 10, and 20 trials OL, compared to 0, 2, 5, 10, and 20 trials IL, all paired adjectives), confirmed previous findings as well as showing that, as OL increases, the greater must the IL level be for maximal relative RI. This was also found by Melton (1941). Further, Briggs reported more significant recall differences across the various IL levels as degree of OL increased. There was no additional information concerning the effects of amount of OL within this period.

PI as a function of List 1 acquisition has been studied by varying the number of trials (Postman & Riley, 1959; Waters, 1942), the number of lists (Underwood, 1945), setting a performance criterion (Atwater, 1953; Underwood, 1949b, 1950a), and analyzing individual item strengths (Runquist, 1957). Two other studies (Greenberg & Underwood, 1950; Werner, 1947) omitted control groups and are not strictly PI designs, and a third (Peixotto, 1947) did not distinguish between learning and retention measures. When significant PI of recall was obtained, all but one of the studies agreed that it was a positive function of the degree or amount of prior learning, and there was even some indication that it leveled off at high degrees of such learning, much as with RI (Atwater, 1953). The one exception (Runquist, 1957) found that PI was not influenced by the degree of the corresponding interfering item strength. The latter is the only study that solely used such analysis and poses an important but separate question concerning the variables determining the retention of individual items per se. Underwood (1950a) found that PI was eliminated at all degrees of prior learning when recall time was extended to 8-sec. intervals. McGeoch and Underwood (1943), using paired-associates lists, found that, when the pairs were presented in fixed order, thus providing the opportunity for serial learning, significant PI was no longer obtained, as opposed to the usual method in which the order of the pairs is varied. A further indication of the sensitivity of PI to slight procedural changes was given in a report that found significant PI in a serial list at a 2-sec. rate of presentation, but not at a 2.3-sec. rate (Underwood, 1941).

One chronic problem which crops up in studies of the degree of prior learning upon PI (and also in RI designs) is that of controlling for practice and warm-up effects. Traditionally, the control group learns only List 2, whereas the experimental group has had prior practice via List 1. Taking List 2 to a common criterion does not insure equal strengths of learning since the rates of acquisition may differ. Although the problem has been recognized (McGeoch & Irion, 1952), it is not dealt with in most PI studies. Young's (1955) is the only experimental effort at such control, wherein the learning was carried to a seven-eighths criterion on the hypothetical next trial, as determined by previous pilot study data.

The only study of PI as a function of the degree of List 2 learning appeared in the extensive investigation by Postman and Riley (1959) who used serial nonsense lists and naive Ss. This part of their work revealed a curvilinear PI (both absolute and relative) function. Maximum PI was obtained at the lowest and highest degrees of List 2 acquisition (5 and 40 trials, respectively) across all levels of List 1 training given (5, 10, 20, and 40 trials). Runquist (1957) found that the degree of PI of any individual list item is unaffected by the acquisition strength of that item—again pointing up the discrepancy between single item retention and overall list retention. The study of PI has not kept pace with the growing knowledge about RI, although recently the greater impact of long-range cumulative effects of prior learning have been brought out strikingly by Underwood (1957) who utilized data from previous retention work and showed that more forgetting is attributable to long-range PI effects than to RI. He found that, although well-practiced Ss forgot about 75 percent over 24 hours, naive Ss (no practice lists) forgot only about 30 percent. This large differential in retention could only be attributed to the strong PI effect of the practice material. Further experimental support was given by Seidel (1959), measuring concurrent PI and RI.

The transitory nature of RI and PI is exemplified in the common observation that these phenomena dissipate after a few relearning trials, sometimes even by the second trial (Osgood, 1948; Underwood, 1945). It follows that recall is the most sensitive measure, whereas if a relearning criterion is used, no interference effects may be demonstrable (McGeoch & Underwood, 1943; Thune & Underwood, 1943; Underwood, 1949b; Waters, 1942).

The rate at which RI dissipates is undoubtedly some function of the degree of learning, or the degree of differentiation of the two response systems involved; but the form of the function is not completely known. Dissipation rate is of importance theoretically and empirically. Melton and Irwin (1940) obtained fastest dissipation at the highest IL level used (40 trials), followed by the next highest level (20 trials). Thune and Underwood (1943) also found rapid dissipation at the highest levels (10 and 20 trials), but there was no difference in rate between them. This latter finding was incompatible with the two-factor theory of Melton and Irwin, in that it could not be explained by reference to the unlearning factor, because the great differences in overt intrusions obtained under the two conditions should have led to different rates of dissipation, favoring the highest level. This point will be considered again in the section devoted to theory. Data from Underwood (1945, Exp. B) also showed much faster dissipation at the high IL level, and the paper by Briggs (1957) suggests that RI dissipates fastest when the interfering material is well learned or overlearned, only at low and intermediate OL levels. RI persistence was generally found to be greatest at the intermediate IL levels used in the four latter studies. Further data on this point as well as comparable figures for rates of PI would be welcome.

SIMILARITY OF MATERIALS

Swenson's (1941) summary of the earlier work on similarity was that "Robinson's theoretical curve is at least roughly accurate" (p. 13). There has since been a definite waning of interest in the Skaggs-Robinson hypothesis as a useful generalization about the effects of similarity upon RI. This is partly because of the failures to duplicate the full theoretical curve within any one experiment (the last attempt at this was made by Kennelly, 1941, and was unsuccessful) and partly because a more heuristic alternative has emerged. The trend within this period may be traced from Boring's (1941) mathematical discussion of communality; Gibson's (1940) more analytical theory reflected in Hamilton's (1943, p. 374) statement that "a two-variable hypothesis should be accepted in preference to the Skaggs-Robinson function"; through Haagen's (1943, p. 44) conclusion that "the hypothesis applies, not to any dimension of similarity, but specifically to the condition in which the continuum of similarity involves a change in the SR relationship of the tasks"; to Osgood's (1949) integration of the literature on RI and similarity in terms of his 3-dimensional transfer and retroaction surface. Ritchie (1954) argued that the Skaggs-Robinson paradox (the statement that the point of maximal OL and IL similarity is simultaneously the condition for greatest interference and also for greatest facilitation) is a pseudoproblem because of an ambiguous scoring procedure. In short, this hypothesis has been superseded by subsequent developments, to which we now turn. Studies of the effects of similarity relationships have been separated into those using paired associates and those using serial lists. The use of paired associates allows specification of the locus of the change in similarity between the lists, an advantage which is not found with serial arrangements. Three classes of change between pair items are possible: response (A–B, A–C), stimulus (A–B, C–B), and both stimulus and response changes (A–B, C–D).

The effect upon retention of learning a new response to an old stimulus has been to produce RI (Bugelski, 1942; Bugelski & Cadwallader, 1956; Gladis & Braun, 1958; Haagen, 1943; Highland, 1949; Osgood, 1946, 1948; Young, 1955) and, also, retroactive facilitation (Haagen, 1943; Parducci & Knopf, 1958). The variable that determined the direction of the effect was the degree of similarity between the two responses. The problem of developing a rigorously objective quantitative scale of meaningful similarity along dimensions feasible for use in verbal form is a serious one, and it has not been adequately met. Usually, adjectives scaled for varying levels of synonymity to standard words were used. These levels were based upon pooled ratings by judges (Haagen, 1949; Osgood, 1946). Parducci and Knopf (1948) used geometric figures varying along some physical dimension with four-digit numerals varying in identity as the verbal responses required. Their OL and recall were visual discrimination tasks, and not really paired associates. The distinction is that the correct response figure and numeral appeared on the stimulus card, whereas in the true paired associates, the response is never a part of the stimulus item. The theoretical rationale of Young's (1955) study deserves some discussion. In the A–B, A–C paradigm, learning A–B also adds to the associative strength of A–C through generalized reinforcement. The magnitude of such generalized reinforcement should be a positive function of the degree of similarity between the B and C response items. In the RI design it was hypothesized that the original list's associative strength (after the IL list was learned) would be the sum of the direct reinforcement gained during its acquisition plus the additional generalized reinforcement gained from the subsequent IL learning. The IL list, on the other hand, would already have gained some generalized reinforcement as a result of the OL training and would thus need less direct reinforcement to achieve criterion during its learning. This would leave the original list with a greater associative strength at recall than the interpolated list, and the magnitude of this difference would be determined by the degree of response similarity between lists. Therefore, it was predicted that, as response similarity between lists increased, RI would decrease and PI would increase. These predictions were tested by Young, using three lists of paired adjectives (to increase the effect) and three levels of response similarity. Results showed that RI as well as overt intrusions decreased as response similarity increased, as predicted. The PI results, as well as a reinterpretation of this entire experiment, will be taken up at the end of this section.

Osgood's (1949) generalization that as response similarity decreases from identity to antagonism, retroactive facilitation should gradually change to increasing RI, was given some empirical support within this period. However, one disturbing finding has emerged. Bugelski and Cadwallader (1956) made a comprehensive attempt to test Osgood's generalizations about similarity

effects, part of which involved the use of Osgood's own word lists
to define four degrees of response similarity—identical, similar,
neutral, and opposed—while keeping the stimuli the same. Results showed decreasing RI with decreasing response similarity.
There was more RI with similar than with opposed responses—a
finding directly contrary to Osgood's prediction, and not in accord
with other data. No explanation was given for these results, but
they cast doubt upon the previous formulation of response similarity. In addition to Osgood's disinclination to use RI control
groups, he has also relied upon an uncommon measure of retention, namely, latency scores. In one of his studies (Osgood, 1948),
the significant drop in RI between opposed and similar responses
was evident only with latency scores, but traditional recall showed
no significant differences. In Osgood's other study (1946) there
were no significant latency differences at recall, but only on the
second and third relearning trials. At no time were the differences
between the neutral and opposed conditions significant. All
things considered, the evidence in favor of the retroaction surface
is less than overwhelming as far as the right half of the response
dimension goes, and indicates that a revision is needed.

Saltz (1953) hypothesized that learning A–C after A–B inhibits B. Assuming that inhibition generalizes less than excitation, presenting a slightly altered A stimulus should again tend
to evoke B. When tested in a straightforward manner, the hypothesis was not confirmed. A second attempt, designed to minimize changes in set, did result in a tendency toward reappearence
of B. No further RI work along these lines has been reported.

There have been two papers on the effects of response similarity on PI. One reported no differential effect (Young, 1955),
although overt intrusions increased with response similarity, and
the other (Morgan & Underwood, 1950) found that PI tended
to decrease as response similarity increased. Osgood (1946, 1948)
reported results couched in terms of PI, but his data are for List
2 acquisition and therefore are measuring negative transfer. A
methodological oversight with consequent possible confounding
of the results of the Young (1955) and Morgan and Underwood
(1950) studies should be pointed out. They both varied similarity along the synonymity of meaning dimension. In terms of A–B,
A–C, the C response varied from very high (i.e., discreet-ailing,

discreet-sickly), to very low similarity, or neutrality with regard to the B response (i.e., noiseless-sincere, noiseless-latent). Each single list had all of the responses at the same similarity level. Thus, it is conceivable that S could "catch on" that the List 2 responses were similar in meaning to those of List 1, and thereby reduce his chances of making errors by restricting his responses to members of the synonym category, with a resulting high positive transfer and low apparent PI. This postulated shift in the pool of responses available to S could be made entirely without his awareness, as several studies of verbal operant conditioning have demonstrated. With lists of low similarity on the other hand, the possibility of such an occurrence would be nil, and therefore no response class restriction would be made, resulting in a drop in positive transfer and higher apparent PI. Since these studies address themselves to rote learning and retention, the possibility of such a form of concept formation is a serious confounding variable. The test of retention may not be of rote recall at all, but actually of reconstruction of the response on the basis of the general concept of synonymity. As would clearly be predicted by such a "categorization" approach, the learning of List 2 was in fact fastest with high response similarity and became progressively slower with decreasing similarity. Both studies stressed the previously discussed response generalization rationale which would lead to increasing PI with increasing similarity, because learning a similar List 2 response would add to the interfering strength of the List 1 response through generalized or "parasitic" reinforcement. These predictions were not in fact confirmed; rather, PI tended to decrease with increasing similarity (although not statistically significant), an expectation consistent with the categorization hypothesis. The magnitude of the effect is probably dependent upon the relative strength of the two lists, as well as upon the number of alternatives in the response classes, which is a task for further empirical work to verify. Such an unintended source of bias may also have been working in the Bugelski and Cadwallader (1956) study, which used a similar list construction technique. Preferably, items at varying levels of response similarity should be included within the same list, so that S would have no opportunity to grasp the concept of the overall list structure. Such a procedure was used for RI by Osgood (1946, 1958) who was aware of this problem. A paper by Twedt and Underwood (1959), which showed that there was no difference in transfer effects between "mixed" and "unmixed" lists, is relevant to lists differing only in formal characteristics, but does not bear upon the question of the general synonymity of the list items as a whole. The lists of the latter study were not varied in degree of meaningful response similarity and thus do not constitute a test of the categorization hypothesis. However, an important paper by Barnes and Underwood (1959) suggested a mediation rationale as another possibility. If A–B is the first list and A–B' the second, there is a possibility of an A–B–B' mediation occurring at recall. In view of these complications, we must conclude that the effects of varying response similarity still have not been unequivocally demonstrated or explained.

The retention effect of learning the same response to a new stimulus was reported in four studies, all of which found retroactive facilitation (Bugelski & Cadwallader, 1956; Haagen, 1943; Hamilton, 1943; Highland, 1949). Similarity was varied either by using geometric figures differing in generalizability (originally developed by Gibson, 1941) or meaningful words scaled for synonymity. The results agreed that retroactive facilitation increased with increasing stimulus similarity. The extreme of similarity is identity, and this produces the most facilitation of all since it amounts to continued practice on the original list. At levels of very low similarity there was some inhibition (Haagen, 1943), and according to Hamilton (1943, p. 375): "When the stimulus forms were of 0 degree generalization there was very little difference in retention in conditions with response identical and with responses different."

No study has ever tested the effects of opposed or antagonistic stimulus relationships while keeping responses the same. Osgood's (1949) retroaction surface does not extend the dimension of stimulus dissimilarity beyond "neutral" or unrelated, although the response dimension does include "antagonistic" relations. The implication is that stimulus opposition is no different in its effects from stimulus neutrality, although no RI evidence is adduced for such a position. It is conceivable, however, that meaningful stimulus opposition or antonymity would actually result in facilitation of recall, based upon a mediation rationale, since such words would be related by *S*'s previous language experience. If response opposition is expected to differ in effect from response neutrality, then stimulus opposition might also. There are no corresponding paired-associates studies upon the PI effects of stimulus variation.

The effect of changing both the stimulus and response members of the interfering list is concisely stated by Osgood (1949, p. 135) : "negative transfer and retroactive inhibition are obtained, the magnitude of both increasing as the stimulus similarity increases." One experiment did not vary stimulus similarity with unrelated responses (Highland, 1949), four studies did vary stimulus similarity with unrelated responses (Gibson, 1941; Haagen, 1943; McClelland & Heath, 1943; Postman, 1958), and another used three degrees of response similarity as well (Bugelski & Cadwallader, 1956). The five latter reports indicate increasing RI with increasing stimulus similarity, and the one study available shows that this holds over all levels of response similarity tested. Two studies from this group will be more fully described since they represent an intriguing departure from the use of the usual physical or meaningful similarity dimension. McClelland and Heath (1943) used as stimulus items for the original and interpolated lists, respectively, a Kent-Rosanoff stimulus word and the most frequent free-association response made to it. Thus an existing prepotent connection was deliberately introduced. Responses were unrelated, and there was no control group. Recall was significantly less under that condition as compared with the case in which there was no association between the stimuli. Since the related words were not similar in appearance or in meaning (e.g., Thirsty-Water) and since a common mediating response could not account for the directionality of the association, the authors concluded that:

> to define the relation between original and interpolated activities which determines the amount of RI, as similarity or as generalization (plain or mediated) is too narrow a conceptionalization, since it does not cover such a learned, uni-directional relation between the two activities as was demonstrated to be of importance here (p. 429).

This study was not carried far enough to prove the point. A third group is needed, for which the related OL and IL stimuli would be interchanged. If this group would display no better recall than the unrelated stimuli group, then the case for the effect of unidirectionality of relationships upon RI would be established. Postman (1958) used geometric figures as OL stimuli. The IL stimuli were either the identical figures, words describing the figures (i.e., "square"), or color names. Responses were unrelated. Both the figure and word groups showed significant RI, with the former having the largest decrement, while the color group did not. These results were explained in terms of the previously learned connections between figures and their names, with formal similarity producing greater interference than mediated equivalence. The influence of unidirectionally prepotent and mediated connections upon forgetting deserves even more attention than it has received. PI is once again slighted, for there are no paired-associates studies concerning both stimulus and response changes.

We turn now to serial list studies, divided into those employing discrete, unconnected items, and those using connected discourse or some approximation thereto. Effects of similarity relations between discrete item lists were reported in three papers which were relatively unrelated as regards their major purposes. Irion (1946) varied the relative serial positions of the original and interpolated adjectives, with some groups learning the identical words for IL, and others learning synonyms. He concluded that similarity of serial position was an effective variable only when identity of meaning was also present. Since several significant differences for IL were reported, we feel that the main variables were confounded with the uncontrolled degree of IL, rendering the results ambiguous. Melton and von Lackum (1941), in a study designed to test an important deduction from the two-factor theory, used two levels of similarity of interpolated items, and found both RI and PI greater under the high similarity condition. Kingsley (1946), with meaningful words, also found poorer retention with interpolated synonyms as opposed to antonyms. Both of the above studies support the generalization that, with serial lists, RI increases with increasing stimulus similarity, along dimensions of both identical elements and meaningfulness.

Ordinary prose or connected discourse has been, until recently, unusually resistant to demonstrable interference effects.

Blankenship and Whitely (1941) studied PI of advertising material (a simulated grocer's handbill) as a function of two levels of judged List 2 similarity. Recall after 48 hours showed greater PI for the more similar condition. Their study actually did not vary degrees of similarity of prose, since one of the two lists was nonsense material, and it may be questioned whether a grocer's handbill resembles prose rather than a list of paired associates. Hall (1955) in an RI design, using a completion test, gave 30 sentences for OL, with IL being more sentences varying in two levels of similarity of topic. Results of that, and of a second, unpublished study, both showed no RI. Deese and Hardman (1954) found no RI for connected discourse under conditions of unlimited response time. Ausubel, Robbins, and Blake (1957), using the method of whole presentation, found no RI. The measure of both learning and recall was a recognition test, largely of substance retention. Peairs (1958) did find RI using a recognition procedure; Slamecka (1959), using grouped Ss, reported that unaided written recall of a short passage was a negative function of the degree of similarity of topic the interfering passage bore to the original passage.

On the whole, these results were rather discouraging about generalizing RI findings from nonsense material to connected discourse and led to the view that prose was not susceptible to RI, or at least to the similarity variable (Miller, 1951, p. 220). We feel, however, that the difficulty was not in the characteristics of connected discourse, but rather in the methods employed. It is noteworthy that all of the above studies employed the less well-controlled techniques of group testing, whole presentation, unlimited recall times, recognition tests, and the like. When, however, connected discourse was presented in the same manner as the traditional serial list, using the serial anticipation method with individually tested Ss, significant RI was obtained, and it was clearly shown to be a function of degree of OL and IL, as well as of similarity of OL-IL subject matter (Slamecka, 1960a, 1960b). Any presumption of the uniqueness of connected discourse with regard to these variables is no longer tenable, and the door is now open for further exploration of this area.

Errors in recognition and recall of a story were shown to be a function of the interference provided by the interpolated presentation of a picture which bore some thematic resemblance to the story (Davis & Sinha, 1950a 1950b). Similarly, Belbin (1950) showed that an interpolated recall test concerning an incidentally present poster interfered with the subsequent recognition of the poster. If the attempted recall is viewed as interfering with the original perceptual trace, then the degree of OL and IL (recall test) similarity was determined by each S's own recall performance.

Lying somewhere between the use of discrete, unconnected items and ordinary prose are two studies employing lists of various orders of approximation to English, constructed according to a method developed by Miller and Selfridge (1950). If RI is a function of contextual constraint, then the use of such materials should be appropriate.

Heise (1956) used an unrelated word list as OL, and five different IL levels of approximation to English. He found recall was best with the greatest dissimilarity between the lists. Thus, the seventh order IL list (close to English text) produced almost no interference, whereas the first order list (same order as OL) produced a great deal, again supporting the generalization concerning greater RI with greater similarity between serial lists. King and Cofer (1958) extended this technique by using OL lists at the zero, first, third, and fifth orders, with four different orders of IL at each of the OL levels. Their intent was to examine similarity effects at various levels of contextual constraint, but the results did not show an overall comprehensive pattern for RI. They suggested that the effects of contextual constraint may prove to be more complex than originally expected, and called for further investigation.

EXTRINSIC FACTORS

In this section are papers focusing upon variables actually extrinsic to the specific items being learned. In most of these studies the groups learned identical materials, and they differed only with regard to such things as the general surround, testing methods, and sets.

The striking effects of altered environment were shown by Bilodeau and Schlosberg (1951). The two groups differed only in the conditions under which IL took place. One group stayed in the same room for all phases, and the other had the IL in a dissimilar room with a different exposure device and a changed posture for S. Recall, done in the OL room, indicated that IL interfered only half as much when associated with a different surround. Elaborating upon this, Greenspoon and Ranyard (1957) also used two different surrounds (different rooms, posture, and exposure devices designated as A and B), in four combinations, and the results, in terms of decreasing order of recall were ABA (AAA, ABB) AAB (those within parentheses not significantly different). Although no controls were used, the findings agree with those of Bilodeau and Schlosberg. These studies support the view that, since recall takes place in some context, the cues governing a response lie not only within the learning material, but also in the general surround, and that the magnitude of RI is a partial function of such context-carried cues. The relative importance of the proprioceptive vs. the exteroceptive cues was not assessed.

Jenkins and Postman (1949) varied testing procedures for OL and IL, using anticipation (A) or recognition (R), in four combinations. Results showed a significant increase in recall when procedures were different, under only one of the comparisons (A–A, A–R). The authors concluded that using a different testing method is a change in set and "helps in the functional isolation of materials learned successively" (p. 72). Postman and Postman (1948) gave four groups the same materials, differing only in the order of the S–R items. Paired syllables-numbers for OL were followed by either paired numbers-syllables or more syllables-numbers. The changed set groups showed better recall. No control groups were used. In the second part of the same report, OL was paired words with either a compatible (doctor-heal) or incompatible (war-peaceful) relation between them. For IL, half the Ss learned a list with the same logical relations, and half learned one with the opposite relations to OL. This latter group showed superior retention, again attributed to the dissimilar sets involved.

Comparing the effects of incidental vs. intentional learning of OL and IL, Postman and Adams (1956) found that, regardless of the OL conditions, intentional IL produced more RI than incidental IL. Both intentional and incidental learning were equally susceptible to RI when followed by IL of the same kind and strength as OL. The authors noted that: "Intentional practice resulted in the learning of a longer number of items during interpolation and hence was a more effective source of interference" (p. 328). Thus, it appears that these conditions were simply the vehicles by which degree of IL, the effective variable, was manipulated. In an earlier paper, Prentice (1943) concluded that incidental learning was more subject to RI than intentional, but when Postman and Adams (1956) corrected Prentice's data by subtracting the respective control group scores, the results agreed with the Postman and Adams findings. If incidental and intentional conditions are construed as providing different sets, or "functional isolation," then an experiment in which the degree of acquisition was equalized should be expected to give different results: the similarly treated groups should display more RI than the changed-set groups. Since this has not been done, we must conclude that the RI effects of incidental vs. intentional conditions per se are not yet known.

The effect of the emotion-arousing characteristic of the IL upon retention is an interesting question, but only one study attempted it within this period and produced inconclusive results (McMullin, 1942), probably because of a confounded experimental design. Among the truly inherent subject variables that have been investigated is the effect of the age of S (Gladis & Braun, 1958; Wywrocki, 1957). The former study divided Ss into three age classes: 20–29, 40–49, and 60–72 years. There was no control group. Although a negative relationship between age and rate of learning was found, the adjusted absolute recall scores revealed no differential RI effects related to age. One might speculate that the decreased learning ability of the older Ss was a PI effect resulting from their many years of previous learning. When the recall scores were "corrected" for this, the actually obtained negative relation between raw recall and age was eliminated. Among the more clinical subject variables, Cassel (1957) reported no differential RI susceptibility between Ss of normal mentality and those with mental deficiency. Sherman (1957) found that psychopaths showed better retention than either neurotics or normals, measured by total forgetting scores. Livson and Krech (1955) reported a moderate positive correlation between recall and scores on the KAE (Kinesthetic Aftereffect Test, which was related to Krech's cortical conductivity hypothesis).

The importance of set factors, generally called warm-up effects, has been recognized (Irion, 1948). Thune (1958) showed that recall was significantly facilitated by a preceding appropriate warm-up. If OL was from a memory drum and IL from a film-strip, then a memory drum warm-up facilitated recall, but a filmstrip warm-up did not. Inappropriate warm-up did facilitate later relearning trials, and Thune concluded that warm-up has both peripheral and central components, with the former more transitory. No RI control groups were used.

The effects of such extrinsic variables upon PI have not yet been investigated. This line of research should be extended, since the magnitudes of interference obtained are often considerable, and probably much of our everyday forgetting is attributable to such context-associated factors.

TEMPORAL EFFECTS

Swenson (1941) summarized the effects of temporal variables as follows:

> [a] ... interpolation immediately adjacent either to original learning or to recall of original learning is more effective in producing retro-active inhibition than is interpolated activity between those two extremes (p. 15). [b] ... the more recent studies suggest an inverse relationship between length of the time interval and relative retro-active inhibition (p. 16).

Subsequent work has called for a modification of those statements.

Examination of the RI paradigm reveals three manipulable temporal intervals: end of OL—start of IL, end of IL—start of RL, and end of OL—start of RL. No single experiment, while keeping the IL learning period constant, can vary only one of these intervals without automatically changing one of the others. When the IL learning period varies (as in studies giving different numbers of IL trials) while the OL–IL and the OL–RL intervals are kept constant, then the IL–RL interval will inevitably vary. Therefore, in the study of any one of these variables, confounding is inescapable. There is no easy way out of this dilemma. The only technique approaching a solution seems to be to do several separate experiments, confounding a different pair of intervals each time, and then evaluating the results of all the experiments by determining which confoundings have no effect. This more elaborate approach has not been used in actual practice; rather, acceptance of such confounding seems to be the rule.

Varying the IL–RL interval allows for measurement of progressive changes in the strength of RI and PI, and deductions concerning the events that occur in that time. Underwood (1948a), using IL–RL intervals of 5 and 48 hr., and Briggs (1954) at 4 min. to 72 hr., report no significant changes in magnitude of RI. Deese and Marder (1957), using unlimited response times, from intervals of 4 min. to 48 hrs., and Peterson and Peterson (1957) from 0 to 15 min., both found no changes in recall. Slight RI decreases were reported by Jones (1953) from .17 to 24 hrs. (with an increase from 24 to 144 hrs.) and by Ishihara (1951). Using the uncommon A–B, C–D design with very high levels of practice, Rothkopf (1957) found an increase in recall from 0 to 21 hrs., but no control groups were used. From the trend of these results, the best conclusion seems to be that RI remains relatively stable over time, at least up to 72 hrs.

In examining the temporal course of PI, Underwood (1949b) found no change from 20 to 75 min., but (Underwood, 1948a) did find a drop in recall from 5 to 48 hrs. (no control groups), and Jones (1953) also reported increasing PI. In a study not explicitly designed to assess PI, therefore lacking control groups, Greenberg and Underwood (1950) also found a significant drop in List 2 recall from 10 min. to 5 hrs. to 48 hrs. In spite of the lack of appropriate controls in some of these studies, the results are in sufficient agreement to allow the conclusion that PI shows a gradual increase through time, which is in accord with logical expectations, as Underwood (1948a) has pointed out.

In comparing the relative strengths of RI vs. PI through time under comparable conditions, Underwood (1948a) found that RI was greater at 5 hrs., but that there was no difference at 48 hrs. Jones (1953) and Rothkopf (1957) reported similar observations. Underwood hypothesized that the failure of List 1 recall to diminish might be due to a process of gradual recovery of OL responses after their unlearning during IL. This led to the use of the modified free recall (MFR) procedure as a method of assessing response dominance. In MFR, S is given a stimulus item common to both lists and asked for the first response that comes to mind. It was felt that such unrestricted, uncorrected recall would provide a fairer estimate of the relative strengths of the competing responses, although it was clearly not intended to be equivalent to the restricted recall required for RI measures. Underwood (1948b) gave MFR at 1 min., 5, 24, and 48 hrs. after IL and found no change in OL responses, a consistent drop in IL responses, and a rise in "other" responses. He concluded that:

> These data are given as further support of the interpretation of unlearning of the first list as being similar to experimental extinction. The fact that no decrease in the effective strength of the first list responses takes place over 48 hrs. suggests that a process running counter to the usual forgetting process is present. It is suggested that this mechanism may be likened to spontaneous recovery (p. 438).

Concerning OL responses, it seems unnecessary to hypothesize two opposing tendencies (recovery vs. "usual forgetting") canceling each other out, as it were, to account for a finding of no change. The usual forgetting curve might not necessarily be expected of OL responses, since the effects of IL could be such as to obliterate, through differential unlearning, more of the weak than the strong responses, leaving the strong, stable ones that are more resistant to the "usual forgetting" process, in the preponderance. List 2 responses, not so selectively eliminated, would be expected to decrease in time. In support of this alternate view we call attention to two relevant bits of evidence. Deese and Marder (1957) found that the number of items recalled after interpolation remained constant over intervals of 4 min., 2, 24, and 48 hours after IL. Also, Runquist (1957) found that resistance to RI was positively related to the degree of an original item's strength. In another MFR experiment, Briggs (1954) did obtain a rise in OL responses between 4 min. and 6 hrs., with subsequent stability through 72 hrs. Because of the discrepancy between these data and those of Underwood (1948b), another study was done in which Briggs, Thompson, and Brogden (1954) found no OL changes between 4 min. and 6 hrs. These authors concluded that "responses from original learning show no change, that responses from interpolated learning tend to decrease with time interval in a fairly regular manner, and that 'other' responses tend to increase . . ." (p. 423). From these MFR data, we tentatively conclude that the processes underlying the temporal stability of RI do not as yet clearly indicate the recovery of unlearned original responses. The spontaneous recovery hypothesis is an attractive one, but more evidence of its validity should be brought forth.

Another problem of interest is the effect of the temporal point of interpolation, which requires keeping the OL–RL interval constant and varying the OL–IL period. Unavoidably, this introduces confounding with the simultaneously varying OL–IL interval, as discussed above.

Houlahan (1941) gave IL either 0, 4, or 8 mins. after OL and found more RI for the immediate interpolation condition. However, there was no direct measure of OL; rather, the performance on some previously learned lists thought to be of equal difficulty to OL was used as a comparison. Within a 16-day OL–RL period, Postman and Alper (1946) gave IL at eight evenly dispersed intervals and found maxima of recall at 1, 8, and 15 days after OL. Degree of acquisition was uncontrolled, since fixed numbers of trials were given; and, since no acquisition data were presented, unequivocal conclusions about the temporal variable cannot be drawn.

Maeda (1951), using short intervals, reported greatest reproduction when IL directly followed OL. Newton (1955) with an A–B, C–B design, and Archer and Underwood (1951) with A–B, A–C, using a 48 hr. OL–RL period with IL at 0, 24, and 48 hrs., concluded that temporal point of interpolation was not an effective variable. Newton and Wickens (1956) noted that the Archer and Underwood study failed to control for differential warm-up, in that the group with IL immediately before RL benefited by warm-up, whereas the other two groups had no comparable advantage. They repeated the Archer and Underwood study with the same materials, but gave a warm-up task to the 0- and 24-hr. groups. No effects of the temporal intervals were obtained, confirming the previous results. However, they also reported two additional experiments, with an A–B, C–D design, with warm-up provided. One study had a performance acquisition criterion, and the other a fixed number of trials. Results of both showed that the 48-hr. group did show significantly more RI than the other two. Those authors state that the A–B, A–C design "is a relationship which is designed to produce a maximum amount of RI, and the intensity of this condition may obscure the RI which can arise from a variable of lesser importance—as the temporal variable may well be" (Newton & Wickens, 1956, p. 153). They especially stressed the importance of generalized competition between lists, a point which shall be developed further in the theoretical section below. We tentatively conclude from the Newton and Wickens (1956) data, supported by Maeda (1951), that RI increases as the OL–IL interval increases and that the effect is thus far specific to the A–B, C–D design.

A comparable PI design would require a constant List 2–RL period, while varying the List 1–List 2 interval. We have been unable to find such an experiment in the literature within this period. Ray (1945) studied List 2 acquisition as a function of the interval since the learning of List 1. Although he speaks of PI, the design is appropriate only to conclusions about negative transfer.

Another temporal variable which has not been studied sufficiently in an RI design is the rate of presentation of the items. The only relevant retention study on this is an unpublished honors thesis by Seeler (1958). OL was a 35-word passage of prose presented via tape recording to a criterion of one perfect unaided written recall, followed by similar memorization of an IL passage, and then by OL recall. OL rates of presentation were $\frac{1}{2}$, 1, and 2 secs., followed by $\frac{1}{2}$; 1; or 2-second counterbalanced rates on the IL. No control groups were used. Results showed that number of trials to mastery of all original and interpolated passages was a direct function of their presentation rates, a finding consistent with acquisition reports based on nonsense materials. There was no influence of either the OL or IL presentation rates, or any of their combinations, upon recall. It might have been supposed that an IL rate different from the OL rate would have served to functionally isolate the original list and produce less forgetting, but that was not the case. The possibility of confounding rate of presentation and strength of associations at the end of OL due to differential acquisition rates (Underwood, 1949a) is not a problem in this study, since unaided recall was used. With the method of serial anticipation, however, the criterial OL trial is also another learning trial, and two groups taken to the same performance criterion may still differ on total associative strength at the termination of the last OL trial. The problem is always present whenever any variable that effects rate of acquisition (such as meaningfulness, similarity, etc.) is used along with the serial anticipation technique. The generalizability of the latter results to unconnected materials as well as the additional independent problem of the RI effects of massed vs. distributed training must await further study.

MAJOR THEORETICAL POSITIONS

In this section we shall discuss the four main theoretical positions which have influenced the period covered by this review. Two major formulations, appearing within a few months of each other (Gibson, 1940; Melton & Irwin, 1940), guided the theoretical aspects of the study of RI within the first few years covered by this review.

Utilizing the classical conditioning principles of stimulus generalization and differentiation, Gibson (1940) presented a set of postulates for verbal behavior that served to lend greater predictive specificity to the transfer or straight competition-of-response view, previously developed by McGeoch and his collaborators. Basic to Gibson's approach is the view that verbal learning and retention are matters of developing discriminations among the items to be learned. She defines her two basic constructs as follows: The construct of generalization is "the tendency for a response R_a learned to S_a to occur when S_b (with which it has not been previously associated) is presented" (p. 204). The construct of differentiation is a "progressive decrease in generalization as a result of reinforced practice with S_a–R_a and reinforced presentation of S_b" (p. 205). A curvilinear growth function of the generalization tendency as practice trials increase is stressed. Essentially, RI is related to the degree of discriminability of the two lists, such discriminability being a positive function of their respective degrees of learning, and a negative function of the time elapsed since learning. Spontaneous recovery of generalization tendencies (wrong responses) through time is assumed. From these postulates, several deductions concerning RI were presented, and

some of these have been tested and confirmed: for instance, RI
as a function of various similarity relations among the items
(Gibson, 1941; Hamilton, 1943), and the curvilinear RI function
obtained as the degree of IL increases (Melton & Irwin, 1940).
Among the deductions tested but not confirmed is one bearing
upon the temporal point of interpolation problem. Gibson feels
that one of the reasons for the disparity of results on this question
lies in the neglect of the importance of the degree of acquisition
of the lists. She predicted that acquisition level would be found
to interact with the temporal point of interpolation because the
spontaneous recovery of generalization tendencies between lists
is a function of time. This prediction was tested by Archer and
Underwood (1951) using three levels of IL acquisition (6/10,
10/10, and 10/10+5 trials) and three OL–IL intervals (0, 24,
and 48 hrs.), but no interaction between them was found. RI
control groups were not used, and in light of the theoretical importance of this study it would seem advisable to re-examine these
variables with a design adaptable to relative RI measures. The
authors themselves expressed dissatisfaction with the outcome
and "felt that a modification of the conditions in our design
would indicate the temporal position to be a factor" (p. 289).

Considering the general reaction toward Gibson's theory
in succeeding RI work, we feel that, on the whole, it has been
favorably received, since it has been given a certain amount of
implicit corroboration by way of being compatible with many
findings (for instance, Briggs, 1957) and has potential for even
further development. It has not, however, stimulated a comprehensive series of experiments aimed at testing the many RI deductions implicit within it. The reason for this is certainly not
any lack of clarity in the postulates. One present weakness seems
to be the lack of direct evidence for a spontaneous recovery process influencing RI.

Melton and Irwin (1940) introduced their two-factor theory
within the framework of a study of RI as a function of the degree
of IL. OL was 5 trials on an 18-item serial nonsense list, followed
by 5, 10, 20, or 40 trials on an IL list. Relying upon a count of
the overt interlist intrusions as an objective index of the degree
of competition between original and interpolated responses at
recall, they found that the curves of amount of absolute RI, and

the number of such intrusions (multiplied by a factor of 2 to do justice to partial intrusions) were not highly correlated. (The theoretical importance of intrusion counts gained its ascendancy with this study.) Rather, interlist intrusions increased to a maximum at intermediate IL levels and then decreased markedly, whereas the curve of RI rose sharply and maintained a relatively high level, declining slightly at the highest degree of IL. That portion of the RI attributable to direct competition of responses at recall was at a maximum when OL and IL were about equal in strength. Therefore, to account for the remainder of the obtained RI not accounted for by overt competition, Melton and Irwin postulated another factor at work, tentatively identified as the direct "unlearning" of the original responses by their unreinforced elicitation or punishment, during IL. The growth of this "Factor X" was assumed to be a progressively increasing function of IL strength. Since Factor X was almost totally responsible for the absolute RI at the highest IL level, and since RI under that condition dissipated most rapidly after a few relearning trials, it was concluded that the effects of such unlearning were quite transitory. This was still a competition of response theory in the sense that the original responses were still assumed to be competing at recall with the interpolated ones, but to that was added the factor of weakening in OL response strength, if not complete extinction, through the process of unlearning.

The presence of confounding between the degree of IL, and the end of IL–start of RL interval was pointed out by Peterson and Peterson (1957) as a possible alternative account of the differences in intrusions obtained by the Melton and Irwin design. With a fixed OL–RL interval the IL–RL interval shortens, with increasing IL trials taking more time. However, another study of the effects of degree of IL did use a fixed IL–RL interval (with a correspondingly varying OL–RL interval—Osgood, 1948) and still found comparable intrusion changes.

A direct deduction from the two-factor theory is that RI, being a result of both unlearning and competition effects, should be greater than PI, which was presumed to be the result of response competition alone. This hypothesis was tested and confirmed by Melton and von Lackum (1941) in a study using five trials on each of two 10-item consonant lists, and has also been

given further general support by others (Jones, 1953; McGeoch
& Underwood, 1943; Underwood, 1942, 1945). Underwood
(1948a) in yet another study also found greater RI than PI at
5 hrs.; but at 24 hrs. they were equal. His resulting postulation
of spontaneous recovery of the OL, and the subsequent developments of that concept have been discussed above.

Later, certain other observations led to some discontent with
the two-factor theory. In an experiment designed to test the generalizability of the Melton and Irwin findings to paired-adjec-
tives lists, Thune and Underwood (1943) used an A–B, A–C design with five OL trials and 0, 5, 10, or 20 IL trials. Their results
confirmed the existence of a negatively accelerated function between RI and degree of IL, as well as the fact that overt intrusions were maximal at the intermediate IL levels (10 trials) and
declined sharply by the 20-trial level, while RI still remained
massive. However, there was no difference in the rate of RI dissipation between the 10 and 20 trial IL levels, and therefore the
transitoriness of RI at these levels could not reasonably be attributable to the unlearning construct. The two-factor theory would
have been forced to predict faster dissipation at the 20 IL level,
since overt intrusions were far less for it than for the 10 IL level.
In addition, the curve of Factor X drawn for the Thune and
Underwood data was quite different in shape from that obtained
by Melton and Irwin, and it was felt to imply rather incongruous
psychological properties for a curve of unlearning. In addition,
an item analysis revealed that almost half of the overt intrusions
took place on items where the original response had never been
reinforced (or correctly anticipated) at all! Therefore, such interlist intrusions could not be legitimate indicators of response
competition, since those responses had never been learned during
OL, and were simply not available to be competing with anything. It is also to be expected that for original responses to be
unlearned they would have to occur during IL in sufficient frequency to be subject to punishment or lack of reinforcement.
Yet, as Osgood (1948) pointed out from his data, the number
of related original list intrusions during IL was "infinitesimally
small" and could not possibly account for much unlearning at
all. This previously observed discrepancy between the assumed
growth of Factor X and the lack of increase in intrusions during

IL as a function of increasing IL trials should be tempered with the possibility that partial intrusions could still play a large role in determining the degree of unlearning obtained, and such intrusions are not easily detected and counted.

Thune and Underwood (1943) suggested that the ratio of overt to covert (and partial) errors need not necessarily remain constant, but may undergo progressive change as a function of the degree of IL, therefore accounting for the drop in overt intrusions by postulating an increase in implicit interference. In a subsequent paper Underwood (1945) elaborated upon this suggestion and formalized his differentiation theory.

The shift in error ratios was interpreted as a resultant of two simultaneous processes: increasing IL associative strength tending to produce more overt intrusions, but being gradually overcome by the growth of differentiation, tending to reduce the intrusions. The magnitude of the differentiation construct was held to be a positive function of the degree of learning of both lists and a negative function of the time between the end of IL and the start of RL. A decrease in overt intrusions was, in effect, the index of increasing differentiation. When the two lists are about equally well learned, intrusions are maximal and differentiation is low; but with increasing disparity between their absolute or relative acquisition levels, intrusions are reduced, indicating increased differentiation. By the same token, a short IL–RL interval should also produce higher differentiation. That this is in fact the case was shown in the Archer and Underwood study (1958) where overt intrusions declined as the IL–RL interval became shorter. The increasing differentiation allows S to recognize and withhold erroneous responses, resulting in fewer interlist intrusions and more covert or omission errors. Differentiation was described phenomenologically by Underwood (1945, p. 25) as being:

> related to the verbally reported experience of "knowing" on the part of the subject that the responses from the interpolated learning are inappropriate at the attempted recall of the OL. Degree of differentiation in this sense is thus an indication of the degree to which the subject identifies the list to which each response belongs.

Empirical support for various aspects of this theory has come from several studies (e.g., Archer & Underwood, 1951; Osgood, 1948; Thune & Underwood, 1943; Underwood, 1945). Further, the fact that intrusion frequencies change but RI still remains constant might be simply a function of the limited recall time (usually 2 sec.) available to S. If this recall time was extended, then perhaps S would have sufficient time both to recognize the erroneous and verbalize the correct response, thus displaying a decrease in RI at high IL (differentiation) levels. Underwood (1950a, 1950b) tested this promising hypothesis, but found no dropping off of the Melton and Irwin effect, and concluded that differentiation does not change as a function of increased (8-sec.) recall time. Unlearning was therefore still retained as a useful concept; but, since it was shown that such response weakening took place only in the first "few" IL trials, as measured by associative inhibition, and because of the relatively great stress put upon the role of differentiation, Underwood's revision of the two-factor theory became an important independent influence upon subsequent RI thinking.

Certain apparent similarities between Underwood's differentiation construct and Gibson's concept of differentiation deserve to be pointed out at this time. For both theorists, differentiation is in part a positive function of degree of reinforced practice on the material, such practice serving to reduce overt intrusion errors. Secondly, temporal relationships also play a large part in determining the strength of both constructs. However, the two positions do differ with regard to certain important aspects of operation of these determiners of differentiation. Underwood's concept refers to the more global process of S correctly assigning the list membership of the responses, whereas Gibson speaks of discrete S–R connections in competition. Furthermore, Underwood's theory is derived from experiments based largely upon the A–B, A–C design, whereas for Gibson, generalization as defined requires that the stimulus members be similar, but not identical. For Underwood, increasing differentiation is marked by a reduction of intrusions and an increase in omissions, but no drop in RI, whereas Gibson implies that increasing differentiation will result directly in improved performance. And finally, Gibson makes spontaneous recovery an integral part of her differentiation concept, while it was not until later that Underwood suggested a spontaneous recovery process, and that was reserved for the unlearning aspect of his theory.

The last theoretical formulation to be considered was put forth by Osgood (1946). It stemmed from his investigations of the RI effects of meaningful opposed responses and involved a hypothesis about reciprocal inhibition of antagonistic reactions, wherein "simultaneous with learning any response the S is also learning not to make the directly antagonistic response" (Osgood, 1948, p. 150). This was clearly an application of the reciprocal inhibition concept of neurophysiology to the area of verbal behavior. In pursuing the tenability of this position, two relevant transfer studies have shown that the learning of both similar and opposed List 2 responses was equally rapid, and much easier than learning neutral responses (Ishihara & Kasha, 1953; Ishihara, Morimoto, Kasha, & Kubo, 1957), thus failing to confirm the hypothesis. Unless further support for the hypothesis is forthcoming, we must conclude that it will not become an important influence in RI work.

With regard to the question of the adequacy of the two-factor theories we are of the opinion that the concept of unlearning is a valuable one, but that an acceptable measure of its magnitude has not yet been devised. Interlist intrusions were proposed only as a partial index, but not as a complete measure of its effects, and the difficulties encountered by such an index have been enumerated above. Instructions calculated to encourage the verbalizing of errors do just that: Morrow (1954) and Bugelski (1948) found that "all that is required to obtain a large number of such errors is to ask for them" (p. 680).

Two interesting proposals have been advanced as methods for distinguishing operationally between effects of competition and effects of unlearning. Postman and Kaplan (1947) spoke of two measures of RI: error scores, and the reaction times for correct responses (residual retroaction). These two measures were found not to be correlated and are thus of necessity measures of two different processes. They suggest that: "It is possible that retention loss (error scores) reflects the effects of unlearning, whereas reaction times may depend primarily on the competition between responses" (p. 143). Their experiment did not include variation of any factor which might be expected to affect unlearning differentially and therefore the usefulness of their proposal has not yet been tested.

Later, Postman and Egan (1948) proposed that the rate of recall of correct responses be a measure of unlearning. Retention was measured by the free recall procedure, and performance was recorded both in terms of number of items recalled, as well as by the rate of emission of correct items, per 3-sec. periods. They state that:

> The two types of measures—amount lost and rate of recall—may be regarded as measures of these two processes (unlearning and competition, respectively). Those aspects of OL which have been unlearned cannot be evoked on retest: unlearning leads to decrement in amount retained. Other aspects suffer competition from the IL but are not unlearned. They are potentially available but "disturbed," and manifest that in a slower rate of recall (p. 543).

These are both valid and constructive formulations deserving of further attention, but no significant efforts have as yet been made to test their usefulness in predicting data crucially relevant to the unlearning factor.

These experiments by Postman point in a new direction, suggesting that such evidence for competition of response is a result of the brief recall times used in RI studies. If competition of response results in increased latencies, then decrements in recall may come when the latency of a response exceeds the 2-sec. interval usually used. Underwood's (1950a) study, which found no PI with an 8-sec. recall interval, supports this possibility.

An experiment by Ceraso (1959) may provide further support for such a hypothesis. With an A–B, A–C design, Ss were asked to recall both the first and second list responses and also to assign these to the proper list. Since a 20-sec. (maximum) recall interval was used, blocking due to competition of response should not be expected. An analysis of the first list responses which were correct on the last trial of OL, and were then scored as incorrect at recall, showed that the reason for the forgetting was simply the unavailability of the response. If the response was available at recall, it was also assigned to the correct list. Since competition of response should reveal itself as a misassignment of the response, it was clear that the forgetting obtained could not be accounted for by competition. Using a technique somewhat related, with an A–B, A–C design, Barnes and Underwood (1959) obtained similar results, and accordingly rejected a competition explanation.

Ceraso also found that in a large number of cases S could give both responses to the stimulus. But does not the unlearning hypothesis imply that learning the second list response entails the unavailability of the first list response? The answer that immediately suggests itself is that unlearning is a function of the degree of first and second list item learning. Therefore, an item analysis of the kind performed by Runquist was undertaken. The result showed that degree of learning of the second list item did not affect the retention of the first list item, thus verifying Runquist's (1957) original finding.

It seems that the latter data pose a real problem for current theories of RI, since the basic mechanism usually postulated requires interaction between associations with similar or identical stimulus items. Both the Runquist and Ceraso findings seem to indicate a nonspecific mechanism. Learning a second list affects the entire first list, regardless of the specific item interactions.

In conclusion, it appears that the major theoretical accounts of RI have remained relatively unchallenged and unchanged for the last ten years, in spite of the accumulation of considerable empirical data. It is hoped that this overview of the current state of the field will help to initiate a more vigorous and sustained effort toward an improved theory of forgetting.

SUMMARY

For a concluding statement we feel it would be appropriate to enumerate some of the pressing problems and empirical gaps currently evident in the status of our knowledge of RI and PI. These points are presented in the order of their appearance in the foregoing review and do not reflect any opinion regarding their relative importance.

1. Reconsideration of the relative merits of RI quantification: absolute RI, relative RI, and total forgetting
2. Determinants of the RI and PI of individual items
3. Determinants of the rate of PI dissipation

4. Development of an objectively quantitative scale of similarity for use in constructing lists of items

5. Reappraisal of the right half of the response dimension of Osgood's retroaction surface

6. Effects of opposed or antagonistic stimulus relations upon RI and PI, with responses the same

7. Effects of varying response similarity upon PI, with the "categorization approach" error eliminated

8. Further study of the RI effects of mediated and unidirectional prepotent association between list items

9. PI as a function of similarity relations within the A–B, C–D design

10. Determinants of the RI and PI of connected discourse

11. Relative importance of proprioceptive vs. exteroceptive extrinsic cues for recall

12. RI effects of incidental vs. intentional acquisition conditions, with degree of acquisition controlled

13. Effects of the affective characteristics of the material upon its RI and PI

14. Better handling of the problem of confounding which arises when temporal intervals are manipulated

15. Further tests of the validity of the spontaneous recovery hypothesis

16. Examination of the point of interpolation problem as a function of other attendant variables

17. RI as a function of presentation rate, and of massing vs. distributing trials

18. Testing of the two-factor theory through an improved measure of the unlearning construct

NOTE

1. This work was supported in part by a grant to the senior author from the National Science Foundation (G-6192).

REFERENCES

Archer, E. J., & Underwood, B. J. Retroactive inhibition of verbal association as a multiple function of temporal point of interpolation and degree of interpolated learning. *J. exp. Psychol.*, 1951, 42, 283–290.

Atwater, S. K. Proactive inhibition and associative facilitation as affected by degree of prior learning. *J. exp. Psychol.*, 1953, 46, 400–404.

Ausubel, D., Robbins, L., & Blake, E., Jr. Retroactive inhibition and facilitation in the learning of school materials. *J. educ. Psychol.*, 1957, 48, 334–343.

Barnes, J. M., & Underwood, B. J. "Fate" of first-list associations in transfer theory. *J. exp. Psychol.*, 1959, 58, 97–105.

Belbin, E. The influence of interpolated recall on recognition. *Quart. J. exp. Psychol.*, 1950, 2, 163–169.

Bilodeau, I. M., & Schlosberg, H. Similarity in stimulating conditions as a variable in retroactive inhibition. *J. exp. Psychol.*, 1951, 41, 199–204.

Blankenship, A. B., & Whitely, P. L. Proactive inhibition in the recall of advertising material. *J. soc. Psychol.*, 1941, 13, 311–322.

Boring, E. G. Communality in relation to proaction and retroaction. *Amer. J. Psychol.*, 1941, 54, 280–283.

Briggs, G. E. Acquisition, extinction, and recovery functions in retroactive inhibition. *J. exp. Psychol.*, 1954, 47, 285–293.

Briggs, G. E. Retroactive inhibition as a function of degree of original and interpolated learning. *J. exp. Psychol.*, 1957, 53, 60–67.

Briggs, G. E., Thompson, R. F., & Brogden, W. J. Retention functions in retroactive inhibition. *J. exp. Psychol.*, 1954, 48, 419–423.

Bugelski, B. R. Interference with recall of original responses after learning new responses to old stimuli. *J. exp. Psychol.*, 1942, 30, 368–379.

Bugelski, B. R. An attempt to reconcile unlearning and reproductive inhibition explanations of proactive inhibition. *J. exp. Psychol.*, 1948, 38, 670–682.

Bugelski, B. R., & Cadwallader, T. A reappraisal of the transfer and retroaction surface. *J. exp. Psychol.*, 1956, 52, 360–366.

Buxton, C. E. List structure as a determiner of amount of retroactive inhibition. *Psychol. Bull.*, 1941, 38, 719. (Abstract)

Cassel, R. H. Serial verbal learning and retroactive inhibition in aments and normal children. Unpublished doctoral dissertation, Northwestern Univer., 1957.

Ceraso, J. An experimental critique of competition of response and specific interference as factors in retroactive inhibition. Unpublished doctoral dissertation, New School for Social Research, 1959.

Cooper, J. B. An attempt to measure the "tension" values of interpolated situations. *J. gen. Psychol.*, 1942, 27, 347–351.

Crannell, C. W. An effective demonstration of retroactive and proactive inhibition. *Amer. J. Psychol.*, 1948, 61, 391–395.

Davis, D. R., & Sinha, D. The effect of one experience on the recall of another. *Quart. J. exp. Psychol.*, 1950, 2, 43–52. (a)

Davis, D. R., & Sinha, D. The influence of an interpolated experience upon recognition. *Quart. J. exp. Psychol.*, 1950, 2, 132–137. (b)

Deese, J., & Hardman, G. W. An analysis of errors in retroactive inhibition of rote verbal learning. *Amer. J. Psychol.*, 1954, 67, 299–307.

Deese, J., & Marder, V. J. The pattern of errors in delayed recall of serial learning after interpolation. *Amer. J. Psychol.*, 1957, 70, 594–599.

Gibson, E. J. A systematic application of the concepts of generalization and differentiation to verbal learning. *Psychol. Rev.*, 1940, 47, 196–229.

Gibson, E. J. Retroactive inhibition as a function of degree of generalization between tasks. *J. exp. Psychol.*, 1941, 28, 93–115.

Gladis, M., & Braun, H. W. Age differences in transfer and retroaction as a function of intertask response similarity. *J. exp. Psychol.*, 1958, 55, 25–30.

Greenberg, R., & Underwood, B. J. Retention as a function of stage of practice. *J. exp. Psychol.*, 1950, 40, 452–547.

Greenspoon, J., & Ranyard, R. Stimulus conditions and retroactive inhibition. *J. exp. Psychol.*, 1957, 53, 55–59.

Haagen, C. H. Learning and retention as a function of the synonymity of original and interpolated tasks. Unpublished doctoral dissertation, State Univer. Iowa, 1943.

Haagen, C. H. Synonymity, vividness, familiarity, and association value ratings of 400 pairs of common adjectives. *J. Psychol.*, 1949, 30, 185–200.

Hall, J. F. Retroactive inhibition in meaningful material. *J. educ. Psychol.*, 1955, 46, 47–52.

Hamilton, R. J. Retroactive facilitation as a function of degree of generalization between tasks. *J. exp. Psychol.*, 1943, 32, 363–376.

Heise, G. Retroactive inhibition as a function of the degree of approximation to English word order. *Amer. Psychologist*, 1956, 11, 450. (Abstract)

Highland, R. W. Retroactive inhibition: Effects of S-R variations in relation to degree of interpolated learning. Unpublished doctoral dissertation, Ohio State Univer., 1949.

Houlahan, F. J. Immediacy of interpolation and amount of inhibition. *J. educ. Psychol.*, 1941, 32, 37–44.

Irion, A. L. Retroactive inhibition as a function of the relative serial positions of the original and interpolated items. *J. exp. Psychol.*, 1946, 36, 262–270.

Irion, A. L. The relation of "set" to retention. *Psychol. Rev.*, 1948, 55, 336–341.

Ishihara, I. The process of retroactive inhibition in retention. *Jap. J. Psychol.*, 1951, 21, 18–25.

Ishihara, I., & Kasha, K. The learning of response words in similar, opposite, or neutral relation: A study on the conditioning principle in verbal learning. *Jap. J. Psychol.*, 1953, 24, 1–12.

Ishihara, I., Morimoto, H., Kasha, K., & Kubo, K. Associative directions and semantic relations in verbal learning. *Tohoku psychol. Folia*, 1957, 16, 7–18.

Jenkins, W. O., & Postman, L. An experimental analysis of set in rote learning: Retroactive inhibition as a function of changing set. *J. exp. Psychol.*, 1949, 39, 69–72.

Jones, W. F., Jr. A comparison of retroactive and proactive inhibition as a function of the time interval between original learning and the measurement of retention. Unpublished doctoral dissertation, Vanderbilt Univer., 1953.

Kennelly, T. W. The role of similarity in retroactive inhibition. *Arch. Psychol.*, 1941, 37, No. 260.

King, D. J., & Cofer, C. N. Retroactive interference in meaningful material as a function of the degree of contextual constraint in the original and interpolated learning. *ONR tech. Rep.*, 1958, No. 21 (Contract NONR 595 (04), Univer. Maryland)

Kingsley, H. L. The factors of similarity and association in retroactive inhibition. *Amer. Psychologist*, 1946, 1, 262. (Abstract)

Livson, N. H., & Krech, D. Dynamic systems, rote learning, and retroactive inhibition. *J. Pers.*, 1955, 24, 2–19.

McClelland, D. C., & Heath, R. M. Retroactive inhibition as a function of degree of association of original and interpolated activities. *J. exp. Psychol.*, 1943, 33, 420–430.

McGeoch, J. A., & Irion, A. L. *The psychology of human learning.* New York: Longmans, Green, 1952.

McGeoch, J. A., & Underwood, B. J. Tests of the two-factor theory of retroactive inhibition. *J. exp. Psychol.*, 1943, 32, 1–16.

McMullin, T. E. A study of the affective nature of the interpolated activity as a factor in producing differing relative amounts of retroactive inhibition in recall and in recognition. *J. exp. Psychol.*, 1942, 30, 201–215.

Maeda, Y. Zur experimentellen Untersuchung über Faktoren der Reproduktionshemming: I. Über Hemmungswirkungen auf die Reproduckton. *Jap. J. Psychol.*, 1951, 21, 1–17.

Melton, A. W. Overt interlist intrusions and retroactive inhibition as a function of the ratio of the degrees of learning of original and interpolated verbal habits. *Psychol. Bull.*, 1911, 33, 575.

Melton, A. W., & Irwin, J. McQ. The influence of degree of interpolated learning on retroactive inhibition and the overt transfer of specific responses. *Amer. J. Psychol.*, 1940, 53, 173–203.

Melton, A. W., & von Lackum, W. J. Retroactive and proactive inhibition in retention: Evidence for a 2-factor theory of retroactive inhibition. *Amer. J. Psychol.*, 1941, 54, 157–173.

Miller, G. A. *Language and communication*. New York: McGraw-Hill, 1951.

Miller, G. A., & Selfridge, J. A. Verbal context and the recall of meaningful material. *Amer. J. Psychol.*, 1950, 63, 176–185.

Morgan, R. L., & Underwood, B. J. Proactive inhibition as a function of response similarity. *J. exp. Psychol.*, 1950, 40, 592–603.

Morrow, M. A. The relation of overt errors during learning to transfer and retroactive inhibition. Unpublished doctoral dissertation, Washington Univer., 1954.

Newton, J. M. Interlist similarities and point of interpolation in retroactive inhibition of verbal associations. Unpublished doctoral dissertation, Ohio State Univer., 1955.

Newton, J. M., & Wickens, D. D. Retroactive inhibition as a function of the temporal position of the interpolated learning. *J. exp. Psychol.*, 1956, 51, 149–154.

Osgood, C. E. Meaningful similarity and interference in learning. *J. exp. Psychol.*, 1946, 36, 277–301.

Osgood, C. E. An investigation into the causes of retroactive interference. *J. exp. Psychol.*, 1948, 38, 132–154.

Osgood, C. E. The similarity paradox in human learning: A resolution. *Psychol. Rev.*, 1949, 56, 132–143.

Parducci, A., & Knopf, N. B. Retroactive facilitation when new responses have been learned to old stimuli. *Amer. J. Psychol.*, 1958, 71, 426–428.

Peairs, R. H. Development and analysis of retroactive inhibition in retention of meaningful connected verbal stimulus material. Unpublished doctoral dissertation, Ohio State Univer., 1958.

Peixotto, H. E. Proactive inhibition in the recognition of nonsense syllables. *J. exp. Psychol.*, 1947, 37, 81–91.

Peterson, L. R., & Peterson, M. J. Intrusions at recall in retroactive inhibition. *Amer. Psychologist*, 1957, 12, 419.

Postman, L. Retroactive inhibition in recall and recognition. *J. exp. Psychol.*, 1952, 44, 165–169.

Postman, L. Mediated equivalence of stimuli and retroactive inhibition. *Amer. J. Psychol.*, 1958, 71, 175–185.

Postman, L., & Adams, P. A. Studies in incidental learning: III. Interserial interference. *J. exp. Psychol.*, 1956, 51, 323–328.

Postman, L., & Alper, T. G. Retroactive inhibition as a function of the time of interpolation of the inhibition between learning and recall. *Amer. J. Psychol.*, 1946, 59, 439–449.

Postman, L., Egan, J. P., & Davis, J. Rate of recall as a measure of learning: I. The effects of retroactive inhibition. *J. exp. Psychol.*, 1948, 38, 535–546.

Postman, L., & Kaplan, H. L. Reaction time as a measure of retroactive inhibition. *J. exp. Psychol.*, 1947, 37, 136–145.

Postman, L., & Postman, D. L. Change in set as a determinant of retroactive inhibition. *Amer. J. Psychol.*, 1948, 61, 236–242.

Postman, L., & Riley, D. A. Degree of learning and interserial interference in retention. *U. Calif. Publ. Psychol.*, 1959.

Prentice, W. C. H. Retroactive inhibition and the motivation of learning. *Amer. J. Psychol.*, 1943, 56, 283–292.

Ray, W. S. Proactive inhibition: A function of time interval. *Amer. J. Psychol.*, 1945, 58, 519–529.

Richardson, J. Retention of concepts as a function of degree of original and interpolated learning. *J. exp. Psychol.*, 1956, 51, 358–364.

Ritchie, M. L. The Skaggs-Robinson hypothesis as an artifact of response definition. *Psycho. Rev.*, 1954, 61, 267–270.

Rothkopf, E. Z. A deduction from an excitation-inhibition account of retroactive inhibition. *J. exp. Psychol.*, 1957, 53, 207–213.

Runquist, W. N. Retention of verbal associates as a function of strength. *J. exp. Psychol.*, 1957, 54, 369–375.

Saltz, E. Act of regression as a special case of retroactive inhibition and functionally related to stimulus generalization. *J. exp. Psychol.*, 1953, 45, 394–400.

Seeler, R. A. Acquisition and retention of verbal materials. Unpublished honors thesis, Univer. Vermont, 1958.

Seidel, R. J. The concurrent effects of proactive and retroactive inhibition. *J. exp. Psychol.*, 1959, 57, 397–402.

Shaklee, A. B., & Jones, B. E. Problems of method and theory in controlling rest activity. *J. gen. Psychol.*, 1959, 60 11–16.

Shaw, F. J. Influence of degree of original learning upon associative and reproductive inhibition. *Proc. Ia. Acad. Sci.*, 1942, 49, 413–417.

Sherman, L. J. Retention in psychopathic, neurotic, and normal subjects. *J. Pers.*, 1957, 25, 721–729.

Shriver, E. L. An artifact of retroactive inhibition. *Amer. Psychologist*, 1953, 8, 435. (Abstract)

Slamecka, N. J. Studies of retention of connected discourse. *Amer. J. Psychol.*, 1959, 72, 409–416.

Slamecka, N. J. Retroactive inhibition of connected discourse as a function of practice level. *J. exp. Psychol.*, 1960, 59, 101–108. (a)

Slamecka, N. J. Retroactive inhibition of connected discourse as a function of similarity of topic. *J. exp. Psychol.*, 1960, 60, 245–249. (b)

Swenson, E. J. Retroactive inhibition: A review of the literature. *Minn. Stud. Educ.*, 1941, No. 1.

Thune, L. E. Reproductive interference following appropriate and inappropriate warm-up activities. *J. exp. Psychol.*, 1958, 55, 535–542.

Thune, L. E., & Underwood, B. J. Retroactive inhibition as a function of degree of interpolated learning. *J. exp. Psychol.*, 1943, 32, 185–200.

Twedt, H. M., & Underwood, B. J. Mixed vs. unmixed lists in transfer studies. *J. exp. Psychol.*, 1959, 58, 111–116.

Underwood, B. J. The effects of punishment in serial verbal learning. *Proc. Ia. Acad. Sci.*, 1941, 48, 349–352.

Underwood, B. J. A test of the two-factor theory of retroactive inhibition by use of the paired-association technique. *Psychol. Bull.,* 1942, 39, 593 (Abstract)

Underwood, B. J. The effect of successive interpolations on retroactive and proactive inhibition. *Psychol. Monogr.,* 1945, 59 (3, Whole No. 273).

Underwood, B. J. Retroactive and proactive inhibition after 5 and 48 hours. *J. exp. Psychol.,* 1948, 38, 29–38. (a)

Underwood, B. J. "Spontaneous recovery" of verbal associations. *J. exp. Psychol.,* 1948, 38, 129–439. (b)

Underwood, B. J. *Experimental psychology.* New York: Appleton-Century-Crofts, 1949. (a)

Underwood, B. J. Proactive inhibition as a function of time and degree of prior learning. *J. exp. Psychol.,* 1949, 39, 24–34. (b)

Underwood, B. J. Proactive inhibition with increased recall time. *Amer. J. Psychol.,* 1950, 63, 594–599. (a)

Underwood, B. J. Retroactive inhibition with increased recall time. *Amer. J. Psychol.,* 1950, 63, 67–77. (b)

Underwood, B. J. Interference and forgetting. *Psychol. Rev.,* 1957, 64, 49–60.

Waters, R. H. The concept of psychological disposition and retroactive inhibition. *Psychol. Bull.,* 1941, 38, 573. (Abstract)

Waters, R. H. Degree of learning and proactive inhibition in retention. *Psychol. Bull.,* 1942, 39, 495–496. (Abstract)

Werner, H. The effect of boundary strength on interference and retention. *Amer. J. Psychol.,* 1947, 60, 598–607.

Wywrocki, E. H. Age difference in retroactive inhibition as a function of the degree of similarity of serial position between the original and interpolated learning. Unpublished doctoral dissertation, Univer. Pittsburgh, 1957.

Young, R. K. Retroactive inhibition and proactive inhibition under varying conditions of response similarity. *J. exp. Psychol.,* 1955, 50, 113–119.

Implications of Short-Term Memory for a General Theory of Memory[1]

ARTHUR W. MELTON, *University of Michigan*

Memory has never enjoyed even a small fraction of the inter-disciplinary interest that has been expressed in symposia, discoveries, and methodological innovations during the last five years. Therefore, it seems probable that the next ten years will see major, perhaps even definitive, advances in our understanding of the biochemistry, neurophysiology, and psychology of memory, especially if these disciplines communicate with one another and seek a unified theory. My thesis is, of course, that psychological studies of human short-term memory, and particularly the further exploitation of new techniques for investigating human short-term memory, will play an important role in these advances toward a general theory of memory. Even now, some critical issues are being sharpened by such observations.

The confluence of forces responsible for this sanguine prediction about future progress is reflected in this AAAS program on memory. Advances in biochemistry and neurophysiology are permitting the formulation and testing of meaningful theories about the palpable stuff that is the correlate of the memory trace as an hypothetical construct (Deutsch, 1962; Gerard, 1963; Thomas, 1962). In this work there is heavy emphasis on the *storage* mechanism and its properties, especially the consolidation

Melton, A. W. Implications of short-term memory for a general theory of memory. *Journal of Verbal Learning and Verbal Behavior*, 1963, 2, 1–21.

process, and it may be expected that findings here will offer important guide lines for the refinement of the psychologist's construct once we are clear as to what our human performance data say it should be.

Within psychology several developments have focused attention on memory. In the first place, among learning theorists there is a revival of interest in the appropriate assumptions to be made about the characteristics of the memory traces (engrams, associations, bonds, $_sH_r$'s) that are the products of experiences and repetitions of experiences. Thus, Estes (1960) has questioned the validity of the widespread assumption (e.g., Hull, 1943; Spence, 1955) that habit strength grows incrementally over repetitions, and has proposed an all-or-none conception as an alternative. More recently, he has examined (Estes, 1962) in detail the varieties of the incremental and all-or-none conceptions and the evidence related to them. Already, some defenders of the incremental concept (Jones, 1962; Keppel and Underwood, 1962; Postman, 1963) have taken issue with Estes' conclusions, and it would appear that this fundamental question about memory will loom large in theory and experiments for some time to come. At a somewhat different level, the revival of experimental and theoretical interest in the notion of perseveration or consolidation of the memory trace (Glickman, 1961), and attempts to embody it in a general theory of learning (Hebb, 1949; Walker, 1958), have also focused attention on a theory of memory as a fundamental component of a theory of learning.

A second strong stimulus to research on memory from within psychology are several findings of the last few years that have forced major revisions in the interference theory of forgetting and consequently a renaissance of interest in it (Postman, 1961). First, there was the discovery by Underwood (1957) that proactive inhibition had been grossly underestimated as a source of interference in forgetting. Then, the unlearning factor as a component of retroactive inhibition was given greater credibility by the findings of Barnes and Underwood (1959). And finally, the joint consideration of the habit structure of the individual prior to a new learning experience, the compatibility or incompatibility of the new learning with that structure, and the unlearning factor (among others) led to the formulation of the interference theory of forgetting in terms that made it applicable to all new learning (Melton, 1961; Postman, 1961; Underwood and Postman, 1960). Thus, this development focuses attention on the interactions of memory traces during learning as well as their interactions at the time of attempted retrieval or utilization in recognition, recall, or transfer.

But perhaps the most vigorous force directing attention within psychology to the need for a general theory of memory is the spate of theorizing and research on immediate and short-term memory during the last five years. In 1958, and increasingly thereafter, the principal journals of human learning and performance have been flooded with experimental investigations of human short-term memory. This work has been characterized by strong theoretical interests, and sometimes strong statements, about the nature of memory, the characteristics of the memory trace, and the relations between short-term memory and the memory that results from multiple repetitions. The contrast with the preceding thirty years is striking. During those years most research on short-term memory was concerned with the memory span as a capacity variable, and no more. It is always dangerous to be an historian about the last five or ten years, but I venture to say that Broadbent's *Perception and Communication* (1958), with its emphasis on short-term memory as a major factor in human information-processing performance, played a key role in this development. Fortunately, many of the others who have made important methodological and substantive contributions to this analysis of short-term memory have presented their most recent findings and thoughts in these Meetings on Memory, and they thus adequately document my assessment of the vigor and importance of this recent development. Therefore I will refrain from further documentation and analysis at this point, since the impact of some of these findings on our theory of memory is my main theme.

THE DOMAIN OF A
THEORY OF MEMORY

A theory of memory is becoming important for a number of different reasons, and somehow all of these reasons properly belong to a comprehensive theory of memory. Its storage mechanism is the principal concern of biochemists and neurophysiologists: the morphology of its storage—whether as a multiplexed trace system with one trace per repetition, or a single trace system subjected to incremental changes in "strength" by repetition—is becoming a principal concern of learning theorists; its susceptibility to inhibition, interference, or confusion both at the time of new trace formation and at the time of attempted trace retrieval or utilization is the concern of forgetting and transfer theorists; and the perhaps unique properties of its manifestation in immediate and short-term retention is the principal concern of psychologists interested in human information-processing performance. One knows intuitively that all of these different approaches emphasize valid questions or issues that must be encompassed by a general theory of memory, but nowhere—with perhaps the exception of Gomulicki's (1953) historical-theoretical monograph on memory-trace theory—will one find explicit systematic consideration of these several different facets of the problem of memory.

Since my present intention is to marshal some data relevant to one of the main issues in a general theory of memory—namely, the question of whether single-repetition, short-term memory and multiple-repetition, long-term memory are a dichotomy or points on a continuum—I feel compelled to discuss briefly what I believe to be the proper domain of a theory of memory and to differentiate it from a theory of learning.

After some exclusions that need not concern us here, learning may be defined as the modification of behavior as a function of experience. Operationally, this is translated into the question of whether (and, if so, how much) there has been a change in behavior from Trial n to Trial $n + 1$. Any attribute of behavior that can be subjected to counting or measuring operations can be an index of change from Trial n to Trial $n + 1$, and therefore an index of learning. Trials n and $n + 1$ are, of course, the presentation and test trials of a so-called test of immediate memory or they may be any trial in a repetitive learning situation and any immediately subsequent trial. By convention among psychologists, the change from Trial n to Trial $n + 1$ is referred to as a learning change when the variable of interest is the ordinal number of Trial n and not the temporal interval between Trial n and Trial $n + 1$, and the change from Trial n to Trial $n + 1$ is referred to as a *retention* change when the variable of interest is the interval, and the events during the interval, between Trial n and Trial $n + 1$. Learning and retention observations generally imply that the characteristics of the task, situation, or to-be-formed associations remain the same from Trial n to Trial $n + 1$. When any of these task or situation variables are deliberately manipulated as independent variables between Trial n and Trial $n + 1$, the object of investigation is *transfer* of learning, i.e., the availability and utilization of the memorial products of Trial n in a "different" situation.

Now, these operational definitions of learning, retention, and transfer are completely aseptic with respect to theory, and I think it is important to keep them so. In part, this is because it is useful to keep in mind the fact that *learning* is never observed directly; it is always an inference from an observed change in performance from Trial n to Trial $n + 1$. Furthermore—and this is the important point for theory—the observed change in performance is always a confounded reflection of three theoretically separable events: (i) the events on Trial n that result in something being stored for use on Trial $n + 1$; (ii) the storage of this product of Trial n during the interval between Trials n and $n + 1$; and (iii) the events on Trial $n + 1$ that result in retrieval and/or utilization of the stored trace of the events on Trial n. For convenience, these three theoretically separable events in an instance of learning will be called *trace formation, trace storage,* and *trace utilization.*

Obviously, a theory of learning must encompass these three processes. However, it must also encompass other processes such as those unique to the several varieties of selective learning and problem solving. Some advantages will accrue, therefore, if the domain of a general theory of memory is considered to be only a portion of the domain of a theory of learning; specifically, that portion concerned with the *storage* and *retrieval* of the residues of demonstrable instances of association formation. This seems to me to fit the historical schism between learning theories and research on memory and the formal recognition of this distinction may well assist in avoiding some misconceptions about the scope of a theory of memory. Historically, our major learning theories have not felt compelled to include consideration of the question whether storage of the residue of a learning experience (Trial n) is subject to autonomous decay, autonomous consolidation through reverberation, or to even consider systematically the memory-span phenomenon. On the other hand, much of the controversy between learning theorists surrounds the question of the necessary and sufficient conditions for association (or memory trace) formation. And even though most learning theories must say something about the conditions of transfer, or utilization of traces, they do not always include explicit consideration of the interference theory of forgetting or alternative theories. As for those who have been concerned with memory theory, they have, following Ebbinghaus (1885), employed the operations of rote learning, thus avoiding in so far as possible the problems of selective learning and insuring the contiguous occurrence of stimulus and response under conditions that demonstrably result in the formation of an association. Their emphasis has been on the storage and retrieval or other utilization of that association, i.e., of the residual trace of it in the central nervous system (CNS), and on the ways in which frequency of repetition and other learning affect such storage and retrieval.

The implication of this restriction on the domain of a theory of memory is that the theory will be concerned with post-perceptual traces, i.e., memory traces, and not with pre-perceptual traces, i.e., stimulus traces. It seems to me necessary to accept the notion that stimuli may affect the sensorium for a brief time and also the directly involved CNS segments, but that they may not get "hooked up," associated, or encoded with central or peripheral response components, and may not, because of this failure of being responded to, become a part of a memory-trace system. This view is supported by the recent work of Averbach and Coriell (1961), Sperling (1960), and Jane Mackworth (1962) which shows that there is a very-short-term visual pre-perceptual trace which suffers rapid decay (complete in .3 to .5 sec.). Only that which is reacted to during the presentation of a stimulus or during this post-exposure short-term trace is potentially retrievable from memory. While it is not necessary to my argument to defend this boundary for memory theory, because if I am wrong the slack will be taken up in a more inclusive theory of learning, it is of some interest that it is accepted by Broadbent (1963) and that it is consistent with a wealth of recent research on "incidental learning" in human subjects (Postman, in press).

What, then, are the principal issues in a theory of memory? These are about either the storage or the retrieval of traces. In the case of the storage of traces we have had four issues.[2] The first is whether memory traces should be given the characteristic of *autonomous decay* over time, which was dignified by Thorndike (1913) as the Law of Disuse and which recently has been vigorously defended by Brown (1958). The antithesis is, of course, the notion that associations, once established, are permanent—a position initially formulated by McGeoch (1932) and incorporated in a radical form in Guthrie's (1935) theory of learning.

The second storage issue is again an hypothesis about an autonomous process, but one involving the *autonomous enhancement* (fixation, consolidation) of the memory trace, rather than decay. The hypothesis was first formulated in the perseveration theory of Müller and Pilzecker (1900), with emphasis on the autonomous enhancement, or strengthening, of a memory trace if it was permitted to endure without interruption. As such, the emphasis was on a property of automatic "inner repetition" if repetition and duration are given a trade-off function in determining the strength of traces. More recently, the hypothesis has been that the memory trace established by an experience *requires* consolidation through autonomous reverberation or perservation, if it is to become a stable structural memory trace in the CNS (Deutsch, 1962; Gerard, 1963; Glickman, 1961; Hebb, 1949). Presumably, the alternative view is that every experience establishes a structural memory trace without the necessity of consolidation through reverberation or perseveration, but also without denying that such reverberation or perseveration, if permitted, may strengthen the trace.

The third issue about storage is the one previously referred to as *morphological* (at the molecular level) in our brief reference to the current controversy about the all-or-none versus the incremental notions of association formation. The all-or-none notion implies that the increment in the probability of response on Trial $n + 2$ is a consequence of establishment of independent and different all-or-none trace systems on Trials n and $n + 1$; the incremental notion implies that the same trace system is activated in some degree on Trial n and then reactivated and strengthened on Trial $n + 1$. It is, of course, possible that both notions could be true.

The fourth issue about trace storage is actually one that overlaps the issues about retrieval or utilization of traces, and is perhaps the most critical current issue. This is the question whether there are two kinds of memory storage or only one. A duplex mechanism has been postulated by Hebb (1949), Broadbent (1958), and many others, and on a variety of grounds, but all imply that one type of storage mechanism is involved in remembering or being otherwise affected by an event just recently experienced, i.e., "immediate" or short-term memory for events experienced once, and that a different type is involved in the recall or other utilization of traces established by repetitive learning experiences, i.e., long-term memory or habit. Since a clean distinction between "immediate" memory and short-term memory is not possible (Melton, 1963), we shall henceforward refer to these two manifestations of memory as short-term memory (STM) and long-term memory (LTM).

Some principal contentions regarding the differences between the two memory mechanisms are that: (a) STM involves "activity" traces, while LTM involves "structural" traces (Hebb, 1949; 1961); (b) STM involves autonomous decay, while LTM involves irreversible, non-decaying traces (Hebb, 1949); and (c) STM has a fixed capacity that is subject to overload and consequent loss of elements stored in it, for nonassociative reasons, while LTM is, in effect, infinitely expansible, with failure of retrieval attributable mainly to incompleteness of the cue to retrieval or to interference from previously or subsequently learned associations (Broadbent, 1958; 1963). On the other hand, the monistic view with respect to trace storage is one which, in general, accepts the characteristics of LTM storage as the characteristics of STM storage as well, and thus ascribes to the traces of events that occur only once the same "structural" properties, the same irreversibility, the same susceptibility to associational factors in retrieval, as are ascribed to LTM.

The bridge to the theoretical problems of trace retrieval and utilization as major components of a theory of memory is obviously wrought by the issue of memory as a dichotomy or a continuum. Those who accept a dichotomy do so on the basis of data on retention, forgetting, or transfer that suggest two distinct sets of conditions for retrieval and utilization of traces; those who accept a continuum do so on the basis of data that suggest a single set of conditions or principles.

The history of our thought about the problems of retrieval and utilization of traces reveals three main issues. The first is the question of the dependence of the retrieval on the completeness of the reinstatement on Trial $n + 1$ of the stimulating situation present on Trial n. Psychologists have formulated several principles in an attempt to describe the relevant observations, but all of them may be subsumed under a principle which asserts that the probability of retrieval will be a decreasing function of the amount of stimulus change from Trial n to Trial $n + 1$. Changes in directly measured and manipulated cue stimuli, like the CS in a classical conditioning experiment, that result in decrement in response probability are generally referred to a sub-principle of stimulus generalization (Mednick and Freedman, 1960); changes in contextual stimuli that result in forgetting are usually referred to a sub-principle of altered stimulating conditions or altered set (McGeoch and Irion, 1952); and stimulus changes that occur in spite of all attempts to hold the stimulating situation constant are referred to a sub-principle of stimulus fluctuation (Estes, 1955). Since these are all principles of transfer, when they are employed to interpret failure of retrieval on Trial $n + 1$, it is clear that all principles of transfer of learning, whether they emphasize the occurrence of retrieval in spite of change or the failure of retrieval in spite of some similarity, are fundamental principles of trace retrieval and utilization. At this moment I see no necessary difference between the dual- and single-mechanism theories of memory with respect to this factor of stimulus change in retrieval, but there may be one implicit and undetected.

The second issue relates to the interactions of traces. Here, of course, is the focus of the interference theory of forgetting which has, in recent years, led us to accept the notion that retrieval is a function of interactions between prior traces and new traces at the time of the formation of the new traces, as well as interactions resulting in active interference and blocking of retrieval. This theory was given its most explicit early expression in the attack by McGeoch (1932) on the principle of autonomous decay of traces, and has been refined and corrected in a number of ways since then (Postman, 1961). In its present form it accepts the hypothesis of irreversibility of traces and interprets all failures of retrieval or utilization as instances of stimulus change or interference. Therefore, it implicitly accepts a one-mechanism theory of memory. However, it has been recognized (Melton, 1961) that the principal evidence for the theory has come from the study of retrieval following multiple-repetition learning, and that the extension of the theory to STM is not necessarily valid. Since dual-mechanism theorists assert that retrieval in STM is subject to disruption through overloading, but not through associative interference, a prime focus of memory theory becomes the question of associative interference effects in STM.

A third important issue related to retrieval is the relationship between repetition and retrieval probability. While the fact of a strong correlation between repetition and probability of retrieval seems not to be questionable, there are two important questions about repetition that a theory of memory must encompass. The first of these is the question of whether repetition multiplies the number of all-or-none traces or whether it produces incremental changes in the strength of a trace. This has already been listed as a problem in storage, but it is obvious that the alternative notions about storage have important implications for the ways in which repetitions may be manipulated to increase or decrease probability of retrieval. The second is the question of whether there is a fundamental discontinuity between the characteristics of traces established by a single repetition and those established by multiple repetitions (or single repetitions with opportunity for consolidation). This appears to be the contention of the dual-mechanism theorists; whereas, a continuum of the effects of repetition in the establishment of "structural," permanent traces seems to be the accepted position of the single-mechanism theorists.

In summary so far, when the domain of a theory of memory is explicitly confined to the problems of the storage and retrieval of memory traces, it becomes possible to formulate and examine some of the major theoretical issues under the simplifying assumption that the formation of the associations or memory traces has already occurred. Then it becomes clear that the conflicting notions with respect to the properties of trace storage and the conflicting notions with respect to the principal determinants of trace retrieval, or failure thereof, converge on the more fundamental issue of the unitary or dual nature of the storage mechanism. My plan is to examine these alleged differences between STM and LTM in the light of some recent studies of human short-term memory, and then return to a summary of the implications these studies seem to have for the major issues in a general theory of memory.

STM AND LTM: CONTINUUM OR DICHOTOMY?

The contrasting characteristics of STM and LTM that have led to the hypothesis that there are two kinds of memory have not, to my knowledge, been considered systematically by any memory theorist, although Hebb (1949), Broadbent (1957; 1958; 1963), and Brown (1958) have defended the dichotomy.

The decay of traces in immediate memory, in contrast to the permanence, even irreversibility, of the memory traces established through repetitive learning, is the most universally acclaimed differentiation. For Hebb (1949) this rapid decay is a correlate of the non-structural, i.e., "activity," nature of the single perception that is given neither the "fixation" effect of repetition nor the opportunity for "fixation" through reverberation. For Broadbent (1957; 1958) and Brown (1958) this autonomous decay in time is a property of the postulated STM mechanism, and attempts have been made (e.g., Conrad and Hille, 1958) to support the notion that time per se is the critical factor in decay. Obviously, this autonomous decay can be postponed by rehearsal—recirculating through the short-term store (Broadbent, 1958)—and Brown (1958) has maintained that such rehearsal has no strengthening effect on the structural trace. However, the decay of a specific trace begins whenever rehearsal is prevented by distraction or overloading of the short-term store (Broadbent, 1957; 1958). A corollary of this last proposition is that the initiation of the decay process, by dislodging the trace from the short-term store, is not dependent on new learning and therefore not on the associative interference principles which account for most if not all of the forgetting of events that reach the long-term store through repetition, reverberation, or both (Broadbent, 1963).

These characteristics contrast sharply with those attributed to LTM by the interference theory of forgetting which has dominated our thinking since McGeoch's (1932) classical attack on the Law of Disuse and which has gained new stature as a consequence of recent refinements (Melton, 1961; Postman, 1961). This theory implies: (a) that traces, even those that result from single repetitions, are "structural" in Hebb's sense, and are permanent except as overlaid by either the recovery of temporarily extinguished stronger competing traces or by new traces; and (b) that all persistent and progressive losses in the retrievability of traces are to be attributed to such associative interference factors, and not to decay or to a combination of nonassociative disruption plus decay. And, as a consequence of these two implications, it is assumed that the effect of repetition on the strength of the single type of trace is a continuous monotonic process. On this basis a continuum is assumed to encompass single events or sequential dependencies between them when these events are well within the span of immediate memory and also complex sequences of events, such as in serial and paired-associate lists, that are far beyond the span of immediate memory and thus require multiple repetitions for mastery of the entire set of events or relations between them.

My discussion of the question: "STM or LTM; continuum or dichotomy?" will therefore examine some experimental data on STM to see (a) whether they are interpretable in terms of the interference factors known to operate in LTM, and (b) whether the durability of memory for sub-span and supra-span to-be-remembered units is a continuous function of repetitions.

The reference experiments that provide the data of interest are those recently devised by Peterson and Peterson (1959) and Hebb (1961), with major emphasis on the former. While a number of ingenious techniques for investigating STM have been invented during the last few years, I believe that the Petersons' method is the key to integration of retention data on immediate memory, STM and LTM. This is because, as you will see, it can be applied to to-be-remembered units in the entire range from those well below the memory span to those well above it, and the control and manipulation of duration and frequency of presentation are essentially continuous with those traditionally employed in list memorization.

In what must have been a moment of supreme skepticism of laboratory dogma, not unlike that which recently confounded the chemist's dogma that the noble gases are nonreactive (Abelson, 1962), Peterson and Peterson (1959) determined the recallability of single trigrams, such as X-J-R, after intervals of 3, 6, 9, 12, 15, and 18 sec. The trigrams were presented auditorily in 1 sec., a 3-digit number occurred during the next second, and S counted backward by 3's or 4's from that number until, after the appropriate interval, he received a cue to recall the trigram. The S was given up to 14 sec. for the recall of the trigram, thus avoiding any time-pressure in the retrieval process. The principal measure of retention was the frequency of completely correct trigrams in recall.

The results of this experiment are shown in Fig. 1. It is noteworthy that the curve has the Ebbinghausian form, even though the maximum interval is only 18 sec., and that there is an appreciable amount of forgetting after only 3 and 6 sec. Other observations reported by the Petersons permit us to estimate that the recall after zero time interval, which is the usual definition of immediate memory, would have been 90 percent, which is to say that in 10 percent of the cases the trigram was misperceived, so that the forgetting is actually not as great as it might appear to be. Even with this correction for misperception, however, the retention after 18 sec. would be only about 20 percent, which is rather startling when one remembers that these trigrams were well below the memory span of the college students who served as Ss.

The rapid deterioration of performance over time is not inconsistent with the decay theory, nor is it necessarily inconsistent with the notion that traces from single occurrences of single items are on a continuum with traces from multiple items learned through repetition. However, additional data with the same method were soon forthcoming. Murdock (1961) first replicated the Peterson and Peterson experiment with 3-consonant trigrams, and then repeated all details of the experiment except that, in one study he used single common words drawn from the more frequent ones in the Thorndike-Lorge word lists, and in another study he used word triads, i.e., three-unrelated common words, as the to-be-remembered unit.

Murdock's results from these three experiments are shown alongside the Petersons' results in Fig. 1. His replication of the Petersons' study with trigrams gave remarkably similar results. Of considerable significance, as we will see later, is his finding that single words show less forgetting than did the trigrams, but that *some* forgetting occurs with even such simple units. Finally, the most seminal fact for theory in these experiments is his discovery that word triads act like 3-consonant trigrams in short-term retention.

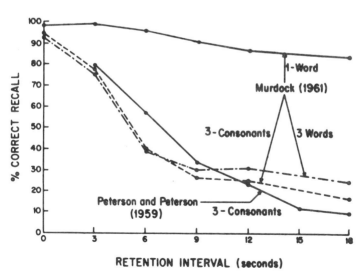

Fig. 1. Percentage frequency of completely correct recall of 3-consonant trigrams (Peterson and Peterson, 1959; Murdock, 1961), and 1-word and 3-word units (Murdock, 1961).

Murdock's data strongly suggested that the critical determinant of the slope of the short-term retention function was the
number of Millerian (1956) "chunks" in the to-be-remembered
unit. Of even greater importance, from my point of view was the
implication that, other things being equal, the rate of forgetting
of a unit presented once is a function of the amount of intra-unit
interference, and that this intra-unit interference is a function
of the number of encoded chunks within the item rather than
the number of physical elements, such as letters, or information
units.

The first of several projected experimental tests of this hypothesis has been completed.[3] The to-be-remembered units were
1, 2, 3, 4, or 5 consonants. The unit, whatever its size, was presented visually for 1 sec., and read off aloud by S. Then .7 sec.
later a 3-digit number was shown for 1 sec. and removed. The
S read off the number and then counted backward aloud by 3's
or 4's until a visual cue for recall, a set of 4 asterisks, was shown.
The delayed retention intervals were 4, 12, and 32 sec., and a
fourth condition involved recall after only .7 sec., hereafter referred to as the zero interval. The Ss were given 8 sec. for the recall of each item. In the course of the experiment each S was
tested four times at each combination of unit size and interval
for a total of 80 observations. Every condition was represented
in each of 4 successive blocks of 20 observations, and there was
partial counterbalancing of conditions within the blocks and of
to-be-remembered units between the blocks. Through my error,
the to-be-remembered units of each specific size were not counterbalanced across the four retention intervals. Thanks only to the
power of the variable we were investigating, this did not, as you
will see, materially affect the orderliness of the data.

The results for the last two blocks of trials are shown in Fig.
2. Again, the measure of recall performance is the percentage
of completely correct recalls of the to-be-remembered unit, i.e.,
the single consonant had to be correct when only one was presented, all five consonants had to be correct and in the proper
order when the 5-consonant unit was presented. The same relationships hold when Ss are not as well-practiced in the task, i.e.,
in Blocks 1 and 2, although the absolute amounts of forgetting
are greater. The data in Fig. 2 are to be preferred to those for

the earlier stages of practice, because all five curves in this figure have their origin very near to 100 percent recall. That is, in all cases it is possible to assume that Ss had, in fact, learned the to-be-remembered unit during the 1-sec. presentation interval.

Aside from the self-evident generalization that the slope of the short-term forgetting curve increases as a direct function of the number of elements in the to-be-remembered unit, two features of these data are worthy of special attention. First, it should be noted that the slope of the curve for the 3-consonant units is not as steep as was reported by both Peterson and Peterson (1959) and by Murdock (1961). We do not know why there is this discrepancy, although it occurs consistently in our work with the Petersons' method.

The other point of interest is the obvious forgetting of the one-consonant unit. This curve looks very much like the one obtained by Murdock for single words. Both findings have signifi-

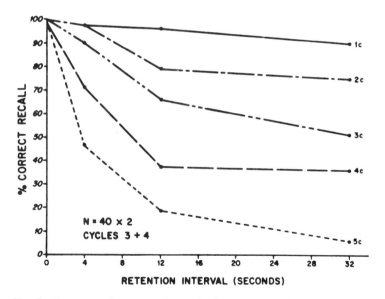

FIG. 2. Percentage frequency of completely correct recall of units of 1 to 5 consonants with well-practiced Ss (Blocks 3 and 4).

cance for theory because they represent instances of forgetting when the intra-unit interference is at a minimum for verbal units. But before giving additional consideration to this point, a further set of data from this experiment needs to be presented and a more general statement of the observed relationships deserves formulation.

If the increased slopes of the forgetting curves shown in Fig. 2 are attributed to an increase in intra-unit interference, it is of some importance to show that the more frequent breakdown of complete recall as one increases the number of letters in the to-be-remembered unit is not merely a breakdown in the sequential dependencies between the letters, but is also reflected in the frequency of correct recall of the first letter of the unit. In Fig. 3 are shown the percentages of first-letter recalls in the last two blocks of our experiment. Although they are lacking in the monotonic beauty of the curves for whole units correct, I am willing to accept the generalization that first-letter recall suffers inter-

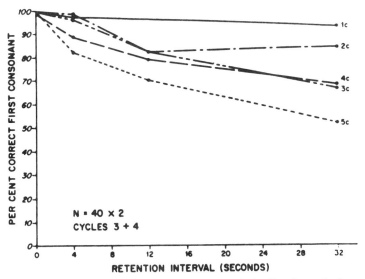

FIG. 3. Percentage frequency of correct recall of the first letter in 1- to 5-consonant units with well-practiced Ss (Blocks 3 and 4).

ference as a function of the number of other letters in the to-be-remembered unit. Thus, what Peterson (1963) has called "background conditioning," and is measured by the recall of first letters, and what he has called "cue learning," and is represented by sequential dependencies in recall, are affected alike by the number of elements in the to-be-remembered unit. This is expected in so far as there is functional parallelism between "free" recall and serial or paired-associate recall with respect to the effect of learning and interference variables (Melton, 1963).

In Fig. 4 the results obtained so far have been generalized

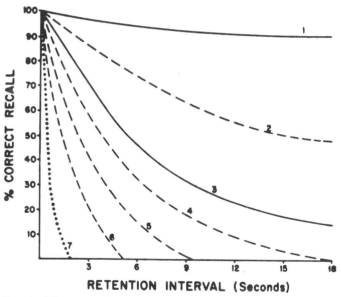

RETENTION INTERVAL (Seconds)

Fig. 4. The expected relationship between the number of recoded units ("chunks") in the to-be-remembered unit, the duration of the short-term retention interval, and the percentage frequency of completely correct recall, when each to-be-remembered unit is presented once, i.e., with just sufficient duration for one completely correct perceptual encoding. The solid-line curves represent some of the empirically determined functions; the dashed lines represent extrapolated functions; the dotted line represents the expected short-term memory function for a to-be-remembered unit that is at memory-span length for the individual S.

and extrapolated. This set of hypothetical curves will be used as the conceptual anchor for three points that are related to the question whether short-term and long-term memory are a dichotomy or points on a continuum. The first, and most obvious, point about the figure is that it reaffirms the notion that intra-unit interference is a major factor in the short-term forgetting of sub-span units, but now the parameter is the number of encoded chunks, instead of the number of physical elements or information units. This is consistent with Miller's (1956) cogent arguments for the concept of chunk as the unit of measurement of human information-processing capacities. It is also the unit most likely to have a one-to-one relationship to the memory trace. Obviously, it is also the concept demanded by the parallelism of the findings of Murdock with 1 and 3 words and our findings with 1 to 5 consonants, even though it cannot, of course, be asserted that the number of elements beyond one in these experiments, be they words or consonants, stand in a one-to-one relationship to the number of chunks. Even though the strings of consonants in our experiment were constructed by subtracting from or combining consonant trigrams of Witmer (1935) association values less than 60 percent, there were surely some easy-to-learn letter sequences and some hard-to-learn letter sequences. That such differences in meaningfulness are correlated with chunkability is well known (Underwood and Schulz, 1960). Also, Peterson, Peterson, and Miller (1961) have shown, although on a limited scale, that the meaningfulness of CVC trigrams is positively correlated with recall after 6 sec. in the Petersons' situation. But perhaps the greatest gain from the use of the chunk as the unit of measurement in formulating the otherwise empirical generalization is a suggestion this yields about how we may get a handle on that intervening variable. It suggests to me that we may be able to establish empirical benchmarks for 1, 2, 3, . . . ,n chunks in terms of the slopes of short-term memory functions and then use these slopes to calibrate our verbal learning materials in terms of a chunk scale.

The evidence that the slope of the short-term forgetting curve increases dramatically as a function of the number of encoded chunks in the unit is evidence against autonomous decay being a major factor, but it does not deny that such decay may occur.

It is evidence against decay as a major factor because: (*a*) a single consonant *was* remembered with very high frequency over a 32-sec. interval filled with numerical operations that surely qualify as overloading and disrupting activities (if one grants that the Petersons' method adequately controls surreptitious rehearsal) ; and (*b*) the major portion of the variance in recall is accounted for by intra-unit interference, rather than time. It does not deny that decay may occur, since there was *some* forgetting of even the single consonant (and of the single word in Murdock's experiment) even though only one "chunk" was involved, and intra-unit interference was at a minimum.

The reason for the forgetting of the single chunk is, I believe, to be found in the other sources of interference in recall in this type of experiment. In the first place, I presume that no one will argue that counting backward aloud is the mental vacuum that interference theory needs to insure the absence of retroactive inhibition in the recall of the to-be-remembered unit, nor is it necessarily the least interfering, and at the same time rehearsal-preventing, activity that can be found for such experiments. However, we must leave this point for future research, because we have none of the systematic studies that must be done on the effects of different methods of filling these short retention intervals, and we also have no evidence, therefore, on the extent to which retroactive interference and intra-unit interference interact.

On the other source of interference which may explain the forgetting of the single chunk—namely, proactive interference (PI) —we do have some evidence. Peterson (1963) has maintained, on the basis of analysis of blocks of trials in the original Peterson and Peterson (1959) study, that there is no evidence for the build-up of proactive inhibition in that experiment, only practice effects. However, this evidence is unconvincing (Melton, 1963) when practice effects are strong, and if it is assumed that proactive inhibition from previous items in the series of tests may build up rapidly but asymptote after only a few such previous items. Such an assumption about a rapidly achieved high steady-state of PI is given some credence by the rapid development of a steady-state in frequency of false-positives in studies of short-term recognition memory (Shepard and Teghtsoonian, 1961).

A second, and powerful, argument for large amounts of PI

throughout the Peterson type of experiment is the frequency of overt intrusions from previous units in the series during the attempt to recall an individual unit. Murdock (1961) found such intrusions in his studies of short-term retention of words, and there was the strong recency effect among these intrusions that is to be expected if the steady-state notion is valid. The analysis of such intrusions in studies involving letters rather than words is limited by the identifiability of the source of the intrusions, but all who run experiments with letters become convinced that such intrusions are very common and usually come from the immediately preceding units.[4]

More systematic evidence for strong PI effects in STM in the Petersons' situation is given by Keppel and Underwood (1962). A representative finding is shown in Fig. 5. A three-consonant item which is the first item in the series is recalled almost perfectly after as long as 18 sec., and PI builds up rapidly over items, especially for the longer retention interval. These data support the notion that there is substantial PI in the Peterson and Peterson experiment on short-term memory for single verbal units. As such, they, as well as the other evidence cited, indicate that the small amount of forgetting of single consonants or single

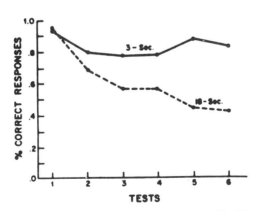

Fig. 5. Percentage frequency of completely correct recall of 3-consonant trigrams after 3 and 18 sec., as a function of the ordinal position of the test in a series of tests. The decline in recall reflects the build-up of proactive inhibition (Keppel and Underwood, 1962).

words over short intervals of time may be partly, if not entirely, attributable to the PI resulting from sequential testing of recall of such items. Keppel and Underwoods' results do not, however, support the view that the PI reaches a steady state in as few as five items, but this does not necessarily deny the steady-state notion. Also, a careful study of these data and the data on intra-unit interference suggests some strong interactions between PI, intra-unit interference (II), and the retention interval, all of which would support the interference interpretation, but discussion of these interactions would be tedious and unrewarding until properly designed experiments have been performed.

My conclusion from all this is that there is sufficient direct or inferential evidence for PI, RI, and II in the short-term retention of single sub-span verbal units, and that the PI and potential RI may account for the observed forgetting of one-chunk units, that is, when II is minimal. So much for interference.

The other line of investigation that needs to be considered before the question of continuum versus dichotomy can be properly assessed has to do with the effect of repetition on the short-term memory for sub-span and just supra-span strings of elements or chunks.

The concept of the memory span is rather important in this discussion because it is the boundary between the number of elements, or chunks, that can be correctly reproduced immediately after a single repetition and the number of elements, or chunks, that require two or more repetitions for immediate correct reproduction. Interestingly enough, the short-term forgetting curve for a unit of memory-span length turns out to be the limiting member of the hypothetical family of curves that has been used to generalize the relationship between the slope of the forgetting curve and the number of chunks in the to-be-remembered unit. The extrapolated forgetting curve for a unit of memory-span length is shown as the dotted-line curve of Fig. 4.

The origin of this limiting curve on the ordinate will, of course, depend on the statistical definition of the span of immediate memory, but in order to be consistent I have placed it in Fig. 4 at or near 100 percent recall after zero interval. It is also assumed that the presentation time for this and all other smaller numbers of chunks is just sufficient for one perceptual encoding of each element, i.e., for one repetition. For a unit of span length it is not surprising that a precipitous decline of completely correct recall to zero is expected when only very short, but filled, delays are introduced before recall begins. No experiment in the literature fits exactly these operational requirements, but the prediction is a matter of common experience in looking up telephone numbers, and we also have Conrad's (1958) evidence that Ss show a radical reduction in correct dialing of 8-digit numbers when required merely to dial "zero" before dialing the number.

At this point we are brought face to face with the question of the effects of repetition of sub-span and supra-span units on their recall. Such data are important for at least two reasons. In the first place, the argument for a continuum of STM and LTM requires that there be only orderly quantitative differences in the effects of repetition on sub-span and supra-span units. In the second place, if repetition has an effect on the frequency of correct recall of sub-span units, such as consonant trigrams, this must certainly have some significance for the conceptualization of the strength of a memory trace—whether it is all-or-none or cummulative.

The effect of time for rehearsal of a set of items before a filled retention interval was first studied by Brown (1958). His negative results led him to the conclusion that recirculation of information through the temporary memory store merely delays the onset of decay, but does not strengthen the trace. However, the original Peterson and Peterson (1959) report on the retention of consonant trigrams included an experiment which showed a significant effect of instructed rehearsal on short-term retention.

Fortunately, we now have available a report by Hellyer (1962) in which consonant trigrams were given one, two, four, or eight 1-sec. visual presentations before retention intervals of 3, 9, 18, and 27 sec. His data are shown in Fig. 6 and require little comment. Obviously, a consonant trigram is remembered better with repetition even though it is completely and correctly perceived and encoded after only one repetition, as judged by the immediate recall of it. The slopes of the retention curves in our hypothetical family of curves based on the number of chunks in the to-be-remembered unit are, therefore, a joint function of chunks and repetitions. Or perhaps a better theoretical statement

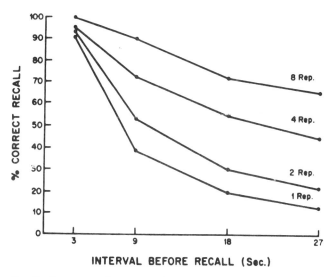

Fig. 6. Percentage frequency of completely correct recall of 3-consonant trigrams as a function of the frequency of 1-sec. presentations of the trigram before beginning the retention interval (Hellyer, 1962).

of this would be to say that repetition reduces the number of chunks in the to-be-remembered unit. This is why one word and one consonant have the same rate of forgetting.

As for the effect of repetition on just supra-span units, we have no data directly comparable to those of Hellyer for sub-span units, but we have data from a much more severe test of the repetition effect. I refer to the method and data of Hebb's (1961) study in which he disproved to his own satisfaction his own assumption about "activity" traces. In this experiment he presented a fixed set of 24 series of 9-digit numbers. Each of the digits from 1 to 9 was used only once within each to-be-remembered unit. The series was read aloud to S at the rate of about 1 digit/sec., and S was instructed to repeat the digits immediately in exactly the same order. The unusual feature of the experiment was that exactly the same series of digits occurred on every third trial, i.e., the 3rd, 6th, 9th . . . 24th, and others varying in a random fashion.

His results are shown in Fig. 7. Hebb considered the rising curve for the repeated 9-digit numbers, when contrasted with

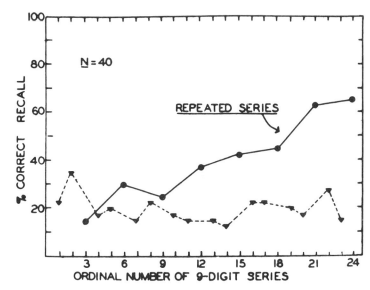

Fig. 7. Percentage frequency of completely correct recall of 9-digit numbers when tested immediately. The "repeated series" was a specific 9-digit sequence that occurred in the 3rd, 6th, 9th ... 24th position in the series of tests. Other points represent nonrepeated 9-digit numbers (Hebb, 1961).

the flat curve for the nonrepeated numbers, to be sufficient basis for concluding that some form of structural trace results from a single repetition of an associative sequence of events. Further, he properly considers this to be a demonstration of the cumulative structural effects of repetition under extremely adverse conditions involving large amounts of RI.

Hebb's method in this experiment may well be another important invention in the analysis of human memory. But I was not completely satisfied with his experiment and the reliability of his findings, for reasons that need not be detailed here. As a consequence of these uncertainties, I have repeated and extended Hebb's experiment by giving each of 32 women Ss two practice numbers and then 80 tests for immediate recall of 9-digit numbers. Within these 80 tests there were 4 instances in which a specific 9-digit number occurred 4 times with 2 other numbers intervening between successive trials, 4 in which a specific number occurred 4 times with 3 intervening numbers, 4 for 4 trials with 5 intervening numbers and 4 for 4 trials with 8 intervening numbers. In addition, there were 16 9-digit numbers that occurred only once. I will not try to describe the interlocking pattern of events that was used to achieve this design, but the design chosen was used in both a forward and backward order for different Ss, and the specific repeated numbers were used equally often under the different spacings of repetitions. Furthermore, within the entire set of 32 different 9-digit numbers used in this experiment, interseries similarities were minimized by insuring that no more than two digits ever occurred twice in the same order. The numbers were presented visually for 3.7 sec. and S recorded her response by writing on a 3 x 5 in. card which contained 9 blocks. Recall began .7 sec. after the stimulus slide disappeared, and 8.8 sec. were allowed for recall.

Unfortunately, my Ss behaved in a somewhat more typical fashion than did Hebb's in that they showed substantial nonspecific practice effects. This complicates the determination of the effects of specific repetition, because later trials on a particular 9-digit number must always be later in practice than earlier trials, and also because this confounding of specific and nonspecific practice effects is more serious the greater the interval between repetitions of a specific number. This confounding has been eliminated, at least to my satisfaction, by determining the function that seemed to be the most appropriate fit to the practice curve based on first occurrences of specific numbers. This function was then used to correct obtained scores on the 2nd, 3rd, and 4th repetitions of a specific number in a manner and amount appropriate to the expected nonspecific practice effect.

A preferred measure of the effect of repetition in this situation is the mean number of digits correctly recalled in their proper positions. In Fig. 8 is shown the mean number of digits correctly recalled, as a function of ordinal position of the first occurrence of a 9-digit number within the experimental session. This merely confirms my statement about practice effects; exhibits the equation used for corrections for general practice effects; and permits observation of the large variability of mean performance in this type of experiment.

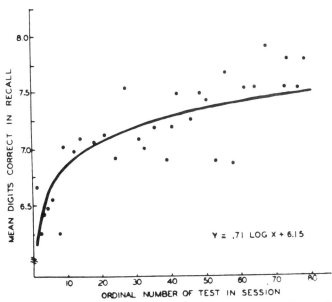

Fig. 8. The nonspecific practice effect in the recall of new and different 9-digit numbers in the course of the experiment.

The principal data from the experiment are shown in Fig. 9. The effect of repetition of a specific 9-digit number is plotted, the parameter being the number of other different 9-digit numbers that intervened between successive repetitions of the specific number. In these curves the points for first-repetition performance are obtained points, and those for performance on the 2nd, 3rd, and 4th repetitions have been corrected for nonspecific practice effects. In Fig. 10 these last data are expressed as gains in performance over performance on the first occurrence of a number. Comparable data for gains in the frequency with which entire 9-digit numbers were correctly recalled show the same relationships.

These data not only confirm the Hebb data, they also add material substance to an argument for a continuum of immediate, short-term, and long-term memory. Just as a continuum the-

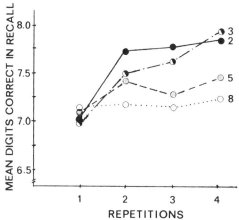

FIG. 9. Mean number of digits correctly recalled, as a function of the number of repetitions of the specific 9-digit number and of the number of other 9-digit numbers that intervened between repetitions. The data points for the first repetition are obtained values; the data points for the second, third, and fourth repetitions reflect corrections for nonspecific practice effects.

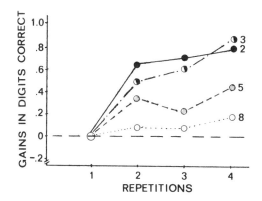

FIG. 10. Mean gains in number of digits correctly recalled, as a function of the number of repetitions of a specific 9-digit number and of the number of other 9-digit numbers that intervened between repetitions. All gain scores have been corrected for nonspecific practice effects.

ory would have predicted Hebb's results with two intervening numbers between repetitions of a specific number, it also would predict that the repetition effect would be a decreasing function of the number of intervening numbers because between-repetition retroactive inhibition is being increased. Even so, I am not sure that any theory would have predicted that one would need to place as many as 8 other 9-digit numbers in between repetitions of a specific 9-digit number before the repetition effect would be washed out. Surely, the structural memory trace established by a single occurrence of an event must be extraordinarily persistent.

With respect to our hypothetical family of retention curves based on the number of chunks in the to-be-remembered unit, we can now with some confidence say that events which contain chunks beyond the normal memory span can be brought to the criterion of perfect immediate recall by reducing the number of chunks through repetition. If this empirical model involving chunks and repetitions to predict short-term forgetting is valid, it should be possible to show that a supra-span 9-chunk unit that is reduced to 7 chunks through repetition, would have the short-term forgetting curve of a 7-chunk unit, and one reduced through repetition to a 3-chunk unit should have a 3-chunk short-term forgetting curve. Even though this prediction is probably much too simple-minded, it now requires no stretch of my imagination to conceive of the "immediate" or short-term memory for single units and the memory for memorized supra-span units, like 12 serial nonsense syllables or 8 paired associates, as belonging on a continuum.

IMPLICATIONS

We may now turn to the implications these data on short-term memory seem to me to have for a theory of memory. I will attempt no finely spun theory, because such is neither my talent nor my interest. Also, I can be brief because, aged Functionalist that I am, I would be the first to admit—even insist—that my inferences are stated with confidence only for the storage and retrieval of verbal material demonstrably encoded by adult human Ss.

The duplexity theory of memory storage must, it seems to me, yield to the evidence favoring a continuum of STM and LTM or else come up with an adequate accounting for the evidence presented here. My preference is for a theoretical strategy that accepts STM and LTM as mediated by a single type of storage mechanism. In such a continuum, frequency of repetition appears to be the important independent variable, "chunking" seems to be the important intervening variable, and the slope of the retention curve is the important dependent variable. I am persuaded of this by the orderly way in which repetition operates on both sub-span units and supra-span units to increase the probability of retrieval in recall, and also by the parallelism between STM and LTM that is revealed as we look at STM with the conceptual tools of the interference theory of forgetting which was developed from data on LTM.

The evidence that implies a continuum of STM and LTM also relates, of course, to some of the other issues about the characteristics of memory storage. While it is perhaps too early to say that the autonomous decay of traces has no part in forgetting, whether short-term or long-term, I see no basis for assuming that such decay has the extreme rapidity sometimes ascribed to it or for assuming that it accounts for a very significant portion of the forgetting that we all suffer continually and in large amounts. On the contrary, the data from both STM and LTM tempt one to the radical hypothesis that every perception, however fleeting and embedded in a stream of perceptions, leaves its permanent "structural" trace in the CNS.

Insofar as I can understand the implications of the consolidation hypothesis about memory storage, I must concur with Hebb's (1961) conclusion that his experiment demonstrates the fixation of a structural trace by a single repetition of an event and without the benefit of autonomous consolidation processes. In fact, I think that our repetition and extension of his experiment establishes that conclusion even more firmly, because it shows that the retrievability of the trace of the first experience of a specific 9-digit number is a decreasing function of the amount of reuse of the elements in the interval between repetitions. Therefore, as far as our present data go, it seems proper to conclude that a consolidation process extending over more than a few seconds is not a necessary condition for the fixation of a structural trace. This does not, of course, deny that consolidation may be a necessary condition in other types of learning or other types of organism, nor does it deny that types of experience (e.g., Kleinsmith and Kaplan, 1963; Walker, 1963) other than the mundane remembering of nonsense strings of letters or words may benefit from such autonomous consolidation processes if they are permitted to occur.

The issue as to whether memory traces are established in an incremental or all-or-none fashion can be refined, but not resolved, on the basis of our observations on short-term memory. In all of the experiments with the Petersons' method, the initial operation was to insure that S encoded, i.e., learned, the to-be-remembered unit in a single 1-sec. presentation of it before the retention interval was introduced. This is "one-trial" learning in a more exact sense than has been true of various attempts to demonstrate the all-or-none principle in associative learning (Postman, 1963). Yet forgetting was rapid and strongly a function of the amount of potential intra-unit interference in the to-be-remembered unit. Also, this unit that was perfectly remembered after one repetition was better remembered after multiple massed repetitions. The proper question in the case of verbal associative learning seems, therefore, to be the characteristics of the trace storage that reflect the effects of repetitions on performance, rather than the question whether such associative connections reach full effective strength in one trial. The question of whether repetitions multiply the number of traces leading to a particular response or produce incremental changes in specific traces seems to me to be subject to direct experimental attack. Perhaps again because of my Functionalist background, I am inclined to believe that future research will show that both the multiplexing of traces and the incremental strengthening of traces results from repetition. Which mode of storage carries the greater burden in facilitating retrieval will depend on the variability of stimulation from repetition to repetition and the appropriateness of the sampling of this prior stimulation at the time of attempted retrieval.

Finally, with respect to the retrieval process, the theory of which is dominated by transfer theory for LTM, it seems that the placing of STM and LTM on a continuum—and the reasons for doing so—forces the interference theory of forgetting to include the prediction of forgetting in STM within its domain. At least, the testing of the theory in that context will extend its importance as a general theory of forgetting, if it survives the tests, and will quickly reveal the discontinuity of STM and LTM, if such is in fact the case.

Whatever may be the outcome of these theoretical and experimental issues in the next few years, of one thing we can be certain at this time. The revival of interest in short-term memory and the new techniques that have been devised for the analysis of short-term memory will enrich and extend our understanding of human memory far beyond what could have been accomplished by the most assiduous exploitation of the techniques of rote memorization of lists of verbal units. In fact, our evidence on STM for near-span and supra-span verbal units suggests that the systematic exploration of the retention of varying sizes of units over short and long time intervals will give new meaning to research employing lists.

Notes

1. This paper comprises, in substance, the author's Vice-Presidential Address to Section I (Psychology) of the American Association for the Advancement of Science, 1962. The author is particularly indebted to the Center for Human Learning, University of California, Berkeley, where a research appointment during the Fall semester of 1962–1963 gave the freedom from academic routine and the stimulating discussions that led to the repetition of the Hebb experiment and also supported the preparation of this paper. Early exploratory studies on short-term memory and the experiment on the recall of different sized verbal units were supported by Project MICHIGAN under Department of the Army Contract DA-36-039-SC-78801, administered by the United States Army Signal Corps. Reproduction for any purpose of the United States Government is permitted.

2. For the purposes of this discussion, I am ignoring the hypothetical property of autonomous, dynamic changes within memory traces in the directions specified by gestalt laws (Koffka, 1935). While the need for such an hypothetical property is not yet a dead issue (Duncan, 1960; Lovibond, 1958), it has had very little support since the classical treatment of the matter by Hebb and Foord (1945).

3. This study and a subsequent one are graduate research projects of David Wulff and Robert G. Crowder, University of Michigan, and will be reported under the title: Melton, A. W., Crowder, R. G., and Wulff, D., *Short-term memory for individual items with varying numbers of elements.*

4. Apparent intrusions from preceding to-be-remembered units were very common in the 1- to 5-consonant experiment reported here, but the experimental design did not counterbalance first-order sequence effects over conditions and nothing meaningful can be said about such intrusions except that they occur with substantial frequency.

References

Abelson, P. H. The need for skepticism. *Science,* 1962, 138, 75.

Averbach, E., and Coriell, A. S. Short-term memory in vision. *Bell Syst. Tech. J.,* 1961, 40, 309–328.

Barnes, J. M., and Underwood, B. J. "Fate" of first-list associations in transfer theory. *J. exp. Psychol.,* 1959, 58, 97–105.

Broadbent, D. E. A mechanical model for human attention and immediate memory. *Psychol. Rev.,* 1957, 64, 205–215.

Broadbent, D. E. *Perception and communication.* New York: Pergamon, 1958.

Broadbent, D. E. Flow of information within the organism. *J. verb. Learn. verb. Behav.,* 1963, 2, 34–39.

Brown, J. Some tests of the decay theory of immediate memory. *Quart. J. exp. Psychol.,* 1958, 10, 12–21.

Conrad, R. Accuracy of recall using keyset and telephone dial and the effect of a 'prefix digit. *J. appl. Psychol.,* 1958, 42, 285–288.

Conrad, R., and Hille, B. A. The decay theory of immediate memory and paced recall. *Canad. J. Psychol.,* 1958, 12, 1–6.

Deutsch, J. A. Higher nervous function: The physiological bases of memory. *Ann. Rev. Physiol.,* 1962, 24, 259–286.

Duncan, C. P. Controlled fixation of the stimulus-figure in a study of autonomous change in the memory-trace. *Amer. J. Psychol.,* 1960, 73, 115–120.

Ebbinghaus, H. *Das Gedächtnis: Untersuchungen zur experimentellen Psychologie.* Leipzig: Duncker & Humbolt, 1885.

Estes, W. K. Statistical theory of distributional phenomena in learning. *Psychol. Rev.,* 1955, 62, 369–377.

Estes, W. K. Learning theory and the new "mental chemistry." *Psychol. Rev.,* 1960, 67, 207–223.

Estes, W. K. Learning theory *Ann. Rev. Psychol.,* 1962, 13, 107–144.

Gerard, R. W. The material basis of memory. *J. verb. Learn. verb. Behav.,* 1963, 2, 22–33.

Glickman, S. E. Perseverative neural processes and consolidation of the memory trace. *Psychol. Bull.,* 1961, 58, 218–233.

Gomulicki, B. R. The development and present status of the trace theory of memory. *Brit. J. Psychol., Monogr. Suppl.,* 1953, Whole No. 29, 94 pp.

Guthrie, E. R. *The psychology of learning.* New York: Harper, 1935.

Hebb, D. O. *The organization of behavior.* New York: Wiley, 1949.

Hebb, D. O. Distinctive features of learning in the higher animal. In J. F. Delafresnaye (Ed.) *Brain mechanisms and learning.* London and New York: Oxford Univ. Press, 1961. Pp. 37–46.

Hebb, D. O., and Foord, E. N. Errors of visual recognition and the nature of the trace. *J. exp. Psychol.,* 1945, 35, 335–348.

Hellyer, S. Supplementary report: Frequency of stimulus presentation and short-term decrement in recall. *J. exp. Psychol.,* 1962, 64, 650.

Hull, C. L. *Principles of behavior.* New York: Appleton-Century-Crofts, 1943.

Jones, J. E. All-or-none versus incremental learning. *Psychol. Rev.,* 1962, 69, 156–160.

Keppel, G., and Underwood, B. J. Proactive inhibition in short-term retention of single items. *J. verb. Learn. verb. Behav.,* 1962, 1, 153–161.

Kleinsmith, L. J., and Kaplan, S. Paired-associate learning as a function of arousal and interpolated interval. *J. exp. Psychol.,* 1963, 65, 190–193.

Koffka, K. *Principles of gestalt psychology.* New York: Harcourt, Brace, 1935.

Lovibond, S. H. A further test of the hypothesis of autonomous memory trace change. *J. exp. Psychol.,* 1958, 55, 412–415.

McGeoch, J. A. Forgetting and the law of disuse. *Psychol. Rev.,* 1932, 39, 352–370.

McGeoch, J. A., and Irion, A. L. *The psychology of human learning* (2nd ed.) New York: Longmans, Green, 1952.

Mackworth, J. F. The visual image and the memory trace. *Canad. J. Psychol.,* 1962, 16, 55–59.

Mednick, S. A., and Freedman, J. L. Stimulus generalization. *Psychol. Bull.*, 1960, 57, 169–200.

Melton, A. W. Comments on Professor Postman's paper. In C. N. Cofer (Ed.) *Verbal learning and verbal behavior.* New York: McGraw-Hill, 1961. Pp. 179–193.

Melton, A. W. Comments on Professor Peterson's paper. In C. N. Cofer and B. S. Musgrave (Eds.) *Verbal behavior and learning: Problems and processes.* New York: McGraw-Hill, 1963. Pp. 353–370.

Miller, G. A. The magical number seven, plus or minus two: Some limits on our capacity for processing information. *Psychol. Rev.*, 1956, 63, 81–97.

Müller, G. E., and Pilzecker, A. Experimentelle Beitrage zur Lehre vom Gedachtnis. *Z. Psychol.*, 1900, 1, 1–300.

Murdock, B. B., Jr. The retention of individual items. *J. exp. Psychol.*, 1961, 62, 618–625.

Peterson, L. R. Immediate memory: Data and theory. In C. N. Cofer (Ed.) *Verbal learning and behavior: Problems and processes.* New York: McGraw-Hill, 1963.

Peterson, L. R., and Peterson, M. J. Short-term retention of individual verbal items. *J. exp. Psychol.*, 1959, 58, 193–198.

Peterson, L. R., Peterson, M. J., and Miller, A. Short-term retention and meaningfulness. *Canad. J. Psychol.*, 1961, 15, 143–147.

Postman, L. The present status of interference theory. In C. N. Cofer (Ed.) *Verbal learning and verbal behavior.* New York: McGraw-Hill, 1961. Pp. 152–179.

Postman, L. One-trial learning. In C. N. Cofer (Ed.) *Verbal learning and behavior: Problems and processes.* New York: McGraw-Hill, 1963.

Postman, L. Short-term memory and incidental learning. In A. W. Melton (Ed.) *Categories of human learning.* New York: Academic Press, in press.

Shepard, R. N., and Teghtsoonian, M. Retention of information under conditions approaching a steady state. *J. exp. Psychol.*, 1961, 62, 302–309.

Spence, K. W. *Behavior theory and conditioning.* New Haven, Connecticut: Yale Univer. Press, 1955.

Sperling, G. The information available in brief visual presentations. *Psychol. Monogr.*, 1960, 74, Whole No. 498.

Thomas, G. J. Neurophysiology of learning. *Ann. Rev. Psychol.*, 1962, 13, 71–106.

Thorndike, E. L. *Educational psychology: II. The psychology of learning.* New York: Teachers College, Columbia Univer., 1913.

Underwood, B. J. Interference and forgetting. *Psychol. Rev.*, 1957, 64, 49–60.

Underwood, B. J., and Keppel, G. One-trial learning? *J. verb. Learn. verb. Behav.*, 1962, 1, 1–13.

Underwood, B. J., and Postman, L. Extraexperimental sources of interference in forgetting. *Psychol. Rev.*, 1960, 67, 73–95.

Underwood, B. J., and Schulz, R. W. *Meaningfulness and verbal learning.* Philadelphia: Lippincott, 1960.

Walker, E. L. Action decrement and its relation to learning. *Psychol. Rev.*, 1958, 65, 129–142.

Walker, E. L. Memory storage as a function of arousal and time. *J. verb. Learn. verb. Behav.*, 1963, 2, 113–119.

Witmer, L. R. The association-value of three-place consonant syllables. *J. genet. Psychol.*, 1935, 47, 337–360.

Unbiased and Unnoticed
Verbal Conditioning:
The Double Agent Robot Procedure[1]

HOWARD M. ROSENFELD and DONALD M. BAER,
University of Kansas

Subjects who were told they were "experimenters" attempted to reinforce fluent speech in a supposed subject with whom they spoke via intercom. The supposed subject was to say nouns, one at a time, on request by the "experimenter," who reinforced fluent pronunciation with points. Actually, the "experimenter" was talking to a multi-track tape recording, one track of which contained fluently spoken nouns, the other track containing disfluently spoken nouns. If the "experimenter's" request for the next noun was in a specified form a word from the fluent track was played to him as reinforcement; requests in any other form produced the word from the disfluent track. Repeated conditioning of specific forms of requests was accomplished with two subject-"experimenters," who were unable to describe changes in their own behavior, or the contingencies applied. This technique improved upon an earlier method that had yielded similar results, but was less thoroughly controlled against possible human bias.

The enduring interest in the conditioning of verbal behavior (Holz and Azrin, 1966) probably is attributable not only to the obvious importance of language in human behavior, but also to the special status accorded language in some non-behavioral or semi-behavioral theories. In this context, a particular body

Rosenfeld, H. M. & Baer, D. M. Unbiased and unnoticed verbal conditioning: the double agent robot procedure. *Journal of the Experimental Analysis of Behavior*, 1970, *14*, 99–107. Copyright 1970 by the Society for the Experimental Analysis of Behavior, Inc.

482

of research (Spielberger, 1965; Spielberger and DeNike, 1966) appears to have demonstrated that when verbal conditioning has proven possible in subjects, it has been accompanied by "awareness" in those subjects: it has occurred only in groups of subjects who could either state or recognize the contingencies of reinforcement applied to them. These results have been interpreted to indicate that changes in verbal responses were not attributable directly to the reinforcing function of the experimenter's contingent verbal approval; rather they were mediated by the discriminative function of private recognitions of the reinforcement contingencies. This inference of a controlling "awareness," derived from probes of introspection, is of course questionable. However, the inference becomes unnecessary if a verbal conditioning situation can be devised in which such probes fail to show any "awareness" to be explained. To facilitate such outcomes the present report describes an improvement on a technique designed by Rosenfeld and Baer (1969) for conditioning verbal behavior without "awareness."

The original technique used by Rosenfeld and Baer required that the subject of the study be recruited for the nominal role of experimenter in a study of social reinforcement. This subject was told that he would interview another person, and in the course of that interview, would socially reinforce some selected response shown by the interviewee. The interviewee was in fact a confederate of the authors—a "double agent"—and served as the true experimenter of the study. The interviewee deliberately displayed a simple hand gesture (rubbing his chin) in a random way. The interviewer attempted to reinforce that gesture by nodding vigorously in consequence. The interviewer was also told that to keep the interviewee "involved" (and hence "conditionable"), it was necessary to prompt him verbally to give fuller answers to the interview question being asked. One interviewer used prompts such as "Yeah" and "Mm-hmm" for this purpose. The interviewee deliberately gave short answers, thus evoking a steady rate of prompting by the interviewer. The interviewee then selectively reinforced one of the prompts ("Yeah") by displaying his gesture (chin rubbing) whenever that prompt occurred. Thus, while the interviewer prompted the interviewee to answer questions fully, and also attempted to reinforce the interviewee's chin-rubs (by nodding at them), the interviewee in fact emitted those chin-rubs as reinforcement for a selected kind of verbal prompt by the interviewer. Conditioning not describable by the interviewer resulted.

A drawback of such interpersonal paradigms is that the experimenter himself is also reinforceable (by success), and thus may purposefully or inadvertently elicit critical responses from the subject by behaviors other than those formally designated as reinforcers. For example, in the original study, "Yeah" or "Mm-hmm" might have been differentially elicited by choice of words, inflection, or facial expression, in addition to being reinforced by experimentally controlled chin rubs. Thus, the human double agent was replaced with a semi-automated mechanism not susceptible to having its own behavior changed by unrecognized contingencies. In addition, such a mechanism requires virtually no training of special personnel and is typically more reliable than the human experimenter.

PROCEDURE

Subjects

The subjects of this report (referred to below as "experimenters") were two undergraduate college girls of 12 students initially contacted. They were asked to participate in a study of what makes people successful in influencing other people. They were offered a minimum payment of $1.00 each to participate, and the possibility of two additional dollars if they could influence another person and explain to the authors exactly what accounted for their success, respectively.

Setting and Instructions

The subject was told by an assistant that she would be the "experimenter" in a verbal conditioning study. She would operate alone in a laboratory room, to guard against accidentally giving "cues" to the supposed subject. Seated at a desk, she was shown her intercom with a manual press-to-talk switch, a pair of lever switches, a pair of counters, and a small light. A tape recorder on her desk played initial instructions, summarized in the following comments.

The "experimenter" was told that the intercom connected her to her "subject" in another, nearby room, that if she pressed the intercom switch she could speak to the "subject" who would speak back to her through the intercom. She was also told that the lever switches produced points on an add-subtract counter located in front of the "subject," one switch adding points, the other subtracting them. Her own counters would record the numbers of correct and incorrect responses that later would be produced by the "subject" (operated by the assistant who would monitor the intercom). The light would signal timeout periods, during which she would rest, make notes, and sometimes receive further instructions.

The "experimenter" was told that she was to attempt to condition the "subject," specifically, some aspect of the "subject's" speech. It was explained that the "subject" had already been told that her task was to emit nouns, when asked, one at a time. The task for the "experimenter," then, was three-fold:

1. Use the intercom to tell the subject when to emit the next word.

2. Use the lever switches to add or subtract points on the counter before the "subject" at any time, to influence her noun-emitting behavior in some specific way.

3. Write down at any time whatever she thought might be responsible for any changes in the "subject's" noun-emitting behavior. (Paper and pencil were supplied.)

The researchers and their apparatus were located in an adjoining room that allowed observation of the "experimenter" through a one-way window. The essential item of apparatus was a multi-channel tape recorder, programmed to play very brief segments of tape at any moment to the "experimenter" through her intercom. On one channel of tape a series of nouns had been recorded, at 3-sec intervals, each fluently enunciated. On a parallel channel, in the corresponding positions of the tape, the same nouns had been recorded, but enunciated in a disfluent manner, typically in the form "Uhh (noun)." Both tracks had been recorded by a professional actress, who read a list of 1000 nouns from a previously free-associated list, simulating the performance of an actual subject. A research assistant, listening to the "experimenter" request the next word from the subject over the intercom, could then play to her the next noun from either channel. (The relay-operated recorder stopped after any word had been played, thus remaining in position to play the next work at any time.)

The Practice Session

The first visit was described to the "experimenter" as a practice session, during which she would become familiar with the situation and the execution of her assignments. More importantly, it allowed an assessment of her typical use of various requests for nouns from the subject, so that one could be chosen for future verbal conditioning. The form of request chosen will be referred to as the "critical request."

After the instructions were completed, the research assistant explained to the "experimenter" that in a moment the assistant would act out the role of the subject, so the "experimenter" could practice.

The assistant then retired to the next room. From there she played over the intercom a tape recording of her own voice (not the actress') which contained a liberal sprinkling of animate and inanimate, singular and plural, and fluent and disfluent nouns. One word at a time was played, following each request by the "experimenter" for the next word. The kind and sequence of these requests were recorded for 30 min. The "experimenter" was then given an appointment to return, to attempt conditioning a "real subject."

Meanwhile, the kinds and relative frequency of her requests for each next word were analyzed. (Typical requests were of the sort "Next," "Next word," "Go ahead, please," "O.K.," or "Now.") One of these requests (*e.g.*, "Next word") was tentatively chosen as the critical request for future verbal conditioning. Criteria for such choice included a moderate frequency of use (not too close to 0 or 100 percent of all requests used), and some evidence of stability over the 30-min session (judged informally).

It should be noted that of 12 potential "experimenters", some produced requests during their practice session that were either too unstable over time, or entirely too stable, to make them acceptable candidates for future conditioning. In these cases, the research assistant sometimes instructed the "experimenter" to be "more interesting." These instructions generally eliminated such problems only briefly. The two "experimenters" described here showed satisfactory baselines of requests during the practice session.

The Experimental Session

Baseline period. When the "experimenter" returned for the second session, she was told that a "real subject" was in the next room, and that it was necessary to gather a baseline of that "subject's" noun emitting behavior, so as to choose some aspect of it to condition. She then was left alone to interact via intercom with the multi-channel tape recording of the actress' voice. A segment of tape was played containing a portion of disfluencies equal to the "experimenter's" baseline proportion of critical requests during the practice session, and her rate of the critical request was checked for its current stability. The criterion for stability was that the rate of this request could vary no more than three responses out of 25, for at least two consecutive blocks of 25 requests each (a "nonsignificant" variation if the sequential requests met the assumptions of the binomial distribution). The rate during this baseline did not have to match the rate of the previous day's baseline session; however, it had to comprise reliably between 20 and 80 percent of the responses per block. If less than 50 percent, it was selected for reinforcement (fluencies); if over 50 percent it was to be followed by disfluent responses. If the critical request did not meet this criterion of stability during the first four 25-response blocks of this session, it was abandoned as a candidate, and other forms of request were examined for stability. If no such request could be found by the sixth block, the subject was considered unsuitable, debriefed, paid, and dismissed. Debriefing was delayed if the subject was recruited from a group in which other members had not yet participated.

Conditioning period. Once a stable critical request had been chosen, the "experimenter's" timeout light was illuminated, and the assistant returned to tell her that the "subject" had a characteristic rate of disfluency that should be a good target for influence through point addition or subtraction. (In case the "experimenter" had not noticed the disfluencies, they were imitated for her.) She was told to use points in any way that would decrease the rate of these disfluencies, and to keep notes about her techniques and their relative success. These notes were to be made whenever the timeout light was illuminated and at any other times that she wished. Further, she was told that the counters before her now would record the cumulative numbers of fluencies and disfluencies emitted by the subject, so that she could see how well her techniques had been working. She was to reset the counters during each timeout, so that they would always show current success or failure.

After these instructions the assistant left and the "experimenter" resumed her interaction with the tape, via intercom. From this point throughout the Conditioning Period, experimental contingencies operated as follows:

1. Each time the "experimenter" used the critical request, the next word played was from the fluent track of the tape; each time she used any other request, the next word played was from the disfluent track of the tape;

2. No more than five consecutive fluent or five consecutive disfluent nouns were played, even though the occasion called for another according to the first rule. (This was to reduce the probability that the "experimenter" would notice the contingency.)

Conditioning by these contingencies continued for at least three blocks of 25 requests each, and until a criterion of conditioning had been met. The criterion required that at least two consecutive 25-request blocks each contain at least enough critical requests to exceed the baseline rates of these requests at the 0.05 level of confidence as specified by tables of the binomial distribution.[2] If conditioning to this criterion was not evident by the end of eight 25-request blocks, the subject was considered a failure, debriefed, paid, and dismissed.

During the Conditioning Period, a timeout was held typically after every third 25-request block to allow the "experimenter" to survey counters, write notes on the effectiveness of her techniques, and re-set the counters.

First reversal period. When the criterion of the Conditioning Period had been met, the contingencies of that period were reversed. Now, in general, it would be true that:

1. Each time the "experimenter" used the critical request, the next word played was from the disfluent track of the tape; each time any other request was used, the next word played was from the fluent track of the tape; *except that:*

2. Fluent nouns were played for only half of the non-critical requests of the first 25-request block of this Reversal Period. (This was to reduce the probability that the "experimenter" would notice an otherwise blatant reversal of the just-prior contingencies.)

3. Subsequent to the first block of 25 requests, no more than five consecutive fluent or five consecutive disfluent nouns were played, even though the occasion called for another according to the first rule.

Otherwise, experimental conditions during the First Reversal Period were similar to those of the Conditioning Period. The criterion of a successful reversal was similar to that of a successful conditioning, except that now performance was compared to that of the last block of the preceding Conditioning Period.

Second reversal period. Given a successful reversal according to the above criteria, the critical request was again subjected to the same contingencies used during the Conditioning Period, plus the qualification that only half of the critical requests of the first 25-request block during this period would be followed by fluent nouns. The same type of criterion for successful reversal was applied as had been used for the First Reversal Period.

Both subjects reports here finished within a single experimental session lasting 90 min. The session took place the day after the practice session.

Interview. At the conclusion of the Second Reversal Period (or on the occasion of earlier dismissal of subjects), an interview was conducted by the assistant to see if the "experimenter" could state the contingencies applied to her or describe the changes that had taken place in her verbal behavior. The interview procedure was adapted from standard procedures employed by Levin (1961) and Spielberger (1962). It began with fairly distant questions asking about what had happened, what techniques were used, and how well they worked, and progressed to increasingly detailed questions about all the contingencies holding between the "experimenter" and her subject.

Recording

The requests made by the "experimenter" were tape-recorded and also recorded verbatim in handwriting by a second assistant in the adjoining room. (Handwritten records allowed the immediate calculation of the rates of the "experimenter's" critical requests, necessary to determine when the criteria of Baseline, Conditioning, First Reversal, and Second Reversal had been met.) Reliability of the handwritten records was established as 96 percent, by comparing them to the tape recordings of requests.

RESULTS

Six of 12 potential subjects examined met the criteria cited for stability of individual baseline within six blocks of 25 responses, during their practice sessions. Of these six subjects, two met all further criteria of successful conditioning, suppression, and reinstatement of the critical response. Inasmuch as variations in several experimental parameters between the subjects could have accounted for the differential successes, the question of generality or of specific conditions for unaware verbal conditioning cannot be answered in this study. The following accounts of the two successful cases are offered as evidence of the possibility of the effect. Of the remaining cases, one conditioned and was aware of the contingencies; two others unknowingly conditioned but failed to reverse; and one failed to condition at all.

Figure 1 displays the rate of critical request for the successful subjects. Subject A displayed several requests in apparently random fashion. The most stable of these was the phrase, "Next word". In the Experimental Session Baseline Period her rate of "Next word" varied from 44 to 48 percent per block and was accordingly chosen as the critical request. The criterion for reliable conditioning was set at 60 percent for two consecutive blocks. This was achieved and surpassed during the sixth and seventh 25-request blocks of the Conditioning Period, as Fig. 1 shows.

The criterion for reliable reversal was set at 80 percent for two consecutive blocks. This criterion excluded the first reversal block, when only half of the non-critical responses produced fluencies, according to the experimental convention designed to avoid awareness. The reversal criterion was met almost immediately,

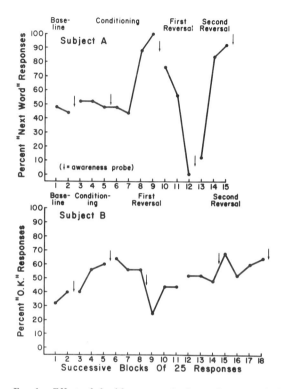

FIG. 1.   Effect of double-agent robot's contingent verbal fluencies on selected verbal responses of two subjects ("Experimenters").

and rate of critical response in fact fell below the criterion, reading 0 percent during the third 25-request block of the First Reversal Period. The Second Reversal Period followed a pattern similar to that of the First Reversal Period, but more quickly: rate of the critical request increased such that the third 25-request block contained 23 critical requests.

In contrast to the variability in baseline responses of Subject A, Subject B emitted only two responses throughout the study ("All right" and "O.K."). In general, her results were similar to those for the first subject in that criteria for conditioning "O.K." and two reversals were met. In this case, changes in rate following changes in contingency were more gradual. Inasmuch as her critical response never exceeded 75 percent of any block, the prescribed one-block 50 percent schedule was not employed.

Subject A wrote notes on her techniques four times after the conditioning phase began. The first of these stated that she supposed "the subject doesn't seem to catch on at all." By the second, Subject A had "produced" a high ratio of fluent responses and commented: "The new strategy seems to have worked much better. At first she seemed to think it was parts of the body but she still did not say 'uh'—even after she went on to other words. She seems to have caught on consciously since she hasn't made one mistake." The next timeout came at the end of a successful reversal, and Subject A wrote: "At first did very badly like at beginning of exp. and then did O.K. again. Once she got going she never reverted back. Did not stick to any subject matter for a great length of time." Virtually the same comments were written during the last opportunity, which followed the final reversal period.

In the terminal interview, carried out by a research assistant, Subject A offered several explanations, illustrated in the following transcriptions:

Assistant: "How effective did you feel you were as an experimenter?"

A: "Hmm, well, I don't think she ever caught on to what it was, so I consider that it was O.K. You know, because it's kind of an unconscious thing."

Assistant: "What strategy were you using?"

A: (Repeated comments written in timeout periods).

Assistant: "And you think it was the point-giving that influenced her?"

A: "I think so. It might have been the words she got on to; but yet it still changes. When she got on to the parts of the body like nose, throat, ear—maybe just because they're sharp words, but when she used other words like 'negotiation' she didn't go 'uh, negotiation.' So I think it must have been the points and not the subject matter."

Assistant: "I see. Did you think that anything else you might have done influenced her in any way?"

A: "Maybe I sound more pleased when she did well. I don't know.
    I didn't try to."
Assistant: "Yeah?"
A: "Maybe my inflection, uh, my own inflection."
Assistant: "Uh-huh, anything else?"
A: "I don't know if my, you know, response would make a differ-
    ence. Like if I would say 'go on' or 'next.' "
Assistant: "Did it seem to?"
A: "I don't think so."
Assistant: "You don't know that it did in any way?"
A: "No."

Subject B wrote only comments on the details of the various
point-giving strategies she had employed. In her interview she
produced no hints at all of any possible awareness that her verbal
responses had any effect on her success.

DISCUSSION

The validity of inferring awareness of elicitation of post-be-
havioral interpretations from subjects is a matter of epistemological preference. Yet on the basis of pervasive evidence of such
"awareness", attempts have been made to diminish the significance of verbal conditioning. Evidence that there are conditions
under which probes do not produce awareness should discourage
such generalizations. More important, the availability of "awareness"-avoiding procedures can further conditioning research
in general by unconfounding instructional and reinforcement
effects.[3]

The apparently successful production of the double-agent
effect in the present study indicates that verbal conditioning
without awareness (as defined here) is a real possibility. Only
one of the subjects even noted the possibility that her verbal behavior might somehow have contributed to her success. Even in
this case the possibility was not stated during the regular within-
experiment probes, but occurred only in response to extreme
prodding and suggestion after the experimental session.

A major advantage of the current automated procedure over
previous methods is that the robot experimenter isolates the subject (the "experimenter") from uncontrolled sources of stimulation that are possible in any human experimenter (Rosenthal,

1966). Despite its artificiality, it nevertheless is apparently accepted by college students as real; all subjects seemed to believe they were dealing with a real person at the other end of the intercom. The use of a professional actress to record the tapes being played was probably an important part of the success of this illusion. She sometimes appeared momentarily at a loss for the next word, or amused by her choice, or curious (presumably about the listener's reaction to the word), or even bored. The words she recorded were realistically balanced for variety and sequence. Thus, the "experimenter" might sometimes develop the hypothesis that the "subject" had fallen into a pattern (such as animal names), but soon would be forced to abandon that hypothesis.

The false leads implicit in the content of the taped noun sequences may indeed contribute to the overall effectiveness of the robot procedure, but it is presumably subordinate to the distraction from awareness provided by the subtle reversal of roles of subject and experimenter. While the effect of the double-agent procedure itself on awareness has not been directly demonstrated (by direct comparison with a control condition), the hypotheses produced by "experimenters" in this and the initial study suggest that they were attending to aspects of their relationship to the "subject" other than the "subject's" attempt to manipulate their verbal behavior.

There probably are numerous other sources of distraction from awareness in interpersonal settings which could be submitted to experimental analysis. On the assumption that schedules of reinforcement are prominent among these possibilities, "experimenters" in the current study typically were allowed to receive only a limited number of consecutive reinforcers. Also, when very high rates of the critical request occurred during the conditioning phase, the contingencies of the subsequent reversal phase were faded in, rather than switched abruptly. While these procedures may have served to prevent awareness, they also may have contributed to a certain ineffectiveness in the reversal procedures, perhaps accounting for those "experimenters" who conditioned but failed to reverse. For example, by effectively putting a fully conditioned response on a fixed-ratio 6 schedule during the fading in of the reversal, that response may have been maintained even in the face of the disfluencies produced by five of every six emissions. Particularly if the disfluencies had no punishing function for the "experimenter," fixed-ratio 6 could prove a reasonable maintenance schedule. Failure to reverse might be eliminated in future research by instructions to do better than one fluency in six; by starting reversals before too extreme a response shift has been produced; by a different convention concerning the number of consecutive reinforcements allowed; or by a different convention concerning the number of reinforceable responses allowed reinforcement during the first 25-request blocks of reversal periods. Thus, a better balance between procedures designed to modify verbal behavior and procedures designed to prevent awareness of these modifications is an important problem for future methodological research.

NOTES

1. The research was conducted at the Bureau of Child Research Laboratories in Lawrence, Kansas, and supported by Program Project Grant HD 00870 from the National Institute of Child Health and Human Development. The authors appreciate the assistance of Pamela Gunnell and Charles Salzberg. Reprints may be obtained from the authors, Department of Psychology, University of Kansas, Lawrence, Kansas 66044.

2. In the absence of a rapid technique for testing for independence of sequential responses, the 0.05 level was used as a guide, not as an accurate estimate of the probability that such results could have occurred by chance.

3. When awareness of reinforcement contingencies has been induced by instructional sets, conditioning has been facilitated (DeNike and Spielberger, 1963).

REFERENCES

DeNike, D. L. and Spielberger, C. D. Induced mediating states in verbal conditioning. *Journal of Verbal Learning and Verbal Behavior*, 1963, 1, 339–345.

Holz, W. C. and Azrin, N. H. Conditioning human verbal behavior. In W. K. Honig (Ed.), *Operant behavior: areas of research and application.* New York: Appleton-Century-Crofts, 1966. Pp. 790–826.

Levin, S. M. The effects of awareness on verbal conditioning. *Journal of Experimental Psychology*, 1961, 61, 67–75.

Rosenfeld, H. M. and Baer, D. M. Unnoticed verbal conditioning of an aware experimenter by a more aware subject: the double agent effect. *Psychological Review*, 1969, 76, 425–432.

Rosenthal, R. *Experimenter effects in behavioral research.* New York: Appleton-Century-Crofts, 1966.

Spielberger, C. D. The role of awareness in verbal conditioning. In C. W. Eriksen (Ed.), *Behavior and awareness.* Durham: Duke University Press, 1962. Pp. 73–101.

Spielberger, C. D. Theoretical and epistemological issues in verbal conditioning. In S. Rosenberg (Ed.), *Directions in psycholinguistics.* New York: Macmillan, 1965. Pp. 149–200.

Spielberger, C. D. and DeNike, L. D. Descriptive behaviorism versus cognitive theory in verbal operant conditioning. *Psychological Review,* 1966, 73, 306–326.

Motivated Forgetting Mediated by Implicit Verbal Chaining: A Laboratory Analog of Repression

Sam Glucksberg and Lloyd J. King, *Princeton University*

After learning an A–B paired-associates list, college students read a list of D words, several of which were consistently accompanied by unavoidable electric shock. The D words were members of implicit B–C, C–D chains, inferred from published word-association norms. In a subsequent recall test of the original A–B list, the B words that were implicitly associated with the shocked D words were forgotten significantly more often than control words.

Are memory items which are specifically associated with unpleasant events more readily forgotten than affectively neutral items? Despite the wealth of empirical and theoretical interest in this question, particularly with respect to the psychodynamic concept of repression, no simple and effective techniques for the study of motivated forgetting have been reported.[1] Our purpose was to demonstrate that forgetting does occur as a function of unpleasant associations.

We adapted Russell and Storms's[2] four-stage mediation paradigm for this purpose. In their study, subjects first learned an *A–B* paired-associates list, where *A* is a nonsense syllable and *B* is an English word. Associations *B–C* and *C–D* were inferred from

Glucksberg, S. & King, L. J. Motivated forgetting mediated by implicit verbal chaining: a laboratory analog of repression. *Science*, 1967, *158*, 517–519. Copyright 1967 by the American Association for the Advancement of Science.

word association norms. For example, if the *A–B* pair were *cef-stem,* then the *B–C* association would be *stem-flower,* and the *C–D* association, *flower-smell; A* and *D* are thus associated by way of the *B–C and C–D* links (see Table 1). Russell and Storms found that learning an *A–B* pair facilitated the subsequent learning of a related *A–D* pair.

TABLE 1
Stimulus words used and inferred associative responses. The *D* words followed by (1) were the experimental words for half the subjects; those followed by (2) were the experimental words for the remaining subjects.

List 1		Inferred chained word	List 2	
A	*B*	*C*	*D*	
CEF	stem	flower	smell	(1)
DAX	memory	mind	brain	(2)
YOV	soldier	army	navy	
VUX	trouble	bad	good	(2)
WUB	wish	want	need	
GEX	justice	peace	war	(1)
JID	thief	steal	take	(2)
ZIL	ocean	water	drink	
LAJ	command	order	disorder	
MYV	fruit	apple	tree	(1)

If such implicit verbal chains do operate, then saying the *B* word implicitly elicits the *C,* and in turn, the *D* words. If the *D* word is associated with an unpleasant event, such as electric shock, then the likelihood of saying, or thinking of, the associated *B* word should be reduced, because the *B* response has an unpleasant consequence, namely, thinking of the *D* word, which presumably elicits fear. Thus, pairing specific *D* words with electric shock should cause differential forgetting of *A–B* pairs learned prior to the *D* word presentations. The *B* words associated with shock-paired *D* words should be forgotten more often than *B* words associated with neutral *D* words.

The stimulus materials we used are shown in Table 1. Note that, as in the Russell and Storms[2] study, the *C* words are never presented, but are assumed to occur as implicit associative responses linking *B* with *D*. Subjects first learned the *A–B* pairs (List 1). After attaining a specified criterion, the *D* words were presented (List 2), with electric shock paired with three of the ten words. Finally, the *A–B* pairs were presented once to test retention.

Sixteen male Princeton University undergraduates served as volunteers. General paired-associates instructions were provided, and subjects learned List 1 by the method of anticipation. The list was presented in three random orders, by use of a slide projector controlled by interval timers. Each nonsense syllable appeared for 1 second, followed, after a 0.75-second slide change, by the syllable and the response word for 1 second. The next syllable appeared immediately after, and 2 seconds elapsed between successive list presentations. List 1 learning continued to one perfect trial in which all pairs were correctly anticipated.

Electrodes were then placed on the third and fourth fingers of the left hand, and a key-operated buzzer was provided for the right hand. Subjects were told that a list of words (List 2) would be projected on the screen, and that each time a word appeared they were to pronounce that word aloud. Some words would be accompanied by shock, and subjects were to press the buzzer key whenever one of these words appeared. The key press did not avoid or escape the shock; it simply indicated that subjects had learned which words led to shock, and which were safe. Each word was presented for 2 seconds, and shock, when presented, occurred during the last second of word presentation. The shock source delivered 1.25 ma at 250 volts a-c, 60 hertz.

For half the subjects, the shock-paired *D* words were *smell*, *war*, and *tree;* for the other half, *brain, good,* and *take.* List 2 presentations, in three random orders, continued until subjects had correctly anticipated shock for three consecutive trials with no incorrect anticipations. The mean number of presentations of List 2 was 7.2, standard deviation = 3.6. Subjects were then given a single relearning trial of List 1, with electrodes left in place. The measure of motivated forgetting was the percentage of shock-associated *B* words forgotten relative to the percentage of control *B* words forgotten. Finally, we asked subjects to state the purpose of the experiment, to recall the words associated with shock, to recall the words of List 2, and finally, to state any connections they could think of between shocked words and List 1 words, and between any List 2 and List 1 words.

Since the two groups of subjects did not differ significantly in any experimental measures, their data were pooled. No subject correctly stated the purpose of the experiment. Recall of the shock-associated D words was perfect, while mean percent recall of the control D words was 71.4. This difference is significant at the .01 level, as evaluated by a Wilcoxon matched-pairs signed-ranks test. This result is to be expected, since subjects' task was to learn which words anticipated shock.

Ten subjects reported that they could not think of any specific connections between any D word and the $A–B$ pairs. Of the remaining six subjects, four reported two correct associations each, but none involved the experimental (shocked) stimuli. The other reported connections were incorrect. These data indicate that any shock-related forgetting is not attributable to verbalizable associations between D and B words, nor to the demand characteristics of the experiment. The original List 1 learning data indicate that any subsequent differences in recall cannot be attributed to differential initial learning. The mean numbers of trials to learn experimental $A–B$ pairs (4.1, S.D. = 2.8) and control $A–B$ pairs (3.4, S.D. = 2.0) did not differ significantly. Similarly, the mean number of correct anticipations (repetitions) of experimental and control pairs did not differ (experimental, 5.1, S.D. = 5.8; control, 5.9, S.D. = 3.1).

We turn now to the recall data relevant to our hypothesis. For the subjects with *smell, war,* and *tree* as the shocked D words, 20.8 percent of the associated $A–B$ pairs were not anticipated correctly, compared to 3.6 percent of the control pairs forgotten. The other group of subjects forgot 37.5 percent of the experimental pairs, and 8.9 percent of the control pairs. A Wilcoxon matched-pairs signed-ranks test applied to the pooled data indicated that the difference in percent retention between experimental and control pairs is significant at the .01 level, T (13) = 5. Three subjects forgot none of the pairs, and only two subjects forgot more control than experimental pairs. No subject substituted an experimental B word incorrectly. Perhaps because of the rapid pacing of the paired-associates list, subjects either anticipated correctly in the recall test or failed to answer.

Pairing of shock with associates of memory items clearly interfered with their subsequent retrieval. Two interpretations of this finding may be considered. First, the shock may have resulted in differential retroactive interference mediated by the superior retention of the experimental D words. If learning a list of such D words between initial learning and recall produces retroactive interference, then the particular form of motivation employed may be irrelevant. The same effect may be obtainable with positive reinforcement, and, indeed, with any operation that produces superior retention of experimental words. This possibility, however, seems unlikely in view of the retroactive facilitation effects reported by Horton and Wiley.[3] Using a three-stage chaining paradigm, they found that, after learning an $A–B$ and a $B–C$ list, learning an $A–C$ list facilitated $A–B$ retention.

Nevertheless, the experiment was repeated with an independent sample of 40 subjects drawn from a different college population: paid volunteers attending summer session at Dickenson College, Carlyle, Pennsylvania. Half of these subjects received shock associated with the experimental D words; the other half received money reward associated with the experimental D words. As in the original experiment, trials to learn List 1 and number of correct anticipations during List 1 learning did not vary as a function of any experimental conditions. Again, as in the earlier experiment, recall of the experimental D words was significantly superior to recall of control D words (100 percent versus 49 percent correct recall for the shock group; 95 percent versus 55 percent of the money group; $P < .01$ in both cases). In terms of these variables, this second experiment replicated the first.

Differential forgetting as a function of shock was similar to the data obtained earlier. Fifteen percent of the experimental $A–B$ pairs were forgotten, compared to 5 percent of the control pairs, and this difference is significant at the .05 level. In contrast, no significant difference in forgetting was obtained between experimental and control pairs in the money-reward condition (10 and 11 percent, respectively). In this money condition, 22 pairs were forgotten, 6 experimental and 16 control. This is very close to the distribution that would be expected by chance, namely 6.6 and 15.4.

These additional data are unambiguous. The differential

forgetting shown is specific to an unpleasant event, shock, and is not attributable to the differential recall of shock-associated words.

NOTES

1. D. W. MacKinnon and W. F. Dukes, in *Psychology in the Making*, L. Postman, Ed. (Knopf, New York, 1962), pp. 662–744; B. Weiner, *Psychol. Bull.* 65, 24, (1966).
2. W. A. Russell and L. H. Storms, *J. Exp. Psychol.* 49, 287 (1966).
3. D. L. Horton and R. E. Wiley, *J. Verbal Learning Verbal Behav.* 6, 36 (1967).
4. Work aided by NIMH grant MH 10742.

Section Five

Physiological Mechanisms
of Learning
and Reinforcement

Considerable research has been done on the physiological bases of learning phenomena (John, 1967; Pribram, 1971). One of the largest areas of research centers around possible physiological substrates of reinforcement. This research basically began in 1954 with the report of Olds and Milner, given in the first reading. Olds and Milner found that electrical stimulation of some subcortical areas of the rat brain would produce a powerful reinforcing effect, often apparently more powerful than other forms of reinforcement. Stimulation of other areas may serve as a punishment. Since the Olds and Milner experiment, the general effect has been demonstrated in a wide range of tasks and with many different types of animals, including man (Bishop et al., 1963).

Many theories have been advanced to explain reinforcing brain stimulation. Olds (1962) generally argues that these areas of the brain are the actual substrates of reinforcement. Similarly, Miller (1961) has shown correlations between the drive reduction theories of reinforcement and reinforcing brain stimulation. That is, areas in the brain where there is a strong reinforcing effect from electrical stimulation, such as the hypothalamus, are also areas concerned with basic drives such as hunger and thirst. Manipulation of the drives often affect how reinforcing the electrical stimulation is. Thus electrical stimulation might be stimulating a reward mechanism usually triggered by drive reduction.

Deutsch (Deutsch and Deutsch, 1966, 122–138; Deutsch and Howarth, 1963) theorizes that in reinforcing brain stimulation the electrical current stimulates both a reinforcement system and a motivation system. Stimulation of the motivation system motivates the animal to make the response that results in reinforcement plus motivation to repeat the response. Hence, the effect is self-perpetuating. This theory explains why there is so little satiation to some reinforcing brain stimulation. It also explains the rapid extinction when the current is shut off, because without stimulation the motivational effect rapidly decays. Critics of Deutsch's theories and experiments often suggest that many of his findings are due to the specific conditions of deprivation and training that Deutsch uses, and that the results don't hold up in more general testing situations (Trowill et al., 1969).

Glickman and Schiff (1967) suggest that "reinforcement evolved as a mechanism to insure species-typical responses to appropriate stimuli". That is, many species of animals have behavior patterns that occur in almost all members of the species. Since these species-typical behaviors are generally important to the species, as in survival value, it is advantageous for these behaviors to become linked with a reinforcement mechanism. This way the behavior will be maintained. Thus, according to Glickman and Schiff, reinforcing brain stimulation is the stimulation and facilitation of a neural system underlying species-typical behaviors.

Following a learning trial there is probably some process, called consolidation, which converts the learning experience into whatever physiological change underlies long-term memory. Many theories, mostly coming from the influence of Hebb (1949), conceptualize this process in terms of memory traces that are activated by the learning experience. This active trace then gradually gives way to a more permanent trace underlying long-term memory. One such model by Walker (1958) is called action decrement. A major assumption of this model is that during the active trace stage there is a tendency against repeating the response related to the active trace. Evidence for this model is presented in the reading by Walker and Motoyoski.

Most of the evidence offered for the existence of a consolidation process utilizes disruptive agents. The disruptive agent, often electroconvulsive shock, is given to the animal immediately after a learning trial. If later it appears the animal has no retention of the learning, it suggests the disruptive agent might have disrupted the consolidation of the learning, preventing the information from going into permanent memory. Almost anything that substantially affects the nervous system seems to function as a disruptive agent. A few of the agents used include electro-convulsive shock, metrazol, carbon disulfide gas, audiogenic seizures, heat narcosis, spreading depression, insulin, polarizing currents, anoxia and subcortical brain stimulation. A difficult question is whether the disruptive agent disrupts the information from being stored or affects the retrieval of the information after it has been stored. The reading by Lewis reviews many of the studies concerned with disruption of consolidation and points out a number of different theoretical interpretations. Reviews by McGaugh and Herz (1972) and by Spevack and Suboski (1969) may be consulted for other theoretical models of the effects of electroconvulsive shock on consolidation.

Other arguments for a consolidation process (e.g., McGaugh 1966; McGaugh and Herz, 1972) appeal to studies on the effects of drugs on learning. If there is a consolidation process, perhaps it can be facilitated by specific drugs such as central nervous system stimulants. Although a number of positive results have been reported, we still need to know a lot more about exactly what the drugs do.

A different approach to the physiology of learning has been based on correlating different aspects of learning with electrical changes in the brain (John, 1967; Morrell, 1961; Pribram, 1971). This can be done with surface electrodes that measure changes of a fairly large number of neurons, as with the electroencephalogram (EEG). This is particularly useful for fairly general states, such as the amount of arousal in the system, but cannot pick up the specificity of other recording techniques where the electrodes are inserted into the brain. These procedures allow recording the activity of a few neurons or a single neuron. The situations in which a neuron is recorded to fire and the pattern in which it fires helps us to map out the functions of the neuron in various activities including learning.

The reading by Pribram, Spinelli, and Kamback shows how much information can be gotten from electrodes in a single area of the brain, in this case the striate cortex, the primary area where visual information is projected.

E. Roy John has been evolving a model in which memory is stored in terms of coherent activity among groups of neurons (cf. John, 1967). Instead of thinking of learning in terms of connections between specific neurons, John argues for a nonconnectionistic model. According to this theory, during learning various sets of neurons are activated and fire together in some coherent nonrandom pattern. Learning results in some change, perhaps in cellular chemistry, which makes it more probable that these neurons will again fire in the same coherent pattern. Memory, then, is stored as a probability of coherence. Pibram, (1969, 1971) has also proposed a nonconnectionistic model. In Pribram's model, based on an analogy with holograms, memory is due to electrical interference patterns in the brain.

Another direction in the physiology of learning has centered around possible biochemical substrates of learning and memory (cf. Gaito and Bonnett, 1971; Ungar, 1970). Most of these studies have been concerned with changes in RNA and proteins that accompany learning. Neural stimulation often results in changes (changes in rate of synthesis, changes in constituent bases) in associated RNA molecules. RNA in turn is involved in producing proteins and some of the proteins affect neural metabolism and firing rate. Some theorists suggest memory is stored in RNA and others suggest it is stored in proteins. Since both RNA molecules and proteins are usually short lived, any memory explanation must have built into it a device to account for long-term memories, perhaps a system that perpetuates itself.

The most controversial area of this biochemical literature concerns the *transfer experiments*. In most of these experiments one animal is trained to make a specific response. This animal is then sacrificed, the RNA extracted from his brain, and the RNA injected into a second animal. The second animal then is trained to make the same response. Several studies have reported that the second animal learns faster if he receives RNA from a trained donor than from an untrained donor. It is sometimes said that memory is transferred from one animal to another via RNA.

There are many critics of the transfer experiments (e.g.,

Luttges et al., 1966). The criticisms hinge on issues such as not being able to replicate the experiments and whether the RNA, which is often injected into the stomach cavity of the receiver, ever even gets to the brain. There are complex, unresolved arguments on both sides of the issues which get into subtleties of training procedures and RNA extraction methods.

Another issue is whether what is transferred is a specific memory or just sensitization, a tendency to simply respond more to certain stimuli. The reading by Jacobson, Babich, Bubash, and Jacobson was part of one of the first series of transfer experiments using rats. They reported transferring a tendency to approach a food dish to the signal of a click or a blinking light. Critics argue that it is not the memory of an association between the light (or click) and food that is transferred, but only a sensitization to light (or click). Thus, the receiver rat is simply more reactive to the light, moves around more, and approaches the food dish more. However, even if only sensitization is transferred, this still appears to be a transfer of learning. For, the acquisition of a sensitivity to a specific stimulus seems to be an example of learning.

The last reading by Albert discusses one of the best controlled transfer experiments. Albert's experiment has a reasonable control for sensitization, and his results suggest something more complex is transferred. Albert is also the first experimenter in transfer experiments to use the same rat as donor and receiver.

Positive Reinforcement
Produced by Electrical Stimulation
of Septal Area and
Other Regions of Rat Brain[1]

JAMES OLDS[2] AND PETER MILNER, *McGill University*

Stimuli have eliciting and reinforcing functions. In studying the former, one concentrates on the responses which come after the stimulus. In studying the latter, one looks mainly at the responses which precede it. In its reinforcing capacity, a stimulus increases, decreases, or leaves unchanged the frequency of preceding responses, and accordingly it is called a reward, a punishment, or a neutral stimulus (cf. 16).

Previous studies using chronic implantation of electrodes have tended to focus on the eliciting functions of electrical stimuli delivered to the brain (2, 3, 4, 5, 7, 10, 12, 14). The present study, on the other hand, has been concerned with the reinforcing function of the electrical stimulation.[3]

METHOD

General

Stimulation was carried out by means of chronically implanted electrodes which did not interfere with the health or free behavior of Ss to any appreciable extent. The Ss were 15 male hooded rats, weighing approximately 250 gm. at the start of the experiment. Each S was tested in a Skinner box which delivered alternating current to the brain so long as a lever was depressed. The current was delivered over a loose lead, suspended from the ceiling, which connected the stimulator to the rat's electrode. The Ss were given a total of 6 to 12 hr. of acquisition testing, and 1 to 2 hr. of extinction testing. During acquisition, the stimulator was turned on so that a response produced electrical stimulation; during extinction, the stimulator was turned off so that a response produced no electrical stimulation. Each S was given a percentage score denoting the proportion of his total acquisition time given to responding. This score could be compared with the animal's extinction score to determine whether the stimulation had a positive, negative, or neutral reinforcing effect. After testing, the animal was sacrificed. Its brain was frozen, sectioned, stained, and examined microscopically to determine which structure of the brain had been stimulated. This permitted correlation of acquisition scores with anatomical structures.

Electrode Implantation

Electrodes are constructed by cementing a pair of enameled silver wires of 0.010-in. diameter into a Lucite block, as shown in Figure 1. The parts of the wires which penetrate the brain are cemented together to form a needle, and this is cut to the correct length to reach the desired structure in the brain. This length is determined from Krieg's rat brain atlas (11) with slight modifications as found necessary by experience. The exposed cross section of the wire is the only part of the needle not insulated from the brain by enamel; stimulation therefore occurs only at the tip. Contact with the lead from the stimulator is made through two blobs of solder on the upper ends of the electrode wires; these blobs make contact with the jaws of an alligator clip which has been modified to insulate the two jaws from one another. A light, flexible hearing-aid lead connects the clip to the voltage source.

The operation of implantation is performed with the rat under Nembutal anesthesia (0.88 cc/Kg) and held in a Johnson-Krieg stereotaxic instrument (11). A mid-line incision is made in the scalp and the skin held out of the way by muscle retractors. A small hole is drilled in the skull with a dental burr at the point indicated by the stereotaxic instrument for the structure it is de-

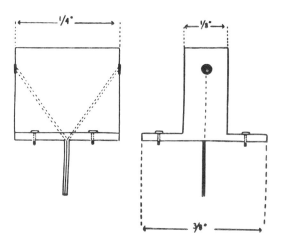

Fig. 1.   Electrode design (see text for detailed description).

sired to stimulate. The electrode, which is clamped into the needle carrier of the instrument, is lowered until the flange of the Lucite block rests firmly on the skull. Four screw holes are then drilled in the skull through four fixing holes in the flange, and the electrode, still clamped firmly in the instrument, is fastened to the skull with jeweler's screws which exceed the diameter of the screw holes in the skull by 0.006 in. The electrode is then released from the clamp and the scalp wound closed with silk sutures. The skin is pulled tightly around the base of the Lucite block and kept well away from the contact plates. A recovery period of three days is allowed after the operation before testing.

Testing

The testing apparatus consisted of a large-levered Skinner box 11 in. long, 5 in. wide, and 12 in. high. The top was open to allow passage for the stimulating lead. The lever actuated a microswitch in the stimulating circuit so that when it was depressed, the rat received electrical stimulation. The current was obtained from the 60-cycle power line, through a step-down transformer, and was adjustable between 0 and 10 v. r.m.s. by means of a variable potentiometer. In the experiments described here the stimulation continued as long as the lever was pressed, though for some tests a time-delay switch was incorporated which cut the current off after a predetermined interval if the rat continued to hold the lever down. Responses were recorded automatically on paper strip.

On the fourth day after the operation rats were given a pretesting session of about an hour in the boxes. Each rat was placed in the box and on the lever by E with the stimulus set at 0.5 v. During the hour, stimulation voltage was varied to determine the threshold of a "just noticeable" effect on the rat's behavior. If the animal did not respond regularly from the start, it was placed on the lever periodically (at about 5-min. intervals). Data collected on the first day were not used in later calculations. On subsequent days, Ss were placed in the box for about $3\frac{1}{2}$ hr. a day; these were 3 hr. of acquisition and $\frac{1}{2}$ hr. of extinction. During the former, the rats were allowed to stimulate themselves with a voltage which was just high enough to produce some noticeable response in the resting animal. As this threshold voltage fluctuated with the passage of time, E would make a determination of it every half hour, unless S was responding regularly. At the beginning of each acquisition period, and after each voltage test, the animal was placed on the lever once by E. During extinction periods, conditions were precisely the same except that a bar press produced no electrical stimulation. At the beginning of each extinction period, animals which were not responding regularly were placed on the lever once by E. At first, rats were tested in this way for four days, but as there appeared to be little difference between the results on different days, this period was reduced to three and then to two days for subsequent animals. Thus, the first rats had about 12 hr. of acquisition after pretesting whereas later rats had about 6 hr. However, in computing the scores in our table, we have used only the first 6 hr. of acquisition for all animals, so the scores are strictly comparable. In behavioral curves, we have shown the full 12 hr. of acquisition on the earlier animals so as to illustrate the stability of the behavior over time.

At no time during the experiment were the rats deprived of food or water, and no reinforcement was used except the electrical stimulus.

Animals were scored on the percentage of time which they

spent bar pressing regularly during acquisition. In order to find how much time the animal would spend in the absence of reward or punishment, a similar score was computed for periods of extinction. This extinction score provided a base line. When the acquisition score is above the extinction score, we have reward; when it is below the extinction score, we have punishment.

In order to determine percentage scores, periods when the animal was responding regularly (at least one response every 30 sec.) were counted as periods of responding; i.e., *intervals of 30 sec. or longer without a response were counted as periods of no responding.* The percentage scores were computed as the proportion of total acquisition or extinction time given to periods of responding.

Determination of Locus

On completion of testing, animals were perfused with physiological saline, followed by 10 percent formalin. The brains were removed, and after further fixation in formalin for about a week, frozen sections 40 microns thick were cut through the region of the electrode track. These were stained with cresyl violet and the position of the electrode tip determined.

RESULTS

Locus

In Table 1, acquisition and extinction scores are correlated with electrode placements. Figure 2 presents the acquisition scores again, this time on three cross-sectional maps of the rat brain, one at the forebrain level, one at the thalamic level, and one at the mid-brain level. The position of a score on the map indicates the electrode placement from which this acquisition score was obtained.

The highest scores are found together in the central portion of the forebrain. Beneath the *corpus callosum* and between the two lateral ventricles in section I of Figure 2, we find four acquisition scores ranging from 75 to 92 percent. This is the septal area. The Ss which produced these scores are numbered 32, 34, M–1, and M–4 in Table 1. It will be noticed that while all of them spent more than 75 percent of their acquisition time responding, they all spent less than 22 percent of their extinction

TABLE 1
Acquisition and Extinction Scores for All Animals Together with
Electrode Placements and Threshold Voltages Used
during Acquisition Tests

Animal's No.	Locus of Electrode	Stimulation Voltage r.m.s.	Percentage of Acquisition Time Spent Responding	Percentage of Extinction Time Spent Responding
32	septal	2.2–2.8	75	18
34	septal	1.4	92	6
M–1	septal	1.7–4.8	85	21
M–4	septal	2.3–4.8	88	13
40	c.c.	.7–1.1	6	3
41	caudate	.9–1.2	4	4
31	cingulate	1.8	37	9
82	cingulate	.5–1.8	36	10
36	hip.	.8–2.8	11	14
3	m.l.	.5	0	4
A–5	m.t.	1.4	71	9
6	m.g.	.5	0	31
11	m.g.	.5	0	21
17	teg.	.7	2	1
9	teg.	.5	77	81

KEY: c.c., corpus callosum; hip., hippocampus; m.l., medial lemniscus
m.t., Mammillothalamic tract; m.g., medial geniculate; teg., tegmentum.

time responding. Thus the electrical stimulus in the septal area
has an effect which is apparently equivalent to that of a conventional primary reward as far as the maintenance of a lever-pressing response is concerned.

If we move outside the septal area, either in the direction
of the caudate nucleus (across the lateral ventricle) or in the
direction of the *corpus callosum,* we find acquisition scores drop
abruptly to levels of from 4 to 6 percent. These are definitely
indications of neutral (neither rewarding nor punishing) effects.

However, above the *corpus callosum* in the cingulate cortex
we find an acquisition score of 37 percent. As the extinction score
in this case was 9 percent, we may say that stimulation was
rewarding.

At the thalamic level (section II of Fig. 2) we find a 36 percent acquisition score produced by an electrode placed again in

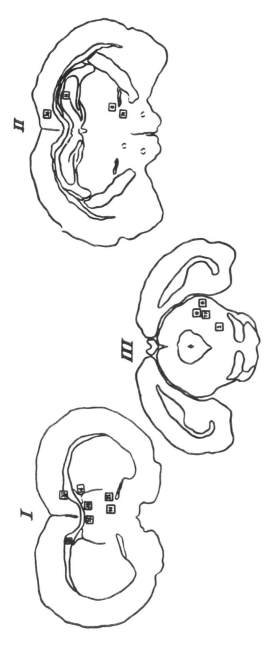

Fig. 2. Maps of three sections. (I) through the forebrain. (II) through the thalamus. (III) through the mid-brain of the rat. Boxed numbers give acquisition percentage scores produced by animals with electrodes stimulating at these points. On section I the acquisition scores 75, 88, 92, 85 fall in the septal forebrain area. On the same section there is a score of 4 in the caudate nucleus, a score of 6 in the white matter below the cortex, and a score of 37 in the medial (cingulate) cortex. On section II the acquisition score of 36 is in the medial (cingulate) cortex, 11 is in the hippocampus, 71 is in the mammillothalamic tract, and 0 is in the medial lemniscus. On section III the two zeroes are in the medial geniculate, 2 is in the tegmental reticular substance, 77 falls 2 mm. anterior to the section shown—it is between the posterior commissure and the red nucleus.

515

the cingulate cortex, an 11 percent score produced by an electrode placed in the hippocampus, a 71 percent score produced by an electrode placed exactly in the mammillothalamic tract, and a zero percent score produced by an electrode placed in the medial lemniscus. The zero denotes negative reinforcement.

At the mid-brain level (section III of Fig. 2) there are two zero scores produced by electrodes which are in the posterior portion of the medial geniculate bodies; here again, the scores indicate a negative effect, as the corresponding extinction scores are 31 and 21 percent. There is an electrode deep in the medial, posterior telgmentum which produces a 2 percent score; this seems quite neutral, as the extinction score in this case is 1 percent. Finally, there is an electrode shown on this section which actually stands 1½ mm. anterior to the point where it is shown; it was between the red nucleus and the posterior commissure. It produced an acquisition score of 77 percent, but an extinction score of 81 percent. This must be a rewarding placement, but the high extinction score makes it difficult to interpret.

Behavior

We turn our attention briefly to the behavioral data produced by the more rewarding electrode placements.

The graph in Figure 3 is a smoothed cumulative response curve illustrating the rate of responding of rat No. 32 (the lowest-scoring septal area rat) during acquisition and extinction. The animal gave a total of slightly over 3000 responses in the 12 hr. of acquisition. When the current was turned on, the animal responded at a rate of 285 responses an hour; when the current was turned off, the rate fell close to zero.

The graph in Figure 4 gives similar data on rat No. 34 (the highest-scoring septal rat). The animal stimulated itself over 7500 times in 12 hr. Its average response rate during acquisition was 742 responses an hour; during extinction, practically zero.

Figure 5 presents an unsmoothed cumulative response curve for one day of responding for rat No. A–5. This is to illustrate in detail the degree of control exercised by the electrical reward stimulus. While this rat was actually bar pressing, it did so at 1920 responses an hour; that is, about one response for every 2 sec. During the first period of the day it responded regularly while on ac-

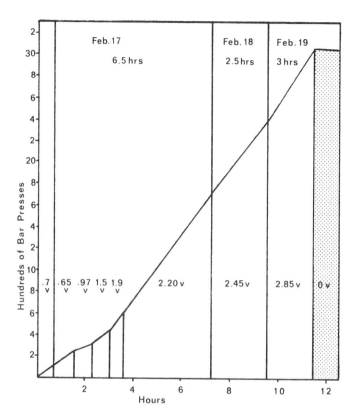

FIG. 3. Smoothed cumulative response curve for rat No. 32. Cumulative response totals are given along the ordinate, and hours along the abscissa. The steepness of the slope indicates the response rate. Stimulating voltages are given between black lines. Cross hatching indicates extinction.

quisition, extinguished very rapidly when the current was turned off, and reconditioned readily when the current was turned on again. At reconditioning points, E gave S one stimulus to show that the current was turned on again, but E did not place S on the lever. During longer periods of acquisition, S occasionally stopped responding for short periods, but in the long run S spent almost three-quarters of its acquisition time responding. During the long period of extinction at the end of the day, there was very little responding, but S could be brought back to the lever quite

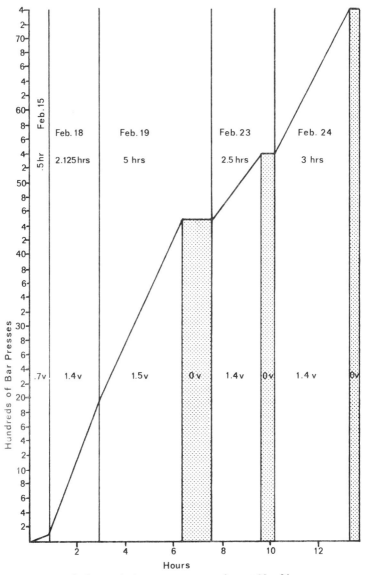

FIG. 4. Smoothed cumulative response curve for rat No. 34.

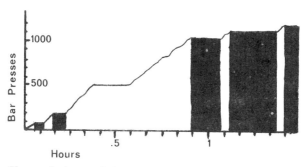

Fig. 5. Unsmoothed cumulative response curve showing about ¾ hr. of acquisition and ¾ hr. extinction for rat No. A–5. Shading indicates extinction.

quickly if a stimulus was delivered to show that the current had been turned on again.

DISCUSSION

It is clear that electrical stimulation in certain parts of the brain, particularly the septal area, produces acquisition and extinction curves which compare favorably with those produced by a conventional primary reward. With other electrode placements, the stimulation appears to be neutral or punishing.

Because the rewarding effect has been produced maximally by electrical stimulation in the septal area, but also in lesser degrees in the mammillothalamic tract and cingulate cortex, we are led to speculate that a system of structures previously attributed to the rhinencephalon may provide the locus for the reward phenomenon. However, as localization studies which will map the whole brain with respect to the reward and punishment dimension are continuing, we will not discuss in detail the problem of locus. We will use the term "reinforcing structures" in further discussion as a general name for the septal area and other structures which produce the reward phenomenon.

To provide an adequate canvass of the possible explanations for the rewarding effect would require considerably more argument than could possibly fit within the confines of a research paper. We have decided, therefore, to rule out briefly the possibility that the implantation produces pain which is reduced by electrical stimulation of reinforcing structures, and to confine further discussion to suggestions of ways the phenomenon may provide a methodological basis for study of physiological mechanisms of reward.

The possibility that the implantation produces some painful "drive stimulus" which is alleviated by electrical stimulation of reinforcing structures does not comport with the facts which we have observed. If there were some chronic, painful drive state, it would be indicated by emotional signs in the animal's daily behavior. Our Ss, from the first day after the operation, are normally quiet, nonaggressive; they eat regularly, sleep regularly, gain weight. There is no evidence in their behavior to support the postulation of chronic pain. Septal preparations which have lived healthy and normal lives for months after the operation have given excellent response rates.

As there is no evidence of a painful condition preceding the electrical stimulation, and as the animals are given free access to food and water at all times except while actually in the Skinner boxes, there is no explicitly manipulated drive to be reduced by electrical stimulation. Barring the possibility that stimulation of a reinforcing structure specifically inhibits the "residual drive" state of the animal, or the alternative possibility that the first electrical stimulus has noxious aftereffects which are reduced by a second one, we have some evidence here for a primary rewarding effect which is not associated with the reduction of a primary drive state. It is perhaps fair in a discussion to report the "clinical impression" of the Es that the phenomenon represents strong pursuit of a positive stimulus rather than escape from some negative condition.

Should the latter interpretation prove correct, we have perhaps located a system within the brain whose peculiar function is to produce a rewarding effect on behavior. The location of such a system puts us in a position to collect information that may lead to a decision among conflicting theories of reward. By physiological studies, for example, we may find that the reinforcing structures act selectively on sensory or motor areas of the cortex. This would have relevance to current S-S versus S-R controversies (8, 9, 13, 16).

Similarly, extirpation studies may show whether reinforcing structures have primarily a quieting or an activating effect on behavior; this would be relevant to activation versus negative feedback theories of reward (6, 13, 15, 17). A recent study by Brady and Nauta (1) already suggests that the septal areas is a quieting system, for its surgical removal produced an extremely active animal.

Such examples, we believe, make it reasonable to hope that the methodology reported here should have important consequences for physiological studies of mechanisms of reward.

SUMMARY

A preliminary study was made of rewarding effects produced by electrical stimulation of certain areas of the brain. In all cases rats were used and stimulation was by 60-cycle alternating current with voltages ranging from $\frac{1}{2}$ to 5 v. Bipolar needle electrodes were permanently implanted at various points in the brain. Animals were tested in Skinner boxes where they could stimulate themselves by pressing a lever. They received no other reward than the electrical stimulus in the course of the experiments. The primary findings may be listed as follows: (a) There are numerous places in the lower centers of the brain where electrical stimulation is rewarding in the sense that the experimental animal will stimulate itself in these places frequently and regularly for long periods of time if permitted to do so. (b) It is possible to obtain these results from as far back as the tegmentum, and as far forward as the septal area; from as far down as the subthalamus, and as far up as the cingulate gyrus of the cortex. (c) There are also sites in the lower centers where the effect is just the opposite: animals do everything possible to avoid stimulation. And there are neutral sites: animals do nothing to obtain or to avoid stimulation. (d) The reward results are obtained more dependably with electrode placements in some areas than others, the septal area being the most dependable to date. (e) In septal area preparations, the control exercised over the animal's behavior by means of this reward is extreme, possibly exceeding that exercised by any other reward previously used in animal experimentation.

The possibility that the reward results depended on some chronic painful consequences of the implantation operation was ruled out on the evidence that no physiological or behavioral signs of such pain could be found. The phenomenon was discussed as possibly laying a methodological foundation for a physiological study of the mechanisms of reward.

NOTES

1. The research reported here was made possible by grants from the Rockefeller Foundation and the National Institute of Mental Health of the U.S. Public Health Service. The authors particularly wish to express their thanks to Professor D. O. Hebb, who provided germinal ideas for the research and who backed it with enthusiastic encouragement as well as laboratory facilities and funds. The authors are also grateful to Miss Joann Feindel, who performed the histological reconstructions reported here.
2. National Institute of Mental Health Postdoctorate Fellow of the U.S. Public Health Service.
3. The present preliminary paper deals mainly with methods and behavioral results. A detailed report of the locus of positive, negative, and neutral reinforcing effects of electrical brain stimulation is being prepared by the first author.

REFERENCES

Brady, J. V., & Nauta, W. J. H. Subcortical mechanisms in emotional behavior: affective changes following septal forebrain lesions in the albino rat. *J. comp. physiol. Psychol.*, 1953, 46, 339–346.

Delgado, J. M. R. Permanent implantation of multilead electrodes in the brain. *Yale J. Biol. Med.*, 1952, 24, 351–358.

Delgado, J. M. R. Responses evoked in waking cat by electrical stimulation of motor cortex. *Amer. J. Physiol.*, 1952, 171, 436–446.

Delgado, J. M. R., & Anand, B. K. Increase of food intake induced by electrical stimulation of the lateral hypothalamus. *Amer. J. Physiol.*, 1953, 172, 162–168.

Dell, P. Correlations entre le système végétatif et le système de la vie relation: mesencéphale, diencéphale, et cortex cérébral. *J. Physiol.* (Paris), 152, 44, 471–557.

Deutsch, J. A. new type of behavior theory. *Brit. J. Psychol.*, 1953, 44, 304–317.

Gastaut, H. Correlations entre le système nerveux végétatif et le système de la vie de relation dans le rhinencéphale. *J. Physiol.* (Paris), 1952, 44, 431–470.

Hebb, D. O. *The organization of behavior.* New York: Wiley, 1949.

Hull, C. L. *Principles of behavior.* New York: D. Appleton-Century, 1943.

Hunter, J., & Jasper, H. H. Effects of thalamic stimulation in unanaesthetized animals. *EEG clin. Neurophysiol.*, 1949, 1, 305–324.

Krieg, W. J. S. Accurate placement of minute lesions in the brain of the albino rat. *Quart. Bull., Northwestern Univer. Med. School*, 1946, 20, 199–208.

MacLean, P. D., & Delgado, J. M. R. Electrical and chemical stimulation of frontotemporal portion of limbic system in the waking animal. *EEG clin. Neurophysiol.*, 1953, 5, 91–100.

Olds, J. A. neural model for sign-gestalt theory. *Psychol. Rev.*, 1954, 61, 59–72.

Rosvold, H. E., & Delgado, J. M. R. The effect on the behavior of monkeys of electrically stimulating or destroying small areas within the frontal lobes. *Amer. Psychologist,* 1953, 8, 425–426. (Abstract)

Seward, J. P. Introduction to a theory of motivation in learning. *Psychol. Rev.,* 1952, 405–413.

Skinner, B. F. *The behavior of organisms.* New York: D. Appleton-Century, 1938.

Wiener, N. *Cybernetics.* New York: Wiley, 1949.

The Effects of Amount of Reward and Distribution of Practice on Active and Inactive Memory Traces[1]

EDWARD L. WALKER, *University of Michigan;* and
RYOJI MOTOYOSHI, *Kyoto University*

Whenever a psychological event occurs such as a reinforced trial in a learning task, it seems highly likely that for a period of time after the trial there is an active trace process. After the disappearance of the active trace phase, there remains an inactive trace variously called permanent trace, permanent memory, or habit strength.

Few modern psychologists will deny the existence of an active trace process, but there is little agreement as to its nature and function. Walker (1958) has spelled out in some detail a mechanism or model for the active trace process. In this model the major function of the active trace is the laying down of permanent memory or habit strength. The active trace also produces a negative tendency against the recurrence of the act it represents. The process which produces this tendency has been referred to as action decrement, and the phenomenon, at least in a simple two-choice situation, has been referred to as alternation tendency.

Walker (1958) has argued, and it has been found empirically that some factors which operate to produce greater learning from a single trial will also operate to produce greater action decrement and thus a greater tendency to alternate. Walker (1956)

Walker, E. L. & Motoyoshi, R. The effects of amount of reward and distribution of practice on active and inactive memory traces. *Journal of Comparative and Physiological Psychology,* 1962, 55, 32–36. Copyright 1962 by the American Psychological Association, and reproduced by permission.

has reported more alternation with a water reward for both alternatives than with no reward for either for thirsty animals. Walker and Paradise (1958) have reported a close relationship between the amount of alternation produced by a given stimulus factor and the rate of learning when these particular stimulus factors are the cues for learning. The present report contains one more demonstration of this principle in showing more alternation for a large reward than for a small reward.

It was also asserted by Walker (1958) that action decrement has biological utility to the extent to which it operates to produce a negative tendency to perform the same act. It thus offers a degree of protection of the active trace process from disturbance before it completes the process of laying down permanent memory. This characteristic seems to involve a pai   x. The mechanism of action decrement protects the organism from further practice and thus from further improvement in performance.

This line of reasoning provides two possible explanations for the well-established efficacy of spaced over massed practice. If action decrement produces alternation, then some of the errors which occur in massed practice should not be attributed directly to less habit strength but should be attributed to a temporary tendency to alternate. If the action-decrement mechanism is a protective device, then immediate repetition of a correct choice should produce some deleterious effect upon the trace and result in lesser habit strength than might have accumulated from the same number of well-spaced trials. The present study was designed to try to isolate these two effects in a simple T-maze learning situation with rats.

To accomplish this objective, each of the two groups of animals tested for alternation with large and small rewards was further subdivided into Spaced and Massed Groups, although the massing in the latter groups was only partial. The two Spaced Groups had only one trial every 12 hr. in a simple T maze. The two Massed Groups had a pair of trials separated by 30 sec. every 24 hr. Assuming that the active trace process has disappeared within a 12-hr. span, we have the following situation: Performance on all trials for the Spaced Groups are a prouct of the permanent trace alone. The first trial of each day for the Massed Groups is also a product of the permanent trace. The second trial, following the first as it does by 30 sec., is the product of the active trace process (which is presumed to be affected also by habit strength), and performance of this trial should reflect the character of the trace. Furthermore, to the extent that such second trials produce a degree of interference of the trace of the first trial of each day, learning in the Massed Group should be slowed. The effects of such interference should be apparent in the performance on the first trial of the day, which is presumed to be a product of the permanent trace alone.

METHOD

Subjects

A total of 32 male albino rats was used. They were a part of a group of 41 animals obtained from Rockland Farms. Nine were eliminated for inactivity during preliminary training. They were approximately 120 days old at the beginning of the experiment.

Apparatus

The apparatus was a simple T maze. The walls were of wood and were 4 in. high. The floor and roof were of hardware cloth. The starting stem and goal arms were 4 in. wide and 18 in. long. Guillotine doors separated the start box from the starting stem and the goal box from the goal stems. The goal boxes were black, and the remainder of the maze was a gray.

Procedure

Preliminary training. The animals were placed on a food-deprivation schedule 10 days before the start of the experiment proper. They were fed 6 gm. twice a day on a schedule which gave them food approximately 1 hr. after each experimental session during the experimental phase. During these 10 days they were handled daily and given a 15-min. period of exploration in a linear runway.

Amount of reward and action decrement. On Day 11 the animals were introduced to the experimental maze for the first time. For half the animals both sides were baited with one small pellet normally used in the Gerbrands-type Skinner box. For the other half both sides were baited with eight small pellets. Each animal was retained in the start box for 5 sec., permitted a free choice, retained in the goal box for 15 sec., and introduced to the start box for a second trial 30 sec. after removal from the goal box. This operation permitted observation of the frequency of alternation as a function of the amount of reward.

Learning phase. Beginning with Day 12 only one side of the maze was baited. For all animals the baited side was the side of first choice—thus the individually preferred side—and the amount of reward was either one or eight pellets as it had been for each animal in the alternation test phase. Half of each of the two groups which differed as to amount of reward was designated at random, with the restriction of equal *N*s, as a Spaced Group and the other half as a Massed Group. A spaced animal had a trial every 12 hrs. A massed-group animal had a pair of trials each day separated by 30 sec., and thus each pair of trials was separated by approximately 24 hrs. Training was continued for 15 days. The animals were run between 7:00 and 10:00 A.M. and again between 7:00 and 10:00 P.M. To control for possible effects of time of day, the "experimental day" began in the morning for half the animals and in the evening for the other half.

RESULTS

Amount of Reward and Action Decrement

The hypothesis was that a large reward would produce more action decrement and thus more tendency to alternate than a small reward. Therefore, there should be more alternation after an 8-pellet reward than after a 1-pellet reward. The results may be seen in Table 1. The difference is in the predicted direction

TABLE 1
Amount of Reward Alternation

Group	Total	Alternation	
	N	N	%
1 Pellet	16	11	68.75
8 Pellet	16	14	87.50

and is as large as could be expected from the theory. Yet the chi square value is 1.61, which is significant at approximately the .20 level. While not statistically significant, the finding constitutes another in a growing body of replications of the basic proposition that a factor which operates to produce greater learning on a single trial will operate to produce greater action decrement and, thus, a greater tendency to alternate.

Massed and Spaced Learning
for Different Amounts of Reward

The results of the learning phase of the study appear in Figures 1 and 2. There is one graph for each of the four groups differing in amount of reward and in conditions of spacing of the trials. In each of the four graphs, the data for the first trial of the day are plotted separately with solid lines. The data for the second trial of the day are plotted in broken lines. Thus, all solid lines and the broken lines in the two graphs of spaced training represent reflections of the permanent trace or habit strength. The broken lines in the massed-training curves reflect the active trace of the first trial of the day, since in the massed-training case, the second trial followed the first by 30 sec., while in spaced training the second trial followed the first by 12 hr.

It will be noted that in the groups with the larger reward (8 pellets), both spaced-training curves and the first-trial curve in massed training appear as normal learning curves. The broken curve in the massed-training group, which is presumed to reflect the active trace process, appears quite atypical. The curves in the small-reward groups are much more variable, but in the last few days, especially in the massed-learning group, the plot of second-trial performance is distinctly inferior to first trial performance. Thus, on visual inspection there appears to be a real difference between performance which is a function of the permanent trace or habit strength and performance which is a function of the temporary active-trace process.

Table 2 presents a variety of numerical analyses relevant to the question of the efficacy of spaced training and the source of the differences between massed and spaced training. In each instance, the t test was used to test the significance of the differences. In both reward conditions the massed-training groups required a significantly greater number of trials to reach the criterion of errorless performance. In both cases the total number of errors was greater in the Massed Group than in the Spaced

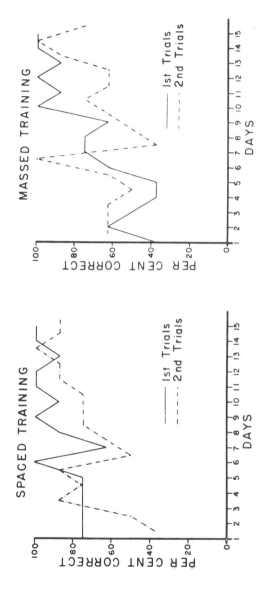

Fig. 1. Graphs showing rate of learning for a 1-pellet reward. (Both solid curves and the broken curve for spaced training are presumed to reflect accumulated habit strength. The broken curve for massed training is presumed to reflect performance as a function of the active trace process.)

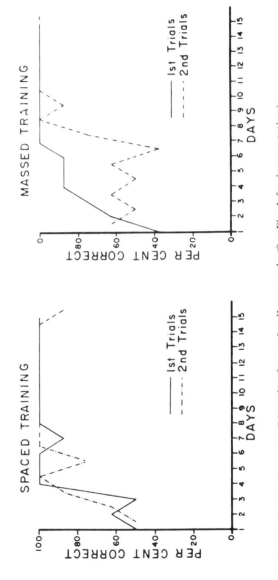

FIG. 2. Graphs showing rate of learning for an 8-pellet reward. (See Fig. 1 for interpretation.)

TABLE 2
Summary of Analyses Relating to Performances of Spaced Versus Massed Groups

Measure	1-Pellet Group			8-Pellet Group		
	Spaced	Massed	P	Spaced	Massed	P
Total trials	16.875	21.875	<.05	6.500	11.500	<.05
Total errors	5.750	9.125	<.05	2.875	4.750	ns
Total reinforcements	5.562	6.375	ns	1.812	3.375	ns
Alternation pairs	3.500	7.875	<.005	1.375	4.250	<.005
Correct-choice repetition pairs		2.625			1.375	
First trials to criterion	4.675	8.000	ns	2.125	2.875	ns
First-trial errors	2.000	4.250	<.02	1.500	1.500	ns

531

Group although in the 8-pellet groups the difference approached, but did not reach, the .05 level. However, there were no significant differences in the number of reinforcements to criterion between Spaced and Massed Groups. If genuine differences in the rates of learning between the massed and spaced conditions, are assumed, the question remains as to the extent to which these differences are attributable to simple alternation and the extent to which they represent significantly slower accumulation of permanent memory or habit strength in the massed-training condition.

If action decrement and the negative bias against repetition of an act is a protective device against interruption of the trace, then the massed condition should produce a greater tendency to alternate between the pair of trials in the day. Table 2 shows the mean number of times that a pair of trials within a day represented alternation. As may be seen, the number of alternation pairs is significantly higher in the massed-training groups as compared with the spaced-training groups. It is, therefore, clear that much of the apparent loss of learning efficiency occasioned by massing of trials can be attributed to the fact that massing produced alternation and thus an artifactual loss in efficiency of learning.

The question remains whether habit strength is being accumulated at a slower rate in the massed-training groups than in the spaced-training groups. If massing produces alternation, if the effect of alternation is to prevent consecutive occurrences of the same choice, and if it is a wholly effective mechanism, then there will be no instance of repetition of the same response on consecutive massed trials and there will be no difference in learning rate between massed and spaced training reflected in the solid curves in Figure 1, which presumably are relatively pure reflections of habit strength.

In Table 2 it can be seen that the number of instances in which the second trial of the pair in massed training represented the same choice as the first trial and, thus, offered an opportunity for trace interruption was in fact quite small, a mean of 2.625 such instances in the 1-pellet group and a mean of 1.375 instances in the 8-pellet group. It would be surprising if such a small number of opportunities for interference with the active trace process produced a significant slowing of the learning process as represented by the first-trial curves. If the first trials of the day are examined independently and the criterion of errorless performance applied to first trials only, it can be seen in Table 2 that the Massed Groups took a greater number of trials to criterion, but the differences are not statistically significant in either case. If the first-trial errors are counted, then the massed 1-pellet group shows a significantly greater number of first-trial errors ($p < .02$), but there is no difference between massed and spaced practice in the 8-pellet groups.

It can therefore be concluded that virtually all the efficacy of spaced training in this simple T-maze learning situation for rats can be attributed to alternation effects produced by massing and that there is little, if any, difference in the rate of accumulation of habit strength under the two conditions. In order to achieve a valid test of the hypothesis that a massed repetition of a particular choice interferes with the trace of the previous trial and thus decreases accumulated habit strength, it would be necessary to achieve a much larger N than the present study provides. This could be achieved simply by running an enormous number of animals, or possibly by massing more than two trials in a two-choice situation, thereby, enforcing repetition of a choice during the active-trace phase.

Summary

A group of 32 male albino rats were given 10 days of preliminary handling and training in a straight runway under 11 hr. of food deprivation. On Day 11 they were given 2 trials, 30 sec. apart, in a simple, enclosed T maze, with half the animals receiving a 1-pellet reward and the other half receiving an 8-pellet reward as a test of the hypothesis that the larger reward would produce more action decrement and thus a greater tendency to alternate than the smaller reward. This expectation was confirmed.

The test of alternation tendency was followed by two learning trials per day for 15 days with the groups at the same reward level, 1 and 8 pellets, as in the alternation test. The side first chosen in the alternation test, thus the preferred side, was the correct side during learning.

Each group was divided into a Spaced and a Massed Group during the learning phase of the experiment. The Spaced Group had one trial every 12 hr. The Massed Group had one pair of trials per day separated by an intertrial interval of 30 sec.

The expectation that the Massed Group would show a greater tendency to alternate was confirmed, and most of the apparent loss in learning efficiency in the massed condition may be attributed to alternation rather than to slower accumulation of habit strength.

NOTE

1. This study was carried out while R. Motoyoshi was a visiting scholar at the University of Michigan in the Spring of 1960. His stay in the United States was made possible by a grant from the Rockefeller Foundation to Kyoto University in Kyoto, Japan. The research was supported in part by a grant to the senior author from the Ford Foundation.

REFERENCES

Walker, E. L. The course and duration of the reaction decrement and the influence of reward. *J. comp. physiol. Psychol.*, 1956, 49, 167–176.

Walker, E. L. Action decrement and its relation to learning, *Psychol. Rev.*, 1958, 65, 129–142.

Walker, E. L., & Paradise, N. E. A positive correlation between action decrement and learning. *J. exp. Psychol.*, 1958, 56, 45–47.

Sources of Experimental Amnesia[1]

Donald J. Lewis, *University of Southern California*

It is pointed out that the notion of consolidation is typically restricted to the fixation of learning and that the performance decrement labeled amnesia can be due to several processes subsequent to fixation on the total input-output memory chain. A review of selected experiments shows the likelihood that at least some experimental amnesias are not due to a failure of fixation. For example, when amnesia for an "old" memory is brought about by means of a single electroconvulsive shock (ECS) it is not likely that consolidation "interruption" is the cause. Also when memory returns following amnesic treatment the source must be sought in a performance variable. Other conditions are discussed in which amnesia does not occur even though the learning-ECS interval is extremely short (less than 1 second). Interpretations of these perplexing findings are suggested.

Following a learning experience, an experimental trauma to the head which produces unconsciousness will frequently result in an amnesia for that learning experience. The amnesia is indexed by a performance decrement in experimentally treated subjects as compared to controls who did not receive the trauma, and the amnesia may be partial or complete. A partial amnesia is present when the experimental animals show more learning

Lewis, D. J. Sources of experimental amnesia. *Psychological Review*, 1969, 76, 461–472. Copyright 1969 by the American Psychological Association, and reproduced by permission.

than animals who did not have the learning experience at all but who still show less memory of the learning experience than animals who experience learning but have no amnesic treatment. Amnesia is defined, then to be a performance decrement, following a learning experience that is produced by trauma to the brain. This definition separates amnesia—an empirical event—from its most common explanation—the interference with consolidation.

This paper gives a review of some recent experimental studies of amnesia and relates the evidence to current theoretical interpretations; but before turning to the experimental data, the author will focus for a moment on the widely held concept of consolidation in the attempt to present a reasonably general consensus concerning its meaning.

CONSOLIDATION

Brief History

Müller and Pilzecker (1900), following in the tradition of Ebbinghaus, attempted to explain why a second list of nonsense syllables caused the forgetting of a first list. They called this forgetting "retroactive inhibition" and said that it occurred because the neural processes set up by the learning of the second list interfered with the perseverating neural processes established during the learning of the first list. Burnham (1903) is given credit for adding the concept of consolidation to perseveration and relating both to the retrograde amnesia (RA) produced by trauma to the head. Although others adopted these ideas, their acceptance was not universal. Lashley (1918) wrote,

> the experimental evidence upon which the belief in gradual fixation of associations is based is far from convincing . . . it all can be explained equally well by other hypotheses, and, in view of the extreme importance of the point for physiological explanation, we should be careful not to accept the assumption of a gradual setting of new functional connections until some real evidence is advanced to support it [p. 363–364].

After a review of the experimental literature on perseverative neural processes and consolidation Glickman (1961) concluded, "In the opinion of the writer, the over-all weight of evidence certainly favors the existence of some mechanism of consolidation . . . [p. 230]." Lewis and Maher (1965), on the other hand, reviewed studies using electroconvulsive shock (ECS) as a source of RA and concluded that the evidence supporting a consolidation process remained unconvincing. This interpretation was contested by McGaugh and Petrinovich (1966), but they were unable to convince Lewis and Maher (1966). McGaugh (1966) has presented a detailed argument favoring a consolidation process and his article, along with that of Glickman (1961), remains the most frequently cited authority for details of the consolidation process.

The present article considers once again some aspects of the consolidation process. Such a consideration seems warranted in view of its continuing importance in stimulating research and the influence it has had in the interpretation of data from a number of different fields.

PROPERTIES OF CONSOLIDATION

A review of the conceptual properties of consolidation can be brief, for they have been stated clearly by those most recently concerned with this notion. Two properties of consolidation seem to be held by all who have treated the subject and a third and fourth probably are held by a majority. The two universal properties have to do with (a) fixation and (b) the time-bound effect. The two properties that are widely but not universally held concern (c) the permanence of the amnesic disruption and (d) the number of memory stages. These are discussed in order.

Memory Fixation

The first point to be made is that consolidation is conceived to refer to memory *fixation* or registration; the two terms are frequently used interchangeably. A few quotations will make this point clear.

> The basic supposition is that reverberatory activity maintains the memory until permanent changes underlying fixation of the trace have been completed [Glickman, 1961, p. 229].
> We do not question the possibility that ECS can interfere with memory trace fixation [Chorover & Schiller, 1966, p. 40].
> The hypothetical process accounting for this development of resistance [to RA] is known as "consolidation" or "fixation of the memory trace" [Weissman, 1967, p. 170].

It was proposed that puromycin caused amnesia by blocking memory fixation (consolidation), i.e., the neural changes inferred to be necessary for lasting or long term memory (Glickman, 1961; McGaugh, 1966) [Davis, 1968, p. 72].
The results support a consolidation theory of memory and indicate that memory fixation requires a relatively long time [Alpern & McGaugh, 1968, p. 265].

Fixation Is Time Bound

The above quotations, among a large number of others that could be chosen, indicate that consolidation refers to the fixation or the input phase of memory. They also substantiate the second point concerning consolidation: that it occurs over a significant period of time and that during this time the trace can be disrupted. Three further quotations should be sufficient on this point.

Electroshock current interferes with relatively long-lasting processes underlying memory storage [McGaugh & Alpern, 1966, p. 665].
Such failure, called retrograde amnesia, seems to imply that memory traces are initially in a relatively vulnerable state, and they require a period to become "consolidated" [Chorover & Schiller, 1965a, p. 1521].
Furthermore, these findings are compatible with the thesis that memory traces are vulnerable for exceedingly long durations, but stabilize progressively with time [Alpern & McGaugh, 1968, p. 267].

Disruption Is Permanent

Another thesis concerning consolidation is that disruption of the trace produces a permanent amnesia. This assumption is stated most forcefully in those studies concerned with recovery of memory following amnesia. Not everyone, however, holds to this assumption (see Deutsch & Deutsch, 1966), but the following recent quotations show that the assumption is not uncommon.

The amnesia did not decrease either as a function of time or as a function of repeated tests. Within the limits of these experiments, amnesia appeared to be permanent. Thus, amnesia produced by ECS continues to be most adequately explained as a consequence of interference with time-dependent processes underlying memory storage [Luttges & McGaugh, 1967, p. 409].
There seem to be at least two stages in the elaboration of mem-

ory: an early labile phase in which representation of information about an experience is susceptible to erasure by perturbations of various kinds, and a later stable phase in which such perturbations have little or no disruptive effect [John, 1967, p. 18].

Memory Stages

A number of theorists, as can be seen from some of the quotations given above, assume several memory stages. The most common assumptions involve simply two stages: an early stage during which memory is susceptible to disruption and destruction, and a later one during which it is not. Others (Barondes & Cohen, 1966) require three stages. The different stages may run consecutively or concurrently. The important point to note about these stages is that they all refer to memory input processes; they all refer to memory fixation.

It should be clear that consolidation theory is a rather loose set of assumptions that are more or less widely held by most of those who do research on experimental amnesia. This paper is not an attempt to characterize any specific individual's notion of consolidation, but rather to present those assumptions that are generally held. There are those who would disagree with any one of the assumptions, but also there are important theorists who would agree with all.

Memory Sequences and the Learning-Performance Distinction

As has been seen, consolidation theory places its emphasis on learning, on the fixation of memories. Input was similarly emphasized by many learning theorists until Tolman insisted on the distinction between learning and performance. The learning-performance distinction reminds us that it is possible for an organism to learn and to remember even though it does not show this learning in any immediate performance. Failure to show learning, after it has occurred, can be due to many causes. Among the most important of these are the lack of appropriate motivation, lack of appropriate incentive, and the effects of extinction and counterconditioning.

If one thinks in terms of the brain processes related to memory, then one can locate the source of amnesia at one or more of several points. First, of course, is registration. It may be that the amnesic agent (AA) prevents the initial registration of whatever brain process underlies that rather permanent change in behavior that is ascribed to learning. If a memory fails to register, there is no possibility of there ever being an expression of that memory. Also, it could be that the memory does register, but that for a period of time fixation is impermanent and susceptible to disruption. This is, of course, one of the assumptions of consolidation theory. But remember that there is more to memory than the fixation of a trace, either through one, or more than one, stage. It can be, for example, that memories are quickly and permanently fixed and that the AAs have their effect on storage[2] processes subsequent to fixation. Presumably, memories can be coded and categorized in some fashion and these categories impart meaning to the memories and determine, at least in part, the manner in which they are stored. Storage is perhaps like a complicated filing system with memories categorized along different dimensions and sorted into appropriate bins. These bins are coded at the time of storage, but after the memory is firmly fixed, they serve only to facilitate retrieval. Tentatively assume that the familiarization procedure (Lewis, Miller, & Misanin, 1968a) manipulates a storage process, but this is discussed later. AAs may introduce so much noise into the system at the time of storage that these categorizations and filing processes are obscured. In a sense, the brain is prevented from organizing memories coherently, although there is no disruption of the actual memory fixation.

There are other processes still farther along in the memory sequence, past fixation and storage. It may be that memories are fixed, categorized, and stored, but that the AA produces its effects on various mechanisms of memory retrieval. A form of dissociation is one such mechanism that results in an interference with retrieval. It could be that the organism remembers and remembers well, but it no longer associates the memory with its original context and, therefore, the memory does not occur when it should. Or it could be that the organism has lost the motivation to express a certain memory. Or, it could be that various forms of suppression, competition, inhibition, which may be applied long after fixation and storage, actively prevent memories from recurring. It should be clear, from this list of alternatives, which undoubtedly does not exhaust all of the possibilities, that it is possible for amnesia to be produced in a variety of ways and at one or more of the various points along the total memory input-output chain. It has been unfortunate, perhaps, that many investigators of experimental amnesia have concentrated their theoretical attention solely on fixation processes. They have tended to attribute the performance decrement that is due to the administration of an AA exclusively to an interference with consolidation during the fixation of a memory. Without denying the very real possibility that it is at the point of fixation that at least some amnesias are produced, it is essential that investigations be open to other possibilities, for the evidence is increasing that at least some amnesic memory failure is due to other causes than failure to consolidate.

Perhaps some theorists maintain that the term consolidation refers to the total memory sequence, but this is a very unanalytic use of the term and it is almost coterminous with the already available "memory." If consolidation is to be used in this way many difficulties are presented, for a separate term for the fixation process will still be needed, and it is still sensible to inquire whether fixation occurs slowly or very rapidly.

Now this paper turns to a selective review of some studies on experimental amnesia which suggest that storage and retrieval processes may be involved. It is not the author's intention to review exhaustively all of the studies in the area; their number is too vast for a paper of this sort. Nor is there a presentation of a theoretical tour de force proving the consolidation theory a failure. But the author points out some problems for consolidation theory and suggests some alternatives to it. The main emphasis is on those processes which the author feels are illuminated by data from his own laboratory.

LEARNING—AA INTERVAL

The magnitude of RA is a function of the time intervening between learning and the administration of the AA. If the interval is short the RA is more complete than if the interval is long, and there is some interval which is long enough so that no RA is produced. This statement summarizes the basic data underlying the first two asumptions of consolidation theory which we discussed earlier in this paper. The fact that RA is greatest when the AA is close to the point of learning affords the basic support for the inference that amnesia is due to interference with fixation. And the fact that RA decreases as the learning-AA interval increases is the basis for the assumption that the memory traces stabilize over time until they are no longer disruptible.

Using multiple ECSs, a number of experimenters have found behavioral deficits even when the temporal interval between learning and the AA was greater than 30 days. Stone and Bakhtiari (1956), for example, gave ECS 30 days after the last learning trial and 70 days after the first and still produced a behavioral deficit. Braun, Patton, and Barnes (1952) found a deficit even when ECS was given 63 days after the completion of a learning experience that had endured over 56 days. Many researchers believe that such learning-ECS intervals are too long to permit the assumption that interference with consolidation is the cause and that in these situations, at least, the behavioral deficit is due to other causes.

Many researchers, using only one ECS do not find amnesia at such long learning-ECS intervals. Heriot and Colman (1962), for example, used an operant chamber and a bar press which was followed by a strong footshock and then ECS at 1, 7, 26, 60, or 180 minutes. The single ECS disrupted behavior up to 60 minutes but not beyond. King (1965) obtained amnesia in a step-through situation with a 5-minute interval separating learning from ECS but not a 15-minute interval. These studies, among a host of others, show the effective amnesic interval to be a matter of minutes, or at most a very few hours. Chorover and Schiller (1965), however, with a step-down apparatus found ECS to be effective at 10 seconds, but not at 30 seconds. A gradient similar to the one reported by Chorover and Schiller (1965) has been found by Quartermain, Paolino, and Miller (1965), in a comparable situation, although their effective amnesic interval extended out to 30 seconds after learning. As a result of their studies, Chorover and Schiller opened the possibility that consolidation occurred quickly within a matter of seconds, and the behavioral deficits reported in many other studies must be due to other processes than failure to consolidate.

Replicating an experiment reported by Bures and Buresová

(1963) in which RA was found even when a 24-hour interval separated learning from ECS used as an AA, Chorover and Schiller (1966) obtained the same results that the original experimenters did, but they also observed that the animals which had received only a single ECS seemed to show considerable fear and that they were also more active. From these observations Chorover and Schiller (1966) hypothesized that ECS was producing its effect not through destruction of the learning trace but because it broke up response inhibition. They reasoned that the footshock, used as the learning stimulus, produced a generalized fear response, indexed by response cessation. ECS served to disinhibit this inhibition of behavior and the animal returned to responding. Thus ECS was assumed to have its effects, in this situation and at long learning-ECS intervals, not on memory, but on response mechanisms.

In a clever series of experiments Chorover and Schiller (1966) showed the plausibility of this interpretation. In one experiment, they administered footshock as the animal entered into the smaller of two compartments, but instead of confining him in this compartment after the shock, as is typical, they allowed him to escape. Under these conditions, when escape was permitted, they found no amnesia even when an interval of only 1 minute separated the footshock from ECS. If, however, subjects were confined in the small compartment, given footshock, and not permitted to escape, then ECS did produce amnesia at the relatively long learning-ECS interval reported by Bures and Buresová (1963).

In another experiment, using a step-down apparatus, they gave ECS 2 minutes after the footshock and found no amnesia, supporting their previous finding that in this situation amnesia did not occur at intervals greater than 20 to 30 seconds. If, however, immediately following the reception of footshock in the step-down apparatus, subjects were confined in a small compartment and given intermittent footshock for 1 minute with ECS following another minute later, there was marked amnesia. Chorover and Schiller concluded that if their animals were allowed to escape from the place where footshock was received, they developed a discriminated avoidance response—an active response—which was not disruptible by ECS. The ECS did disrupt, however, a passive avoidance response which was a nondiscriminated fear response.

This interpretation of the effects of ECS on passive avoidance responding has a great deal of intellectual appeal. Unfortunately, there are data which may not be consistent with this point of view. A recent experiment by Kopp, Bohdanecky, and Jarvik (1966), using a two-compartment, "step-through" apparatus patterned for mice instead of rats, had ECS follow footshock at intervals of 5, 20, 80, 320 seconds, and 1 and 6 hours. Their animals were also allowed to escape from the small compartment where they had received the footshock, since this was considered crucial by Chorover and Schiller (1966). Another group received no ECS at all. The authors found a significant amnesia even at 6 hours. They also gave a tailshock to another group of mice outside the experimental apparatus. These animals showed no effect of tailshock. The conclusion the experimenters drew was that the experimental animals had learned a discriminated avoidance response in this situation as shown by the avoidance behavior of those shocked inside the compartment and not by those shocked outside. Also, even with a learned discriminated avoidance, amnesia appeared at a 6-hour learning-ECS interval.

That a discriminated avoidance was learned seems clearcut and at the same time it is not completely conclusive to the issue. The animals could well have discriminated the environment outside of the apparatus as different from the environment inside without discriminating any of the features inside the experimental apparatus. Therefore within the apparatus there would be a generalized fear response rather than a discriminated avoidance response. This would mean, following Chorover and Schiller (1966), that an ECS should have a long-term amnesic effect on the generalized conditioned emotional response inside the apparatus, and thus the data of Kopp et al. (1966) may pose no serious problem.

Lewis, Miller, Misanin, and Richter (1967) report data giving some difficulty to Chorover and Schiller's (1966) interpretation. They used a step-down situation, but gave footshock on the raised platform rather than the floor of the apparatus. Thus the subjects learned to step off the platform rather than to avoid stepping off as is conventional in this situation. When ECS followed this discriminative, active, avoidance response, an effective amnesia was produced. The familiarization time given the animals in the Lewis et al. (1967) experiment, however, was not as great as that given by Chorover and Schiller.

Comparison of Amnesic Agents

An initial and plausible simplifying assumption seems to have been that the basic neurochemical events underlying learning were fairly similar for different kinds of learning experiences, and that different AAs would have fairly similar effects. This assumption, never strongly held and certainly not crucial to the consolidation point of view, has been found wanting in a number of aspects. It is now clear that the amount of amnesia is a function at least of the species used, the type of AA, its intensity and duration, and the learning situation, in addition to the learning-AA interval. Pearlman, Sharpless, and Jarvik (1961), for example, found amnesia due to ether and pentobarbital limited to a learning-AA interval of 10 minutes, but metrazol would produce amnesia at least 4 days following learning. They tended to think, however, that the response deficit produced by metrazol was due to other causes than the interference with consolidation.

Paolino, Quartermain, and Miller (1966) compared different durations of CO_2 with different intensities of ECS. They found no RA when CO_2 was administered for only 10 seconds. When CO_2 was administered for 15 seconds, the RA gradient extended to 1 minute, and it extended to 4 minutes with 25 seconds of CO_2. The effective RA gradient for ECS extended to only 30 seconds, and they found that intensity of the ECS current in milliamperes produced no differential effect. They concluded that there are qualitatively different steps in consolidation which are differently affected by different AAs.

McGaugh (1966) reported that he could get RA at a learning-ECS interval of 1 hour using a current enduring for 200 milliamperes. This interval could be extended to 3 hours with a current of 400 milliamperes, but no further extension of the interval occurred at 600 milliamperes. This finding was later confirmed by Alpern and McGaugh (1968), Miller (1968), and others.

These findings clearly indicate that the duration of the AA can be a determiner of the amount of RA. It now seems, in fact, that some of the conflicts noted above are due either to the degree of original learning (Ray & Bivens, 1968), or to the intensity of the AA (Jarvik & Kopp, 1967; Lee-Teng, 1969; Miller, 1968; Ray & Barrett, 1969). The amnesia gradient can probably be described in part by a family of curves in which these variables figure as parameters. Even so, interference with consolidation is not the necessary explanation for these effects, since whatever effect an AA has will depend on its strength of the memory.

We may note that most, if not all, of the AAs also have convulsant properties. Many anesthetics produce seizures and are in fact convulsants. Trifluoroethyl, which Alpern and Kimble (1967) found so effective as an AA, is a convulsant at all ordinary temperatures. Add to their convulsant properties the fact that anesthetics can have an inhibitory effect on brain activity and we again have a pattern of neural spiking followed by electrical inhibition. This pattern seems to be part of the RA syndrome, and it has been investigators' conjecture that inhibition plays a crucial role in producing RA. Such spiking and inhibition may, as most have conjectured, have their effect on the input (consolidation) of the memory trace, but because there are other plausible sources one must be wary of unvaryingly attributing every deficit to interference with consolidation.

Extremely Short Learning—AA Intervals

With a few notable exceptions, most of the studies considered so far have varied the learning-AA interval within moderate limits. Pearlman et al. (1961) found RA at 4 days with metrazol but attributed it to performance factors rather than to consolidation interference. Alpern and Kimble (1967) did the same with their performance decrement at 24 hours due to potentiated ether. At the short end (less than 10 seconds) of the continuum RA has always been found, and it is just this closeness of learning and the AA that has been the firmest basis for the inference that RA is due to a consolidation failure.

Lewis et al. (1968a), however, report a case in which RA either does not occur or is greatly reduced, even when the ECS follows immediately upon the termination of the learning experience. They administered a 5-second footshock as the rat stepped off the small raised platform. Then ECS was given at the instant that the footshock terminated. Under these standard conditions almost total RA was produced. Another group of animals was given considerable familiarization experience in the apparatus before the experimental treatment was initiated. They were placed in the apparatus and allowed to explore for a total of 5 minutes on each of three different occasions. On the fourth trial they received footshock immediately by ECS. These animals showed very little RA. In another experiment (Lewis et al., 1968a) RA was demonstrated to be a function of the amount of familiarization. The important point is that very little, if any, RA was shown by familiarized animals for whom zero time intervened between learning and ECS.

If, however, the learning-ECS interval is defined as the time intervening between the *on*set of the footshock and the ECS, then a total interval of only 5 seconds was involved in this experiment, scarcely long enough for "long-term" consolidation to be complete. And yet the data show that it was. To explore this interval more completely, the duration of the footshock was manipulated in another experiment (Lewis, Miller, & Misanin, 1969) with groups of subjects receiving footshock for .5-, 2½-, and 5-seconds duration followed immediately by ECS. Those subjects that received prior familiarization (a total of 15 minutes) again showed very little RA. Thus, even with only .5 second intervening between learning and ECS no RA was produced. At least, if there was RA, it was not statistically reliable and was not retrograde over the intervals that were employed.

It is the author's tentative view that fixation (learning) is almost instantaneous with information input (registration) and that ECS and other AAs have their effects on processes occurring subsequent to fixation. The use of a familiarized situation into which a relatively simple piece of new information is introduced allows one to study a memory trace in simple form. The attempt to reduce the learning situation to a simple one was, of course, the reason for the introduction of the one-trial apparatus. Familiarization further simplifies the situation in that the animal has already explored the situation sufficiently so that he knows where the corners are, the grids, the platform, and so forth.

The introduction of footshock represents, then, a relatively "simple" stimulus which is easily integrated into an existing cognitive complex. The subject does not need to spend much time in thought about what has happened and where it has happened and we find that fixation time approaches the speed of neural transmission. This indicates that at least in this simple situation consolidation time is reduced to just about the time it takes for information penetration.

It still may be true that there is an interference with consolidation that occurs for more complex information but another interpretation takes a different track. The author proposes that the familiarization operation has its effect on the coding of information for storage subsequent to an extremely rapid consolidation process. Familiarization gives the subject a ready tag, or code, for the input which can then be stored or filed in a manner that makes it quickly accessible. In a more complex situation, information will still penetrate and consolidate rapidly, but the subject may not have the use of this information. An AA will thus work on the storage process—on the "subprogram" that labels information for easy retrieval—and retrieval is made difficult. Of course, to make this interpretation meaningful, operations must be specified that will result in retrieval following amnesia. This problem will be discussed in the section on Memory Return.

Another study that manipulates the effective learning-AA interval in an instructive way is that of Miller, Misanin, and Lewis (1969). The subjects drank in an operant chamber until their lick rate was fairly steady. Then one group was presented with a tone as the conditioned stimulus (CS) which was followed immediately by footshock. Three seconds following the termination of footshock they were given ECS. When the CS was presented again, subjects tended to continue to lick, an indication of RA. For another group, during training, the tone CS and footshock occurred just as with the first group, but the 3-second interval between footshock and ECS was filled by a blinking light. Significantly more RA was produced under this condition. The time interval between CS and ECS was identical in both cases, and there is no reason to suppose consolidation speed should differ. Nevertheless, the two conditions differed in the amount of RA that was produced. It is possible that filling the interval between CS and ECS with another stimulus somehow made the coding of the CS more difficult; successive compound stimuli require more trials to learn than do single stimuli. Much more work needs to be done on this problem, however, and on a complexity variable in general, before its properties are clear.

Long Learning—AA Intervals

Thus far the effects of ECS given at short intervals following learning have been discussed. Now some recent studies in which longer intervals have been examined are discussed. Schneider and Sherman (1968), using a situation which ordinarily does not produce RA at learning-ECS intervals greater than 2 or 3 minutes at the most, gave footshock followed 6 hours later by a second footshock and ECS 30 seconds thereafter, and they found RA. They also gave a first footshock, followed by another one 30 seconds later with ECS following an interval of 6 hours, but got no RA. RA at this long interval was a feature of the second footshock immediately preceding the ECS. They reasoned that footshock produces (a) learning and (b) arousal; and that ECS disrupts the second property of footshock and not the first. Thus ECS has its effect on the retrieval of a memory and not on its fixation.

A similar notion may be contained in the two-part theory of memory consolidation expressed by Ray and Bivens (1968). They found that the amount of RA was a function of the intensity of the footshock used to produce learning. With longer intervals between learning and ECS, RA could be produced only with decreasing footshock intensities. They conjectured that there may be a CS-UCS (unconditioned stimulus) connection based on simple contiguity which is not subject to disruption by ECS. The second component, perhaps solely a performance one, varies with footshock intensity and is susceptible to disruption.

In an experiment somewhat similar to that of Schneider and Sherman (1967), Misanin, Miller and Lewis (1968) produced RA with an interval of 24 hours separating learning from ECS. The response they worked with was a cessation of drinking brought about by pairing a CS with footshock while the subject was drinking. They showed that if the sequence was CS, followed immediately by footshock, followed immediately by ECS, a great deal of RA occurred. If, however, 24 hours separated the CS and footshock from the ECS there was no RA. These are expected findings of the kind typically taken to support consolidation theory. However, RA could also be produced 24 hours following learning if the CS immediately preceded the ECS. The rationale that led to this experiment holds that ECS is an inhibitor (Lewis & Maher, 1965) for those processes which it follows closely. Thus if an old memory could be rather precisely reactivated and followed immediately by ECS, an amnesia producing inhibition should result. The prediction was confirmed. This study, as well as the one by Schneider and Sherman (1968), indicates that ECS inhibits those memory processes with which it is contiguous, independent of whether these memories are new or old.

Two stages of memory can be distinguished (Misanin et al., 1968) although it should be clear that these two stages have little to do with fixation. One stage of memory is that of the "specious present," the memory that is in momentary awareness, that is being immediately used. This is the "active memory state." The other kind of memory consists of all other memories that lie outside of awareness. This is the "inactive memory state." It is investigators' conjecture, not yet adequately tested, that memories in transition from one state to another are susceptible to inhibition by AAs, although it may be that memories in the active state, whether in transition or not, can be inhibited. This means that the time between learning and the AA is of importance only to the degree that the memory is in the active state, which it usually is when learning is occurring. To the extent that the subject turns to something else so that a memory "recedes" to the inactive state, a time-bound effect will appear until a point is reached at which RA will not occur. A great deal more research will be required to test the implications of this simple conjecture.

MEMORY RETURN

As has been noted, one common (Luttges & McGaugh, 1967) but not universal (Deutsch & Deutsch, 1966) assumption by consolidation theorists is that the memory trace is physically destroyed by amnesia. This is why experiments showing spontaneous recovery (Kohlenberg & Trabasso, 1968; Miller, 1968; Zinken & Miller, 1967) have such importance. At the moment, however, the preponderance of the evidence (Chevalier, 1965; Greenough, Schwitzgebel, & Fulcher, 1968; Herz & Peeke, 1967; Luttges & McGaugh, 1967) indicate that there is no spontaneous recovery. The issue is perhaps not yet resolved, and the importance of the topic warrants still further investigation.

If it is assumed that the structural change making up an "item" of memory occurs in a relatively short period of time, probably less than 1 second, then most amnesias are not due to an interference with a consolidating engram, but to an interference with memory access. This means that the memory remains but it is unavailable for expression. Lewis, Miller, & Misanin (1968b), in a series of experiments, attempted to return the memory to expression by using a simple reminder.

In their first experiment they used four groups of animals in a step-down situation. One group received footshock alone; one group received footshock followed by ECS; a third group received ECS alone; and a fourth group received no treatment. Tests on the following day showed that the footshock alone had produced a great amount of fear and that when this footshock was followed by ECS the fear was largely removed. The ECS alone had no effect. Four hours later in another room, in another apparatus, all of the animals were given a "reminder shock." The purpose of the second footshock was to remind the animals of the first. Then 24 hours later they were returned to the original footshock situation for a retention test. The data showed a significant amount of memory return in the amnesic groups. This finding was confirmed in three other experiments. A similar finding was reported by Koppenaal, Jagoda, and Cruce (1967), and by Geller and Jarvik (1968), although both of these studies lacked the control groups necessary to make their data convincing. Memory return has also been reported by Flexner and Flexner (1968), who found amnesia due to an intracranial injection of puromycin and a return of memory following a later intracranial injection of saline. Insofar as the memory returned, the Flexners concluded, as the author has, that the amnesia was caused by an interference with memory expression and not its destruction.

The general conclusion to be drawn from these studies is that memories are tougher than has been previously claimed. They may be obscured, and their retrieval may be prevented, but they are present and appropriate means can be found to recover them.

THEORETICAL CONCLUSIONS

The main burden of this paper has been to point out alternatives to consolidation theory. The typical procedure in RA experiments has been to have an animal experience a simple learning task, wait varying time intervals, and administer an AA. Any resulting amnesia has commonly been attributed to the failure of the memory trace to fixate (Glickman, 1961; McGaugh 1966) ; to a failure in learning. But there is no necessary reason always to attribute a response decrement following learning and an AA to failure at the input end. There is a great deal going on subsequent to fixation as the learning-performance distinction has always made clear. And there is nothing in the design of amnesia experiments that demands that a response (output) failure be always attributable to a failure to fix the input.

Certainly the author is not denying now, nor before (Lewis & Maher, 1965), that perhaps some amnesias can be due to the failure of fixation. The author does, however, think that there are other alternatives that need to be explored before consolidation theory becomes firmly fixed as accepted fact, and believes that considerable evidence points to other processes along the total input-output channel as among the sources of amnesia. At least some of these sources lie at the retrieval end of the continuum, actively preventing a fixed and present memory from being expressed. Much of the evidence that leads us to this conclusion has been detailed here. Some of this evidence comes from studies in which no, or greatly reduced, amnesia is found even at a .5-second interval between learning and ECS. Other evidence shows that amnesia will occur at long intervals between learning and ECS if the memory is reactivated. Still other evidence suggests that the memory is still present even though the subject behaves in an amnesic fashion.

How do these amnesic retrieval failures occur? It was Lewis

and Maher's (1966) notion that ECS produced a massive inhibition which was conditioned to the stimuli of the situation in which the ECS occurred, or to them through a temporal stimulus generalization gradient. This latter would account for the "time-bound" effect. The studies to which this version of "inhibition theory" was applied involved both multiple learning trials and multiple ECSs, and these multiple ECSs permitted the conditioning of inhibition as experimentally verified by Adams and Lewis (1962). But such conditioning is not as likely in experiments which involve only one ECS. Inhibition does, nevertheless, occur, in the author's conception, and it is "time bound" in the sense that it applies to those memory processes which it is closest to. Thus ECS can inhibit either new memories or old ones (Misanin et al. 1968). The age of the original learning trace is not important, but the temporal distance between the trace, of whatever age, and the ECS is. That ECS is basically an inhibition of traces rather than a destroyer of them is shown by the several reminder studies mentioned in this paper.

It is also a tentative conjecture that other AAs work in a similar inhibitory way to ECS. Most AAs have both a spiking component and a subsequent period of decreasing electrical activity (inhibition). This pattern is shown by anesthetics, ECS, spreading depression, and is reported for many protein synthesis inhibitors. Acetoxycycloheximide may be an exception to this generalization, but its effects are still too contradictory to permit a firm conclusion.

NOTES

1. This paper was supported by National Institute of Mental Health Grants MH-07129 and MH-15861. The author wishes to thank Norman Richter for his assistance. Work was begun on this paper while the author was at Rutgers University, and all of the research reported here was performed in the Psychology Laboratory at Rutgers University.
2. Please note that the term "storage" here refers exclusively to processes subsequent to fixation. In its typical usage it refers either to a combined memory location and fixation process or to fixation alone. The present usage conforms to that proposed by Melton (1963, p. 3).

REFERENCES

Adams, H. E., & Lewis, D. J. Electroconvulsive shock, retrograde amnesia, and competing responses. *Journal of Comparative and Physiological Psychology,* 1962, 55, 299–301.

Alpern, H. P., & Kimble, D. P. Retrograde amnesic effects of diethyl ether and bis (trifluoroethyl) ether. *Journal of Comparative and Physiological Psychology,* 1967, 63, 168–171.

Alpern, H. P., & McGaugh, J. L. Retrograde amnesia as a function of duration of electroshock stimulation. *Journal of Comparative and Physiological Psychology,* 1968, 65, 265–269.

Barondes, S. H., & Cohen, H. D. Puromycin effect upon successive phases of memory storage. *Science,* 1966, 151, 594–595.

Braun, H. W., Patton, R. A., & Barnes, H. W. Effects of electroshock convulsions upon the learning performance of monkeys: I. Object-quality discrimination learning. *Journal of Comparative and Physiological Psychology,* 1952, 45, 231–238.

Braun, J. J., Meyer, P. M., & Meyer, D. R. Sparing of a brightness habit in rats following visual decortication. *Journal of Comparative and Physiological Psychology,* 1966, 61, 79–81.

Bures, J., Buresová, O. Cortical spreading depression as a memory disturbing factor. *Journal of Comparative and Physiological Psychology,* 1963, 56, 268–272.

Burnham, W. H. Retroactive amnesia: Illustrative cases and tentative explanation. *American Journal of Psychology,* 1903, 14, 382–396.

Chevalier, J. A. Permanence of amnesia after a single posttrial electroconvulsive seizure. *Journal of Comparative and Physiological Psychology,* 1965, 59, 125–127.

Chorover, S. L., & Schiller, P. H. Short-term retrograde amnesia in rats. *Journal of Comparative and Physiological Psychology,* 1965, 59, 73–78.

Chorover, S. L., & Schiller, P. H. Reexamination of prolonged retrograde amnesia in one-trial learning. *Journal of Comparative and Physiological Psychology,* 1966, 61, 34–41.

Davis, R. E. Environmental control of memory fixation in goldfish. *Journal of Comparative and Physiological Psychology,* 1968, 65, 72–78.

Deutsch, A. J., & Deutsch, D. *Physiological psychology.* Homewood, Ill.: Dorsey Press, 1966.

Flexner, L. B., & Flexner, J. B. Intracerebral saline: Effect on memory of trained mice treated with puromycin. *Science,* 1968, 159, 330–331.

Geller, A., & Jarvik, M. E. Electroconvulsive shock induced amnesia and recovery. *Psychonomic Science,* 1968, 10, 15–16.

Glickman, S. E. Perseverative neural processes and consolidation of the neural trace. *Psychological Bulletin,* 1961, 58, 218–233.

Greenough, W. T., Schwitzgebel, R. L., & Fulcher, J. K. Permanence of ECS-produced amnesia as a function of test conditions. *Journal of Comparative and Physiological Psychology,* 1968, 66, 554–556.

Heriot, J. T., & Colman, P. D. The effects of electroconvulsive shock on retention of a modified "one-trial" conditioned avoidance. *Journal of Comparative and Physiological Psychology,* 1962, 55, 1082–1084.

Herz, M. J., & Peeke, H. V. S. Permanence of retrograde amnesia produced by electroconvulsive shock. *Science,* 1967, 156, 1396–1397.

Jarvik, M. E., & Kopp, R. Transcorneal electroconvulsive shock and retrograde amnesia in mice. *Journal of Comparative and Physiological Psychology,* 1967, 64, 431–433.

John, E. R. *Mechanisms of memory.* New York: Academic Press, 1967.

King, R. A. Consolidation of the neural trace in memory: Investigation with one-trial avoidance conditioning and ECS. *Journal of Comparative and Physiological Psychology,* 1965, 59, 283–284.

Kohlenberg, R., & Trabasso, T. Recovery of a conditioned emotional response after one or two electroconvulsive shocks. *Journal of Comparative and Physiological Psychology,* 1968, 65, 270–273.

Kopp, R., Bohdanecky, Z., & Jarvik, M. E. Long temporal gradient of retrograde amnesia for a well-discriminated stimulus. *Science,* 1966, 133, 1547–1549.

Koppenaal, R. J., Jogoda, E., & Cruce, J. A. J. Recovery from ECS produced amnesia following a reminder. *Psychonomic Science,* 1967, 9, 293–294.

Lashley, K. S. A simple maze: With data on the relation of the distribution of practice to the rate of learning. *Psychobiology,* 1918, 1, 353–367.

Lee-Teng, E. Retrograde amnesia in relation to subconvulsive and convulsive currents in chicks. *Journal of Comparative and Physiological Psychology,* 1969, 67, 135–139.

Lewis, D. J., & Maher, B. A. Neural consolidation and electroconvulsive shock. *Psychological Review,* 1965, 72, 225–239.

Lewis, D. J., & Maher, B. A. Electroconvulsive shock and inhibition: Some problems considered. *Psychological Review,* 1966, 73, 388–392.

Lewis, D. J., Miller, R. R., & Misanin, J. R. Control of retrograde amnesia. *Journal of Comparative and Physiological Psychology,* 1968, 66, 48–52. (a)

Lewis, D. J., Miller, R. R., & Misanin, J. R. Recovery of memory following amnesia. *Nature,* 1968, 220, 704–705. (b)

Lewis, D. J., Miller, R. R., & Misanin, J. R. Selective amnesia in rats produced by electroconvulsive shock. *Journal of Comparative and Physiological Psychology,* 1969, in press.

Lewis, D. J., Miller, R. R., Misanin, J. R., & Richter, N. G. ECS-induced retrograde amnesia for one-trial active avoidance. *Psychonomic Science,* 1967, 8, 485–486.

Luttges, M. W., & McGaugh, J. L. Permanence of retrograde amnesia produced by electroconvulsive shock. *Science,* 1967, 156, 408–410.

McGaugh, J. L. Time-dependent processes in memory storage. *Science,* 1966, 153, 1351–1358.

McGaugh, J. L., & Alpern, H. P. Effects of electroshock on memory: Amnesia without convulsions. *Science,* 1966, 152, 665–666.

McGaugh, J. L., & Petrinovich, L. F. Neural consolidation and electroconvulsive shock reexamined. *Psychological Review,* 1966, 73, 382–387.

Melton, A. W. Implications of short-term memory for a general theory of memory. *Journal of Verbal Learning and Verbal Behavior,* 1963, 2, 1–21.

Miller, A. J. Variations in retrograde amnesia with parameters of electroconvulsive shock and time of testing. *Journal of Comparative and Physiological Psychology,* 1968, 66, 40–47.

Miller, R. R., Misanin, J. R., & Lewis, D. J. Amnesia as a function of events during the learning-ECS interval. *Journal of Comparative and Physiological Psychology,* 1969, 67, 145–148.

Misanin, J. R., Miller, R. R., & Lewis, D. J. Retrograde amnesia produced by electroconvulsive shock after reactivation of a consolidated memory trace. *Science,* 1968, 160, 554–555.

Müller, G. E., & Pilzecker, A. Experimentelle beiträge zur lehre vom gedächtnis. *Zeitschrift für Psychologie*, 1900, Suppl. No. 1.

Paolino, R. M., Quartermain, D., & Miller, N. E. Different temporal gradients of retrograde amnesia produced by carbon dioxide anesthesia and electroconvulsive shock. *Journal of Comparative and Physiological Psychology*, 1966, 62, 270–274.

Pearlman, C. A., Jr., Sharpless, S. K., & Jarvik, M. E. Retrograde amnesia produced by anesthetic and convulsant agents. *Journal of Comparative and Physiological Psychology*, 1961, 54, 109–112.

Quartermain, D., Paolino, R. M., & Miller, N. E. A brief temporal gradient of retrograde amnesia independent of situational change. *Science*, 1965, 149, 1116–1118.

Ray, O. S., & Barrett, R. J. Disruptive effects of electroconvulsive shock as a function of current level and mode of delivery. *Journal of Comparative and Physiological Psychology*, 1969, 67, 110–116.

Ray, O. S., & Bivens, L. W. Reinforcement magnitude as a determinant of performance decrement after electroconvulsive shock. *Science*, 1968, 160, 330–332.

Schneider, A. M., & Sherman, W. Amnesia: A function of the temporal relation of footshock to electroconvulsive shock. *Science*, 1968, 159, 219–221.

Stone, C. P., & Bakhtiari, A. B. Effects of electroconvulsive shock on maze relearning by albino rats. *Journal of Comparative and Physiological Psychology*, 1956, 49, 318–320.

Weissman, A. Drugs and retrograde amnesia. *International Review of Neurobiology*, 1967, 10, 167–198.

Zinken, S., & Miller, A. J. Recovery of memory after amnesia induced by electroconvulsive shock. *Science*, 1967, 155, 102–103.

Electrocortical Correlates of
Stimulus Response and Reinforcement

KARL H. PRIBRAM and D. N. SPINELLI, *Stanford University School of Medicine;* and MARVIN C. KAMBACK, *University of California*

Three patterns of electrical response were identified in the occipital cortex of rhesus monkeys making a differential discrimination: an input pattern that identifies which stimulus has been displayed; a reinforcement pattern that indicates whether the outcome of the differential response was rewarded or in error; and an intention pattern that occurs prior to the response and predicts which response the monkey is about to make. Neither the reinforcement nor the intention pattern is present while the monkeys perform at chance; at this time, only the differences due to input can be distinguished. These results suggest that more than simple input transmission is occurring in the primary visual mechanism. The influence of the experience of the organism is apparently encoded in the averaged electrical potentials recorded from the striate cortex.

To combine the techniques of electrophysiology with those of behavioral analysis of organisms subjected to cerebral ablations (1), we recorded potential changes that occur in the striate cortex of rhesus monkeys at various instants in a trial during which a visual discrimination is made. We placed a monkey in a restraining chair in front of, and within easy reach of, a 20- by 20-cm translucent panel split vertically down the center. Each

Pribram, K. H., Spinelli, D. N., & Kamback, M. C. Electrocortical correlates of stimulus response and reinforcement. *Science*, 1967, *157*, 94–96. Copyright 1967 by the American Association for the Advancement of Science.

half of the panel could be independently depressed; pressure closed a microswitch which sent a pulse to be recorded on magnetic tape (1.3 cm). The pulse also activated a circuit designed to deliver a food pellet into a cup placed under the panel whenever a correct response was made.

In front of the monkey, there was, attached to the chair, a small lever which, when pulled, activated a stimulus display. Thus there was reasonable assurance that the monkey would attend (make an observing response) to the display. Initially, during "shaping," the display covered the entire translucent panel until the animal pressed it; but the duration of exposure was gradually shortened until it lasted for only 0.01 msec. This short duration—in essence a flash—ensured that a transient response occurred in the visual pathways. A transient response was chosen because the techniques of analysis of neuroelectric phenomena are considerably more advanced at present for transients than for changes in steady state. Two stimulus patterns (vertical stripes and a circle) equated for area were generated in a relatively random sequence by slides in a modified Kodak Carousel projector facing the back of the panel. The order of the display of the two patterns was determined in advance, so that the report of the response would be collated by the reinforcing circuit with the pattern displayed. This collation determined whether the response made was correct or incorrect. The occurrence of reinforcement was also recorded on the magnetic tape.

Once "shaped," the monkeys were trained to press the right half of the panel whenever the circle was displayed and to press the left half of the panel whenever the vertical stripes were displayed. One monkey failed to learn the task (a difficult one because of the short duration of the display), and the other two monkeys reached a criterion of 85 percent correct in 200 consecutive trials after 1800 and 2800 trials. Two hundred trials were given daily 6 days a week.

The sequence of events that constitutes a trial is therefore as follows: (i) The monkey pulls a lever which initiates a pulse recorded on magnetic tape and (ii) turns on a stimulus display which lasts 0.01 msec. One of two patterns (vertical stripes or circle) is displayed; a pulse to indicate which display is flashed is reported to a reinforcing circuit and recorded on magnetic tape.

(iii) After a variable period, the monkey depresses either the right or left half of the display panel. This pressure also initiates a pulse which is recorded on magnetic tape and reported to the reinforcing circuit. This circuit then delivers a food pellet whenever the vertical-stripe display is followed by a press of the left panel and whenever the circle display is followed by a press of the right side of the panel. Reinforcement is also recorded on the tape.

Recording of electrical activity from the brain was continuous over sample sessions of 200 trials and, of course, coincided with the recordings of the behavioral events. The sessions chosen were (i) at the beginning of training, after the monkey had been conditioned to press but while he was performing at chance, and (ii) after criterion performance was established. Recordings were made from 12 placements in the striate cortex. All were bipolar (depth of cortex to surface) from an insulated nichrome wire (300 μ in diameter). The electrical brain signals were adequately amplified before they were recorded on magnetic tape.

The tape-recorded results were processed on a small general-purpose digital computer (PDP-8). Brain activity was digitized by an A-to-D converter, and the results of conversion were stored on digital magnetic tape. We devised programs to average the digitized electrical activity forward in time from the onset of the stimulus display (the pulling of the lever) and from the response (the depression of either half of the display panel). Averages were also obtained by running the tape backward from the two time markers; these records indicated what was going on in the monkey's brain just prior to his turning on the display and making the differential response. Programs were also developed to equate records obtained from unequal numbers of trials, so that correct and incorrect performances could be compared at criterion. Finally, routines to smooth the curves were adapted for photographing the results.

For each of the samples recorded, compilations were made of the brain activity (i) after stimulus display, (ii) preceding differential response, and (iii) after differential response. These compilations were then broken down into three categories: circle as opposed to vertical stripes, right as opposed to left panel, and correct as opposed to incorrect outcomes. Reliable differences (2) can be ascertained in the configuration of the brain record evoked by a stimulus display of 0.01 msec (3). In this instance, the circle generated a downward deflection; the two peaks of this deflection are more nearly equal than those generated by the vertical stripes. In the response to stripes, the amplitude of the second peak always exceeded the first. This difference did not change appreciably between the sample taken before learning occurred and the one taken at criterion performance.

The records obtained before and after differential response are essentially flat before learning of the problem takes place. No characteristic deflections occur constantly. At criterion, however, a marked difference routinely characterizes correct and incorrect outcomes; nonreinforcement is accompanied by a marked burst of activity in the record (approximately 40 cycles per second). At this time, a difference can also be seen in the brain recording made just prior to the differential response. From this difference, one can predict whether the monkey is going to press the right or the left side of the panel (regardless of whether this will prove to be correct or incorrect). Because this difference in the record prior to response was never observed when the monkey was performing at chance, differences in movement per se probably cannot account for differences in the neuroelectric response.

Three types of brain activity were discerned: an input pattern related to the stimulus display and present before as well as after learning, a reinforcement pattern indicating correct or incorrect outcome of the trial, and an intention pattern which occurs prior to the differential response once it has become meaningful.

All the brain patterns were not recorded from all 12 electrode placements in the striate cortex. From some, input patterns were obtained best; intention patterns were derived from others, and reinforcement patterns were best obtained from still others. Yet all these brain patterns did occur in the striate cortex—the end station of the anatomically homotopic tracts originating in the retina. These findings suggest that much more than simple input transmission occurs in the primary visual mechanism. At the striate cortex, the neuroelectric signals encode the influence of experience not only with respect to input differences, but also

with respect to the organism's intentions to respond and the outcome of behavior.

Notes

1. Neurobehavioral studies of the functions of the posterior "association"
   and frontolimbic formations of the forebrain have produced a wealth of
   evidence [K. H. Pribram, *Can. Psychol.* 7, 326 (1966) ; _____, in *Advances in the Study of Behavior* (Academic Press, New York, in press) ;
   _____, A. Ahumada, J. Hartog, L. Roos, in *The Frontal Granular Cor-
   tex and Behavior* (McGraw-Hill, New York, 1964), p. 28]. Despite this
   abundance, or perhaps in part as a result of it, a series of dilemmas in
   regard to interpretation has arisen. Part of the problem has been the
   limited repertoire of techniques, consisting primarily of ablation of neural
   tissue and experimental analysis of behavior before and after surgery.
   Interpretation (as opposed to description) of results is always ambiguous
   when there is only one mode of presentation of data. Recently, additional
   methods of neuro-behavioral study have become available, largely as the
   result of application of computer technology to analysis of electrophysiological recordings of the brain. The pioneering observations of D. B.
   Lindsley [in *Electrical Stimulation of the Brain* (Univ. of Texas Press,
   Austin, 1961), p. 331] and of E. R. John and K. F. Killam [*J. Nerv.
   Ment. Dis.* 131, 183 (1960)] have paved the way for experiments in which
   behavior of the brain, as well as of the organism, during problem solving
   can be studied. Perhaps, by monitoring some internal as well as external
   responses of unoperated and lesioned primate solvers of problems, the
   choice among interpretations may be narrowed.
2. R. Spehlmann, *Electroencephalogr. Clin. Neurophysiol.* 19, 560, (1965) ;
   E. R. John, R. N. Herrington, S. Sutton, *Science* 155, 1439 (1967) ; S. Sutton, P. Tueting, J. Zubin, E. R. John, *ibid.*, p. 1436.
3. To determine quantitatively whether reliable differences existed between
   wave forms in the records, we used the following system of analysis of
   data. The record was averaged and displayed on the oscilloscope of a PDP-8
   computer system. A vertical line was then positioned by a computer program at each inflection point of the displayed wave pattern; these lines
   then served as break points for analysis of data. The amplitude values of
   the raw data of the segment of the wave between two break points was
   then averaged and stored. By this device, the relative amplitude of comparable segments of different waves could be statistically compared by
   using Student's *t* test. This method allows some estimate of the reliability
   (in the face of variability) of the difference between segments of the
   waveform, though, of course, it does not determine whether a total waveform is significantly different from another. When reported, a waveform
   differs from its control at least by $P < .05$.
4. Supported by NIMH grant MH 12970 and research career award MH
   15,214 to K.H.P.

Differential-Approach Tendencies Produced by Injection of RNA from Trained Rats

ALLAN L. JACOBSON, FRANK R. BABICH, SUZANNE BUBASH, and ANN JACOBSON, *University of California*

Two groups of rats were trained in a Skinner box to approach the food cup when a discriminative stimulus (click or blinking light) was presented. Ribonucleic acid was extracted from the brains of these two groups of rats and injected into two groups of untrained rats. The untrained two groups then manifested a significant tendency (as compared with one another) to react differently to the two stimuli. On the average, the response appeared to be specific to the stimulus employed during training.

When RNA was extracted from the brains of rats trained to approach a food cup and was injected intraperitoneally into untrained rats, the rats so injected made significantly more approaches to the food cup than did controls (rats injected with RNA from brains of untrained rats). (1) We now present evidence that this effect is specific rather than general. Our new experiment is similar to our earlier one, except that we used two experimental groups, each trained to respond to a different discriminative stimulus.

Initially, 16 male Sprague-Dawley rats, aged 50 to 60 days, weighing 220 to 240 g. received magazine training in a standard Grason-Stadler Skinner box; that is, they were trained to ap-

Jacobson, A. L., Babich, F. R., Bubash, S., & Jacobson, A. Differential approach tendencies produced by injection of RNA from trained rats. *Science*, 1965, *150*, 636–637. Copyright 1965 by the American Association for the Advancement of Science.

proach the food cup when a discriminative stimulus was presented. For eight rats, the discriminative stimulus was the distinct click (1). For the other eight rats, the discriminative stimulus was a blinking light. The latter stimulus was produced by blinking the 10-watt house light (within the Skinner box) three times in succession, the three blinks taking a total of approximately 1 second.

For the click-trained rats, magazine-training was accomplished in the same fashion as in our earlier study (1).

The blinking light proved to be a somewhat more difficult stimulus to establish as a signal, and accordingly, minor modifications in the magazine-training procedure were made. After early training, the rats did not respond to the blinking light but they did run to the cup upon hearing the slight noise produced by the pellet's dropping into the cup. As training progressed, on more and more trials we withheld the pellet until the rat responded to the light alone. Thus, we essentially transferred dis-

TABLE 1.
Total number of responses per animal on the 25 test trials with click and on the 25 test trials with light.

| Stimulus | | Score (C-L) |
Click	Light	
Injection with RNA-C		
2	3	− 1
3	4	− 1
5	2	3
5	2	3
6	1	5
7	1	6
7	0	7
11	2	9
Injection with RNA-L		
0	7	− 7
0	7	− 7
0	3	− 3
1	3	− 2
0	2	− 2
0	2	− 2
0	1	− 1
7	5	2

criminative control of the approach response from the noise of the descending pellet to the blinking light.

Each of these 16 rats was trained to the stimulus as described (1). By the end of training, each rat in both groups approached the food cup promptly and swiftly from any part of the box when the appropriate discriminative stimulus (click or blinking light) was presented, and rarely or never approached the cup in the absence of that stimulus.

Upon completion of the training, each rat was killed with ether, and the brain was taken out as quickly as possible. A cut was made on a line joining the superior colliculus to the rostral end of the pons. The tissue posterior to this cut was discarded, as was the tissue of the olfactory bulbs. RNA was extracted from the remaining tissue (1.3 g, average weight) and was dissolved in 2.0 ml of isotonic saline. Approximately 8 hours after extraction, the RNA from each of the rats, light-trained or click-trained, was injected intraperitoneally with a 1.9 cm 22-gauge needle into an adapted untrained rat (1). During adaptation, most animals initially made slight startle responses to the click, but few or no startle responses occurred to the blinking light. By the end of the adaptation series, no animal made any visible response to either the click or the blinking light.

Thus eight animals received RNA (RNA-C) from click-trained rats and eight received RNA (RNA-L) from light-trained rats. All were assigned code letters and tested "blind" (1).

A session of testing for a given animal consisted of placing that animal in the Skinner box, permitting one minute to elapse, and then delivering a series of ten stimuli (five clicks and five lights in a mixed order, as described below). The stimuli were spaced at least 30 seconds apart. Five such testing sessions were given (1). During the first three test sessions, the order of presentation of stimuli was LCCLLCCLLC; during the last two sessions, the order was CLLCCLLCCL. Each test animal thus received a total of 25 click and 25 light trials. At the beginning of testing, all rats had been deprived of food for approximately 24 hours. After the third test session, all rats were fed 4 to 5 g of Purina Lab Chow. The method of testing and the criterion of response were identical to those used in our first experiment.

A comparison of the two judges' tallies revealed that they

agreed on 790 out of 800 trials, that is, on 98.7 percent of the judgments.

Each rat received a difference score (C-L) which was obtained by subtracting number of responses to light (L) from number of responses to click (C) for that rat. The Mann-Whitney U test (2) was performed to test the null hypothesis that the C-L scores of the two groups did not differ from each other. The test indicated that the difference between groups injected with RNA-C and RNA-L was significant ($P < .001$, one-tailed test). The difference in response to click for the two groups was significant by a Mann-Whitney U test ($P < .002$, one-tailed test).

We may conclude on the basis of the statistical analysis of C-L scores that the two groups differed in their tendencies to react differentially to click and blinking light. The average difference score for the group injected with RNA-C is positive (3.9), whereas the average difference score for the group injected with RNA-L is negative ($- 2.8$), although the test used compares these scores with each other rather than with zero. A further conclusion is that RNA-C rats responded more to click than did the RNA-L rats. The differences between the groups in response tendencies may be attributed to the RNA preparation injected into the test rats, and hence presumably to the effects which original training produced upon the RNA of the donor animals. Since handling, nutrition, and adaptation to the Skinner box were matched for the two groups, the transfer effect cannot be attributed to these factors. Thus, the new results support our original finding that a response tendency can be transferred by RNA injection, and they further suggest that this effect is to a substantial extent specific rather than general.

Notes

1. F. R. Babich, A. L. Jacobson, S. Bubash, A. Jacobson, *Science* 149, 656 (1965).
2. S. Siegel, *Non-parametric Statistics for the Behavioral Sciences* (McGraw-Hill, New York, 1956).

Memory in Mammals:
Evidence for a System Involving
Nuclear Ribonucleic Acid*

D. J. ALBERT,† *Mental Health Research Institute,*
University of Michigan

The learning of an avoidance response was confined to one hemisphere in rats by starting cortical spreading depression in the other. Removing the medial (but not anterior or posterior) cortex of the trained hemisphere impairs retention of the learning. If the medial tissue is intraperitoneally injected back into the donor animal, there is savings in relearning with the untrained hemisphere. This savings seems to be specific to the previously learned task and the effect occurs only when the tissue from the trained hemisphere is removed after consolidation of the learning has progressed for several hours. Ribonucleic acid molecules located in the nucleus of some group of cortical cells seem to mediate the savings effect. These results suggest that the effect of injecting the tissue from the trained cortex is to allow ribonucleic acid molecules which have coded the information about the learned response to migrate to the untrained hemisphere and function there as stored learning.

1. INTRODUCTION

The changes in the central nervous system which constitute learning have generally been thought to consist of changes

---

*Most of this work was done at McGill University, Montreal, Canada, where it was supported by a USPH Predoctoral Fellowship to the author. It has also been supported by a grant to the Mental Health Research Institute (NIH M7417-04).
†Postdoctoral fellow.

Albert, D. J. Memory in mammals: evidence for a system involving nuclear ribonucleic acid. *Neuropsychologia,* 1966, *4,* 79–92.

limited to the synapse, which alter the functional relations between nerve cells and neural circuits [8, 13, 18]. There are, however, several lines of evidence which suggest that this conceptualization is at least an oversimplification. First, Morrell [14] has shown that learning may involve transcortical pathways connecting different parts of the cortex and has concluded that it is unlikely that the changed functional relations between parts of such a complex network could be accounted for by a simple chain of synaptic modifications. More recently, Albert [2, 3] has shown that the processes which occur during the consolidation, or fixation, of learning in the rat do not suggest that new morphological synaptic changes are being strengthened, but rather that more stable temporary changes, such as new macromolecular templates, are involved in forming the permanent retention mechanisms. Finally, experiments with planaria seem to show that learning in this more primitive species is coded in macromolecules [21].

The present experiments consider the possibility that macromolecular changes are central to the information storage system in the rat brain. The experiments parallel those done with planaria where evidence was found that learning could be transferred chemically by injecting ribonucleic acid from a trained planarian into an untrained planarian [21]. The design of the present experiments is also to transfer stored information chemically, but the transfer is not between animals, but instead, between one hemisphere and the other in the same animal. Such an intraanimal transfer of learning seemed particularly advantageous because it involves fewer biological assumptions. (Since these experiments were done, however, two reports [4, 7] have appeared describing what appears to be inter-animal chemical transfer of learning in rats, and these studies will be considered in the discussion.)

Restriction of the learning to one hemisphere is obtained by using cortical spreading depression to make the other hemisphere nonfunctional during training. A simple avoidance task is used which is known from previous experiments to be easily learned when only one hemisphere is functional [2].

The first step in these experiments is to locate the region in the trained hemisphere where the memory of the avoidance response is stored. It is found that a lesion in the medial (but not anterior or posterior) region of the cortex impairs retention, which suggests that the learning may be stored there. To further test the possibility that the learning is stored there and that a chemical storage mechanism is involved, a second experiment is done in which the tissue from the medial cortex is removed and intraperitoneally injected back into the donor animal. When these animals are tested on the avoidance task using the untrained hemisphere, they show savings in relearning while uninjected control animals do not. To demonstrate more clearly that the savings effect is due to the injection of molecules from the trained tissue which have coded the avoidance learning, several additional experiments are presented which show that the savings in relearning is specific to the previously learned task and that the molecules mediating the effect have the characteristics which existing evidence and intuitive reasoning require for a macromolecular information coding system.

2. METHOD

The experiments all follow a single schedule with minor variations. The subjects were naive, male hooded rats weighing 225–275 g from the Quebec Breeding Farm and Maxfield Animal Supply. Cannulas for starting spreading depression were first implanted in the antero-lateral parietal bone over each hemisphere. On the following day (day 1), the animals were trained on an avoidance task while one hemisphere had cortical spreading depression. It is known that spreading depression disturbs the functioning of the affected hemisphere and that with this task, the learning that occurs while one hemisphere is depressed is recorded mainly in the normal hemisphere [2].

On day 2, the animals were again subjected to surgery and this time the tissue from the medial region of the trained cortex (which seems to be the area storing the learning) was removed. The procedure differs at this point depending on the purpose of the experiment. If the tissue was to be injected back into the animal, it was kept ice cold as it was removed. When surgery was complete, any desired manipulations of the tissue were made and it was then injected intraperitoneally back into the donor animal.

On day 3, the trained hemisphere was depressed and the animal was tested for savings in relearning with the untrained hemisphere. If the injected tissue has no effect, the animal should require as many trials to relearn as in the original learning, but if there is some positive transfer of learning, the animal should relearn in fewer trials. Groups of 6–8 animals were usually sufficient to establish reliable estimates of the effect of the injected tissue.

Most of this procedure has been described in detail previously [2] and will be presented only generally here. Unilateral spreading depression was started and maintained for training and testing by 12 per cent potassium chloride (KCl) placed in the polyethylene cannula over one cortex (for details of the cannulas, see Albert [2]). The presence of spreading depression was confirmed by noting a hypesthesia of the body contralateral to the depressed hemisphere. The KCl was left in the cannula for as long as spreading depression was wanted on the cortex and then removed by flushing the cannula with sterile 0.9 per cent NaCl.

The avoidance apparatus was a box (10×36×18 in. deep) with white and black halves separated by a sliding partition. The animal was first placed in the black side for 1 min, and then placed at the end of the white side, facing the white end. If the animal returned to the black side within 5 sec, the trial was counted as an avoidance; if not, the animal was shocked intermittently until it moved to the black side. There was a 1 min. intertrial interval during which the animal remained in the black compartment. This procedure was the same for both the first learning and the test for savings in relearning, except that in the savings test, the animals were purposely shocked as little as possible to avoid making them freeze.

Approximately 15 per cent of the animals were discarded in the course of training and retraining. The major reasons for discarding animals were: too rapid (less than 10 trials) or too slow (more than 30 trials) first learning; development of localized motor seizures which interfered with performance.

2.1 Removal and handling of tissue
from the trained cortex

Tissue from the trained cortex was removed using a suction technique. A 10 ml syringe provided the suction and an attached 15 gauge curved hypodermic needle (whose diameter [1.75 mm] is about the thickness of the cortex) was worked gently into the brain tissue and, in places, under the skull to remove the cortical tissue. When the lesion was finished, gelfoam was slipped into the empty space.

Figure 1 shows the location and similarity in size of the anterior, medial, and posterior lesions. The lesions frequently removed the underlying white matter (corpus callosum) but seldom invaded other subcortical structures. The medial lesions gave the most important effects and these began 3–4 mm from the posterior cortical tip and 1–2 mm from the midline and extended about 4 mm anterior and laterally to within 1–2 mm of the rhinal fissure.

If the cortical tissue was to be injected without any experimental changes, it was placed in about 5 ml of ice cold 0.9 percent NaCl as it was removed. Following surgery, it was broken into small pieces (though this was not necessary) by briefly manipulating it by hand in a teflon and glass homogenizer. The tissue was then intraperitoneally injected using a 10 ml syringe and an 18 gauge hypodermic needle, care being taken to avoid getting the fluid into the intestines.

In some experiments, the tissue was separated into subcellular components in order to determine the intracellular location of the molecules causing the savings in relearning. In this case, the tissue was placed in ice cold 0.25 molar (M) sucrose

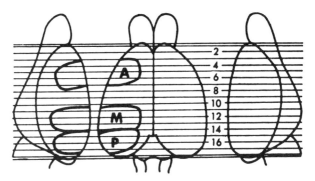

FIG. 1. A Lashley diagram of the rat brain showing the approximate location and size of the unilateral anterior (A), medial (M), and posterior (P) cortical lesions.

as it was removed and then homogenized using an electric motor drive. To separate the cell nuclei [9, 17] the homogenate was layered over 5 ml of 0.32 M sucrose in a 15 ml centrifuge tube and centrifuged for 10 min at about 800 g in an International Centrifuge bucket rotor (No. 241). To inject the isolated nuclei, the nuclear pellet on the bottom of the centrifuge tube was resuspended in 5 ml of ice cold 0.25 M sucrose.

To separate the soluble and solid portions of the nuclear fraction, the isolated nuclei were resuspended in distilled water (8 ml, 0°C) to break them open. The solid material was then sedimented by centrifuging at 100,000 g for 60 min in a Spinco Ultracentrifuge (No. 40 head).

A preliminary identification of the kind of molecules mediating the savings in relearning was established using enzymes which selectively break down certain kinds of molecules. Protein was broken down using trypsin. The trypsin used was sterile, lyophilized, 3 times recrystallized (Worthington Biochemicals). Ribonuclease was used to destroy ribonucleic acid and this was 5 times recrystallized (National Biochemical Company).

3. Results

3.1 The Locus of Information Storage

The first step in this research is to locate the region in the trained hemisphere where the information about the avoidance response is stored. Previous experiments using the same task seemed to show that if the information is made to transfer from the trained to the untrained hemisphere (by giving the animal one avoidance trial with the trained and untrained hemispheres functional), the information is received in the medial region of the untrained cortex [2, 3]. It seemed reasonable, therefore, that in the trained hemisphere at least part of the learning is localized in the homotopic medial cortex.

To test this hypothesis, the animals were given a retention test after the medial cortex of the trained hemisphere was removed. The lesions were made on the day after avoidance training, and on the following day, the animals ($N = 10$) were tested for savings in relearning the avoidance task while the untrained hemisphere was nonfunctional with cortical spreading depression. Two control groups of 6 animals each were treated in the same way except that the lesions were in the anterior or posterior region of the trained cortex (see Fig. 1 for the locus of the lesions).

The animals with lesions in the medial cortex took almost as many trials to relearn (13.5 trials) as in the first learning. In contrast, the animals with anterior or posterior lesions showed significant ($P < 0.05$; all statistics are two-tailed rank tests) savings, reaching criterion in 4.2 and 5.1 trials, respectively. (There were no differences between groups in original learning in this or subsequent experiments.)

These results support the suggestion that some of the learning involved in the avoidance task is stored in the medial cortex of the trained hemisphere, but of course, they are not conclusive since the lesions may have interfered with recall rather than removing the stored information.

TABLE 1.
The effect of a lesion in the anterior, medial, or posterior cortex of the trained hemisphere on the retention of an avoidance response. Both the first learning and the retention test are given while one cortex has spreading depression.

| Locus of lesion | N | Mean trials to learn | |
		First learning	Retention test
Anterior	6	12.3 ± 4.2	4.2 ± 2.8*
Medial	10	14.4 ± 6.4	13.5 ± 5.9
Posterior	6	13.0 ± 2.7	5.1 ± 2.3*

*Significantly different from first learning ($P < 0.05$).

3.2   Injecting the Tissue from the Trained Cortex.

To test the possibility that the memory of the avoidance response is chemically coded, the tissue from the medial region of the trained cortex was removed and intraperitoneally injected back into the same animal. The line of reasoning behind this procedure was that when the tissue which is thought to contain the learning is injected, some of the molecules which code the learning may enter the blood vessels and be transported to and into the brain. The molecules are assumed to be structurally labelled with respect to their region of origin in the brain (medial cortex) so that once in the brain they are absorbed and alter only the similarly labelled cells in the homotopic region of the untrained cortex.

There are, of course, many assumptions in this argument, but those that make it most "biologically unlikely" concern the possibly of getting the molecules into the brain and to the right spot. The main obstacle to getting the molecules into the brain is the blood–brain barrier, and there is evidence that some kinds of large molecules (antibodies) can get through [19]. In addition, the lesion in the trained hemisphere will disturb the blood–brain barrier and should greatly increase the ease of penetration into the brain [11]. As to getting the molecules to the right spot, this seems to require the assumption that the molecules are labelled, but there is evidence that this kind of labelling can occur and that such molecules could migrate to specific regions of the brain. This is shown most clearly in an experiment where antibodies formed to a specific brain tissue (caudate nucleus) and injected intraventricularly, subsequently attacked and disturbed only this specific structure [12].

Two groups of 15 animals each were trained on the avoidance task with one hemisphere depressed and on the following day, the medial cortex of the trained hemisphere was removed. In the experimental group, this tissue was intraperitoneally injected back into the donor animal as soon as the surgery was complete; in the control group, there was no injection. Both groups of animals were tested the following day for savings in relearning with the trained hemisphere depressed.

The results are clear (Table 2). The animals injected with the tissue from the medial cortex relearning significantly faster (5.0 trials, $P < 0.01$) than in the first learning. They also learned faster than the no-injection control group (18.8 trials, $P < 0.01$) which was slightly slower than in the first learning. To control for the possibility that the faster learning in the experimental group was due to the injection of the cortical tissue but not specifically to the medial tissue where the learning is thought to be stored, another control group was injected with tissue from the posterior region of the trained cortex (Fig. 1). In this group, relearning required 12.1 trials, not significantly better than the first learning or the control group with no injection.

TABLE 2.
The effect of injecting tissue from the medial region of the trained cortex on relearning with the untrained hemisphere.

| | | Mean trials to learn | |
Group	N	First learning	Relearning with untrained hemisphere
Medial lesion, tissue injected	15	18.4 ± 5.0	5.0 ± 1.9*
Medial lesion, no injection	15	15.4 ± 7.1	16.7 ± 5.8
Posterior lesion, tissue injected	8	15.9 ± 7.9	12.1 ± 4.4
Medial lesion†, tissue injected	8	15.4 ± 4.8	7.4 ± 2.9‡
Medial lesion†, no injection	8	17.4 ± 5.3	13.1 ± 6.3

*Significantly different from first learning ($P < 0.01$).
†Groups run blind.
‡Significantly different from first learning ($P < 0.05$).

To control for experimenter bias as a source of error, the medial injection group and the no-injection control group were repeated blind. The results were the same (Table 2): the animals ($N = 8$) injected with the tissue from the medial cortex of the trained hemisphere showed significant savings in relearning (7.4 trials) while the no-injection group ($N = 8$) did not (13.1 trials, $P < 0.05$).

The results support the hypothesis that at least part of the memory of the avoidance response is chemically stored in the medial cortex and that when the coded molecules are removed and injected back into the same animal, they can alter the untrained hemisphere so as to make relearning faster.

3.3 The Specificity of the Injection Effect

In order to show more conclusively that the effect of the injected tissue is to actually transfer chemically stored information rather than to simply facilitate learning or performance in general, a slightly different task was given on the relearning day. In this new task, an animal which had previously learned to avoid the white side was put down just over the middle of the box onto the white side (see Fig. 2). The animal now had a choice; it could avoid the shock by running to the black side as previously learned or by running into the far half of the white side. If the effect of the injected tissue from the trained cortex is not specific, about the same number of injected and uninjected animals should learn each response; but if, instead, the injected material actually carries information about the previous learning to the untrained hemisphere, the injected animals should show a greater tendency to relearn the previously acquired task.

One hemisphere was depressed and the animals trained to avoid the white side; on the following day, the tissue from the medial cortex of the trained hemisphere was removed and injected back into the animals of the experimental group but not those of the control group. The next day, the trained hemisphere was depressed and the animals were trained on the modified avoidance task in which they could avoid shock by moving to the black side or to the end of the white side (Fig. 2). The procedure was the same as in the first training with several exceptions: the animals were put down in the white side, half facing the black and half facing the white side; when the animal chose the white side, the partition separating the black and white sides was not replaced during the intertrial interval, and in order for the movement to be considered a response, the animal had to remain in that end for at least 15 sec; the animal was required

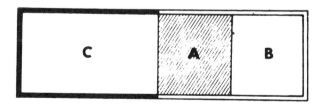

Fig. 2. The floor plan of the modified avoidance apparatus used in testing the specificity of the savings effect. The animal is put down in zone A and can avoid shock by moving to the white (B) or black (C) end.

to reach a criterion of 7 out of 8 consecutive trials to one side without shock instead of 9 out of 10.

The results (Table 3) : the animals that were injected with the lesioned tissue all (8) moved to the side of the box (black) that had been safe during the first learning. In the uninjected group, only 3 out of the 8 animals chose this side; the others went to the end of the white side.

TABLE 3.
The effect of injecting the cortical tissue from the trained hemisphere on the animal's choice of approaching the previously avoided or approached sides. The trained hemisphere is depressed during the choice test.

Group	Number of animals avoiding each side in relearning	
	Black	White
First trained to avoid white side		
Injected	0	8*
Uninjected	5	3
First trained to avoid black side		
Injected	7	1*
Uninjected	2	5

*Combined groups ($P < 0.01$).

To control for any side preferences, the experiment was repeated with the white side safe during the first learning. The results were the same. Seven out of eight injected animals went to the white side compared to 2 out of 7 uninjected animals.

It is clear that the animals injected with the tissue from the trained cortex chose to relearn the previously learned task more frequently than the uninjected animals ($P < 0.01$; combined groups). This seems to show that specific chemically coded information about the learned avoidance response is transferred to the untrained hemisphere by molecules in the injected tissue.

3.4 The Length of the "Consolidation" Period

Since the evidence up to this point strongly supported the conclusion that the memory of the avoidance response is chemically coded, additional experiments were done to relate the molecules causing the savings to existing evidence and intuitive requirements for a molecular information storage system. The first of these experiments considers the length of time following training required for the formation of the molecules mediating the savings. If these molecules are a part of the permanent information storage system in the brain, there should be a consolidation, or fixation, period of several hours after training before the synthesis is complete.

The animals were trained with one hemisphere depressed and then at varying times afterward, the medial cortex of the trained hemisphere was removed and injected back into the donor animal. Twenty-four hours later, the trained hemisphere was depressed and the animals were tested for savings in relearning.

The results are shown in Fig. 3. When the tissue from the trained cortex was removed at 2 or 4 hr after training, the injec-

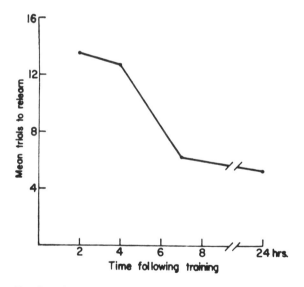

FIG. 3. The number of trials required to relearn when the injected tissue from the trained cortex is removed at varying times following training. The average scores of 6 animals determine each point. The 2- and 24-hr groups were run blind.

tion did not give rise to savings in relearning (13.5 and 12.6 trials, respectively). By about 7 hr, however, there was significant savings (6.2 trials, $P<0.05$) and the amount was not significantly less than that of a 24-hr group (5.2 trials). (The 2- and 24-hr groups were run blind. The first learning scores for these groups were 13.8 and 15.0 trials, respectively; the relearning of the 24-hr group was significantly [$P<0.05$] faster than that of the 2-hr group.)

A period of over 4 hr following training is required for the formation of the molecules mediating the savings in relearning. This interval is somewhat longer than the 1–2 hr period that has generally been found for the consolidation of learning, but approaches very closely the 5–10 hr interval that Albert [3], using a new method, has obtained. The finding of an appropriate "consolidation period" for the savings effect clearly suggests that the molecules mediating the savings are a part of the permanent information storage system that is formed following learning.

3.5 Intracellular Origin of the Molecules
       Mediating the Savings

One would expect that as with other biological functions, information storage in the nervous system would be associated with a particular place or structure. The grossest physical localization of the critical molecules that could be made with the present preparation would be with respect to the cortical layers and the kind of cell, neuron or glia, but these experiments pose numerous difficulties and so were postponed. An equally important experiment is the subcellular localization of the active molecules within the cortical tissue and this is a comparatively simple problem using the well-known technique of differential centrifugation [9, 17].

Following some preliminary experiments which indicated that the active molecules were in the cell nuclei, the following experiment was carried out blind. The animals were first trained; the medial region of the trained cortex was then removed, and the tissue homogenized in ice cold 0.25 M sucrose. The cell nuclei were separated from the homogenate by centrifugation (see Method) and suspended in 0.25 M sucrose. Half the animals (6) were injected with the nuclei and half with the rest of the cellular homogenate. The next day the trained hemisphere was depressed and the animals were tested for savings in relearning.

Table 4 shows the results. The animals injected with the isolated nuclei showed savings in relearning (8.4 trials) while the animals injected with the rest of the homogenate did not (12.3 trials, $P<0.05$).

TABLE 4.
The effect of injecting various parts of the tissue from the medial region of the trained cortex on the relearning of the untrained hemisphere.

Fraction of tissue homogenate	N	First learning	Relearning with untrained hemisphere
Cell nuclei*	6	13.0 ± 1.7	8.4 ± 2.4†
Homogenate minus cell nuclei*	6	12.5 ± 2.2	12.3 ± 2.4
Part of cell nuclei			
Solid	6	19.7 ± 6.6	4.3 ± 1.8†
Soluble	6	12.4 ± 1.0	11.4 ± 5.6

*Groups run blind.
†Significantly different from first learning ($P<0.05$).

A second experiment was done to determine whether the active molecules were in the solid or soluble portion of the cell nuclei. The method was to first isolate the nuclei and break them open by suspending them in distilled water. The solid material was then separated into a pellet by centrifuging at high speed (see Method). The pellet of solid material was suspended in distilled water and injected into half the animals and the soluble material (the supernatant) was injected into the others. The animals were tested for savings in relearning with the untrained hemisphere the following day.

Savings in relearning (Table 4) was shown by the group injected with the solid nuclear material (4.3 trials) but not the group injected with the soluble portion (11.4 trials, $P<0.05$).

The results seem clear: the critical molecules for the savings effect are located in the solid material of the nucleus, presumably the nucleolus. Although this conclusion may appear somewhat uncertain in view of expected cytoplasmic contamination of the isolated nuclei [9], the nuclear material, as isolated, appears to contain the full savings effect and the only subcellular particle which would be almost entirely present there are the nuclei.

3.6 Characteristics of the Molecules Mediating the Savings

The chemical characteristics of the molecules which seem to be storing and transferring the learned response are examined in this final group of experiments. These begin by testing the possibility that the chemical is a macromolecule since this would seem to be necessary to both code the learning and allow selective migration to a specific region of the brain.

In the first experiment, the cortical tissue was heated in a water bath at 100°C for 10 min, which is enough heat to destroy the structure and biological activity of most large molecules. The homogenate was then cooled and injected back into the donor animal.

These animals $(N = 6)$ did not show savings in relearning with the untrained hemisphere (16.8 trials; Table 5), which supports the hypothesis that a macromolecule is mediating the savings effect.

TABLE 5.
The effect of changing the injected cortical tissue in various ways on the savings in relearning with the untrained hemisphere.

		Mean trials to learn	
Treatment	N	First learning	Relearning with untrained hemisphere
Heat (100°C)	6	16.7 ± 7.0	16.8 ± 4.0
Cross animals	5	16.8 ± 7.1	16.4 ± 7.2
Incubation in:			
Ribonuclease	6	17.2 ± 7.2	15.2 ± 5.9
Trypsin	4	15.8 ± 4.4	3.8 ± 1.1*
0,9% NaCl	3	21.3 ± 5.4	4.0 ± 0.8*

*Combined groups, significantly different from first learning ($P < 0.05$).

A second experiment considers the effect of injecting the tissue across animals. It seemed possible that the macromolecular coding of the learning might be chemically specific to each animal, or that the macromolecules mediating the effect might be destroyed as a foreign substance when injected across animals. The procedure was simply to inject the tissue from the trained cortex of one animal into another animal which had also been trained and lesioned.

When these animals ($N=5$) were tested the following day with the trained hemisphere depressed, there was no savings in relearning (16.4 trials, Table 5).

This result also suggests that a large organic molecule is mediating the chemical transfer of learning.

To establish a preliminary identification of the specific kind of molecule mediating the savings, a final experiment was done using enzymes to selectively destroy either protein or ribonucleic acid. The tissue from the trained cortex was homogenized and the solid part of the cell nuclei isolated by centrifugation. This material was suspended in 6 ml of a 0.9 percent NaCl solution to which was added 1 mg/ml of trypsin (to break down protein) or 1 mg/ml ribonuclease (to break down ribonucleic acid). The suspensions were incubated for 60 min at 37°C in a water bath, cooled, and injected back into the donor animal. The animals were tested for savings in relearning the following day.

The results suggest that the critical molecule is a ribonucleic acid (Table 5) since the savings was blocked when the tissue was incubated in the ribonucleic acid destroying enzyme (15.2 trials, $N = 6$). Destroying protein did not impair the savings in relearning (3.8 trials, $N = 4$) and these animals were about the same as a control group whose tissue was incubated in 0.9 percent NaCl alone (4.0 trials, $N = 3$).

4. Discussion

Injection of the tissue from the medial cortex of the trained hemisphere causes savings in relearning with the untrained hemisphere and there is a clear relation between the savings effect and the previous learning. The savings seems to be due to a specific tendency to perform the previously acquired response (Table 3), and the effect occurs only when the tissue is removed from the trained cortex after consolidation of the learning has progressed for several hours (Fig. 3). Further, the ribonucleic acid molecules which seem to be mediating the effect are located only at a specific site in the cell, the nucleus (Table 4). These results suggest that the effect of injecting the trained cortical tissue is to allow ribonucleic acid molecules which have coded the learned response to migrate to the untrained hemisphere and function there as stored learning.

On the basis of present knowledge about learning and information storage, the most important criticism of the present experiments seems to be that the effect of the injection may be to stimulate the natural interhemispheric transfer of the avoidance response in some way. The evidence, however, does not support this interpretation. For example, when the tissue from the medial cortex is removed, the animal cannot recall the learning with the trained hemisphere (Table 1) so that it seems unlikely that there could be a spontaneous interhemispheric transfer of the learning. Also, there is no effect of the injection when the tissue is removed within 4 hr after learning (Fig. 3). It is true that lesioning within about 1 or 2 hr of training would cause cortical disturbances such as spreading depression which might interfere with consolidation taking place in other parts of the brain; however, these kinds of disturbances are known to be ineffective in interfering with the consolidation processes that occur during the next 2 hr [3], and yet the removal and injection of the medial cortical tissue during this time still does not cause savings in relearning.

In addition, the conclusion that information is being transferred chemically is supported by the simultaneous discovery of evidence for interanimal chemical transfer of learning by Fjerdingstad, Nissen and Roigaard-Petersen [7] and Babich, Jacobson, Bubash and Jacobson [4]. The failure to obtain interanimal transfer in the present experiments would seem to be due either to the possibility that the interanimal effects are smaller and, therefore, went unobserved, or that they occur only when the ribonucleic acid is isolated before being injected.

The evidence that chemically coded changes are involved in information storage in the mammalian nervous system is clearly important for the understanding of learning but it far from specifies the nature of the actual changes that occur. It does not rule out the possibility of synaptic changes which occur along with the nucleic acid change, particularly since there is considerable evidence that chemicals can determine synaptic connections [20]. However, in agreement with Morrell [14], the present results suggest that it is unlikely that information is stored in multisynaptic pathways connecting separate areas of the brain. If this were the case, it would be necessary to conclude that in the present experiments, the injected material reaches specific cells and alters their connections. A more likely possibility would seem to be that certain areas of the brain are equipotential and that the injected molecules need only migrate to a certain region of the brain. This implies that the altered functional relations between parts of the brain following learning do not result from direct neural connections, but rather, that they may be effected through changes in the reception or emission of temporally patterned neural activity. (See Morrell [14], Brazier [5], Hydén [10], and Adey Dunlop, and Hendrix [1] for examples and evidence about the various forms such temporal activity might assume.)

The biochemical characteristics of the storage mechanism are slightly clearer than the functional changes they cause. Since the ribonucleic acid molecules which seem to code the learning are in the nucleus, far from where they would directly affect electrochemical membrane changes, these molecules probably could not alter the behavior of neural cells directly. Rather, consistent with the other known functions of ribonucleic acid molecules as templates, it seems likely that here again their function would be to dictate the construction of molecules, such as protein, which actually effect the functional changes in the cell.

There is evidence that the injected ribonucleic acid in the present experiments could work this way. For example, it has been shown in biochemical experiments [6, 15, 16] that ribonucleic acid can penetrate some kinds of cells and dictate the formation of particular proteins. Further, the evidence also indicates that the changes which this entering ribonucleic acid induces may be permanent since it seems to cause the cell nucleus to establish a biochemical process for permanently producing the new proteins [16].

Finally, these speculations and results on the nature of information storage are highly significant for experiments on the process of consolidation, or fixation, of learning. Albert [3] has suggested that during the one or two minutes following a learning trial, the molecules are formed (or released) that constitute the templates (or stimulants) for the rest of the consolidation process and that this is followed first by a physical chemical process and then by a process of biochemical synthesis. It now seems an interesting possibility that the physical chemical process may consist of a migration of the template molecules from their original position (perhaps at the neural axon hillock or dendritic membrane) to the cell nucleus and that the synthetic processes would consist of the formation of the appropriate nuclear ribonucleic acid and afterwards protein.

Acknowledgements—The author is indebted to the staff and students of the Neurochemistry Department of the Montreal Neurological Institute for help with some of the experiments.

NOTES

1. Adey, W. R., Dunlop, C. W. and Hendrix, C. E. Hippocampal slow waves. *A. M. A. Archs Neurol.* 3, 74–90, 1960.
2. Albert, D. J. The effect of spreading depression on the consolidation of learning. *Neuropsychologia* 4, 49–64, 1966.
3. Albert, D. J. The effect of polarizing currents on the consolidation of learning. *Neuropsychologia* 4, 65–77, 1966.
4. Babich, F. R., Jacobson, A. L., Bubash, S. and Jacobson, A. Transfer of a response to naive rats by injection of ribonucleic acid extracted from trained rats. *Science, N.Y.* 149, 656–657, 1965.
5. Brazier, M. A. B. Long-persisting electrical traces in the brain of man and their possible relationship to higher nervous activity. In *Moscow Colloquium on Electroencephalography of Higher Nervous Activity,* Jasper, H. H. and Smirnov, G. D. (Editors), *Electroenceph. clin. Neurophysiol.* suppl. 13, 347–358, 1960.
6. Cohen, E. P. and Parks, J. J. Antibody production of nonimmune spleen cells incubated with RNA from immunized mice. *Science, N.Y.* 144, 1012–1013, 1964.
7. Fjerdingstad, E. J., Nissen, Th. and Roigaard-Petersen, H. H. Effect of RNA extracted from the brain of trained animals on learning in rats. *Scand. J. Psychol.,* 6, 1–6, 1965.
8. Hebb, D. O. *The Organization of Behavior.* Wiley, New York, 1949.
9. Hogeboom, G. H. Fractionation of cell components of animal tissues. In *Methods in Enzymology,* Vol. 1, Colowick, S. P. and Kaplan, N. O. (Editors), pp. 16–19, Academic Press, New York, 1955.
10. Hyden, H. Biochemical changes in glial cells and nerve cells at varying activity. In *Biochemistry of the Central Nervous System,* Vol. 3, *Proc. 4th Intern. Congr. Biochem.,* Brucke, F. (Editor), pp. 64–89, Pergamon Press, London, 1959.

11. Lajtha, A. The "brain barrier system." In *Neurochemistry*, Elliott, K. A. C., Page, I. H. and Quastel, J. H. (Editors), pp. 399–430, Thomas, Springfield, 2nd edition, 1962.

12. Mihailovic, Lj. and Jankovic, B. D. Effects of intraventricularly injected anti-n. caudatus antibody on the electrical activity of the cat brain. *Nature, Lond.* 192, 665–666, 1961.

13. Milner, P. M. Learning in neural systems. In *Self-Organizing Systems*. Yovits, M. C. (Editor), pp. 190–200, Pergamon Press, New York, 1959.

14. Morrell, F. Effect of anodal polarization on the firing pattern of single cortical cells. *Ann. N. Y. Acad. Sci.* 92, 860–876, 1961.

15. Niu, M. C., Cordova, C. C., and Niu, L. C. Ribonucleic acid-induced changes in mammalian cells. *Proc. natl. Acad. Sci. U.S.A.* 47, 1689–1700, 1961.

16. Niu, M. C., Cordova, C. C., Niu, L. C. and Radbill, C. L. RNA-induced biosynthesis of specific enzymes. *Proc. natl Acad. Sci. U.S.A.* 48, 1964–1969, 1962.

17. Potter, V. R. Tissue homogenates. In *Methods in Enzymology*, Vol. 1, Colowick, S. P. and Kaplan, N. O. (Editors), pp. 10–15, Academic Press, New York, 1955.

18. Rank, J. B. Synaptic "learning" due to electroosmosis: A theory. *Science, N.Y.* 144, 187–189, 1964.

19. Sherwin, A. L., Richter, M., Cosgrove, J. B. R. and Rose, B. Studies of the blood-cerebrospinal fluid barrier to antibodies and other proteins. *Neurology* 13, 113–119, 1963.

20. Sperry, R. W. Problems in the biochemical specification of neurons. In *Biochemistry of the Developing Nervous System*, Waelsch, H. (Editor), pp. 74–84, Academic Press, New York, 1955.

21. Zelman, A., Kabat, L., Jacobson, R. and McConnell, J. V. Transfer of training through injection of "conditioned" RNA into untrained planarians. *Worm Runner's Digest* 5, 14–19, 1963.

Further Reading

GENERAL TEXTS

Adams, J. A. *Learning and memory: an introduction.* Homewood, Ill.: Dorsey Press, 1976.

Hall, J. F. *The psychology of learning.* Philadelphia: J. B. Lippincott, 1966.

Hulse, S. H., Deese, J., & Egeth, H. *The psychology of learning.* New York: McGraw-Hill, 1975.

Karen, R. L. *An introduction to behavior theory and its applications.* New York: Harper & Row, 1974.

Mikulas, W. L. *Concepts in learning.* Philadelphia: Saunders, 1974.

THEORIES OF LEARNING

Bolles, R. C. *Learning theory.* New York: Holt, Rinehart, Winston, 1975.

Goldstein, H., Krantz, D. L. & Rains, J. D. (eds) *Controversial issues in learning.* New York: Appleton-Century-Crofts, 1965.

Hilgard, E. R., & Bower, G. H. *Theories of learning.* Englewood Cliffs, N.J.: Prentice-Hall, 1975.

Hill, W. F. *Learning: a survey of psychological interpretations.* Scranton: Chandler, 1971.

Lefrancois, G. R. *Psychological theories and human learning.* Belmont, Calif.: Wadsworth, 1972.

Marx, M. (ed) *Learning: Theories.* New York: Macmillan, 1970.

Sahakian, W. S. *Psychology of learning.* Chicago: Markham, 1970.

OPFRANT CONDITIONING

Catania, A. C. (ed) *Contemporary research in operant behavior.* Glenview, Ill.: Scott, Foresman, 1968.

Honig, W. K. (ed) *Operant behavior: areas of research and application.* New York: Appleton-Century-Crofts, 1966.

McGinnies, E., & Ferster, C. B. (eds) *The reinforcement of social behavior.* Boston: Houghton Mifflin, 1971.

Reynolds, G. S. *A primer of operant conditioning.* Glenview, Ill.: Scott, Foresman, 1975.

Skinner, B. F. *Science and human behavior.* New York: Macmillan, 1953.

Whaley, D. L., & Malott, R. W. *Elementary principles of behavior.* New York: Appleton-Century-Crofts, 1971.

Williams, J. L. *Operant learning: procedures for changing behavior.* Belmont, Calif.: Wadsworth, 1973.

RESPONDENT CONDITIONING

Beecroft, R. S. *Classical conditioning.* Goleta, Calif.: Psychonomic Press, 1966.

Black, A. H., & Prokasy, W. F. (eds) *Classical conditioning II: Current research and theory.* New York: Appleton-Century-Crofts, 1972.

Prokasy, W. F. (ed) *Classical conditioning: a symposium.* New York: Appleton-Century-Crofts, 1965.

VERBAL LEARNING AND RETENTION

Dixon, T. R., & Horton, D. L. (eds) *Verbal behavior and general behavior theory.* Englewood Cliffs, N.J.: Prentice-Hall, 1968.

Hall, J. F. *Verbal learning and retention.* Philadelphia: J. B. Lippincott, 1971.

Kausler, D. H. *Psychology of verbal learning and memory.* New York: Academic Press, 1974.

Postman, L., & Keppel, G. (eds) *Verbal learning and memory*. Baltimore: Penguin Books, 1969.

Slamecka, N. J. (ed.) *Human learning and memory: selected readings*. New York: Oxford Univ. Press, 1967.

PHYSIOLOGY OF LEARNING

Deutsch, J. A. (ed.) *The physiological basis of memory*. New York: Academic Press, 1973.

Grossman, S. P. *A textbook of physiological psychology*. New York: John Wiley, 1967.

John, E. R. *Mechanisms of memory*. New York: Academic Press, 1967.

McGaugh, J. L., & Herz, M. J. *Memory consolidation*. San Francisco: Albion, 1972.

Pribram, K. H. *Languages of the brain: experimental paradoxes and principles in neuropsychology*. Englewood Cliffs, N.J.: Prentice-Hall, 1971.

Pribram, K. H., & Broadbent, D. E. (eds) *Biology of memory*. New York: Academic Press, 1970.

Ungar, G. (ed) *Molecular mechanisms in memory and learning*. New York: Plenum Press, 1970.

BEHAVIOR MODIFICATION

Bandura, A. *Principles of behavior modification*. New York: Holt, Rinehart, & Winston, 1969.

Mikulas, W. L. *Behavior modification*. New York: Harper & Row, 1978.

O'Leary, K. O., & Wilson, G. T. *Behavior therapy: application and outcome*. Englewood Cliffs, N.J.: Prentice-Hall, 1975.

Rimm, D. C., & Masters, J. C. *Behavior therapy: techniques and empirical findings*. New York: Academic Press, 1974.

REFERENCES

Ausubel, D. P., Stager, M., & Gaite, A. J. H. Retroactive facilitation in meaningful verbal learning. *Journal of Educational Psychology*, 1968, *59*, 250–255.

Bandura, A. *Principles of behavior modification*. New York: Holt, Rinehart, & Winston, 1969.

Bishop, M. P., Elder, S. T., & Heath, R. G. Intracranial self-stimulation in man. *Science*, 1963, *140*, 394–396.

Broadbent, D. E. Flow of information within the organism. *Journal of Verbal Learning and Verbal Behavior*, 1963, *2*, 34–39.

Campbell, B. A., & Church, R. M. (eds) *Punishment*. New York: Appleton-Century-Crofts, 1968.

Church, R. M. The varied effects of punishment on behavior. *Psychological Review*, 1963, *70*, 369–402.

Deutsch, J. A., & Deutsch, D. *Physiological psychology*, Homewood, Ill.: Dorsey Press, 1966.

———, & Howarth, C. I. Some tests of a theory of intracranial self-stimulation. *Psychological Review*, 1963, *70*, 444–460.

Dunham, P. J. Punishment: method and theory. *Psychological Review*, 1971, *78*, 58–70.

Gaito, J., & Bonnett, K. Quantitative versus qualitative RNA and protein changes in the brain during behavior. *Psychological Bulletin*, 1971, *75*, 109–127.

Glickman, S. E., & Schiff, B. B. A biological theory of reinforcement. *Psychological Review*, 1967, *74*, 81–109.

Guthrie, E. R. *The psychology of learning*. New York: Harper, 1935.

Hall, J. F. *Verbal learning and retention*. Philadelphia: J. B. Lippincott, 1971.

Hebb, D. O. *The organization of behavior*. New York: John Wiley, 1949.

Hendry, D. P. (ed) *Conditioned reinforcement*. Homewood, Ill.: Dorsey Press, 1969.

Hodos, W., & Campbell, C. B. G. Scala Naturae: Why there is no theory in comparative psychology. *Psychological Review*, 1969, *76*, 337–350.

Hull, C. L. *Principles of behavior*. New York: Appleton-Century-Crofts, 1943.

John, E. R. *Mechanisms of memory*. New York: Academic Press, 1967.

John, E. R. Switchboard versus statistical theories of learning and memory. *Science*, 1972, *177*, 850–864.

Jones, J. E. Contiguity and reinforcement in relation to CS–UCS intervals in classical aversive conditioning. *Psychological Review*, 1962, *69*, 176–186.

Kellogg, W. N. Chimpanzees in experimental homes. *Psychological Record*, 1968, *18*, 489–498.

Landauer, T. K. Reinforcement as consolidation. *Psychological Review*, 1969, *76*, 82–96.

Luttges, M., Johnson, T., Buck, C., Holland, J., & McGaugh, J. An examination of "transfer of learning" by nucleic acid. *Science*, 1966, *151* 834–837.

Martin, E. Verbal learning theory and independent retrieval phenomena. *Psychological Review*, 1971, *78*, 314–332.

Masters, W. H., & Johnson, V. E. *Human sexual inadequacy*. Boston: Little, Brown, 1970.

McGaugh, J. L. Time-dependent processes in memory storage. *Science*, 1966, *153*, 1351–1358.

———, & Herz, M. J. *Memory consolidation*. San Francisco: Albion, 1972.

Mikulas, W. L. *Behavior modification: an overview*. New York: Harper & Row, 1972.

Miller, N. E. Implications for theories of reinforcement. In Sheer, D. E. (ed) *Electrical stimulation of the brain*. Austin, Texas: Univ. Texas Press, 1961.

———. Some reflections on the law of effect produce a new alternative to drive reduction. *Nebraska symposium on motivation*, 1963, *11*, 65–113.

Morrell, F. Electrophysiological contributions to the neural basis of learning. *Physiological Reviews*, 1961, *41*, 443–494.

Olds, J. Hypothalamic substrates of reward. *Physiological Reviews*, 1962, *42*, 554–604.

Pomerantz, J. R., Kaplan, S., & Kaplan, R. Satiation effects in the perception of single letters. *Perception & Psychophysics*, 1969, *6*, 129–132.

Premack, D. Toward empirical behavior laws: I. Positive reinforcement. *Psychological Review*, 1959, *66*, 219–233.

_____. Reinforcement theory. *Nebraska symposium on motivation*, 1965, *13*, 123–180.

_____. A functional analysis of language. *Journal of the Experimental Analysis of Behavior*, 1970, *14*, 107–125.

Pribram, K. H. The neurophysiology of remembering. *Scientific American*, 1969, *220* No. 1, 73–86.

_____. *Languages of the brain: experimental paradoxes and principles in neuropsychology*. Englewood Cliffs, N.J.: Prentice-Hall, 1971.

Sheffield, F. D. A drive-induction theory of reinforcement. In Haber, R. N. (ed) *Current research in motivation*. New York: Holt, Rinehart, & Winston, 1966a.

_____. New evidence on the drive-induction theory of reinforcement. In Haber, R. N. (ed) *Current research in motivation*. New York: Holt, Rinehart, & Winston, 1966b.

Sherman, J. A., & Baer, D. M. Appraisal of operant therapy techniques with children and adults. In Franks, C. M. (ed) *Behavior therapy: appraisal and status*. New York: McGraw-Hill, 1969.

Spence, K. W. *Behavior theory and conditioning*. New Haven: Yale Univ. Press, 1956.

Spevack, A. A., & Suboski, M. D. Retrograde effects of electroconvulsive shock on learned responses. *Psychological Bulletin*, 1969, *72*, 66–76.

Spielberger, C. D., & DeNike, L. D. Descriptive behaviorism versus cognitive theory in verbal operant conditioning. *Psychological Review*, 1966, *73*, 306–326.

Trowill, J. A., Panksepp, J., & Gandleman, R. An incentive model of rewarding brain stimulation. *Psychological Review*, 1969, *76*, 264–281.

Ungar, G. (ed) *Molecular mechanisms in memory and storage*. New York: Plenum Press, 1970.

Verhave, T. The pigeon as a quality control inspector. *American Psychologist*, 1966, *21*, 109–115.

Walker, E. L. Action decrement and its relation to learning. *Psychological Review*, 1958, *65*, 129–142.

Waugh, N. C., & Norman, D. A. Primary memory. *Psychological Review*, 1965, *72*, 89–104.

Wilson, G. T., & Davison, G. C. Processes of fear-reduction in systematic desensitization: Animal studies. *Psychological Bulletin*, 1971, *76*, 1-14.

Wolpe, J. *Psychotherapy by reciprocal inhibition*. Stanford: Stanford Univ. Press, 1958.

Dr. William Lee Mikulas is an associate professor of psychology at the University of West Florida at Pensacola. He is an author and college professor who has contributed widely to learning theory. His other published works include *Behavior Modification: An Overview,* published in 1972 and *Concepts in Learning,* published two years later. In addition to these he has contributed extensively to the literature of learning theory, behavior modification, and related topics with articles in *Psychological Reports, Canadian Psychologist, Psychological Record,* and other professional and academic journals and periodicals.